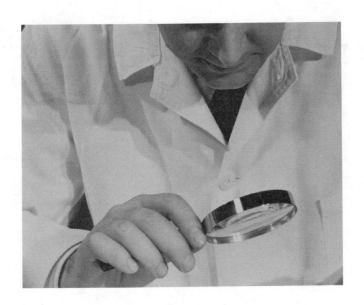

Developing Applications with Visual Studio.NET

Richard Grimes

Addison-Wesley

Boston • San Francisco • New York • Toronto • Montreal
London • Munich • Paris • Madrid
Capetown • Sydney • Tokyo • Singapore • Mexico City

4/4/2002 Borders 49.99

The publisher offers discounts on this book when ordered in quantity for special sales. For more information, please contact:

Pearson Education Corporate Sales Division
201 W. 103rd Street
Indianapolis, IN 46290
(800) 428-5331
corpsales@pearsoned.com

Visit AW on the Web: www.aw.com/cseng/

Library of Congress Control Number: 2002100855

Pearson Education, Inc.
Rights and Contracts Department
75 Arlington Street, Suite 300
Boston, MA 02116
Fax: (617) 848-7047

0-201-70852-3
Text printed on recycled paper
1 2 3 4 5 6 7 8 9 10—CRS—0605040302
First printing, February, 2002

To my father,
Norman William Grimes,
who died just before I completed this book.

Contents

4 Interoperation and COM+   **347**

Preface

.NET is a whole new way to program. It has taken me a while to get used to using it, but now I feel that .NET is the future of developing code. The two main features that .NET brings are the runtime and the Framework Class Library. The runtime executes all .NET code and provides a secure environment. The Framework Class Library is available to all .NET code regardless of the language that is used to create that code. The library is a culmination of all the libraries that Win32 developers are accustomed to using, and some APIs are provided through a new paradigm, but others are mere mirrors of the Win32 APIs that they replace. The significant point is that all of the APIs are accessed in the same way, so the application developer no longer has to learn multiple ways to access libraries (DLL exported functions, class libraries, template libraries, COM). The intention is to put more focus on using the APIs than on accessing them.

I have spent a considerable amount of time determining how .NET works and how the various classes in the library are related. On occasion it was a joy to see how .NET had provided a new API that put more power in the hands of the developer, and on a few occasions I was frustrated to see that .NET had provided a solution that reduced the facilities offered to the developer. In this book I want to give you the benefit of my odyssey through .NET. I will enthuse when .NET does it right, and I will tell you straight when .NET does it wrong.

One thing is clear: .NET is here to stay. Expect in the future that Microsoft will put more and more emphasis on .NET. Your future as a developer will be intimately entwined with .NET, and by becoming familiar with .NET now, you'll ensure that you'll be ready for whatever Microsoft decides to release in the future.

Intended Audience

I have deliberately decided to target C++ Win32 developers. This book has no VB.NET code and only the barest minimum of ASP.NET. If you want to develop in VB.NET, or you want to develop Web applications with ASP.NET, there are other excellent books that will suit you better than this one.

I also make no excuses about the fact that this book is packed full of details, and in places it touches on tough concepts. I have worked hard to glean the information that I present in this book. I didn't have access to privileged knowledge. What you see here is the result of writing many hundreds of test applications, of pouring over IL generated with ILDASM, and of single-stepping through code with the .NET debuggers. Where I present code, you can be assured that what you see is code that I have written and tested. When I describe how an API works, you can be assured that I have determined that behavior by actually trying out the code. I have worked hard to write this book, and I expect you to work hard as you read through it. That way you'll have the enlightening learning experience that I had.

What to Expect

My intention when writing this book was to give you a grand tour of developing applications with Visual Studio.NET. As with all grand tours, you have to do a lot of preparation before you can start. For this reason the book is split into three parts: The first four chapters describe the .NET Framework, Chapters 5 through 7 describe the tools in Visual Studio.NET that you can use to develop applications, and Chapters 8 and 9 explain how to develop and debug applications.

The chapters follow a logical progression from a basic description of the .NET Runtime, through a description of the framework and the tools to develop .NET executables and libraries, to developing applications with the Visual Studio.NET design environment. I made a deliberate choice to leave an introduction of Visual Studio.NET until Chapter 5 because much of the development that you can do with .NET can be done with a simple text editor like Notepad (indeed, I urge you to use Notepad as you work through the first few chapters). However, at the point that your project grows larger than a handful of files, at the point that you move away from trivial resources and XML files to use more real-life files, you'll start to realize that you need a more accomplished editor and tools to help you develop your application.

It is at *this* point that you'll need to use Visual Studio.NET. If you use VS.NET before you've gone through the details of .NET's facilities, you won't appreciate the tools that VS.NET provides. I also want to give you the impression that there is a life beyond wizard-generated code.

The following is a brief description of what to expect in the chapters of this book.

Chapter 1: .NET Runtime

In this chapter I start exactly where I should: right at the beginning with a description of the .NET Runtime. The runtime executes *all* .NET code, so in this chapter I describe the basic concepts of the runtime and how it locates and runs code. I describe the languages that you can use and various .NET features used to generate events, to provide error information, and to access code outside of the current code module. Then I describe the .NET facilities for adding type information to a code module, and how you can add custom type information. Finally, I explain how code is packaged and the new mechanism for locating and loading that code.

Chapter 2: Framework Class Library

I use this chapter to give an overview of what I consider to be the "core" library. The framework library is available to all .NET languages and can be considered to be a culmination of the various APIs that Win32 developers are accustomed to using. The Framework Class Library contains many classes, and I have chosen to explain just a few. These are the classes that you are most likely to use—the classes without which you are unlikely to be able to do any .NET development.

I explain threading, basic input/output using streams to files and to the console, the debugging classes, and collection classes. Once I have made the foundation with the fundamental classes, I follow up with a description of the user interface classes to allow you to create windows and draw in those windows. Finally, I describe what I call the "other" classes. Strictly speaking, they are not core classes, but they are important for application development, so I give an overview of these classes and how to use them.

Chapter 3: Contexts and Remoting

.NET provides a new level of code isolation: application domains, which I introduced in Chapter 1. In this chapter I explain how code in one application domain can access code in another domain: .NET remoting. .NET defines an idea called context—domain membership is one property of a context—and .NET needs to take special action to allow calls to be made across contexts. I explain how cross-context calls are made and how you can change the way that .NET manages these calls.

This chapter explains in detail how .NET remoting works, the types of objects that can be accessed remotely, how long they live, and the security aspects of accessing those objects. Finally, the chapter has a description of asynchronous programming, including how exceptions and return values are handled when a call is made asynchronously.

Chapter 4: Interoperation and COM+

Interoperation is required to allow your .NET code to access native code. In this chapter I cover all aspects of interoperation from accessing DLLs, through Platform Invoke, to accessing COM and COM+ components. I start by describing how Platform Invoke works and contrast this to how you can access native C++ code from managed C++. I also explain marshaling nonsimple types, how exceptions are handled, and "unsafe" code.

In the second half of the chapter I explain how interoperation with COM and COM+ is achieved. .NET provides tools to allow you to use COM objects in .NET code and to use .NET objects in COM code. I show you how to use these tools and describe how COM concepts like events, aggregation, and registration are achieved. The final part of the chapter explains the .NET classes that allow you to write COM+ classes.

Chapter 5: Visual Studio.NET Environment

By this point in the book you should have a good grounding in the facilities that .NET offers and the classes that you can use. In this chapter I introduce you to the facilities in Visual Studio.NET that you can use to develop .NET code. I start with a general description of the user interface: the various windows and toolbars that are provided. I then give a brief description of the code-generating wizards and the UI features of VS.NET that you can use to change the code that is generated.

In the latter half of the chapter I explain how to manage your code and the tools that you can use to search in your code and to get help. Finally, I explain the Toolbox and how to use external tools.

Chapter 6: Creating and Building Solutions

In this chapter I look in detail at how you create and build solutions. A solution is a collection of projects, and a project contains source files that are compiled to create an output. I start this chapter by explaining the various project types that you can add to a solution and the various classes that you can add to those projects. Following the general theme of this book, I explain only C++ and C# classes, but I do include a description of the C++ projects that create native code.

In the second half of the chapter I explain how to build and deploy solutions. I describe how to start a compilation, and how to customize it. I also explain how you can deploy the outputs from a solution and the various project types that are provided to do this.

Chapter 7: Visual C++.NET

C++ is the most flexible of the .NET languages. Visual C++ allows you to develop both native and managed code, as well as a mixture of the two. I start this chapter by describing the new features in ATL, beginning with a description of Visual C++ attributes and an explanation of how these help your development. Then I explain ATL Server, which is used to write ISAPI extensions for Web applications and Web Services.

The rest of the chapter is concerned with managed code, and I explain how managed C++ differs from native C++ in declaring classes and in handling interfaces, arrays, and strings.

Chapter 8: Application Development

This chapter is concerned with two main subjects: developing UI controls and forms, and localizing resources. In the first half of the chapter I explain components and controls and lead you through the process of developing a control that is integrated with the Visual Studio.NET **Toolbox** and **Properties** windows. In the second half of this chapter I describe .NET resources and how you can use the Visual Studio.NET tools to create localized resources.

Chapter 9: Debugging

After you have designed, written, and built your application, the next step will be to check that it does what it is designed to do, and to correct code that is in error. That is, you will have to debug your application. Visual Studio.NET allows you to debug both native and managed code, and even to step from the managed to the unmanaged world and vice versa. In this chapter I explain all the facilities that you can use to debug your code: how to set breakpoints, how to use the debugging windows, and how to debug more than one process.

Acknowledgments

Like all other books, this one involved the help of many people without which the book would not have been possible. This book would not have happened without Don Box. Don persuaded me to write for the DevelopMentor series at Addison-Wesley, and he was instrumental in the initial ideas about the main content and focus of this book. My thanks go to Don for his guiding hand. My thanks also go to the editors at Addison-Wesley: to Gary Clarke, who got the project started; to Kristin Erickson, who helped me through the initial part of the book; and finally to Stephane Thomas, who took over the reins from Kristin and helped me through the majority of the book. I would also like to thank the reviewers who helped ensure that what you read here is technically correct.

I would also like to thank those people at Microsoft who helped me during the writing of this book. Although this book is primarily about Visual Studio.NET, I have had the most amount of help from the Visual C++ team, and therefore I can wholeheartedly recommend their work. I have had help from many people on the C++ team, but I would particularly like to recognize the help of Walter Sullivan and Mike Dice from the libraries team, and Ronald Laermans, Mike Hall, and Jeff Peil.

Richard Grimes

Kenilworth, United Kingdom

September 2001

Chapter 1

.NET Runtime

At first glance the .NET Framework appears to be a new departure for Microsoft. The old way—compiling source code to x86 native code, which is then executed by the computer's processor—is being replaced by a mechanism by which source code is compiled to tokens that are executed by a runtime. However, much of what you see in the .NET Framework (including aspects of the runtime) has its roots in many technologies that have come from Redmond over the last 20 years or so. Therefore, the .NET Framework can be viewed as a collection of technologies and libraries that is a natural culmination of Microsoft's technologies in a bold attempt to unify Windows development.

.NET can be treated as composed of three general parts: the Framework Class Library, .NET languages, and the runtime. The Framework Class Library can be considered a collection of two types of classes: those that provide a new paradigm to program applications, and those that are essentially a version of the Win32 API that is divided into components. I will have more to say about the Framework Class Library—its structure and design—in the next chapter.

In this chapter I will address the .NET Runtime and in the process talk about some of the language aspects. Throughout this book I will use two of the .NET languages: C# and managed extensions for C++. I will talk about aspects of both languages in this chapter in the context of describing the .NET Runtime, and I will give a more detailed description of managed extensions for C++ in Chapter 7.

1.1 .NET Features

The .NET Runtime executes code written in .NET languages and compiled to Microsoft intermediate language (IL). All .NET code is executed by the runtime, which will ensure that the correct code is run. That is, the called code must have the exact signature that the calling code specifies, and checks are performed to ensure that all code has the permission to perform its actions. This means that there are several important issues that the runtime must address—issues like security, memory management, and interoperation with non-.NET code—which I will cover in this section.

1.1.1 .NET Languages

.NET applications are made up of code that calls methods on framework types and custom types. .NET language compilers range from those that merely compile scripting code (*.NET consumers*) to those that allow you to write your own types and extend an existing type (*.NET extenders*). .NET language compilers compile your source code to intermediate language opcodes that are just-in-time (JIT) compiled at runtime and executed by the .NET executable engine.

To a large extent .NET development does not differ much from Win32 development: You identify the problem that you are trying to solve, design your code, write the code using services provided by the operating system (and other libraries), and then compile that code to a binary that is executed by the system. The differences become apparent when you take a closer look at this process.

At the heart of .NET is the *Common Type System* (CTS), which defines reference and value types as a standard that all languages must follow when compiling .NET code. The Common Type System defines certain specifications that new types must follow, which may or may not be mapped to a language feature. Types written in one language (and compiled to IL) can be used in source code written in another language. The base set of features that a language compiler must support to allow types to be used and extended by other languages is defined in the *Common Language Specification* (CLS). If a tool obeys this set of rules—and therefore is CLS compliant—the types it generates can be used by code generated by another CLS-compliant tool.

It is for this reason that Microsoft calls the .NET Runtime the *Common Language Runtime* (CLR). However, I want to make it clear that the .NET Runtime executes the opcodes of only one language—intermediate language; the term *CLR* comes from the fact that the IL can be *generated* from any language.

Microsoft explains that this feature allows you to develop applications in multiple languages. Although I agree that this is possible, in practice individual developers will be more likely to learn and use just one language rather than many. The reason I say this is that developers write code that uses library code, and if the library code is compiled to IL and is CLS compliant, the developer is able to use the language most familiar to her, effectively becoming monolingual. This contrasts sharply with traditional Win32 development, which almost made multilingualism a requirement with respect to code because different languages produced different types of libraries that were accessed in different ways.

To a certain extent the IL generated by the various .NET compilers is more or less the same, so the language used to create the types could be regarded as irrelevant (this is the impression that Microsoft is keen to convey). Of course, this is not strictly true because the C++ compiler performs some optimization on the IL that it produces, so the code generated from the managed C++ compiler will perform better than code generated from C# or VB.NET. Furthermore, some languages have features that provide conveniences to the developer that result in extra IL. For example, VB.NET allows developers to use late binding, which will involve IL that is called at runtime to locate and load the requested code. However, such details will be ignored by many software houses because their emphasis will be on rapid and economic development, and one of the most important factors here is to reuse existing skills—skills that the workforce is comfortable using—and reduce training costs.

IL is just one part of the data used in a .NET type. Just as important as IL is information called *metadata*. Every .NET extender must generate metadata for all the types that it generates. Metadata describes types in .NET—a vitally important function because it allows the runtime to check if the code that it is being asked to load is the same type as the code that the calling code expects to call. Intermediate language is explicit about the method and the number and type of the parameters that the method takes. The runtime compares the IL in the calling code with the metadata of the corresponding method on the type requested, and if they do not match exactly the type will not be called. This comparison protects users from security violations and protects memory from corruption.

1.1.2 Executing Code

Figure 1.1 shows a schematic of how code is executed in .NET. All .NET code is contained in deployment packages called *assemblies*. These include the IL of the types that they contain and the metadata that describes those types. Each assembly also has information about the assemblies that its types use so that when the code calls a type in another assembly, the runtime can locate and load the assembly and finally load the type. When the runtime has loaded the type, it replaces the entry point of every method with a piece of stub code. When the method is called, the stub code executes the just-in-time (JIT) compiler on its IL. The JIT compiler generates code that is native to the platform where the assembly is run and caches this code in memory somewhere. The stub code on the type's method is now changed to point to this native code so that subsequent calls to the method will execute the native code without the JIT step.

This jitted code remains in memory and is discarded when the type is unloaded. Another option (called *prejitting*) is to compile the IL to native code when installing an assembly. Prejitting extends the time it takes to install the assembly, but it means that the first execution of each type is quicker because the JIT step is no longer required. The Framework Class Library assemblies are all prejitted, and you can choose to prejit your own code with the `ngen.exe` tool.

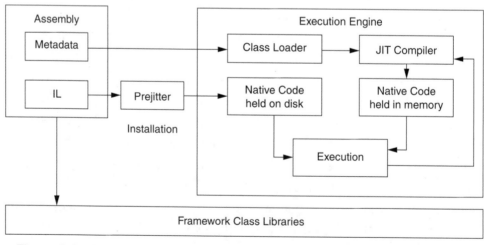

Figure 1.1 Schematic of code execution by the .NET Runtime

DEVELOPING APPLICATIONS WITH VISUAL STUDIO.NET

Jitted code will always involve the extra JIT step, so doesn't it make the code slower compared to conventional compiled code? Possibly not. The JIT compiler has the advantage of running on the machine where the code will be executed. This means that a JIT compiler can examine metrics like the processor and the amount of memory installed in the machine and use this information to tune the native code that is produced.

Conventional compilers do not have this advantage; either they generate general-purpose (one size fits all) code, or the developer has to create several versions optimized for different parameters (e.g., look at the C++ compiler's /G3, /G4, /G5, and /G6 switches to optimize for various processors). The pre-jitter suffers from this problem too because the code that it generates is based on the machine's state when and where the prejitter is run. The optimized native code generated by the prejitter is created according to the machine configuration, and this configuration is read at install time, *not* execution time. If the configuration changes (perhaps more memory is installed), the prejitter will have to be reapplied to take advantage of this change.

One of the problems with Win32 native libraries was that different languages (and different vendors of the same language) used different memory allocators. Some languages allowed items to be allocated, and the language would then clean up; others required explicit cleanup to be performed. These differences led to another level of complication in attempts to make a library language neutral, inevitably leading to memory leaks. .NET provides a single source of allocated memory—the .NET managed heap—and one way to manage that memory, the garbage collector.

1.1.3 Interop

Since the advent of NT 3.1, many millions of lines of code have been written for 32-bit Windows. From what I have already told you about .NET—IL, the JIT compiler, and the execution engine—it may appear that these millions of lines of code are now legacy and will no longer be used. This is not the case because many of the classes that are present in the Framework Class Library are based on Win32 APIs—presenting a .NET face to a well-known facility. Furthermore, even classes in the framework that appear to offer a new paradigm depend on

Win32 native code (e.g., Windows Forms is based on GDI+, a new graphics library for Windows, but this library is itself based on the Graphical Device Interface [GDI] code that we have been using throughout the lifetime of Windows). The reason is pretty clear: Windows has had a long period of evolution, and as in many cases the result has been efficient code, Microsoft did not want to start this evolution process all over again.

So if Microsoft uses Win32 code, there must also be a way for you to use native Win32. Indeed there is; in fact, Microsoft could hardly avoid allowing you to access native code because then moving over to .NET would be a sudden movement either involving writing applications afresh or porting them to the new platform. Porting is never a happy experience, and it always produces "ported" code—that is, code that is written for one platform or library and "bent" to use another platform or library. It is far better to use the code in the environment where it was originally designed and where it has been tested and tuned.

Thus there is a requirement for interoperation between .NET code and native, non-.NET code that Microsoft could not ignore. .NET has four technologies (more details will be given in Chapter 4):

- Platform Invoke
- It Just Works
- COM Interop
- Manual Marshaling

Platform Invoke (P/Invoke) allows you to call methods in libraries that have been compiled for a specific platform, and on Windows this means calling functions exported from Dynamic Link Libraries (DLLs). The developer has to identify the library that contains the method and may have to provide some hints (like the character set that should be used in conversions of managed strings to unmanaged strings). However, to a large extent the developer still does not have to worry about the conversion of parameters.

The only potential problem occurs if the developer wants to pass a record of data to a function via P/Invoke. Records (or value types) in .NET are managed by the runtime, and by default there is no guarantee of the absolute location of a field within the type. However, .NET does provide a mechanism for indicating that the fields in a record should be at an absolute location. Again it involves writing more code (but not much more).

It Just Works (IJW) is a special case of P/Invoke, and as a technology it is available only in the managed extensions for C++. Managed extensions allow you to have garbage-collected (managed) classes in the same source code as C++ heap- and stack-allocated (unmanaged) classes, and it even allows you to link to static linked libraries (more details will be given in Chapter 7). IJW allows you to call this code largely without worrying about whether the data types used by the unmanaged classes are compatible with the types used in managed code. You don't have to worry about this conversion because *it just works!*

The Component Object Model (COM) has become a phenomenally successful technology because it allows you to divide code into components. A lot of library code can be accessed only as COM objects; indeed, some Windows APIs use COM (or COM-like) code (e.g., DirectX and the Windows Shell). .NET provides a technology called COM Interop to allow you to call COM objects from .NET and to call .NET objects via COM. This is illustrated in Figure 1.2.

For a .NET type to call a COM object, the developer must generate a wrapper .NET class. The .NET Framework provides a tool called `tlbimp.exe` for this purpose. `tlbimp` takes a type library, or a file that has a type library

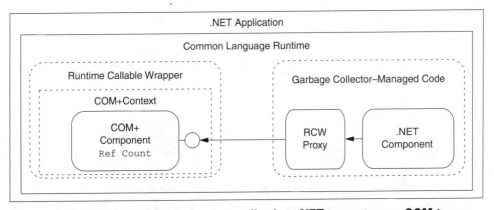

Figure 1.2   Runtime callable wrapper allowing .NET types to use COM types. The lifetime of the COM object is determined by its reference count. The garbage collector determines the lifetime of a .NET object, so the RCW will adjust the COM object's reference count when the proxy is no longer being used.

bound as a resource, and generates an assembly that has the necessary wrapper classes (runtime callable wrappers, or RCWs) that the .NET code calls.

A corresponding tool called `tlbexp.exe` reads an assembly and generates a type library from the types in the assembly. A superset of `tlbexp.exe` is `regasm.exe`, which generates a type library containing the wrapper classes that allow COM to call .NET code (COM callable wrappers, or CCWs, Figure 1.3) and adds registry entries so that the .NET code is accessible through normal COM code (via `CoCreateInstance()`, `CoGetClassFactory()`, and so on).

COM Interop is very important for another reason. More Win32 coders use Visual Basic than any other programming language. This represents a huge number of programmers and a vast amount of Visual Basic code compiled to unmanaged native code. Visual Basic.NET is totally different from Visual Basic 6, principally because VB.NET (like all other .NET languages) uses the Framework Class Library. If that weren't enough, VB.NET also adds features alien to VB programmers, like threads and exceptions. All of this represents a huge shift in the information that VB6 programmers have to assimilate before they become productive.

What can be done with all of that "legacy" VB6 code? Porting is one option, but as I mentioned earlier, porting is likely to generate a lot of work and will produce code that runs on a platform where it was not originally designed to run.

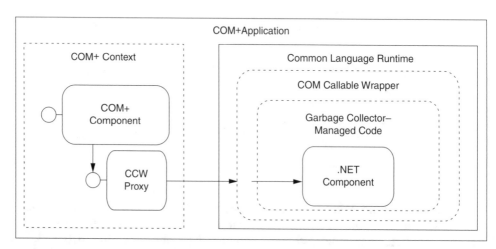

Figure 1.3 The COM callable wrapper used to allow COM and COM+ components to access .NET types

DEVELOPING APPLICATIONS WITH VISUAL STUDIO.NET

There has to be another way. Visual Basic does not allow you to create DLL-exported functions, but it does make it very easy to create COM objects (it is as simple as creating a Visual Basic public class). Thus, to reuse Visual Basic COM components, the best option is simply to use COM Interop. Furthermore, because the process to convert Visual Basic code to COM classes is straight-forward, there will probably be a well-paid community of Visual Basic programmers who will do no more than this—just to allow VB6 code to be used by .NET through COM Interop.

Finally, if all else fails, you can manually marshal calls from .NET to native unmanaged code. The framework comes with many classes to allow you to do this. You can convert from managed types to unmanaged types, you can use unmanaged interfaces in managed code and vice versa, and you can even pass references of managed objects to unmanaged code.

1.1.4 Garbage Collector

As I mentioned earlier, .NET manages memory through a garbage collector. Types in .NET can be described as either *reference types* or *value types*. Reference types (sometimes called classes) are allocated on the runtime managed heap. This heap is implemented as a high-performance heap where allocations are relatively cheap. The heap is managed by the garbage collector (GC) that tracks object usage. When there are no longer any references to an object, the GC will mark the memory used by the object as available for reuse (which again is a relatively cheap process). Later the GC will clean up the heap and reuse the memory that is no longer being used; it may also compact the heap and, in the process, move existing objects around in memory. This is the most expensive part of using the GC. The Framework Class Library has classes that allow you to alter how the GC works, and even to initiate this compaction process perhaps when your application is idle.

Because the GC may move objects around in memory during compaction, it has to adjust any pointers that object references in your code use to access existing managed objects. Thus if your language allows object pointers, you should treat them as special because you cannot rely on their absolute values. If the absolute value is important (e.g., if you have passed the pointer to unmanaged code) you can "pin" the pointer to indicate to the GC that the object to which it refers must not be moved in memory.

Using a garbage collector insulates the developer from the details of memory allocation and frees the developer from the responsibility of releasing memory. The same applies to strings and arrays because the framework provides classes that manage strings and arrays. The bounds of arrays are checked on every access so that your code can never call an array beyond its bounds.

The .NET GC performs garbage collection using a generational mechanism, in which objects that survive one collection are promoted to an older generation. The GC can optimize its work only by performing garbage collection on the earlier generations. This optimization is based on empirical evidence that younger objects are more likely to be short-lived, so garbage collection on younger objects will yield more free space than garbage collection on older objects.

The managed heap is essentially a block of memory allocated by the runtime and treated like a stack. When code calls the managed heap with the `new` operator, the runtime knows the size of the object required and reserves memory at the end of the heap by moving the heap pointer to accommodate the size of the object. The reserved memory can then be initialized by a call to the object's constructor. The pointer to this memory is returned to the code as the reference of the type requested; this object is said to be in generation 0. If the type has a destructor (in C# and C++), the `new` operator will recognize this and queue the object for finalization, which I will explain later.

When there is no more space on the managed heap, a call to the `new` operator will result in the GC performing a garbage collection. Garbage collection is a mechanism by which unreachable objects are discarded. An object is *unreachable* when it is no longer possible to reach that object from a reference from another object. The JIT compiler and runtime keep a list of *roots*, from which all reachable objects can be accessed. These roots are things like static objects—that is, object references currently on the stack or held in CPU registers.

During garbage collection this list is passed to the GC, which builds a graph of the objects to which the roots refer directly or indirectly (see, for example, Figure 1.4). Any object on the heap that is not in this graph is unreachable, and the memory that such objects occupy can safely be reused. Thus the GC can

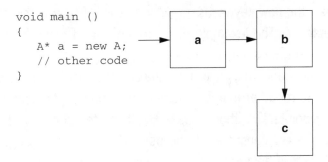

```
void main ()
{
    A* a = new A;
    // other code
}
```

Figure 1.4   Object graph from a root

move reachable objects in the heap to fill in the gaps left by discarded objects and change the object references in your code.

This works fine if the only access to these objects are through references that the GC knows about. However, this is not always the case. If you pass a pointer to memory within a managed object to code that is not tracked by the GC (code marked as `unmanaged` in C++ or as `unsafe` in C#), then when the GC moves objects around during garbage collection it will not be able to update those pointers and they will become invalid. To get around this problem, you can *pin* a pointer. C++ and C# diverge on how they do this. First, here is the C++ code:

```
// C++
#using <mscorlib.dll>
using namespace System;
#include <stdio.h>
__gc struct A { int i; };

#pragma unmanaged
void UseIt(int* p)
{
    printf("pointer is at %x\n", p);
}
#pragma managed

void main()
{
    A* a = new A;
    int __pin* p = &a->i;
    UseIt(p);
}
```

I will explain the new keywords __gc and #using later in this chapter and in depth in Chapter 7. This example has an unmanaged function, UseIt(); the developer uses the unmanaged pragma to ensure that the code is compiled as native code. The code that calls this unmanaged function passes an *interior* pointer to an int member that is a member of a managed object (Chapter 7 will explain interior pointers). Although UseIt() uses the pointer to the embedded int member, the GC cannot track the pointer and cannot change the value of the pointer while it is being accessed by the native code in UseIt(). The only option is to tell the GC that it should not move the object in memory; this is the reason for creation of the pinned pointer, indicated by the __pin keyword. The lifetime of the pinned pointer in the main() function determines how long the object should be pinned, so once the pointer goes out of scope (or if the pinned pointer is assigned to zero), the object is unpinned and can be moved by the GC the next time it does a collection.

C# has two mechanisms for pinning. First, it defines unsafe code, which is code that is allowed to use direct pointers; second, it allows you to obtain pointers and pin objects in fixed blocks (I will explain C# classes and the entry points to applications later in this chapter):

```csharp
// C#
using System;
class A { public int i; }
class App
{
    static unsafe void UseIt(A a)
    {
        fixed (int* p = &a.i)
        {
            Console.WriteLine(
                "pointer is at {0:x}", (int)p);
        }
    }
    static void Main()
    {
        A a = new A();
        a.i = 0;
        UseIt(a);
    }
}
```

Here the method `UseIt()` is marked as `unsafe`, so the code must be compiled with the `/unsafe` command-line switch. The pointer to the embedded data member is created in the `fixed` statement, which pins the object during the scope defined by the following code block.

We can optimize garbage collection by targeting just short-lived objects—generation 0—and performing garbage collection only on later generations if the collection does not achieve enough free space on the heap. You can force a collection by calling `GC.Collect()`. This function can force collection either up to a specific generation or of all generations. Any object remaining on the heap after a collection is promoted to an older generation, up to a maximum of `GC.MaxGeneration`.

During garbage collection, unreachable objects that are mentioned in the finalization queue are scheduled for finalization. A reference to each one is placed into another queue, called the *freachable* queue. Because there is now a root that has a reference to the object, the finalizable object is treated as reachable—and remains on the heap. This object's generation is increased to the next generation.

Each process has a separate thread, called the *finalization thread,* that goes through the freachable queue and calls the `Finalize()` method on each object. `Finalize()` calls the "destructor" code defined for the object (it will become more apparent later what I mean by this). The "destructor" code is used to clean up the object, so the finalized object on the heap is now in an uninitialized state and its memory will be released only during the next GC cycle for this generation.

Finalization appears to be useful, but bear in mind that finalized objects live longer on the heap than nonfinalized objects and that you cannot control when `Finalize()` will be called. So-called deterministic finalization does not exist in .NET. Although at first this may appear to be a facility removed from the developer's armory, it is not a huge problem. .NET developers have to change how they code to accommodate this. .NET provides the `IDisposable` interface, and disposable components implement a `Dispose()` method for the cleanup code. The developer has the responsibility to call this method when he knows that the object will be used no more. C# defines a construct based on the using statement to scope a variable and call the `Dispose()` method at the end of this scope (I will give more details of this construct later in this chapter).

When you identify a resource that your object uses and that you think needs to be placed in the `Dispose()` method, think again. It may be possible to change the code so that resources are not retained needlessly long—for example, as follows:

```csharp
// C#
class Logger : IDisposable
{
    TextWriter tw;
    public Logger()
    {
        tw = File.AppendText("log.txt");
    }
    public void Write(string s)
    {
        tw.Write(s);
    }
    public void Dispose()
    {
        tw.Close();
    }
}
```

This trivial code illustrates the point I am trying to make: The `TextWriter` class allows you to write text to a file (I'll explain this in more depth in the next chapter), but once `Logger` has opened a file for writing, it has an exclusive lock on the file. An instance of the `Logger` class can be used with C# `using` blocks because it defines a `Dispose()` method. This ensures that the `tw` object is closed, which removes the exclusive lock on the file. If this code were put in the destructor of the C# class, then it would be called only when the finalization thread called the finalizer. This could happen at any time.

Placing the cleanup code in `Dispose()` rather than in the destructor has the effect of reducing the time that a `Logger` object holds on to the resource. But why stop here? It makes far more sense to hold on to the resource only for the period that it is being used—for example, as follows:

```
// C#
public void Write(string s)
{
    TextWriter tw = File.AppendText("log.txt");
    tw.Write(s);
    tw.Close();
}
```

As this code illustrates, if you restructure your code so that it holds on to resources only as long as they are needed, it is possible to reduce the need for finalization methods. In this code I have ignored the situation of an instance of Logger being shared by many other objects that might even call the instance from other threads. I will leave a solution to this problem to the next chapter.

The garbage collector does a lot of work for you, and in most cases you'll be happy to let it do its work in the way that it chooses. Sometimes, however, you will want to give the GC a bit of help. One such situation is a circular reference, as illustrated in Figure 1.5. In this case object a has a reference to object b, which has a reference to object c. If this is merely the case, there is no problem because when a is no longer reachable (e.g., a variable goes out of scope), the GC will mark the object as available for garbage collection. In doing so, the GC will see that objects b and c are also unreachable and hence should also be collected. Nothing changes if object c has a reference to object b, a circular reference, because the garbage collector will still realize that objects b and c are unreachable. In COM, however, circular references were a problem. You had to be careful in COM, particularly when interfaces were used to provide callbacks.

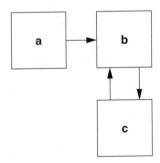

Figure 1.5   A simple circular reference

In Figure 1.6 the situation is complicated further because another object, object d, has a reference to object c. This means that when object a becomes unreachable, objects c and b will still be reachable through d. Eventually d will become unreachable, and so will objects b and c.

This is fine, and no object becomes everlasting because at some point in time objects b and c will become unreachable. However, b may be an object that is not intended to be long-lived, so when a becomes unreachable, b should also be removed because c can always create another instance of b if needed. The short lifetime of b is prevented by the circular reference with c.

.NET allows you to break this circular reference with a *weak reference*. A component that holds a weak reference to another component can continue to access that component while it is still alive, but the weak reference does not keep the object alive. When a weak reference is created for an object, the *target* of the weak reference is added to the *weak-reference list*. When the garbage collector performs a collection, it searches the weak-reference list for objects in the graph of reachable objects. If the weak references cannot be found in this graph, the object can be treated as unreachable.

Creating a weak reference is straightforward:

```
// C#
class C
{
    private WeakReference b = null;
    public C(B bref)
    {
```

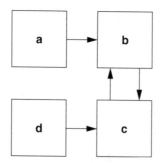

Figure 1.6   A circular reference containing a reference to a short-lived object

DEVELOPING APPLICATIONS WITH VISUAL STUDIO.NET

```
    b = new WeakReference(bref);
    }
    public void UseB(); // see later
}
```

This code shows the class c constructor, which is passed a reference to a B object. Code in the c class uses this object, so an instance of c holds on to a weak reference by creating an instance of the `System.WeakReference` class based on the b instance. The garbage collector does not treat the member `c.b` as a reference to a B object because it is a *weak* reference. Of course, the whole point of holding on to this reference is to allow a c object to access the B object. We accomplish this by creating a strong reference from the weak reference:

```
// C#
public void UseB()
{
    B bref = (B)b.Target;
    // use bref...
}
```

In this code I get a strong reference by casting the `Target` member of the `WeakReference` object to the B type. This generates a strong reference in the local variable `bref` and hence is scoped to the `UseB()` method. This means that I can access the object during the method, but the strong reference disappears once the method returns.

1.1.5 Security

Win32 security is based on threads obtaining an access token and then performing an action on a secured "object" (e.g., a file). The function that performs the action does an access check on the access token against an access control list (ACL) that has been created for the object. By and large, your code will not make explicit access checks because most of the things that you want to do will have a Win32 API that does the access check for you and then returns a handle to the object if the access succeeds.

This works fine as long as the code that is being executed can be guaranteed to be from a trusted source and therefore will not attempt to do something it shouldn't. The problem is that in this world of components, your application may use a component obtained from a source that you cannot control. This suspect code will be run under your access token, which means that it will get the access that has been granted to you and—crucially—the actions that it performs will be audited to you.

COM/COM+ presented one solution: the ability to run components in another process that could be configured to run under an identity with just enough privileges to perform the work that the component was supposed to do. However, this approach required action from an administrator and meant that the component was accessed through interprocess communication (IPC). Further, remotely accessed components also presented a problem because a remote user could try to mimic a valid user and attempt to perform actions as that user. Win32 prevents this situation with authentication: The remote user has to prove that he is who he says he is.

.NET security sits on top of Win32 security, so you always get Win32 access checking and authentication. In addition, you get *code access security (CAS)*. CAS enforces security on the basis of the identity of the code, not that of the user. So if you run code on your machine using your account, you may have access to your hard disk through Win32 access permissions, but .NET checks the source of the code (i.e., where it originates) and uses this information to determine whether to give that code permission to access your hard disk.

The criteria that .NET uses to determine permissions are called *evidence*: the directory where the code resides, the URL from which the code was downloaded, the security zone, the strong name of the assembly, and the publisher of the assembly. (A strong name is a cryptographic public key and is embedded in an assembly; I'll come back to this later.)

From the evidence, .NET uses a security policy to create a *permission set,* a group of permissions to perform certain actions. These actions are performed by the Framework Class Library, which is implicitly trusted by the system. The framework classes initiate the security checks to see if code has the permissions to perform the action. The basic idea is that the permissions given correspond to how trusted the code is.

However, the evidence does not involve just your code. The .NET security system gathers evidence from all the code in the stack. So if your code—written by you and installed on your machine—tries to access the hard disk, the security system will check against the security policies set for the machine to see if your code is allowed to do this. If it is, the security system will then check the code that called your code, determining its evidence and checking for the corresponding permissions. If calling code in the stack comes from an untrusted site, the permissions granted to *your* code will be reduced accordingly. This process is repeated for all the code in the call stack.

The permissions granted are based on the security policy. This policy is determined on three levels: machine settings, user settings, and domain settings (a domain is a unit of isolation within a process that hosts the .NET Runtime; I'll talk more about domains later in this chapter). The user and machine settings are stored in administrative files and configured with Framework SDK tools. The domain settings are specified at runtime in code.

The permissions granted to your code are not automatically passed to the calling code, and thus the calling code is not implicitly allowed to do any more than it is trusted to do. However, because permissions are determined on the basis of the evidence gathered from all code in the stack, your code may not have the permissions to do the work that it needs to do. .NET gives your code the ability to specify that it needs a certain permission, regardless of the trust level of the code that calls your code, in effect saying that the stack trace check should not be performed farther up the stack.

It is your responsibility to specify just the permissions that your code requires and give no more permissions. Furthermore, if your code calls utility code, you can specify the permissions that you are willing to allow that utility code to have. You have the documentation of the utility code, you know what that code should do, and hence you can protect your code from the utility code's performing an action it should not need to do. Because you specify these permissions in code at runtime, they are specific to the current application domain; these are the domain permissions.

Most Win32 developers are used to access token access checks (usually based on user identity), and if they are COM+ developers they are used to access checks being performed through COM+ roles. The good news is that you can still do this within your code. Figure 1.7 shows the relationship between

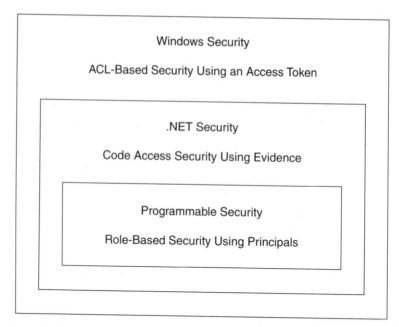

Windows Security

ACL-Based Security Using an Access Token

.NET Security

Code Access Security Using Evidence

Programmable Security

Role-Based Security Using Principals

Figure 1.7   Relationship of security checks in .NET managed code

Windows security and .NET security. The Framework Class Library provides classes to perform checks for a user's principal, and to check for NT group membership. In addition, you can apply attributes to classes and methods to specify the principals that have permission to execute that code.

1.2   Types

.NET extenders allow you to create your own types, and to make these types available to other code. Types are called *reference types* or *value types*, depending on how they are created and how their memory is maintained.

1.2.1   Classes

In general, classes are reference types.[1] Classes have features that are familiar to C++ developers: They can have constructors, methods, operators, and data

---

1. C# classes are reference types; however, managed C++ uses the __gc and __value modifiers to determine if a type is a reference or value type, which means that a class can be a value type and a struct can be a reference type.

members (fields), and members of classes have access specifiers that determine which code can access them. .NET classes are different from C++ classes in many respects. .NET classes support only single-implementation inheritance; they do not support the C++ concept of destructors (although they do support a "finalization" mechanism that is initiated through a managed C++ destructor or a C# destructor) and they do not support friends. In addition, .NET classes support events—a notification mechanism whereby other code can "register" that it wants to be notified when an event occurs.

.NET classes are similar to C++ classes in that they support multiple-interface inheritance, in which the class is responsible for implementing specific functionality. They support virtual methods and abstract classes so that you can support polymorphism. Finally, .NET classes—like all other features in .NET—are completely self-describing.

Typically .NET languages declare a .NET reference type as `class`. Here are examples from C# and managed C++:

```
// C#
class csPerson
{
    private ushort age = 0;
    private string name = null;
    public csPerson(){}
    public csPerson(ushort a, string s)
    { age = a; name = s; }
    public void Walk()
    { /* other code */ }
    // other code omitted
}
// managed C++
__gc class cppPerson
{
private:
    unsigned short age;
public:
    String* name;
    cppPerson() : age(0), name(0)
    { }
    cppPerson(unsigned short a, String* s)
                : age(a), name(s)
```

```
    { }
    void Walk();
    // other code omitted
};
```

How classes are declared is a language issue. Note, however, that in managed C++ a class declared without __gc will be an unmanaged class, and that to ensure that the class is a reference type you have to use the __gc modifier. __gc means that objects of the class are managed by the garbage collector. Objects of an unmanaged class are created on the unmanaged heap. "Unmanaged" in terms of classes does not mean that the code is native because all code in a source file that is compiled as managed code will be compiled to IL.[2] I have shown a managed class, but you can also have managed structs, meaning that the members of the garbage-collected type default to public access.

Note that C# does not have a concept of a scope resolution operator with respect to classes. This means that you have to provide the code for the C# class methods in line, rather than outside of the class as with C++. This makes sense because .NET types are described by metadata, which is imported into other assemblies that use these types. The equivalent in unmanaged C++ is to put class definitions in header files, thereby allowing the compiler to check against class member prototypes, and to have the class implementations in separate .cpp files.

Compared to the other .NET languages, managed C++ allows for finer-grained interoperation between managed or unmanaged code and data. Indeed, managed C++ allows you to have pointers to unmanaged objects in managed objects, and vice versa (which requires some special handling that I'll talk about in Chapters 4 and 7).

In the previous code I showed that the two classes have constructors—methods that are called when an instance of the class is created. In IL, constructors all have the same name—.ctor—but are differentiated by the class to which they belong and by the parameters that they take. All .NET classes are created on the managed heap, and .NET languages show this by requiring the use of a new operator:

---

2. This is specifically the case when you compile a file with the /clr switch. There are exceptions, which I will outline in Chapter 7.

```
// C#
csPerson richard = new csPerson();
richard.Walk();
// managed C++
cppPerson* richard = new cppPerson;
richard->Walk();
```

Again, language issues are showing: C# uses the dot operator (.) to access members of the class, and it requires that the parentheses be included when the default (parameterless) constructor is called. C++ allows you to call the default constructor without specifically giving a pair of empty parentheses, and it treats the value returned from the `new` operator as a pointer, so you must use pointer syntax (i.e., declare a pointer variable and access members with the arrow operator ->).

Although I understand this approach, I think it could cause a brief moment of confusion because the C++ mind might think that an instance of the class could be created on the stack:

```
cppPerson richard;
```

This example looks like good C++ code, but it is bad .NET code. The cppPerson class is marked with __gc and hence is managed by the garbage collector and *must* be created on the managed heap. You *cannot* create __gc classes on the stack.

.NET classes support overloading, so a class can have several methods that have the same name and differ only by their parameter lists. .NET classes also support conversion operators (conversion to different types) and what C++ programmers call *operators*—things like equality, greater than, and increment. Operators are essentially methods with a defined name (e.g., op_Equality, op_GreaterThan, op_Increment) that languages can map to operator symbols (in these cases ==, >, ++).

Data in .NET classes is stored in items called *fields*. A field can be a value type, in which case the data the field contains is stored in the memory allocated for the object on the managed heap, or it can be a reference to a reference type, in which case a pointer to the embedded object that is also allocated on the managed heap is stored in the object. .NET allows a syntactic feature called *properties*. Properties are accessed with the same syntax as fields, but they do not necessarily represent storage. A property is implemented through `get` and `set` methods, and the absence of one or the other leads to read-only and write-only properties. The fact that a property does *not* represent storage is important when you consider interfaces.

A class can also contain *events*. Events look like but are not data items; they are a metadata device to allow a class to generate events through calls to a *delegate*. A delegate is an object that contains information about a method to call, and it works similarly to C function pointers. Delegates are multicasting, which means that they can contain information about several methods; thus when code invokes a single delegate, many methods may be called. Because an event does not represent storage, events can also be part of an interface.

.NET classes support object-oriented concepts like polymorphism; they allow you to specify that a method is bound at runtime, using virtual methods. In managed C++, virtual methods are declared and overridden just as they are in unmanaged C++. In C#, a derived virtual method has to be marked with the `override` or `new` keywords. `override` means that the derived-class method should override the base-class method and thus be allowed to be called through a base-class reference, as is the case in C++. `new`, on the other hand, means that the derived class method is new, so it is hidden if it is called through a base-class reference.

Finally, .NET supports the notion of *abstract classes*, those that cannot be created at runtime and hence *must* be used as a base class. Abstract classes can contain code, so they allow you to provide a partial solution. Making the class abstract tells developers that they *must* provide some of their own code to use your code. In C#, methods can also be marked as abstract, and an abstract method is equivalent to a C++ pure virtual method:

```
// C#
abstract class csSomeCode
{
    public int ReturnZero(){ return 0; }
    public abstract int ReturnOne();
}
sealed class csTheRest : csSomeCode
{
    public override int ReturnOne(){return 1;}
}
```

```
// C++
__abstract __gc class cppSomeCode
{
    public:
    int ReturnZero(){ return 0; }
    virtual int ReturnOne() = 0;
};
__sealed __gc class cppTheRest : public cppSomeCode
{
public:
    int ReturnOne(){return 1;}
};
```

`csSomeCode.ReturnOne()` is marked as `abstract`, so that method is
not implemented in the class. The derived class has to provide that code.

The antithesis of abstract classes is *sealed classes*. A sealed class represents the final development of the type; hence, it cannot be used as a base
class. In the previous code `csTheRest` and `cppTheRest` are sealed classes,
so you cannot derive from either of them.

When you create an instance of a reference type, you get a pointer to the
instance. Some languages, like C++, make this obvious through the C++
pointer syntax; other languages, like C# and VB.NET, use object references.
When this pointer is passed as a method parameter, it is passed by value, but as
with pointers in C++, this means that you can access the reference that was
created outside of the method:

```
// C++
void cppUseIt(cppTheRest* p)
{
    int i = p->ReturnOne();
}
// use this code
cppTheRest* p = new cppTheRest;
cppUseIt(p);
```

In this code the object is created outside of `cppUseIt()`, but the pointer is
used within the method. If you want to create the object in the method and return
it, you can do this with a method that returns a pointer to another pointer:

```
// C++
void cppCreateIt(cppTheRest** p)
{
    *p = new cppTheRest;
}
// use this code
cppTheRest* p = 0;
cppCreateIt(&p);
```

C# object references are passed by value as well, but C# also gives you the ability to return an instance through a parameter. The equivalent of the previous two methods is as follows:

```
// C#
void csCreateIt(ref csTheRest p)
{
    p = new csTheRest();
}
static void csUseIt(csTheRest p)
{
    int i = p.ReturnOne();
}
// use this code
csTheRest p = null;
csCreateIt(ref p);
csUseIt(p);
```

The `ref` keyword means that data is passed from the caller to the method; the method could access the reference before creating a new instance. In this case that makes no sense, but I have used this keyword because it replicates the same code as in managed C++. In this example it makes better sense to use the C# `out` modifier, which indicates that the variable in question is intended to be only an `out` parameter and thus has to be created in the method.

1.2.2 Managed and Unmanaged C++ Classes

In managed C++ you have the option of determining whether a class is managed or unmanaged: A managed class has the `__gc` modifier; an unmanaged class, the `__nogc` modifier or no modifier. When you compile a source file with the `/clr` switch, all code will be compiled to IL whether or not the `__gc` modifier is used. There are exceptions, of course, as outlined in Chapter 7, but basically some C++ code, as well as functions that you have marked with appropriate pragmas, will always compile to native code.

In .NET the terms *managed* and *unmanaged* refer to how the storage for instances of the type are maintained. A managed type is always created with the .NET `new` operator, and always on the GC-managed heap. In managed C++, an unmanaged type can be created on the stack, but if it is created on the heap, the unmanaged version of `new` will be used and thus it will be created on the unmanaged C++ heap. Because unmanaged types are created on the unmanaged heap, you still have to use the unmanaged `delete` operator when you are finished with the object.

1.2.3 Value Types

Instances of value types are typically created on the stack. The rationale behind value types is that they are small types that are frequently created and freed, and the process of allocating and accessing these types on a heap would make them extremely inefficient. Most of the primitive types in .NET are value types—for example, the 16-bit integer type:

```
// C#
ushort age = 36;
csPerson me = new csPerson(age, "Richard");
```

When you declare an instance of a value type like this, space is allocated on the stack. A more compact way of writing the same thing is:

```
// C#
csPerson me = new csPerson(36, "Richard");
```

By default, parameters are passed to methods by value in C#, so a copy of the `ushort` value will be passed to the `csPerson` constructor. If the `ushort` type were a reference type, you would have to create an instance of it on the managed heap, and this would be an inefficient usage of memory because the `age` variable would be a pointer to a small amount of memory allocated on the managed heap, and the pointer actually takes up more storage than the value to which it points.

The csPerson class has two data members: a string member called name, and a ushort member called age. string is a reference type, so the class member is a pointer to the managed heap where the string is allocated. This is more obvious when you look at the managed C++ version, in which the data member is explicitly a pointer (String*). The ushort member is a value type, so it is not a pointer to storage on the managed heap. However, it *is* stored on the managed heap. The reason is that csPerson is a reference type, so instances have to be created with new. The new operator determines how much memory the object needs, including storage for its fields. For the name field the new operator allocates space for a pointer, but for age it allocates the actual space required for the ushort member (16 bits). This is shown in Figure 1.8.

In C# there are two categories of value types, enum and struct—for example:

```
// C#
public enum csSex : byte {unknown, Male, Female}
```

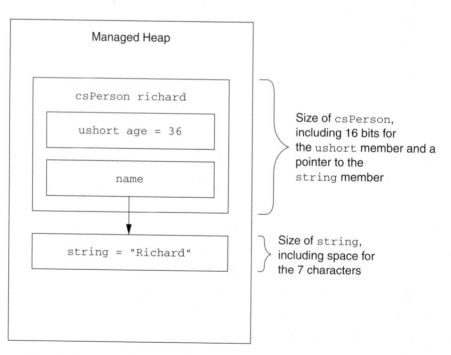

Figure 1.8   Reference types, value types, and the managed heap

DEVELOPING APPLICATIONS WITH VISUAL STUDIO.NET

```
public struct csAppearance
{
    public Color hairColor;
    public Color eyeColor;
}
```

Enums are implicitly derived from `System.Enum`, whereas structs are implicitly derived from `System.ValueType`. Note that you are allowed to specify the base type for the enum; this facility is also available in managed C++. Managed C++ is not as prescriptive as C#; a value type is any type that is marked with __value:

```
// C++
public __value enum cppSex : unsigned char
{ unknown, Male, Female };
public __value struct cppAppearance
{
    Color hairColor;
    Color eyeColor;
};
```

The C++ `enum` declaration will appear a little odd to C++ developers, but again it illustrates that C++ code compiled with the `/clr` switch follows different rules than code compiled without the switch.

C# and managed C++ disagree about what `struct` means. In C#, `struct` is a value type, but you still need to indicate the access of each member; in managed C++, `struct` can be a reference or a value type, but like unmanaged C++ all the members are implicitly public and hence accessible from code outside of the class.

The C# and C++ primitive types, all of which are value types, are summarized in Table 1.1. All value types are derived from `System.ValueType`, which means that they support the `ToString()` method. So although the following code looks odd, it does compile:

```
// C#
int i = 42;
string str1 = i.ToString();
string str2 = 43.ToString();

// C++
int i = 42;
String* str1 = i.ToString();
String* str2 = 43.ToString();
```

Table 1.1 .NET types

C# Type	C++ Type	Size (bits)	.NET Type
bool	bool	8	Boolean
char	wchar_t	16	Char
byte	unsigned char	8	Byte
sbyte	char	8	SByte
short	short	16	Int16
ushort	unsigned short	16	UInt16
int	long*	32	Int32
uint	unsigned long	32	UInt32
long	__int64	64	Int64
ulong	unsigned __int64	64	UInt64
float	float	32	Single
double	double	64	Double
decimal	– †	64	Decimal

*It is interesting that for managed C++ on a 32-bit system, int and unsigned int are 32 bits each, but that on all systems the C++ long type is always 32 bits. This contrasts with C#, in which int is always 32 bits and long is always 64 bits.
†C++ does not have a native decimal type.

All value types are implicitly sealed; this means that they cannot be used as base classes. There are three ways to initialize a value type:

1. Create an instance, and then initialize each member individually.
2. Create an instance, and pass values to a constructor.
3. Create an array, and use an initializer list for it.

If you are creating many items or if the value type has many members, the first method can involve writing lots of code:

```
// C#
csAppearance richard;
richard.hairColor = Color.Black;
richard.eyeColor = Color.Brown;
```

DEVELOPING APPLICATIONS WITH VISUAL STUDIO.NET

Here I allocate the value type on the stack, so `new` is not called. The C# compiler creates a local `csAppearance` variable and then calls the `initobj` IL opcode, which zeros all the members of the value type. After that I explicitly initialize the members to the values I want to use.

The second method reduces the amount of code but needs a constructor:

```
// C++
public __value struct cppAppearance
{
    cppAppearance(Color h, Color e)
    {
        hairColor = h; eyeColor = e;
    }
    Color hairColor;
    Color eyeColor;
};
cppAppearance GetAppearance()
{
    return cppAppearance(Color::Black, Color::Brown);
}
```

Managed C++ allows you to call the constructor of a value type when it is created on the stack. In this code I am creating a `cppAppearance` object on the stack and initializing it through its constructor. The method returns a `cppAppearance` object, again via the stack, so a copy is made.

C# does not allow you to call the constructor of a value type like this; the equivalent code in C# requires that you use the `new` operator. The following code defines a function that creates and initializes a managed array:

```
// C#
public struct csAppearance
{
    public csAppearance(Color h, Color e)
    {
        hairColor = h; eyeColor = e;
    }
    Color hairColor;
    Color eyeColor;
}
csAppearance[] GetGrimesAppearances()
{
```

```
        csAppearance robin;
        robin = new csAppearance(Color.Wheat, Color.Blue);
        csAppearance rosemary;
        rosemary = new csAppearance(Color.LightYellow,
            Color.Blue);
        csAppearance richard;
        richard = new csAppearance(Color.Black, Color.Brown);
        csAppearance rebecca;
        rebecca = new csAppearance(Color.Brown, Color.Green);
        return new csAppearance[]
            {robin, rosemary, richard, rebecca};
    }
```

The initial four lines of the function `GetGrimesAppearances()` make it *look* like you are creating instances on the managed heap. However, the C# compiler knows that `csAppearance` is a value type and treats the call to `new` as your indication that you want to call a constructor, and *not* that you want to create the value type on the managed heap.

I find this usage a little confusing and inconsistent because on the one hand you create a value type instance on the stack without calling `new`, but on the other hand you call `new` specifically to create a reference type instance on the managed heap. The requirement of calling `new` so that you can call a constructor is inconsistent. Incidentally, managed C++ will give you an error if you attempt to create a value type using the managed `new` (although if you choose, you can create a value type on the unmanaged C++ heap with the unmanaged `new` operator).

In the `GetGrimesAppearances()` method I created an array of `csAppearance` objects. Managed arrays are reference types, so they must be created with the `new` operator. I do not give the size of the array because I have used an initializer list showing the third way to initialize a value type with a value. C# deduces the size of the array from the size of the initializer list. Notice that items in the initializer list are created on the stack, but the actual array object is returned from the method to code where this stack frame no longer exists. In this code the values in the individual `csAppearance` objects are copied by value into the memory allocated for the array.

A more convenient way to do the same thing is to combine the creation of the array with an initializer list that has the call to the `csAppearance` constructors:

```csharp
// C#
csAppearence[] GetGrimesAppearances()
{
    return new csAppearance[]
    {
        new csAppearance(Color.Wheat, Color.Blue),
        new csAppearance(Color.LightYellow,
                        Color.Blue),
        new csAppearance(Color.Black, Color.Brown),
        new csAppearance(Color.Brown, Color.Green)
    };
}
```

Again new is called merely to ensure that the appropriate constructor is used. Managed C++ also supports the creation of initializer lists for arrays (I will cover the syntax for C++ managed arrays in Chapter 7):

```cpp
// C++
cppAppearance GetGrimesAppearances() []
{
    cppAppearance grimesSiblings[] = {
        cppAppearance(Color::Wheat, Color::Blue),
        cppAppearance(Color::LightYellow,
                     Color::Blue),
        cppAppearance(Color::Black, Color::Brown),
        cppAppearance(Color::Brown, Color::Green)
    };
    return grimesSiblings;
}
```

This code makes more sense than the C# equivalent in the respect that you do not need to apply new to the value type to call its constructor. I find, though, that it is odd insofar as grimesSiblings *looks* like it is being allocated on the stack while the compiler actually creates it on the managed heap.

Like reference types, value types can have methods, properties, events, and fields. They can even have virtual methods. However, value types are always sealed, so no types can be derived from them. Value types have virtual methods to support derivation from interfaces (whose methods are *always* virtual) and to allow you to override the System.ValueType methods.

1.2.4 Boxing

Consider this code in managed C++:

```
// C++
Console::WriteLine(S"the value is {0}", 42);
```

This seemingly innocuous code will not compile. The reason is that the static method `Console::WriteLine()` has many overloaded forms, but none that take a string and an integer. The nearest form looks like this:

```
static void WriteLine(String*, Object*);
```

The format string is passed in the `String*` parameter, but the second parameter is an instance of `Object`. This is an example of a frequent situation that occurs when a reference type is required but the variable that you wish to use is a value type. There must be a mechanism to convert a value type to a reference type and vice versa. .NET obliges here with mechanisms called *boxing* and *unboxing*. Boxing is the conversion of a value type to a reference type. It involves creating an object on the managed heap that has the same fields as the value type. The runtime creates this object and initializes its fields with the values in the value type. The term *boxing* comes from the fact that the runtime creates a new instance of the value type wrapped ("boxed") by a runtime-created wrapper. This process is illustrated in Figure 1.9.

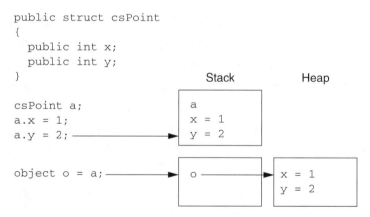

Figure 1.9   Boxing

DEVELOPING APPLICATIONS WITH VISUAL STUDIO.NET

In C#, boxing occurs automatically. However, because boxing involves creating a new object on the managed heap, C++ requires that you use the __box keyword so that it is clear that a new object is being created:

```
// C++; use the public type defined previously
csPoint a;
a.x = 1; a.y = 2;
Object* o = __box(a);
```

The boxed object acts as a wrapper—a copy of the value type—and has all the members that the value type has (those inherited from `ValueType` and any other members the value type defines), but it is created *on the managed heap.* Because it has all the methods of the value type, if you obtain the type using `GetType()` for both the boxed and unboxed objects, the type object returned will refer to the same type.

Boxing is potentially dangerous because a copy by value is made to create the boxed type, yet in C# it looks as if a reference assignment is made:

```
// C#
csPoint a;
a.x = 1; a.y = 2;
object o = a;
((csPoint)o).x = 42; ((csPoint)o).y = 43;
if ((((csPoint)o).x == a.x)
        && (((csPoint)o).y == a.y))
    Console.WriteLine("boxing hasn't worked!");
```

The assignment to the reference type `o` results in the creation of a new object (*but the* `new` *operator is not used!*), so changing its members has no effect on the value type on which it is based. A novice seeing a reference type being assigned to an object will assume that the assignment to a reference is made, and thus changing the members of a reference changes the members of the object to which it refers. In this respect, managed C++ is far clearer about what you are doing and makes the code far easier to understand.

Unboxing involves creating a value type from a reference type, so you need to tell the runtime what value type you want. The preceding code shows an example.

1.2.5 Managed Arrays

I have already shown some examples of using managed arrays, and I will discuss the new syntax of managed arrays in managed C++ in Chapter 7. In this
section I want to make a few general comments about arrays.

The Framework Class Library has an abstract class called `System.Array`;
this is the base class for the arrays that you can use in .NET. A look at the IL
generated when you use arrays shows that there are IL instructions for single-
dimensional arrays (called *vectors*) and multidimensional arrays. When you
create an array, the compiler uses the appropriate IL. Vectors always have zero-
based indexes, whereas the multidimensional-array syntax allows you to specify
a lower bound other than zero. C# and C++, however, require that all lower
bounds, for both vectors and multidimensional arrays, are always zero.

When you declare a vector or array, you have to identify how many elements
are required. The compiler creates an instance of the array on the managed
heap that has sufficient space for all of the elements needed. So if you create an
array of a value type, sufficient space is allocated on the heap for all of the elements, and the values are copied to this buffer:

```
// C#
int[] tens = new int[2];
tens[0] = 10;
tens[1] = 20;
```

When you allocate an array of reference types, space is reserved for
pointers to the type that you specify, so you have to allocate those objects
yourself:

```
// C#
Uri[] dotneturls = new Uri[2];
dotneturls[0] = new Uri("http://www.microsoft.com/net");
dotneturls[1] = new Uri("http://www.grimes.demon.co.uk");
```

Accessing array elements involves specifying an index. The IL opcodes that
access vector and array members implicitly perform a bounds check and will
throw `IndexOutOfRangeException` if the index is out of bounds. You cannot
treat a managed array as just an indexed access to a buffer of memory as you
can in C.

All arrays implicitly derive from `System.Array`, so you can call any of the methods defined for this class. Thus, to get the total number of elements in an array, you can access the `Length` property; and to get the number of elements in a dimension, you can call the `GetLength()` method. `System.Array` implements `IList`, so you have random access to items through an *indexer* (a property that takes one or more indices and typically is accessed through the square-bracket syntax). `Array` also implements `IEnumerable`, which means that you can have serial access to its members using an *enumerator,* typically through the C# or VB.NET `foreach` construct.

1.2.6 Member Access

Members of each type have a defined access specification. .NET has seven levels of access, as shown in Table 1.2. C++ is far more expressive than C# because it allows you to use all seven levels, whereas C# allows you to use only six.

The C++ syntax may appear a little odd to hardened C++ programmers, but once you know the rules it becomes simple. The first part of the C++ access specifier determines the access granted to types within the current assembly; the second part gives the access granted to types outside of the assembly. Thus `public protected` means that any type within the current assembly can access the member, but in external assemblies only types derived from the current type can access the member. `protected private` means that only types in the current assembly and types derived from the current type have access to the member.

The CLS defines derived types as `family` and types in the same assembly as `assem`. The last access level in Table 1.2—`privatescope`–is interesting. It is generated automatically for static variables in methods. Consider this code:

```
// C++
public __gc class Incrementer
{
private:
    static int m_x = 0;
public:
    int Inc()
```

```
    {
        static int x;
        x++;
        return x;
    }
};
```

The single method, `Inc()`, has a static variable, `x`. In effect, this variable is a class static member because if you create several instances of `Incrementer` and call `Inc()` on each instance, the same variable will be incremented. In

Table 1.2   Member access levels in .NET

CLS Equivalent	C#	C++	Meaning
public	public	public public or public	Accessible by any code
famorassem	protected internal	public protected	Accessible by types in the same assembly, or by types derived from the containing type, whether in the same assembly or not
assem	internal	public private	Accessible by code in the same assembly
family	protected	protected protected or protected	Accessible by code in types derived from the containing type, whether in the same assembly or not
famandassem		protected private	Accessible by code in types derived from the containing type only if they are in the same assembly
private	private	private private or private	Accessible only by code in the containing type
privatescope	(used on method static variables)	(used on method static variables)	Accessible only by code in the method where the static variable is declared

fact, the static variable x in Inc() is essentially the same as the private static member m_x, except that x is accessible only in the scope of the method Inc(), whereas m_x can be accessed by any code in the class. For this reason the compiler marks x as privatescope, and it marks the class static member m_x as private.

1.2.7 Common Language Specification

The Common Language Specification (CLS) is a set of suggestions that allow types written in one language to be used by code in other languages. On the surface the mere existence of the CLS may appear to imply that .NET is not language neutral—because, the argument goes, if it were language neutral, the IL created by any language compiler would be executed by the runtime. In fact, that statement is true, with or without the CLS, because as I have already mentioned, the .NET Runtime executes only one language: IL. The point of the CLS is to allow you to write code that has certain language features (features that do not have a direct correspondence to IL) that will be usable in code written in other languages.

Let me give a quick example. Implementation inheritance is part of IL, and all languages must recognize inheritance (even if the language does not use inheritance itself). Inheritance is not mentioned in the CLS because a language that does not recognize all the benefits of inheritance (virtual methods, polymorphism, and so on) loses so much that it cannot be a .NET language.

On the other hand, the keywords that a language uses are specific to that language. They have no effect on the IL produced (because the whole point of a compiler is to translate these language keywords to IL), so there is nothing sacred about the keyword that a specific language uses. Hence, to be CLS compliant, a language must have a mechanism to allow it to use, and to create types that have members that use, names that are keywords in that language. Consider this C# enum:

```
// C#
public enum friend {ENEMY, ACQUAINTANCE, BUDDY}
```

friend is a keyword in C++ (although it is not used by the managed extensions), but to allow the C# friend type to be used in C++, there must be a way to indicate to the C++ compiler that `friend` is a type and not a C++ keyword. And there is: the `__identifier` operator:

```cpp
// C++
void MeetPerson(String* name, __identifier(friend) relation)
{
    switch(relation)
    {
    case __identifier(friend)::ENEMY:
        Ignore(name);
        break;
    case __identifier(friend)::ACQUAINTANCE:
        SayHi(name);
        break;
    case __identifier(friend)::BUDDY:
        Hug(name);
        break;
    }
}
```

As you can see, the identifier `friend` can be used in C++ as a type name. The excessive use of the `__identifier` operator makes this code look a little ugly, but it is certainly usable. C++ provides the `__identifier` operator so that the code complies with CLS Rule 4: "CLS-compliant languages [must] supply a mechanism for referencing identifiers that coincide with keywords."

There are 41 rules in the Common Language Specification—all documented in the .NET SDK. A type that follows these rules is called *CLS compliant*. Thus, to allow a compiler to determine which types it can safely use, you should mark public compliant types with the `[CLSCompliant]` attribute (I'll explain attributes later). If all types in an assembly are CLS compliant, you can apply `[CLSCompliant]` as an assembly-level attribute. This is a voluntary action, and when you apply this attribute you must check that the type to which you apply it is indeed compliant; your compiler will not do the check for you.

If a type is marked with `[CLSCompliant(true)]` (or the assembly is marked with this and the type is not `[CLSCompliant(false)]`), any members of the type that are not CLS compliant must be marked with `[CLSCompliant(false)]` and a compliant alternative should be offered.

The CLS is a subset of the Common Type System (CTS). The CTS describes the basics of how to define types, stating rules governing names, members, and qualities. Again, these rules are well documented in the .NET Framework SDK, but unlike the CLS, compilers must follow these rules; otherwise the types created will not be .NET types.

1.3 Other .NET Features

The previous section outlined the basic features of .NET. In this section I will cover some more features that, although important, are not quite as fundamental.

1.3.1 Interfaces

Interface programming is a very powerful technique. Interfaces describe behavior; they do not represent data storage, nor do they represent implementation. Implementation is the responsibility of classes.

Imagine that you have an interface called `IStorage` that defines the behavior of storing data. You could have some classes that store data to a disk—a floppy disk or a hard disk. These classes are all related because they represent "storage," so they could be part of a class hierarchy (perhaps a base class `Disk` would have common code used to access both floppy and hard disks). Equally, you could have a compact flash or smart media device, both of which represent ways to store data, but they are certainly *not* disks and so should not be involved in the `Disk` hierarchy. A compact flash device has the same storage behavior as a hard disk, but a compact flash device is not a disk and a hard disk is not a memory device. This means that there is no common base class to allow you to treat instances of these storage types polymorphically.

Interfaces solve this problem because they simply indicate a behavior that a type must implement. This means that a type can derive from many interfaces without violating the .NET requirement that a type can derive from only a single class. So you could provide an interface, `IStorage`, with methods `Read()` and `Write()` representing data access in the storage device. You could provide classes like `Memory` and `Disk` that would derive from this interface and would implement these methods for a generic type of storage. Furthermore, you could derive from these base classes for specific devices, like `HardDisk`,

FloppyDisk, and CompactFlash, and yet all of these entities would have their storage behavior defined by the IStorage interface.

A great example of interfaces can be found in the .NET collection classes (see Figure 1.10). You have a choice here about how you access the data in the collection and how the data is stored internally. The IList interface gives random access to data in a collection, and thus you can access individual items by their index. Three general-purpose classes can be accessed in this way: Array, which represents an array of a fixed size; ArrayList, whose size is dynamically increased as needed; and StringCollection, which is a dynamically sized array specifically for strings.

If random access is not important to you because you will always read items in the collection in a specified order, you can use a collection that implements an IEnumerable interface. This interface gives access to an enumerator object that can be used to access members serially from beginning to end.

However, you may decide that you want to keep a collection of associated name/value pairs, in which case you can use either one of the dictionary classes (HashTable, SortedList, StringDictionary, or ListDictionary) or the NameValueCollection class. The dictionary classes implement IDictionary, which gives access to an enumerator that implements IDictionaryEnumerator, which gives serial access to name/value pairs. The NameValueCollection class provides random access to the data, through an indexer.

The power of interfaces here is that the consumer of data in a collection does not care how the information is stored. The consumer is concerned only with the access interface on the collection. Here is an example of a consumer:

```
// C#
public void DumpData(IEnumerable container)
{
    foreach(object o in container)
        Console.WriteLine(o.ToString());
}
```

The C# foreach construct calls GetEnumerator() on the container object to return an IEnumerator interface reference. The construct uses this

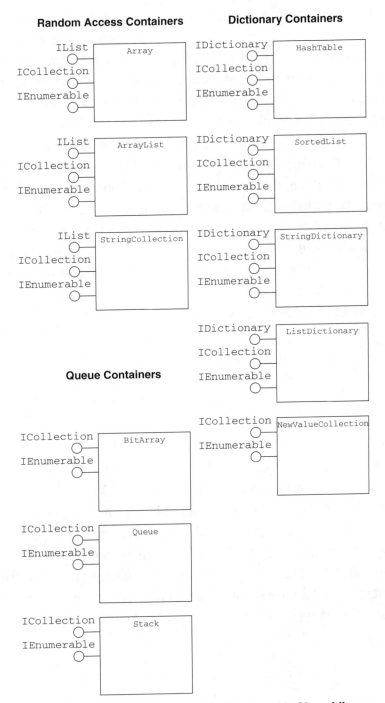

Figure 1.10 Collection classes in the .NET Framework Class Library

interface to access the members in the `container` object by accessing `IEnumerator.Current` and calls `IEnumerator.MoveNext()` to determine if the `foreach` loop should continue and fill the `Current` property with the next item.

The `DumpData()` method just prints out data; it does not take an object reference because in this context it is irrelevant whether the data is stored in an array or a queue. On the other hand, the producer of the data is concerned with how the data is stored. So if the producer knows how many items to pass to `DumpData()`, it can use the `Array` class, which has the advantage that a single allocation is performed. If the producer does not know how many items it will store when it first creates the container, it can create an instance of `ArrayList` and indicate an initial allocation, but when the collection's capacity has been exceeded it will resize itself. Because the `IEnumerable` interface is passed to the `DumpData()` method, this method has no knowledge (nor does it need any) about how the data was stored.

Now consider the following example:

```
// C#
string[] beatles = new string[4];
beatles[0] = "John";
beatles[1] = "Paul";
beatles[2] = "Ringo";
beatles[3] = "George";
DumpData(beatles);
```

In this case the C# language implicitly casts the `beatles` array instance to an `IEnumerable` interface pointer. In addition, C# allows you to perform the cast explicitly using the `as` keyword, and because the array is derived from `IEnumerable`, the cast in this example will always succeed.[3] However, if you have a base-class reference and you are not sure whether the object it refers to implements the interface that interests you, then the `as` keyword will either cast to the interface or return `null` if the cast fails. The `as` keyword, as in the following example, is equivalent to the `dynamic_cast<>` operator in managed C++:

---

3. The type of `beatles` is `String[]`, a vector of `String` objects. Vectors are an IL type derived from `Array`.

```csharp
// C#
public void UseBand(object band)
{
    IEnumerable e = band as IEnumerable;
    if (e != null) DumpData(e);
}
// use the method
UseBand(beatles);
```

Interfaces do not contain storage, but they can contain properties. Properties are a syntactic device for presenting members of a type to a user as if the members were fields. Properties can be part of an interface because they are implemented through methods. This means that the data that properties change or return can be sourced from locations other than the current object (e.g., from a file or a database), or they can even be generated dynamically.

In addition, interfaces can contain events. When an event is part of an interface, it does not represent storage. Instead, it means that as part of the behavior of the object that implements the interface, when something happens in the object, an event may be generated and another object can "register" to receive this event. Types that implement the interface must provide storage for the event.

As you use the .NET Framework Class Library, you'll become aware that many classes have methods that take interface parameters or are extended by implementation of an object with a specified interface. Interfaces are clearly useful in terms of implementations. Interfaces are also useful as notation devices. In this case the interface does not contain any members, and the idea is that when presented with an object, code can check the type of object passed to it by checking for a specific interface. For example, here's a class hierarchy:

```csharp
// C#
public interface IPrintablePublicly {}
public class Document
{
    public Print(){ /* print the doc */ }
}
public class PublicDocument : Document, IPrintablePublicly
{
    public PublicDocument(Stream docdata)
    { /* store stream */}
```

```
      // data that can be printed
}
public class SecretDocument : Document
{
    public SecretDocument(Stream docdata)
    { /* store stream */}
    // data that must not be printed
}
```

Using one of the collection objects shown in Figure 1.10, you can pass a collection of `PublicDocument` and `SecretDocument` objects. However, because most of them contain `System.Object` references, the container will have base-class references:

```
// C#
ArrayList docs = new ArrayList();
docs.Add(new PublicDocument(strProductList));
docs.Add(new PublicDocument(strPriceList));
docs.Add(new SecretDocument(strEmployeeSalaries));
PrintForPublication(docs);
```

A function like `PrintForPublication()` must be able to distinguish between documents that are printable and those that are not. One way to do this is to check for the `IPrintablePublicly` interface by using the C# `is` statement:

```
// C#
public void PrintForPublication(IEnumerable docs)
{
    foreach (object o in docs)
    {
        Document doc = (Document)o;
        if (doc is IPrintablePublicly)
        {
            doc.Print();
        }
    }
}
```

The `is` keyword checks whether a cast will be successful without performing the cast. The beauty of this technique is that the code is clean and clear. The abstract base class has the code to print documents whether the intended

```
```

audience is the general public or a restricted subset. Because this code is the same for all audiences of the print run, it makes no sense to put it in a virtual method. The decision in `PrintForPublication()` is made according to whether the document has been marked as publicly available or not. Another way to do the same thing would be to use an attribute, but the disadvantage is that the reflection API is more complicated than the simple `is` check, as you'll see shortly.

1.3.2 Metadata and Attributes

The most important feature of .NET is metadata. The .NET Runtime is based on and cannot function without metadata. Metadata underpins the type checking built into the runtime, which in itself is an integral part of the security system. Metadata is used by the runtime to determine the facilities that a type requires and to determine the context in which the object should run. Native code typically relies on compile-time checking, but with managed code the runtime uses metadata to perform its checks. And because metadata can describe *everything* in .NET, the runtime always knows what it is loading and running.

When you compile an assembly, the compiler adds into a part of the assembly (called the *manifest*) a list of the assemblies that your code will use. The IL statements that make up your types describe exactly the members of the other types they call. When your code is executed, the .NET type system reads the type that you require, loads the requested assembly (after the required security and version checks have been performed), and reads the metadata of the member that your code wants to call. If this description does not match the description of the member that your code wants to call, the type will not be loaded. Your code will never call code that it does not intend to call.

Microsoft has defined the metadata specification, covering everything thought to be needed to define types. However, because Microsoft's developers recognize that they are neither infallible nor psychic, they allow you to extend metadata so that you can accommodate types that they have not envisioned. You extend metadata with classes called *custom attributes*.

Table 1.3 `AttributeTargets` enumerated values

Assembly	Event	Parameter
Class	Field	Property
Constructor	Interface	ReturnValue
Delegate	Method	Struct
Enum	Module	All

Custom attributes can be applied to any item in a source file. Table 1.3 shows the values in the `AttributeTargets` enumeration, which indicate the items to which attributes can be applied.

Using an attribute is straightforward. The general format is to give the name of the attribute in square brackets in front of the item to which the attribute will be applied. Attributes can be applied to assemblies and to modules (the files that make up assemblies, as explained later), and because there is no "item" in the source file that represents these entities, languages provide a mechanism to explicitly mention whether the attribute is for the assembly or the module. In addition, in some situations applying an attribute is ambiguous. For example, in the following code it is not clear whether the attribute is applied to the method itself or to the return value of the method:

```
// C#
class ExampleClass
{
    [Info] public int ReturnZero(){return 0;}
}
```

Languages provide a mechanism that uses a prefix to disambiguate attributes. C# and C++ differ in the exact form of some prefixes (see Table 1.4).

C++ is more expressive than C# (it has a prefix for each of the individual attribute targets in the `AttributeTargets` enumeration). There are no prefixes in C# for interfaces and constructors (basically because there is nothing that could be confused with these items). C# uses `type` for classes, structs, and enums, whereas C++ explicitly says which type, even though that distinction is not strictly necessary:

DEVELOPING APPLICATIONS WITH VISUAL STUDIO.NET

Table 1.4 Prefixes used to disambiguate attributes

C#	C++
assembly	assembly
—	constructor
—	delegate
event	event
field	field
—	interface
method	method
module	module
param	parameter
property	property
return	returnvalue
type	class, struct, enum

```
// C#
[type: MyClassAttr] class csMyClass {}
[type: MyStructAttr] struct csMyStruct{}
[type: MyEnumAttr] enum csMyEnum{}

// C++
[class: MyClassAttr] __gc class cppMyClass {};
[struct: MyStructAttr] __gc struct cppMyStruct{};
[enum: MyEnumAttr] __value enum cppMyEnum{};
```

Note that by convention, attribute classes have the suffix `Attribute`. However, C# and C++ allow you to omit the suffix, so in the example here, `[MyClassAttr]` is implemented by a class called `MyClassAttrAttribute`.

1.3.2.1 Types of Attributes

Attributes add metadata through an IL directive called `.custom`, and for this reason they are called *custom attributes*. There are three types of custom attributes: custom attributes, distinguished custom attributes, and pseudo custom attributes.

Pseudo custom attributes are custom attributes because they have the general syntax (square brackets, mandatory and optional parameters), but they are called *pseudo* because unlike other custom attributes, they do not extend metadata. Instead they change existing metadata. Two good examples are the attributes `[Serializable]` and `[NonSerialized]`, which are used to indicate whether the fields in a class are serialized.

Microsoft recognized that serialization of types is a necessity, so it included a flag in metadata called `tdSerializable` that can be applied to types and indicates that the fields of the specified type should be serialized. The `[Serializable]` attribute merely turns on this flag for all fields in a type. If the type contains fields that the developer does not want serialized, she can apply the `[NonSerialized]` attribute to those fields, which has the effect of attaching the `fdNotSerialized`[4] metadata flag to the field—for example:

```
// C#
[Serializable]
public class csSquare
{
    private int width;
    private int height;
    [NonSerialized] private int area = -1;
    public csSquare(int w, int h)
    { width = w; height = h; }
    public int Area
    {
        get{ if (area == -1) area = width * height;
            return area; }
    }
}
```

This reference type can be serialized, but in that case only the `width` and `height` fields will be serialized. The `area` field has been marked with `[NonSerialized]`, so it will not be serialized. The reason is that the area is obtained through the `Area` property, which will calculate the area at runtime if it has not already been set.

---

4. Note the inconsistency here: The `[NonSerialized]` attribute changes the `fdNotSerialized` flag.

The C# compiler will generate the following IL:

```
// IL
.class public auto ansi
    serializable beforefieldinit csSquare
    extends [mscorlib]System.Object
{
    .field private int32 width
    .field private int32 height
    .field private notserialized int32 area
    .method public hidebysig specialname
        rtspecialname instance void
        .ctor(int32 w, int32 h) cil managed;
    .method public hidebysig specialname instance
        int32 get_Area() cil managed;
    .property instance int32 Area()
    {
        .get instance int32 csSquare::get_Area()
    }
}
```

This code is generated by the `ildasm.exe` tool being run on the assembly that contains this class. This tool reads all the metadata in the assembly and displays the types and their members, as well as the IL code in the methods. It is worth pointing out that in IL a class is identified by its assembly and namespace, so `[mscorlib]System.Object` refers to the `System.Object` class in the `mscorlib` assembly. As I mentioned earlier, custom attributes are identified by the `.custom` directive. In this example the `.custom` directive does not appear because the attributes are pseudo custom attributes that add the `serializable` IL modifier to the class and the `notserialized` modifier to the `area` field. Another pseudo custom attribute of note is `[DllImport]`. This attribute affects an IL modifier called `pinvokeimpl`, which specifies that a method is implemented not by a class member, but by a method exported from a native DLL. I will talk more about this attribute in Chapter 4.

The second type of custom attribute is called a *distinguished custom attribute*. Such attributes do not correspond to metadata defined by Microsoft. Distinguished custom attributes have data that is stored in the assembly alongside the items to which they apply. In IL, distinguished custom attributes are indicated by the .custom keyword. However, even though there is no specific metadata flag for the attribute, the runtime knows about it and acts on it. It is a *custom* attribute because metadata has been extended to take the attribute into account, but *distinguished* because the runtime knows about it.

An example of a distinguished custom attribute is [OneWay], which can be found in the System.Runtime.Remoting.Messaging namespace. [OneWay] indicates to the runtime that a method does not have any return values, or any out or ref parameters; as a consequence, callers of the method are not interested in any return from the method (including any exceptions thrown by the method). You simply "fire and forget" the method. When you call the method in another domain (defined in a later section), .NET remoting will be used. The .NET remoting infrastructure knows about the [OneWay] attribute and will act on it. Here's an example of using [OneWay]:

```
public class Listener
{
   [OneWay] public void InformMe(string action){}
}
```

Here's the IL generated for the class:

```
.class public auto ansi beforefieldinit Listener
       extends [mscorlib]System.Object
{
   .method public hidebysig specialname rtspecialname
    instance void .ctor() cil managed;
   .method public hidebysig instance
    void InformMe(string action)
    cil managed
   {
    .custom instance void
     [mscorlib]System.Runtime.Remoting.Messaging
       .OneWayAttribute::.ctor() = ( 01 00 00 00 )
     // other code
   }
}
```

The important feature is the .custom line, which allocates space for the custom attribute. The name, assembly, and namespace of the attribute—as well as the name of the constructor on the attribute class and any data that should be passed to the constructor (in this case no value is passed to the constructor; the four byte values indicate that there are no constructor parameters)—are stored as metadata.

DEVELOPING APPLICATIONS WITH VISUAL STUDIO.NET

When this class is loaded, the runtime can read the metadata attached to the class, by using the `GetAttributes()` static method on the `System.ComponentModel.TypeDescriptor` class. When `GetAttributes()` is called, the attribute objects for the attributes that have been applied to the class will be created and the appropriate constructor will be called on each attribute object. The important point here is that the attribute objects will be created only when the reflection API is called. You do not incur the overhead of the attribute objects if the reflection API is not called.

1.3.2.2 *Writing Attributes*

The final type of attribute is called simply *custom attribute*. Custom attributes also add metadata through the `.custom` IL keyword, but unlike distinguished custom attributes, these attributes mean nothing to the runtime.

The Framework Class Library contains many custom attributes, and you can define your own as well. Defining your own custom attribute is straightforward: All you have to do is create a class derived from `System.Attribute` and mark it with the `[AttributeUsage]` attribute to indicate the items to which your attribute can be applied. In addition, `[AttributeUsage]` indicates whether your attribute can be applied more than once to a single item and whether the attribute is inherited when it is applied to a class that is a base class for another class. The items to which you can apply an attribute are described in the `AttributeTargets` enumeration in Table 1.3.

Attributes can have mandatory parameters or named, optional parameters. *Mandatory parameters* are implemented through constructor parameters on the attribute class; named, *optional parameters* are applied through fields or properties on the attribute class—for example:

```
// C#
[AttributeUsage(AttributeTargets.Class,
                Inherited = false,
                AllowMultiple = true)]
public class CommentAttribute : Attribute
{
    private string comment;
    private bool isImportant = false;
    public CommentAttribute(string str)
```

```
    { comment = str; }
    // read only
    public string Comment { get{ return comment; } }
    public override string ToString()
    {
        string s = comment;
        s += (isImportant ? ": Important!!"
                            : ": Ignore me");
        return s;
    }
    public bool IsImportant
    { set{ isImportant = value; } }
}
```

The `CommentAttribute` class can be applied to classes only because I have used the `AttributeTargets.Class` enumerated value. Compilers read the attribute usage of an attribute before applying the attribute to an item, and they will issue an error if the attribute is being applied to an inappropriate item. If you omit `[AttributeUsage]` from an attribute class, the default target `All` will be used.

Because parameters passed through constructors are unnamed, the order in which they appear is important (sometimes they are called *positional* parameters). In general, unnamed parameters should be treated as mandatory parameters. You can provide overloaded constructors that provide default values for some unnamed parameters—for example:

```
// C#
public CommentAttribute()
{ comment = "no comment"; }
```

However, if you consider the usage of such an attribute, it is not clear what an attribute user should or should not use as parameters. The convention that unnamed parameters are mandatory and named parameters are optional makes the attribute usage much clearer.

Named parameters are implemented through public fields or properties on the attribute class. The choice of using a field or a property is determined by whether you want the parameter to be read-only (in which case a property with a `get` accessor is the appropriate choice) or read/write (in which case a field is appropriate). Of course, properties are implemented through methods, which means that when they are accessed, code can be run, so you may decide to do more in the property accessor than merely setting or getting a value. The IsImportant property on the [Comment] attribute is a named parameter and can be used like this:

```
// C#
[Comment("FirstClass")]
class FirstClass{}
[Comment("SecondClass", IsImportant = false)]
class SecondClass{}
[Comment("ThirdClass", IsImportant = true)]
class ThirdClass{}
```

In this code, FirstClass and SecondClass have the unimportant comments of "FirstClass" and "SecondClass", respectively, whereas the comment "ThirdClass" applied to ThirdClass is considered important. Here are the appropriate .custom tags from the IL for these classes:

```
// IL
.class private auto ansi beforefieldinit FirstClass
    extends [mscorlib]System.Object
{
    .custom instance void
     CommentAttribute::.ctor(string)
    // ...FirstClass..
     = ( 01 00 0A 46 69 72 73 74 43 6C 61 73 73 00 00 )
    .method public hidebysig specialname
    rtspecialname instance
    void .ctor() cil managed;
}
.class private auto ansi beforefieldinit SecondClass
    extends [mscorlib]System.Object
{
    .custom instance
     void CommentAttribute::.ctor(string)
    // ...SecondClass..
    // T..IsImportant.
     = (
         01 00 0B 53 65 63 6F 6E 64 43 6C 61 73 73 01 00
         54 02 0B 49 73 49 6D 70 6F 72 74 61 6E 74 00 )
    .method public hidebysig specialname
    rtspecialname instance
    void .ctor() cil managed;
```

```
    }
    .class private auto ansi beforefieldinit ThirdClass
        extends [mscorlib]System.Object
    {
        .custom instance
         void CommentAttribute::.ctor(string)
        // ...ThirdClass..T
        // ..IsImportant.
        = (
            01 00 0A 54 68 69 72 64 43 6C 61 73 73 01 00 54
            02 0B 49 73 49 6D 70 6F 72 74 61 6E 74 01 )
        .method public hidebysig specialname
         rtspecialname instance
         void .ctor() cil managed;
    }
```

These tags indicate that the constructor on the `CommentAttribute` class is called when the attribute object is created. Take a closer look at the embedded data. In the case of `FirstClass` the data looks like this:

```
( 01 00 0A 46 69 72 73 74 43 6C 61 73 73 00 00 )
// ...FirstClass..
```

The string that is passed to the constructor is ten characters long. Prefixed by its length (`0x0A`), this string[5] can be seen in the embedded data. The attribute data is then suffixed with two NUL bytes.

In the other two cases, the embedded data contains the string passed to the constructor, followed by `0x01` to indicate that there is one named parameter. This is followed by an indication of whether the parameter is a property (`0x53`) or a field (`0x54`), followed by the type of the parameter (`0x02` is a `bool`). Finally there is the parameter's name (prefixed with the length of the name) and its value (`0x01` for true and `0x00` for false).

From the data embedded as part of `.custom`, you can deduce the actions that should be performed at runtime to create and initialize the custom attribute. Indeed, the custom attribute data is essentially a list of instructions and the data that those instructions take—in contrast to object serialization. Serialization is effectively a bitwise copy of the fields in an object. Custom attribute data is not

---

5. Note that this string is made up of single byte characters.

serialized because attribute parameters can be passed through properties, and properties do not necessarily mean data storage. Consider this implementation of the IsImportant property:

```
// C#
public bool IsImportant
{
    set
    {
        isImportant = value;
        if (isImportant)
        {
            File f = new File("classes.log");
            StreamWriter sw;
            sw = new StreamWriter(
                    f.Open(FileMode.Append));
            sw.Write(comment);
            sw.Close();
        }
    }
}
```

This is the code to give the property a value; the data passed to the property is available through the implicit value item. This code basically tests whether the comment is important, and if so, it appends the comment to a log file. This example highlights the fact that properties represent code and not necessarily storage.

However, here is a dilemma: When is the property setter called? At first glance, the logical occasion is the application of the attribute to an item, which appears to occur when the code is compiled. Of course, this cannot happen! Instead, the property setter will be called when the attribute is read by the reflection API *and* the usage of the attribute results in the property's being set. Because properties are used for optional parameters, the property setter may never be called. If you have constructors on your attribute class, you may think at least one of them will be called. However, all that attributes do is add metadata to an item—a blob of data—and to make this metadata mean anything you have to read the attribute with the reflection API. The lesson here is that you should not expect your attribute to be called unless you provide the code to explicitly call it. I will show examples later.

In the preceding example, the `CommentAttribute` class may be defined in the same assembly as the items to which it is applied, and because it is `public`, it can be applied to items in other assemblies. If your attribute can be applied to assemblies or modules, you must define it in a separate assembly. If you attempt to define an assembly attribute class in the same assembly, the compiler will see the usage of the attribute before it sees the attribute class, and you'll get an error. I will explain assemblies and modules, and how to build them, later in this chapter.

1.3.2.3 Reading Attributes

Attributes are read with the reflection API. There are several ways to read the attributes on a type, depending on whether you are reading the attribute on an instance of the type or through type metadata. If you have an instance, you can create an instance of the `System.Reflection.TypeDelegator` class and call `GetCustomAttributes()` to get an array of attributes:

```
// C#
MyAttributedClass myclass = new MyAttributedClass();
TypeDelegator td = new TypeDelegator(myclass.GetType());
foreach (object o in td.GetCustomAttributes(true))
{
    Console.WriteLine(o.ToString());
}

// C++
MyAttributedClass* myclass = new MyAttributedClass;
TypeDelegator* td;
td = new TypeDelegator(myclass->GetType());
IEnumerator* e;
e = td->GetCustomAttributes(true)
            ->GetEnumerator();
while (e->MoveNext())
{
    Console::sWriteLine(e->Current->ToString());
}
```

The difference between the C# and C++ code is mainly the lack of the `foreach` statement in C++ for iterating through an enumerator obtained on a class that implements `IEnumerable`. There are two overloads for `GetCustom-`

`Attributes();` I have used the first one in the preceding code where the parameter indicates whether the array should contain the attributes that the object has inherited from its base class. The second overload also takes a `Type` parameter, and the method will filter the custom attributes and return only those with the specified type, as follows:

```
// C#
object[] attrs;
attrs = td.GetCustomAttributes(
        typeof(CommentAttribute), true);
```

```
// C++
Object* attrs[];
attrs = td->GetCustomAttributes(
        __typeof(CommentAttribute), true);
```

The `typeof()` (or `__typeof()`) operator returns a `Type` object for the specified type (which is a *singleton* object—there is only one instance of it). Note that you must use the entire name of the attribute class; you cannot omit the `Attribute` suffix because the operator requires a *class* name and not an *attribute* name.

The `GetCustomAttributes()` method is called—delegated—to the appropriate class for the item. If you have the type object for an item, you can then access the nested items in that type (e.g., the methods in a class) and call `GetCustomAttributes()` on the class (e.g., `MethodInfo`) that describes the nested item. The reason you can do this is that the `Reflection` namespace classes for each item are derived from `MemberInfo`, which defines this method.

1.3.2.4 *Attribute Scenarios*

Attributes extend metadata, but what use is that to you? You can use attributes in several ways, a few of which I'll mention in this section. First, the metadata that you add is out of band, and it is not read by the runtime. It is your responsibility to provide code that reads metadata using the reflection API and to act on that data.

One pattern that the Framework Class Library uses frequently is to associate an attribute class with an abstract class. When you use the attribute on a class, you *must* derive that class from the specified abstract class. (The canonical example is `[AttributeUsage]` and `Attribute`. If you use the former, you *must* derive from the latter; however, you can use the latter without the former.)

This pattern means that the abstract class provides code that reads the attribute, gets information from the attribute's properties and fields, and acts on that information—for example:

```
// C#
public enum CatalogLevelType {None, Basic, All};
[AttributeUsage(AttributeTargets.Class,
                Inherited = true,
                AllowMultiple = false)]
public class CatalogAttribute : Attribute
{
    private string name;
    public CatalogAttribute(string fileName)
    { name = fileName; }
    public CatalogLevelType Level
        = CatalogLevelType.None;
    public string Comment = "";
    public string Name
    { get{ return name;} }
}
```

The attribute defined by this class has a mandatory parameter that is accessed through a read-only property called Name. This property indicates the name of a file that should be used for logging access to the class to which the attribute is applied. In addition, the class has two optional parameters (implemented through fields) that identify how much information about the class should be logged and a comment about the class. A class that uses the [Catalog] attribute should derive from Catalogable:

```
// C#
public abstract class Catalogable
{
    public Catalogable()
    {
        TypeDelegator td;
        td = new TypeDelegator(this.GetType());
        Type t = typeof(CatalogAttribute);
        object[] attr;
        attr = td.GetCustomAttributes(t, true);
        if (attr.Length == 1)
        {
            CatalogAttribute cat;
```

```
        cat = (CatalogAttribute)attr[0];
        if (cat.Level == CatalogLevelType.None)
            return;
        // catalog information about the object
        if (cat.Name.Length != 0)
        {
            StreamWriter dump = null;
            try
            {
                // exception if the file does not exist
                dump = File.AppendText(cat.Name);
            }
            catch(FileNotFoundException)
            {
                dump = File.CreateText(cat.Name);
            }
            dump.WriteLine("an instance of "
                        + GetType().ToString()
                        + " has been created");
            if (cat.Level == CatalogLevelType.All)
                dump.WriteLine("\t" + cat.Comment);
            dump.Close();
        }
    }
  }
}
```

The constructor of this class reads the attributes of the class and uses this information to open and write to a log file. Because this class is the base class of classes that use [Catalog], when instances of those classes are created the information will be logged. The TypeDelegator class is initialized with this.GetType(), where this is an instance of a class that uses the [Catalog] attribute. I use TypeDelegator to get an array of CatalogAttribute objects from the class. Because CatalogAttribute is defined by the statement AllowMultiple=false, the array will have a maximum of one entry. The attribute and the class are used like this:

```
// C#
[Catalog("objects.txt",
        Level = CatalogLevelType.All,
        Comment = "First Class")]
```

```
class ClassOne : Catalogable { }
[Catalog("objects.txt",
        Level = CatalogLevelType.Basic,
        Comment = "Second Class")]
class ClassTwo : Catalogable { }
[Catalog("objects.txt")]
class ClassThree : Catalogable { }
```

When instances of `ClassOne` are created, the name of the class and the comment are logged. When instances of `ClassTwo` are created, just the name of the class is logged. And when instances of `ClassThree` are created, no information is logged.

In another pattern used by the framework, a separate class reads attributes and acts on them. Continuing from the `[Catalog]` attribute example, here is a container class that holds objects:

```
// C#
public class CatalogContainer : System.Collections.ArrayList
{
    public override int Add(object value)
    {
        TypeDelegator td;
        td = new TypeDelegator(this.GetType());
        Type t = typeof(CatalogAttribute);
        object[] attr;
        attr = td.GetCustomAttributes(t, true);
        if (attr.Length == 1)
        {
            CatalogAttribute cat;
            cat = (CatalogAttribute)attr[0];
            if (cat.Level == CatalogLevelType.None)
                return base.Add(value);
            if (cat.Name.Length != 0)
            {
                StreamWriter dump = null;
                try
                {
                    dump = File.AppendText(cat.Name);
                }
                catch(FileNotFoundException)
                {
                    dump = File.CreateText(cat.Name);
```

```
            }
            dump.WriteLine("an instance of "
                            + value.ToString()
                            + " has been added "
                            + "to the container");
            if (cat.Level == CatalogLevelType.All)
                dump.WriteLine("\t" + cat.Comment);
            dump.Close();
        }
    }
    return base.Add(value);
}
}
```

If the object being added to the container has the `[Catalog]` attribute, this information is logged to the appropriate file. In this case the class does not have to derive from `Catalogable` because the functionality of logging is now in the container class.

A final pattern in this roundup of attribute usage is merely to use attributes as a notation device. The attribute indicates that there is something special about the item to which it is applied. A separate class uses the reflection API to check for the attribute and then do some special processing on the item. An example is the `[Browsable]` attribute in the `System.ComponentModel` namespace. This attribute has a single property that indicates whether a visual designer should show the item. If the attribute's `Browsable` property is set to `false`, the item should not be shown. If the attribute is not used or the `Browsable` property is set to `true`, the item can be shown. The attribute does nothing else; it has no other data.

If the item to which such an attribute is applied is a class, it is simpler to use an empty interface to do this, as explained earlier. However, the `[Browsable]` attribute can be applied to the members of a type, for which the interface technique cannot be used.

1.3.3 Exceptions

The single most important rule that all COM developers have learned to follow is that whatever you do, do not allow exceptions to leak unhandled out of your component. The reason is that with COM, exceptions are language specific: A C++ exception is different from a structured exception handling (SEH) exception, and many languages (in particular Visual Basic) do not have complete exception support.

COM components can be housed in essentially three contexts: an in-process server, an out-of-process server, or a host. If the component is in-process and throws an exception, the client application that loaded the DLL has to handle the exception, which typically doesn't happen because the client code does not expect exceptions. In this case the client process shuts down, displaying the ugly **Application Error** dialog generated by the system. This gives the users of the client the impression that the client is what is buggy, rather than the component, which is the real culprit.

The alternative is to load the component into a host process, such as `dllhost.exe`. If the component throws an exception, the host process is shut down and the client process will merely get an HRESULT error when it tries to access the component through an interface proxy (of course, you always check HRESULT errors and act on them, don't you?). COM+ components running in server applications run under `dllhost`. If an exception is thrown by a component running in a COM+ application, all activities in the application will be shut down as the instance of `dllhost` is shut down.

The final package is a COM executable (EXE) server. This is a process that maintains its own COM apartments to run the class factories and the objects that they create. If a component in an EXE server throws an exception that is not caught, the entire process is shut down and again the interface proxy to the object will return an HRESULT error.

The solution in COM was to wrap as much code as possible in exception handling and then convert caught exceptions into HRESULT errors. However, HRESULT errors are not user-friendly because they are just 32-bit numbers, and it is the responsibility of the client developer to try to work out what these cryptic numbers mean. As COM evolved, another solution appeared: error objects. These could be described as "pseudoexception objects" because the COM marshaling layer knows how to marshal an error object from the component apartment to the calling apartment, and it does this automatically and silently as out-of-band information. Error objects contain a description of the error that has occurred, which helps client developers, particularly those of the Visual Basic persuasion.

However, there are still problems with error objects. The API for generating error objects is not particularly developer-friendly, and it requires objects that issue an error object to implement a specific interface (`ISupportErrorInfo`). If an object does not implement this interface, then if the client is written according to Microsoft recommendations it will ignore any error objects issued.

One final problem is that if there is a chain of components—one calling another—and an error object is created somewhere in this chain, this error object applies to all of the components. Error objects are considered immutable once created, so components farther down the stack have the option of either allowing the original error object to be propagated unaltered, or to replace it completely. There is no mechanism for the error object to be "adjusted" to take additional error information. Extended error objects were provided with OLE DB, and these do allow you to add more than one record of information to an error object, but they require writing more C++ code and have not gained popularity.

In .NET, errors are handled exclusively by exceptions. .NET code can throw an exception when an "exceptional" condition has occurred—something that the current code cannot handle. This condition could have made the data in the current stack frame invalid, so stack "unwinding" occurs where local value types are discarded and references go out of scope (and if the objects that they refer to have no other references, they will be available for garbage collection). Functions farther up the stack could depend on the results from the errant code, and thus the stack unwinding can propagate through these functions, too.

Some exceptions may not be so serious as to affect all of the stack, in which case the developer can just guard the sensitive code with a `try` block. In this case the developer is asserting that only the guarded section of code is affected by the exception, and that the rest of the code in the remaining part of the method, and in the stack, is unaffected. Allowing exceptions to propagate like this simplifies both client and component code:

```
//C#
void Calculate(int x)
{
    if (x <= 0)
```

```
      throw new Exception(
         "parameter must be greater than zero");
      // use x here...
   }
```

Notice that this method does not return a value. Microsoft recommends that you do not use return values to return errors; exceptions should be used instead. Error return values result in more complicated client code, as well as the nightmare of maintaining pages of error codes in your component's documentation. Furthermore, because constructors do not return values, there is no way to indicate why a constructor has failed unless the constructor throws an exception.

I have chosen to use an instance of the `Exception` class for the exception in the preceding example, but you can use any of the exception classes in the Framework Class Library, or you can define your own exception class derived from `Exception`. Indeed, it makes sense to develop a class hierarchy of exception classes (but sadly, the VS.NET IDE does not recognize this, as you'll see when I talk about the **Exceptions** dialog in Chapter 9).

C# and C++ use similar syntax to throw exceptions, to guard blocks of code that can possibly throw exceptions, and to catch the exceptions:

```
// C#
try
{
   myObj.DoSomething();
}
catch (Exception e)
{
   Console.WriteLine(e.ToString());
}

// C++
try
{
   myObj->DoSomething();
}
catch (Exception* e)
{
   Console::WriteLine(e->ToString());
}
```

The only difference here is in the different operators that each language uses to access object members. Notice that exceptions are objects, and thus they are always caught through pointers. (Although it looks like normal C++ exception handling, you are not allowed to catch exceptions by value or through C++ references.)

The curly braces in this context are required; you cannot ignore them in the single-line case as you can with, for example, the `if` statement. You can use multiple `catch` statements to provide handles for different exceptions. If you do this, however, be careful to put the handlers for more general exceptions (those classes higher in the exception class hierarchy, like `Exception`) *after* the handlers for more specific exceptions. C# will issue an error if a general exception handler appears above a specific one, but C++ will issue only a warning. If you want to suppress an exception without handling it, then in both languages you should provide a `catch` clause for the exception type without a variable:

```
// C#
try
{
    myObj.DoSomething();
}
catch (MyException e)
{
    Console.WriteLine(e.ToString());
}
catch (Exception)
{
    // don't want to handle other exceptions or
    // allow them to propagate
}
```

In addition, both C++ and C# allow you to rethrow an exception from a `catch` handler. To do this you merely use the `throw` statement without a parameter, and the original exception will be rethrown even if the handler caught it as its base class.

If your method is intended to return a calculated value (or has `out` or `ref` parameters) and it throws an exception, the method farther up the call stack will not get a return value. This is precisely why exceptions are propagated up the call stack: to indicate to other functions that the data generated by the errant code should be considered suspect. However, neither the compilers nor the runtime does any more than this—for example:

```
// C#
class ErrorApp
{
    static void Main()
    {
        int j = 0;
        try
        {
            Errant(out j);
        }
        catch (Exception)
        {
        }
        Console.WriteLine("j has the value {0}", j);
    }
    static void Errant(out int i)
    {
        i = 99;
        throw new Exception("ignore my results");
    }
}
```

C# uses the `out` keyword to indicate that data is returned through the parameter. This code will print out `j has the value 99` at the command line. You have to be careful about code like this and enforce a discipline saying that results that come back from code that generates exceptions should not be used.

The `System.Exception` class looks like this:

```
// psend 0 C# generated from IL
public Exception : ISerializable
{
    public Exception();
    public Exception(string msg);
    public Exception(String msg, Exception inner);
    public virtual string HelpLink {get; set;}
    protected int HResult {get; set;}
    public virtual Exception InnerException {get;}
    public virtual string Message {get;}
    public virtual string Source {get; set;}
```

```
public virtual string StackTrace {get;}
public virtual Exception GetBaseException();
public override string ToString();
// ISerializable methods
public virtual void GetObjectData(
   SerializationInfo info, StreamingContext ctx);
public Exception(SerializationInfo info,
               StreamingContext ctx);
}
```

The class derives from `ISerializable` (which is why it implements both `GetObjectData()` and the constructor with the `SerializationInfo` and `StreamingContext` parameters[6]), which means that instances of `Exception` can be serialized and passed via a remoting channel.

Take a look at the properties of this class: In addition to `Message`, `Source`, `StackTrace`, and `HelpLink`, which do just as their names suggest, the class contains a property called `InnerException`, a constructor that takes an `Exception` instance, and the method `GetBaseException()`. These members allow you to create and access a chain of exceptions. When a component calls code that throws an exception, the component can catch the exception and add information to it before rethrowing the exception:

```
// C#
void f()
{
   try
   {
      myObj.DoSomething();
   }
   catch (Exception e)
   {
      Console.WriteLine(e.ToString());
      throw new Exception("I caught this too!", e);
   }
```

6. `ISerializable` indicates that the object supports custom serialization. There are two halves to serialization: On the one hand, the object has to be serialized to a stream, and thus a class has to support `GetObjectData()`; on the other hand, a class that supports serialization must allow instances to be created from data serialized to the stream. Objects are initialized through constructors. `ISerializable` is an *interface,* and interfaces do not have constructors. This is one of the few interfaces that *requires* a specific constructor to be implemented when you implement the interface.

```
    }
void g()
{
    try
    {
        f();
    }
    catch (Exception e)
    {
        Console.WriteLine(e.ToString());
        while ((e = e.InnerException) != null)
            Console.WriteLine(e.ToString());
    }
}
```

Exceptions are thread based, so you should be careful to catch them on the thread where the function that generates them is called. There is no metadata for indicating the possible exceptions that a method can throw, and consequently compilers cannot check whether exception handling would be prudent.

The AppDomain class has an event called UnhandledException that generates the event through an UnhandledExceptionEventHandler delegate when an exception has been thrown and has not been caught (I'll explain events and delegates later):

```
// C#
public delegate void UnhandledExceptionEventHandler(object
sender,
    UnhandledExceptionEventArgs e);
public class UnhandledExceptionEventArgs : EventArgs
{
    public UnhandledExceptionEventArgs(
        object exception, bool isTerminating);
    public object ExceptionObject {get;}
    public bool IsTerminating {get;}
}
```

You can supply a handler through this event to ensure that when an exception is uncaught by other code in your application, you are informed that something has happened. Of course at this point it is most likely useless to continue execution (hence the IsTerminating property), but at least you can log the exception. The most important advice I can give is that you should *always* use exception handling, whether or not the documentation for the classes you are using says that exceptions can be thrown.[7]

As I mentioned earlier, exceptions are serializable. This is why I said you should catch the exception "on the thread where the function that generates them is called" rather than "on the thread where the exception is generated." If you make a remote call and an exception is generated in the remote object, the exception will be serialized and passed back to the calling thread and rethrown there. If you call a method asynchronously through a delegate (as described later), the exception is treated as output data from a method. Therefore, the exception is thrown in the calling thread when that thread harvests results from the delegate by calling the `EndInvoke()` method. If the method that is called asynchronously is marked with the `[OneWay]` attribute, no data—not even exceptions—is returned to the calling thread.

Finally (pun intended), it is possible to perform postprocessing for a `try` guarded block. I have to stress that this is not exception handling, although because a `try` block is used, postprocessing can be combined with exception handling. The processing can be carried out in a `finally` clause to a `try` guarded block. The idea of `finally` is that when the flow of execution leaves the `try` block, the code in the `finally` block is called. The flow of execution may leave the `try` block through a `return` statement, by an exception being thrown, or simply by all the code in the `try` block being executed.

In C#, the postprocessing occurs in a block marked with the `finally` keyword, but in C++ the `__finally` keyword is used. Beware, however, because this keyword is also used with structured exception handling (with a block guarded with the `__try` keyword in unmanaged code). So whereas a C# program has `try`/`finally` code, C++ has `try`/`__finally` code. One use of `finally` is to provide so-called deterministic finalization (DF) in the current version of .NET, to mirror how the stack-based objects with destructors are used in unmanaged C++:

---

7. Following the grand tradition of technical writers, I will omit exception handling for practically all the code I give in this book. The reason is that Addison-Wesley uses the same error correction ink to print this book that was used to print Don Box's May 1999 "House of COM" column in *Microsoft Systems Journal.*

```
// C#
TextWriter tw = null;
try
{
    tw = File.AppendText("results.txt");
    string results = DoSomeProcessing();
    tw.Write(results);
}
finally
{
    if (fs != null) fs.Close();
}
```

This code creates a new file to write out some results. Once this file is open, an exclusive lock on the file prevents any other thread from accessing the file until `TextWriter.Close()` is called to close the stream (and the underlying file). This code ensures that however the `try` block is left, the `finally` block will always be called. So if `DoSomeProcessing()` throws an exception, the file will still be closed. This code is cumbersome, so C# has a mechanism to simplify the code.

C# allows you to define a `using` block of code that defines the scope of a single object. Once the object goes out of scope, a special cleanup method will be called:

```
// C#
using (TextWriter tw = File.AppendText("results.txt"))
{
    string results = DoSomeProcessing();
    tw.Write(results);
}
```

This code effectively does the same as the previous code. When the `tw` variable goes out of the scope determined by the curly braces, the `Dispose()` method will be called, and this method calls the `Close()` method.

The code in the `using` statement should be an object declaration of a class that derives from the `IDisposable` interface (and hence implement a `Dispose()` method), and the object must be initialized (to `null` is OK). You can declare only one variable in a `using` statement, but you are allowed to nest `using` statements.

Note that `using` does not destroy the object; it merely determines when `Dispose()` will be called. `Dispose()` should be used to release resources, and the onus is on the developer to make sure that the object is not used after `Dispose()` is called, or to make sure that if the object is reused, its resources are re-created—for example:

```
// C#
TextWriter tw = File.AppendText("results.txt");
using (TextWriter tw1 = tw)
{
    string results = DoSomeProcessing();
    tw1.Write(results);
}
tw.Write("oops!");   // the file has been closed!
```

1.3.4 Delegates

A common problem in C and C++ programming comes from the facility in these languages to cast pointers to virtually anything you like using C-style pointers. Here is some pretty useless code that illustrates the casting of function pointers:

```
// unmanaged C++
typedef size_t (*FPTR)(const char*);
void PrintStringLen(const char* str)
{
    FPTR length = (FPTR)strlen;
    printf("%s is %d characters long\n",
           str, length(str));
}
```

The cast to an `FPTR` pointer is performed whether or not the function has the same signature as the function pointer. In the following code an invalid cast is made:

```
// unmanaged C++
void PrintStringLenBadly(const char* str)
{
    FPTR length = (FPTR)strcat;
    printf("%s is %d characters long\n",
           str, length(str));
}
```

The call through the `length` pointer will result in `strcat`'s reading two `char*` pointers from the stack, whereas only one will be present. This code will compile fine because the compiler sees that you have made the cast, so you are happy that the strcat() function is called in this way. When the code is run, there is no runtime check, and this code will most likely throw an exception.

If I take the cast out of PrintStringLenBadly(), the compiler will indicate that there is a problem. However, often I cannot do this, so a runtime check is the only way to confirm that the developer knows what he is doing. Consider the Win32 GetProcAddress() function. You pass two parameters to this function. The first is an HMODULE of a DLL that you have loaded, and the second is an identifier of the exported function that you want to call (the name as a string, or an ordinal). The function returns a function pointer to the exported function. Because this is a general-purpose function, it returns a void* value that you have to cast to the function signature you expect. There is no choice; you have to cast. This requirement has led to many bugs.

Indeed, it can be argued that one of the reasons for COM was to solve this very problem, because a DLL COM server exports code through coclasses, and the only way to access code on a coclass is through an interface. The interface is a contract between the coclass and the client, and when the client requests an interface by name (IID) and the object implements the interface, the interface pointer that the object returns *must* be valid and contain valid pointers for all of the methods on the interface. The reason that you have to cast the out parameter on QueryInterface() from a pointer to a void* value to a pointer to the interface that you require is that QueryInterface() is a general-purpose method, so it must be able to return any interface pointer. However, Query-Interface() behaves very much like the C++ dynamic_cast<> operator in that the cast is performed at runtime: The out parameter of QueryInterface() is either a valid interface pointer of the type requested or a NULL pointer.

.NET takes another approach. Delegates are essentially smart function pointers; they hold information about a method (or more than one if they are multicast), and like all .NET items, delegates are completely described by metadata. Because this metadata can be read at runtime, the .NET Runtime will ensure that when it calls a method through the delegate, the method has *exactly* the signature that the delegate requires. If not, the runtime will generate an exception.

To declare the delegate, you need to give the signature of the method that will be called:

```
// C#
public delegate void CompletedAction(string msg);

// C++
public __delegate void CompletedAction(String* msg);
```

In both cases (C# and C++), the compiler generates a class with the same name as the delegate. Here is the IL that the C# compiler generates:

```
// IL
.class public auto ansi sealed CompletedAction
        extends [mscorlib]System.MulticastDelegate
{
    .method public hidebysig specialname
     rtspecialname instance void
     .ctor(object 'object',
            native unsigned int 'method')
            runtime managed
    { }
    .method public hidebysig virtual instance void
        Invoke(string msg) runtime managed
    { }
    .method public hidebysig newslot virtual instance
     class [mscorlib]System.IAsyncResult
        BeginInvoke(string msg,
            class [mscorlib]System.AsyncCallback callback,
            object 'object') runtime managed
    { }
    .method public hidebysig newslot virtual instance void
        EndInvoke(
            class [mscorlib]System.IAsyncResult result)
            runtime managed
    { }
}
```

The first thing to note is that these methods are empty and are marked with the `runtime` modifier. `runtime` means that the implementation is provided not by the developer, but by the .NET Runtime. The class is sealed (meaning that you cannot derive from it), and it is derived from `MulticastDelegate`. Do not be tempted to write your own delegate class because if you do, the C# compiler will generate error CS0644: `cannot inherit from special class "System.MulticastDelegate."` Similarly, the C++ compiler will generate error C3375 if you try to derive from `Delegate` or `MulticastDelegate`. Clearly something about the delegate classes deserves closer attention.

Now look at the methods that the compiler provides. I will come back to the constructor in a moment; the other three methods are `Invoke()`, `BeginInvoke()`, and `EndInvoke()`. These methods are used to invoke the method(s) to which the delegate refers. `Invoke()` will call the method(s) synchronously; that is, they will be called by the current thread, which will block until the method(s) have been called serially and have completed. `BeginInvoke()` and `EndInvoke()` are provided to allow the method(s) to be called asynchronously; that is, when `BeginInvoke()` is called, the runtime will create a new thread and call the delegate's method(s) on this new thread. This means that the calling thread is not blocked and thus can do other work. When the calling thread knows that the asynchronous delegate call has completed, it can call `EndInvoke()` to complete the call and harvest the results.

These invocation methods have no special knowledge about the methods that they will call, yet they give you the option of calling a method either synchronously or asynchronously. I will cover asynchronous calls in more depth in Chapter 3.

Creating a delegate is straightforward. First you need a class that has a method with the same signature as the delegate:

```
// C#
public class ActionDone
{
   public static void OnCompletedS(string action)
   {
      Console.WriteLine(
         "the {0} has completed", action);
   }
   public void OnCompleted(string action)
   {
      Console.WriteLine(
         "the {0} has completed", action);
   }
}
```

This class has two methods—one static method and one instance method. I have deliberately implemented these two methods to illustrate that the method called through a delegate can be an instance or a static method. To do this you must create an instance of the delegate class and pass information about the method to the constructor of that class. The IL given previously shows that the constructor takes a reference to an object and an `unsigned int` value. The reference is the object that implements the method (or `0` if the method is static), and the `unsigned int` value is the address of the method that will be called. The C# compiler helps because all that you, as a C# developer, have to do is pass the method to call to the delegate constructor in your code, and the compiler ensures that the right values are passed to the class:

```
// C#
CompletedAction ac1 = new
    CompletedAction(ActionDone.OnCompletedS);
ActionDone ad = new ActionDone();
CompletedAction ac2 = new CompletedAction(ad.OnCompleted);
```

The first line creates a delegate that will call the static method `OnCompletedS()`, whereas the last line creates a delegate that will call the instance method `OnCompleted()` on the object `ad`. The C++ compiler is not so helpful; in this case you must call the constructor with the object and method pointer parameters:

```
// C++
CompletedAction* ac1
ac1 = new CompletedAction(0,
         &ActionDone::OnCompletedS);
ActionDone* ad = new ActionDone;
CompletedAction* ac2;
ac2 = new CompletedAction(ad,
         &ActionDone::OnCompleted);
```

Because `OnCompletedS()` is static, there is no associated object; hence the object parameter is `0`. Next we need to be able to tell the delegate to call the method(s) to which it refers:

```
// C#
ac1.Invoke("called method");

// C++
ac1->Invoke(S"called method");
```

In fact, the C# and C++ compilers help here, too, because rather than using the cumbersome code of calling through `Invoke()`, you can call the delegate instance as if it were a method:

```
// C#
ac1("called method");

// C++
ac1(S"called method");
```

Just bear in mind that when you use this form, the code does not mean that you are calling a method called `ac1()`. Instead, you are calling the `Invoke()` method on the delegate `ac1`, and the delegate will call the method(s) that `ac1` contains.

The delegate class derives from `MulticastDelegate`, which implies that the delegate can hold more than one method. To create a multicast delegate, you have to create a delegate object that is the combination of one or more delegates. The `System.Delegate` class (the base class of `MulticastDelegate`) has a static method called `Combine()` that will return a new delegate object based on the delegates you pass as parameters. Thus a delegate class acts as a container of delegate objects, and you can access these by calling the `GetInvocationList()` method.

Here is the code for combining delegates in C++. Because `Combine()` returns a `Delegate` object, I have to perform a cast, and because I know that the delegate is a `CompletedAction` instance, I can use `static_cast<>`:

```
// C++
ActionDone* ad1 = new ActionDone;
CompletedAction* d = 0;
d = static_cast<CompletedAction*>(
        Delegate::Combine(new CompletedAction(
            ad1, &ActionDone::OnCompletedAction), 0));
ActionDone* ad2 = new ActionDone;
d = static_cast<CompletedAction*>(Delegate::Combine(
        new CompletedAction(
            ad2, &B::OnCompletedAction), d));
d->Invoke(S"called method");
```

Calling `Combine()` is tedious, so the C++ and C# compilers help again by providing a `+=` operator for multicast delegates, and the compiler converts this operator to `Combine()`:

```csharp
// C#
ActionDone ad = new ActionDone();
CompletedAction ac = null;
ac += new CompletedAction(ad.OnCompleted);
ac += new CompletedAction(ActionDone.OnCompletedS);
```

```cpp
// C++
ActionDone* ad = new ActionDone;
CompletedAction* ac = null;
ac += new CompletedAction(ad, &ad->OnCompleted);
ac += new CompletedAction(0, &ActionDone::OnCompletedS);
```

The `ac` variable now holds two delegates—one based on an instance method, and the other based on a static method. When the delegate is invoked (through `ac()`), both methods will be called, and they will be called serially in the order in which they were combined (in this case `OnCompleted()` will be called first). If one of the methods throws an exception, the invocation will be stopped. It is important, therefore, that you design the methods so that they do not throw exceptions.

As you have seen, the delegate is invoked as if it were a method, but what happens if the method that is called returns a value? The delegate class generated by the compiler takes this eventuality into account. If `Completed-Action` returns a value or has `out` or `ref` parameters, the `Invoke()` method will also have a return value and the same `out` and `ref` parameters. However, what if the delegate is multicast? In this case only the return values from the last invoked method will be returned; all the other values will be ignored. If you are really interested in the return values, you can write a `foreach` loop on the array of delegates returned from `Delegate.GetInvocationList()` and invoke each method individually. This is also one way to recover from one of the methods throwing an exception:

```csharp
// C#
Delegate[] arr = ac.GetInvocationList();
foreach (Delegate d in arr)
{
    CompletedAction ca = (CompletedAction)d;
    try
    {
        ca("called method");
```

```
        }
        catch (Exception) // I don't use the exception
        {
            Console.WriteLine("{0} on {1} failed",
                d.Method, d.Target);
        }
    }
```

Because `GetInvocationList()` returns an array of `Delegate` objects, it must be cast to the delegate I want to call. However, if the delegate is not of this *exact* type, the cast will fail at runtime with `InvalidCastException`. The runtime uses metadata associated with the delegate objects to ensure that the cast is correct. In no case will a cast to a different type succeed.

In general, it makes little sense for a delegate that will be used in a multicast situation to have return values. If you have a delegate like `CompletedAction` that returns no data, you can make the call to the delegate more efficient (in particular, in the remote case) by marking the method with the `[OneWay]` attribute. This means that nothing will be returned to the caller, and if the method is called on another thread and throws an exception, then not even the exception will be propagated back to the caller.

Delegates can be used to call a method asynchronously, and this does not depend on how the method is implemented. You do not have to write a method specifically to allow it to be called asynchronously, and you have to do very little in the client code to call the method asynchronously. But I will leave the details until Chapter 3, where I will describe the .NET remoting infrastructure.

The Framework Class Library also makes good use of delegates; the most obvious use is with threads. The `System.Threading.Thread` class gives access to threads, and the constructor of this class takes a delegate to the procedure to be executed by the thread:

```
// C#
public Counter
{
    private int x;
    private Thread t;
    public Counter(int i)
    {
```

```
        x = i;
        t = new Thread(new ThreadStart(ThreadProc));
        t.Start();
    }
    void ThreadProc()
    {
        for (int i = 0; i < x; i++)
        { Console.WriteLine(i) }
    }
}
```

This code creates a thread based on the thread procedure `ThreadProc()`, which merely prints out a series of numbers to the console. The `ThreadStart` delegate takes no parameters, nor does it return any values. The `Counter` class shows one way to pass data to the thread (via an instance variable). I will investigate threading in more detail later in this book.

Another important use for delegates is as a notification mechanism. In this case one class has a delegate field, and other classes are able to "register" to receive the notification by combining a new delegate in the notifier's delegate field. When something happens in the notifier class, it merely has to call the delegate to notify all the registered objects.

Delegate fields represent storage in a class, but the notification use that I just mentioned is a behavior implemented by delegates. Behaviors are described by interfaces, which cannot have storage and so cannot have delegate fields. There must be another way to use an interface to describe that a class can generate notifications. There is, and it involves class and interface members called *events*.

1.3.5 Events

A .NET event is a metadata device. An event can be part of an interface, which means essentially that if a class implements the interface, it supports certain methods, and it supports generating a notification (the event) to classes that choose to accept this notification. However, when a class derives from an interface, it *must* provide the behavior represented by the interface, which means that it must provide an implementation of all of the methods, properties, and events in the interface. Thus the class must also declare an event. When the compiler sees an event in a class, it generates a class to handle the event and adds a field to the class.

Both C# and C++ have a keyword to allow you to declare an event based on a delegate:

```
// C#
public interface IcsDoAction
{
    void Action(int x);
    event CompletedAction Completed;
}

// C++
public __gc __interface IcppDoAction
{ .
    void Action(int x);
    __event CompletedAction* Completed;
};
```

This interface says that the class that implements this interface can perform this action and generate the `CompletedAction` event when the action completes. When compiled, this interface generates the following IL:

```
// IL
.class interface public abstract auto ansi IcsDoAction
{
    .method public hidebysig newslot
        virtual abstract instance
        void Action(int32 x) cil managed { }
    .method public hidebysig newslot specialname
        virtual abstract instance
        void add_Completed(class CompletedAction 'value')
        cil managed synchronized { }
    .method public hidebysig newslot specialname
        virtual abstract instance
        void remove_Completed(
            class CompletedAction 'value')
        cil managed synchronized { }
    .event CompletedAction Completed
    {
        .addon instance void IcsDoAction::add_Completed(
                class CompletedAction)
        .removeon instance void
            IcsDoAction::remove_Completed(
                class CompletedAction)
    }
}
```

As you would expect for an interface, the methods are implicitly public, and they are abstract. Adding an event to the interface has two effects: First, two methods are added: `add_Completed()` and `remove_Completed()`. Second, the `.event` tag is added to the IL to associate these methods with their actions through the `.addon` and `.removeon` directives. The event also adds some extra methods to the interface.

Now, when you derive from this interface, you *must* implement the members of the interface, which means that you have to add the event to your class:

```
// C#
public class csActions : IcsDoAction
{
    public event CompletedAction Completed;
    public void Action(int x){ /* see later */}
}

// C++
public __gc class cppActions
    : public IcppDoAction
{
public:
    __event virtual CompletedAction* Completed;
    void Action(int x){ /* see later */}
};
```

As you would expect, adding the event to a class has the effect of adding the `CompletedAction` delegate field to the class as a private member, and the `add_Completed()` and `remove_Completed()` methods as public members.[8] This means that code outside the class can combine delegates with the event delegate but cannot raise the event; only code in the class can raise the event.

Because the delegate is a private member, clients that handle the event cannot access it directly. Instead they call the `add_Completed()` method, which is a public member of the class. To make it more obvious that in the client code the handler is being added to the delegate that the event uses, the C# and

---

8. The C++ compiler adds the `raise_Completed()` method as a *protected* member so that you can call this method only in the class or a derived class.

C++ compilers allow you to write code as if you were combining the handler delegate with the event:

```
// C#
ActionDone ad = new ActionDone();
Actions actions = new Actions();
actions.Completed += new CompletedAction(ad.OnCompleted);
actions.Completed += new CompletedAction(ActionDone.OnCompletedS);
```

Don't be fooled by this; you do not have direct access to the `Completed` event. The C# and C++ compilers just translate this code to call `add_Completed()`. An event is generated just as with a delegate:

```
// C#
public void Action(int x)
{
    string str;
    str = String.Format(
        "Action number {0} has completed", x);
    Completed(str);
}
```

If you write a class that has an event member and you do not fire the event, the C# compiler will issue a warning. The C++ compiler does not do this. The C++ compiler also accepts the `+=` syntax to add handlers to an event, and it allows you to raise an event by calling through the event member of the class. In addition, it allows you to raise an event in the class using the `__raise` keyword, which appears to be largely redundant:

```
// C++
void Action(int x)
{
    String* str = String::Format(
        S"Action number {0} has completed", __box(x));
    Completed(str);           // can do this...
    __raise Completed(str);   //...or this
}
```

The two lines here that raise the event produce the same IL.

When either compiler sees that a class contains an event, it will add the appropriate `add_` and `remove_` methods to the class (and the `raise_` method for

C++). The default implementation for the `add_` method calls `Delegate.Combine()`, the default implementation for the `remove_` method calls `Delegate.Remove()`, and the default implementation for the `raise_` method calls `Invoke()` on the delegate. If you choose, you can provide your own implementations for these methods. C# and C++ provide different ways to do this. In C# you provide the implementations of the `add_` and `remove_` methods like this:

```csharp
// C#
public class csActions : IcsDoAction
{
    protected CompletedAction del;
    public event CompletedAction Completed
    {
        add    { del += value; }
        remove { del += value; }
    }
    public void Action(int x)
    {
        string str;
        str = String.Format(
            "Action number {0} has completed", x);
        del(str);
    }
}
```

The `add` handler code will be used for the `add_` method, and the `remove` handler code will be used for the `remove_` method. Because this code is provided, you cannot generate the event by calling through the event member. Instead, I have provided a separate delegate. In this code I merely replicate the code that the C# compiler would have generated for me; however, I could have put any code in there.

C++ takes a different approach from that of C#. Here is the C++ equivalent:

```cpp
// C++
public __gc class cppActions
    : public IcppDoAction
{
    CompletedAction* CompletedDel;
public:
    cppActions() : CompletedDel(0) {}
```

```
void Action(int x)
{
    String* str = String::Format(
        S"Action number {0} has completed", __box(x));
    Completed(str);
}
__event void add_Completed(CompletedAction* d)
{ CompletedDel += d; }
__event void remove_Completed(CompletedAction* d)
{ CompletedDel -= d; }
protected:
    __event virtual void raise_Completed(String* s)
    { if (CompletedDel) CompletedDel(s); }
};
```

Take a look at the last three methods. These have been marked with the __event keyword to indicate to the compiler that they should be used to implement the event. The name of the event is Completed. I have used a separate delegate called CompletedDel as storage for the delegates.

The Framework Class Library makes widespread use of events. In particular, it is the basis of message handling in the Windows Forms API. Here is an example using the FileSystemWatcher class. This class watches a file or directory and generates events when something happens to the item that is being watched:

```
// C#
public class FileWatcher
{
    private FileSystemWatcher fsw = null;
    public void Change(object sender,
                       FileSystemEventArgs args)
    {
        Console.WriteLine("{0} {1}",
            args.ChangeType.ToString(), args.Name);
    }
    public FileWatcher(string s)
    {
        fsw = new FileSystemWatcher(s);
        fsw.Changed +=
            new FileSystemEventHandler(Change);
        fsw.EnableRaisingEvents = true;
    }
}
```

In this class I allow the user to specify a file or folder as the constructor parameter. The class passes this parameter to the constructor of `FileSystemWatcher` and then adds the `Changed` delegate on this object before starting to watch by setting the `EnableRaisingEvents` property to `true`.

`FileSystemEventHandler` is the type of *all* the events generated by this class: `Changed`, `Created`, `Deleted`, `Error`, `Renamed`. This is a pattern used by many of the classes in the Framework Class Library; it allows you to write a generic handler that handles similar events. The parameters of the `FileSystemEventHandler` delegate are an instance of `object`, which indicates the object that generated the event, and an instance of `FileSystemEventArgs`, which has details about the event that was generated.

This means that you have two choices: Either you write an event handler to handle all of the `FileSystemWatcher` events and use a switch in the handler to check `FileSystemEventArgs.ChangeType` to see which event was generated, or you provide a separate handler for each of the events that can be generated. You use the first method if your event handlers have large portions of common code, and the second method if the event handlers are significantly different.

I should point out that the `FileSystemEventArgs.ChangeType` property is one of the enumerated values in `WatcherChangeTypes`. However, `WriteLine()` does not have an overloaded version that takes an enumerated value from `WatcherChangeTypes` as a second parameter. In this situation the C# compiler checks if the type has a `ToString()` method and if so (as it does in this case), automatically calls it. I don't like compilers calling code on my behalf without telling me, so in this example I explicitly call `ChangeType.ToString()`.

1.4 Packaging and Deployment

One of the design goals of .NET was to end "DLL hell." This phrase has an interesting history, and it has resurfaced several times during the evolution of Windows—most often when Microsoft was promoting a new technology to solve this very problem. There have been many attempts, and I'll outline some of these later. None of these technologies completely solved DLL hell because even though they were initially well thought out, later a problem always surfaced that rendered the solution useless. .NET provides a new solution: new versioning, new code location strategies, and side-by-side assemblies. These innovations address many of the problems that caused DLL hell. Only time will tell if they actually solve the problem.

1.4.1 Assemblies and Modules

The base unit of deployment is the assembly. An assembly contains types, which means that it contains the IL and the metadata that describes those types. Assemblies can also contain resources like localized strings and bitmaps. When I say "can contain," however, I don't necessarily mean all in one file. One of the goals of .NET is to enable the network deployment of assemblies, and a file stuffed with rarely used code and resources will take up valuable network resources when it is deployed. Instead, an assembly can be composed of several files, which means that when an assembly is deployed, only the frequently used code and resources are passed over the network. When client code uses a type or resource that is not in the downloaded files, the .NET Runtime can download the required files.

The data that the assembly contains—in the manifest—is the metadata for the assembly itself. The manifest has information about all the files that make up the assembly, whether they are other DLLs or resource files like bitmaps. The manifest also contains a list of the assemblies used by the current assembly. Figure 1.11 shows the contents of a sample manifest. The identity of an assembly—which is as unique as possible—is made up of the name, version, culture, and (if used) strong name. I'll cover strong names later, but essentially a strong name is a public key that together with the private key (held by the publisher of the assembly) is used to sign and identify the assembly.

When you use a type in your assembly that is defined in another assembly, the compiler creates a *static link* to the assembly of that type. The manifest of your assembly contains a table that has the identity (name, version, culture, strong name) of all the assemblies to which your assembly is statically linked, to allow the system to load the correct assembly at runtime.

Every assembly must link to the `mscorlib` assembly because `mscorlib` contains the basic types that you use in your .NET code. The C++ compiler requires you to specify explicitly that you are using this assembly by placing the following line at the top of each source file compiled with the `/clr` switch:

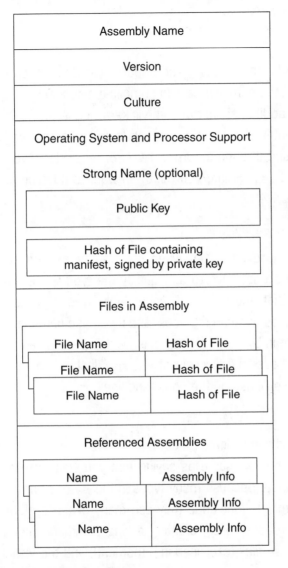

| Assembly Name |
| Version |
| Culture |
| Operating System and Processor Support |

Strong Name (optional)

| Public Key |
| Hash of File containing manifest, signed by private key |

Files in Assembly

File Name	Hash of File
File Name	Hash of File
File Name	Hash of File

Referenced Assemblies

Name	Assembly Info
Name	Assembly Info
Name	Assembly Info

Figure 1.11   Sample manifest contents

```
#using <mscorlib.dll>
```

This statement looks similar to the C++ directive #import, and although it is similar, it does more. This line does the work of the following lines for an equivalent unmanaged C++ application:

```
#include <windows.h>
#pragma comment(lib, "user32.lib")
#pragma comment(lib, "kernel.lib")
```

In other words, the `#using` line imports the description of types from an assembly so that the compiler can do compile-time checking (equivalent to using a header file). In addition, it instructs the linker to generate tables in the final executable that identify the libraries the code will use (equivalent to the linker instructions passed through the `#pragma comment` directive).

If you use a `#using` line, you will often want to have an associated `using namespace` line:

```
using namespace System:
```

This C++ feature says that when you use types defined in the `System` namespace, you do not have to fully qualify the type name with its namespace name. Beware that there is not necessarily a one-to-one correspondence between assemblies and namespaces, and if you use unmanaged C++ headers, the types brought in by `#using` may clash with types declared in the headers.

C# does not have an equivalent of `#using`. Instead you have to mention the assemblies that you'll use on the command line:

```
csc myfile.cs /r:System.dll
```

This command line indicates that `myfile.cs` refers to types in the `System` assembly (this is not the same as saying that you want to use the types in the `System` *namespace*, because many types in the `System` *namespace* are in the `mscorlib` assembly). Your code may use many of the system assemblies and many of your own assemblies, creating a long command line. The C# compiler helps with *response files* (explained in a moment), and the Visual Studio.NET IDE helps by allowing you to build up a list of the assemblies to which you will refer.

You may use the `using` statement in the C# source file, but this is equivalent to the `using namespace` statement in C++. By default the `mscorlib` assembly is always referred to, and you do not have to use the `/r` switch with this assembly. Furthermore, the C# compiler allows you to use response files containing the command-line options that you want. You can refer to these on the command line with the `@` symbol:

DEVELOPING APPLICATIONS WITH VISUAL STUDIO.NET

```
csc myfile.cs @myfile.rsp
```

Here, `myfile.rsp` could contain a line with `/r:System.dll`. If you do not give the name of the response file on the command line, the compiler will look for a file called `csc.rsp` in the same directory where `csc` is invoked or in the folder that contains the framework assemblies (`%systemroot%\Microsoft. NET\Framework\<version>`, where `<version>` is the version of the .NET Runtime). This means that you do not have to provide lines of references on the command line when you compile your applications.

I mentioned earlier that assemblies can be made up of several files; Figure 1.12 shows a sample schematic. An assembly called `one.dll` is made up of four separate files. The main file is `one.dll`, which is a portable executable (PE) DLL that contains the manifest for the entire assembly. The short name of the assembly is the name of this file without the extension, so this is assembly `one`.

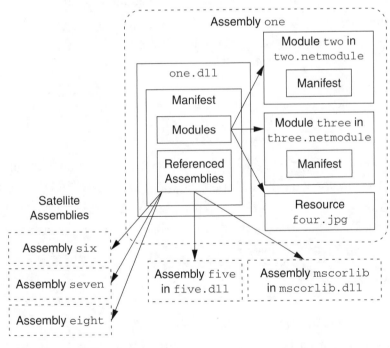

Figure 1.12   Assemblies

The assembly manifest indicates that the assembly contains three other files. Two of these are modules `two` and `three`, contained in the files `two.netmodule` and `three.netmodule`, which contain types. A third file in the assembly is a resource (`four.jpg`). In addition, the assembly has references to two other assemblies—`mscorlib` and `five`—which will contain types and resources, possibly in separate modules. At runtime, the .NET system will use this information to locate these extra assemblies. (I will explain how later, but basically the system looks in the application's folder or in a special folder called the global assembly cache (GAC).)

Finally, on the left-hand side I indicate that the assembly uses localized resources in satellite assemblies. These are resource-only assemblies, one of which (the one that is appropriate for the current locale) is loaded at runtime by an object called `ResourceManager`.

If assembly `one` is downloaded over the network, the physical file `one.dll` will be downloaded, but not necessarily the other modules. Only if your code refers to one of the other modules in `one`, or uses the resource, will these files be downloaded.

As a simple example, take a look at this code:

```
// C#
Assembly assem;
assem = Assembly.LoadFrom(
    "http://localhost/Assem/one.dll");
object o1 = assem.CreateInstance("ClassOne");
```

If `ClassOne` is a type in assembly `one`, then when this code is run the file `one.dll` is downloaded from the specified URL. This file will end up in a special folder, `Assembly\Download`, in your `%SystemRoot%` folder (typically `C:\WINNT`). The other modules in the assembly will not be downloaded. If you use another type—for example,

```
// C#
object o2 = assem.CreateInstance("ClassTwo");
```

and this type is in another module, `two`, then this module's file (`two.netmodule`) will be automatically downloaded from the URL that you specified as the address of the assembly.

This new module will be downloaded to the same special folder; however, if you use Windows Explorer to look at this folder, you'll see only the assembly name. The reason is that Microsoft has provided a namespace extension to view the downloaded assemblies, and the extension shows the *assemblies* and not the *modules* that make up the assemblies. (If you want to verify that the modules are being downloaded, look at the log files for Internet Information Services [IIS] on the server.) .NET provides several ways to determine where code is located, and it even allows you to change this location through configuration files.

To create a module you need to call the C# compiler with the `/target:module` switch or, if you are compiling C++, pass the `/NOASSEMBLY` switch to the linker (you also need to indicate that the linker should create a DLL with the `/LD` compiler switch or `/DLL` linker switch). Here is an example:

```
csc two.cs /t:module /out:two.netmodule
cl /clr /LD two.cpp /link /NOASSEMBLY /OUT:two.netmodule
```

Modules, too, have a manifest, but it is rather sparse: It includes details about the assemblies (in particular `mscorlib`) that the module uses, as well as a few flags. A module cannot be loaded by itself; it can be loaded only as part of an assembly

To create an assembly, you have to link together all the modules you have created. In C# you use the `/target:library`, `/target:exe`, or `/target:winexe` switch (depending on the type of assembly you want to create; I'll talk about these in the next section) to create an assembly. To add a module to this assembly, you must use the `/addmodule:<modulename>` switch, where `<modulename>` is the name of the module.

In C++ the option to create an assembly is similar, except that you need to inform the linker. You can do this with the `/DLL` linker switch to create a library assembly, or you can use the `/SUBSYSTEM` switch with `CONSOLE` or `WINDOWS` to create an EXE module (the `/LD` compiler switch will automatically link as a DLL, and with no switch the assembly will automatically link as a console EXE module[9]). To

---

9. Furthermore, using the `/SUBSYSTEM:CONSOLE` or `/SUBSYSTEM:WINDOWS` switch is redundant because the linker will select the appropriate subsystem depending on whether your entry point is `main()` or `WinMain()`.

add a module to an assembly, you should use the /ASSEMBLYMODULE linker switch:

```
csc /t:library one.cs /addmodule:two.netmodule
cl /clr /LD one.cpp /link /ASSEMBLYMODULE:two.netmodule
```

In this case the manifest for the assembly contains the following information:

```
// IL
.file two.netmodule
  .hash = (82 DB F8 EA 3C 4B BE 68 73 4C 57 22 C0 14 87 EA
           96 10 40 3A )
.class extern public ClassTwo
{
  .file two.netmodule
  .class 0x02000002
}
.module one.dll
// other flags
```

Notice that this metadata contains the names of the external modules that are part of the assembly and also lists the types in that module. In other words, these types are available only through the assembly. Multimodule assemblies are a great way of streamlining how your code is distributed, but unfortunately they are not supported by the Visual Studio.NET IDE. If you want to create multi-module assemblies, you have to write your own makefiles.

Assemblies are the deployment unit in .NET, but as you have already seen, they also act as an umbrella unit that defines a boundary for the types they contain. Public types are those that the developer has decided should be available outside of the assembly. Internal (or private) types are available only to types within the assembly, regardless of the module where the type is contained. This arrangement allows you to split the implementation of your code over several classes, but to present a public face to the type that could be just one class. In C#, a public type is marked with the public keyword, whereas a private type (one that is not available outside of the assembly) either does not have this keyword or is explicitly marked with internal:

```
// C#
public class csExternallyAvailable {}
```

```
internal class csUnavailable {}
class csUnavailableToo {}
```

C++ is similar, except that it uses the keyword `private` instead of `internal`:

```
// C++
public __gc class cppExternallyAvailable {};
private __gc class cppUnavailable {};
class __gc cppUnavailableToo {};
```

Note that if you compile these two sections of code as is and look at the metadata with the Intermediate Language Disassembler (ILDASM), the C# assembly will contain all three types, with two of them marked `private`. The C++ assembly will show only the externally available class. The reason? If a private type is not used in the assembly where it is defined, the C++ linker will not add it to the assembly, but the C# linker is not as smart. Because the assembly defines the type boundary, it also defines the versioning and security boundary.

1.4.1.1 Assembly Types

The compiler (for C#) or linker (C++) allows you to determine the main entry point for an assembly. Table 1.5 shows the types of assemblies that you can create.

Whatever you can do in C# you can also do in C++. The difference between the two languages is tool support: C# is accepted by the Windows Forms and Web Forms designers; C++ is not. This means that although it is possible to build a GUI application in C++, you do not get a rapid application development (RAD) tool with drag-and-drop support.

The first three types in Table 1.5 are EXE modules, meaning that in addition to containing .NET types and metadata, they have to have code specific to the target operating system to start the .NET Runtime and pass execution to the assembly entry point. At the moment, this means that these types of assemblies are platform specific because the operating-system loader specifically loads them via their PE entry point. In the future, an operating-system loader may be able to detect that an EXE contains a .NET assembly and in response initialize the .NET execution engine, step through the PE header until reaching the IL, and then start executing. At this writing, however, this capability does not exist.

Table 1.5 Command line switch and classes used for various application types

Type	C++	C#
GUI	Define `WinMain()` and use `System.Windows.Forms` classes.	Use `/t:winexe` and define a class with a `Main()` method and use `System.Windows.Forms` classes.
Console	Define `main()`.	Use `/t:exe` and define a class with a `Main()` method.
NT services	Define `WinMain()` and use `System.ServiceProcess.ServiceBase`.	Use `/t:winexe` and `System.ServiceProcess.ServiceBase`.
ASP.NET	Apply the `/LD` switch and use `System.Web.UI` classes.	Use `/t:library` and use `System.Web.UI` classes.
Web Services	Apply the `/LD` switch and use `System.Web.Services` classes.	Use `/t:library` and use `System.Web.Services` classes.
Library	Apply the `/LD` switch.	Use `/t:library`.

The NT service type is even more platform specific because an NT service is a mechanism to extend the NT operating system, in particular to create code that can run under the LOCALSYSTEM account, which has the highest security on the local machine (i.e., trusted computing base, or permission to "act as part of the operating system"). Clearly NT services can run only on NT systems.

ASP.NET assemblies are library assemblies that can be created in C# through the Visual Studio.NET Web Forms designer to create browser-accessible Web applications. ASP.NET assemblies can be written in C++, but you do not have the *code-behind* facility that is available with C# and VB.NET. Code-behind allows you to split the user interface (`.aspx` file) and the code for a page (code-behind file), When the page is accessed, a new class is created by combination of the code-behind with the instructions in the `.aspx` file, and this new class is dynamically compiled and executed. This dynamic compilation allows you to change the user interface independently of the code, but it requires .NET classes that can compile the source code. Such classes are not available for C++.

Web Services are an extension of ASP.NET that allow you to expose function-ality through methods accessible over Simple Object Access Protocol (SOAP, an XML-based remote procedure call [RPC] that at the moment is implemented over HTTP). Both of these types of assemblies use features of IIS and thus can be run only on Windows systems that have IIS and the ASP.NET Internet Server API (ISAPI) installed.

The only assembly type that can be described as truly platform independent is the library assembly type. This type is in a standard PE format. Library assembly types have IL and metadata and contain a manifest, but because they don't necessarily contain native code to operate, other operating systems can access the types in the assembly.

On a language level, C# assemblies must have a `Main()` method if the assembly is a GUI, NT service, or console application. This method must be a static method of a class and is typically public (which is logical, because external code calls the method). However, you do not need to make it explicitly public because the compiler specifically looks for this method, and when the compiler sees this method it will mark it as an entry point. Indeed, the class that has the `Main()` function does not even have to be a public class. You can have multiple classes in an assembly with a `Main()` method, but in this case you must identify to the compiler which type has the `Main()` method that is used as the entry point with the `/main` switch. The entry point of a C# application is always `Main()`, regardless of whether the application is GUI or console based. If the application is GUI based, the `Main()` method has the responsibility of creating the first form in the application.

Here is an example of `Main()`:

```
// C#
static int Main(string[] args)
{
    foreach (string s in args)
        Console.WriteLine(s);
    return 0;
}
```

You are allowed to omit the arguments and/or the return value (i.e., make the method return `void`). `args` is a zero-based string array that contains the arguments from the command line.[10]

C++ entry points are slightly different, and I'll cover these in more depth in Chapter 7. Part of the problem is that C++ .NET applications can contain native unmanaged code (written in line or linked in from a static library), as well as managed code. Unmanaged C++ needs to initialize the C runtime library to enable you to use global objects (whether or not those objects use the C runtime library [CRT]). Managed C++ overcomes this problem by creating a separate entry point that does this initialization and then calls your designated entry point.

As with unmanaged code, managed C++ applications have different entry points depending on whether or not the application is GUI-based. If the application runs from the console, it must have a `main()` entry point. This looks just like an unmanaged version:

```
// C++
int main(int argc, char* argv[], char* envp[])
{
   // get the command-line arguments
   for (int x = 0; x < argc; x++)
      Console::WriteLine(argv[x]);
   // get the environment variables
   while (*envp)
   {
      Console::WriteLine(*envp);
      envp++;
   }
   return 0;
}
```

Notice that the arguments are passed through *unmanaged* types. Also be aware that the arguments are C-like; that is, the first entry in `argv` is the name of the application. If you link with the unmanaged code `setargv.obj`, you will get command-line argument expansion just as you would expect to get with unmanaged C++. As with unmanaged code, you can choose to ignore the environment parameter and the command-line arguments and return `void`.

---

10. Note that for C# applications, the first argument is the first argument that you give on the command line (or the **Run** command from the **Start** menu) after the application name. This is a contrast to native applications, in which the first command-line argument is the name of the executable.

GUI-based applications require that you define a `WinMain()` method. If you do this, the compiler will automatically indicate that this is the GUI entry point and that you need the `/SUBSYSTEM:WINDOWS` linker switch:

```
// C++
#using <mscorlib.dll>
#using <System.Windows.Forms.dll>

int WinMain(int instance, int previnstance,
            char* cmdline, int show)
{
    System::Windows::Forms
        ::MessageBox::Show("Hello");
}
```

This code will create a GUI-based application that will show a message box. No console is created when you run this application.

One final type of assembly that I have not covered yet is the *dynamic assembly*. Dynamic assemblies can be created in code as a memory resource, compiled at runtime, and if you choose, either persisted to disk or run from memory.

1.4.1.2 Assembly Names

As I mentioned earlier, all assemblies have simple text names. Each text name is the name of the file that contains the manifest, but without the extension (e.g., `one.two.dll` contains the assembly called `one.two`). However, you cannot guarantee that your name is unique and that no one else will use the same name. .NET has a solution in *strong names.* A strong name is a public/private key pair: The developer keeps the private key, and the compiler provides the public key and a hash signed by the private key in the assembly manifest.

The name of an assembly is not just the simple text name; it consists of the concatenation of the simple name, the version, the culture, and the public key (if the assembly has a strong name). Assemblies are loaded into application domains. The following code will print out the names of all the assemblies in the current domain:

```
// C++
Assembly[] assemblies;
assemblies = AppDomain.CurrentDomain.GetAssemblies();
foreach(Assembly a in assemblies)
   Console.WriteLine(a.FullName);
```

I will explain domains in more detail later. This code will generate the following output:

```
mscorlib, Version=1.0.3200.0, Culture=neutral,
    PublicKeyToken=b77a5c561934e089
app, Version=0.0.0.0, Culture=neutral,
    PublicKeyToken=null
```

This output shows that the domain contains the assemblies `mscorlib` and `app`, which is the assembly that printed this output. The assembly `mscorlib` has a public-key token of `0xb77a5c561934e089`. This is not the public key itself, but rather a hash generated from the key (which should still be unique).

When you refer to a type in an assembly in your code, the complete name of the referred assembly is stored in your assembly's manifest, including the strong name. When your assembly is loaded, the system checks the list of assemblies that you use and for each one locates the physical file and loads it. If an assembly has a public key, the loader compares this public key of the referred assembly with the expected public key that is held in the referring assembly. This is one of the checks that .NET performs to ensure that it loads the correct assembly (the section on versioning later in this chapter explains the complete mechanism). The loader can then create the hash of the assembly and, using the public key, decrypt the signed hash in the manifest of the loaded assembly and compare the two. This provides a mechanism for the loader to determine if the loaded assembly has been tampered with after the assembly developer has created it.

By default, assemblies are treated as private; that is, an assembly should be used only by a single application and is typically located in the same directory as the application. Library code that is intended to be used by other code is often known as a *shared assembly*. A shared assembly has to be located in a place where all other assemblies on your machine can access it. The Windows system directory is *not* the correct place for these assemblies because it contains the Windows system files.

Instead .NET provides the *global assembly cache* (GAC) to contain shared assemblies that have a strong name. The GAC is not simply a directory that all users on your machine can access. If it were a simple directory, then when different vendors provided DLLs with the same name and installed these in the

DEVELOPING APPLICATIONS WITH VISUAL STUDIO.NET

GAC, the older version would be overwritten with a newer version. Instead, the GAC is implemented as a hierarchy of directories. When you install the .NET Framework on your machine, the setup program will install a namespace extension for the `assembly` folder that shows all the shared assemblies, regardless of their version. It hides the folder hierarchy that is needed to support multiple versions of a single assembly.

To add a strong name to an assembly, you first have to generate the name. The Framework SDK provides a tool called `sn.exe` that generates a public/ private key pair that can be saved in a file:

```
sn -k app.snk
```

This command line will generate a public/private key pair in the file `app.snk`. The file contains binary data, so the strong-name utility gives you some options for viewing this data:

```
sn -o app.snk pub.txt
sn -t app.snk
sn -tp app.snk
```

The first line extracts the public key and writes it as a series of comma-separated values to the file `pub.txt`. The second line extracts the public key and prints the public-key token (the hash of the public key) on the command line. The final example prints the public-key token and a string version of the public key.

The public key is added to an assembly through the following assembly attribute:

```
[assembly: AssemblyKeyFile("app.snk")]
```

The `[AssemblyKeyFile]` attribute (in the `System.Reflection` namespace) indicates to the appropriate compiler or linker that when it generates the manifest for the assembly, the public and private keys are in the specified file. In addition, the strong-name utility can store public and private keys in a "container" in the cryptographic service provider that generates the key using the `-i` switch to `sn.exe`. This container essentially stores the keys using a friendly name, and you can use the name to apply the key to an assembly as follows:

```
[assembly: AssemblyKeyName("MyAppKey")]
```

Once you have built an assembly with a strong name, .NET versioning can be applied (as explained later), and you can make the assembly a shared assembly by putting it in the GAC. You can interact with the GAC using two tools: the command-line tool `gacutil.exe` and the shell namespace extension `shfusion.dll`. The command-line tool allows you to add and remove assemblies from the GAC, as well as to get a complete list of all the shared assemblies in the GAC. The namespace extension is essentially a user interface version of `gacutil.exe` that appears as a folder under the `%systemroot%` directory called `assembly`. Currently there is no official way to interact programmatically with the GAC; however, the `fusion.dll` library does export COM objects to interact with the GAC, and there is an example in the Framework SDK samples (called comreg) that shows how to use these objects.

Figure 1.13 shows the view of the GAC on my machine. The GAC is divided into two parts: the general GAC that contains assemblies that have been installed on this machine through install programs (in this case assemblies are installed as part of the Visual Studio.NET installation), and the `Download` folder. The `Download` folder contains the assemblies that have been downloaded from the network.

Figure 1.13 also shows the complete names of the shared assemblies, including the version and public-key token in each case, and it also indicates whether the assembly as been prejitted.

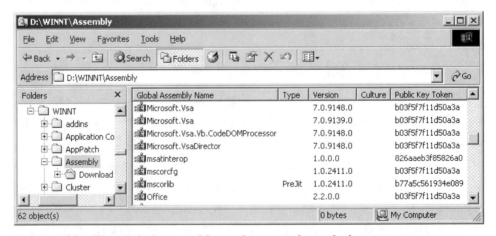

Figure 1.13   The global assembly cache seen through the `shfusion.dll` **namespace extension**

Strong names and the GAC have another use. .NET component services like transaction support are provided by COM+ component services. COM+ requires a component to be installed in a COM+ application so that it can run in the required context. For .NET components to be put into a COM+ application, they must be contained in assemblies that have strong names and have been put in the GAC. The types that use .NET component services must derive from `System.EnterpriseServices.ServicedComponent`, and when the runtime sees such a component for the first time, it creates a COM+ application and adds the component. The global unique identifiers (GUIDs) that are used for the application and component are generated from the public key—the strong name—of the assembly. (I will return to this in Chapter 4.)

1.4.2 Versioning before .NET

Versioning has always been a problem in Win32, and although various ways of easing the problem have been tried, they have proved largely ineffectual. From its inception, Windows was designed to use shared libraries called Dynamic Link Libraries (DLLs). The name does not necessarily mean that the library is explicitly loaded and the entry points are dynamically linked at runtime, although this is one way to do it. The name derives from the fact that the code module containing the library code need not be present at compile time. Instead the developer either writes explicit code to load the appropriate DLL (the API `LoadLibraryEx()`) and bind to the function at runtime (the API `GetProcAddress()`), or else links to a static linked library—an import library—that inserts thunks in the code that resolve to an import table. In this latter case, when the application is loaded, the system reads the required DLLs from the import table, locates and loads the DLLs, and then adjusts the import table to ensure that the thunks point to the correct virtual addresses.

Dynamic binding to a function at runtime with `GetProcAddress()` has an implicit danger, as mentioned earlier. This function returns a `void*` pointer to the required function, and the developer has the responsibility of casting it to the correct function pointer. If the developer does not cast to the *exact* function signature, the stack will be misinterpreted and an exception is likely to occur. As I mentioned earlier, .NET solves this problem through delegates that perform runtime checking to make sure that when you call a function through a pointer, the pointer identifies the correct function.

In both cases there must be a mechanism to locate the DLL. If the developer uses `LoadLibraryEx()`, either she can give an absolute path, which clearly restricts the installation options, or she can give just the name of the DLL and allow the system to locate the DLL at runtime. If the developer accesses the DLL through an import library, the DLL is loaded when the application is loaded (or optionally, when a function in the DLL is first used). In this case the developer has no option about the location of the DLL; the application is at the mercy of Windows. This is the main source of the eponymous "DLL hell."

The DLL location algorithm used by `LoadLibraryEx()` looks like this:

- The list of currently loaded DLLs to see if a DLL has the same name as the one requested
- The folder where the application's EXE is installed
- The folder where the application was invoked
- The system directory (the folder returned by `GetSystemDirectory()`)
- The 16-bit Windows directory
- The Windows directory (the folder returned by `GetWindowsDirectory()`)
- The folders in the `PATH` environment variable

The problem is that when the system cannot find a DLL, it widens its range more and more, so it could end up loading a completely different DLL. The system loads DLLs by name alone; it makes no attempt to check the code in the DLL.

An astute developer could use the Win32 `VERSIONINFO` resource on the loaded DLL to check the version of the DLL. `VERSIONINFO` holds a version and is obtained as a resource of the DLL; the developer can read this resource to check that the version of the DLL is correct. However, the Win32 `VERSIONINFO` API is very primitive, requiring the developer to traverse structures of data doing appropriate pointer arithmetic. (If you have gone through the pain of the Win32 `VERSIONINFO` API , you'll be pleased to see that the equivalent in the .NET Framework Class Library, `System.Diagnostics.FileVersionInfo`, makes this process far easier.)

The `LoadLibraryEx()` search strategy could easily pick up a different DLL with the same name. To avoid this problem, two solutions were developed in tandem: One solution was to bypass the search strategy altogether and allow an application to load only a DLL from its own folder. This meant that the DLL was private to this application, so eventually several copies of the same DLL could exist on the same disk. The other solution was to allow applications to share DLLs, but to solve the location problems by registering the location of the DLL with the system cross-referenced to a versioned identifier, and load the DLL using an API that checked this list of registered DLLs. As you'll see, the .NET solution is essentially a combination of these two. But I am getting ahead of myself.

1.4.2.1 Application-Specific Private DLLs

To ensure that a Win32 application uses just private copies of a DLL, you have to use a redirection file. This file has the same name as the application loading the DLL, but it has the extension `.local` (so if your application is called `myapp.exe`, you create a file called `myapp.exe.local`). The redirection file is totally empty and serves as a marker to the system so that the application's directory is always searched first for the DLL. If the developer gives a path as a parameter to `Load-LibraryEx()`, the system extracts the DLL's name and ignores the rest of this path.

Of course, this mechanism makes the DLL application specific, which may not be the behavior you want. You may have several EXEs in your application, each in a different folder, or you may use a DLL provided by a third party and stored in a separate directory. A major source of DLL hell was developers' placement of their DLLs in the system directory, for two reasons: First, a DLL could be overwritten with the same name, which could be a different version of the DLL or could be a different DLL entirely. Second, the DLL is placed high up in the `LoadLibraryEx()` search strategy, making it more likely to be loaded by mistake.

Even if the new DLL replaces a previous version of the same DLL, there is another potential problem: uninstallation. A good application cleans up when it is uninstalled. However, if the installation program replaces an existing DLL and the application it installs is removed, it will remove a DLL used by another application, rendering that application useless. Let's see how these issues were addressed in Windows 2000.

1.4.2.2 Windows File Protection

Windows 2000 solves the problem of loading the wrong DLL in several ways. Again, you'll see aspects of these solutions in .NET's solution. If you know that the DLL is likely to be used by more than one application, you can register it as a shared DLL in the system registry in the following key:

```
HKLM\Software\Microsoft\Windows\CurrentControlSet\SharedDlls
```

Shared DLLs are installed in the `SharedDlls` folder, a special folder whose path you can obtain by passing `CSIDL_PROGRAM_FILES_COMMON` to `SHGet-FolderPath()`. When an installer tries to copy a DLL to the hard disk, it first checks if the DLL is a shared DLL, and if so it installs the DLL only if it is a newer version. In any case, the installer increments a reference count of the DLL held in the registry. When an uninstaller tries to remove a shared DLL, it first consults the registry, and if the DLL is registered there it decrements the DLL's reference count. If the reference count falls to zero, the uninstaller can remove the DLL from the hard disk.

Of course, allowing a later version to overwrite an earlier version can cause problems. Some applications are written to exploit undocumented "quirks," and there is no guarantee that a later version will have these quirks. Windows 2000 and Windows 98 solve this problem with side-by-side DLLs, which I'll talk about later.

Windows 2000 protects its own DLLs with Windows File Protection (WFP) by making the system directory a special folder. By default, Windows 2000 will hide the system folder in Windows Explorer, but even if you do configure Windows Explorer to show the system folder (or indeed use the command line), you'll find that replacing a system DLL is not possible. Windows 2000 takes the attitude that the operating system should be changed only when a service pack is installed. When the operating system is installed (or updated with a service pack), the installer makes a copy of the system files in a directory called `%systemroot%\system32\dllcache`, and when it detects that a protected file has been replaced, it checks if the replacement is allowed. If not, it restores the DLL from the cache.

A solution to the DLL location problem came with COM. Indeed, you could argue that COM is just a DLL management technology.[11] COM code is supplied as

---

11. *You* could argue this, but *I* would also point out that COM does more than this. However, I would agree with you that DLL management is the most important of COM's features.

DEVELOPING APPLICATIONS WITH VISUAL STUDIO.NET

classes packaged in DLLs. A class is accessed via a single DLL (although its code may be packaged in other DLLs), and the location of the DLL is registered with the system under the class's name—a 128-bit unique integer called a CLSID (class ID). Code using the class does not need to know the location of the DLL; it just needs to know the class's name and pass this to COM, which will locate and load the DLL.

A COM class implements one or more interfaces, so in a way the class name is a named implementation of these interfaces. If a developer wants to update a class, providing a more up-to-date version of these same interfaces, he has no choice but to provide a new class name (CLSID). Using the old class name may break older code that depends on the old functionality. Versioning in COM, therefore, depended on the proper management of CLSIDs and the names of the interfaces used (IIDs). The versioning of DLLs (through `VERSIONINFO` resource) was ignored by COM.

If the developer followed the rules and made sure that new versions of classes and interfaces always had new names, and if administrators made sure that once registered, they kept COM DLLs in the same location, COM would work well. The trouble with that last statement is that there are a lot of ifs, and emphasis is put on developers and administrators to follow rules—something, typically as a species, they do not want to do.

1.4.2.3 *Side-by-Side Components*
Side-by-side COM components are components for which two or more versions exist on the same machine and each version can run at the same time in different processes. Strictly speaking, COM should not allow side-by-side components because different versions of coclasses should have different names. In practice, however, you will always come across the situation in which a component needs to be updated to fix a bug, and you do not want to have to update the clients that use instances of this coclass.

Components designed to be run side by side have the same CLSID (they are the same component—just different versions of it). This means that the same key in the registry will be used for component registration, so the new version of the component must make take this into account, as follows:

* Add a reference count key to the component's key. When a side-by-side component is registered, it should increment this value, and it should

decrement it when that component is unregistered. The registry key can be deleted when the reference count falls to zero.

- The path to the component's DLL should *not* be absolute. Instead a relative path should be used so that the application will pick up the DLL server from its own directory.

- The original DLL must be moved to a shared folder so that when an application tries to load a coclass in it and does not have a copy of the DLL in its folder, the shared version will be loaded through the DLL load strategy.

Another solution is to use redirection for COM components—that is, to install your DLL files in the same direction as the application and provide a `.local` redirection file, as explained earlier, which will ensure that the system loads only DLLs from the application directory. When COM loads a component's DLL—whether or not the `InprocServer32` registry key gives a full path to the DLL—COM will first look in the application's directory for the DLL. This means that even if a component with the same CLSID has been previously installed on the same system with a full path given in the registry, this version will be ignored in preference to the component in the local application folder.

If there is no version of the DLL in the application's directory, the registered version is used instead. Because you want to keep the registry the same (so that existing applications that use the component do not break), it stands to reason that you should not register the side-by-side component's COM server. Only the original server should be registered.

1.4.3 Locating and Versioning .NET Assemblies

Now that you have seen some of the earlier technologies used to solve the DLL location and versioning problem, let's look at how .NET improves on them.

1.4.3.1 *Fusion*

Fusion is the internal name of the project at Microsoft to try to eliminate the problems of sharing DLL code. The Windows File Protection and side-by-side components can be regarded as early versions of Fusion. Indeed, .NET has support for side-by-side components built in. The concept of redirection files (`.local`) is the default behavior of .NET: All assemblies are by default private and must be loaded from the local directory; code from other locations can be loaded through the configuration file for an application (`.config`).

On the other hand, the GAC can be seen as an evolution of the `dllcache` folder used by WFP. The GAC operates as a repository of code used by all processes, but unlike `dllcache`, the GAC allows administrators to install their own code there, and it respects multiple versions and cultures of the code. Thus you get the benefit of file protection *and* side-by-side code. The GAC was previously called the *Fusion cache,* and it is implemented by `fusion.dll`. The view of the GAC in Windows Explorer is a shell namespace extension implemented by `shfusion.dll`. In addition, the Framework SDK comes with a tool called the Fusion Log Viewer (`FusLogVW.exe`) that shows details about all the binding actions carried out through Fusion.

By "binding action" I mean Fusion's mechanism for locating the assemblies used by an application, and then loading them. Fusion uses three policies when binding:

1. **Application policy**. These policies apply to a specific application and are contained in a configuration file in the application directory that has the name of the application with the `.config` extension.

2. **Publisher policy**. These policies are generated by the publisher of an assembly and are used to make compatibility changes on shared components. They are provided as assemblies (compiled through the assembly builder utility, `al.exe`) and are installed in the GAC.

3. **Administrative policy**. These policies are machine settings (for a specific version of .NET Framework) and are contained in a file called `machine.config` in the `config` directory (`%systemroot%\Microsoft.Net\Framework\<version>\config`, where `<version>` is the version of the .NET Framework).

A configuration file can contain information other than binding information. Configuration files all have the same format, which I'll cover later.

If you are using an application configuration file or a publisher policy file to manage side-by-side versions of an assembly, that assembly must have a strong name. If the assemblies to which these files refer have been copied to the wrong directory, you can use the Fusion Log Viewer mentioned earlier to resolve the problem. This viewer shows the results of the binding that occurs as each policy is applied (from top to bottom in the list above), and if any policy fails it indicates the reason why.

The Fusion project extends further. A version of Fusion is supplied with Windows XP even if you do not install the .NET Framework. This version adds to the concepts of .NET Fusion in two important ways. Because Fusion supplies protection for the code files copied when a new application is installed, it removes the need to reboot the machine, and it also removes the possibility that an installation could break other applications. The second property of Fusion in XP is that the features we see in .NET will be applied to native Win32 code.

The version of Fusion in Windows XP introduces its own concept of a manifest describing native code to the system. Like the .NET manifest, the native manifest contains information about the dependencies of an application—the DLLs it requires and the versions of those DLLs. XP uses the manifest to ensure that it will load only the application with the specified version of the DLLs. Native manifests are XML files that have the name of the application with the extension `.manifest`. For example, the following is the manifest provided for the Windows log-on process (`winlogon.exe.manifest`), which indicates the version of `comctl32.dll` that should be used:

```
<assembly[12] manifestversion="1.0"
         name="Winlogon" version="1.0.0.0"
         languageid="0000"
         description="Windows Logon User Interface"
         processorarchitecture="X86">
    <dependency assemblyname="comctl32"
     version="6.0.0.0" languageid="0000" />
</assembly>
```

1.4.3.2 Configuration Files

.NET configuration files are XML files that give information to the runtime, to Fusion, or to your application. They have the same general format:

```
<configuration>
   <configSections>
      <!—description of each section -->
```

---

12. It is interesting that the native DLLs in these files are referred to as *assemblies*.

```
    </configSections>
    <!-- sections -->
</configuration>
```

You can add your own collections by including an entry to the `<configSections>` collection, which identifies the classes that can be used to configure the appropriate section in this file. Here's an example from the `machine.config` file on my machine:

```
<configSections>
    <sectionGroup name="system.net">
        <section name="authenticationModules"
         type="System.Net.Configuration.
            NetAuthenticationModuleHandler,System"
            />
        <!-- other sections -->
    </sectionGroup>
    <system.net>
        <authenticationModules>
            <add type="System.Net.DigestClient" />
            <add type="System.Net.KerberosClient" />
            <add type="System.Net.NegotiateClient" />
            <add type="System.Net.NtlmClient" />
            <add type="System.Net.BasicClient" />
        </authenticationModules>
        <!-- other sections -->
    </system.net>
    <section name="appSettings"
            type="System.Configuration
                .NameValueSectionHandler,System" />
</configSections>
```

This file indicates that there are configuration sections called `system.net` and `appSettings`. The values in the `appSettings` section are read using the general-purpose handler class `NameValueSectionHandler` (in the `System` assembly). This information is used by the `ConfigurationSettings` class (in the `System.Configuration` namespace), as I'll show in a moment, and the handlers define the items that you can add to the named section. The `appSettings` section is a single-level section in that it has only a child node, and the values are given as `Key` and `Value` attributes of the XML node—for example:

```
<appSettings>
    <add key="BackColor" value="White" />
    <add key="ForeColor" value="Black" />
</appSettings>
```

This information defines two values—BackColor and ForeColor—that can be read at runtime.

On the other hand, system.net is described with a <sectionGroup> tag, which means that the system.net section has nested sections. Each of these is described by a <section> tag, and I have shown the settings for only one: authenticationModules.

You can create your own handlers if you want to add your own sections in your configuration files. To do this you need to implement IConfiguration-SectionHeader (in the System.Configuration namespace). The application and publisher files "inherit" the <configSections> section from machine.config and can have their own sections.

At runtime an application can read its settings with the static AppSettings property of ConfigurationSettings:

```
// C#
foreach(string key in ConfigurationSettings.AppSettings)
{
    Console.WriteLine("{0} = {1}",
        key, ConfigurationSettings.AppSettings[key]);
}
```

So if my application had a configuration file with the <appSettings> section shown previously, the BackColor and ForeColor items and their values would be printed out. ConfigurationSettings also has a static method called Get-Config() that takes the name of a configuration section and returns a collection object appropriate for the configuration object for that section. For example, <appSettings> returns a NameValueCollection object:

```
// C#
NameValueCollection keys = null;
keys = (NameValueCollection)
    ConfigurationSettings.GetConfig("appSettings");
```

A shared assembly—one that has a shared name and is installed in the GAC—can also be configured by a publisher policy file. Publisher policy files follow the same format as application configuration files, but they are installed into the GAC as assemblies. Such installation means that you need to embed the configuration file in a resource-only assembly with `al.exe`:

```
al /embed:changesv1.config
   /out:changesv1_0.dll /keyfile:key.snk
```

The assembly created by this command line can then be installed into the GAC with `gacutil`.

1.4.3.3 .NET Versioning

Before I describe the details of .NET versioning, it is worth reiterating that version checking occurs only with assemblies that have strong names. As I mentioned earlier, an assembly identity is not just the assembly name, but also the version, culture, and strong name. Versioning in .NET is applied only at the assembly level, and a developer has to do it deliberately.

Thus we avoid the binary compatibility issues that Visual Basic COM developers suffered, when the compiler would change GUIDs during the development cycle of a component unless the developer changed the IDE settings to prevent this. However, when a developer changes a type in one of the source files that make up the assembly, the developer *must* update the version of the assembly. There's a shortcut, though, as I'll describe in a moment.

The assembly version is added through the `[AssemblyVersion]` assembly-level attribute (in the `Reflection` namespace). This attribute takes a string parameter in the following format:

```
<major>.<minor>.<build>.<revision>
```

If you provide the `<major>` and `<minor>` versions, you can provide an asterisk for `<build>`, which means that the build will be generated at compile time as the number of days since January 1, 2000, and the revision will be generated as the number of seconds since midnight (modulo 2). Or you can specify your own build number, in which case you can use an asterisk for the revision and the revison will be generated for you at compile time—for example:

```
// both C# and C++
[assembly: AssemblyVersion("1.0.*")]
```

The attribute indicates that this is version 1.0 of the assembly, and it allows the compiler to generate the build and revision number. This is a safe and useful way to version assemblies because every time you compile the assembly the revision *at least* will be updated, so you can track the versions of an assembly being built.

At runtime the assembly loader uses the version to determine which assembly to load. You may decide that the exact version is not necessary, in which case you can use configuration files to specify which versions are acceptable. This is done with the `<bindingRedir>` item in the `<runtime>` section of a configuration file:

```
<configuration>
   <runtime>
      <bindingRedir Name="myassembly"
         Version="*" VersionNew="2.0.0.0">
      </runtime>
</configuration>
```

This information indicates that in spite of the version of `myassembly` that is held in the application's manifest, Fusion will load version 2.0.0.0.

In addition, you can specify the culture of the assembly, to localize it. This is done with the `[AssemblyCulture]` attribute that has the culture in RFC 1766 form:

```
// both C# and C++
[assembly: AssemblyCulture("en-US")]
```

1.4.3.4 Satellite Assemblies

One thing that complicates the versioning scheme just described is the situation in which it is applied to so-called satellite assemblies that are used to provide localized resources to another assembly. For example, imagine you have an assembly with types that return string values, and you want those strings to be localized to the locale of the machine. To facilitate this localization, the developer should move the literal strings out of the assembly and create localized versions of these strings—each string associated with a culture-neutral identifier. The original assembly is now called the *main assembly,* and the localized resources will each make up a *satellite assembly.*

The string/identifier pairs for a specific culture can then be compiled as a resource with the `resgen.exe` utility, and the resource can be embedded as a named resource as part of a culture-specific assembly with the `al.exe` assembly builder tool. At runtime, code uses `ResourceManager` (in `System.Resources`) to load the resource from the satellite file. This class loads the appropriate assembly according to the current culture (more detail about using resources will be given in Chapter 8).

The assembly builder tool takes the culture and a version as command-line switches, but this means that satellite assemblies are separate files from the main assembly, and they could have different versions changing at a different frequency from that of the main assembly. This presents a versioning problem because there must be a mechanism to allow the satellite assemblies to be versioned independently from the main assembly in a safe way. To do this the main assembly specifies a *base version* for the satellite assembly that it uses. It does this with an assembly-level attribute:

```
[assembly: SatelliteContractVersion("1.0.0.0")]
```

Unlike versions applied through `[AssemblyVersion]`, the base versions must have all four parts. The satellite assembly can be versioned independently from the main version, and the changes can be reflected in the application's configuration file or, if the application is installed in the GAC, through a publisher policy file.

The binding process for satellite assemblies differs slightly from that applied to other assemblies. When a `ResourceManager` object is created, it initiates loading of the satellite assembly, in which case the runtime first looks in the GAC for the satellite assembly with the correct culture and checks if it has the resource. If not, the runtime then checks the current directory to see if the resource is in a culture-specific assembly, and if not, it starts the search again. This time, however, it searches for an assembly that has the appropriate "fallback" culture—first in the GAC and then in the current directory.

Each culture will have a fallback culture that will be searched in this way, until finally the runtime will attempt to locate the resource in the default resources for the assembly, which will be in the main assembly. If this search fails, the resource cannot be found and an exception will be thrown.

1.4.3.5 Binding and Probing

When an application is loaded, the runtime must locate and load the assemblies that the application uses. *Probing* is the process that the runtime uses to determine the location of the assemblies, and once an assembly is located it is *bound* to the assembly that uses it. By default, assemblies are private, which means that an assembly is not intended for wide use; instead it is intended for use by just one application. In this case, when a type in a private assembly is referred to, the loader looks in the application base (AppBase, the root directory of the application) for the assembly. AppBase is the place where the runtime's searches for private assemblies start. By default, Fusion will check the App-Base folder and then AppBase\<assem>, where <assem> is the name of the assembly that it is trying to locate (it searches for the assembly packaged both as a DLL and as an EXE).

You may decide that it is better to install your application such that assemblies are placed in specific subfolders within the application's folder. To do this you provide information in the policy configuration files mentioned earlier through a probing element that indicates a semicolon-delimited list of the sub-directories to check for the assembly:

```
<configuration>
   <runtime>
    <assemblyBinding
     xmlns="urn:schemas-microsoft-com:asm.v1">
       <probing privatePath="bin;dlls"/>
    </assemblyBinding>
   </runtime>
</configuration>
```

This application configuration file indicates that when the system tries to locate private assemblies, it should add the subdirectories bin and dlls to the search path. You can probe directories only under the application's directory.

Furthermore, the current locale is taken into account: Fusion will look for a subdirectory with the name of the current locale and perform the probing process there, too.

Assemblies do not have to be located on the hard disk; they can be located on a remote server. In this case the URI for the assembly can be specified in a `<codeBase>` element in the assemblies collection in the configuration file. The `<codeBase>` element can also be used to load the assembly from a directory other than the application's directory and subdirectories, as long as the assembly has a strong name.

You can load assemblies dynamically using the `Assembly.LoadFrom()` method (in the `System.Reflection` namespace). If you do this, the assembly will be placed in the `Download` directory mentioned earlier. However, this highlights an interesting problem. On the surface, .NET appears to be shifting away from the COM and RPC interface-based paradigm to a VB-like object-based paradigm. Indeed, as you'll learn in Chapter 3, you can access .NET remotely without the use of interfaces—a feat that is not possible with COM. However, the more I use .NET the more I realize that interface programming has not died; it is merely hidden from general view, and it appears in hours of need (somewhat like the legend of King Arthur, except that interfaces come to the rescue more often—well, actually, the difference is that interfaces *do* come to the rescue).

Here is an example. To demonstrate that classes can be dynamically downloaded from a Web site, I wrote this code:

```
// C#
Assembly assem = Assembly.LoadFrom(
    "http://MyServer/MyAssemblies/one.dll");
object o = assem.CreateInstance("MyClass");
MyClass myclass = (MyClass)o;
```

The first line gets the assembly from my server. Next I create an instance of a public type in the assembly that I downloaded (`MyClass`), and so that I can call the members of that type, I cast it to the class. This code looks fine, and you would expect to be able to call the `MyClass` members on the `myclass` reference.

Here my problems begin. To be able to do the cast, I had to reference the assembly that defined `MyClass` on the command line of the C# compiler, which put information about the assembly at compile time in the referring assembly. This information includes the *exact* version of the `one.dll` assembly that was referred to at compile time, so if this is different from the version on the Web site, I have a problem: They are different assemblies. Even if they are exactly the same assembly, the cast will fail because the runtime distinguishes between the dynamically loaded assembly and the statically linked assembly: They are two different assemblies if only because the statically linked assembly is a private assembly in the same directory and the downloaded assembly is in the `Download` folder.

The solution lies in using an interface in a separate assembly. Versioning is performed on the assembly level, and as long as the assembly version remains the same, it can be treated as immutable. The `object` reference obtained by dynamic loading of the type from a downloaded assembly may be cast to this interface, and if the type supports the interface, the cast will succeed (remember that the assembly defining the interface is *not* downloaded) and the methods can be called.

1.4.4 Application Domains

Win32 uses processes and threads for execution contexts. Processes are used to provide memory protection; each process has its own memory space and cannot touch the memory used by another process.[13] Within each process, threads execute the code, and thus every process has to have at least one thread. This scheme is good because each process is protected from rogue processes (those that try to tamper with other processes) and from badly written processes (those that have a habit of corrupting their own memory and then dying a horrible death).

Components are code that you invite into your process. Windows controls and COM components are packaged in DLLs. To use these components, you load the DLL into your process, giving the components complete access to your process's memory. If a component is badly or maliciously written, it can access the work you are doing and do something nasty with it (such as forward to your

---

13. Of course, *cannot* is a word that developers seldom want to use, so there are ways to provide shared memory between processes as long as both processes agree. For this discussion, however, assume that I am talking about isolated, unrelated processes.

boss all the job application letters you write), or it may simply write over your memory, corrupt your data, and kill your process. COM solves this problem by using Windows memory protection, which provides a surrogate process called `dllhost.exe` that the administrator uses to host a component. If the component tries to scribble on memory outside of itself, it is the memory managed by `dllhost.exe`, and not the application process, that is corrupted; if the component causes the process to die, that process is `dllhost.exe`.

The downside of the surrogate process is that it is a separate process, and thus when you talk to your chosen component this conversation has to occur through an IPC (interprocess communication) mechanism, which will always be many times slower than the in-process case. IPCs such as COM use proxy code that looks like the code that a process is trying to access. The proxy packages method parameters into data structures to be transmitted to the external process, either by copying data by value or by providing information that the external process can use to create a proxy to access objects by reference. What is needed is a mechanism to isolate code within a single process.

A side effect of using processes shows up when you debug them. The debugging API has the annoying behavior that once you have attached the debugger to a process, there is no way to detach it without shutting down that process. This is fine if you are debugging to investigate an exception that would otherwise kill your process, but it is irritating if you are investigating a minor bug or a bug in a component loaded in the process. What is needed here is a debugger that can gracefully remove itself from a process without killing the process, and one that can debug just one isolated section within the process without affecting the other sections of the process.

.NET introduces the concept of *application domains* to overcome these problems. Each host .NET process has at least one domain that contains threads executing IL code. You can create additional domains in a process, but each one is isolated from all others. All IL is verified by the type system before it is executed to ensure that the correct code is called and that the code does not perform invalid memory operations. This verification is performed by the runtime in addition to the memory protection applied at the process level by the operating system. Thus the verification is applied at a subprocess level within the domain.

Similar to IPC, communication between domains requires marshaling of data and object reference through proxies. However, when the two domains that are communicating are within the same process, the mechanism is very much faster than IPC (though the use of proxies makes it slightly slower than intradomain access) and thus gives you the advantage of fast component access while still maintaining isolation.

The analogy of domains being subprocesses within a process is useful. Traditional NT processes apply configuration settings like security at the process level. Developers could often tweak these settings in code on a per-thread basis. *Application settings* in .NET are applied at the domain level, so if you have multiple domains in one process, they can be configured independently of each other—either in a configuration file or by code. When you change the way that code access security works, to assert a permission that your code requires, the change is relevant to only the single domain.

When you load an assembly into a domain, the assembly is specific to that domain. It cannot directly access objects in any other domain, and thus it cannot access the memory used by other domains. If more than one domain loads the same assembly, a new copy of the assembly is loaded unless the assembly is loaded as *domain neutral*. The core system assembly, `mscorlib`, will be used by all domains and is always loaded as domain neutral. Domain-neutral assemblies can be private assemblies or shared assemblies; the point is that just one copy of the code is loaded in each domain in a process.

Typically .NET hosts create domains. The current way to write a host is to write a native application that loads the execution engine with a call to `CorBind-ToRuntimeEx()`.[14] This method returns the COM interface `ICorRuntimeHost`, which has a method called `CreateDomain()`. A call to `CreateDomain()` returns a pointer to `System.AppDomain()` through COM Interop, and the host process can use the methods on this class to load assemblies into the domain.

The `CreateDomain()` method is also available to managed code as a static method on the `AppDomain` class—for example:

---

14. The prefix `Cor` is a legacy of the evolution of .NET from various technologies within Microsoft. The original suggestion of a runtime was announced at the 1997 Professional Developer Conference, where it was called the `Component Object Runtime`.

```csharp
// C#
using System;
using System.Reflection;
using System.Runtime.Remoting;

public class DomainMember : MarshalByRefObject
{
    public string GetLocation()
    {
        return "I am in "
            + AppDomain.CurrentDomain.FriendlyName;
    }
}

public class App
{
    public static void Main()
    {
        // create object in default AppDomain
        DomainMember c1 = new DomainMember();
        Console.WriteLine("first object: {0}",
            c1.GetLocation());
        // create a new AppDomain
        AppDomain ad;
        ad = AppDomain.CreateDomain(
                "Second Domain", null);
        // load the current assembly to get its full name;
        // in this case mscorlib.dll will be the
        // first assembly
        Assembly[] assemblies;
        assemblies = AppDomain.CurrentDomain.
            GetAssemblies();
        // create an instance of our class in the
        // new AppDomain
        ObjectHandle h;
        h = ad.CreateInstance(
                assemblies[1].FullName, "DomainMember");
        DomainMember c2 = (DomainMember)h.Unwrap();
        Console.WriteLine("second object: {0}",
            c2.GetLocation());
    }
}
```

This code creates instances of `DomainMember` in the default domain, as well as in a domain that I create, called `Second Domain`. The `App-Domain.CreateInstance()` method takes the name of the assembly that contains the type. As explained earlier, this isn't merely the simple text name of the assembly; instead, the full display name is required. To get this I access the assembly and use the `FullName` property. The first assembly loaded into the domain is `mscorlib`, so to get the current assembly I access the second item in the array. (I could get the current assembly also by calling the static `Assembly.GetExecutingAssembly()`.)

Threads are not domain specific. They are not members of a single domain; they are members of the process. However, typically you use a thread only in a single domain because the Framework Class Library does not provide the classes to share threads across domains. When you create a thread object, you create it in a specific domain, and this means that the thread object (and thus the thread to which it is attached) will be used in that single domain. `System.Threading.Thread` is not serializable, so `Thread` objects cannot be passed between domains. The `Thread` class has a member called `Get-Domain()`, which will return information about the domain in which the thread is *currently* running.

Again, however, threads are not domain specific. This can be shown when you consider the `Threading.ThreadPool` class, which gives access to the *process's* thread pool. Any domain can queue work on threads in the thread pool, and the same thread could do work in any of these domains.

1.4.5 Administering Security

I mentioned earlier that all code is subject to code access security applied by the runtime through a security policy. This policy is determined in three ways: through machine settings, user settings, and domain settings applied through code.

The machine settings and user settings are administered through a command-line tool called `caspol.exe` and a Microsoft Management Console (MMC) snap-in called the Microsoft .NET Framework Configuration (the file `mscorcfg.msc`), which the .NET installer will add to your machine's Administrative Tools Start Menu folder. These tools give access to data in the configuration files in the CONFIG directory of the framework folder. The machine.config file has a section that specifies the trust levels defined for the system. My machine is a workstation machine and has these settings:

```
<securityPolicy>
  <trustLevel name="Full" policyFile="internal" />
  <trustLevel name="High"
   policyFile="web_hightrust.config" />
  <trustLevel name="Low"
   policyFile="web_lowtrust.config" />
  <trustLevel name="None"
   policyFile="web_notrust.config" />
</securityPolicy>
```

This information indicates how these levels of trust are resolved by use of other files in the CONFIG directory. These files specify permissions grouped together in permission sets, and code is given a permission set based on a set of rules called *code groups*. web_hightrust.config has the following code group:

```
<CodeGroup class="FirstMatchCodeGroup" version="1"
           PermissionSetName="Nothing">
  <IMembershipCondition class="AllMembershipCondition"
     version="1"/>
  <CodeGroup class="UnionCodeGroup"
     version="1" PermissionSetName="ASP.Net">
    <IMembershipCondition
     class="UrlMembershipCondition"
     version="1" Url="$CodeGen$/*"/>
  </CodeGroup>
  <!-- other code groups -->
</CodeGroup>
```

Note that the FirstMatchCodeGroup group contains other code groups. I have shown just one child code group. Each child group can also have its own child group; thus a tree of groups forms. Each code group contains membership conditions, and if code meets the criteria, the specified permission set is considered for the final permission set for the code, with the permissions for one child group combined with the permissions assigned to its parent. For example,

UnionCodeGroup says that if the URL of a piece of code is the URL given in $CodeGen$, it will get the permissions given in the permission set called ASP.Net *and* in the permission set in its parent, called Nothing.

As their name suggests, permission sets contain one or more permissions that the code can perform, so in web_hightrust.config the permission set called ASP.Net looks like this:

```
<NamedPermissionSets>
    <PermissionSet class="NamedPermissionSet"
        version="1" Name="ASP.Net">
        <IPermission class="EnvironmentPermission"
          version="1"
          Read="TEMP;TMP;USERNAME;OS;COMPUTERNAME" />
        <IPermission class="FileIOPermission"
         version="1" Read="$AppDir$"
         Write="$AppDir$" Append="$AppDir$"
         PathDiscovery="$AppDir$" />
        <!--other permissions omitted -->
    </PermissionSet>
    <!--other permission sets omitted -->
</NamedPermissionSets>
```

These items mean that (in addition to the permissions that I have omitted) the code granted this permission set has restricted access to only those environment variables listed and has read, write, and append access to files in the directory identified by $AppDir$ (which is the application's directory). They also indicate the framework permission classes (in System.Security.Permission) that are used to configure these permissions programmatically. When the system has performed a code access check, it will generate the permission set by creating instances of these classes. The attributes within the <IPermission> tags give the values that will be passed to the constructor of the specified permission class.

Thus, in the preceding example, when creating the ASP.Net permission set, the runtime will create an instance of the FileIOPermission class. This class has a constructor that takes a FileIOPermissionAccess enumeration (AllAccess, NoAccess, Append, Read, Write) and a string that lists the files or directories where the access is allowed.

I mentioned earlier that your application domain can also affect the security policy; it does this by creating permission sets at runtime. For example, your code may want to have specific permissions—for example, to access a specific file—and if these permissions are not given, your code will not work. It would be very unhelpful indeed if your code received that permission in the security policy but code farther up the call stack did not have the same permissions. To avoid these problems, your code can indicate that it needs a particular permission and that code farther up the call stack should not be considered for code access security. To do this your code must create a permission (or a permission set) and then call `Assert()`:

```csharp
// C#
try
{
    FileIOPermission fiop;
    fiop = new FileIOPermission(
        FileIOPermissionAccess.Write,
        "results.txt");
    fiop.Assert();
    // write stuff to the file
}
catch(SecurityException se)
{
    Console.WriteLine("cannot access this file");
}
```

When you assert a permission like this, you are telling the runtime not to check code access farther up the stack, so the code that calls your code can have any level of trust. Of course, your code must have the specified permission according to the machine and user policies; by calling `Assert()`, you don't simply get the permission you request. In addition, the Win32 security system may have an access control list on a secured object affected by the permission asserted, so the permission granted will also depend on the access token of the thread having a principal that has been granted access permissions in the ACL.

On the other hand, your code could call code in an assembly that you have not written. In this case you may have documentation saying what this assembly will do, but do you trust that this code will not try to do something else? To guard against this possibility, you can create a permission set of the permissions that you think the utility code *should* need and no more. You do not give this code more permissions than those that the security policy has given your code, but you can restrict those permissions. To do this your code creates a permission set and then adds individual permissions to it, up to the level that you want to allow the utility code to have. Before you call the utility code, you call `PermitOnly()` on this permission set to give the called code those permissions. (You can also call `Deny()` if you want to impose restrictions rather than giving specific permissions.)

The security API also supports the application of assertion through attributes. Each permission class has a corresponding attribute class—for example:

```
// C#
[FileIOPermission(SecurityAction.Assert, Write="results.txt")]
public void WriteResultsOne()
{
   // write data to results.txt
}
public void WriteResultsTwo()
{
   FileIOPermission fiop;
   fiop = new FileIOPermission(
     FileIOPermissionAccess.Write,
     "results.txt");
   p.Assert();
   // write data to results.txt
}
```

These two methods assert the same permission. `WriteResultsOne()` is clearer than `WriteResultsTwo()` but suffers from two problems. First, when you make an assertion in code, you can protect that code with a `try` block (as shown earlier) and handle the exception within the method where the assertion is performed. If you apply the assertion through an attribute and this fails, the exception will propagate to the calling code. Second, any parameters used in the assertion (in this case the name of the file that will be written to) are hard-coded when you use an attribute, but it can be determined at runtime whether the assertion is performed in code.

1.5 Summary

.NET represents a new way of programming. The most important change is the way in which types are located and loaded. All types are housed in assemblies, and when a type is used in an assembly, information about that type and its assembly is stored in the referring assembly's manifest. This is static linking in that the referring assembly knows the *exact* assembly that should be loaded at runtime. However, at runtime the assembly is located in a dynamic way, according to default search rules that the administrator can change through configuration files.

All types are described by metadata, and the security system uses this information to ensure that the type loaded and executed is the type that the referring code requested. Metadata can be extended by attributes that developers can use to add information about how the type should be used and even to add some behavior to the type. The runtime recognizes some attributes and can change how it uses the type on the basis of its attributes, and you can write your own code to read and act on attributes.

All .NET code is compiled to intermediate language that is JIT-compiled at runtime. .NET compilers translate code into IL and metadata and package them in assemblies. A .NET consumer tool imports types as IL code and has no knowledge about the original language used to write the type. IL is language neutral, meaning that developers can use any .NET language to write .NET code. Thus developers will use the language with which they are most comfortable.

To a certain extent, many of the things that you can do in .NET, and the ways that you can do them, have their roots in Win32. Some parts of the Framework Class Library present new paradigms of programming, but others are simple wrappers around Win32 APIs, dividing those APIs into more components, and may be simpler to use. In the next chapter I will investigate the framework classes and show how using the framework differs from using the Win32 API, and how it can be just the same.

Chapter 2

Framework Class Library

However wonderful an operating system is, it is useless if developers cannot access its facilities. However wonderful a language is, it is useless without a good runtime library. The library that comes with a language has as much influence on your choice of a development language as do the facilities in the language. I explained in Chapter 1 that the .NET Framework comes with a runtime that does wonderful things for you, but this would be of little use if it did not come with a library.

Microsoft has provided the Framework Class Library, a collection of assemblies that are installed on your machine when you install .NET. These assemblies are available to every application, so they are installed in the machine's GAC. The Framework Class Library contains the basic classes that you need to build your applications and in general provide a wrapper over Win32.

In this chapter I will outline the main parts of the Framework Class Library, and I will describe most of the important namespaces. With most of the Framework Class Library, Microsoft has taken the opportunity to step back from the Win32 API, abstracting the functionality that it wants to provide. Consequently, many of the classes in the Framework Class Library bear little resemblance to their equivalents in Win32. The framework classes are more object oriented, and by and large they are easier to use and understand. However, Win32 is a huge library, and clearly Microsoft has not had enough time to complete this process of abstraction over the entire library. As a result, some parts of the Framework Class Library appear as mere wrappers over Win32.[1] This is a

---

1. Of course, this could mean that the Win32 way was the best way to perform the specific action, but it could also mean that Microsoft merely hasn't had the time to develop a new paradigm.

pity because this is the first opportunity since NT 3.1 was released for a complete rethinking of the Windows API. Another opportunity will not come along for many years.

2.1   The Win32 API

Before I describe the Framework Class Library, I want to put the library into context and describe the Win32 API to give you a better understanding of why the Framework Class Library is structured in the way it is. The first version of NT essentially contained user, kernel, GDI, networking, and security DLLs. This functionality was provided as DLL-exported functions, essentially making Windows a C API. At that time most Windows applications were written in C, although C++ was gaining popularity. It took several years for 32-bit VB to arrive, and during this time NT was extended with new functionality. Every time this happened, the API provided was a C API—consisting of exported functions from a DLL.

Visual Basic gained popularity because it made Windows programming simple by providing Win32 functionality through VB intrinsic objects. To get the text in an edit box and to make sure that the string buffer is the correct size, you access the `Text` property of the text box object rather than calling `GetWindowTextLength()` and then `GetWindowText()`. This approach is great, but it suffers from one main drawback: Every time NT is extended by a new API, VB has to have a new intrinsic object. This is far from satisfactory.

VB allows programmers to access exported functions using the `Declare` statement, but this means that the VB programmer has to use the (essentially) C-based parameters provided through the API. Of more concern is the fact that many Win32 APIs are related and act on a system resource identified by an opaque handle. VB intrinsic objects hide these handles from the developer by wrapping such APIs as objects (e.g., a `ListBox` object holds the list box's `HWND` handle, which is used to send messages to the list box when the user accesses the `ListBox` properties), which could validate these handles. By accessing APIs through the `Declare` statement, we lose this advantage.

OLE automation came along (initially on 16-bit Windows) and changed things. Rather than importing a whole load of functions from a DLL, the automation developer merely imports an `Application` object and then makes requests either for methods implemented by that object or for other objects with the required functionality. Automation is based on COM, but in general, automation programmers ignore interfaces because to a VB programmer, methods are implemented by objects. This is an important point, and it clearly influenced .NET. As new APIs appeared on NT, they began to appear as exported DLL functions *and* through automation objects. The VB library could be extended without VB itself having to be changed because an automation object appeared in VB code as if it were a VB intrinsic object.

Automation requests are made with locale-specific text requests. Automation objects are requested to convert text strings to locale-independent identifiers at runtime by the automation clients, and then the code is invoked with these identifiers being passed. This is called *late binding;* it is used extensively, but it has some considerable problems, principally because the invocation always requires a lookup to convert a text string to the member identifier. This means that the check of whether an object supports a member is carried out at runtime, even though the developer should have all the information at compile/development time to determine what the object can do. A simple spelling mistake of an object's member name in an automation script may not appear until months after the script has been deployed.

Of course, the lookup could be performed by a tool (the unmanaged Visual Basic 6 IDE does this), but this inherent weakness is part of automation. Furthermore, because automation is based on text identifiers, the developer's job is more difficult because the method that converts the text identifiers to the member identifiers is locale dependent, which means that a different version is required for every locale where the code is intended to be sold.

Automation is based on COM. COM is interface based, interfaces are immutable, and all methods are accessed through interface pointers. Object-based automation circumvents this rule because automation objects implement `IDispatch`, which follows COM's rules, but it allows the immutability of interfaces to be bypassed by allowing dynamic invocation through `GetIDsOfNames()` and `Invoke()`. Classes implement interfaces, but the class is largely incidental to the COM programmer because all access is through interface pointers and the class name (its CLSID) is mentioned only briefly in the call to `CoCreateInstanceEx()`. This is logical because interfaces represent behavior, and once a developer has selected the particular implementation of the behaviors she requires (by selecting a CLSID), the rest of the code is concentrated on using that behavior.

COM offered a bright light—a way of unifying API access in an object-oriented way. You can write a COM class with all COM clients in mind by providing its functionality through `[oleautomation]` interfaces (for scripting clients and those that use type library marshaling) and RPC-like "custom" interfaces (for C and C++ clients). This means that a library can be encapsulated by classes that can be accessed by all developers. Of course, existing APIs have to be converted to COM objects, and all new APIs should be provided as COM objects, too, but once the work has been carried out, Win32 could be a complete, unified API.

Is this really possible? It is a noble aim, but there are some tough problems to overcome. The Win32 API has been developed over many years, through the use of different paradigms and even different mechanisms for basic things like passing data and handling errors. The task of wrapping all the APIs as a unified library is not trivial. As an example, let me explain how memory allocation and error handling—two of the most important features that a library should provide—are managed in Win32.

2.1.1 Memory Allocation

Many Win32 APIs return large amounts of data, so with a C-based API someone has to take responsibility for managing that memory. Some APIs define a fixed-length record and ask the developer to allocate it (typically as a stack-based `auto` variable). For example, `GetSystemInfo()` receives information about the current system in a `SYSTEM_INFO` structure that you allocate and pass through a pointer. The data in this structure has a fixed length, so the system has no problems. Other APIs return variable-length data and require that you allocate a buffer large enough to hold the returned data. For example, `GetComputerName()` returns the NetBIOS name of a machine up to a maximum of `MAX_COMPUTERNAME_LENGTH` (plus 1 for the `NUL` terminator). You can create a buffer of this size, or you can take potluck and pass a smaller buffer. The API has a parameter for the length of the buffer that you provide, and if this is too small, it will return to you the minimum size that it needs.

DEVELOPING APPLICATIONS WITH VISUAL STUDIO.NET

Other APIs are odder still. Take, for example, `ReadEventLog()`. This API asks you to allocate a buffer that it will fill with an event log record (`EVENT-LOGRECORD`) if the buffer is large enough. However, it is an extremely "helpful" API because if it sees that your buffer is large enough to take more than one instance of `EVENTLOGRECORD`, it will fill the remaining space with extra records! This is a nightmare from a programming point of view because you can never guarantee how many records will be returned on each call to `ReadEventLog()`, and as a consequence your code becomes horribly complicated because you have to cache the buffer that you use. Furthermore, the API returns variable-length records, but rather than being helpful and structuring these so that string parameters are accessed through string pointers, it just dumps the bytes on you and gives you offsets to those strings.

Isn't Windows clever enough to allocate memory itself? Of course it is! Windows has a plethora of APIs to manage memory, and other APIs that take advantage of these memory APIs show yet another way to pass data through method parameters. Many APIs will allocate memory for you using `LocalAlloc()`,[2] their documentation stating that you ought to free the memory when you are finished with the buffer. Examples can be seen in the cryptographic APIs, the access control APIs, and `FormatMessage()`. In addition, some APIs will allocate memory for you but will not tell you how they do it, and they issue a dire warning in their documentation that you should not free the memory yourself. Examples can be seen in the Local Security Authority (LSA) security APIs and the network APIs, which provide methods to clean up the buffers that they allocate.

Finally, in some cases Windows simply gives up and admits that it does not know how much data will be returned. In such cases the API is accessed through enumeration where your code provides a callback function that Windows calls with each piece of information it has. (One example is the `EnumWindows()` API.)

---

2. Win32 inherited the names `GlobalAlloc()` and `LocalAlloc()` from Win16, but the two are actually the same.

As you can see, memory can be allocated in many ways: by the client as a fixed structure, by the client as a variable structure with the function checking the size of the buffer, by the function's use of a known allocator (`LocalAlloc()`) with the client taking responsibility for deallocation, and finally by the function's use of its own allocator with the client being required to call another API to deallocate the buffer.

For COM to be used for the basis of a unified library, it had to hide all of these complexities. To a certain extent it did so by providing a set of rules stating who had the responsibility of allocating and deallocating memory, and by handling cross-process calls through proxy objects that hid most of the allocations that made it look as if memory were being allocated locally. However, COM still wasn't completely straightforward, so the result was code that could leak interface reference, `BSTR`, `VARIANT`, and `SAFEARRAY` values if the authors forgot (or weren't aware) that they had to release those items. If developers followed COM's rules, there would be no problems. However, COM's rules were frequently ignored, and for this reason COM was not used as the basis of a unified library.

.NET solves the memory allocation problem in a very simple way: Applications never allocate or deallocate memory; instead, the garbage collector (GC) is responsible for all memory.

2.1.2 Error Handling

Now let's take a look at errors. Some APIs will return an error code indicating what has occurred. For example, the registry APIs (`RegOpenKey()`, `RegQuery-Value()`, and so on) do this and return a value that is documented in `winerr.h`. These are mere numbers, and to get a human-readable string describing the error, you can pass the error code to `FormatMessage()`. Other APIs return an error value that is private to the API. With network APIs (`lm.h`) and RPC APIs (`rpcdce.h`), for example, you are given a status value and it is your responsibility to sort out what it means (typically by reading through the documentation or the header files). Other APIs return a `BOOL` value to indicate whether the function (e.g., `GetComputerName()`) was successful, and if a value of `FALSE` is returned, you can call either `GetLastError()` to get a status code (again, documented in winerror.h) or `FormatMessage()` to get a formatted string describing the error. Finally, some Win32 APIs even use exceptions: The `HeapCreate()`, `HeapAlloc()`, and `HeapRealloc()` functions can throw an SEH exception (SEH stands for *structured exception handling*) if the functions fail. Although these APIs document that throwing exceptions is optional, it represents yet another way to indicate an error condition.

In an attempt to make some sense of this mess, COM started by introducing a unified error reporting mechanism using 32-bit codes called `HRESULT` results. The original documentation cryptically mentioned that 16 bits of each status code could be a "handle" to further error information, but this idea was never developed further. As a consequence, developers were sent back to the bad old days of maintaining lists of error codes. Error handling improved with error objects and OLE DB extended error objects, but the main focus was still on status codes.

As an application developer, you have to take into account all of these different ways of indicating errors. Of course, it does not help that in C++ a value of `true` is nonzero, so the following code:

```
// unmanaged C++
if (RegOpenKey(HKEY_LOCAL_MACHINE,
            "Software", &hKey))
{
    puts("cannot open HKLM\\Software");
}
```

will always generate an error because `RegOpenKey()` returns a status code, not a `BOOL` value, where a return value of `0` indicates success.

Clearly a unified library would have to provide a coherent error reporting mechanism. .NET does this through exceptions. Exceptions are part of the runtime, so *all* .NET languages understand them. This means that when a class written in one lanuage generates an error by throwing an exception, that error can be caught by a class written in a totally different language. COM could not do this because the term *exception* meant different things to different languages: It meant C++ exceptions to C++, SEH exceptions to C, and the **Application Error** dialog to VB.

2.2   Framework Class Library

The Framework Class Library was created to provide a unified approach to the collected Windows APIs. You could argue that the Framework Class Library is made up of two sets of classes: the core library and the rest. The core library is implemented mainly in the `mscorlib` assembly and is contained largely in the `System` namespace. If Microsoft ports .NET to other platforms, the core library is clearly the priority. The rest of the Framework Class Library consists of classes that give access to services provided by Windows. These classes are more difficult for Microsoft to port to other platforms, either because those platforms do not have the services or because their implementation on other platforms is totally different from the implementation of their equivalents in Windows.

Some of the Framework Class Library APIs follow new paradigms. Notable are the `System.Windows.Forms` namespace and the `System.IO` namespace used for windowing and file stream access, respectively. Both of these namespaces provide mechanisms that differ considerably from their equivalents in Win32. These new paradigms are logical and (by and large) offer a platform-neutral mechanism. Other classes do not fare as well.

2.3   The Core Library

I have to stress that the following sections are the classes that I consider the core library. Microsoft may provide a different collection of classes if it ports .NET to other platforms. My list consists of the Framework Class Library classes that could be ported to other platforms and the classes that I think should be ported. Some namespaces I have not covered either because I will cover them in later chapters (like the runtime services) or because other texts do them more justice (e.g., the ASP namespaces and the security namespaces).

2.3.1   General-Purpose Classes

The `System` namespace contains essentially two groups of classes, which I have called general-purpose classes and system classes. I will cover system classes in the next section. General-purpose classes are those that you need for day-to-day programming tasks, so in this group I include the collection classes in `System.Collection` and `System.Collection.Specialized`.

2.3.1.1 Manipulating Primitive Types

I will start with the value types used to manage data types, which were given in Table 1.1 in Chapter 1. As I mentioned then, even literal values in your code are instances of these value types, so the following statement is perfectly legal:

```
// C#
string str = 42.ToString();
```

In this case, `42` is an instance of `Int32`, and `Int32.ToString()` will return the string version of the number. C# also allows you to access the static members of the value type through the C# primitive type. For example, `short` is the value type `Int16`, which has a static method called `Parse()` to construct an `Int16` object from a string. C# allows you to call `Parse()` through `short`, as well as through `Int16`:

```
// C#
short s1 = Int16.Parse("42");
short s2 = short.Parse("42");
```

There is no C++ equivalent to this last line. You cannot call the methods of Framework Class Library classes through primitive types in this way (this is not a great problem here because in this case you can call the methods on `Int16`). C# will automatically box a value type that you pass as a parameter to `Console.WriteLine()`, so you can write the following:

```
// C#
int x = 42;
Console.WriteLine("Value is {0} {1}", x, 42);
Console.WriteLine("Value is " + x + " " + 42);
```

In the first case, C# boxes the two `Int32` instances and passes them to the version of `WriteLine()` that takes two object parameters (and a format string). These `Int32` instances will eventually be passed to `String-Builder.Format()`, which will create the string by calling `ToString()` on the boxed parameters and inserting the results of those calls into the formatted string. This string will then be passed to the current stream output object.

The second version takes a more straightforward approach, stitching the string together with a call to `String.Concat()` before calling the current stream output object. In this simple case the first example involves calling more code than the second, and the first case should be used only when you specifically want to format a value with values other than the default.

C++ does not do quite as much work for you; in fact, it makes you explicitly specify that you want to box a value. C++ enforces this requirement because the boxing process creates a new object, giving the user control over the performance implications:

```
// C++
int x = 42;
Console::WriteLine(S"Value is {0} {1}",
    __box(x), __box(42));
String* str = String::Concat(S"Value is ",
    __box(x), S" ", __box(42));
Console::WriteLine(str);
```

There are a couple of interesting points to make here. First, `String` does not have a + operator; C# has its own string + operator, which C++ does not. This means that you have to do the concatenation yourself in C++. (I have used the version that takes four `Object*` pointers. If you need to concatenate more strings, you will need to call the version that takes an array of `Object*` pointers.) All the parameters to this overload must be `Object*` pointers. Hence, the value types must be boxed, and interestingly, the string literals must be given as .NET strings with the `S` prefix, which generates the IL code to treat the literal as a .NET string rather than an array of `char` values. (Remember, C++ allows you to use both .NET types and native unmanaged C++ types.)

Considering that the concatenation version is quicker than the version that uses `StringBuilder.Format()`, it is a pity that C++ does not have an equivalent to C#'s + string operator because a format string seems far more natural to a C++ developer and is more likely to be used than the concatenation version.[3] However, managed C++ developers have taken the (correct) stance that classes define operators, and because `String` does not have a + operator, the language should not provide one.

---

3. To be fair, however, although my tests show that the concatenation version is consistently quicker, it is only marginally so (by 0.5 percent).

DEVELOPING APPLICATIONS WITH VISUAL STUDIO.NET

All of these types have a method called `GetTypeCode()` that returns a value from the `TypeCode` enumeration.

Most of the types have `MaxValue` and `MinValue` constant properties to indicate the range of values allowed and to enable checking of the range. The Framework Class Library has an exception type called `OverflowException` that can be thrown. By default, overflows are not detected in C#, so to turn on this feature you must use either the `/checked` switch on the compiler or the `checked` statement to define checked blocks.[4] (Conversely, if the source file is compiled as checked code, you can define unchecked blocks with `unchecked`):

```
// C#
// compiled without /checked
static void Main()
{
    short s1 = Uint16.MaxValue;
    // no overflow checking performed
    s1++;
    short s2 = Uint16.MaxValue;
    // turn on checking for this code
    checked{s2++;}
}
```

This code will throw `OverflowException` on the last statement; incrementing `s1` merely discards the overflow. Overflow checking is performed for the operators +, − (the binary operator), and * because overflow checking can be performed on the IL for these operators. In addition, overflow checking can be performed on conversions between the integral types. Although these overflow checks are performed by IL and are not a language feature, turning them on is a language feature—one sadly lacking from this version of the C++ compiler. In C++ you have to perform overflow checks yourself.

The primitive value types have methods appropriate to the data types that they represent. The integer and floating-point types have essentially just `Parse()` and `ToString()` methods because little that is interesting can be determined from

---

4. IL has two versions each of the operators +, −, and * (but not /): one that has the `ovf` suffix (e.g., `add.ovf`), which checks for overflows, and one that does not. The `/checked` switch and checked blocks determine which version is used.

these data types. Other types have more interesting values, so methods are provided to check these values. `Char`, for instance, represents a character, so it has a method to check what type of character it is: Is it a letter, a digit, or white space? Is it uppercase or lowercase?

The Framework Class Library also has classes to allow you to manipulate date values; they are `DateTime` and `TimeSpan`. A point in time is represented by `DateTime`, which is the number of 100-nanosecond intervals since 00:00:00 on the first of January 0001, according to the Gregorian calendar (which is the default calendar). A `DateTime` instance can be initialized to use another calendar, which can be found in the `System.Globalization` namespace. Although the actual date is held as an `Int64` value, the class provides properties to get information like the day, month, and year, and even the day of the week (through a locale-independent enumeration called `Day-OfWeek`; I'll explain how to get the locale-dependent day name later). In addition, `DateTime` has a static property called `Now` that you can use to get the current time and date. The `DateTime` class also supports conversions to and from two other time types that Win32 supports: `FILETIME` and automation's `DATE`.

`DateTime` has operators and methods that allow you to perform time and date arithmetic. You can add hours, minutes, seconds, and so on to a `DateTime` instance, and you can subtract one `DateTime` instance from another. However, subtracting one date from another results not in another date, but in a time interval, which in .NET is represented by the `TimeSpan` class. `TimeSpan` has properties that allow you to access the time interval in terms of various time units (number of seconds, minutes, days, and so on).

There is one more class in this roundup: `Uri`. As its name suggests, this class is used to hold information about a Uniform Resource Identifier. Instances of this class are initialized with a string that represents the URI, which can include the protocol, domain name, port, resource path, and query string or anchor. The class has properties that return these various constituent parts. The class also has methods that allow you to check the validity of the URI, and to escape the string.

2.3.1.2 Collections

The `System.Collection` and `System.Collection.Specialized` namespaces contain the standard .NET collection classes. `System.Collection` defines four interfaces for collections—`ICollection`, `IList`, `IEnumerable`, and `IDictionary`—as well as classes with standard implementations of the behaviors represented by these interfaces.

`ICollection` is the most basic. Its only collection-relevant member is the `Count` property, which returns the number of items in the collection. Collections that implement this interface typically also implement one of the other interfaces to give access to the collection data in a useful way.

The `IList` interface gives random access to data in the collection via an index. `IEnumerable` gives access to an enumerator object that can be used to access members serially from beginning to end in the collection. Three general-purpose classes can be accessed in this way: `Array`, which represents an array of a fixed size; `ArrayList`, whose size is dynamically increased as needed; and `StringCollection`, which is a dynamically sized array specifically for strings.

If random access is not important to you because you will always read items in the collection in a specified order, you can use a collection that implements an `IEnumerable` interface. This interface gives access to an enumerator object that can be used to access members serially from beginning to end. `IDictionary` gives access to an enumerator that implements `IDictionaryEnumerator`, which in turn gives serial access to key/value pairs. I described the various collection classes in Chapter 1.

2.3.1.3 Converting Types

An instance of one type can be converted to an instance of another type if an appropriate conversion operator is provided. If you define your own types, conversion is carried out when you define an `op_Implicit()` or an `op_Explicit()` operator on the type (which I'll explain in a moment).

For the primitive types, the Framework Class Library provides the `Convert` class. Some conversions are symmetrical; some are not. This class has a general-purpose method called `ChangeType()` that takes the object to be converted and an indication of the type to which it should be converted, which can be either a `Type` object (which you can obtain through the C# `typeof()` or the C++ `__typeof()` operator) or a `TypeCode` enumerated value (which is a property of all the primitive value types). In addition, you can pass the `IFormatProvider` interface on a formatter object. `IFormatProvider` provides culture-specific formatting information. I will talk about formatters later.

In the following code I convert a 16-bit integer to a string and specify the base of the number to use in the conversion. In this case I want the hex format of the string to be printed:

```
// C#
short s = 255;
Console.WriteLine("0x"
    + Convert.ToString(s, 16));
```

You can also use the `Convert` class to convert binary data to and from base64:

```
// C#
byte[] arr = new byte[10];
for(byte b = 0; b < arr.Length; b++)
    arr[b] = b;
string s = Convert.ToBase64String(arr);
```

The Framework Class Library provides a class called `FormatterConverter` (in `System.Runtime.Serialization`) that combines a serialization formatter with the `Convert` class. I will talk about serialization in Chapter 3.

If you write your own types, you can provide your own conversion operators by implementing the `op_Implicit()` and `op_Explicit()` operators on your type. These operators are not CLS compliant, but the .NET languages provided with VS.NET support conversions using these operators. The difference between the two is that `op_Implicit()` is called when a conversion is performed without a cast, in which case the conversion should be completed without any loss of information or any possibility of an exception being thrown. The developer performs an implicit conversion because he is sure of the implication, and typically the types being converted are related.

On the other hand, when the developer attempts to coerce the conversion of a value from one type into another type, information could be lost, or worse still, the values could be so incompatible that the conversion could fail. In this case the cast has to be explicit, acting as an indicator to the developer that the cast may fail.

These operators are implemented as static operators that take as a parameter the type that is being cast and return a new instance of the type to which the cast is being made:

```
// C#
public class Celsius
{
    private float temperature = 0;
    public float Temperature
    {
        get{ return temperature; }
        set
        {
            // absolute zero is -273.15 degrees Celsius
            if (value <= -273.15f)
                throw new ArgumentOutOfRangeException(
                    "impossible temperature!");
            temperature = value;
        }
    }
    public Celsius(float x)
    { Temperature = x; }
    public static explicit operator Celsius(float x)
    { return new Celsius(x); }
    public static implicit operator float(Celsius x)
    { return x.Temperature; }
}
```

The `Celsius` class represents a temperature in Celsius. The minimum value possible is –273.15°C. The laws of physics say that no temperature is possible at or below –273.15°C; this value is known as absolute zero. Thus `Celsius` checks if the value passed as the temperature is less than or equal to absolute zero. I have added an explicit conversion operator to convert a `float` type into a `Celsius` type, so I can create instances of the class in two ways:

```
// C#
Celsius roomTemp = new Celsius(18.0f);5
Celsius boiling = (Celsius)100.0f;
```

It is important to understand what is happening here. The first line calls the constructor and passes a `float` value to it; the second line calls the explicit conversion operator, which indicates that the cast is required.

The `Celsius` class also has an implicit operator to convert from a `Celsius` value to a `float` value. This conversion is implicit because it should always succeed:

```
// C#
float b = boiling;
```

2.3.1.4 Formatting Types

I have already mentioned `Parse()`, which is used to convert a string to the appropriate data type. The string must be in a format appropriate to the type that is being called. If it isn't, `FormatException` will be thrown. Each primitive type's value type has a `ToString()` method that returns a string version of the value the instance holds.

Most types have two versions of `ToString()` (some have more)—one with no parameters that provides default formatting, and another with an `IFormat-Provider` parameter. The `IFormatProvider` interface has a single method called `GetFormat()` that returns a format string for the type that is passed as a parameter. `IFormatProvider` is implemented by a formatter class. The Framework Class Library provides two formatter classes: `NumberFormatInfo` and `DateTimeFormatInfo` (both in the `Globalization` namespace). When this second version of `ToString()` is called, it in turn calls `GetFormat()`, passing its type, and the formatter class returns the format for the current locale, as well as the settings that the user may have selected through the Control Panel.

---

5. Note that `f` in this code indicates that the literal is a `float` value; it has nothing to do with an antiquated, non-SI (Système International) temperature scale.

This formatting mechanism is especially useful for the `DateTime` class, which I introduced earlier and will talk about in more detail later. You can get the number formatter for the locale by calling `NumberFormatInfo.CurrentInfo`, and the date formatter by calling `DateTimeFormatInfo.CurrentInfo`.

If you call the parameterless `ToString()` on an object, the formatter class for the current locale is used. If you want to format for another locale, you need to create a `CultureInfo` object for that locale, as illustrated here:

```
// C#
foreach (CultureInfo ci
        in CultureInfo.GetCultures(
            CultureTypes.AllCultures))
{
    Console.WriteLine(ci.Name + "("
        + ci.NativeName + ") "
        + DateTime.Now.ToString(
            "F", ci.DateTimeFormat));
}
```

The static `DateTime.Now` property returns a `DateTime` object for the current time and date. `CultureInfo.GetCultures()` will return all the requested cultures, and in this case I have used the enumerated value `AllCultures` to get all the cultures on my machine. `CultureInfo.DateTimeFormat` returns the data format for the selected culture. I can pass this as the parameter to `ToString()` for the `DateTime` object, but by default the "general" date format (e.g., "04/04/2001 14:47:46" for my locale, which is UK English) will be returned. It is more interesting to use another overload, which takes a format parameter, and in the code example here I have specified that I want the full format (e.g., "04 April 2001 14:47:46") by using the string `"F"`.

This code prints out the culture name (in ISO 639-2 format [three-letter language name] or ISO 3166 format [three-letter country/region name]), the name of the locale (in the language of that locale), and then the date and time in long format. Characters that cannot be printed in the language of the current locale will be printed as queries (?). Table 2.1 shows the standard formats, and Table 2.2 shows the characters that you can use to create a custom format.

Table 2.1 `DateTime` **formatting strings**

String	Pattern*	DateTimeFormatInfo†
d	MM/dd/yyyy	ShortDatePattern
D	dddd, MMMM dd, yyy	LongDatePattern
f	dddd, MMMM dd, YYYY HH:mm	
F	dddd, MMMM dd, YYYY HH:mm:ss	FullDateTimePattern
g	MM/dd/yyyy HH:mm	
G	MM/dd/yyyy HH:mm:ss	
m, M	MMMM dd	MonthDayPattern
r, R	ddd, dd MMM yy HH:mm:ss GMT	RFC1123Pattern
s	yyyy-MM-dd HH:mm:ss	SortableDateTimePattern
S	yyyy-mm-DD hh:MM:SS GMT	
t	HH:mm	ShortTimePattern
T	HH:mm:ss	LongTimePattern
u	yyyy-MM-dd HH:mm:ss	UniversalSortableDateTimePattern
U	dddd, MMMM dd, yyyy HH:mm:ss	UniversalSortableDateTimePattern

*Patterns are described in Table 2.2.
†The property of `DateTimeFormatInfo` that returns the specified pattern.

2.3.1.5 Streams

The `System.IO` namespace defines an abstract class called `Stream`, which is the base class for the various stream classes used for input and output. The `System.IO` namespace is concerned mainly with input/output to the file system, but streams are used to access other sources of data as well. The main stream classes are shown in Table 2.3.

The `Stream` base class defines the basic functionality that these classes ought to implement. It has properties to determine what you can do to the stream (is it readable? writable? does it support random access?), as well as

Table 2.2 `DateTime` **formatting strings**

Pattern	Description
d	Numeric day of the month without a leading zero
dd	Two-digit numeric day of the month (with a leading zero if necessary)
ddd	Three-letter day of the week
dddd	Full name of the day of the week
ff, fff, ffff, fffff, ffffff, fffffff	Fraction of a second; the number of *fs* gives the precision as the number of digits
gg	Period or era string
h	Hour in 12-hour format without a leading zero
hh	Hour in 12-hour format with a leading zero
H	Hour in 24-hour format without a leading zero
HH	Hour in 24-hour format with a leading zero
m	Minute, without a leading zero
mm	Minute, with a leading zero
M	Numeric month without a leading zero
MM	Two-digit numeric month (with leading zero if necessary)

Table 2.3 The main stream classes in the Framework Class Library

Class	Description
`BufferedStream`	Wrapper class that adds buffering to an existing unbuffered stream
`FileStream`	Buffered stream based on a disk file
`IsolatedStorageFileStream`	Buffered stream to a file within isolated storage
`MemoryStream`	Stream based on memory
`NetworkStream`	Unbuffered stream based on a socket

information about the size of the stream and the current position in the stream. In addition, there are methods to read and write single bytes and arrays of bytes, and if you choose to read or write arrays of bytes, you can do this synchronously or asynchronously (I will cover asynchronous programming in Chapter 3).

I will discuss how to get hold of a stream in a moment. First, however, I want to show how to access data through streams, so I will assume that there are two methods—GetInputStream() and GetOutputStream()—that return stream references:

```
// C#
using (Stream outStr = GetOutputStream())
{
    byte[] outBuf = new byte[7]
        {82, 105, 99, 104, 97, 114, 100};
    outStr.Write(outBuf, 0, outBuf.Length);
}

byte[] inBuf = null;
using (Stream inStr = GetInputStream())
{
    inBuf = new byte[(int)inStr.Length];6
    inStr.Read(inBuf, 0, inBuf.Length);
}
// use inBuf here
```

In this code it does not matter what the stream is based on (it could be a file or a socket, for example); the same methods are used. I have used C# using blocks to ensure that the stream is open only as long as it is needed. At the end of the using block the Dispose() method will be called on the stream; Dispose() will call the Close() method. If the outStr reference is a stream based on a file, the file will be open until Close() is called. Typically this will mean that there will be an exclusive lock on the file, preventing other code from accessing it. On a buffered file stream there is another reason for calling

---

6. Because Stream.Length is a long type, whereas the value used to create an array is an int type, I have to do an explicit cast.

`Close()`, in which case data will not be written to the file until the stream is flushed, which happens when `Close()` is called.

Instances of the stream classes shown in Table 2.3 are created either by a call to their constructors or through separate objects. For example, I can create a `FileStream` object as follows:

```
// C#
FileStream fs1 = new FileStream(
    "test.txt", FileAccess.Read);
FileStream fs2 = File.OpenRead(
    "test.txt");
```

In both cases the code opens a file for read access. Dealing in bytes is a nuisance when the data that you are using is in a format other than `byte` arrays. In the example I gave earlier, the `outBuf` array contains the ASCII characters for the string `"Richard"`. The `System.String` class has a method called `ToCharArray()`, but it is of no use when you are writing data to strings because `char` and `byte` are not the same. `byte` is the `System.Byte` type, which represents a single, unsigned byte; `char` is the `System.Char` type, which is a 16-bit Unicode character.

The `System.Text` namespace has a class called `Encoding` that allows you to interconvert `char`, `byte`, and `string` values. There are several encoding classes, used to convert to ASCII, Unicode (big-endian and little-endian), and Unicode Transformation Format (UTF-7 and UTF-8). The `Encoding` class has static properties that will return references to these classes. For example, if you want to convert an array of `byte` values that represents an ASCII string to one that represents a `System.String` object, you can use the `ASCII` property of `Encoding` to return a reference to an `ASCIIEncoding` class:

```
// C#
byte[] bufFore = new byte[7]
    {82, 105, 99, 104, 97, 114, 100};
string strFore =
    Encoding.ASCII.GetString(bufFore);
string strSur = "Grimes";
byte[] bufSur = new byte[strSur.Length];
Encoding.ASCII.GetBytes(strSur.ToCharArray(),
    0, strSur.Length, bufSur, 0);
```

In this code, `strFore` will be initialized with the string `"Richard"`, whereas the buffer `bufSur` will have the ASCII characters for the string `"Grimes"`. However, although this code represents a mechanism to convert strings to and from a format that can be passed to a stream, it is still rather cumbersome, and it does not take into account other data types.

The `System.IO` namespace contains classes based on streams called readers and writers that provide a friendlier face to stream access; these classes are shown in Table 2.4. The class names are a little misleading because although only some of them contain the word `Stream`, all of these classes are used with streams, and they convert between binary data and .NET data types. The `StreamReader` and `StreamWriter` classes allow you to treat a stream as a series of characters arranged in lines. Thus, given a stream reference in the variable `stm`, you can do this:

```
// C#
using (StreamReader reader =
    new StreamReader(stm, Encoding.ASCII)
{
    string str;
    do
    {
```

Table 2.4   Reader and writer classes

Class	Base Class	Description
BinaryReader	Object	Allows data to be read from a stream as the various base-class data types.
BinaryWriter	Object	Allows data to be written to a stream as the various base-class data types.
StreamReader	TextReader	Allows data to be read from a stream as lines or characters; you can specify the encoding or allow the class to determine it. The class can also open a stream based on a file.
StreamWriter	TextWriter	Allows data to be written to a stream as lines or characters. The class can also open a stream based on a file.

```
      str = reader.ReadLine();
      Console.WriteLine(str);
   } while (str != null);
}
```

The `StreamReader` class has many constructors. The one I have chosen takes a stream and an encoding class. The `StreamReader` class doesn't have to be created on a stream; indeed, you can create the object based on a file by giving the name of the file, as shown here:

```
// C#
StreamReader file;
file = new StreamReader("test.txt");
```

This code opens the file `test.txt` and provides access to it via `Stream-Reader`. I will return later to the issue of opening a stream based on a file. If you want, you can allow the `StreamReader` class to determine the encoding of the stream. To do this you should call the constructor that takes four parameters:

```
// C#
StreamReader file;
file = new StreamReader("test.txt",
   Encoding.ASCII, true, 1024);
```

The first parameter is either an existing stream or the name of the file (as in this example), the second parameter is the default encoding that should be used if the class cannot determine the encoding to use, the third parameter is a Boolean value, and the final parameter specifies the size of the buffer for buffered access. If the Boolean parameter is `true`, the `StreamReader` class will read the first 3 bytes of the stream to determine the encoding to use. If it cannot determine the encoding, it uses the default that you pass to the constructor. `StreamWriter` works similarly. The writer class, however, allows you to write data as lines, characters, or strings to the stream.

The `BinaryReader` and `BinaryWriter` classes are created only on streams, so if you want to base them on a file, you have to open a stream on a file using `IO.File.OpenRead()` or `IO.File.OpenWrite()`. The `BinaryReader` and `BinaryWriter` classes have a plethora of read and write methods—one for each of the .NET basic data types.

The `BinaryWriter` class writes strings using an overloaded version of `Write()`. This method writes the string using the class's encoding and prefixes it with the length of the string. The interesting thing about the length value is that as few bytes as possible are used to hold this size; it is stored as a type called a 7-bit encoded integer. If the length does not exceed 7 bits, a single byte is used. If the length is greater than this, the high bit on the first byte is set and the value is shifted by 7 bits to create a second byte. This process is repeated with successive bytes until there are enough bytes to hold the length. This mechanism is used to make sure that the length does not become a significant portion of the size taken up by the serialized string. `BinaryReader` and `BinaryWriter` have methods to read and write 7-bit encoded integers.

Reader and writer classes are used to read and write the various .NET primitive data types to and from streams. However, they do not take into account perhaps the most important data types to pass through a stream: objects. One option would be to add a `ToString()` method to your object that would convert the object's state to a string by converting each field to a string and then concatenating the strings. You could then use `BinaryWriter.WriteString()` to serialize the object's state to a stream.

To read an object from a stream, you will have to have a constructor on the object that takes a `System.String` parameter and in this constructor extract the values from the string to initialize the object's fields. There are three main problems here: First, the constructor will have to parse the string to extract the field values, and this is not a trivial task. Second, this process uses up a constructor and the `ToString()` method, so a naïve user could try to pass her own string to the constructor or pass the object to a method that required a string, like `Console.WriteLine()`, which would trigger a call to `ToString()`. In both cases your code will not be used in the way it is intended.

The final problem arises when your object has a field that is a reference to another object. In that case the object—and any object it references—must be serialized. Your serialization code needs to build up an entire graph of objects that should be serialized, and this graph must take into account the situation when two objects refer to the same object: When the base object is

DEVELOPING APPLICATIONS WITH VISUAL STUDIO.NET

deserialized, only one instance of this shared object should be created. In Chapter 3 I will explain how this is accomplished.[7]

Finally, note that `Stream` has methods for asynchronous access. To a certain extent, these are superfluous because *any* method that uses a delegate can be called *asynchronously*. However, there are valid reasons for these methods to be here. Having these methods on the class makes it immediately obvious to developers that the stream *can* be accessed asynchronously, so they will not overlook this useful mechanism. In addition, implementers of streams can implement the asynchronous methods specific to the type of stream that is being accessed rather than relying on the general-purpose delegate mechanism. Asynchronous calls will be covered in Chapter 3.

2.3.1.6 *Console Input and Output*

Command-line applications need a console. When you compile an application as a console application, the compiler adds the following to the manifest:

```
.subsystem 0x00000003
```

This statement indicates that when the application starts, the system must provide a console window. Either the console is the command line from where the application was started, or the system will create a new console. Such applications receive input either through the command-line arguments (which I described in Chapter 1) or through the static `Read()` and `ReadLine()` methods on the `Console` class. Output to the console also comes through the `Console` class.

The `Console` class gives access to a `TextReader` object and two `TextWriter` objects, which are provided as static properties. The `In` property is used to get console input; the `Out` and `Error` properties give access to the console output and error output streams, respectively. `Console` provides static methods that give access to the `In` and `Out` objects:

---

7. Object serialization is supported in .NET because it is the mainstay of the remoting APIs, so I will defer discussion until the next chapter.

```
// C#
Console.WriteLine("Printed on the console");
string line = Console.ReadLine();
if (line != null)
{
    // use the string
}
```

These method calls are passed to `Out.WriteLine()` and `In.ReadLine()`. To write to the error stream, you have to call the `Error` object directly; by default, this output will appear on the console. There are two ways to redirect the output: by using redirection at invocation or in code. For example, this code:

```
// C++ test.cpp
void main()
{
    Console::WriteLine(S"Normal output");
    Console::Error->WriteLine(S"Error output");
}
```

can be invoked in the following ways:

```
test
test > out.txt
test 1>out.txt 2>err.txt
```

In the first case, both strings appear on the command line. In the second case, the normal output (from `Out`) will be redirected to a file, and the error output will appear on the command line. In the third case, the `1` indicates that normal output will be sent to `out.txt`, and the `2` indicates that error output will be sent to `err.txt`. `Out` and `Error` behave like the `cout` and `cerr` objects in the C++ standard library.

You can change these output objects programmatically by calling the `SetOut()` and `SetError()` methods, each of which takes a `TextWriter` reference. You change the input stream by calling `SetInput()` and passing a `TextReader` object—for example:

```
// C++
Console::SetOut(new StreamWriter(S"out.txt"));
```

```
Console::WriteLine(S"Normal output");
// ... other code
Console::Out->Close();
```

`StreamWriter` derives from `TextWriter`, which I pass here to `SetOut()`. From this point on, the output from all code that uses the output methods of `Console` (regardless of the assembly in which that code is located), will go to this file. However, there is a problem: `StreamWriter` objects give buffered access to a file, so before the application shuts down you must make sure that the buffer is flushed. In this code I call the `Close()` method, which will flush the buffer before closing the underlying file.

Input from the command line is read by a call to `Console.ReadLine()`. This method will block until the user presses the **Enter** key, and then it will return the string without the terminating new-line character. If the input is a string, you have no problem, but if the string holds numeric data or several parameters, you will have to parse it. `System.String` has methods that allow you to search through the string for substrings. After you have obtained these substrings, you can use `Convert` or the appropriate `Parse()` method to get the types you require. For example, if the input is a three-dimensional point in the format (x, y, z), you can use this code:

```
// C#
string line = Console.ReadLine();
if (line != null && line.Length > 0)
{
    string[] p = line.Split(new Char[]{','});
    if (p.Length < 3)
      throw new Exception("provide three numbers");
    double x, y, z;
    x = Convert.ToDouble(p[0]);
    y = Convert.ToDouble(p[1]);
    z = Double.Parse(p[2]);
    // use values here
}
```

Here I check that there is a string from the input (the user may have terminated the input stream by pressing **Ctrl-Z** or may have entered no values and simply pressed **Enter**). Then I split it into the substrings indicated by each comma. Next I convert to `double` values, using `Convert.ToDouble()` for two of the strings and `Double.Parse()` for the third, to indicate how to use this alternative.

The `Write()` and `WriteLine()` methods can take individual parameters, or they can take multiple parameters and a format string. The format string contains numbered placeholders that can contain the field width and formatting information. If a field width is given, the field is padded with spaces on the left—for example:

```
// C#
Console.WriteLine("<{0,5}{1,5}>", 123, 45);
// prints <  123   45>
```

To control how numbers are formatted, you can use the specifiers summarized in Table 2.5. When a type is passed to `WriteLine()` or `Write()` (or to `String.Format()`), the method will check if the type implements the `IFormattable` interface. If it does, it will call its version of `ToString()`:

Table 2.5 Format specifiers for number types[*]

Format String	Description
`{n:C}`	Currency format. The number is printed with the currency symbol, separator, and decimal places set for the current locale.
`{n:Dm}`	Integer with m digits.
`{n:Em}`	Scientific format; m gives the precision.
`{n:Fm}`	Fixed format; m gives the number of decimal places.
`{n:Gm}`	General format, either fixed or scientific. This is the default format.
`{n:Nm}`	Number format. Thousands are grouped with the locale-specific grouping character (a comma, for example) and m decimal places.
`{n:R}`	Round-trip format. The resulting string can be converted back to the value without loss of data.
`{n:Xm}`	Hexadecimal with m digits.

[*]*Note:* Here n is the placeholder's number, and m is a parameter that controls the format.

DEVELOPING APPLICATIONS WITH VISUAL STUDIO.NET

```csharp
// C# syntax
public interface IFormattable
{
    string ToString(string format, IFormatProvider fp);
}
```

The type has the responsibility of returning a formatted string. The first parameter is the format string supplied in the placeholder, and the type can interpret this string however it wishes. The second parameter provides access to the locale-specific format objects, so the type that implements this method can call `IFormatProvider.GetFormat()`, for example, and ask for the number format object to get the locale-specific format for the group separator or the negative symbol. The value types for all the primitive types implement `IFormattable.ToString()` according to the comments in Table 2.5, but you can provide your own format string for your types.

If the formats in Table 2.5 do not cover your formatting requirements, you can specify your own custom format string. This string is made up of literal characters plus combinations of the characters 0, #, and %. 0 and # are digit placeholders; if there is no digit, then 0 indicates that a zero digit should be given. % means that the number should be treated as a percentage—that is, multiplied by 100. Commas can be used in the format string, in which case they have one of two meanings: If they appear immediately to the left of a decimal place, they act as a prescaler; that is, the number is divided by 1,000 for every comma before being formatted. Otherwise the number is printed with thousand separators. Here are some examples:

```csharp
// C#
Console.WriteLine("{0:000.00}", 1.1);
// prints 001.10
Console.WriteLine("{0:###.00}", 1.1);
// prints 1.10
Console.WriteLine("{0:###%}", 0.1);
// prints 10%
Console.WriteLine("{0:#,.####}", 12345.67);
// prints 12.3457
Console.WriteLine("{0:#,#}", 1234567);
// prints 1,234,567
```

Finally, if you want to provide different formatting strings for positive, negative, and zero numbers, you can separate them with semicolons:

```csharp
// C#
Console.WriteLine("{0:#.00;(#.00);none}", 12.34);
```

The first format is for positive numbers, the second for negative numbers (e.g., -44 would be printed as `(44.0)`), and last one for zero.

Enumerated values are useful in code because they have a recognizable name, and you use this name rather than the number that it represents—for example:

```csharp
// C#
public enum MyColors
{Red = 0xff0000, Green = 0xff00, Blue = 0xff}
```

If I want to pass a value to indicate red, I can use either `MyColors.Red` or the actual value `0xff0000`, but the former is far more readable. Enumerations can also be printed with format strings, in which case you have the option of printing either the value of the item or the name:

```csharp
// C#
Console.WriteLine("{0:G} {1:X}",
    MyColors.Red, MyColors.Red);
```

This code will print out the following:

```
Red 00FF0000
```

You can use the `IFormattable` interface to provide your own mechanism to format your types. Remember that `IFormattable` allows you to use a format provider to get information about the format. You can write your own format provider that implements `IFormatProvider`. This provider can be passed to methods that take a format provider and an object to format, and your provider will be used to format the object. This mechanism allows you to provide your own code to format existing types.

2.3.1.7 Mathematical Functions

The `System.Math` class contains static members that allow you to perform the most common mathematical operations. `Math` also has two static fields—`E` and

PI—which have the values of the mathematical symbols e and π. Table 2.6 gives the trigonometric methods, Table 2.7 the logarithmic methods, and Table 2.8 the remaining arithmetic methods of the Math class.

Pseudorandom numbers can be generated through the Random class. You can create an instance using an Int32 seed value. If you use the constructor without a seed, it still does *not* return the same sequence of pseudorandom numbers (unlike the CRT rand() method). You can access the random numbers in three formats: Int32, Double, or Byte. If you want an Int32 random number, you can specify the upper and lower bounds of the range. If you want a Double number, the value returned is greater than or equal to 0 and less than

Table 2.6 Trigonometric functions*

Member	Description
Cos, ACos	Cosine and inverse cosine
Cosh	Hyperbolic cosine
Sine, ASin	Sine and inverse sine
Sinh	Hyperbolic sine
Tan, ATan, ATan2	Tangent and inverse tangent (ATan2 has the angle as the quotient of its two parameters)
Tanh	Hyperbolic tangent

*Note: Angles are given in radians.

Table 2.7 Logarithmic functions

Member	Description
Exp	Exponential; Exp(x) returns e^x
Log	Logarithm base e
Log10	Logarithm base 10
Pow	Power; Pow(x, y) returns x^y
Sqrt	Square root

Table 2.8 **Other functions**

Member	Description
Abs	Absolute value of the parameter.
Ceiling	Smallest whole number greater than or equal to the parameter.
Floor	Largest whole number less than or equal to the parameter.
IEEERemainder	Remainder; IEEERemainder(x, y) returns the remainder from x/y.
Max	Maximum of two values.
Min	Minimum of two values.
Round	Rounded value; Round(x) returns the whole number nearest to x, rounding up or down. If x is halfway between two numbers, it is rounded to the nearest even number.
Sign	Sign of the parameter. It returns −1 for negative numbers, 1 for positive numbers, and 0 otherwise.

1. Finally, you can obtain an array of random bytes by creating a byte array big enough to hold the number of bytes that you want.

2.3.2 System Classes

In this section I want to outline the various classes in the System namespace that are used to give access to higher-level functionality that you'll use when implementing your applications. By and large these classes wrap Win32 functionality.

2.3.2.1 General-Purpose Values

Environment is a general-purpose class to hold methods that give access to information about the current machine and the invocation of the application. Essentially the members of this class fall into two groups: information about the current application and information about the system.

When you start an application, it may be invoked with some command-line parameters (this is true of GUI applications as well as console applications).

These are available either through the parameters of the `Main()` (or `main()`) function, as I mentioned in Chapter 1, or via the `Environment` class. You have the option of getting these parameters either as an array of strings through `GetCommandLineArgs()` or as a concatenated string through the property `CommandLine`. Note that in both cases the command line is treated like the C command line; that is, the first item on the command line is the name of the application. This contrasts with the parameter to the C# `Main()` function, in which case the array of strings does not include the name of the application.

Every application is invoked with access to environment variables. Environment variables are accessible through three methods on `Environment`. You can access a specific environment variable with `GetEnvironment-Variable()`, which will return the value of the variable you mention, or a `null` reference if the variable is not set. In addition, you can call `GetEnvironment-Variables()`, which will return the `IDictionary` interface on a collection that contains all the set environment variables. The following code produces output equivalent to typing "SET" at the command line:

```
// C#
IDictionary env;
env = Environment.GetEnvironmentVariables();
foreach(string s in env.Keys)
    Console.WriteLine(s + "=" + env[s]);
```

The final method for accessing environment variables is `ExpandEnvironmentVariables()`. This method takes a string that contains the names of environment variables (in the form `%<name>%`, where `<name>` is the variable's name) and returns a string that has the environment variables' names replaced with their values:

```
// C#
string system32;
system32 = Environment.ExpandEnvironmentVariables(
    @"%windir%\System32");
```

This code puts the full address of the system's `System32` folder in the variable `system32`. Notice that I use C#'s `@` symbol to allow me to turn off escaping in the string so that I can use backslashes without escaping them. (Incidentally, you can obtain the system directory through the `Environment.SystemDirectory` property.) One directory that is not represented by an environment variable is the directory from which the application was invoked (which is *not* necessarily the same as the application directory). This directory is obtained through the `CurrentDirectory` property of the `Environment` class.

The `Environment` class also gives you access to certain diagnostic information (more diagnostics are available in the `System.Diagnostics` namespace, as I'll explain later). The `WorkingSet` property returns the amount of memory that the process is using, and `StackTrace` returns a string that has the names of the methods in the call stack (note, however, that this is the stack when the property is *called* and hence includes the methods used to access the property).

Finally, your application can return a status code (known to the system as an *error level*). This value is returned from the application's `Main()` (or `main()`) function. However, anywhere in your application you can access your intended value through the `ExitCode` property. Note that the status code will *always* be the value returned from `Main()` (and if `void` is returned, the value returned will always be `0`). Thus if you use `ExitCode`, make sure that your `main()` (or `Main()`) method returns the correct value:

```
// C++
int main()
{
    MyAppClass* c = new MyAppClass;
    c->Run();
    return Environment::ExitCode;
}
```

This code creates an instance of `MyAppClass` containing the application code that may set the application's status code. This code may also call `Exit()` to stop the application immediately without throwing an exception. `Exit()` takes the exit code as its parameter.

The `Environment` class also gives access to certain machinewide values. The NetBIOS name of the machine is accessed through the `MachineName` property. The operating system that the machine is running is obtained through the `OSVersion` property, which returns an `OperatingSystem` object that gives the operating-system type, as well as its version, through an enumeration. Incidentally, the `Version` property returns the version of the CLR (Common Language Runtime) that is installed on your machine.

I mentioned in Chapter 1 that configuration policies can be given in a machine-wide file. The path to this file can be obtained through the `SystemConfigurationFile` property. The final member that I want to mention is `GetLogicalDrives()`, which I think would be more logically placed in the `System.IO` namespace. This method returns a string array in which each item is the name of a drive on the system, in the format `D:\` where `D` is a drive letter.

2.3.2.2 CLR Classes

I mentioned `AppDomain` in Chapter 1. Let's take a closer look at this class and the garbage collection class. Through calls to the methods `CreateInstance()` and `CreateInstanceFrom()`, `AppDomain` allows you to create domains in the current process and types within those domains. If you want to create types in the current domain, you can use the `Activator` class, which has similar named methods. These methods return an `ObjectHandle` object, which is essentially a wrapper object that holds information about an object that could be in another domain and even in another process. To use this object, you must "unwrap" it first by calling `ObjectHandle.Unwrap()`. I will come back to this in Chapter 3.

The other class that I want to talk about in this section is `GC`. This class gives access to how the garbage collector works. The GC performs garbage collection using a generational mechanism: Objects that survive one collection are promoted to an older generation, and the GC can optimize its work by performing garbage collection only on the earlier generations. This optimization is based on empirical evidence that younger objects are more likely to be short-lived, so garbage collection on those will yield more free space than garbage collection on older objects would.

The `GC.MaxGeneration` property gives the maximum number of generations that the system supports, and the `GC.Collect()` method allows you to initiate a garbage collection either on a specific generation or on all generations.

If you are interested in the generation of a specific object, you can pass the object to `GC.GetGeneration()`, and if you would like to see the amount of memory allocated, you can call `GC.GetTotalMemory()`.

The other methods of `GC` allow you to control finalization: `SuppressFinalize()` prevents finalization and is typically called when you have explicitly decided to clean up an object's resources. For example, in a C++ destructor, if you later decide that the finalizer should be called, you can call `ReRegisterForFinalize()`. `KeepAlive()` prevents the GC from garbaging-collecting an object within the current method (it is used for objects that are passed through interop). `WaitForPendingFinalizers()` ensures that a thread blocks until all finalizers have been called; this method is typically called before an application finishes.

2.3.2.3 Contexts

I will cover contexts in greater depth in Chapter 3. In this section I will introduce the concepts and the general classes that the Framework Class Library provides. A *context* is an execution environment that a component requires to run. If the context does not exist, the component will not function the way that its author intended.

A component's context is created by the runtime. If the runtime cannot create the context, the type will not be loaded. A component that must remain in a particular context is referred to as *context bound.* Such a component can be accessed by components in other contexts as long as marshaling is used. This intercontext communication can be between contexts within the same application domain, within the same process, on the same machine, or between different machines, as illustrated in Figure 2.1.

Not all components are context bound; most components are domain bound, so they can be accessed from components in the same domain without marshaling, and from components in other domains with marshaling. Domain-bound components are context agile: They are created in one context but are accessed directly by code in another context.

By default, all components are context agile but not marshalable. This means that if you create your object in one context, you can pass a reference to that object to another object running in a different context. If your component

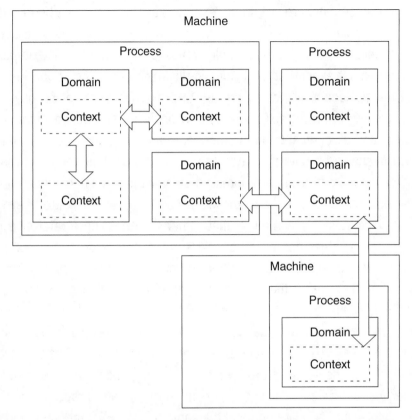

Figure 2.1   Contexts. Contexts exist within domains, and context-bound components can interoperate with components in other contexts through marshaling. This interoperation includes contexts in the same domain, in other domains, in other processes, or on other machines.

has a specific context requirement—for example, it must always be called on the same thread—you can derive the class from `ContextBoundObject` and use an attribute to specify the context. When you pass a reference to such a component to another context, the runtime steps in and makes sure that a proxy is created in the receiving context. The proxy and the `ContextBoundObject` base class ensure that the call from the out-of-context object is made in the correct context. In some cases a type may have methods and fields that are not context bound but a field that is context bound. In this situation the field should be marked with the `[ContextStatic]` attribute.

Some components are not so context sensitive and thus can be called from any context within the domain. However, such a component may be created as domain specific; that is, the data it holds must reside in the specific domain and its methods must execute in that domain, in which case when code in another domain needs access, it gets it through a proxy. Domain-specific objects are derived from `MarshalByRefObject`. The object is said to be *marshaled by reference,* and all context-bound components are marshaled by reference (but objects marshaled by reference are not necessarily context bound). If the component can be created in one domain but can be passed to and run within another domain, it should have the `[Serializable]` attribute. `[Serializable]` indicates to the runtime that rather than passing a reference of the component to another domain, it should serialize the fields of the component and pass these to the code in the other domain, where the runtime will create a clone of the object using the serialized fields. Such an object is referred to as *marshaled by value.*

The other context class that you'll find in the `System` namespace is `ServicedComponent`. This is a special type of context-bound object for which the context includes the services provided by .NET component services (also known as *enterprise services*). .NET component services are provided by COM+. Indeed, COM+ and .NET are one and the same thing: .NET represents the client-side runtime; COM+ represents the server-side runtime and provides the services that are used on the server. Thus it makes sense to call COM+ component services *.NET component services.*

Components that use the services provided by .NET component services are marked with the attributes that can be found in the `System.EnterpriseServices` namespace and are summarized in Table 2.9. In Chapter 4 I will explain how to use these.

2.3.3 Tracing and Debugging

I will cover debugging and use of the Visual Studio.NET debuggers in greater depth in Chapter 9. In this section I will outline the classes that the Framework Class Library provides. The `System.Diagnostics` namespace has classes

Table 2.9 Component-services attributes

Attribute	Description
`ApplicationAccessControl`	Allows you to set the security of a component-services application.
`ApplicationActivation`	Indicates whether the components are created in the creator's process.
`ApplicationID`	Gives the GUID for the application.
`ApplicationName`	Gives the application's name.
`ApplicationQueuing`	Enables queuing support for the application.
`AutoComplete`	Indicates that when a method completes successfully, the context should reflect this.
`ComponentAccessControl`	Enables security checking on access to the component.
`COMTIIntrinsics`	Allows passing of the context properties from the COM transaction integrator to the COM+ context.
`ConstructionEnabled`	Indicates that the component will be passed a construction string when created.
`Description`	Describes the application.
`EventClass`	Identifies the event class.
`EventTrackingEnabled`	Enables event tracking on the component.
`ExceptionClass`	Identifies the queuing exception class.
`IISIntrinsics`	Allows access to IIS intrinsic values.
`InterfaceQueuing`	Enables queuing support on the specified interface.
`JustInTimeActivation`	Specifies just-in-time activation support.
`LoadBalancingSupported`	Determines whether the component supports load balancing.
`MustRunInClientContext`	Indicates that the component must be created in the creator's context.
`ObjectPooling`	Indicates that the component will be created in an object pool and configures the size of the pool.

(continued)

Table 2.9   (continued) Component-services attributes

Attribute	Description
SecurityRole	Indicates the security role that will have access.
Synchronization	Indicates the activity membership of the component.
Transaction	Indicates the transaction support required by the component.

that can be split into five groups: tracing, debugging, performance monitor, event log, and process information. The performance monitor and event log are specific to NT; I have delayed description of the Framework Class Library classes for these services until later in this chapter because I don't really regard them as a "core" part of the Framework Class Library. The reason I say this is not that I think such facilities are not an important part of the core of a library— far from it, I think that they are vital in a class library; it is just that the classes provided as part of the Framework Class Library (particularly those for the event log) are mere wrappers around Win32.

If your algorithm has a bug, you often have little choice but to single-step through that algorithm in the debugger using test data and check line by line that the correct results are being produced. Single-stepping through code is a good exercise because it gives you an idea of *code coverage;* that is, you can see which code is called and which code is baggage. You also get an idea of the code that is called repeatedly and is a candidate for optimization. However, single-stepping is tedious, and as a mechanism to get intermediate results it is inefficient. A much better mechanism is to add code to the algorithm to output intermediate results, which you can analyze later.

During the testing phases of an application you want to catch all possible bugs. If your application generates data using a complicated algorithm, then using accurate test data and precalculated results is vital because a bug in an algorithm will not necessarily generate an exception. If you do not have test data—perhaps because it is not possible to obtain such data—there must be an alternative mechanism for checking that the algorithm is working correctly. One approach is to break down your algorithm into small sections of code and check for pre- and postconditions and invariants.

By *preconditions* I mean the assumptions that the function makes before it starts processing. For example, if you have a string manipulation function, one of the preconditions is that the string is not `null`. If the string is `null`, the function cannot work. When the function returns, some conditions must be `true`; these are *postconditions.* For example, a method that has an `out` parameter must initialize this parameter; if the method returns without initializing the parameter, the postcondition has failed.

Finally, classes can have conditions that should always be *true—invariants.* For example, if your class has an array of a fixed size, one of the invariants is that the index to this array must always be greater than zero and less than the number of elements in the array. Some invariants should always be upheld; others may be violated within a method but must remain invariant when the method returns.

Pre- and postconditions and invariants can be traced. However, violation of one of these invalidates everything else the algorithm does, so there is little point in continuing if a violation has occurred. These conditions are handled with *assertions.* An assertion checks a condition, and if the condition fails, the assertion will generate an assertion dialog.

The Framework Class Library provides tracing and assertion capabilities in the `Debug` class; your application must be compiled specifically to use this class. To do this you have to define the DEBUG symbol, which the C# and C++ compilers allow you to do with the `/d` switch (for C#) or `/D` (for C++), or in source code with `#define` (symbols can be undefined with `#undef`). If the DEBUG symbol is *not* defined, all traces of `Debug` are removed from the final binary. By default, Visual Studio.NET defines DEBUG for debug builds.

The `Debug` class has two types of methods to generate trace messages. `Write()` and `WriteLine()` look like the equivalent methods accessed through the `Console` class. However, they do not take format strings; you must make sure that strings you pass to these are correctly formatted. In addition to a string, you can pass a category string that can mean whatever you like it to mean, so you can categorize trace messages on a scale of importance, for example. The other type of message is conditional; the methods in this case are `WriteIf()` and `WriteLineIf()`. The overloaded versions of these methods have a Boolean as the first parameter, and this parameter determines whether the message should be traced. These methods allow you to replace code like this:

```
// C#
if (items == 0)
    Debug.WriteLineIf("there are no items");
```

with code like this:

```
// C#
Debug.WriteLine((items==0),
    "there are no items");
```

If both lines of code are compiled with DEBUG *not* defined, the former runs a check and then does nothing, even if the check evaluates to true. In the second case, when DEBUG is not defined no code is generated.

Filling your code with trace messages makes good sense for keeping track of intermediate values so that you can check that your algorithm is working the way that you require. Assertions are more immediate; when an assertion fails, the tester should be informed immediately. Debug.Assert() takes a Boolean, which is the condition that you are asserting. If this fails, the assertion action will occur. The default implementation of Assert() is supplied by Default-TraceListener (as you'll see later), and this will give a dialog informing the user that the assertion failed, along with an optional descriptive string and an optional detailed string. The following code, for example,

```
// C#
Debug.Assert(items>0, "there are no items");
```

will generate the dialog shown in Figure 2.2.

As Figure 2.2 shows, the dialog contains a useful key to the meaning of the buttons in the title bar.[8] If you click on **Abort**, the application will be immediately aborted, giving you the option of editing the source code to solve the problem. If

---

8. Clearly Microsoft decided that the buttons **Abort**, **Retry**, and **Ignore** were confusing. What is not clear is why the developers decided to provide a key in the title bar rather than replacing the button captions with **Quit**, **Debug**, and **Continue**.

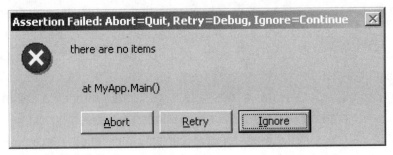

Figure 2.2   Default Assertion Failed dialog

you would like to see the context of the failed assertion, you can click on **Retry**, which will run the currently registered debugger on your system. You should always pause before clicking **Ignore** because doing so continues execution. Your code has asserted that a condition must be `true` for the code to work correctly, so if the condition is `false`, the code will not work correctly, so why bother continuing? If the condition that you assert is not required for the correct running of the code, your code should not have made the assertion.

The `Debug` class has a useful facility for indenting messages. Each time you call `Debug.Indent()`, subsequent messages will be indented by additional `Debug.IndentSize` spaces. You can use this facility to distinguish visually between messages created by methods within the call stack, as illustrated here:

```
// C#
public class MyClass
{
    public void DoSomething()
    {
        Debug.Indent();
        Debug.WriteLine("DoSomething called");
        DoWork();
        Debug.Unindent();
    }
    private void DoWork()
    {
        Debug.Indent();
        Debug.WriteLine("DoWork called");
        Debug.Unindent();
    }
}
```

The fact that `DoWork()` is private means that any messages generated in this method will be indented at one level more than the messages generated by the public methods (because private methods can be called only by other methods in the class).

When an assertion fails or a message is generated through a call to one of the `Write()` methods or the `Fail()` methods, the assertion or message is passed to listeners registered for the current application domain. It is the responsibility of these listeners to decide what to do with these messages. When the application domain is created, an instance of the `Default-TraceListener` class is added to this list of registered listeners. This list is held in the static property `Debug.Listeners`, which is a collection that allows you to add and remove items. If you do not want the default listener, you can remove it and add a better listener to this list. Every listener class derives from the abstract base class `TraceListener`.

The framework supplies two other listeners: `TextWriterTraceListener` and `EventLogTraceListener`. As the names suggest, the first class writes trace messages to a file, and the second writes them to the event log—for example:

```
// C#
Debug.Listeners.Add(
    new TextWriterTraceListener(Console.Out));
```

Either you can add this object to the `Listeners` collection through code, or you can use a configuration file.

An alternative to the `Debug` class is the `Trace` class. `Trace` has the same methods and properties as `Debug`, but the code is called only if you define the `TRACE` symbol. Visual Studio.NET defines `TRACE` for C# projects created with the project wizards, but thankfully not for C++ projects. The documentation says that this is a feature; I consider it a fault. The documentation offers the following argument for defining `TRACE` in release builds: Once your application has been debugged and tested and finally deployed, you may receive a report from one of your customers that a problem has occurred, so you can tell your customer to use a trace tool to gather the trace messages, which your engineers can use to determine the source of the problem.

My argument *against* defining TRACE in release builds is twofold: First, the code that generates these trace messages takes up space in your binary, and for downloaded assemblies it is *always* a good idea to reduce the size of your binary. Second, these trace messages are being generated (but not collected) even when the application is running correctly; because each trace message will take time, they will have an effect on the performance of your application (a small effect, perhaps, but still an effect).

More troublesome is the fact that using trace messages effectively couples your application to the process used to monitor the trace messages: debug monitors. When your application (or your library code) runs on a customer's machine, you have no control over the other processes running on that machine. As a consequence, the customer may run a badly written debug monitor that takes a long time to handle each debug message. If such a message is generated through the Win32 DebugOutputString() method, which is the case with the default trace message listener (DefaultTraceListener, as explained earlier), your call to log a trace message will *block* until the debug monitor has completed its handling of the trace message.

So merely by adding trace messages to your code, you are suddenly at the mercy of the writer of a debug monitor—an appalling situation to be in. Furthermore, if your code has assertions through the Trace class, defining TRACE will mean that the assertions will still be active in your code, with the possibility that your customers will see a modal assertion dialog. Worse yet, if your code is run in a window station other than the interactive window station, no one will be able to dismiss the assertion dialog! The message is clear: *Do not allow your release code to be compiled with TRACE defined.*

In addition, if you leave trace messages in your release build, you will need them because you have not fully tested your code, and you should *never* distribute code that has not been fully tested. Of course, there is the counterargument: What do you do if something unexpected does appear in a release build? My reply is that reporting problems in a release build is different from reporting them in debug builds. In release builds, such unexpected errors are *exceptional,* and you should use the event log, which is written by Microsoft as an efficient mechanism to log important event messages and does not have the deficiencies of debug monitors that I have mentioned. I'll have more to say about the event log later in this chapter.

Incidentally, if you find that a process on your machine has been compiled with TRACE defined and it generates assertion dialogs needlessly,[9] you can turn off this facility through a configuration file. To do this you need to add the following node:

```
<configuration>
   <system.diagnostics>
      <assert assertuienabled="false"
              logfilename="asserts.log">
   </system.diagnostics>
</configuration>
```

If you turn off the assertion user interface like this, it makes sense to redirect the assertion messages to a separate log file so that a record of assertion failures is maintained.

I mentioned earlier that to use the Debug class, you must define the DEBUG symbol on the compiler command line (C# uses the /d switch, and C++ the /D switch, to do this). The reason this works is that the methods on the Debug class are marked with the [Conditional] attribute—for example:

```
// C#
[Conditional("DEBUG")]
public static void WriteLine(string message);
```

The interesting thing about this attribute is that it does not affect how the assembly that contains this method is compiled. That assembly will still have the IL in it; however, the attribute will be read by compilers compiling code that references this code. So if your code calls this method and has DEBUG defined, the compiler will put the code in your assembly to call this method. If your assembly is compiled without the DEBUG symbol defined, the compiler will ignore all code that calls this method. Consider the following code:

---

9. A while ago I suffered from such a problem: A library provided by a well-known database vendor had a switch statement that handled the default case with a modal dialog saying that it could not handle the case. My code ran under IIS and merely hung whenever this dialog was shown.

```
// C#
public class Test
{
    [Conditional("DEBUG")] pubic void f()
    { Console.WriteLine("called me"); }
    public void g()
    { f(); }
}
```

If this code is compiled with DEBUG defined, it can call g() and the string will be printed on the console. However, if this code is compiled with DEBUG undefined, the class will still have a method f(), but g() will be empty. This means that another assembly compiled with DEBUG defined can call either f() or g(), but only f() will generate output. This behavior is different from C++ and C# conditional compilation, in which the symbol controls whether the code will be added to the final binary file.

One final way of diagnosing problems in your code is to turn tracing code on or off with a global value. In this case you can globally turn on tracing (by defining DEBUG), but you protect tracing code with a conditional check—for example, as follows:

```
// C#
if (bTraceOn)
    Debug.WriteLine("Called MyObject");
```

The problems with this approach are how to set the bTraceOn variable, and where to get the information to determine whether it should be true or false. The natural place for the value of such a variable is a configuration file, and to access this file the Framework Class Library provides the BooleanSwitch class. This class accesses a Boolean value set as a value in the application configuration file. It is used like this:

```
// C#
class Use
{
    public void DoSomething()
    {
        BooleanSwitch bUseIt;
        bUseIt = new BooleanSwitch(
```

```
            "AdvancedFeatures",
            "Use advanced features");
        if (bUseIt.Enabled)
            Console.WriteLine(
                "these are the advanced features");
        else
            Console.WriteLine(
                "these are the basic features");
    }
}
```

The constructor takes the name of the switch and a description. At runtime the bUseIt variable is initialized with values in the application's configuration file; this class changes its behavior according to this switch. The configuration file has an entry for the AdvancedFeatures switch and looks like this:

```
<configuration>
    <system.diagnostics>
        <switches>
            <add name="AdvancedFeatures"
                value="1"/>
        </switches>
    </system.diagnostics>
</configuration>
```

The value of 1 corresponds to a value of true for bUseIt.Enabled; a value of 0 corresponds to a false switch value. In the <switches> node you can add switches, remove a particular switch (using <remove/> with a name attribute), or even remove all switches (with <clear/>). Note that using BooleanSwitch does not depend on compiling with any specific symbol.

The System.Diagnostics namespace also contains a switch called TraceSwitch. The name is a little deceiving because it does not have to be used with the Trace or the Debug class. The TraceSwitch class has a Level property that is one of the TraceLevel enum values: Error, Warning, Verbose, Info, and Off. In addition, it has four Boolean properties that correspond to whether Level is set to one of these values (e.g., TraceError is true if Level is TraceLevel.Error). In your code you create and check a TraceSwitch object to determine the amount of information to trace; whether you decide to do this with the Trace class is up to you.

DEVELOPING APPLICATIONS WITH VISUAL STUDIO.NET

Both classes—`BooleanSwitch` and `TraceSwitch`—derive from the `Switch` class, and you can create your own switch class by deriving from this class. Your switch can access integer values only from the configuration file; however, it is free to expose those values as any type you like: The `Boolean-Switch` exposes the configuration value as a `bool` value—for example:

```
// C#
class DaySwitch : Switch
{
    public DaySwitch(string display, string desc)
        : base(display, desc){}
    public string Day
    {
        get
        {
            DayOfWeek day = (DayOfWeek)SwitchSetting;
            string d;
            d = DateTimeFormatInfo.
                    CurrentInfo.GetDayName(day);
            return d;
        }
    }
}
```

The configuration file should have an entry for the switch that has a value between `0` and `6`. When the switch is used, the `Day` property accesses the value in the configuration file by calling the `SwitchSetting` protected property on the base class. `SwitchSetting` returns an `int` value, which is why you can put only integer values in the configuration file. In this code I use the `DateTime-FormatInfo` class to return the day name according to the current locale.

2.3.4 Net

Transmission Control Protocol/Internet Protocol (TCP/IP) is the mainstay of the Internet and of corporate networks. The classes that you'll find in the `System.Net` namespace are based one way or another on IP—and TCP/IP in particular; you'll find no NetBIOS classes here. There are two Net namespaces: `System.Net` and `System.Net.Sockets`. I'll give an overview of both namespaces here because they are interrelated.

The basic units of TCP access are defined in the `System.Net.Sockets` namespace. An application that exposes an interface to the network does so through an *end point* (a port at a particular address). The application's thread listens on this end point and blocks until a client makes a connection. The connection to the client is through a `Socket` object, and read and write operations are carried out through the passing of `byte` arrays. As I mentioned earlier in this chapter, strings in .NET are not `byte` arrays (although they can be accessed as `char` arrays). However, the `NetworkStream` class can be based on a `Socket` object, which allows you to use a reader or writer class so that you can read or write data through the socket as .NET data types.

Now let's look at this from the client end. The client creates a `TcpClient` object and attempts to make a connection using the server's end point. Once the server has accepted the connection, the client gets a `Socket` object through which it can read data from and write data to the server.

You can install Simple TCP/IP Services through the Windows 2000 setup, which will install five utilities: chargen (character generator), daytime, discard, echo, and qotd (quote of the day). In the following code I connect to the echo service:

```
// C#
static void Main()
{
    const int echo = 7;
    const string localhost = "127.0.0.1";
    Socket s = new Socket(
        AddressFamily.InterNetwork,
        SocketType.Stream, ProtocolType.Tcp);
    s.Connect(new IPEndPoint(
        IPAddress.Parse(localhost), echo));
    byte[] write = Encoding.ASCII.GetBytes(
        "this is some data");
    s.Send(write);
    byte[] read = new byte[write.Length];
    s.Receive(read);
    Console.WriteLine(Encoding.ASCII.GetString(read));
}
```

This code shows basically all there is to the client side of TCP connections: You make the connection, write data to the server, and read replies from the server. The `Socket` class has methods to allow it to be used for a variety of socket types. I have chosen to use TCP/IP through the parameters of the `Socket` constructor. After that I connect to the appropriate server by supplying an instance of `System.Net.IPEndPoint`, which needs an `IPAddress` object (essentially a 64-bit number, which is converted from the dotted-byte format) and a port number. Then I write some data to the server and read its reply. Because the data being sent to the server consists of ASCII characters, I have to convert the string using the `Encoding.ASCII` class. When I read the data back again, I get a `byte` array, so I convert this back to a string.

As you can see, socket access is straightforward. The majority of code using sockets is concerned with the protocol of the service being accessed—that is, the format of the data being sent, and the format of the data returned.

The `System.Net.Sockets` namespace provides higher-level classes for accessing TCP and UDP (User Datagram Protocol) servers: `TcpClient` and `UdpClient`, respectively. Here is the echo client using `TcpClient`:

```
// C#
static void Main()
{
    const int echo = 7;
    TcpClient tcpc = new TcpClient();
    tcpc.Connect("localhost", echo);
    StreamWriter w;
    w = new StreamWriter(tcpc.GetStream());
    w.Write("this is some data\n");
    w.Close();
    StreamReader r;
    r = new StreamReader(tcpc.GetStream());
    Console.WriteLine(r.ReadLine());
    r.Close();
    tcpc.Close();
}
```

This code shows use of the higher-level `System.IO` classes to simplify access to the socket. Actually, I have cheated a little because I have made sure that the data sent to the echo server is terminated by a new-line character so that I can use `ReadLine()`. The server side is similarly straightforward:

```
// C#
static void Main()
{
    const int echo = 7;
    Socket sin = new Socket(
        AddressFamily.InterNetwork,
        SocketType.Stream, ProtocolType.Tcp);
    sin.Bind(new IPEndPoint(
        System.Net.IPAddress.Any, echo));
    while (true)
    {
        sin.Listen(0x7fffffff);
        Socket s = sin.Accept();
        while (s.Available == 0) Thread.Sleep(10);
        byte[] b = new byte[s.Available];
        s.Receive(b);
        s.Send(b);
    }
}
```

Again, I have shown how to implement the code using raw sockets: First I create a socket of the correct type; then I bind it to a port. The socket is put into a listening state, which means that it will block until a request is received, at which point I create a new socket to handle the request by calling `Accept()` and then do the actual action. Because the server needs to get a string from the client, first I enter a `while` loop, polling the `Socket.Available` property until it is nonzero. If you were to write a TCP server, it would make sense to create a new thread after the call to `Accept()` and pass the socket to this thread. This would free the main socket to listen on the port again, making the server more available.

The Framework Class Library provides the `TcpListener` class to wrap up some of the less elegant listening code:

```
// C#
static void Main()
{
    const int echo = 7;
```

```
    TcpListener tcpl = new TcpListener(echo);
    tcpl.Start();
    while (true)
    {
        Socket s = tcpl.AcceptSocket();
        while (s.Available == 0) ;
        byte[] b = new byte[s.Available];
        s.Receive(b);
        s.Send(b);
    }
}
```

In the code in this section, I have used some of the end point and address classes in `System.Net`. Machines on the Internet each have a unique 32-bit number called an *IP address*. IP addresses are typically quoted as four dotted bytes expressed in decimal format. In the future, IP addresses will be extended to 64 bits, so the `IPAddress` class is used to hold a 64-bit IP address. This class allows you to convert an IP address to (via `ToString()`) and from (via `Parse()`) dotted-byte format, and it acts as a generic class for data conversion.

The preceding code reads data through a socket by calling `Accept-Socket()`. The `TcpListener` class also has a method, called `AcceptTcp-Client()`, that returns a `TcpClient` object through which you can access a `NetworkStream` object to read data from and write data to the client.

Different machines treat multibyte integers differently in terms of the order of the bytes that make up the integer. So that different machines can interoperate using binary data (as opposed to string representations of numbers), there is a standard order of bytes: the network order. `IPAddress.NetworkToHostOrder()` allows you to convert an integer from one machine to the order that the current machine uses; `IPAddress.HostToNetworkOrder()` does the conversion in the opposite direction. These methods are overloaded for all of the integer types: `Int16`, `Int32`, and `Int64`. The final use for `IPAddress` is that it defines constants that are useful: I have already shown `Any`, which is used by a listener to bind to a socket. In addition, there are `Broadcast` and `Loopback`, which is the address of `localhost`. The combination of an address and a port is an end point, represented by `IPEndPoint`.

The dotted-byte representation of addresses provides addresses that are only slightly more memorable than 32-bit numbers. Domain names are much easier to remember because they are strings. However, the Internet works on IP addresses, which means that there must be a way to convert from a domain name to an IP address, and this is the reason for the `Dns` class.

`GetHostName()` returns the name of the current machine, and `Resolve()` obtains the `IPAddress` object for a domain name. `Resolve()` may involve querying a Domain Name System (DNS) server on the Internet, which can take time, so this method is provided in both a synchronous form and an asynchronous form. A domain name may refer to more than one IP address, and if this is a possibility for the domain name that you are trying to resolve, then a call to `GetHostByName()` will return an instance of `IPHostEntry` that has an array of `IPAddress` objects.

The rest of the classes in `System.Net` build on the basic classes that I have already described. `System.Net.WebRequest` and `System.Net.Web-Response` are abstract classes that represent, respectively, a request to and a response from a server. The concrete classes `HttpWebRequest` and `HttpWeb-Response` define, respectively, the requests to and responses from an HTTP server. However, you do not create the instances of these classes directly; instead, you call `WebRequest.Create()` with a URI, and this method inspects the requested protocol and returns an instance of the appropriate class:

```
// C#
string uri = "http://www.microsoft.com/";
WebRequest req = WebRequest.Create(uri);
WebResponse result = req.GetResponse();
StreamReader rs;
rs = new StreamReader(result.GetResponseStream());
while (rs.Peek() != -1)
{
    Console.WriteLine(rs.ReadLine());
}
rs.Close();
```

In this case the protocol is HTTP, so the `WebRequest` and `WebResponse` references are `HttpWebRequest` and `HttpWebResponse` objects. If you change the URI to a local file—for example, as follows:

```
string uri = Environment.ExpandEnvironmentVariables(
    "file://%systemroot%\\odbc.ini");
```

then `FileWebRequest` and `FileWebResponse` objects will be created. These objects contain 183183information about the actual operation. For example, if you make a call to a Web site, the response will have information about the headers and the cookies that were returned with the response through the `HttpWebResponse.Headers` and `HttpWebResponse.Cookies` properties.

You can also call servers that require authentication. To do this you initialize the `WebRequest.Credentials` property, which is an `ICredentials` interface, and the namespace provides a class called `CredentialCache` that allows you to add individual `NetworkCredential` objects (domain, name, password) for an authentication type (e.g., Basic and Digest), and a site.

If all you want to do is get a page or send data to an HTTP server, you can use the `WebClient` class. `WebClient` uses `WebRequest` and `WebResponse` objects in its implementation and exists to give a friendly face to these classes. Here is an example:

```
// C#
WebClient req = new WebClient();
req.DownloadFile("http://localhost/default.htm",
                 "defaultpage.txt");
Stream stm = req.OpenRead(
    "http://localhost/default.htm");
```

2.3.5 Threading

The `System.Threading` class contains the basic classes for threading. .NET threads are represented by the `Thread` class. Note that this is a logical thread; it may be based on a native thread provided by the operating system, or it may be implemented by software.[10] When you create a thread, you have to pass a delegate to the constructor that will be the thread procedure—for example:

---

10. Basically what I am saying is that `Thread` is not equivalent to `ProcessThread` in the `System.Diagnostics` namespace. However, in tests in which I have monitored the number of `ProcessThread` objects created when I created `Thread` objects, the two numbers have seemed to correlate, indicating to me that they are based on the same underlying operating-system object in Windows.

```
// C#
void Factorial()
{
    long fact = 1;
    for (long i = 1; i <= 20; i++) fact *= i;
    Console.WriteLine("factorial is " + fact);
}

// use the thread
Thread t = new Thread(new ThreadStart(Factorial));
t.Start();
```

This code performs the factorial of 20 and then prints out the value. The thread that calls `Start()` is free to perform another task while the `Factorial()` function is being called. If your machine has more than one processor, the thread that runs `Factorial()` could run on a different processor from the one that created the thread, so the two can run in parallel. In most cases, however, the two threads will run on the same processor, which means that each thread will get a quantum of time to execute before it is preempted to allow another thread to execute.

Each thread will grab some memory for its stack and other aspects of its thread context. When the system switches between threads, this thread context must be stored along with the current CPU register values, and the thread context and register values of the next thread will be loaded before it is run. This means that during a thread context, switch time is taken up for the switch that could have been used to execute thread procedure code. In other words, adding new threads to your application will not improve the performance. As a rule, it is best to keep the number of threads as small as possible.

In general, threads are useful for two reasons: They allow you to divide your code into isolated sections that can be performed concurrently. They also give your code more availability, by which I mean that applications that service client connections could create a thread for each connection, which would prevent the client from timing out when it attempted to make a connection. Threads will not necessarily allow you to service the entire request more quickly, but they give the client the impression that you are not ignoring it.

DEVELOPING APPLICATIONS WITH VISUAL STUDIO.NET

The call to the `Thread` constructor is equivalent to (but not necessarily the same as) a call to the Win32 `CreateThread()` function with a value of `CREATE_SUSPENDED`, and a call to `Start()` is equivalent to the Win32 `Resume-Thread()` function.[11] `Thread` objects can be in one of the states identified by the `ThreadState` enumeration and accessed through the read-only `Thread.ThreadState` property. To change the state of a thread, you call one of the methods on the `Thread` class, as indicated in Table 2.10.

Note that `ThreadState` is a bitmask. The reason is that `Thread` objects can be in multiple states at the same time. For example, a thread could be

Table 2.10 Thread states

State	Description	Thread Method
Aborted	The thread has aborted.	
AbortRequested	The thread has been told to abort; `ThreadAbortException` is raised in the thread.	`Abort()`
Background	The thread is running in the background.	
Running	The thread is running.	`Start()`
Stopped	The thread has stopped.	
StopRequested	The thread has been told to stop.	
Suspended	The thread has been suspended.	
SuspendRequested	The thread has been told to suspend.	`Suspend()`
Unstarted	The thread object has been created, but not started.	`Thread` constructor
WaitSleepJoin	The thread is blocked.	`Join()`, `Sleep()`, or `Wait()` on a synchronization object

11. I have to stress that the `Thread` constructor may not be implemented in this way, but I find it helpful to think of it like this.

waiting when it is told to abort, in which case it will be in the `WaitSleepJoin |`
`AbortRequested` state.

A `Thread` object is in the `WaitSleepJoin` state when it has decided to
sleep (`Sleep()`), when it is waiting for another `Thread` object to stop
(`Join()`), or when it is waiting on a synchronization object by calling
`Monitor.Wait()`. The `Sleep()` method can be called only on the current
`Thread` object. The parameter determines how many milliseconds the `Thread`
object wants to sleep, and if this value is zero, it indicates that the `Thread`
object will relinquish the remainder of the time slice allocated to it (so it will not
execute again until the `Thread` object is rescheduled to run). If the `Thread`
object calls `Thread.Sleep(Timeout.Infinite)`, the `Thread` object enters
long-term sleep and can be awakened only by another `Thread` object calling
`Thread.Interrupt()`. This causes `ThreadInterruptedException` to be
thrown in the sleeping `Thread` object. You can use this as a basic thread communication mechanism:

```
// C#
public void SleepyThread()
{
    while(true)
    {
        try
        { Thread.Sleep(Timeout.Infinite); }
        catch(Exception) { }
        DoMyWork();
    }
}
```

The `Thread` object that uses this thread procedure will sleep until another
`Thread` object calls `Interrupt()`, at which point it will wake up, do its work
(with `DoMyWork()`), and then return to a deep sleep. The previous code is
never-ending; there is no obvious way to break this loop, although you could use
a synchronization object as will be described later, or you could tell the thread to
abort, as illustrated here:

```
// C#
Thread t = new Thread(
    new ThreadStart(SleepyThread));
```

```
t.Start();
for (int i = 0; i < 10; i++)
{
    DoSomeLengthyWork();
    t.Interrupt();
}
Thread.Sleep(SOMEDELAY);
t.Abort();
```

This code creates a thread, and in a loop it performs some work. Every time `DoSomeLengthyWork()` completes, it calls `Interrupt()` to tell the `Thread` object to do its work (I am assuming that `DoSomeLengthyWork()` takes a lot longer than `DoMyWork()`). After ten loops the work has completed. The code waits to allow the newly awakened thread to do its work, and then it calls `Thread.Abort()` to tell the thread to die. `Abort()` is equivalent to the Win32 `TerminateThread()` method, except for one important point: The `Thread` object knows that it is being aborted. The system aborts the `Thread` by throwing `ThreadAbortException` in the thread. The `Thread` object code can catch this exception and perform cleanup in the exception handler. However, once the exception handler has completed, the `Thread` object dies. Your handler can override this behavior by calling `ResetAbort()`, but it needs to have the `ControlThread` permission to do this. Rarely, however, does it make much sense to do this; if a `Thread` has been told to abort, then it really should abort.

`Sleep()` can be called only on the current thread; however, you can suspend another thread by calling `Suspend()`. This method puts the thread into the `ThreadState.Suspended` state, which can be awakened by a call to `Resume()`. When a thread is asked to suspend, the system marks it as `SuspendRequested` and waits for a safe point in the thread's code to suspend it. "Safe" here means that the garbage collector is happy for the suspension to occur.

`Thread` objects can represent foreground or background threads. A foreground thread keeps the process alive, even when the main thread has died. Foreground threads are the default for threads. A background thread will not keep the process alive, so when the foreground threads have died, the runtime will shut down all of the background threads and die itself. To make your thread a background thread, you need to set `IsBackground` to `true`.

The combination of `Sleep()` and `Interrupt()` is a way to perform one basic type of thread communication: to instruct a `Thread` object to perform some work. Communication the other way around—to indicate that a `Thread` object has performed its work—is accomplished by a call to `Join()`. This method is equivalent to the Win32 `WaitForSingleObject()` function on a thread handle. The `Thread` object that calls `Join()` will block until the other `Thread` object has stopped:

```
// C#
Thread t = new Thread(
    new ThreadStart(Factorial));
Console.WriteLine("Starting work");
t.Start();
t.Join();
Console. WriteLine("Completed work");
```

This example is trivial code, of course, but if the called `Thread` object generates some data that the calling `Thread` object depends on, `Join()` will ensure that the called `Thread` object has finished its work before continuing.

The delegate, `ThreadStart`, that the `Thread` object uses does not have any parameters, nor does it return any values—unlike the Win32 equivalent, `THREAD_START_ROUTINE`, which takes a `void*` pointer through which you can pass a pointer to any data type or structure. This brings up the question of how you pass data to a thread, or get data from it. The answer is to use a class instance—for example:

```
// C#
public class CFactorial
{
    private long m_i;
    public long result = 0;
    public CFactorial(long i)
    {
        if (i > 20)
            throw new ArgumentOutOfRangeException(
                "parameter too large!");
        if (i <= 0)
            throw new ArgumentOutOfRangeException(
                "parameter must be > 0!");
```

```
        m_i = i;
        result = 1;
        Thread t;
        t = new Thread(
            new ThreadStart(DoFactorial));
        t.Start();
    }
    public void DoFactorial()
    {
        for (long i = 1; i <= m_i; i++)
            result *= i;
    }
}
```

In this code the results are returned through a public member. However, this member can be accessed by both the calling and the called threads, so we have a thread synchronization issue. The most immediately important issue is how the calling thread knows that the called thread has completed its work. I will investigate this issue later.

If my application needs to perform many calculations, many threads will need to be created. As I mentioned earlier, creating many threads is rarely a good idea; a better solution is to queue the work on a pool of threads. The Threading.ThreadPool class gives access to a pool of threads maintained by the runtime. There is only one thread pool in each process, and it is created the first time that ThreadPool.QueueUserWorkItem() is called. A process can have many application domains, but the ThreadPool class ensures that the queued work is performed in the right domain. The QueueUserWorkItem() method has a WaitCallback delegate as a parameter. When a thread becomes available in the thread pool, WaitCallback is invoked—for example, as follows:

```
// C#
public class CFactorial2
{
    public long result = 0;
    public CFactorial2(long i)
    {
        if (i > 20)
            throw new ArgumentOutOfRangeException(
                "parameter too large!");
```

```
        if (i <= 0)
            throw new ArgumentOutOfRangeException(
                "parameter must be > 0!");
        result = 1;
        ThreadPool.QueueUserWorkItem(
            new WaitCallback(DoFactorial), i);
    }
    public void DoFactorial(object o)
    {
        long fact = (long)o;
        for (long i = 1; i <= fact; i++)
            result *= i;

    }
}
```

The `WaitCallback` delegate has an `object` parameter that can be used to pass data to the method. When the method in the delegate has completed, the thread does not finish; it goes back into the thread pool, where it becomes available to call another `WaitCallback` delegate. You have no control over the thread that performs the work or the size of the thread pool.

Thread pools are more efficient than individual threads. First, you do not have the continual overhead of creating and destroying threads because in the best case the threads are created once by the system and sit in the thread pool until the process dies. Second, threads are kept as busy as possible because an idle thread takes up resources. When a thread pool thread has completed its work, it becomes immediately available to do other work.

In Chapter 1 I talked about the problem of performing work with shared objects. I mentioned that if you want to use scarce resources, it is best to hold on to these resources for as short a time as possible. If a resource is used by multiple objects, you can make it accessible by making it a shared resource. However, the problem with this approach is that the shared object could be used across multiple threads, which could present a thread synchronization issue because the nature of the shared scarce resource is that it should be used by only one thread at a time.

A thread pool can solve the problem here:

```
// C#
class Logger
{
```

```
    static public void Write(string s)
    {
        ThreadPool.QueueUserWorkItem(
            new WaitCallback(WriteString), s);
    }
    static private void WriteString(object s)
    {
        TextWriter tw = File.AppendText("log.txt");
        tw.Write(s);
        tw.Close();
    }
}
```

Here the client code calls a method to log a string. This call queues the request to write to the file into the thread pool, which, when a thread becomes available, calls `WriteString()` to access the scarce resource and write the string. The thread pool is free to run more than one thread, so two threads could handle `WriteString()` requests in the thread pool. In this situation, the call to `File.AppendText()` will fail with an exception if another thread already has the file open. This particular problem can be handled like this:

```
// C#
static private void WriteString(object s)
{
    TextWriter tw = null;
    while (true)
    {
        try
        { tw = File.AppendText("log.txt"); }
        catch (Exception)
        {
            Thread.Sleep(0);
            continue;
        }
        break;
    }
    if (tw != null)
    {
        tw.Write(s);
        tw.Close();
    }
}
```

`ThreadPool` has a method called `RegisterWaitForSingleObject()`, which is passed a delegate, a waitable object, and a timeout. The delegate is called when either the timeout occurs or the waitable object becomes signaled. *Waitable objects* are instances of classes derived from the `WaitHandle` or `Timer` class (see Table 2.11). The final parameter of `RegisterWaitForSingleObject()` indicates whether the delegate is called just once or repeatedly. If an instance of `AutoResetEvent` is used, once the event is signaled the delegate will be called and the event will be reset, so the waiting thread will sleep until the event is signaled again.

`RegisterWaitForSingleObject()` returns a `RegisteredWaitHandle` reference. If you decide that you no longer want to wait on the object that you registered, you can call `Unregister()` on it.

`AutoResetEvent` and `ManualResetEvent` are used for thread synchronization. An event can be in two states—signaled or unsignaled—and your code

Table 2.11 Waitable classes

Class	Description
`AutoResetEvent`	When a call to one of the `Wait()` methods returns, either through a timeout or because the event is signaled, the event object is automatically reset to unsignaled. If multiple threads are waiting on a single instance of AutoResetEvent, only one thread will see that the event became signaled.
`ManualResetEvent`	Events of this type are signaled and unsignaled by calls to `Set()` and `Reset()`. Once the state of the event has changed, the event remains in this state until it is manually changed. This means that if multiple threads wait on an event, they will all be released when the event becomes signaled.
`Mutex`	This class is used to allow a shared resource to be used by one thread at a time. When one thread "owns" a `Mutex` object, subsequent calls to one of the `Wait()` methods will block other threads.
`Timer`	A `Timer` object is created with a timeout value, and it becomes signaled when the timeout interval has expired.

changes this state by calling `Set()` or `Reset()` on the event object. When a single `Thread` object waits on an `AutoResetEvent` event, the `Thread` object will block until either the event is signaled or the timeout occurs. If the event is signaled (i.e., if another `Thread` object calls `Set()`), the system automatically is reset to unsignaled. This means that if multiple threads wait on a single instance of `AutoResetEvent` and the event becomes signaled, only one thread will be released from the wait state because once one thread is released the event is reset and the other threads see an unsignaled event. In effect, if you have *n* threads waiting on an instance of `AutoResetEvent` using `WaitOne()`, you have to call `Set()` *n* times. This is not the case with `ManualResetEvent`; if multiple threads are waiting on such an event, all of those threads will be released when the event is signaled.

If an object is shared by two threads, you have a potential problem: The two threads could access thread-sensitive code, or try to access the shared object fields, at the same time. Synchronization objects and contexts can be used to prevent this from happening. The default for .NET objects is *no* synchronization, so if an object is to be used by more than one thread, you *must* apply synchronization to your code.

If the shared object has a 32-bit or 64-bit field, this field can be accessed in a thread-safe way through the `Interlocked` class—for example:

```
// C#
class Counter
{
    public int Count = 0;
    public int Increment()
    { return Interlocked.Increment(ref Count); }
}
```

You can create an instance of this class and use it with multiple threads. Each thread can call `Increment()` safely because `Interlocked.Increment()` increments the parameter passed by reference in a thread-safe way. That is, if two threads call this method at the same time, the increment calls are atomic and the value will be incremented by two.

A `Monitor` object can be used to protect a section of code:

```csharp
// C#
class Counter
{
    public int Count = 0;
    public int Increment()
    {
        Monitor.Enter(this);
        Count++;
        Monitor.Exit(this);
        return Count;
    }
}
```

The ++ operator is not an atomic operator, so without synchronization two threads could call the operator, with the effect that one thread could be pre-empted before ++ has written its result back to storage. The second thread could perform the entire increment operation, but this would be in vain because when the first thread runs again it writes its result back to storage.

The calls to `Monitor.Enter()` and `Monitor.Exit()` mark a section of code that can be run by only one thread at a time: While one thread is in this block of code, another thread will be blocked at the `Enter()` statement. Note that you cannot create `Monitor` objects, so you cannot pass instances of them to another object. Also note that because I pass the `this` reference to `Enter()`, the *entire* object is monitored, so if you have another guarded section of code in the same class, other threads will be locked out of this code too. You can prevent this problem by passing a waitable object, such as an instance of `ManualResetEvent`:

```csharp
// C#
ManualResetEvent mre;
mre = new ManualResetEvent(false);
public int Increment()
{
    Monitor.Enter(mre);
    try     { Count++; }
    finally { Monitor.Exit(mre); }
    return Count;
}
```

This code is protected by the fact that the manual reset event is being held as an instance field. It cannot be a local variable because then every time the method was called, a new synchronization object would be used. If your method is static, you cannot use an instance field. Instead, you can use the type object, which is obtained by a call to `typeof()` in C# (or `__typeof()` in C++):

```
// C#
public static void MyMethod()
{
    Monitor.Enter(typeof(MyClass));
    try     { /* thread-sensitive code */ }
    finally { Monitor.Exit(typeof(MyClass)); }
}
```

I have used `try` and `finally` to make this code more generic. The code in the `try` block could consist of more than one line (although you should try to keep the amount of code short), and however this guarded block is exited, the `Monitor.Exit()` code must be called. The C# `lock()` statement will generate similar code; the following is equivalent to the previous method:

```
// C#
public int Increment()
{
    lock(mre)
    { Count++; }
    return Count;
}
```

If a thread is waiting to enter a guarded block at `Monitor.Enter()`, it will be in a `WaitSleepJoin` state. Such a thread can be interrupted with a call to `Thread.Interrupt()`, which, as I mentioned earlier, will cause `ThreadInterruptedException` to be thrown. A call to `Abort()` elicits different behavior: The exception will be thrown when the thread wakes from the wait. As I mentioned earlier, a blocked thread is a thread that is not doing any work, so you should always try to prevent a thread from being blocked. `Monitor.TryEnter()` allows you to determine if a call to `Enter()` will succeed or block.

The `Mutex` object can be used to protect a section of code. In this case the "ownership" of the object is passed between threads: The thread that "owns" the mutex is allowed to execute, and the other threads that want to own the mutex will block:

```csharp
// C#
Mutex mutex = new Mutex(false);
public int Increment()
{
    mutex.Wait();
    try     { Count++; }
    finally { mutex.ReleaseMutex(); }
    return Count;
}
```

`Mutex` objects can be named. If one process creates a named `Mutex` object and another process on the same machine tries to create a `Mutex` object with the same name, the two processes will get access to the same underlying kernel object and thus will be able to perform synchronization.

So far, the methods I have shown have protected the write access to the instance member, but they have left the read access unprotected. Of course, you can always lock the section of code that reads the value, but this code starts to get complicated. The reason is that using the same locking object for both reading and writing to a value is inefficient when multiple threads try to read the value at the same time: Because the value does not change, *all* reading operations should be allowed simultaneously. However, when a single thread writes to the value, all threads—readers and writers—should be blocked until the operation completes. The Framework Class Library provides the `ReaderWriterLock` class to encapsulate all of this functionality:

```csharp
// C#
private int count = 0;
ReaderWriterLock wrl;
wrl = new ReaderWriterLock();
public int Count
{
    get
    {
        int i;
        wrl.AcquireReaderLock(Timeout.Infinite);
        try     { i = count; }
```

```
        finally { wrl.ReleaseReaderLock(); }
        return i;
    }
    set
    {
        wrl.AcquireWriterLock(Timeout.Infinite);
        try    { count = value; }
        finally { wrl.ReleaseWriterLock(); }
    }
}
public int Increment()
{
    Count++;
    return Count;
}
```

Again, this is a fairly trivial problem, but now the code has been complicated to make it thread safe. As you can see, I have implemented `Count` as a property, and I protect both read and write access with the `ReaderWriterLock` object.

The `System.Runtime.Remoting.Contexts` namespace has a class-level attribute called `[Synchronization]`, which is relevant to this discussion of synchronization and thread-sensitive code. This context attribute indicates to the runtime that when you share an instance of the class with this attribute across contexts, only one thread will be able to access the instance at any one time. `[Synchronization]` effectively locks the instance so that when one thread has access to the object the lock is applied and other threads are prevented access to any members of the class. The attribute can take a Boolean to its constructor to indicate whether the class is reentrant; that is, if code in the synchronized class makes a call out of the class, another thread can make a call into the class. If reentry is not allowed, then a thread must complete a method before another thread can access the class. The `[Synchronization]` attribute constructor can also take a flag to indicate the type of synchronization required. These are public fields in the class (see Table 2.12). An object that is synchronized in this way can be accessed by multiple threads, but by only one thread at a time.

Synchronization access across objects (`Synchronization.REQUIRED`) is effectively an extension of the idea of marking a section of code to be used by

Table 2.12 Synchronization flags

Flag	Description
NOT_SUPPORTED	Synchronization is not applied.
SUPPORTED	Synchronization is applied if an instance is used by another object that has a synchronization lock.
REQUIRED	Synchronization must be applied, but if an instance is used by another object that has synchronization, that synchronization lock will be used.
REQUIRES_NEW	Synchronization must be applied; a synchronization lock will always be created for each instance of this class.

only one thread at a time. This idea is extended across code in several objects rather than applying to just a section of code within a method. This means that other threads will be blocked from entering several objects, and as I mentioned before, a blocked thread is a thread doing no work.

In many cases your threads will create the objects that they use, in which case the data in a particular object will be specific to the associated thread. In other cases an object could be shared by different threads so that those threads share the data. If the data is writable, you have to apply synchronization as I described earlier. There is also an intermediate option: A class may have both data that is shared between threads and data that is specific to each thread. This flexibility requires that the thread-specific data be in *local data storage*. Local storage applies to contexts in general; that is, when you allocate local data storage, the data is accessible only from the context that placed it there.

The Thread class has a method called AllocateDataSlot(), which allocates local storage to be used by every thread and returns a Local-DataStoreSlot object to identify this storage. Any thread can pass this identifier and thread-specific data to SetData(), which places the data into storage allocated for this specific thread. If a thread calls GetData(), the method will get the data that that particular thread put there, even though another thread may have called SetData() with another value.

Local data slots may be named, but they are always identified by `Local-DataStoreSlot` objects. To allocate a named data slot, you call `Allocate-NamedDataSlot()`, which returns a `LocalDataStoreSlot` object. However, you can always get such an object for a named data slot by calling `GetNamed-DataSlot()`; effectively, the thread maintains a map of names to `Local-DataStoreSlot` objects. When you no longer need a named data slot, you can remove it from this map by calling `FreeNamedDataSlot()`.

The final point to make about threads is that exception handling is thread specific. If an exception is thrown from a thread and it is not caught, the thread will die. The runtime will write a message to `Console.Out` stating that an exception has occurred, and it will dump exception information. You can add a delegate to an application domain through the `AppDomain.UnhandledException` event that will be called if an exception is not caught.

As the name suggests, this event is quite generic; it handles all uncaught exceptions within the specific application domain. The event passes an `UnhandledExceptionEventArgs` object, which you can use to determine the exception that was thrown. Of course, this event handler is effectively the last line of defense, so it may not be possible to rectify the problem. The `UnhandledException-EventArgs` object has a property called `IsTerminating` that specifies that the process will terminate (in particular, if the exception was thrown by the main thread).

Thus you should protect your thread routines to ensure that exceptions do not leak out. One exception is special: If `ThreadAbortException` is raised, another thread has told your thread to die by calling `Abort()`. Your thread can catch this exception and perform cleanup work, but once the catch handler has completed, the thread will die.

2.3.6 Reflection

The reflection namespace is one of the most important APIs in .NET because it gives access to the metadata in an assembly, and it is metadata that the runtime uses for type checking. Let's start at the beginning: assemblies. The `System.Reflection` namespace contains the assembly-level attribute classes that you can use to provide information about the assembly. These attribute classes are shown in Table 2.13.

Table 2.13 Assembly attributes

Attribute	Description
`AssemblyAlgorithmIdAttribute`	The cryptographic algorithm that is used to hash the files in an assembly.
`AssemblyCompanyAttribute`	The name of the publishing company.
`AssemblyConfigurationAttribute`	The assembly configuration (e.g., Retail or Debug).
`AssemblyCopyrightAttribute`	The copyright statement.
`AssemblyCultureAttribute`	The culture of the assembly; this is used by satellite assemblies that provide locale-dependent resources.
`AssemblyDefaultAliasAttribute`	A friendly name for the assembly; this is useful when the assembly name is lengthy or unmemorable.
`AssemblyDelaySignAttribute`	An indicator that the assembly was not signed (perhaps because the author did not have the key), but there is space for the signature to be added later.
`AssemblyDescriptionAttribute`	A description of the Win32 file that contains the assembly; if this is not set, the assembly version is used.
`AssemblyFileVersionAttribute`	The version of the assembly.
`AssemblyFlagsAttribute`	The object's support for side-by-side execution.
`AssemblyInformationalVersionAttribute`	Extra version information, not used by the runtime.
`AssemblyKeyFileAttribute`	The file that contains the public/private key for signing the assembly.
`AssemblyKeyNameAttribute`	The name of the key stored with the cryptographic service provider.
`AssemblyOperatingSystemAttribute`	The operating system for which the assembly was built.

(continued)

Table 2.13   (continued) Assembly attributes

Attribute	Description
AssemblyProcessorAttribute	The processor for which the assembly was built.
AssemblyProductAttribute	The name of the product to which this assembly belongs.
AssemblyTitleAttribute	A friendly name for the assembly.
AssemblyTrademarkAttribute	A trademark for the assembly.
AssemblyVersionAttribute	The version of the assembly.

Information about an assembly is accessed through the `Assembly` class. You can get the `Assembly` objects for the current application domain (one for each assembly loaded into the domain) by calling `GetAssemblies()`:

```
// C#
Assembly[] assemblies;
assemblies = AppDomain.CurrentDomain.GetAssemblies();
foreach (Assembly a in assemblies)
{
    Console.WriteLine("Assembly: ");
    Console.WriteLine("\tFullName " + a.FullName);
    Console.WriteLine("\tCodeBase " + a.CodeBase);
    Console.WriteLine("\tLocation " + a.Location);
    Console.WriteLine("\tEntryPoint " + a.EntryPoint);
    Console.WriteLine("\tEvidence " + a.Evidence);
}
```

This code will provide information for all the assemblies loaded in the current application domain. If you want to get the assembly that contains the current type, you can call the static `GetExecutingAssembly()` or `GetCallingAssembly()` method on the `Assembly` class, which will return the assembly that called the current assembly. You can call the static `GetAssembly()` method and pass a `Type` object to get the assembly that contains that particular type. The `Assembly` class also has a static member called `GetEntryAssembly()` that returns the assembly that contains the entry point where the application started. In addition, you can call the static `Load()` method to tell the Fusion binding and probing mechanism to load a specified assembly, or if you know the file path to an assembly you can pass it to `LoadFrom()`.

When an assembly is loaded into an application domain, the `App-Domain.AssemblyLoad` event is generated. The delegate for this event has an `AssemblyLoadEventArgs` parameter that has a member that called `Loaded-Assembly`, which is the `Assembly` object of the assembly that is loaded. You can use this event to track the assemblies that are loaded into your process.

Once you have an `Assembly` instance, you can call `GetExported-Types()` to get all the public types in the assembly, as illustrated here:

```
// C#
static void Main(string[] args)
{
    if (args.Length == 0)
    {
        Console.WriteLine(
            "You must supply a file name");
        return;
    }
    Assembly assembly;
    assembly = Assembly.LoadFrom(args[0]);
    Console.WriteLine("This assembly exports:");
    foreach (Type t in assembly.GetExportedTypes())
        Console.WriteLine(t.ToString());
}
```

Assemblies can be made up of several files or associated with several files. To get the modules in the assembly you can call `GetModules()`, which will return an array of `Module` objects. If the current assembly has satellite assemblies, for culture-specific resources, a specific assembly can be obtained by a call to `GetSatelliteAssembly()` identifying the satellite with a `CultureInfo` object.

I mentioned in Chapter 1 that the name of an assembly includes its short name, version, culture, and strong name. Once you have an `Assembly`, you can call `GetName()` to get an `AssemblyName` object that contains this information. The `FullName` property of an `Assembly` object gives the string version of the assembly name.

As you can see, there are multiple ways to load an assembly, and you do not need to rely on Fusion to do it for you. Once you have loaded an assembly, you can instantiate a type in that assembly by calling `CreateInstance()`. After you have created an instance, you can call members on that instance. All of this can be done at runtime, and the instructions indicating which assembly and type to load and which members to be called can be held in some kind of script. In essence, what I am describing is late binding. C# and C++ do not support late binding as part of the language; indeed, the code to dynamically load and call members can become very complicated. VB.NET does support late binding as part of the language,[12] for backward compatibility to VB6. However, late binding is rarely a good idea; it is almost always better to allow the compiler to check your code for you.

Let's look at how late binding works. Once you have loaded an assembly, you can use `Assembly.CreateInstance()` to create the instance, and then obtain the type object so that you can get information about the type. The type object is an instance of `System.Type`, and it has methods to access all the members of the type. I'll come back to this class in a moment. Once you have accessed the member that interests you, you can call `Invoke()`. In the following code I load the assembly passed on the command line and then call the entry point of the assembly assuming that the entry point takes no arguments:

```
// C#
static void Main(string[] args)
{
    Assembly a;
    a = Assembly.LoadFrom(args[0]);
    MethodInfo mi = a.EntryPoint;
    object o = a.CreateInstance(
        mi.DeclaringType.Name);
    mi.Invoke(o, null);
}
```

---

12. The VB compiler calls code in `Microsoft.VisualBasic.Helpers.LateBinding` to do the late binding at runtime.

The `Assembly.EntryPoint` property returns information about the entry point method in a `MethodInfo` object. `DeclaringType` is the type object of the class that contains the entry point. I then call `Invoke()`, passing the method instance and an array of parameters. Because I assume that the entry point takes zero parameters, I pass `null` for the parameter array. The compiler is happy about this code because it has no idea about the assembly that I will want to load until runtime. However, if I run this code with an assembly that has parameters on its entry point (e.g., the assembly that contains this code), `TargetParameterCountException` will be thrown. There are two important points here: First, the runtime does not allow you to execute a method with the wrong number (or type) of parameters, which is a good thing. Second, the check is performed *at runtime*. Because the check is done at runtime, you do not get the security blanket of the compiler making these checks for you. This is why I say that late binding is rarely a good thing.

The `System.Reflection` namespace contains classes describing the various members that can appear on a type (including nested types). You can access all of these through the type object either by mentioning the particular member (e.g., `GetMethod("Main")`) or by calling the more generic method that returns all members of the same type (e.g., `GetMethods()`) and then choosing the one you want. The `Type` class gives access to constructors, methods, events, properties, fields, interfaces, and any nested types defined in the type; it also gives access to the attributes defined on the type. In addition, you can initialize an instance of the `TypeDelegator` class with the type whose members you are interested in determining.

2.4 GDI+ and Windows

Windows XP provides a new graphics library called GDI+. This library is provided in `gdiplus.dll` and is built on `gdi32.dll`, so in this respect it is treated as an addition to the operating system rather than an update. GDI+ is also provided for other platforms through the .NET framework.[13] There is nothing particularly

---

13. I have to be careful here because Microsoft goes to great lengths to explain that .NET does not update the operating system, saying that you do not have a newer version of Windows 2000 or Windows Millennium Edition when you install the .NET Framework.

.NET about GDI+; indeed, it can be called by unmanaged code, through a whole slew of exported functions that start with the prefix `Gdip` (e.g., `GdiplusStartup()` and `GdipCreatePath()`). Indeed, the Platform SDK even provides a series of header files containing C++ classes that make accessing these functions simpler.

.NET provides classes to perform most graphics actions that you will need to do. These classes are in namespaces with names that start with `System.Drawing`. However, .NET does *not* provide classes to perform three-dimensional transformations, so there is no equivalent of OpenGL; it also does not provide animation routines, so there is no equivalent of DirectX. In addition, the Framework Class Library provides classes to manipulate windows and the various controls that are provided on Windows. These classes treat windows as containers of controls called *forms*, and the namespace is called `System.Windows.Forms`.

As the name suggests, `System.Windows.Forms` is closer to the VB6 way of generating applications (scripting together controls on a form) than the Microsoft Foundation Classes (MFC) way (the document-view-controller paradigm). Indeed, you cannot regard Windows Forms as an *application framework* because it lacks even the basic document-handling code that is present in MFC.

2.4.1 System.Drawing

The `System.Drawing` namespace contains the basic tools to perform drawing in a window. The basic window code is actually in `System.Windows.Forms`, and the `Paint` event is called by the system to allow you to paint your window's client area. The `Paint` event handler is passed a `PaintEventArgs` parameter that has a `Graphics` member. The `Graphics` class has the methods that you use to draw on a window:

```
// C#
using System;
using System.Windows.Forms;
using System.Drawing;
class AppForm : Form
{
```

```
    protected override void OnPaint(
       PaintEventArgs e)
    {
       e.Graphics.FillRectangle(
          Brushes.Red, e.ClipRectangle);
       base.OnPaint(e);
    }
    static void Main()
    {
       AppForm form = new AppForm();
       Application.Run(form);
    }
}
```

This simple code will create a window and paint it red. There is a lot going on here. The `Main()` method creates a new form and passes it to the static `Run()` method. I could have called `ShowDialog()` on the form object, but using the `Application` class means that a standard message loop is created for each form created in the application.

When Windows tells the application that it wants the window to paint itself, it calls `OnPaint()` and passes it a `PaintEventArgs` parameter that has two properties: `ClipRectangle`, which has the area that needs painting (in device units); and `Graphics`, which gives access to what could be described as the graphics context, and this is the subject of the rest of this section. The default implementation of the `OnPaint()` method inherited from `Control` generates the `Paint` event, so if you do not override this method (or you call it explicitly), you can add `Paint` event handlers:

```
// C#
public AppForm()
{
    Paint += new PaintEventHandler(MyPaint);
}
protected void MyPaint(
    object sender, PaintEventArgs e)
{
    e.Graphics.FillRectangle(
       Brushes.Red, e.ClipRectangle);
}
```

The Windows Forms designer uses this last mechanism when you add paint handlers to your class.

The `Graphics` class allows you to do basic drawing operations like drawing lines (straight lines, arcs, curves, and Bézier curves) and shapes (pies, polygons, rectangles, and ellipses). These operations are carried out similarly to how they would be in Win32 GDI, except that you pass the drawing object that you want to use (pen or brush) to the method, rather than "selecting" the object into the device context, as you do in GDI. Another refreshing change with the .NET drawing mechanism is that the coordinate system is a lot easier to understand. You no longer have to worry about obscure concepts like mapping modes and viewports.

Drawing in the `Graphics` class goes like this: The sizes and positions of windows and controls are expressed in device units, which are pixels. Your code can draw in pixels, or it can set `Graphics.PageUnit` to one of the members of `GraphicsUnit` (see Table 2.14). In effect, these units define a scaling going from the units you specify (called the *World*) to the units that are used to plot on the device (*Device* units). If you have units in one, you can convert to the other using `Graphics.TransformPoints()`, which takes an array of points and an indication of the source and destination coordinate systems (`CoordinateSpace`: `Device`, `Page`, or `World`). So if you had a window and you

Table 2.14   GDI+ coordinate units

Enumeration	Unit Size
Display	1/75 inch
Document	1/300 inch
Inch	25.4 millimeters
Millimeter	1 millimeter
Pixel	A device pixel
Point	A printer's point, 1/72 inch
World	World unit

wanted to work in `Millimeter` units to draw a rectangle 20 millimeters square in the center,[14] you would use the following code:

```csharp
// C#
e.Graphics.PageUnit = GraphicsUnit.Millimeter;
PointF[] center = new PointF[]
   { new PointF(ClientSize.Width/2,
                ClientSize.Height/2)};
e.Graphics.TransformPoints(
   CoordinateSpace.World,
   CoordinateSpace.Device, center);
// the first two float values give the position
// of the rectangle; the other two are
// its width and height
e.Graphics.DrawRectangle(Pens.Black,
   center[0].X-10f, center[0].Y-10f,
   20f, 20f);
```

By default, the x coordinate extends from left to right, the y coordinate extends from top to bottom, and the top left-hand point is (0, 0), as Figure 2.3 shows. However, this configuration is not always convenient; you may want the axes to point in different directions (e.g., the y axis to point upward), and you

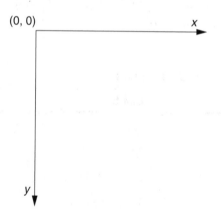

Figure 2.3   Default `System.Drawing` **coordinates**

---

14. Note that the square will not be exactly 20 millimeters on your monitor, but it will be when printed on paper. Monitors exaggerate dimensions; for example, my laptop screen shows a 20-millimeter square 14 percent bigger.

DEVELOPING APPLICATIONS WITH VISUAL STUDIO.NET

may want the origin to be in a different position (e.g., the center of the window). To do this you need to apply a *GDI+ transformation.*

A GDI+ transformation is a `Matrix` object containing information about the transformation that will be performed on the two-dimensional coordinates and a translation (or movement) of the points. Matrix multiplication on a two-dimensional point can scale the point, skew it, mirror it, or rotate it about a point; a translation will move a point the specified units in the x or y direction. The matrix for the transformation is given as a two-by-two array of numbers:

$$\begin{bmatrix} m_{11} & m_{12} \\ m_{21} & m_{22} \end{bmatrix}$$

The first row is applied to the point being transformed and produces the new x coordinate; the second row is applied to the point being transformed and produces the new y coordinate. So if a point (x, y) is represented as a one-dimensional vector, the transformation is applied by multiplication of the vector by the matrix:

$$\begin{bmatrix} m_{11} & m_{12} \\ m_{21} & m_{22} \end{bmatrix} \bullet \begin{bmatrix} x \\ y \end{bmatrix} = \begin{bmatrix} m_{11}x + m_{12}y \\ m_{21}x + m_{22}y \end{bmatrix}$$

Figure 2.4 shows some standard transformations that you can apply. Note that these transformations are performed with respect to the origin. A *translation*—a movement by an absolute amount—cannot be represented by a matrix transformation because it is simply an addition of vectors:

$$\begin{bmatrix} x \\ y \end{bmatrix} + \begin{bmatrix} a \\ b \end{bmatrix} = \begin{bmatrix} x + a \\ y + b \end{bmatrix}$$

The combination of matrix multiplication and vector addition can represent any transformation. This is why `Matrix.Elements` has six `float` values; the first four are the matrix, and the final two are the translation (which can also be accessed through `Matrix.OffsetX` and `Matrix.OffsetY`).

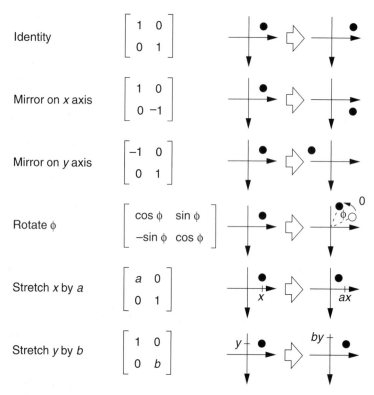

Identity	$\begin{bmatrix} 1 & 0 \\ 0 & 1 \end{bmatrix}$	
Mirror on x axis	$\begin{bmatrix} 1 & 0 \\ 0 & -1 \end{bmatrix}$	
Mirror on y axis	$\begin{bmatrix} -1 & 0 \\ 0 & 1 \end{bmatrix}$	
Rotate ϕ	$\begin{bmatrix} \cos\phi & \sin\phi \\ -\sin\phi & \cos\phi \end{bmatrix}$	
Stretch x by a	$\begin{bmatrix} a & 0 \\ 0 & 1 \end{bmatrix}$	
Stretch y by b	$\begin{bmatrix} 1 & 0 \\ 0 & b \end{bmatrix}$	

Figure 2.4   Common matrix transformations

The `Graphics` object has a property called `Transform`, which is a `Matrix` object and represents the transformation performed on the coordinates that you apply before they are converted to device units when used by the various graphics methods. Figure 2.3 shows the default directions of the coordinates, but if you would prefer the y axis to be mirrored—that is, to point upward—you can apply a transformation that has a mirror as the x axis. If, in addition, you want the origin to be in the center, you need a translation to shift all your points half the width of the window left and half the height of the window downward. To do all of this, all you have to do is initialize the `Transform` property as follows:

```
// C#
e.Graphics.Transform =
    new Matrix(1, 0, 0, -1,
```

DEVELOPING APPLICATIONS WITH VISUAL STUDIO.NET

```
ClientSize.Width/2,
ClientSize.Height/2);
```

`ClientSize` is a property of a `Form` object, and it gives a `Size` object with the window's width and height in pixels. By default, the `Transform` property is the identity transformation; that is, the matrix is the identity matrix shown in Figure 2.4, and the translation is 0 units in both directions.

You can apply multiple transformations by applying multiple `Matrix` objects, one after the other. There are two ways to do this. First, you can create a `Matrix` object and apply various transformations on it, and then assign the `Transform` property to this `Matrix` object. The transformations that you can apply include rotation by an angle in radians (where $360° = 2\pi$ radians), stretch by a specified amount in the x or y direction, shear, and translation. These transformations are represented by the methods `Rotate()`, `Scale()`, `Shear()`, and `Translate()`, respectively. There is also a generic function called `Multiply()`, to which you supply another `Matrix` object that represents the operation to be applied to the existing one. This option is useful if you want to hold the matrix as a form variable.

The other option is to apply these transformations directly to `Transform` by calling the various transformation methods on the `Graphics` object: `RotateTransform()`, `ScaleTransform()`, and `TranslateTransform()` to rotate, stretch, and translate, respectively; and `MultiplyTransform()` to perform a transformation represented by a `Matrix` object. You can always set the `Transform` property back to identity by calling `ResetTransform()`.

The order in which you apply two operations to a point is often important. Translating by 10 pixels in the x direction and then rotating by 30° is not the same as rotating by 30° and then translating by 10 pixels in the x direction. For this reason, all the transformation methods (on `Matrix` and on `Graphics`) are overloaded. One version has a `MatrixOrder` parameter, which indicates which operation comes first—the one in the existing matrix or the one represented by the parameter to the method. The other version assumes that the operation in the parameter is applied first.

In my earlier examples, I used pens and brushes. The `System.Drawing` namespace has two classes—`Pens` and `SystemPens`—that hold default pens you can use. `Pens` contains over 140 pens as static properties with various named standard colors. Note that each of these pens has a width of one unit (the unit, of course, depends on `Graphics.PageUnit`), so if you have set the unit to `Inch`, you will have a very wide pen! The `SystemPens` class has static properties that are named according to the various system colors. Using these pens, you can ensure that the drawing agrees with the color scheme set for the current machine.

If you want to create a pen with a custom color and pen width, you can use the `Pen` class. In addition, you can set the alignment—that is, whether the pen draws along the line (`Center`, the default) or to the left, to the right, or (for a curve) on the inside or outside. Pens can be used to draw multiple lines, and you can alter how these lines join using `LineJoin`. You can also change the start and end point appearance with `StartCap` and `EndCap`. Finally, you can create a dashed pen, and you can select the dash type with `DashStyle`, the space between dashes with `DashOffset`, and the ends of the dashes with `DashCap`. You can define your own dash pattern by providing an array of `float` values:

```
// C#
Pen p = new Pen(Color.Red);
p.DashStyle = DashStyle.Custom;
p.DashPattern = new float[]{5f, 2f, 1f, 2f};
e.Graphics.DrawRectangle(p, 10, 10, 200, 200);
```

Here I have used the static member of the `Color` class called `Red`. You can also use this class to create your own colors. In addition, the namespace has a class called `SystemColor` that contains the colors of the appropriate system colors set on the current machine. If you have a color used on an HTML page (and hence held as a string) or in the Win32 RGB format or the OLECOLOR format, you can use `ColorTranslator` to convert these to a `Color` value.

A brush is used to provide the color or pattern when a shape is filled; the Framework Class Library provides several classes that allow you to use a pre-created brush or to create your own. The `Brushes` class contains static properties that are solid brushes of named colors. `SystemBrushes` has static properties that are named after the user interface items that they are used to paint; it uses the currently set system colors. If you want to define a custom color, you can use `SolidBrush`; this and the other two classes I have mentioned here are solid brushes. However, you can use `TextureBrush` and base it on an image; the brush will repeat the image in the region it is used to paint.

If you want to fill an area with a hatch pattern, you can use a `HatchBrush` object. This class actually appears in `System.Drawing.Drawing2D`, but it applies to the current discussion. The constructor of the `HatchBrush` class takes a member from the `HatchStyle` enumeration, which determines the type of hatch that is used, You can also specify the foreground and background colors of the hatch. There are two other brush types in the `System.Drawing.Drawing2D` namespace, but I will defer a description of those until the next section.

The `System.Drawing` namespace also has classes that allow you to manipulate images and icons. The `Icon` class allows you to load icons from files or streams (e.g., from a resource) and convert them into `Bitmap` objects if necessary. The `Graphics` class has a `DrawImage()` method that allows you to draw `Image` objects; the `Bitmap` class is derived from `Image`.

You can also create graphics paths using the `GraphicsPath` class. `GraphicsPath` has methods similar to those of the `Graphics` class, except that they add a graphical instruction to the graphics path that can be played back later through `Graphics.DrawPath()` and `Graphics.FillPath()`. `GraphicsPath` also has a `Transform()` method, which you can use to supply a `Matrix` object and a `Warp()` method so that the class can distort the image, through the array of floating-point values passed as a parameter.

In a similar way, you can define clip areas and regions. The `Region` class has methods that allow you to build up an area made of `Rectangle` and `GraphicsPath` objects. As the name suggests, a region is an area on the screen where you can draw. The interesting thing about regions is that they can have irregular outlines that you can construct by combining regions, by taking one region away from another, or by determining the space occupied by one region but not by another. These combinations are summarized in Figure 2.5.

You can test this yourself with the following code:

```
// C#
GraphicsPath gpA = new GraphicsPath();
gpA.AddEllipse(10, 10, 100, 100);
```

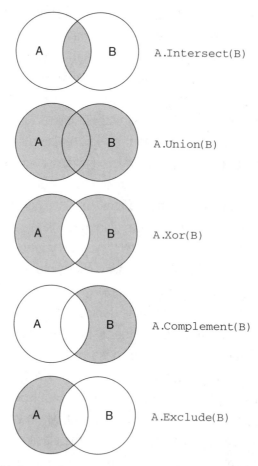

A.Intersect(B)

A.Union(B)

A.Xor(B)

A.Complement(B)

A.Exclude(B)

Figure 2.5 Combining regions. The shaded area illustrates the combining of two regions.

```
Region A = new Region(gpA);
GraphicsPath gpB = new GraphicsPath();
gpB.AddEllipse(60, 10, 100, 100);
Region B = new Region(gpB);
A.Intersect(B);   // find the intersection
e.Graphics.FillRegion(Brushes.Red, A);
```

Finally, you can manipulate strings on-screen. There are a few steps to this manipulation: First you need to select a font, then you need to determine the size of the string, and then you have to draw the string. There are several ways

DEVELOPING APPLICATIONS WITH VISUAL STUDIO.NET

to select a font. For example, you can use the constructors and properties of `Font` to specify precisely the font that you need, but this approach carries with it the danger that the precise font does not exist. Alternatively, you can provide a few clues to the type of font you want (e.g., its size and whether it is a serif or sans serif font), and the system will select the font nearest to the one you specify. Finally, you can query the system for all of the fonts that are installed and select an appropriate font.

Fonts of a similar type are grouped together in families. You can get a family of fonts through the `FontFamily` class, and the families that are installed on your machine are accessible through the static `FontFamily.GetFamilies()` method. Once you have a `FontFamily` object, you can provide it to a `Font` constructor along with other information that will better identify the font you want. Drawing a string involves calling `Graphics.DrawString()`. In addition to the string and font, you need to provide a position where you want the string drawn. This means that you need to calculate the area on the window that the string of the specified font will fill. To do this you can call `Graphics.Measure-String()`, which will return a `SizeF` value type with the height and width of the area that the string will occupy in the window.

Once you have determined the minimum area that the string will occupy, you can use this information to create a rectangle where you want the string to appear. You can use the `StringFormat` class to indicate how the string should be placed in the rectangle, so you can indicate if the string is left-, right-, or center-justified (`StringAlignment`) and specify how the string is trimmed if it is bigger than the area (`StringTrimming`). `StringFormat` also has information about the tab stops that will be used, which you can set by passing an array of `float` values to `SetTabStops()`. Finally, you can pass the string, the font, the rectangle, and the string format to `Graphics.DrawString()` to draw the string on the screen.

The final point of this discussion is that the `System.Drawing` namespace has the value types needed to hold information about areas, points, and sizes of objects on-screen. These classes are used by the `System.Windows.Forms` namespace too, and they come in two formats: an integral and a float version.

As an example, look at the size structure; there are two versions: `Size` and `SizeF`. `Size` is initialized with width and height expressed as `int` values. This is fine for most of the units that you can use in your drawing routines (e.g., `Pixel`), but it makes little sense for the larger units, like `Inch` (if this were so, the smallest possible size in this case would be 1 inch). The `SizeF` structure contains members similar to those of `Size`, but the values are held as `float` values, which means that you can have a size that is the fraction of a unit.

2.4.2 System.Drawing.Drawing2D

I mentioned many members of the `System.Drawing.Drawing2D` namespace in the previous section (e.g., `GraphicsPath` and `Matrix`). The remaining classes in this namespace take advantage of the *alpha blending* facilities that GDI+ offers. Alpha blending treats a color as having four values: the red, green, and blue components, and the alpha component. The alpha component determines how transparent the color will be.

In the following code I create a red-filled rectangle and draw over the top of it with a series of 1-pixel-wide green rectangles. For an alpha value of 0, which represents complete transparency, the green would not appear; for a value of 255, which represents complete opacity, the underlying color would not be seen at all. The effect of this code will be to generate a gradient rectangle going from red to green and giving all the combinations of red and green in between:

```
// C#
e.Graphics.FillRectangle(
   Brushes.Red, 0, 0, 256, 50);
for (int x = 0; x < 256; x++)
{
   Color color = Color.FromArgb(x, Color.Green));
   e.Graphics.FillRectangle(
      new SolidBrush(color, x, 0, 1, 50));
}
```

Building a color gradient like this is cumbersome and inefficient. A better solution is to use `LinearGradientBrush`. This class allows you to specify the colors that will be used in the gradient. Of course, to be able to create the gradient, the class also needs to know the length over which the gradient will be applied, which is given by the first two parameters to the constructor:

```
// C#
LinearGradientBrush brush = null;
brush = new LinearGradientBrush(
    new Point(0, 0), new Point(255, 0),
    Color.Red, Color.Green);
e.Graphics.FillRectangle(brush, 0, 0, 256, 50);
```

Note that in this code, the two points are on a line. In this case the gradient occurs linearly along this line. However, if you specify a rectangle and a `Line-arGradientMode` value, you can specify that the gradient be performed horizontally, vertically, or diagonally:

```
// C#
LinearGradientBrush brush;
brush = new LinearGradientBrush(
    new Rectangle(0, 0, 256, 256),
    Color.Red, Color.Green,
    LinearGradientMode.ForwardDiagonal);
e.Graphics.FillRectangle(brush, 0, 0, 256, 256);
```

The blend that is used by `LinearGradientBrush` is accessed through the `Blend` property, which is an instance of the `Blend` class. You can change this property to alter how the blend is applied, and even provide a `Matrix` object to apply a transformation to the gradient.

2.4.3 System.Windows.Forms

The Windows Forms library could occupy a whole chapter on its own, so in this section I will just outline the basic classes. Bear in mind that the Windows Forms library is just that—a basic library to manage forms. It is not intended to be an application framework like MFC. This means that there are no classes for managing documents or for document objects (doc-objects), and you do not get MFC-style command routing. If you add a menu to your form, it is isolated. You do not get MFC-style *command UI updates*, which automatically update the checkmarked and enabled status of menu items; you do not get the automatic status bar update when a menu item is highlighted; and there is no mechanism to connect a menu to a toolbar. If you want any of these features, or any of the other application framework features offered by MFC, you have to write them yourself. This is not trivial.

My point is that Windows Forms is not a replacement for MFC. If you are currently considering MFC for your next project, then you are unlikely to choose Windows Forms instead. Windows Forms is for the type of user interface project for which previously you would have considered consider using VB6.

In the previous few sections I explained basic drawing; to draw, however, you need to have a window. Windows, and the controls that can be added to them, are the purpose of the `System.Windows.Forms` namespace. Each thread in a Windows application has a message queue. The application reads messages in the queue in a message pump and dispatches messages to the windows created on the thread. Typically the message pump loops in the main thread of the application so that when the message pump stops looping, the main thread dies and the application goes away. A modal dialog has its own message pump, so the function creates the dialog blocks while the dialog is showing. If this is the main thread, then, this function will prevent the main thread from returning.

With this basic information in mind, let's look at the .NET windowing classes. As I've shown already, `Form` is the basic class for creating user windows. The following code creates a blank form:

```
// C#
class App
{
    static void Main()
    {
        Form form = new Form();
        form.ShowDialog();
    }
}
```

`ShowDialog()` creates a modal dialog, and the main thread will loop in the dialog procedure provided by this method. When the method completes, the main thread will end and the application will die. If the modal dialog creates modeless dialogs, its message loop will dispatch messages to these new windows.

DEVELOPING APPLICATIONS WITH VISUAL STUDIO.NET

If you replace ShowDialog() with Show(), a modeless dialog will be created; however, there is no message loop in this case, so the thread will not be blocked and the application will die.

There is an alternative to ShowDialog(), as I showed earlier. This is the Application.Run() method, which will create a message pump for you. Because it implements a message pump, this method will block. What is the difference between Form.ShowDialog() and Application.Run()? On initial inspection there is not much of a difference because both methods end up calling the same code. However, Run() provides a "back door" into the message loop for the Microsoft Office (MSO) Component Manager, which is a component that allows user interface components to interact with each other to show modal and nonmodal dialogs. Calling Run() with a form reference indicates that this form is the main form of the application, so when this form closes the application should go away. Calling Run() without a form will create a loop that will continue to live even if there are no windows. This means that the MSO Component Manager will still be able to talk to the application.

This code will show a window, but when you close the window the application will still run (which you can verify with Task Manager):

```
// C#
class App
{
    static void Main()
    {
        Form form = new Form();
        form.Show();
        Application.Run();
    }
}
```

In this case, if you want to close the application when the form closes, the form should catch the Closed event and call Application.Exit(). In general, it is best to indicate a main form and allow that to define the lifetime of the application. The Application class generates events when the application thread is idle, or when the thread or the application exits. Thus you can provide idle handling.

The two main classes involved in forms are the `Form` class and its ancestor, `Control`. These two classes have the majority of the methods that you will need to call on your window. The classes declare the events generated by the message handlers given in the class; for example, the click message is handled by the `OnClick()` method that generates the `Click` event.

`Form` and `Control` have events for the most often generated Windows messages; if you want to handle other messages, you have to intercept them yourself. To do this you should override `Form.WndProc()`. This method takes a reference to a `Message` object, which encapsulates a Windows message. Because this parameter is passed by reference, you can handle one message by changing it to another message. Otherwise you can write appropriate message handling by referring to the Windows SDK. For example, the following code creates a window without a caption bar, but you can move this window by treating the entire window as a caption bar (click and hold down the left mouse button and move the mouse). The `WM_NCHITTEST` message is what tells the system that the entire window should be treated as a caption bar:

```csharp
// C#
class CaptionlessForm : Form
{
    const int HTCAPTION = 2;
    const int WM_NCHITTEST = 0x84;
    public CaptionlessForm()
    { ControlBox = false; }
    protected override void WndProc(ref Message m)
    {
        if (m.Msg == 0x84) // WM_NCHITTEST
        {
            m.Result = new IntPtr(HTCAPTION);
            return;
        }
        base.WndProc(ref m);
    }
}
```

Note that this version of `WndProc()` overrides the version in the base class, but you must call the base-class version because otherwise other messages will not be handled correctly. Whatever values are passed through the WPARAM and LPARAM parameters, the handler code for the WM_NCHITTEST message returns the same value: HTCAPTION. Because the Message parameter is passed by reference, you can change it, so you return values through the Message.Result member.

The System.Windows.Forms namespace provides wrapper classes for all of the Win32 controls and custom controls. These are derived from Control and are added to the Controls property of the parent form through Add() (or AddRange() to add several controls):

```
// C#
class UseButton : Form
{
    public UseButton()
    {
        ClientSize = new Size(150, 40);
        Text = "Test";
        Button button = new Button();
        button.Location = new Point(40, 10);
        button.Text = "Click Me";
        button.Click +=
            new EventHandler(ClickedButton);
        Controls.Add(button);
    }
    public void ClickedButton(object sender, EventArgs e)
    { MessageBox.Show("you clicked me"); }
}
```

This code creates a form that has a single button with the caption **Click Me**, and a click handler implemented by the Form class in a method called Clicked-Button(). The handler shows a message dialog by calling one of the overloaded static methods of the MessageBox class. In addition, the Framework Class Library provides classes for the common dialogs, which are accessed more or less like they are in Win32. That is, you decide initial values for the dialog, show the dialog, and then when the dialog is closed, read the values that were set.

The Control and Form classes will generate events when windows are created and closed. When a window is first created, it will be sent the

`Form.Load` event just before it is shown. To a large extent this is superfluous because form initialization should occur in the form's constructor. This event was added to the `Form` class as a security blanket to placate the VB6 developers who felt left out when they discovered that VB.NET was not VB6.NET.

When a user clicks on the close button, the `Form.Closing` event is generated. This is a `CancelEventHandler` delegate that is passed a `CancelEventArgs` object, which has a `Cancel` property. The handler for the `Closing` event can set the `Cancel` property to `true` to indicate that the window should not close. Your code can implement the `Closing` event to query the user if form data should be saved. Typically this query is posed in a yes/no/cancel dialog in which the **Cancel** button means that the user has decided not to close the window. If the user does decide to close the form, the `Form` object gets the `Form.Closed` event to indicated that the window has closed.

When a window comes to the front, it gets the `Form.Activated` event. At this point you know that the user wants to use the window, so you should update the form. If the user presses **Alt-Tab** to go to a window, or if a minimized window is restored, it is activated. On the other hand, a window that is minimized is deactivated (as is the window that the user leaves when pressing **Alt-Tab**), and a deactivated window gets the `Form.Deactivate` event. In addition to these two events, the events `Control.GotFocus` and `Control.LostFocus`, respectively, occur when a window gets or loses the focus. These events make sense to controls and multiple-document interface (MDI) child windows, as I'll explain later.

Normally you would write code like this using the Visual Studio.NET Windows Forms designer, which is a RAD tool that allows you to drag and drop controls onto a form. The Windows Forms designer generates the code for the controls added through drag-and-drop, but as you can see, it is straightforward to write this code yourself. If you use C++ as your development language, you have no option because there is no support for C++ in the Windows Forms designer. The following is equivalent C++ code for the previous example:

```
// C++
#using <mscorlib.dll>
#using <system.windows.forms.dll>
```

```
#using <system.drawing.dll>
#using <system.dll>
using namespace System;
using namespace System::Windows::Forms;
using namespace System::Drawing;

__gc class UseButton : public Form
{
    public:
    UseButton()
    {
        ClientSize = System::Drawing::Size(150, 40);
        Text = S"Test";
        Button* button = new Button();
        button->Location = Point(40,10);
        button->Text = S"Click Me";
        button->Click +=
            new EventHandler(this, ClickedButton);
        Controls->Add(button);
    }
    void ClickedButton(Object* sender, EventArgs* e)
    { MessageBox::Show(S"you clicked me"); }
};
void WinMain(int, int, char*, int)
{
    UseButton* w = new UseButton();
    Application::Run(w);
}
```

In general, converting a C# class generated by Windows Forms designer into C++ is relatively straightforward. So if you intend to use C++ as your GUI development language, it is best to decide which controls you want to use and which events you want to handle, and to use the Windows Forms designer to generate the required C# code. Once you have done this, you can convert the code to C++ and implement the event handlers.

When the C++ compiler sees that an application has a `WinMain()` method, it tells the linker that it should use the `/SUBSYSTEM:WINDOWS` switch, so compiling the previous code is as simple as giving `/clr` and the name of the source file to the compiler. Although I have a `using namespace` statement for the `System::Drawing` namespace, I have to give the fully qualified name for `Size` because `Form` has a `Size` property, so I need to disambiguate between the two. In addition, note that members like `ClientSize` are *properties,* so if you want to change them you should change the entire property. Compare the previous code with the following:

```
// C++
ClientSize.Width = 150;
ClientSize.Height = 40;
```

which is equivalent to this code:

```
// C++
get_ClientSize().Width = 150;
get_ClientSize().Height = 40;
```

The `set_ClientSize()` method is not called, and this is a problem because `set_ClientSize()` makes the call to change the size of the window.

Since I have mentioned sizes, it is worth pointing out the various size and position properties available through `Form` (and its base classes). `Control.Bounds` is the bounding rectangle of the window, in pixels, on the screen. These bounds are also available as `Control.Left`, `Control.Top`, `Control.Right`, and `Control.Bottom`, and the position that can be deduced from `Control.Left` and `Control.Top` is available through `Control.Location`. In addition, `Control.Width` and `Control.Height` can be deduced from the bounds, as can `Control.Size`, the total size of the window.

In general, changing these properties will eventually lead to a call to `Control.SetBounds()`. `Form.ClientSize` gives the width and height of the area within the form where you can paint (i.e., inside of the sizing border and caption). This data is also available through `Form.ClientRectangle`. The various properties of a form are shown in Figure 2.6.

In addition, `Form.DesktopBounds` and `Form.DesktopLocation` are equivalent to `Control.Bounds` and `Control.Location`, except that they take the taskbar into account (see Figure 2.7). You can change the size of a window relative to the current size by calling `Control.Scale()` with a `float` value that indicates how much bigger or smaller the window should be.

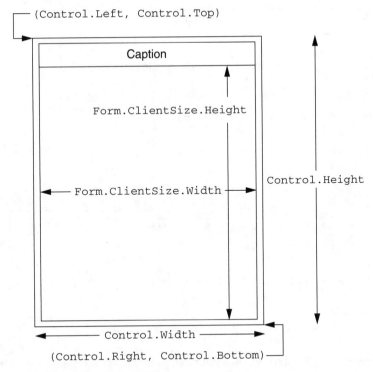

Figure 2.6 Window size properties

Because these various properties are interrelated, naturally the events generated when they change are also interrelated. When the `Size` property changes, the `Control.SizeChanged` event is generated; when the form is actually resized, the `Control.Resize` event is generated. Because resizing a window changes the `Size` property, a `SizeChanged` event will always follow a `Resize` event. Similarly, the `Move` event is generated when a window is moved, and this changes the `Location` property, which in turn generates the `LocationChanged` event.

The default window arrangement is VB-style forms; that is, the first form (the *main form* if you pass a reference to it to `Application.Run()`) creates other forms—modal or modeless—that float aimlessly around the screen. For a bit more order, you can write to the so-called multiple-document interface (MDI) layout. In MDI, there is one main window (the MDI parent), and the child windows it

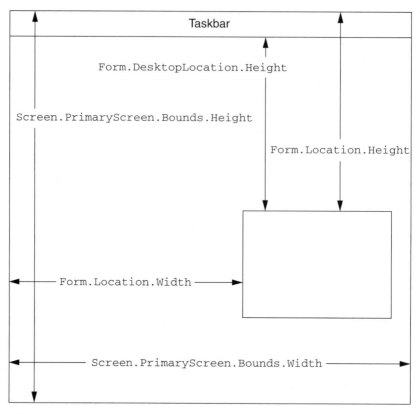

Figure 2.7 Window location properties

creates (MDI children) are constrained to its bounds. An MDI application is allowed to create modal and modeless forms, but now they have specific meanings: A modal form is used to get information from the user and is temporary, whereas modeless forms are used to gather information through toolbars.

Creating an MDI application is straightforward. The MDI parent form sets its `IsMdiContainer` property to `true`, and the child form sets its `MdiParent` property to the MDI parent form:

```
// C#
class Child : Form
{
    public Child()
    { Click += new EventHandler(OnClick); }
```

```
    // create a new child when a child is clicked
    public void OnClick(object o, EventArgs e)
    {
        Child c = new Child();
        c.MdiParent = this.MdiParent;
        c.Show();
    }
}
class Parent : Form
{
    public Parent()
    {
        IsMdiContainer = true;
        Child c = new Child();
        c.MdiParent = this;
        c.Show();
    }
}
```

A form can check its IsMdiContainer and IsMdiChild properties to see if it is being used as an MDI parent or child. An MDI parent can access its children through the MdiChildren property, which will return an array of Form objects. In addition, the parent can call LayoutMdi() to rearrange child windows; this method takes an MdiLayout value.

MDI children are not activated or deactivated, so they do not get the Activated and Deactivate events. Instead they get Form.MdiChildActivate, as well as the GotFocus and LostFocus events.

In general, your application will be made up of Form objects that have all of the standard embellishments. If you want, however, you can paint your own embellishments (e.g., by overriding WndProc()). To do this you must use the standard window styles set for your machine. Information about these settings can be found in the SystemInformation class through static properties. If you want to get information about the monitor that is being used, you can call the Screen class.

Windows can have menus—either through a menu bar beneath the caption bar, or as a floating pop-up menu. The System.Windows.Forms classes support both types through the MainMenu and ContextMenu classes. Every form has a Menu property, which identifies the menu that will be displayed beneath the caption. This property is an instance of the `MainMenu` class, which is a container for `MenuItem` objects. Unlike Win32, in which menus are typically stored as resources, `MainMenu` instances are built up at runtime. This means that you have the responsibility to check the locale and load the appropriate assembly resource through a `ResourceManager` instance (or via a satellite assembly).

Creating a menu is straightforward: Both `MainMenu` and `MenuItem` derive from `Menu`, which has a member called `MenuItems`; this means that an instance of `MenuItem` can be a member of a menu and can itself contain menu items. Adding a menu to your window involves building up submenus of menu items and then adding these to other menu items until you reach the top level, which is a `MainMenu` instance:

```csharp
// C#
public MyForm()
{
    MenuItem menuFile = new MenuItem();
    menuFile.Text = "File";
    MenuItem menuFileExit = new MenuItem();
    menuFileExit.Text = "Exit";
    menuFileExit.Click +=
        new EventHandler(OnMenu);
    menuFile.MenuItems.Add(menuFileExit);

    MenuItem menuHelp = new MenuItem();
    menuHelp.Text = "Help";
    MenuItem menuHelpAbout = new MenuItem();
    menuHelpAbout.Text = "About";
    menuHelpAbout.Click +=
        new EventHandler(OnMenu);
    menuHelp.MenuItems.Add(menuHelpAbout);

    Menu = new MainMenu();
    Menu.MenuItems.AddRange(
        new MenuItem[] {menuFile, menuHelp});
}
public void OnMenu(object o, EventArgs e)
{
    MenuItem mi = (MenuItem)o;
    MessageBox.Show(mi.Text);
}
```

This code creates two menu items on the main menu: **File** and **Help**. Each of these has a submenu item that is added through the `Add()` method of the `Menu-Items` property. Multiple menu items can be added to a menu at one time by the `AddRange()` member, which I have used here to add the submenus to the main menu. Menus generate several types of events, perhaps the most important one being the `Click` event that is generated when the menu item is clicked. The code here shows an example of handling the `Click` event for the **Exit** and **About** menu items. You can handle menus either by implementing individual handlers or, as I have done, by using a general handler. If you have a general handler, the `object` parameter of the handler will be the menu item that generated the event, and you can use this information to perform the specific action.

If the menu item has set the `OwnerDraw` property to `true`, you take the responsibility to draw the item. When the parent menu is shown, the `Mea-sureItem` event for the owner-draw menu item will be generated. You can use this event to indicate how much space you need to draw the item:

```
// C#
MenuItem menuColor = new MenuItem();
menuColor.Text = "Colors";
for (int x = 0; x < 3; x++)
{
    MenuItem menuColorItem = new MenuItem();
    menuColorItem.OwnerDraw = true;
    menuColorItem.MenuID = x;
    menuColorItem.Click +=
        new EventHandler(OnMenu);
    menuColorItem.MeasureItem +=
        new MeasureItemEventHandler(OnMeasure);
    menuColorItem.DrawItem +=
        new DrawItemEventHandler(OnDraw);
    menuColor.MenuItems.Add(menuColorItem);
}
```

The handlers look like this:

```
// C#
public void OnMeasure(
    object o, MeasureItemEventArgs e)
{ e.ItemHeight = 20; e.ItemWidth = 50; }
```

```
public void OnDraw(object o, DrawItemEventArgs e)
{
    Brush b = Brushes.Black; // default value
    MenuItem mi = (MenuItem)o;
    switch(mi.MenuID)
    {
    case 0: b = Brushes.Red;   break;
    case 1: b = Brushes.Blue;  break;
    case 2: b = Brushes.Green; break;
    }
    e.Graphics.FillRectangle(b, e.Bounds);
}
```

In addition to drawing your own menu items, you can indicate that an item has a check mark. There are two types: ticks and radio buttons. If `Radio-Checked` is `true`, radio buttons are used. To show the check mark, you set the `Checked` property to `true`. Note that these are mere embellishments to the menu; the logic (that a radio button is part of a radio button group, of which only one is selected) is entirely up to you. Here's a class that does this work for you:

```
// C#
public class RadioGroup
{
    private ArrayList items = new ArrayList();
    public void Select(int index)
    {
        if (index < 0 || index > items.Count)
            throw new ArgumentOutOfRangeException(
                        "out of range");
        foreach(MenuItem mi in items)
        {
            ((MenuItem)mi).Checked = false;
        }
        ((MenuItem)items[index]).Checked = true;
    }
    public void Add(MenuItem mi, bool selected)
    {
        mi.RadioCheck = true;
        int index = items.Add(mi);
        mi.Click += new EventHandler(OnClick);
        mi.Index = index;
        if (selected || index == 0) Select(index);
```

DEVELOPING APPLICATIONS WITH VISUAL STUDIO.NET

```
    }
    public MenuItem[] GetItems()
    {
        MenuItem[] mis = new MenuItem[items.Count];
        for(int x = 0; x < items.Count; x++)
            mis[x] = (MenuItem)items[x];
        return mis;
    }
    protected void OnClick(object o, EventArgs e)
    { Select(((MenuItem)o).Index); }
}
```

RadioGroup maintains a list of MenuItem objects, one of which (by default, the first item) must be checked. As RadioGroup adds an item to the list, it adds a Click handler that calls the member method Select(). This method clears the Checked property of all the items and sets the Checked property of the item that was clicked. Select() is public, so the developer can also check a specific item. Use it like this:

```
// C#
Menu = new MainMenu();
MenuItem items = new MenuItem("Items");
RadioGroup group = new RadioGroup();
// first item is selected by default
group.Add(new MenuItem("One",
    new EventHandler(OnMenu)), false);
group.Add(new MenuItem("Two",
    new EventHandler(OnMenu)), false);
group.Add(new MenuItem("Three",
    new EventHandler(OnMenu)), false);
menuCount.MenuItems.AddRange(group.GetItems());
Menu.MenuItems.Add(menuItems);
```

The Control class has a property called ContextMenu; this is the menu that is shown when the user right-clicks on the control or form. This property is an instance of the ContextMenu class, which can be constructed from an array of MenuItem objects:

```
// C#
this.ContextMenu = new ContextMenu(
    new MenuItem[]
    { new MenuItem("One", new EventHandler(OnMenu)),
```

```
        new MenuItem("Two", new EventHandler(OnMenu)),
        new MenuItem("Three", new EventHandler(OnMenu))
    }
);
```

One problem in form-based applications is the validation of controls. If a modal form contains controls, to gather data you typically want to validate the values in the controls before the dialog is removed. If the values are not valid, the user should be reminded of why the values are incorrect. In Windows Forms, an `ErrorProvider` control provides this reminder.

Such a control does not have a user interface until an error is generated. An error is generated by a call to the error provider's `SetError()` method, with a reference to the control that has the invalid data and an error string passed in. If the error string has more than zero characters, an icon (`ErrorProvider.Icon`) is displayed next to the control. This icon has a tool tip that shows the error string, as Figure 2.8 illustrates.

The form in Figure 2.8 validates the text in the text box when the **Validate** button is clicked. Here is the code for this form:

```
// C#
class MyForm : Form
{
    ErrorProvider errorProvider ;
    errorProvider = new ErrorProvider();
    TextBox txtName;
    public MyForm()
    {
        errorProvider.DataMember = null;
        errorProvider.ContainerControl = this;
        txtName = new TextBox();
        txtName.Location = new Point(60, 10);
```

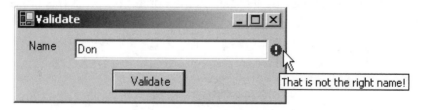

Figure 2.8   A form with an error provider

```
txtName.Size = new Size(200, 20);
Button btnValidate = new Button();
btnValidate.Location = new Point(100, 40);
btnValidate.Text = "Validate";
btnValidate.Click +=
    new EventHandler(OnValidate);
Label label = new Label();
label.Location = new Point(10, 10);
label.Size = new Size(50, 25);
label.Text = "Name";
ClientSize = new Size(275, 70);
Controls.AddRange(
    new Control[]
        {btnValidate, label, txtName});
this.Text = "Validate";
}
protected void OnValidate(object o, EventArgs e)
{
    if (txtName.Text.Length == 0)
        errorProvider.SetError(txtName,
            "You must provide a name!");
    else if (txtName.Text != "Richard")
        errorProvider.SetError(txtName,
            "That is not the right name!");
    else
        errorProvider.SetError(txtName, "");
}
}
```

The `HelpProvider` control works in a similar way. This control shows help text when the **F1** key is pressed. The help string that is displayed depends on the control that currently has the input focus. For example, you could add the following to the end of the `MyForm` constructor:

```
// C#
HelpProvider helpProvider = new HelpProvider();
helpProvider.SetHelpString(txtName,
    "Enter here the name that you want validated");
helpProvider.SetHelpString(btnValidate,
    "Click here to validate the name");
```

This code generates the pop-up window shown in Figure 2.9. If you want more detailed help, you can set the `HelpNamespace` property to the name of

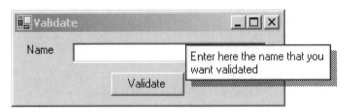

Figure 2.9 A form with a help provider

an HTML or compiled HTML (CHM) file, and then you can use the `SetHelp-Keyword()` method to associate a control with an anchored keyword (using the `<A>` tag) in the help file. `HelpProvider` is a friendly front end for the `Help` class that wraps the HTML 1.0 help engine.

2.5   Other Framework Class Library Classes
The classes in the remaining Framework Class Library namespaces will be important to you when you develop your Windows applications. By their nature, however, they are tied to the Windows operating system.

2.5.1   Event Log
The NT event log is a persistent store of important application messages. You should *not* use the event log for messages that make sense only during your debugging and testing phase. You should also refrain from reporting messages like *The process has started* because such events always happen and thus are not *eventful*. Instead, you should use the event log to save information that will be important diagnostics if something exceptional happens—for example, if you try to open a file that should exist and the operation fails.

The event log is a wonderful facility because it collates event messages from processes on a single machine, and the API allows administrators to access the event log on other machines. So a central event log could hold messages from processes in a distributed application. Sadly, the .NET classes for accessing the event log have rather debased the facility, as you'll see later in this section.

Using the event log is straightforward. To read the `Application` log on the current machine you need to create a new `EventLog` object:

```
// C#
EventLog ev = new EventLog("Application");
foreach(EventLogEntry e in ev.Entries)
    Console.WriteLine(e.Source + " " + e.Message);
```

This code accesses an array of entries in the `Application` event log at the time the call is made. Each instance of `EventLogEntry` has all the information for each entry in the log. When the call to access the `Message` property of `EventLogEntry` is made, the message is formatted according to three pieces of information: `EventID`, the `ReplacementStrings` array, and the message resource file registered for the `Source` property of the message. The path to the message resource file is obtained from the following key:

```
HKEY_LOCAL_MACHINE\System\CurrentControlSet\Services\EventLog
```

This key contains keys for each of the current event logs (usually `Application`, `System`, and `Security`), and these keys contain a key for each source that can generate events in that log. Within each key is a value called `EventMessageFile` that contains the path to the source's message resource file. These files are resource-only DLLs that contain a MESSAGETABLE resource. The code that formats the event message uses `EventID` to get a format string from the message table resource and `ReplacementStrings` to fill in the placeholders in the format string with the actual values. So far, so good.

This mechanism of generating the message at runtime may seem complicated, but it is deliberate and useful for two reasons. First, the final message can be as long and as descriptive as you like, but the information that is stored in the event log is small: just `EventID` and `ReplacementStrings`. Long replacement strings are an indication that the event itself is too general and that you are using the replacement strings to distinguish between dissimilar messages with the same `EventID` values. If done correctly, the information for the message in the event log is small. A small event log is a good thing for multiple reasons, which I'll explain in a moment.

The other reason why this mechanism is good is that the message is formatted when the event is read. This means that a locale-specific event message file is used on the machine *where the event message is formatted*. So the Windows XP machine JEAN could be located in Paris and run under the French locale, and the Windows XP machine JOHN could be located in London and run under the UK English locale. I could copy the event log from JEAN (either by remote access or physically as a disk file) and read it on JOHN. The events generated on JEAN will appear as English when read on JOHN, even though they are generated in French. In a multicultural, multinational world, this is a great facility.

Here are the two important reasons for keeping the event log small: First, if you want to access the event log of a machine over a network, you want to ensure that the number of bytes passed over the network is kept to a minimum, thereby making the reader application appear more responsive. Second, the event log has a facility to limit the size of the physical disk files that are used to hold the event log information. When this maximum size is exceeded, the older events are discarded. Because events are *eventful* and therefore important, you do not want them to be discarded without first being read. Keeping event log entries as small as possible will ensure that this rarely happens. I'll explain how .NET writes to the event log in a moment, but as you'll see, it does it in the worst possible way.

The event log has a rather arcane Win32 API: When you read events (as I mentioned earlier), you actually pass a buffer and the event log fills the buffer with as many event log records as it can squeeze into it (it does not even tell you how many records it has returned). This makes sense when you access the event log remotely, but it makes the reader code complicated. There is definitely room for improvement here, and as the code I gave earlier shows, .NET uses array syntax to give access to the event log, so it gets a gold star there.

The other problem with the event log is the generation of the resource files. The format messages are items in a MESSAGETABLE binary resource in a DLL. To create this resource you generate a script and compile it with the message resource compiler, mc.exe. Visual Studio has editors for things like string tables and VERSIONINFO, but it has never had (and still doesn't) an editor for MESSAGETABLE resources. As a consequence, projects that include these resources are more complicated then they need to be. .NET has failed miserably to solve this issue.

When writing an event, EventLog.Write() copies your message *in its entirety* to the event log. This means that the developer has the responsibility of formatting the message string according to the locale where the message was generated. From this point onward, then, that message will always be read in that locale-specific form. So if you are a developer working on an application that will be distributed across multiple locales, you have two choices: One possibility is to format the event log messages according to the locale in which you expect the support engineer to work (but can you *really* determine this at design time?), in which case local users will see the message in a locale different from the one they are used to reading. The alternative is to format the event using the local machine's locale, in which case you have to hope that there are support engineers for that locale. Tough choice.

I said earlier that a message resource file is used to format a message. How does this fit into the way that `EventLog` works? When .NET is installed on a machine, a file called `EventLogMessages.dll` is installed into the GAC (global assembly cache) associated as a message resource file (`.mresource`) with part of the `System` assembly. This file has 65,535 entries, each of which looks like this:

```
%1
```

In other words, for every possible `EventID`, the entire format string is a placeholder, which means that the `ReplacementStrings` array has just one entry: the entire message. So the two most important reasons for the event log's behavior have been totally ignored by the .NET designers. The designers of the .NET classes had a golden opportunity to make the event log easy to use, and to augment its functionality, but instead they have removed some of its best functionality. This is why I say that the NT event log has been debased by .NET. With this in mind, let me now explain how to use the .NET classes.

The first thing to mention about `EventLog` is that the same class is used to read and write to the event log. I think it would have been better to have provided two classes—a reader and a writer—because you will rarely want to do both things at the same time. When you read from the event log, you obtain an `EventLogEntryCollection` object on the specified log. This object is dynamic, so if an event is added to the log after you've obtained this object, the log will show up when you enumerate through it—for example, as follows:

```
// C#
EventLog ev = new EventLog("Application");
EventLogEntryCollection elec = ev.Entries;
foreach(EventLogEntry e in elec)
   if (e.Source == "Test")
     Console.WriteLine(e.Message);
EventLog.WriteEntry("Test", "Test Message");
foreach(EventLogEntry e in elec)
   if (e.Source == "Test")
     Console.WriteLine(e.Message);
```

Here I read the entries in the event log for the `Test` source; then I write a message with this source and use the same collection to read the event log again. The new message will appear in the second enumeration. In the code I access the `Application` event log; to get a list of the logs installed on your machine (or another machine), you can call `GetEventLogs()`. You may decide that once you have read from the event log, you want to remove the event records. To do this you call `Clear()`.

One event message that you should be aware of is warning message 2013 from the `Srv` source. This message indicates that a specified disk is at or near capacity—that is, that you've used up 90 percent of that disk. If your machine generates this event, it makes sense to delete any temporary files that may be on this disk, so your application should clean up the temporary files for which it is responsible. How do you know that this event message—or any NT event log event message—has been generated? The answer is a .NET event called `EventLog.EntryWritten`. Your application can provide a handler like this:

```
// C#
EventLog ev = new EventLog("Application");
ev.EnableRaisingEvents = true;
ev.EntryWritten +=
   new EntryWrittenEventHandler(Handler);
```

Notice that you have to enable event generation specifically by setting `EnableRaisingEvents` to `true`. The problem is that all events from this log will be sent to the handler, regardless of whether the event is created for a specific source. Thus the handler must filter to items passed to it. These come in as

`EntryWrittenEventArgs` objects, which have a property called `Entry` that is an instance of `EventLogEntry`:

```
// C#
void Handler(object sender,
    EntryWrittenEventArgs e)
{
    if (e.Entry.Source == "Svr"
            && e.Entry.EventID == 2013)
    {
        DeleteMyTempFiles();
    }
}
```

You write to the event log using `WriteEntry()`. This method is confusingly overloaded with instance and static methods. The rule to bear in mind is that the methods that take a source parameter are static. The instance methods do not have this parameter, but you have to call them through an `EventLog` instance that has been initialized either with the overloaded constructor that takes a source name, or with a source that you have set by accessing its `Source` property directly. The `Source` property identifies the application that generated the event. If your application is distributed between processes and machines, you can use the same `Source` property for all; it allows you to easily filter the event log for events for a specific application.

There are two ways to create a source: The first is simply to call `WriteEntry()` for a source that does not exist, in which case the class will merely create the source for you. The second way is to explicitly call `CreateEventSource()`, which also gives you the ability to create a source on a remote machine, as long as it is called from a principal that has administrator privileges on the remote machine.[15] To test whether a source exists, you can call `SourceExists()`; and if you decide that you no longer want the source, you can call `DeleteEventSource()`.

Every message will have a type and a category. If you do not specify the type (one of the values shown in Table 2.15), the default `Informational` will

---

15. In addition, the remote machine must have the .NET Framework installed because the event source will use the `EventLogMessages.dll` file provided by .NET.

Table 2.15 Event log message types

Event Type	Meaning
Information	General-purpose message.
Warning	Warning; the administrator must take action.
Error	A critical error has occurred.
Success audit	A secured object has been accessed.
Failure audit	Access to a secured object has been denied.

be used. The audit types will be used only for messages sent to the `Security` log. The `Security` and `System` logs can be written to only by code running as a service under the `LOCALSYSTEM` account. This helps the user sort event messages, but a finer level is achieved through categories.

Categories are determined by applications, and a few of the overloaded versions of `WriteEntry()` take a category parameter. However, I advise you not to use this option because at best the category will appear in the event log viewer as a number, and at worst it will be formatted as one of the default values contained in `eventlog.dll`. The standard categories are listed in Table 2.16.

This is yet another area where .NET falls short of the equivalent in Win32. The problem is the inability to write and register a message resource file. In

Table 2.16 Standard categories

Category Number	Category Name
0	Devices
1	Disk
2	Printers
3	Services
4	Shell
5	System events
6	Network

DEVELOPING APPLICATIONS WITH VISUAL STUDIO.NET

Win32 you simply register the values of `CategoryCount` and `CategoryMessageFile` in the source's entry in the registry, and the event log viewer will display the category read from the registered file.

By default, every machine will have three logs: `Application`, `System`, and `Security`. Of these three, you will be interested only in the `Application` log; however, you may decide that you want to create your own log. To do this you set the `EventLog.Log` property before you read or write events (either directly or by calling the constructor that takes a log name). To check whether a log exists, you can call `Exists()`; and if you want to remove a log, you can call `Delete()`. Each source is specific to a log, and you can call `LogNameFromSourceName()` to get the log associated with a source.

What is my verdict about the event log classes in the Framework Class Library? If you want to read the event log, these classes are fine. If you want to generate events, however, my advice is to avoid them. You will be better off writing the code to access the event log as unmanaged code that uses the Win32 API. This way you can use message resource files and avoid filling the event log with an excessive amount of data. You can call this unmanaged code from your application using P/Invoke. If you do this, you can watch as your competitors fill event logs needlessly, overwrite events, and annoy their customers while your software uses the event log the way it was intended.

2.5.2 Performance Counting

I have already mentioned that the event log API is arcane, and that .NET could have improved on it significantly but instead has merely provided a weak alternative. The Win32 performance monitor API is also arcane, and it is also complicated, but in this case the .NET designers have provided a much better solution. To provide even the simplest performance monitor counter, you have to write a sharable DLL that manipulates the system registry and creates some complicated, multinested structures. The other side of the coin—reading performance counter—is even stranger: You have to read the registry! Even when you've got the data from the performance hive in the registry, you must still perform some complicated structure and memory management to get anything meaningful.

I have good news about the .NET performance-monitoring classes: They make creating and accessing performance counters straightforward and simple. The basic performance counter classes are `PerformanceCounterCategory` and `PerformanceCounter`. The performance monitor Microsoft Management Console (MMC) snap-in allows you to select a counter (some performance data) on an instance of a "performance object." The term *performance object* is a little misleading because it refers to the type of performance data that you want to view—for example, memory or thread. Instead of *performance object,* the .NET classes use the term *category,* which makes more sense.

`PerformanceCounterCategory` allows you to access existing categories or to create new ones. To test whether a category exists, you can call `Exists()`; and if the required category does not exist, you can create it with `Create()`. Counters and categories are intimately entwined, so when you create a category you have to give the counters that the category contains. You do this either by passing the name of the counter to `Create()`, or if the category contains several counters, by passing a reference to a `CounterCreationDataCollection` object, which is a collection of `CounterCreationData` objects. If you use `CounterCreationData` objects, you can specify the type of each performance counter (e.g., if the counter tracks a rate or an instantaneous value); otherwise the counter is `PerformanceCounterType.NumberOfItems32`—that is, an instantaneous value:

```
// C#
if (!PerformanceCounterCategory.Exists("MyCategory"))
{
    PerformanceCounterCategory.Create(
        "MyCategory", "My category counters",
        "MyCounter", "My performance counter");
}
```

As you can see, when you create categories and counters you also have to give a help string, which will be shown in the performance monitor. Typically you'll make this call in the start-up routine of your application or in the installation program. This call changes a key in the system registry, so you'll want to remove these values when your application is uninstalled. To do this you simply call `Delete()`.

DEVELOPING APPLICATIONS WITH VISUAL STUDIO.NET

The `PerformanceCounterCategory` class also allows you to get information about the categories and counters installed on the current machine (or on another machine):

```csharp
// C#
PerformanceCounterCategory[] cats;
cats = PerformanceCounterCategory.GetCategories();
foreach(PerformanceCounterCategory cat in cats)
{
    string[] names = cat.GetInstanceNames();
    if (names.Length == 0)
    {
        foreach(PerformanceCounter c
                in cat.GetCounters())
        {
            Console.WriteLine(
                c.CategoryName
                + "." + c.CounterName);
        }
    }
    else
    {
        foreach(string name in names)
            foreach(PerformanceCounter c
                    in cat.GetCounters(name))
            {
                Console.WriteLine(c.CategoryName
                    + "." + c.CounterName
                    + " [" + name + "]");
            }
    }
}
```

Some counters are associated with an "instance." For example, the Processor category supplies counters associated with each of your processors. If your machine has more than one processor, there will be an instance of each counter for each processor. You can get the instances associated with each category by calling `GetInstanceNames()`, and you can pass the name of an instance to `GetCounters()` to get the counters associated with that instance. The preceding code will print out the names of all counters on your machine. If you know the name of an instance (e.g., the name of a process in the Process category), you can check whether the instance exists by calling `Instance-Exists()`.

If a counter exists (which you can test with a call to `Performance-CounterCategory.CounterExists()`), you can access it by creating an instance of `PerformanceCounter`. This class is used to read the value of a counter and to write values to a counter. I think this is a bit of a mistake; it would have made more sense to have a class representing read-only counters because the counters that your process creates are always read/write, but the counters created by other processes are read-only, and if you write to a read-only counter, an exception will be thrown. `ReadOnly` is a property of `Performance-Counter`, as are general properties of the counter, such as its name, a help string, and the category, instance, and machine where the counter is obtained.

If you are reading performance data, you need to know what type of data will be returned. `CounterType` gives the property type as a member of the `PerformanceCounterType` enumeration, as shown in Table 2.17. The type of

Table 2.17 Types given by `PerformanceCounterType`

Type	Description
AverageCount64	Average number of bytes per operation
AverageTimer32	Average amount of time per operation
CounterDelta32	Difference between two 32-bit counters
CounterDelta64	Difference between two 64-bit counters
CounterMultiTimer	Average sampling among items
CounterMultiTimer100Ns	Average sampling among items over a 100-nanosecond period
CounterMultiTimer100NsInverse	The inverse of the timer for multiple but similar items over a 100-nanosecond period
CounterMultiTimerInverse	The inverse of the timer for multiple but similar items
CounterTimer	The most common timer
CounterTimerInverse	The inverse of the timer

(continued)

Table 2.17 (continued) Types given by `PerformanceCounterType`

Type	Description
`CountPerTimeInterval32`	The number of items queued or waiting using 32-bit values
`CountPerTimeInterval64`	The number of items queued or waiting using 64-bit values
`ElapsedTime`	Time elapsed between operations
`NumberOfItems32`	Instantaneous counter value using 32-bit values
`NumberOfItems64`	Instantaneous counter value using 64-bit values
`NumberOfItemsHEX32`	Instantaneous counter value intended to be displayed as a hexadecimal number using 32-bit values
`NumberOfItemsHEX64`	Instantaneous counter value intended to be displayed as a hexadecimal number using 64-bit values
`RateOfCountsPerSecond32`	The number of counts per second using 32-bit values
`RateOfCountsPerSecond64`	The number of counts per second using 64-bit values
`RawFraction`	Instantaneous value, to be divided by the base data
`SampleCounter`	A count that is either 1 or 0 on each sampling interrupt
`SampleFraction`	A count that is either 1 or 0 on each sampling interrupt, displayed as a percentage
`Timer100Ns`	Average sampling among items, expressed as a percentage
`Timer100NsInverse`	The inverse of the timer for multiple but similar items, expressed as a percentage

performance data determines how the performance monitor and your application should display the data, and whether the raw data in the counter is sufficient to display the value.

Some of the counter types (`AverageCount64`, `AverageTimer32`, `Counter-MultiTimer`, `CounterMultiTimer100Ns`, `CounterMultiTimer100NsInverse`, `CounterMultiTimerInverse`, `RawFraction`, and `SampleFraction`) can be used only if divided by another value called a *base value*. The base value is provided by another counter, and the counter base types are shown in Table 2.18. However, you do not have to worry about reading this base value because the .NET classes will do it for you. For the types mentioned earlier, use `NextValue()` instead of the `Raw-Value` property on the counter. If the type does not require a base value, then calling `NextValue()` will return the same thing that `RawValue` returns.

In addition, if you want to calculate a trend in the counter value, you can take a value at particular point in time and compare it with a value taken at another time. To do this you call `NextSample()`, which will return a `CounterSample` value type that holds information about the value read, including the raw value, the base value, and the time when the sample was taken. To get the value of the sample, you can call `CounterSample.Calculate()`; an overloaded version takes two samples and calculates their average.

If you are writing your own performance counter, you have two options: You can either write the value to the counter directly via its `RawValue` property or increase the value—by 1 by calling `Increment()` or by a specified value by calling `IncrementBy()`, both of which take negative values.

The underlying performance monitor extension that provides performance monitor counters does this through a block of data, as I mentioned at the beginning of this section. When a single counter is read, the entire buffer of

Table 2.18 Base counters

Type	Description
`AverageBase`	Used as the base data in the computation of time or count averages.
`CounterMultiBase`	Used as the base data for the multicounters.
`RawBase`	Used as the base data in the computation of time or count averages.
`SampleBase`	Used as the base data for the sample counters.

DEVELOPING APPLICATIONS WITH VISUAL STUDIO.NET

performance counters for the specified instance is read. So if you read more than one counter in a category, it is more efficient to access the entire buffer. The buffer is accessed in its entirety by a call to `PerformanceCounterCategory.ReadCategory()`, which returns an instance of `InstanceDataCollectionCollection`. As its name suggests, this is an associated collection of `InstanceDataCollection` objects; each item is associated with a counter name. Each `InstanceDataCollection` object associated with a counter is a collection of `InstanceData` objects; that is, there is one `RawValue` object for each instance.

2.5.3 Process Information

You can also read information about a running process. I mentioned at the start of this chapter that .NET has a new class that allows you to read the version information in a file. This class, `FileVersionInfo`, works with both assemblies and unmanaged code because it reads `VERSIONINFO` resources. When you use the assembly attributes in the `Reflection` namespace to add version and other information to an assembly, this information is also added to a `VERSIONINFO` resource in the assembly. The `FileVersionInfo` class gives access to the various items in the `VERSIONINFO` resource through properties, as the following example illustrates:

```
// C#
[assembly: AssemblyVersion("1.0.*")]
class App
{
    static void Main()
    {
        FileVersionInfo fvi;
        Assembly assembly;
        assembly = Assembly.GetExecutingAssembly();
        fvi = FileVersionInfo.GetVersionInfo(
            assembly.Location);
        Console.WriteLine("From VERSIONINFO "
            + fvi.FileVersion);
        Console.WriteLine("From Assembly "
            + assembly.GetName().Version);    }
    }
}
```

This code depends on the fact that the path to the main assembly file is returned from the `Assembly.Location` property. If you run this code, you'll see that the two versions are the same. You can also access running processes by using the `Process` class:

```
// C#
foreach (Process p in Process.GetProcesses())
    Console.WriteLine(p.ProcessName);
```

In addition to the process name, you can get lots of information that in Win32 took a fair amount of code to obtain. For example, the `Threads` property will return a collection of the threads running in the process. Note that this is a collection that contains `ProcessThread` objects, not `Thread` objects, and the two types are not directly related.[16] The `ProcessThread` class gives read access to things like the thread state and the time the thread has run in user and kernel mode, and read/write access to the thread's priority:

```
// C#
foreach (ProcessThread t
        in Process.GetCurrentProcess().Threads)
{
    Console.WriteLine(t.Id + " " + t.ThreadState
        + " " + t.PriorityLevel);
}
```

Each process can load libraries (DLLs or EXEs), which are known as modules. Note that these are Win32 modules and are not the same as the modules that make up an assembly. The `Process` class gives access to the modules through a collection of `ProcessModule` objects. The following code gives the name of the executable that contains it, and all of the DLLs loaded by that executable:

```
// C#
foreach(ProcessModule m
        in Process.GetCurrentProcess().Modules)
{
    Console.WriteLine(m.ModuleName);
}
```

---

16. Indeed, when you install .NET on your machine, performance counters will be installed. These contain a category called `.NET CLR Threads` that has two counters: `# of current logical Threads` and `# of current physical Threads`.

Included among the executables here are `kernel32.dll`, `user32.dll`, `mscoree.dll`, and `mscorlib.dll`.[17]

2.5.4 Data

There are essentially two ways to get data from a data source: as a disconnected `DataSet` object or through a data reader. `DataSet` is a structured object that is based on XML and has complete information about the data it contains. A data reader allows you to query a data source, getting data one row at a time and accessing the columns individually. The two types of data access allow you to program either in an ActiveX Data Objects (ADO) fashion or in an OLE DB fashion. The data namespaces are shown in Table 2.19.

However you access the data, you need to establish a connection to the data source. There are two ways to do this: The generic way is through the classes in `System.Data.Oledb`, whereas the classes in `System.Data.Sql-Client` are specifically for access to SQL Server.

To connect to an OLE DB data source, you use `OleDbConnection` and provide a connection string. If you choose to, you can create transactions through a call to `BeginTransaction()`, which will return an `OleDbTransaction` object. You can use the methods on this object to start the transaction and to commit or abort it. To perform a particular action, you must create a

Table 2.19   Data namespaces

Namespace	Description
System.Data	Basic ADO.NET classes
System.Data.Common	Common classes used by data providers
System.Data.Oledb	Classes for the .NET OLE DB provider
System.Data.SqlClient	Classes for the SQL Server provider
System.Data.SqlTypes	Data types used with SQL Server

17. And lots of other DLLs, including `msvcrt.dll` and `msvcr70.dll`, indicating that the runtime—or the Framework Class Library—is written in C++.

command either by passing the command SQL and the connection object to the `OleDbCommand` constructor, or by calling `CreateCommand()` on the connection object and then setting the `CommandText` property. After you have done this, the connection can be opened with a call to `Open()`, and you are ready to read the results.

Connecting to a SQL Server data source is similar, except that instead of using `OleDbConnection` you use `SqlConnection`, and instead of using `OleDbCommand` you use `SqlCommand`. In the remainder of this section I will describe only how to use the OLE DB classes. Here is an example of opening a connection:

```
// C#
OleDbConnection conn = new OleDbConnection(
    "Provider=SQLOLEDB;Data Source=localhost;"
    + "Integrated Security=SSPI;"
    + "Initial Catalog=northwind");
OleDbCommand command = new OleDbCommand(
    "SELECT CustomerID, CompanyName "
    + "FROM Customers", conn);
conn.Open();
```

Now you have a choice: Do you access the results a row at a time, or do you use a `DataSet` object? Let's look at the first option:

```
// C#
OleDbDataReader reader = command.ExecuteReader();
while (reader.Read())
{
    Console.WriteLine("{0} {1}",
        reader.GetString(0),
        reader.GetString(1));
}
reader.Close();
conn.Close();
```

If the command does not return any results, you can call `OleDb-Command.ExecuteNonQuery()`. You can execute stored procedures, but to do so you first have to add the parameters to the command using an `OleDbParameter` object:

```csharp
// C#
OleDbCommand command;
command = new OleDbCommand("CustOrderHist", conn);
command.CommandType = CommandType.StoredProcedure;
OleDbParameter custID;
custID = new OleDbParameter(
    "@CustomerID", OleDbType.VarChar);
custID.Value = "CHOPS";
command.Parameters.Add(custID);
conn.Open();
```

To use a `DataSet` object, you have to use an adapter class—for example, `OleDbDataAdapter`. This class has a property, `SelectCommand`, that you use to set the command. Next you create a `DataSet` object and call the `Fill()` method to have the adapter fill that object. Once you have done this, the `DataSet` object will have the results from executing the command, as well as schema information:

```csharp
// C#
OleDbDataAdapter adapter;
adapter = new OleDbDataAdapter();
adapter.SelectCommand = command;
DataSet data = new DataSet();
adapter.Fill(data);
```

The beauty of a `DataSet` object is that it can be serialized to XML (through `GetXml()`) and passed to another process that uses XML, or it can be passed as a parameter to a remote object and it will be serialized as a stream of XML nodes and passed by value. If you are passed an XML stream from another process (it may not be a .NET process), you can use that stream to create a `DataSet` object with `ReadXml()`. The XML in a `DataSet` object has the information and the schema, so it can be used totally disconnected from the data source that was used to generate it.

2.5.5 Message Queuing

Message queuing is an appropriate name for the technology that I will describe in this section. You create a message and post it to Microsoft Message Queuing (MSMQ), where it sits in a queue until another process takes it out. Message queuing is distributed; the process that posts the message could be on a machine separate from the one containing the process that reads the message.

The message can also be posted when the two machines are not connected because MSMQ stores messages locally and forwards them when the two machines are connected to the same network. MSMQ guarantees delivery; it just does not guarantee when that delivery will happen. The message can be posted when the reader process is not running, and it can be read well after the posting process has shut down.

This situation encourages a different style of programming: fire and forget. In this scenario a process should not expect an immediate reply to a message it posts.

The starting point of an MSMQ application is the `MessageQueue` class, which contains static methods for general queue management and instance methods for accessing a specific queue. To determine the queues on a machine, you can use `GetPublicQueuesByMachine()` and `GetPrivateQueuesByMachine()` and specify the machine name. You can query the local machine for its public queues by calling `GetPublicQueues()` to get all public queues, or by setting the criteria using a `MessageQueueCriteria` object to get specific queues.

If you already know the name of a queue, you can test whether the queue exists by calling `Exists()`. If the queue does not exist, you can create it with `Create()`, and you can remove an existing queue with `Delete()`—for example:

```
// C#
string path = @"HELIOS\Orders";
if (!MessageQueue.Exists(path))
    MessageQueue.Create(path);
```

This code tests whether the queue `Orders` exists on the machine `HELIOS`, and if it doesn't exist the code creates it. To post a message to a queue you must access a specific queue, which you do by creating an instance of `MessageQueue` and passing the queue name to the constructor:

```
// C#
MessageQueue mq = new MessageQueue(path);
```

After this you can send a message to the queue using `Send()`. This method takes an object parameter, which means that you can pass any data type. Of course, if the data is a value type, you have to box it first. If you want to send a reference type, be aware that reference types are passed by reference; that is, a *reference* to the object is passed.

Because the object will be on the managed heap in the calling process and hence lives there, there is no guarantee that the object will still be alive when the listening process reads the message. Instead, the object must be passed by value; that is, the object should be serialized. I will talk about serialization in more detail in Chapter 3, but basically an object called a *formatter* reads the serializable object and writes the object's fields and information about the object's type to the body of a message. To make an object serializable, you use the `[Serializable]` attribute:

```
// C#
[Serializable]
public class Order
{
    public Order(){}
    public Order(string c, string p, int i)
    { Customer = c; Product = p; Count = i; }
    public string Customer = null;
    public string Product = null;
    public int Count = 0;
}
```

Note that the object has a default constructor; I'll explain why later. You use the object like this:

```
// C#
Order order;
order = new Order("Richard", "100Mb Zip Disk", 4);
mq.Send(order);
mq.Close();
```

At this point the sender process loses all responsibility for the object. The message will be placed in an outgoing queue of the current machine, and eventually the local MSMQ service will pass the message to the target MSMQ server, where the message will be placed in the specified public queue. There is no indication to the sending process that this mechanism is successful, and because the local MSMQ service has the responsibility of passing the message to the target machine, `Send()` blocks only as long as it takes to put the message in the local outgoing queue.

The formatter used when a message is being sent is accessed via the `MessageQueue.Formatter` property. By default, this will be an instance of the `XmlMessageFormatter` class, which serializes the object as XML. Here is the body of the message that contains the `order` object I created in the preceding code example:

```
<?xml version="1.0"?>
<Order xmlns:xsi="http://www.w3.org/2000/10
                 /XMLSchema-instance"
       xmlns:xsd="http://www.w3.org/2000/10
                 /XMLSchema">
  <Customer>Richard</Customer>
  <Product>100 Mb Zip Disk</Product>
  <Count>4</Count>
</Order>
```

The listening process also needs to access the named queue, and the `MessageQueue` object must use the same formatter as the sender, which should be initialized to understand the data types that the sender sends. The formatter initialization depends on the type of formatter used (which I'll talk about in Chapter 3). For the default formatter, `XmlMessageFormatter`, the listener needs to pass an array that indicates the types that could be in the message:

```
// C#
MessageQueue mq = new MessageQueue(@".\Orders");
XmlMessageFormatter formatter;
formatter = (XmlMessageFormatter)mq.Formatter;
formatter.TargetTypeNames =
    new string[]{"Order, orderassem"};
```

In this case the listener will handle only messages that contain serialized `Order` objects (in the `orderassem` assembly), so the string that is passed to `TargetTypeNames` is the name of the type followed by the name of the assembly that contains the type. Now you have two options: You can read the queue either synchronously or asynchronously. In the first case you call

`Receive()`, which blocks until a message is read from the queue; the data is returned as a `Message` object. The `Body` property of the message contains the object that was sent, so you can cast this to the appropriate object type:

```
// C#
Message m = mq.Receive();
Order o = (Order)m.Body;
Console.WriteLine("Message: \n\t"
    + o.Customer + " ordered "
    + o.Count + " " + o.Product);
```

When you set `TargetTypeNames` on the XML formatter, a `HashTable` instance of `XmlSerializer` objects will be created—one serializer for each member in the array. These serializers know how to deserialize the specified type. The accessor for `Message.Body` loops through each of these serializers and passes it the XML in the body of the message. If a serializer understands the data in the XML, it deserializes the data; that is, it creates an uninitialized instance of the class and then initializes the fields using the XML.

Because it creates an uninitialized instance, the object type must have a default constructor. This new object is returned as an `object` instance, which the code then casts to the appropriate type. `Receive()` removes the message from the queue; however, you can use `Peek()` to access the message without removing the message. This method allows you to inspect the object to determine if you can handle it, or you can leave it there for another process to read.

The message can be passed as clear text, or it can be encrypted. For the message to be encrypted, the queue must have its `EncryptionRequired` property set to `Body` or `Optional`. In addition, you must explicitly set the `UseEncryption` property of the message:

```
// C#
MessageQueue mq = new MessageQueue(mqPath);
mq.EncryptionRequired = EncryptionRequired.Body;
Order order;
order = new Order("Richard", "100 Mb Zip Disk", 4);
Message msg = new Message(order);
msg.UseEncryption = true;
mq.Send(msg);
```

In Chapter 3 I will talk about methods for reading messages aynchronously; here I will give the basics for reading messages. `MessageQueue` has two methods: `BeginReceive()` and `EndReceive()`. `BeginReceive()` immediately returns an `IAsyncResult` interface. This interface has information about the asynchronous operation. It includes a property called `IsCompleted`, which your code can occasionally poll.

On the other hand, if your code has completed its work and really does need to access the message (and is happy to block while this occurs), it can access `IAsyncResult.AsyncWaitHandle` and call `WaitOne()`, which will block until the receive operation has completed. At this point the code can call `EndReceive()`, passing `IAsyncResult`. This method returns the `Message` object that was read. In both of these cases, `EndReceive()` is called on the same thread that called `BeginReceive()`.

There is another option: When you call `BeginReceive()`, a separate thread is selected to make the call to `MessageQueue.Receive()`. When this synchronous method completes, the `IsCompleted` property on the `IAsyncResult` interface is set to `true`, `AsyncWaitHandle` is signaled, and an event called `ReceiveCompleted` is generated. Of course, when an event is generated, the thread that generates it will call the handlers that were registered for the event. Here is an example:

```
// C#
public static void OnReceiveCompleted(
   Object source,
   ReceiveCompletedEventArgs asyncResult)
{
   Order o =
      (Order)asyncResult.Message.Body;
   Console.WriteLine("Message: \n\t"
      + o.Customer + " ordered "
      + o.Count + " " + o.Product);
}
```

The first parameter of the event handler is the `MessageQueue` object that generated the event. The second parameter gives access to the `IAsyncResult` interface that `BeginReceive()` returned, as well as to the message that was read. Be careful about what you do in the event handler because, as I mentioned earlier, exception handlers are thread specific, so if an object is contained in the message other than the type that was specified to the formatter, an exception will be thrown. If you do not wrap the `Message.Body` access with exception handling, the exception will be eaten and you will never see it. Therefore, always use exception handling and log an error. Of course, you really should not get a message with an unknown object type.

2.6 Summary

The Framework Class Library was created with a tough design goal in mind: a library based on the Win32 APIs that hides all of the ugly features of Win32 and encapsulates the functionality in an object-oriented way that allows that functionality to be used on other platforms by developers not familiar with Win32's peculiarities. I hope this chapter has conveyed the impression that the Framework Class Library has largely achieved this aim, but not completely.

The fact that the Framework Class Library falls short of its goal is a disappointment because an opportunity to review and rewrite the Win32 API will not occur again. I am not saying that the Framework Class Library is a failure. In fact, I believe the opposite: The Framework Class Library is a bold undertaking that has come very close to software development nirvana: a truly universal library. It's just that if Microsoft had taken a little more time to develop the Framework Class Library, this nirvana could have been achieved. Instead, we have been given a fine library that sits among other fine libraries that can be used for Windows development.

Chapter 3

Contexts and Remoting

One of the goals of .NET is to provide a component technology for tomorrow's software solutions. Components are designed to run in a specific context—the runtime requirement—without which they will not work. .NET gives you facilities that you can use to indicate the context in which a component should run and to allow your code to access the context to configure it.

The current feverish expansion into the Internet suggests that businesses view the Internet as the next frontier. Microsoft's existing component technology for networks—Distributed Component Object Model (DCOM)—works well on intranets, but it has been proven to be problematic when extended to the Internet. A new component technology needs a new way to access remote components: interoperation with other machines.

.NET provides several ways to access remote objects. The most flexible is .NET *remoting*, which gives the client access to a remote object through a proxy that has access to the object's context. This means that the remote machine has to run .NET. The Framework Class Library also allows you to write Web Services clients and servers that use standard protocols and hence can be accessed by (and can access) machines that do not have .NET.

These ideas—modes of interoperation between machines and between contexts—are the subject of this chapter.

3.1 Contexts

Different components have different requirements of their environment. These requirements define the context in which a component will run. *Contexts* are not a new concept, but as component development has moved from COM through

Microsoft Transaction Server (MTS) and COM+, contexts have become more important and more visible. I will go into more detail about COM+ component services in Chapter 4, but as an introduction to contexts in general, let me take COM+ as an example.

Among other things, COM+ provides automatic transaction enlistment through contexts: A component can be marked to indicate to COM+ that it uses resource managers that must be enlisted into a transaction—that is, that it can run only if there is a transaction it can use. The existence of such a component without a transaction makes no sense, so COM+ will make sure that a transaction exists and that when the component's code is run, any resource managers used by the component are enlisted into the transaction. The component does not do the enlistment itself; it merely uses a resource manager, and that resource manager is automatically enlisted. The component's context contains the transaction.

This is not the only way to use transactions. A component that does not use COM+ can create a transaction and enlist all the resource managers within that transaction. There is nothing special about COM+ in this respect, but the advantage of the COM+ component is that the enlistment is automatic, occurring because the component has been marked to indicate that it can run only if a transaction exists. If the component uses another component that requires a transaction, the transaction will flow to that object, too. Transactions require code to run in isolation, so COM+ ensures that all components that use the same transaction are synchronized; that is, there is only one thread of execution so that it is not possible for two components in a transaction to be executing at the same time. Synchronization is added automatically for components that use transactions.

.NET uses COM+ for its component services, as I'll explain in Chapter 4, but it broadens the idea because components that use contexts do not have to use COM+. As with most things in .NET, your code indicates the services it requires—and hence the context in which it should be run. Using attributes, the runtime ensures that the appropriate context exists when the object is created. Context attributes are understood by the runtime because it is the runtime that creates the context. In addition, some attributes require the classes to which they are applied to be derived from a specific class. This class provides runtime support for the component.

3.1.1 Context Bound and Context Agile

.NET components can be context bound or context agile. By default, objects are *context agile,* which means that the context in which they are used does not matter. Thus they can be accessed through direct references when they are accessed from within the application domain where they are created—irrespective of the context of the object making the call.

A component that is *context bound* must run in a specific context. To indicate its context requirements, the object's type has a specific context attribute or derives from a specific base class (usually `ContextBound-Object`). If the context of the object's creator is suitable, the runtime will create the object there; otherwise it will create a new context for the new object. A context-bound object remains in the context for life.

You can obtain the `Context` object for the default context of the application domain by calling `Context.DefaultContext`, and for the current thread by calling `Thread.CurrentContext`. The `Context.ContextProperties` property gives access to all of the context properties, which in turn give access to an instance of `IContextProperty`. Through this interface you can access the name of the context property. The property may also implement other interfaces, some of which are summarized in Table 3.1. I will get back to these properties later, when I talk about the various context sink chains.

You may decide that your context-agile object needs to have data specific to the context in which it is run. A simple example is a context-agile object that can be called by different threads. You may decide that the object's data should be specific to the thread that calls it, and put the data into thread-local storage. The generic way to do this is through *data slots.*

Once you have the current context, you can call methods on the `Context` class to access data slots: `AllocateDataSlot()` returns an unnamed data slot (a `LocalDataStoreSlot` object); `AllocateNamedDataSlot()` allocates a data slot and associates it with a string name that you can use to access the data slot later with `GetNamedDataSlot()`. The named data slot can be freed with a call to `FreeNamedDataSlot()`.) The object can store data in the data slot using `Context.SetData()`—passing the data and the `Local-DataStoreSlot` object—and retrieve this data later with `GetData()`.

Table 3.1   Context property interfaces

Interface	Description
`IContextAttribute`	Implemented by attributes that define contexts.
`IContextProperty`	Used to provide a name for the context.
`IContextPropertyActivator`	Implemented by context properties used in activation.
`IContributeClientContextSink`	Used to contribute an interception sink on the client side.
`IContributeDynamicSink`	Implemented by properties that want to get information about when a method call starts and ends.
`IContributeEnvoySink`	Implemented by context properties that contribute to the envoy sink chain.
`IContributeObjectSink`	Implemented by properties that want to contribute to the object sink chain.
`IContributeServerContextSink`	Used to contribute an interception sink on the server side.

Context-agile components can be subdivided into three types: those that are not marshaled, those that are marshaled by value, and those that are marshaled by reference. Those that are not marshaled can be accessed from any context within a single application domain, but they cannot be accessed by code from outside of the domain. Marshaled components can be accessed by code outside of the domain where they are created, but they are still context agile because the context in which this code runs does not matter. There are two types of marshaling: marshaling by reference and marshaling by value. It is worth taking a detour to discuss parameter marshaling.

3.1.2   Passing Parameters by Reference and by Value

By default, primitive data types are *passed by value,* which means that the actual value is placed on the stack and a method is called. The method has access to the stack and can obtain the values placed there. If the called code alters such a parameter, it is the value on the stack that is altered, and because the stack frame lives only as long as the method call, this changed value is discarded when the method returns.

Recall from Chapter 1 that .NET defines application domains that are a unit of isolation within a .NET process. A primitive type can be passed by value through method calls within an application domain and across application domain boundaries.

This is true in both C# and C++, but both languages provide a mechanism to change the marshaling semantics to marshal by reference. In C# this mechanism is the `ref` keyword; in C++, making the parameter a `__gc` pointer achieves this mechanism:

```
// C#
void csTimesTwo(ref int i)
{
    i *= 2;
}
void csUseTimesTwo()
{
    int iLocal = 2;
    csTimesTwo(ref iLocal);
}

// C++
void cppTimesTwo(int __gc* i)  // or Int32*
{
    *i *= 2;
}
void cppUseTimesTwo()
{
    int iLocal = 2;    // or Int32
    cppTimesTwo(&iLocal);
}
```

This code indicates that the data being passed by value is a *pointer*, which means that by dereferencing the pointer, the called code gets access to the storage in the calling code. The parameter is said to be *passed by reference*. If this call is made across process or machine boundaries, the access is across those boundaries. Both C# and C++ can restrict how such pointer parameters are used: C#

uses the out keyword; C++ uses the System::Runtime::InteropServices::OutAttribute attribute:

```
// C#
void csTwo(out int i)
{
    i = 2;
}
void csUseTwo()
{
    int iLocal = 0;
    csTwo(out iLocal);
}

// C++
void cppTwo([Out] int __gc* i) // or Int32*
{
    *i = 2;
}
void cppUseTwo()
{
    int iLocal = 0;    // or Int32
    cppTwo(&iLocal);
}
```

The runtime assumes that all parameters passed through pointers are in/out parameters unless [OutAttribute] is used to indicate that data is returned only through the pointer. The C# out keyword adds this attribute to the IL for the parameter.

What happens if the parameter itself is a reference type? The answer is in the question; that is, reference types are passed by reference. Indeed, this is immediately obvious when you look at C++ code, which requires that reference types be passed through pointers. This is true for all reference types when passed as parameters within the same application domain. So in the following code, a reference to an instance of a class called AValue is passed to a function called TimesTwo():

```
// C#
class AValue
{
    public int x = 0;
```

```
        public AValue(int i){ x = i; }
    }
    class UseValue
    {
        public void TimesTwo(AValue a){a.x *= 2;}
        public void UseIt()
        {
            AValue a = new AValue(2); // a.x is 2
            TimesTwo(a);             // a.x is 4
        }
    }
}
```

Notice that I do *not* use the `ref` keyword. If I did, it would be the reference that was passed by reference, which means that the method could replace the reference with a reference to another object. The syntax of C# makes it looks like the parameter is passed by value; it isn't, and I think this is an inconsistent aspect of C# syntax. Because objects are passed through pointers in C++, C++ is far clearer about what is being passed and what type of access the method has to the object.

Reference types *can* be passed by value, as long as they are written to support this capability. A reference type that is passed by value is serialized to a stream of bytes, and it is this stream that is passed to the method. The runtime creates an uninitialized instance of the object and uses the stream of bytes to initialize it. In effect, this means that the runtime freeze-dries the object, moves it to the new context, and then rehydrates it.

3.1.3 Marshaling Objects between Contexts

When you pass an object across an application domain or a context boundary, you have to explicitly tell the runtime how the object should be marshaled: Is the most important point of the object its location or its state? If the location is important—that is, the object must be accessed from a specific context—then the object should be marshaled by reference. If the location is not important, the object can be marshaled by value. Of course, there are other criteria to take into account—the size and type of the object's state, for example—but you should always use the object location as the first criterion. For example, a remote object should execute in a particular context, in a specific application domain.

Such an object must be marshaled by reference so that it runs in the domain where it was created, but it can be accessed from another domain.

An object that must run in a specific context should have `MarshalByRef-Object` within its class hierarchy; that is, it should be derived either from this class directly or from `ContextBoundObject`. As the name suggests, if a reference to such an object is passed to another context, access to that object will be across the context boundary and hence marshaling has to be used. Figure 3.1 shows how this works. An object that is derived from `MarshalBy-RefObject` can be accessed through a direct pointer by an object within the same context, whereas an object in another context can access the marshalable object only through a proxy.

When the object reference is marshaled, an `ObjRef` object is created in the server domain for the object that has been registered for remoting. The client application domain obtains the `ObjRef` object (I'll describe the details later) and creates a proxy object (called `TransparentProxy`) from `ObjRef`. The `ObjRef` object contains information about the out-of-context object— specifically its location, its type information, and information about the *channel* and envoy chain used to access it (which I will explain later). The information in the `ObjRef` object locates the out-of-context object and indicates how the object is accessed. Compare this with the DCOM `OBJREF` packet (which is explained in the section on remoting).

You can view an `ObjRef` object as a serialized representation of an object reference. The exporting context contains a map that associates an `ObjRef`

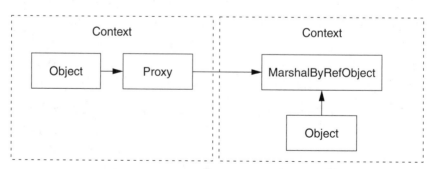

Figure 3.1   Accessing marshal-by-reference objects

DEVELOPING APPLICATIONS WITH VISUAL STUDIO.NET

object with the actual object so that when it receives a call it can dispatch the call to the right object. The `ObjRef` class can be extended, giving you the ability to piggyback your own information onto message calls.

The client code can also pass the reference to the out-of-context object to another context. In such cases the `ObjRef` object is passed to the new context, which can then use the information in `ObjRef` to create a proxy to the object.

The contexts in Figure 3.1 may be in the same process and may even be in the same application domain. Using a proxy in the in-domain case may appear to be overkill, but the proxy object is optimized for this case: The importing object gets the lightweight `TransparentProxy` object, which tests whether the object is in the same application domain, in which case `TransparentProxy` will call the object through a direct pointer. If the object is in another application domain, the remoting layer will trap the call through `TransparentProxy` and obtain a `RealProxy` object from `ObjRef`.

The `RealProxy` object has the code to make cross-domain calls, as shown in Figure 3.2. I will come back to proxies when I cover .NET remoting later. You can determine whether the reference you have is a direct reference or a reference through `RealProxy` by calling the static method `RemotingServices.GetObjRefForProxy()`. If the object is in the domain, a `null` reference will be returned; otherwise you will get the `ObjRef` object used to locate the object.

Objects that are not domain specific can be marshaled by value to another domain and used there. An object that is designed to be marshaled by value has to provide a mechanism for the runtime to extract its state. The `[Serializable]` attribute provides this mechanism by indicating to the runtime that it should extract the state from the object's fields. If a field is considered temporary—particularly if it can be calculated from other fields—it can be marked with `[NonSerialized]`.

When a marshal-by-value object is passed to another domain, the state of the object is extracted and put into a serialization stream that also has information about the object it represents (its type and assembly). When the object is unmarshaled into the importing domain, the runtime reads the serialization stream to determine the type of the object. It then creates an uninitialized instance of this type by calling the default constructor, and it initializes the instance by writing the values held in the serialization stream directly into the fields of the object.

There are a couple of significant points here: A serializable class *must* have a default constructor, but it does not need any other constructors. The runtime initializes the object by writing to the object's fields. It does not matter what access specifier you have used on these fields; the runtime is all-powerful and is able to read and write private fields. You can change how a type is serialized by

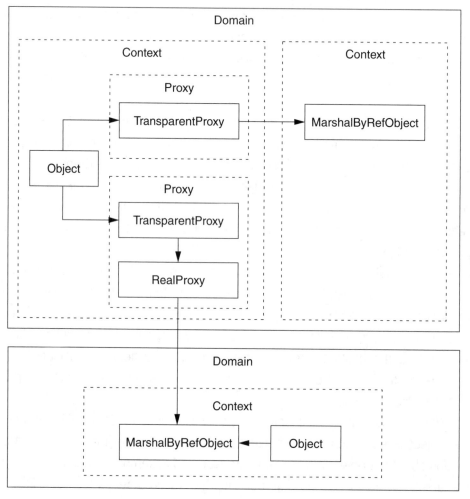

Figure 3.2　Cross-context and cross-domain calls

implementing `ISerializable`. I will talk about serialization in more depth later in this chapter.

Some objects are specific to a context, which means that direct access to the object is allowed only from objects within the same context; all access by objects in other contexts is through proxies. Figure 3.3 shows the situations in which proxies are used, for the types of objects summarized in Table 3.2; Table 3.3 shows how such objects are accessed.

Note that marshaling occurs only when code accesses instance members; static members are always agile and can be accessed without marshaling. This means that if you have a static data member, the data will exist in the context where the member is accessed.

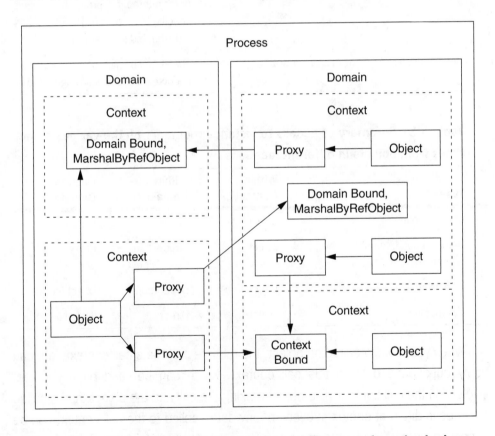

Figure 3.3 Context- and domain-bound objects. The use of proxies in these situations is summarized in Table 3.3.

Table 3.2 Object types

Context	Base Class	Description
Not marshaled, but agile	`Object`	Can be used in any context within the domain through a direct reference.
Marshaled by value, agile	May use `Serializable`; may also derive from `ISerializable`	State flows to another domain, where the object is accessed through a direct reference. There is no distributed identity.
Domain bound, agile	`MarshalByRefObject`	Object is bound to a specific application domain but can be accessed by objects in another domain through a proxy. The state is specific to a domain. The object has a distributed identity.
Context bound	`ContextBoundObject`	The state specific to a context; out-of-context access is through a proxy.

Table 3.3 Summary of access to instance members on the various object types from objects in different locations

Type	Within Context	Within Domain	Outside of Domain
Context bound	Direct	Proxy	Proxy
Domain bound, marshaled by reference	Direct	Direct	Proxy
Marshaled by value	Direct	Direct (copy)	Direct (copy)
Not marshaled	Direct	Direct	(Not allowed)

When you make a call to an object, the runtime creates a call context. You can apply out-of-band data to this call context, which can be read by any object involved in the call context. The object making the call and the object that is called could be in different contexts; even so, any data applied to the call context can be accessed by all the objects involved. This is illustrated in Figure 3.4, where an object in Context B accesses a context-bound object in Context A; the runtime

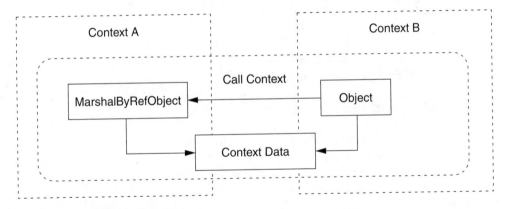

Figure 3.4 Call contexts

creates the call context whenever a method is called on the context-bound object. The calling and the called objects have access to the call context and its data, so, for example, you can pass a marshal-by-value object as out-of-band data.

The call context acts like a logical thread, so the marshal-by-value class must derive from `ILogicalThreadAffinative` to indicate that it should be accessed only on this logical thread. The Framework Class Library provides a class called `CallContext` that gives access to the call context through static methods. The call context has named data slots that are specific to the particular call, so the client can call `CallContext.SetData()` to store an `ILogicalThreadAffinative` object in a named data slot, and the object can call `CallContext.GetData()` to retrieve the out-of-band data. In addition, the call context can contain an array of objects called *headers* that have name/value pairs. These can be set through the `SetHeaders()` method with an array of `Header` objects and retrieved by the object with a call to `GetHeaders()`. The value object used in a header must be serializable, but it does not have to have affinity with the logical thread.

For example, the following is a marshal-by-value object that has a logical thread affinity:

```
// C#
[Serializable]
public class ThreadAffinityObj
    : ILogicalThreadAffinative
{
```

```csharp
    public string str=null;
    public ThreadAffinityObj()
    {
        str = "\tCreated in " +
            AppDomain.CurrentDomain.FriendlyName;
    }
    public void GetLocation()
    {
        Console.WriteLine("ThreadAffinityObj in "
            + AppDomain.CurrentDomain.FriendlyName);
        Console.WriteLine(str);
    }
}
```

To test this code, I need an object in another context, so I will create an object in a new application domain and call it. This object must be `MarshalByRefObject`:

```csharp
// C#
public class CrossCtxObject
    : MarshalByRefObject
{
    public void GetLocation(string dataslot)
    {
        Console.WriteLine("CrossCtxObject in "
            + AppDomain.CurrentDomain.FriendlyName);
        ThreadAffinityObj a;
        a = (ThreadAffinityObj)
                CallContext.GetData(dataslot);
        a.GetLocation();
    }
}
```

To use the object, I create a new application domain and then activate an instance of `CrossCtxObject` in that domain:

```csharp
// C#
class App
{
    public static void Main()
    {
        AppDomain ad;
        ad = AppDomain.CreateDomain(
            "Second AppDomain", null);
```

```
    Assembly assembly;
    assembly = Assembly.GetExecutingAssembly();
    ObjectHandle oh;
    oh = ad.CreateInstance(
        assembly.FullName, "CrossCtxObject");
    CrossCtxObject b;
    b = (CrossCtxObject )oh.Unwrap();
    CallContext.SetData(
        "Test", new ThreadAffinityObj());
    b.GetLocation("Test");
    }
}
```

After creating the `CrossCtxObject` object and receiving a proxy, I set a data slot called `Test` with a marshal-by-value object and call through the proxy. `GetLocation()` obtains the marshal-by-value object from the data slot and prints out the name of the executing application domain, as well as the fact that the object in the data slot was created in the default application domain, which will have the name of the process.

3.1.4 Context Sink Chains

A context is a conglomeration of individual contexts. You may have a context made up of one subcontext that applies synchronization and another subcontext that applies additional security checks. As calls are made into or out of a context, they are intercepted by the subcontexts that make up the context so that appropriate action can be taken. In .NET parlance, the segments of code that perform this appropriate action are called *sinks*.

Contexts contain two chains of sinks: On the client side the proxy calls through an *envoy sink chain*, which then calls through the *client context sink chain*, after which the channel is called to transmit the call to the server. On the server side the channel calls the *server context sink chain*, which calls the *object sink chain*, which eventually calls an object called the *stack builder* that constructs the stack before calling the object. This process is summarized in Figure 3.5.

The context sinks are used to process messages as they enter or leave the context. Context sinks implement the `IMessageSink` interface and are created in response to a call to a context property. To create a context property, you

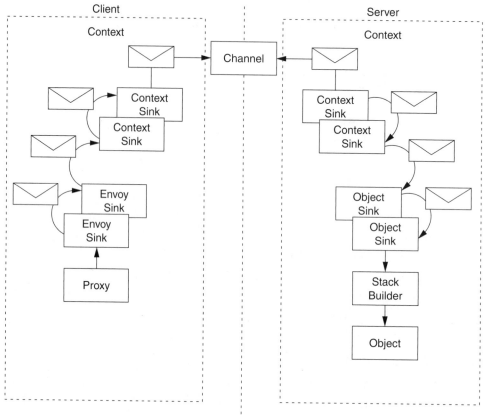

Figure 3.5   Context sink chains

derive an attribute from `ContextAttribute` and implement either `ICon-tributeClientContextSink` or `IContributeServerContextSink` (or both), and then apply this attribute to the class that needs to use the custom context. The runtime calls `GetClientContextSink()` or `GetServerContextSink()` to create the context sink; both methods are passed a reference to the chain of the sinks created so far. Your custom context sink will be called by the runtime when a call is made across a context boundary, and your sink should carry out its action before calling the next sink in the chain.

Envoy sinks on the client side are called within the context before the context sink chain is called; in effect this is the client-side representation of the server context. As with context sinks, envoy sinks and object sinks implement the `IMessageSink` interface. On the server side the context property that provides the sink implements `IContributeObjectSink`; on the client side, the property should implement `IContributeEnvoySink`. These interfaces each have a method to create the appropriate sink (`GetObjectSink()` and `GetEnvoySink()`, respectively), which is called by the runtime. The runtime passes the chain of sinks constructed so far, and as with context sinks, the sink that you return should hold on to this sink chain; and when a sink is called, it should do its work and then call the next sink.

Envoy sinks are available through the proxy for the object. The proxy holds the `ObjRef` instance for the object, and `ObjRef` has a property called `EnvoyInfo`, which is an `IEnvoyInfo` reference. This interface has a single property, called `GetEnvoySinks`, which is the `IMessageSink` reference for the first sink in the envoy chain. There are a couple of ways to get this sink chain: You can pass the proxy to `RemotingServices.GetObjRefForProxy()` to get the `ObjRef` object, or you can call `RemotingServices.GetEnvoyChainForProxy()` to get the first sink in the chain:

```
// C#
// an object in another context
MyObject myObj = new MyObject();
Console.WriteLine("The envoy sink chain is:");
IMessageSink ms;
ms = RemotingServices.GetEnvoyChainForProxy(myObj);
while (ms != null)
{
    Console.WriteLine(
        ms.GetType().ToString());
    ms = ms.NextSink;
}
```

3.1.5 Dynamic Properties and Sinks

You can create your own sinks and persuade the runtime to call them, as I mentioned earlier. Context, envoy, and object sinks should be considered part of the context; the context will not work without them. So if you want to temporarily add a sink to the chain at runtime—perhaps for debugging or logging—context sinks are not the way to do it. To perform this action, the .NET Runtime offers dynamic sinks, available through dynamic context properties. These dynamic properties can be registered and unregistered at runtime. They do not take part in the context chain; they are just observers that add nothing to the context, and they are called when a message crosses a context or application domain boundary. Figure 3.6 illustrates these concepts.

To write a dynamic property, you should create a class that implements (1) `IDynamicProperty`, which gives access to the dynamic property's name, and (2) `IContributeDynamicSink`, which has a method, `GetDynamicSink()`, that returns a reference to an object that implements `IDynamicMessageSink`. Because the dynamic sink does not contribute to the context, it does not implement `IMessageSink`. Instead, `IDynamicMessageSink` allows the sink to have access to the message merely to see what the message contains. In the following code I have combined the property and the sink in one class:

```
// C#
// implements both the property and the sink
```

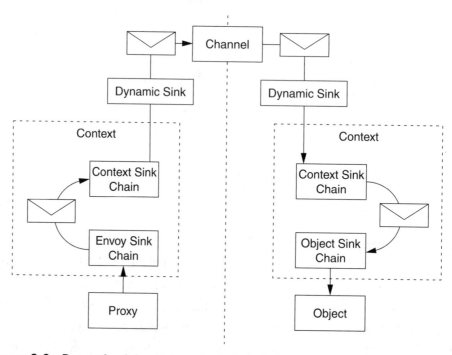

Figure 3.6   Dynamic sinks and context sink chains

DEVELOPING APPLICATIONS WITH VISUAL STUDIO.NET

```
class Spy : IDynamicProperty,
            IContributeDynamicSink,
            IDynamicMessageSink
{
    // IDynamicProperty
    public string Name
    { get { return "Spy"; } }
    // IContributeDynamicSink
    public IDynamicMessageSink GetDynamicSink()
    { return this; }
    // IDynamicMessageSink
    public void ProcessMessageStart(
        IMessage reqMsg,
        bool bCliSide, bool bAsync)
    {
        Console.WriteLine("start> {0} {1} ",
            bCliSide ? "client":"server",
            bAsync ? "async" : "sync");
        foreach(string s in reqMsg.Properties.Keys)
            Console.WriteLine("\t" + s + " = "
                + reqMsg.Properties[s]);
    }
    public void ProcessMessageFinish(
        IMessage replyMsg,
        bool bCliSide, bool bAsync)
    {
        Console.WriteLine("finish> {0} {1} ",
            bCliSide ? "client":"server",
            bAsync ? "async" : "sync");
        foreach(string s in replyMsg.Properties.Keys)
            Console.WriteLine(
                "\t" + s + " = "
                + replyMsg.Properties[s]);
    }
}
```

`ProcessMessageStart()` is called when the call is made over a context boundary; `ProcessMessageFinish()` is called when the function call returns. To indicate to the runtime that the dynamic sink should be used, you must register it with the runtime using `Context.RegisterDynamicProperty()`. Similarly, when you no longer want to use the sink, you should unregister the property with `Context.UnregisterDynamicProperty()`.

The parameters passed to `RegisterDynamicProperty()` allow you to determine if the sink will be applied to a specific object or to a context. If the second parameter is non-`null`, the sink will be applied to a specific object (either a proxy or an object); in this case the third parameter must be `null`. If the third parameter is non-`null`, a context will be monitored, so the second parameter must be `null`. If both parameters are `null`, *all* calls into or out of *all* contexts are monitored.

In the following example I define a context-bound object and use the `[Synchronization]` attribute to identify a context requirement of the object (in this case, to ensure that all out-of-context calls are synchronized so that only one call is active at a time). To make sure that the object is called from another context, I create the object on the main thread and then create a new thread that calls the object:

```
// C#
[Synchronization]
public class App
    : ContextBoundObject
{
    static void Main()
    {
        Context.RegisterDynamicProperty(
            new Spy(), null, null);
        App a = new App();
        Thread t;
        t = new Thread(
            new ThreadStart(a.CtxBoundMethod));
        t.Start();
        t.Join();
    }
    public void CtxBoundMethod()
    { Console.WriteLine("In CtxBoundMethod"); }
}
```

If you test this code yourself, you'll see the properties that are created as part of the cross-context call. You'll see that you have start and finish message calls for the constructor (called `.ctor`) and the method call. In addition, you'll get information about the method that is called and its parameters. For example, here is the output for the call to `CtxBoundMethod()` (I give just the output from `ProcessMessageStart()`):

```
start> server sync
    __Uri =
    __MethodName = CtxBoundMethod
    __MethodSignature = System.Type[]
    __TypeName = App, byrefsix,
        Version=0.0.0.0, Culture=neutral,
        PublicKeyToken=null
    __Args = System.Object[]
    __CallContext = System.Runtime.Remoting
                    .Messaging.LogicalCallContext
In CtxBoundMethod
```

3.1.6 Tracking Handlers

When a context-bound object is accessed across a context boundary, a proxy is used. The proxy is created from an ObjRef object, which, among other things, identifies the location of the object. The operation of creating an ObjRef object from an actual object is called *marshaling*, and the process of creating a proxy from an ObjRef object is called *unmarshaling* (see the section on marshaling later in this chapter).

You can define and create a *tracking handler* to monitor these calls to marshal and unmarshal ObjRef objects. A tracking handler implements ITrackingHandler and is registered (and unregistered) through the TrackingServices class:

```
// C#
class Tracker : ITrackingHandler
{
    public void DisconnectedObject(object obj)
    {
        Console.WriteLine(
            "disconnected \n\t"
            + obj.ToString());
    }
    public void MarshaledObject(
        object obj, ObjRef or)
    {
        Console.WriteLine(
            "marshaled \n\t"
            + obj.ToString()
            + " \n\t" + or.URI);
```

```
    }
    public void UnmarshaledObject(
        object obj, ObjRef or)
    {
        Console.WriteLine(
            "unmarshaled \n\t"
            + obj.ToString()
            + " \n\t" + or.URI
            + "\n\t" + or.TypeInfo.TypeName);
    }
}
// in the code that uses the tracker
TrackingServices.RegisterTrackingHandler(
    new Tracker());
```

3.2 Serialization

I mentioned in the previous section that marshal-by-value objects need to be serialized. In other words, their state is obtained in a form that can be transmitted to
another context, where it can be used to initialize a new instance of the same
class. This creates the illusion that an object is actually moving from one context
to another because the client that accesses the marshal-by-value object will
access it within its own context, even though the object was created in another
context. I say "illusion" because, of course, the client sees a new object with the
same state as the marshal-by-value object that it requested—a "clone", if you like.

Serialization is important for contexts and remoting for many reasons, as I
have mentioned already and will talk about in the next subsection. But serialization is important in other areas too. For example, a marshal-by-value object
can be stored in a file or a database, and serialization is required to pass objects
through MSMQ (Microsoft Message Queuing) calls. I will outline the general
details of serialization in this section.

3.2.1 Serializing Objects

The serialization process extracts the state of an object and places it in a
stream that can be transmitted to another context. A couple of things are
implied here: First, there must be some way to identify the fields in an object that
constitute its state and a mechanism to extract the values in these fields.

Second, there must be some code that can convert this data into a format the stream can hold.

As you may have guessed, the information about what items constitute the object's state is held in metadata inserted by the attributes `[Serializable]` and `[NonSerialized]`. The `[Serializable]` attribute can be applied to classes, delegates, enums, and structs, and it effectively sets the serializable metadata for all fields in the item to which it is applied. Not all fields contain the "state" of the object; some fields may hold temporary or intermediate values that can be calculated or deduced from the other fields. It does not make sense to serialize these fields, so you can turn off the serializable metadata by applying the `[NonSerialized]` attribute to the field, as illustrated here:

```csharp
// C#
[Serializable]
public class Point
{
    private double xVal;
    private double yVal;
    [NonSerialized]
    private double len = 0;
    public Point(int x, int y)
    { xVal = x; yVal = y; }
    public double x{get{return xVal;}}
    public double y{get{return xVal;}}
    public double Length
    {
        get
        {
            if (len == 0)
                len = Math.Sqrt(x*x + y*y);
            return len;
        }
    }
}
```

This code defines a read-only class that represents a point. It has three properties: x and y for the x and y coordinates, and Length for the length of the vector from the origin to the point. These properties are based on three fields: xVal, yVal, and len. When the Length property is accessed, the code checks if it is zero, in which case, the length is calculated and cached in the field `len`. Because the vector length is calculated, there is no reason to serialize it, so it is marked with the `[NonSerialized]` attribute.

Note that the `[Serializable]` attribute is not inherited, which means that if a class is marked as serializable, derived classes are not automatically serializable. This makes sense because the derived class could have members that are not serialized. On the other hand, the `[NonSerialized]` attribute is inherited.

3.2.2 Formatters

When a serializable object is passed by value across a context boundary, the runtime will serialize it using a *formatter*. The Framework Class Library provides several formatters, with the base classes in the `System.Runtime.Serialization` namespace. A formatter should implement the `IFormatter` interface:

```
// C#
public interface IFormatter
{
    SerializationBinder Binder
    {get; set;}
    StreamingContext Context
    {get; set;}
    ISurrogateSelector SurrogateSelector
    {get; set;}
    void Serialize(Stream serializationStream, object graph);
    object Deserialize(Stream serializationStream);
}
```

The `Serialize()` and `Deserialize()` methods do as their names suggest: The former takes a serializable object and writes its state to a stream in the appropriate format; the latter takes a stream and returns an object created from the data in the stream. Notice that the `object` parameter to `Serialize()` is called `graph`. This is intentional because although the parameter may simply be a primitive value type or an instance of a simple reference type, it may also be an object with embedded objects. Consider the following code:

```
// C#
[Serializable]
public class OddClass
{
    private string s1;
    private string s2;
    public OddClass()
    { s1 = s2 = null; }
    public OddClass(string s)
    { s1 = s2 = s; }
}
```

When you create an instance of this class with the second constructor, the constructor assigns both of the private members to the same string. If this instance is serialized, what should be sent to the stream? Of course, the state of the string that was passed to the constructor should be serialized, but Odd-Class holds two references to this object, so should two copies be serialized? What happens if the connection between items is more complicated? For example, if you have a doubly linked list, what should be serialized then? The object that is serialized represents a *graph* of objects with various interconnections, so the serialization infrastructure must be able to take this into account. I will leave discussion about this to later in this section. For now let's get back to IFormatter.

The properties of the formatter affect how it behaves. The Context property has information about the destination of the data when an object is being serialized or the source of the data when it is being deserialized. Context.State is an enumerated value that indicates this information, and Context.Context contains any additional information about the source or destination of the data. When an object is serialized, the formatter should write complete information about that object, including the full name of its type and the full name of the assembly that houses it, so that an uninitialized instance of the type can be created during deserialization and initialized with the serialization stream. In some cases (e.g., if a newer but compatible version of the class exists in the destination context), the formatter deserialization code may change the class to be loaded, which it does with the Binder property. Finally, the SurrogateSelector property is an object that contains the surrogates that may be used to do the serialization. Each surrogate is specific to a particular type, so a formatter can have code that is specific for particular types, as well as generic code for all objects.

The framework provides two standard formatters: `SoapFormatter` and `BinaryFormatter`. Using a formatter is straightforward:

```
// C#
Point p = new Point(1, 2);
BinaryFormatter bf;
bf = new BinaryFormatter();
Stream stm;
stm = new FileStream("data.dat", FileMode.Create);
bf.Serialize(stm, p);
stm.Close();
```

In this code, `stm` is a stream based on a file. The `BinaryFormatter` object reads the metadata on the fields of an object, and if the serializable metadata is set, the field is serialized to the stream. What is interesting is that the fields can be private, yet the `BinaryFormatter` class (indeed, any formatter class) can still obtain the value of the field and serialize it.

Reading an object from a stream also involves a `BinaryFormatter` object:

```
// C#
Point p = null;
BinaryFormatter bf;
bf = new BinaryFormatter();
Stream stm;
stm = new FileStream("data.dat", FileMode.Open);
p = (Point)bf.Deserialize(stm);
stm.Close();
```

The `Deserialize()` method creates an instance of the object that was serialized into the stream by calling the default constructor. It then initializes the fields that are not marked with `[NonSerialized]` with the serialized values. Again, the fields of the class can be private, yet the `SoapFormatter` is still able to write to them. How does `Deserialize()` know what class the stream holds? The `Serialize()` method places in the stream the name of the assembly, the complete name of the class and its version, the names of the fields that are serialized, and finally the values of those fields. To see the formatted data without having to resort to a hex viewer, you can change the formatter used to `SoapFormatter`:

```csharp
// C#
Point p = new Point(1, 2);
SoapFormatter sf;
sf = new SoapFormatter();
sf.AssemblyFormat = FormatterAssemblyStyle.Full;
Stream stm;
stm = new FileStream("data.xml", FileMode.Create);
sf.Serialize(stm, p);
stm.Close();
```

I have explicitly specified that the XML should have the full assembly name. The `data.xml` file has the following content:

```xml
<SOAP-ENV:Envelope
 xmlns:xsi="http://www.w3.org/2001/XMLSchema-instance"
 xmlns:xsd="http://www.w3.org/2001/XMLSchema"
 xmlns:SOAP-ENC="http://schemas.xmlsoap.org/soap/encoding/"
 xmlns:SOAP-ENV="http://schemas.xmlsoap.org/soap/envelope/"
 xmlns:clr="http://schemas.microsoft.com/clr/1.0">
 SOAP-ENV:encodingStyle="http://schemas.xmlsoap.org
                          /soap/encoding/"
   <SOAP-ENV:Body>
      <a1:Point id="ref-1"
       xmlns:a1="http://schemas.microsoft.com
       /clr/assem/pointer%2C%20Version%3D0.0.0.0%2C%20
       Culture%3Dneutral%2C%20PublicKeyToken%3Dnull">
         <xVal>1</xVal>
         <yVal>2</yVal>
      </a1:Point>
   </SOAP-ENV:Body>
</SOAP-ENV:Envelope>
```

The assembly is called `pointer`, and the version of this assembly is `0.0.0.0`. `SoapFormatter` creates an element in the SOAP (Simple Object Access Protocol) body for the serialized type, and then embedded members and their values are child elements. The `OddClass` example I gave earlier shows that the SOAP formatter handles the case of multiple references to the same object by using `href` (simplified to remove the namespace attribute of the `a1` element):

```
<SOAP-ENV:Body>
   <a1:OddClass id="ref-1">
      <s1 id="ref-3">hello</s1>
      <s2 href="#ref-3"/>
   </a1:OddClass>
</SOAP-ENV:Body>
```

As I've indicated, the serialization infrastructure is powerful because it has access to nonpublic members in your class. You, too, can access such members, using the `FormatterServices` class, but your code must have the `SecurityPermissionFlag.SerializationFormatter` permission. This class has a method called `GetObjectData()` that will return all the values of the specified members. So for our `Point` class, I can get the values in the private fields with the following code:

```
// C#
Point p = new Point(1, 2);
MemberInfo[] mi;
mi = p.GetType().GetFields(
   BindingFlags.NonPublic|BindingFlags.Instance);[1]
object[] objs;
objs = FormatterServices.GetObjectData(p, mi);
foreach(object o in objs)
{ Console.WriteLine(o.ToString()); }
```

The call to `GetFields()` gets the field information (`FieldInfo`) for all of the nonpublic fields in the class. `MemberInfo` is the base class of `FieldInfo`. This array is then passed to `GetObjectData()`, which returns an array containing the values of the specified members. `GetObjectData()` is quite a powerful method.

On the other hand, you may decide that you want to initialize an object. `FormatterServices` has a method called `GetUninitializedObject()` that will create an object *without calling any of its constructors*. After you have created this "empty" object, you can fill its fields with a call to `PopulateObjectMembers()` that passes the object, an array of `MemberInfo` to indicate the members to initialize, and an array of objects that have the data. Again, access specifiers mean nothing to this method!

---

1. Note that if you ask for nonpublic members, you have to specify whether you are interested in static or instance members.

3.2.3 Object Manager

During deserialization the formatter needs to know if an object in the stream has already been deserialized (a *back reference*) or not (a *forward reference*). When an object is being deserialized, the formatter can ask a runtime object called `ObjectManager` if it knows about that object by passing it a reference ID to a function called `GetObject()`. If `ObjectManager` knows about the object being deserialized, it will return the object's value; otherwise it will return `null`. If `ObjectManager` does not know about an object, the formatter can deserialize the object and pass it and the reference ID to `RegisterObject()` so that it is known to the `ObjectManager` for future reference.

The IDs passed to `ObjectManager` are generated by another class (`ObjectIDGenerator`), which generates IDs that are unique for the lifetime of the formatter.

3.2.4 Custom Serialization

If you want to control the data that is put into the stream and read out of the stream—essentially bypassing the use of the serialization metadata—you can implement the `ISerializable` interface on your object. This interface has a single method called `GetObjectData()`, which allows you to determine the information that is serialized to the stream:

```
// C#
void GetObjectData(
    SerializationInfo info,
    StreamingContext context);
```

`StreamingContext` contains information about the source and destination of the data in the stream. The `SerializationInfo` parameter is essentially a property bag; it contains named values. Your implementation of `GetObjectData()` should write the data that it wants serialized into the `SerializationInfo` object—for example, as shown here:

```
// C#
public class MyObject
    : ISerializable
{
```

```
// details of constructors will be shown later
private string str;
public void GetObjectData(
    SerializationInfo info,
    StreamingContext context)
{ info.AddValue("__str", str); }
}
```

The value in the member `str` is written to the stream and given a name of `__str`. However, this is only part of the story because there has to be a mechanism for the data in a stream to be used to initialize an object when the object is deserialized. `ISerializable` is unusual because it requires your class to implement both the items in the interface *and* a specific constructor. .NET interfaces do *not* contain constructors, so you just have to remember this. For the sample class, the constructor should look like this:

```
// C#
internal MyObject(
    SerializationInfo info,
    StreamingContext context)
{
    str = info.GetString("__str");
}
```

This constructor takes the `SerializationInfo` reference containing the values that were serialized, and you extract the objects from this stream by name. I have marked the constructor with `internal` to indicate that yet again, the almighty serialization infrastructure has complete access to the members of your object, and it does not respect the access specifiers that you use. When you write data into the `SerializationInfo` object or read data out, you do not have to worry about the graph of objects or the format of the data; all of this is handled for you by the formatter and `ObjectManager`.

3.2.5 MSMQ Serialization

In Chapter 2, I spoke about Microsoft Message Queuing (MSMQ). The MSMQ concept allows messages to be passed between disconnected processes. When the client application generates the message, the server process does not have to be running. Indeed, the server process may read the message hours or days after the message was generated. Messages sent via MSMQ contain a body that is just a buffer of bytes. It is up to the server to interpret what those bytes mean, but clearly the messages must be written in a format that the server can understand.

When you pass an object through an MSMQ message, you must send the *state* of the object in the message, and the server must initialize an instance of the same class with this state. As you have seen, the way to do this is to make the class serializable with the `[Serializable]` attribute or to use custom serialization.

The formatter is accessible through the `Formatter` property of the `MessageQueue` class, which is an object that implements `IMessageFormatter`. If you do not set this property, an instance of `XmlMessageFormatter` will be created when the property is first accessed. The `XmlMessageFormatter` class is loosely coupled in that the server-side code registers a collection of types that it expects to be sent through its `TargetTypes` property.

When you read a message through the `MessageQueue` object, `MessageQueue` returns a `Message` object with the message in its `Body` property. When you access the `Body` property, the accessor calls the `Read()` method of the formatter. The version of this method in `XmlMessageFormatter` creates a list of `XmlSerializer` objects—one for each of the possible types in `TargetTypes`—and then asks each of these if it can deserialize an object from the message.

The other two formatters that the Framework Class Library supplies are `ActiveXMessageFormatter` and `BinaryMessageFormatter`. The former is compatible with the unmanaged MSMQ ActiveX formatter and thus allows you to interoperate with existing MSMQ code. Like `BinaryMessageFormatter`, `ActiveXMessageFormatter` sends the message as binary data; thus the messages are smaller than those created by `XmlMessageFormatter`. Don't be too worried by the size of the message, unless your messages are enormous (by this I mean hundreds of kilobytes). It is more important to look at the *number* of network calls being made than at the size of the messages.

Whereas `ActiveXMessageFormatter` formats the message itself, `BinaryMessageFormatter` uses `System.Runtime.Serialization.Formatters.Binary.BinaryFormatter`, which reads the stream to see the types that are passed. This means that with `BinaryMessageFormatter` the server is tightly coupled to the client in that the server must know about the type that the client will send, and must access it accordingly.

3.3 Remoting

Before I explain the facilities of .NET remoting, it is worth devoting a few words to Microsoft's existing distributed technology: DCOM. DCOM is implemented over Microsoft's implementation of the Distributed Computing Environment (DCE) RPC. Every machine that can serve DCOM objects will have an RPC server (the COM Service Control Manager [SCM]) that takes object activation requests through RPC interfaces. This server sits on UDP and TCP port 135.

When the SCM activates a COM server, it dynamically assigns the server's process a UDP and TCP port somewhere in the range 1024 to 65535. The SCM then constructs a structure called `OBJREF`, which contains information about the server (`OXID`), the object that was activated (`OID`), and the interface requested on the object (`IPID`). `OXID` contains information used to find the server on the network—that is, the server's network address and end point.

The client is given the `OBJREF` structure, which it unmarshals to gain a proxy object. To the client, the proxy looks like the object that it wants to access in that it supports the interfaces implemented by the object. If the client passes the interface pointer to another apartment, the interface pointer is marshaled again by the passing of `OBJREF` to the importing apartment. Thus, when an interface pointer is passed between apartments, it is actually `OBJREF` that is passed; when an `OBJREF` structure is unmarshaled, a new proxy is created that is specific to the apartment where the proxy is created. This means that proxies always refer to the actual object, and you can never have a proxy to a proxy.

DCOM is based on RPC, which means that RPC security is applied. That is, a client makes a call using a particular security principal, and the server can give access to the client according to the principal's authorization. To prevent hackers from mimicking principals, RPC allows several levels of authentication (how often the server authenticates that the client is who it says it is) and can support several types of authentication. The higher levels of authentication allow you to configure the packet encryption on the reasoning that if you cannot authenticate a client, encryption is useless. Of course, without authentication, authorization is also useless.

There are several problems with DCOM. On the Internet the main problem is DCOM's use of ports. Typically, corporate firewalls expose HTTP port 80 and possibly HTTPS port 443, but nothing else. Using DCOM over the Internet first involved persuading the network administrator to open port 135—hardly an easy task of persuasion. Once you did that, you had the even more difficult task of persuading the network administrator to open ports 1024 to 65535 for the DCOM servers' end points!

To play down this monumental request, you could restrict DCOM to a range of end points, but even so, network administrators rarely allowed ports to be opened. Another problem with DCOM is that RPC authentication is used. Clients that access servers across the Internet are typically unauthenticated anonymous clients, or if authentication is required, there is a problem of how it is performed. Authenticated DCOM calls typically time out while authentication is being performed.

Even on an intranet, DCOM isn't perfect. Servers should be within a firewall to prevent any problems with dynamically allocated ports, and the machines should be all in the same domain—or in trusted domains—to prevent security problems. Most developers could get the hang of DCOM authentication—NT4 provided a GUI application that allowed you to create access control lists (ACLs)—but often they were tripped up by authentication, particularly because both the client and the server had to set the authentication level or the default values would be used.

Of greater concern, of course, is the fact that the client and the server code effectively can run only on Windows machines and are written for the Win32 API. Initiatives like EntireX did allow DCOM to be implemented on Solaris, and Microsoft's own Java SDK allowed Java objects to be exposed as COM objects if they were run on Windows, but these products hardly achieved market saturation. DCOM was (and is) stigmatized with the accusation of its detractors that it is a Windows-only technology.

One final issue—which is a problem with DCOM on the Internet and intranets—is that by default, objects are accessed by reference. When a client activates a remote object, the interface that is returned is usually a reference to the remote object, which means that all access to the object involves a network call. Often the developer is happy to have this behavior because the object is designed to run on the remote machine. Of greater concern, however, is the case in which a client passes data to the remote server via an object because that object will live on the *client* machine. To access this data, the server would have to make a network call.

This problem was compounded by VB-style property access. There are ways to solve this problem with DCOM.[2] The simplest is to make objects marshal by value; that is, the state of the object is passed via DCOM, but when the interface is unmarshaled the proxy is initialized with the object's state so that the client accesses the object's state locally (i.e., a network call is not required). This is similar to .NET's idea of serializable objects, with one crucial difference: You have to implement the serialization of the object and provide a custom proxy object that deserializes the state.

DCOM gave some flexibility to the developer: The DCOM specification allows DCOM packets to be extended through an undocumented mechanism called *channel hooks,* and DCOM itself used this mechanism for passing errors as out-of-band data. In addition, Windows 2000 provides many new features that allow you to make your intermachine calls more efficient, but the architecture of COM and DCOM is still effectively a closed technology.

The Microsoft Developer Network (MSDN) documents the COM architecture as consisting of components, and it lists the interfaces that the various components (proxies, stubs, channels) implement. But the complete detail of how the technology is implemented is missing, and extending COM by inserting your own interception layers is far from straightforward.[3]

---

2. For details, see my article in the September 2000 edition of *MSDN Magazine:* "Marshaling Your Data: Efficient Data Transfer Techniques Using COM and Windows 2000," available at http://msdn.microsoft.com/msdnmag/issues/0900/DataTrans/DataTrans.asp.
3. It is possible to intercept COM by writing your own proxy-stub DLLs, but because the Microsoft Network Data Representation (NDR) API is not documented, it is difficult to use DCOM. You can use your own protocol (for example, Martin Gudgen's Pluggable Channel Architecture, www.develop.com/marting/pca.html), but that is hardly a perfect solution.

3.3.1 .NET Remoting

Now let's take a look at how remoting is handled in .NET. There are three ways to access a .NET component remotely:

1. **.NET remoting**. Components are exposed through .NET channels and use distributed garbage collection. Components can be activated by the client (one component per client) or by the server (singleton, or single call) and then accessed by the client.

2. **Web Services**. Essentially these are singleton components, accessed through a well-known Web Service "interface." The transport protocol is HTTP, and the data is typically formatted according to SOAP.

3. **COM+ component services**. .NET components are packaged in COM+ applications and can be accessed through DCOM or HTTP/SOAP. Typically components use just-in-time activation.

I will cover Web Services later in this chapter and COM+ in Chapter 4; in this section I will focus on .NET remoting. The choice of the type of remoting is based on several criteria. .NET components that use COM+ component services can be accessed remotely when the proxy COM+ application is installed on a local machine. This adds an extra deployment cost: You must export the proxy application and then install it on the machine where you want to access the component. However, you do get component services, which means that your components can use COM+ events, transactions, and synchronization.

Web Services abstract the user from components. The user does not see a component; instead, the user sees just a collection of methods. These methods are usually referred to as the "interface" of the Web Service, but it is not an interface in the same sense as a COM or .NET interface. The client does not access the Web Service through an interface reference; it merely calls whichever method it is interested in calling. Web Service methods can return objects, but those objects will always be returned by value. Web Services are accessed through HTTP, which is stateless, so if you want to save session state between calls, you must use a mechanism for saving session state, such as, for example, `HttpSessionState`.

In general, both COM+ and Web Services give you remoting free of charge. They allow you to configure the remoting so that you can control things like authentication, but you cannot extend the remoting protocol. This is where .NET remoting comes in. The architecture is completely open; you can control how the data is serialized and you can change how the data is transmitted. Of course, such flexibility does come with some complexity.

3.3.2 .NET Remote Components

.NET remoting gives you two ways to access components: *client activated* and *server activated.* Client activated means that a client asks for an object and the server will create an object specifically for that client. The client may decide to share that object with other objects, but the point is that the object owes its existence to the client's request for it to be activated. Client-activated objects present a lifetime issue: The client has a reference, but the object lives on the server. The server has to find some way to track when the client has finished with the object. This is a perennial problem with distributed objects, and different component technologies have taken different approaches. Client-activated objects use lease objects to solve the problem, as I'll explain later.

Server-activated objects are also known as *well-known objects.* However, there are no facilities in .NET to make them more "well known" than client-activated objects. The term appears to come from the fact that the end point of the server-activated object must be known by the client before the client can get access (with a client-activated object this end point is generated when the object is activated). I think it is more appropriate to call them server-activated objects.

There are two types of server-activated objects: Either just one object is provided by the server and all clients access just this *singleton* object, or the server creates an instance of the object merely to service a *single call* to one of the object's methods and then the object is destroyed. The nature of server-activated objects means that they cannot be created with constructor parameters. If you want to create objects using constructor parameters, you must create client-activated objects.

Client-activated objects and server-activated objects also differ in how the proxy is created. For a client-activated object, `ObjRef` is passed to the client application domain, and the remoting layer creates the `TransparentProxy` object from `ObjRef`. Server-activated objects, on the other hand, are not created by the client, so for the client to have access to an object, it must already know where the object is. The remoting layer can use this information on the client side to create an instance of `ObjRef` without having to access the server.

Both server and client code can identify an object that should be accessed remotely in two ways: using code or using configuration files. In general, configuration files make the code far cleaner, but I will show both methods here. The first thing a server needs to do is create the channel that will be used later to access the object and, if the object is client activated, to activate that object. This is simple; you just call `RegisterChannel()`:

```
// C#
ChannelServices.RegisterChannel(
    new TcpServerChannel(4000));
```

The static `RegisterChannel()` method takes an `IChannel` reference on an instance of a channel object. The main channels in the Framework Class Library are based on TCP and HTTP. They differ not only in the transport that is used, but also in the formatter. By default, TCP channels use a binary formatter, whereas HTTP channels use a SOAP formatter, but this can be changed if necessary.

The TCP and HTTP channels come in three types: client, server, and bidirectional. In the preceding example I use a server channel because I merely want the server to listen for connections from a client. `TcpServerChannel` should be given details of the port on which to listen and optionally the name of the channel. The name of the channel should be unique on the machine; the default name for TCP channels is `tcp`.

If the remote object uses a callback (e.g., generates an event in the client), the client must register a channel for this callback. This channel must be on a different port from the channel that is used to access the server. If there is no callback to the client, the client need not explicitly register a channel; you'll see why in a moment. The server needs to register the types that can be accessed and indicate whether they are client-activated objects or server-activated objects. To access an object that is activated and running on a remote machine (whether it is client or server activated), the class must derive from `MarshalBy-RefObject`.

3.3.2.1 Client-Activated Objects

Client-activated objects are registered as such by `RegisterActivatedServiceType()`:

```csharp
// C#
ChannelServices.RegisterChannel(
    new TcpServerChannel(4000));
RemotingConfiguration
    .RegisterActivatedServiceType(
        typeof(MyClass));
Console.WriteLine(
    "press ENTER to stop server...");
Console.ReadLine();
```

The static `RegisterActivatedServiceType()` method is passed the type object of the class that can be created remotely. The remoting infrastructure adds information about this class to an internally maintained table. Then when a request comes on the channel, the framework can check whether the requested type is registered and, if so, create the object. The object is then assigned a URI, and information about this URI is returned to the client, where the remoting structure will create an instance of `ObjRef`, as you'll see later. The client does not see the URI; it sees just a proxy object. Your object can access the URI by calling the static `RemotingServices.GetObjectUri()` method.

The four lines of code shown here are all that is needed for a server, other than the code for the class `MyClass`. The remote object class can be implemented in a separate assembly, as long as the assembly metadata is available during compilation and the assembly is accessible at runtime. The code here contains a call to `Console.ReadLine()` to block the main thread; without this call the application will finish and the channel will stop listening. Requests for object activation will come in through the process thread pool, so they will be handled on a thread other than the main thread.

When a class is registered on the server, the runtime adds it to the list of registered classes that it maintains. You can access this list by calling `RemotingConfiguration.GetRegisteredActivatedServiceTypes()`, which returns an array of `ActivatedServiceTypeEntry` objects. Each of these objects has information about the class type and assembly, as well as a list of the context attributes of the type.

If the remote class is in a separate assembly, the client-side administration is easy: All you have to do is make that assembly accessible to the client assembly so that the client has access to the metadata. However, the remote object is designed to run in a different domain from the client, and you may also decide that you do not want to allow the client code access to the remote object's assembly (e.g., because you want to protect the IL in the assembly from snooping eyes). If distributing the remote object's assembly to the client machine is a problem, you have two options: First, you can run the SOAPSUDS utility on the assembly to create a new assembly that has just the public metadata for the remote object (the actual code is not added to this assembly). This assembly can be distributed to the client machine. The other option is to change your object design so that its methods are available through an interface defined in another assembly. This interface assembly can be distributed to the client machine.

The client needs to activate the object, and to do this it must specify the location of the object. RegisterActivatedClientType() does this by associating a type with the URI where the object can be found:

```
// C#
RemotingConfiguration
    .RegisterActivatedClientType(
        typeof(MyClass), "tcp://TESTMACHINE:4000");
MyClass c = new MyClass();
c.CallYou();
```

Of course, this address is the activation address of the object; it is the end point where the server is listening, ready to create object instances. Now that the type MyClass has been associated with the activation URI, when you use the managed new operator on the type the runtime will make the activation request through the specified channel. When the server has created an instance, the object will have a unique URI beneath the activation URI, and this URI will be returned through an ObjRef instance (for server-activated objects this information is already available on the client side, so the ObjRef instance can be created without a call to the server). As I mentioned before, you can access this URI through the `GetObjectUri()` method:

```
// C#
MyClass c = new MyClass();
Console.WriteLine("called on "
   + RemotingServices.GetObjectUri(c));
c.CallYou();
```

This code will print out a URI like this:

```
called on /2bb32eb7_9ab3_4979_883f_8e82b9701246/1.rem
```

Of course, the complete URI includes the host name, channel, and port. You can get this information by calling `RemotingConfiguration.GetRegisteredActivatedClientTypes()` and iterating until you get the `ActivatedClientTypeEntry` object for the specific type. This object will have an `ApplicationUrl` property. Again, your client does not need to know about this URI because it is hidden in the `ObjRef` instance in the proxy object. Once you have activated an object in this way, you can call the client's methods through the proxy.

Both the client and the server registration of client-activated objects can be achieved through configuration files. Configuration files are not automatically loaded, so you have to tell the runtime which file to use. The name of the configuration file can be anything you like; however, you may decide to use the application configuration file, which you can get with the following call:

```
// C#
string configfile =
   AppDomain.CurrentDomain
      .SetupInformation.ConfigurationFile;
```

Here's an example of a server-side configuration file:

```
<configuration>
   <system.runtime.remoting>
      <application name="Server">
         <service>
            <activated
              type="MyClass, MyAssem" />
```

```
        </service>
        <channels>
            <channel
                type="System.Runtime.Remoting
                    .Channels.Tcp.TcpChannel,
                    System.Runtime.Remoting"[4]
                port="4000" />
        </channels>
    </application>
  </system.runtime.remoting>
</configuration>
```

This code indicates that the application identified by `Server` has a TCP channel on port 4000 and will allow clients to activate instances of `MyClass` in the `MyAssem` assembly. This is most of the information provided by the code in the previous server example. The new version of this server looks like this:

```
// C#
RemotingConfiguration.Configure(
    "myserver.config");
Console.WriteLine(
    "press ENTER to stop server...");
Console.ReadLine();
```

Because the information about the types that will be available through the server is given by the configuration file, the server can be compiled without the object metadata. This means that you can write a generic server and determine the available classes at deployment time. This server code looks very sparse because most of the work is done by `Configure()` through the configuration file; this is intentional, as you'll see later.

All the `Configure()` method does is read the configuration file and use the information to call the appropriate `RemotingConfiguration` method. The remoting team did this deliberately so that you can use whatever mechanism you choose for determining which objects are available as remote objects. Configuration files are convenient when there are just a few classes to configure. However, a system that makes many objects available could store the information in a database and register them in code.

---

4. Luckily for me and the layout editor of this book, white space is allowed in attributes.

On the client side, the configuration file is similar:

```
<configuration>
    <system.runtime.remoting>
        <application name="Client">
            <client url="tcp://localhost:4000">
                <activated type="MyClass, MyAssem" />
            </client>
        </application>
    </system.runtime.remoting>
</configuration>
```

This time we do not need to use the channel collection because the `url` attribute of the client specifies enough information for the runtime to create the channel to the server activator object. The client code is straightforward:

```
// C#
RemotingConfiguration.Configure(
    "myclient.config");
MyClass c = new MyClass();
c.CallYou();
```

When the object is created in the server, the server creates an `ObjRef` object that is returned to the client to allow the client to find the actual object. The server maintains a map containing references to all of the objects that are accessed remotely, and the `ObjRef` objects that are used to access them. When a method request comes in, it will contain the information from the client `ObjRef`, and the remoting framework can use this map to ensure that the request goes to the correct object. When the server process dies, all the registered channels and objects will be released and will no longer be available.

3.3.2.2 Server-Activated Objects

The difference between client-activated objects and server-activated objects is clearly the initiation of the activation request: Server-activated objects are created by the server. With client-activated objects, the request is made to an activator on the server, and the activator returns information that identifies the activated object and is used in the client to create the `ObjRef`.

Server-activated objects do not need this step because the server creates the remote object. However, because server-activated objects do not use this extra step, the client cannot get the URI of the object from the server. One option could be to allow the client to query the server for the URI of the type that it wants to access, but this approach involves a network call. The alternative—used by .NET—is to register the type on the server as being activated at a specific URI. This URI is known to both the server and the client, and because the client developer knows this URI, she can use it to access the server-activated object.

There is no API for a discovery mechanism to ask a server for the URIs of all its registered classes, so I would not regard these objects as "well known." To use server-activated objects, however, you *do* have to have specialized knowledge about the object's URI (which is more knowledge than you need for client-activated objects), so I would regard server-activated objects as "developer known" rather than "well known."

As the name suggests, server-activated objects are activated by the server, and there are two types:

1. **Singleton**. A single instance of the object is created when a client makes a request for the object and then lives as long as the server application. All clients have access to the same object instance.

2. **Single call**. The object exists only when a client makes a call. When the client calls a method on the object, the server activates an instance of the class; and when the call completes, the object is destroyed.

The singleton object makes sense for an object that represents a single server resource. Note, however, that although all clients will have access to the same object, this is not a complete bottleneck because the runtime uses a thread pool to service calls to a singleton (the analogy to COM is a multi-threaded-apartment [MTA] singleton). This means that you must write your singleton code to take into account the fact that two threads could be calling the same method at any one time. Any thread-sensitive code or data should be protected with synchronization objects (but keep this protected code as short as possible because synchronized code has an adverse affect on scalability). The advantage of a singleton is that it can hold data in the object between client calls. Singleton objects are created under lifetime control: If the object is not used, after five minutes of inactivity it will be destroyed.

Single-call objects can also be used to access server resources. However, the actual instance of the object lives only for the duration of the call, so you cannot hold object data between client calls. Neither singleton nor single-call classes can have constructor parameters.

The server should register the channel and the class:

```csharp
// C#
ChannelServices.RegisterChannel(
    new TcpServerChannel(4000));
RemotingConfiguration.RegisterWellKnownServiceType(
    typeof(MyClass), "MyClassURI",
    WellKnownObjectMode.SingleCall);
Console.WriteLine("Press ENTER to stop server");
Console.ReadLine();
```

This code registers the class for the single-call object. Because this object is "well known," you also have to provide a URI for the class—in this case MyClassURI. If you prefer, you can use a configuration file:

```xml
<configuration>
    <system.runtime.remoting>
        <application name="Server">
            <service>
                <wellknown
                 mode="SingleCall"
                 type="MyClass, MyAssem"
                 objectUri="MyClassURI" />
            </service>
            <channels>
                <channel port="4000"
                 type="System.Runtime.Remoting
                     .Channels.Tcp.TcpChannel,
                     System.Runtime.Remoting" />
            </channels>
        </application>
    </system.runtime.remoting>
</configuration>
```

DEVELOPING APPLICATIONS WITH VISUAL STUDIO.NET

On the client side you have three options, which I will show here. The first option is to use `Activator.GetObject()`:

```csharp
// C#
MyClass c;
c = (MyClass)Activator.GetObject(
            typeof(MyClass),
            "tcp://localhost:4000/MyClassURI");
c.CallYou();
```

As before, because I am creating a single object, I do not need to register a channel; calling `GetObject()` will do that. If I want to create more than one instance of the class, I need to register a channel that will be shared by all the objects. The `GetObject()` call will send a request to the server at the specified URI, and a proxy will be returned through which you can call the object.

The second option is to register the object on the client side as a well-known object:

```csharp
// C#
RemotingConfiguration.RegisterWellKnownClientType(
    typeof(MyClass),
    "tcp://localhost:4000/MyClassURI");
MyClass c = new MyClass();
c.CallYou();
```

Registering the client type means that you can create an instance by using the managed `new` operator.

Finally, the third option is to use a configuration file:

```xml
<application name="Client">
    <client>
        <wellknown
          type="MyClass, MyAssem"
          url="tcp://localhost:4000/MyClassURI" />
    </client>
</application>
```

The call to `Activator.GetObject()` or `new` does not activate the object; instead, the client code gets a proxy object. The network connection is made only when a method is called through the proxy, and if the object is a single-call object, it is destroyed after the call is completed.

3.3.2.3 Remote Callbacks

When you register a client channel, it is just that—a channel used to send messages to a server. If the server object makes callbacks to the client, the client itself acts as a server and must register a server channel. The following example uses the class I mentioned earlier:

```csharp
// C#
public delegate void CallBack(string s);
public class MyClass
    : MarshalByRefObject
{
    public void CallYou(){}
    public void CallYou(CallBack d)
    { d("you called me"); }
}
```

For a client-activated object, the client configuration file must have a <channels> collection in the <application> node. If the client is run on the same machine as the server, it must have a different port from that of the server object:

```xml
<channels>
  <channel port="4001"
           type="System.Runtime.Remoting
                 .Channels.Tcp.TcpChannel,
                 System.Runtime.Remoting" />
</channels>
```

The client code could look like this:

```csharp
// C#
public class CalledObject
    : MarshalByRefObject
{
    static public void CallMe(string s)
    {
        Console.WriteLine(
            "called me with: " + s);
```

```
    }
    public static void Main()
    {
        RemotingConfiguration.Configure(
            "remote.config");
        MyClass c = new MyClass();
        b.CallMe(new CallBack(
            CalledObject.CallMe));
        // do something else
    }
}
```

3.3.2.4 *Remote Objects and Exceptions*

I mentioned in Chapter 2 that exceptions are serializable. This means that when an exception is generated in an application domain, it is transmitted by value from the application domain where it is generated to the calling application domain where it is rethrown. As a consequence, you will have two call stack dumps: one on the server side and one on the client side. There are several important ramifications here.

First, you should write your classes to be as bulletproof as possible; however, you cannot guarantee that third-party classes will be as robust as yours. What you can guarantee is that if such third-party code throws an exception, it will not kill your server even if you do not use exception handling throughout your code. This solves the irritating problem with COM and COM+ that if a remote object throws an exception, the entire process is shut down, killing any other objects used by other clients. Serializing exceptions in this case is a good thing.

Second, having two call stack dumps has the odd effect that a client process on one machine will get an exception thrown by an object (that the client application developer may not have written) running in another process on another machine. Such an exception may have little relevance to the client that called the object, so your client code must make some intelligent decisions. An exception that was caused by the client's passing an invalid argument is a legitimate exception to log on the client machine or to return to the user. An exception that occurred because of an internal error in the object will make no sense to the user on the client machine. Indeed, it makes *more* sense to log the error on the server machine. These issues highlight again the importance of proper exception handling.

Note that the remote exception is caught on the thread where the object is executing before being serialized and returned to the client. This means that you cannot use the `AppDomain.UnhandledException` event on the server side to catch the exception.

3.3.2.5 *Hosting Remote Objects in IIS*

Earlier in this section I showed the minimal code for a remote server. It looked rather sparse, with just a call to `RemotingConfiguration.Configure()` and a call to `Console.ReadLine()` to prevent the server from finishing early. Because the configuration file has all the information about the channels to register and the objects that will be available as remote objects, it seems that there ought to be a standard server process that exists simply to call `RemotingConfiguration.Configure()`. Such a process is the ASP.NET process.

To get IIS to host remote objects, you have to name the configuration file `web.config` because ASP.NET looks specifically for this file in the folder that is mapped to the virtual directory. The file should have a `<service>` collection specifying all the classes that can be used for remote objects. The channel used will be an HTTP channel, but you can use whatever port you choose (as long as it is greater than or equal to 1024). The assemblies that contain the classes that can be remoted should be in a subfolder called `bin`.

I will come back to `web.config` when I cover Web Services later.

3.3.2.6 *Proxies*

When a client gets a reference to an object of a class derived from the `MarshalByRefObject` class, it actually gets a proxy object. This is true when the object is on a different machine from the client, or even if it is in a different application domain in the same process. Clearly, cross-machine, cross-process, and cross-domain calls have different requirements as far as the remoting infrastructure is concerned, but the developer does not need to worry about this because the JIT compiler and the .NET Runtime take this into account.

When a client makes an activation call, or calls a method that returns an object reference, what it will actually get is a reference to an object called a *transparent proxy.* The transparent proxy looks exactly like the remote object that is requested, but when the client makes a call through the transparent proxy, the runtime determines if the `MarshalByRefObject` object is in the same application domain as the client, and if so, the call goes directly to that object. If the object is in another application domain, the call is converted to a message (an object with an `IMessage` interface) and is passed to a `RealProxy` object. This object forwards the message to the `MarshalBy-RefObject` object through the appropriate channel. This process is summarized in Figure 3.7, which shows a conceptual view; in actuality, the transparent proxy is a field in the `RealProxy` class.

Note that if the object is server activated, no network calls are made to obtain the reference to the transparent proxy. The only time that network calls

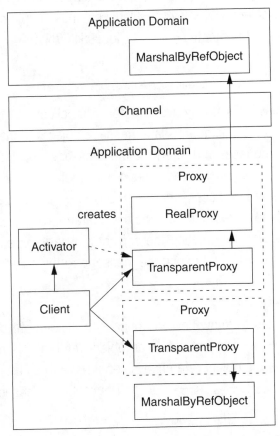

Figure 3.7 Conceptual view of calling remote objects through a proxy

are made is when the client accesses the object through a method call or a property access. For client-activated objects the transparent proxy is returned from an activation request, which of course requires a call to the remote application domain. The transparent proxy is not extendable, but the `RealProxy` class is. You can determine if a reference is a transparent proxy by calling the static method `RemotingServices.IsTransparentProxy()`, and you can access the `RealProxy` object from a transparent proxy by calling the static method `RemotingServices.GetRealProxy()`.

The framework is extendable, and you can write a custom proxy class to replace `RealProxy` (but not the transparent proxy). Such a custom class must derive from `RealProxy`, which provides all the standard methods that a proxy should have, including a private field for the transparent proxy. This class has an abstract method called `Invoke()`, which you must implement to send the message to the remote object. `Invoke()` looks like this:

```
// C#
public abstract IMessage Invoke(IMessage msg);
```

Clearly `Invoke()` is not convenient for your clients to call because the client will have to create the appropriate message objects to make the activation and method call requests and interpret the messages returned. To help you here, the `RealProxy` constructor takes a parameter that is the type of the remote object that will be accessed. The `RealProxy` class uses the type information from this type object to create the transparent proxy, and the transparent proxy does all the work of creating the correct message type and initializing it, and finally calling `Invoke()` to send the message to the object.

3.3.3 Marshaling

The proxy object has to know how to connect to the remote object, so it consults data in an `ObjRef` object. When an object reference is passed across a remoting boundary, the object reference is serialized into an `ObjRef` object by a call to `RemotingServices.Marshal()`. The `ObjRef` class looks like this:

```
// psuedo C# generated from IL
class ObjRef
```

```
    : IObjectReference, ISerializable
{
    public ObjRef();
    public virtual IChannelInfo ChannelInfo
    {get; set;}
    public virtual IEnvoyInfo EnvoyInfo
    {get; set;}
    public virtual IRemotingTypeInfo TypeInfo
    {get; set;}
    public virtual string URI
    {get; set;}
    public bool IsFromThisAppDomain();
    public bool IsFromThisProcess();
    // methods needed for ISerializable
    public ObjRef(SerializationInfo,
        StreamingContext);
    public void GetObjectData(
        SerializationInfo, StreamingContext);
    // method needed for IObjectReference
    public virtual object GetRealObject(
        StreamingContext);
}
```

The fact that some of these methods are virtual implies that you can extend ObjRef to hold custom marshaling data—yet another place where the remoting infrastructure is extensible.

As you can see, ObjRef contains a URI that uniquely locates the remote object. This URI is used to make the connection when the proxy object is created by unmarshaling the ObjRef with a call to RemotingServices.Unmarshal(). Connecting to a remote object requires more than just the URI; the remote connection goes through a channel object that transmits method requests as messages, and information about this channel is held in the ChannelInfo property. The EnvoyInfo property holds information about the envoy chain, which, as you learned earlier, is a representation of the server context. The proxy, of course, contains a transparent proxy that should look like the remote object, and metadata is needed for creation of the transparent-proxy object. This is the reason for the TypeInfo property.

3.3.4 Leases and Lifetime

The server has no knowledge of the lifetime of a client-activated object. The client could hold on to the object reference for a short time or a long time, or it could pass a reference to another object, meaning that the lifetime of the object is determined by two references. When the server creates the object, it does not know which of these situations is appropriate. To complicate things further, a remote object could be accessed over a network that could be unreliable, so what might appear as a long object lifetime could actually be a broken network link.

.NET solves this issue of lifetimes with *leases*. Each application domain has a lease manager that acts as the root for the lease and for remote objects as far as the garbage collector is concerned. Each remote object has a lease with an expiration time, and the lease manager has the responsibility of checking each lease to see if it has expired. It does this by maintaining a list of the leases in the order of the amount of time left. When a lease expires, the lease manager contacts the *sponsors* of the lease to see if they want to renew. If they do not want to renew, the lease manager releases its reference on the lease and the object, thus allowing the garbage collector to collect them. The time between each check performed by the lease manager is set with the static property `LifetimeServices.Lease-ManagerPollTime` (the default is 10 seconds).

There are several ways to set the lease time for an object. First, each application domain has default values for leases, which are set in the server by a call to the `LifetimeServices` object:

```
// C#
// set the default lease time to 60 seconds
LifetimeServices.LeaseTime = TimeSpan.FromSeconds(60);
```

When any client-activated object is created, the remoting infrastructure automatically creates a lease for it using this default value.

An object can also set its own lease time: All client-activated objects must derive from `MarshalByRefObject`, which has a method called `GetLifetimeService()` that will return the lease for the object. To specify the lease time, you should override this method, call the base implementation to get the lease object, and set the timeout values. Lease objects can be in one of five states, which are listed in Table 3.4.

The lease timeout value can be set only when the lease is in the `Initial` state:

```csharp
// C#
public class MyClass
    : MarshalByRefObject
{
    public override Object
        InitializeLifetimeService()
    {
        ILease lease = (ILease)base
                        .InitializeLifetimeService();
        if (lease.CurrentState
                == LeaseState.Initial)
        {
            lease.InitialLeaseTime
                = TimeSpan.FromSeconds(30);
        }
        return lease;
    }
    // other methods
}
```

Table 3.4 Values in the `LeaseState` enumeration

State	Meaning
Null	The lease has not been initialized.
Initial	The lease has been initialized but is not yet active.
Active	The lease is active.
Renewing	The lease has expired and is ready for renewal by a sponsor.
Expired	The lease has expired and cannot be renewed.

Another way to set these values is to use a remoting configuration file:

```
<system.runtime.remoting>
  <application>
    <lifetime leaseTime = "60S"/>
    <activated type = "MyClass,MyAssem">
      <lifetime leaseTime = "30S"/>
    </activated>
  </application>
</system.runtime.remoting>
```

Here I indicate that the lease time for `MyClass` is 30 seconds, and for all other objects the lease time is 60 seconds. The timeout value can be in seconds (`S`, as shown here), milliseconds (`MS`), minutes (`M`), hours (`H`), or days (`D`).

Finally, a client can explicitly renew a lease by accessing the lease object and calling the `Renew()` method. If the time passed to this method is less than `CurrentLeaseTime` for the lease, the call is ignored.

When the timeout expires, the lease manager contacts the sponsors of the lease to see if they want to renew. A sponsor is a separate object that implements `ISponsor`. It could be a remote object, which would mean that the lease manager would have to make a network call. There are two important issues here: First, the network may not be reliable, so the lease manager could use a timeout value to determine if the sponsor was accessible and if it wasn't, contact the next sponsor on the lease's sponsor list. Second, if the sponsor is remote, the application that hosts the sponsor must provide a channel to allow the lease manager to call back to the sponsor.

As you might imagine, there are several ways to set the sponsor timeout: You can use the default value set by `LifetimeServices.Sponsorship-Timeout` or by the property of the same name on the object's lease object, or you can set these values through the `sponsorshipTimeOut` attribute of the `<lifetime>` node in the remoting configuration file. If no sponsor can be contacted, the object with the lease will be garbage-collected.

The Framework Class Library supplies a class called `ClientSponsor` that you can use as is for a sponsor. As the name suggests, this class is intended to be used on the client side, as illustrated here:

```csharp
// C#
MyClass obj = new MyClass();
ILease lease = (ILease)RemotingServices
    .GetLifetimeService(obj);
lease.Register(
    new ClientSponsor(
        TimeSpan.FromMinutes(5)));
```

This code indicates that when the lease expires, the lease manager will call `ClientSponsor`, which will indicate that the lease should be extended to 5 minutes. Here the sponsor is running in the same application domain as the client. This is not a requirement; the sponsor could live on another machine—possibly one on the same subnet as the remote object to make the lease manager's access to the sponsor more reliable.

Using sponsors to keep a client-activated object alive means that the machine that has the sponsor is contacted only when the lease has expired. This is an improvement on the ping packet used by DCOM, but it still involves periodic network access, and it presents the developer with the dilemma of how big to make the lease time.

Another option is to assume that if a client calls the object, the network connection to the client still exists and therefore the lease should remain until the next client call. This option is called *renew on call,* and it works like this: When a client makes a call, the lease time is set to the value of the property `ILease.RenewOnCallTime` (or is left at its current value if the value of the `ILease.CurrentLeaseTime` property is greater).

In determining the value to use for `RenewOnCallTime`, the developer has to weigh keeping the object alive too long (if `RenewOnCallTime` is too big) against requiring renewal sponsor calls (if `RenewOnCallTime` is too small). As before, you can set a default value for `RenewOnCallTime` or specify a value for a specific class; in both cases you can do this programmatically or in a configuration file. If `RenewOnCallTime` is zero, renew on call will not be used.

3.3.5 Message Sinks and Channels

Objects are called through messages sent via channels. Messages package method requests through the transparent proxy, which passes the message to the `RealProxy` object through its `Invoke()` method. `RealProxy` passes the message to the remote object via the channel, and in the process the message passes through message sinks, which are extensibility points. This process is illustrated in Figure 3.8.

In effect, the transparent proxy serializes the stack resulting from the client call to a message object, and this stack is passed to the first message sink, which processes the message and then passes it to the next message sink in the chain (obtained through `IMessageSink.NextSink`). On the server side, the final message sink in the chain is the stack builder that deserializes the message and constructs a stack frame to call the remote object.

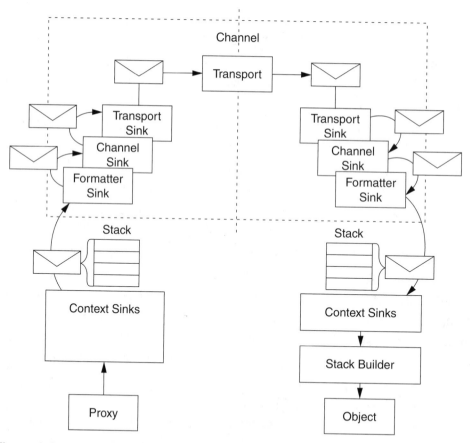

Figure 3.8   Calling a remote object through a channel

DEVELOPING APPLICATIONS WITH VISUAL STUDIO.NET

Message objects are passed from sink to sink as `IMessage` interface references, but they support other interfaces as well, depending on the type of message and how it is called. The standard message interfaces are listed in Table 3.5.

Information can be added to a message through a message sink, which implements the `IMessageSink` interface. Each sink object has a reference to the next sink in the chain, so it can perform its manipulation of the message—or another action—before passing the message to the next message sink. Sink objects pass messages by calling `IMessageSink.SyncProcessMessage()` for synchronous calls and `AsyncProcessMessage()` for asynchronous calls. On the client side, the *first* sink must implement `IClientFormatterSink` (a conglomeration of `IMessageSink` and `IClientChannelSink`), which takes incoming messages and converts them into streams. The last sink before the channel is the *transport sink*. .NET allows you to add your own code between the first message sink and the transport sink.

Channels and their sinks have to be registered before they can be used. As I described earlier, channels can be registered through either `ChannelServices.RegisterChannel()` or a configuration file passed to `RemotingConfiguration.Configure()`:

Table 3.5 Standard message interfaces

Interface	Description
IMessage	Basic standard message interface
IConstructionCallMessage	Interface implemented by a message that makes the activation request for an object
IConstructionReturnMessage	Interface implemented by a message that is returned after an activation request
IMethodCallMessage	Interface implemented by messages that are used for method calls, and to pass arguments that are passed to the remote object
IMethodReturnMessage	Interface implemented by messages that return results from method calls

```
<configuration>
    <system.runtime.remoting>
        <application name="Server">
            <channels>
                <channel
                    type="System.Runtime.Remoting
                        .Channels.Tcp.TcpChannel,
                        System.Runtime.Remoting"
                    port="4000" />
            </channels>
        </application>
    </system.runtime.remoting>
</configuration>
```

This file indicates that the TCP transport protocol will be used. The `TcpChannel` class implements the `IChannelReceiver` interface, so it has methods to control the listening of the channel object. This channel object will listen for messages from the client. At the client end, a TCP channel object will implement the `IChannelSender` interface, which has methods for creating the message sink chain. Channel sinks and formatters can also be registered through the configuration file:

```
<channel type="System.Runtime.Remoting
            .Channels.Tcp.TcpChannel,
            System.Runtime.Remoting"
        port="4000">
    <serverProviders>
        <formatter
          type="System.Runtime.Remoting.Channels.
              SoapServerFormatterSinkProvider,
              System.Runtime.Remoting">
            <properties TypeFormat="TypesAlways"
                    AssemblyFormat="Simple"/>
        </formatter>
        <provider
          type="MyChannelSinkProvider,
              MyChannelSinks" />
    </serverProviders>
</channel>
```

Sinks are configured through *properties*, which can be applied as child nodes to the sinks in the configuration file. The names of these properties are

DEVELOPING APPLICATIONS WITH VISUAL STUDIO.NET

the properties of the formatter class. In the preceding example I indicate that the formatted stream will contain descriptions of the types of all objects that are serialized and that the name of the assembly will be the simple name (as opposed to the full assembly name).

The classes that you mention in the `<serverProviders>` and `<client-Providers>` nodes are not the actual sink classes; they are classes used to create providers. The server sink providers (both formatters and providers) implement `IServerChannelSinkProvider`, while the client sink providers implement `IClientChannelSinkProvider`. Both of these interfaces have a method called `CreateSink()` that is called by the runtime to create the sink.

3.3.6 Channels

The Framework Class Library contains two channel classes: `HttpChannel` and `TcpChannel` (both client and server versions). The channels implement `IChannel` and either `IChannelReceiver` or `IChannelSender`. When a remote object is activated, a sink capable of communicating with the remote object is retrieved from the channel by a call to `IChannelSender.Create-MessageSink()`. This sink implements `IMessageSink`, which is called by the remoting infrastructure to perform synchronous (`SyncProcessMessage()`) or asynchronous (`AsyncProcessMessage()`) calls. These methods handle the message as appropriate before passing it to the next sink in the chain.

3.3.7 Extending the Remoting Framework

.NET remoting has been built with extensibility in mind. On the server side you can customize the `ObjRef` object (the distributed, serialized representation of the object), as well as the message sinks, channel sinks, formatters, and the channel itself (see Figure 3.9).

A custom channel implements `IChannelReceiver`, which is called by the runtime to start listening on the custom channel (`StartListening()`) and then to stop listening (`StopListening()`). The channel should listen for client connections, and when a connection is made, handle the request. In addition, the receiver channel should provide access to its properties so that the runtime

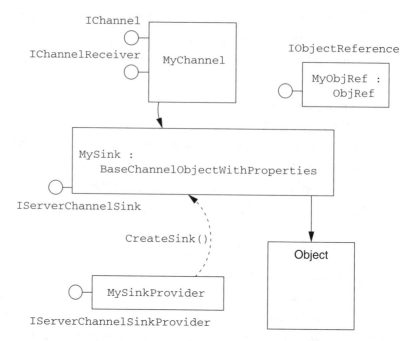

Figure 3.9 Extensibility points on the server side

can query and set property values. To do this the channel must implement the `IDictionary` interface. To help, the Framework Class Library provides `BaseChannelWithProperties`, which has a basic dictionary implementation.

On the client side you can customize the proxy, message sinks, channel sinks, formatters, and the channel itself (see Figure 3.10). As with a receiver channel, the sender channel needs to give access to its properties, so you can use `BaseChannelWithProperties` to get a basic implementation. In addition, you have to provide an implementation of `CreateMessageSink()`. This method is called by the framework when the client attempts to activate the object. The object that is created will have a URI, and this and the message sink are returned from `CreateMessageSink()`.

Channel sink providers should have constructors with two parameters: an instance of `IDictionary` that has the attributes of the provider tag in the configuration file, and an instance of `ICollection` that contains the information added through property child notes for the provider in the configuration file.

DEVELOPING APPLICATIONS WITH VISUAL STUDIO.NET

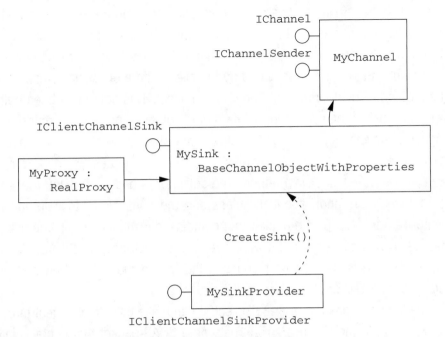

Figure 3.10 Extensibility points on the client side

3.3.8 SOAP

`HttpChannel` uses the SOAP formatter by default. It is interesting to use a tool like Network Monitor to sniff the packets being passed when requests are made to activate and call remote objects. Here is a simple class:

```
// C#
public class MyClass
    : MarshalByRefObject
{
    int x;
    public MyClass(int i){ x = i; }
    public string CallYou(int i)
    {
        return "you called me with "
            + i.ToString()
            + " and I have "
            + x.ToString();
    }
}
```

This class has a single constructor that takes one parameter, and one other method that returns a string based on the parameter passed to the constructor and the parameter passed to the method. Figure 3.11 shows the messages that are sent when the object is activated by the client with a constructor parameter and a method is invoked through the HTTP channel. This figure has been edited to remove most of the superfluous data that is not relevant to this discussion.

When the client makes a call to activate the object, the call goes through a service called `RemoteActivationService`, and a request is made for the `IActivator.Activate()` method. The activator is passed a SOAP message that contains information about the class and the constructor to call, and the activator returns a response packet that contains information about whether the construction was successful. If it was, it returns an instance of `ObjRef`. Among other things, the `ObjRef` object contains the URI to the object that was activated (this is a GUID; in the figure I call it `uri`).

Once the client has the `ObjRef` object, it can make calls to the client through POST requests to the URI in `ObjRef`, passing a SOAP packet that contains information about the method and any parameters it has. Because the URI in `ObjRef` uniquely identifies the object on the server, the request will go to the specific object; the `OBJREF` structure behaves as the distributed identity of the object.

3.3.9 Security

Remote objects present a whole series of security problems. Imagine the possible calls. A client activates an object on a remote machine through a remoting channel: Is the client authorized to make the connection through the channel? to configure the channel? to activate the object? The client then makes a call on the client: Is it authorized to call the specific method on the object? The client may make a call that involves code in an assembly that is downloaded from another machine: Should the object allow that code to run? Let's look at how security is managed in the remoting situation.

You could argue that a remoting channel is a "hole" through which external code can access your machine. Therefore, it is very important that that hole be carefully regulated and that security be enforced to prevent entry by an attacker. If you decide to download and execute code from a Web site, how can you be

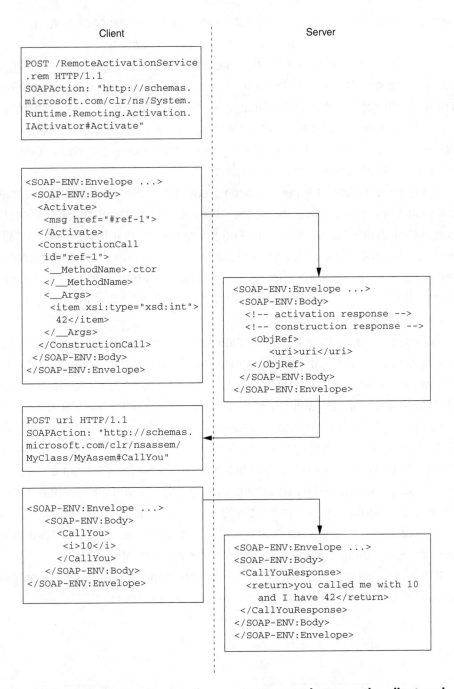

Client   Server

```
POST /RemoteActivationService
.rem HTTP/1.1
SOAPAction: "http://schemas.
microsoft.com/clr/ns/System.
Runtime.Remoting.Activation.
IActivator#Activate"
```

```
<SOAP-ENV:Envelope ...>
 <SOAP-ENV:Body>
  <Activate>
   <msg href="#ref-1">
  </Activate>
  <ConstructionCall
   id="ref-1">
   <__MethodName>.ctor
   </__MethodName>
   <__Args>
    <item xsi:type="xsd:int">
     42</item>
   </__Args>
  </ConstructionCall>
 </SOAP-ENV:Body>
</SOAP-ENV:Envelope>
```

```
<SOAP-ENV:Envelope ...>
 <SOAP-ENV:Body>
  <!-- activation response -->
  <!-- construction response -->
   <ObjRef>
    <uri>uri</uri>
   </ObjRef>
 </SOAP-ENV:Body>
</SOAP-ENV:Envelope>
```

```
POST uri HTTP/1.1
SOAPAction: "http://schemas.
microsoft.com/clr/nsassem/
MyClass/MyAssem#CallYou"
```

```
<SOAP-ENV:Envelope ...>
   <SOAP-ENV:Body>
    <CallYou>
     <i>10</i>
    </CallYou>
   </SOAP-ENV:Body>
</SOAP-ENV:Envelope>
```

```
<SOAP-ENV:Envelope ...>
 <SOAP-ENV:Body>
  <CallYouResponse>
   <return>you called me with 10
    and I have 42</return>
  </CallYouResponse>
 </SOAP-ENV:Body>
</SOAP-ENV:Envelope>
```

Figure 3.11 Schematic showing the messages sent between the client and server during a remote client activation and method call

guaranteed that the code will not create a remoting channel back to its Web site and transmit your data? The answer is *code access security.*

The framework class libraries that are involved in setting up and configuring remoting channels (`RemotingConfiguration`, `ChannelServices`, `Context`) all make code access checks. In effect, code that has full trust on your machine or on your local intranet has permission to configure only channels and remote types, whereas only code that is fully trusted by the entire system can add code to the channel, message, and context sink chains.

Once the remoting channel has been created, the client will attempt to make activation calls, which travel along the channel. The channel should be secure enough that the call is not hijacked. And if you decide that the activation call is sensitive, you should take steps to ensure that eavesdroppers cannot determine what calls you are making. To enforce these security measures, you have several choices: To ensure that a call is not hijacked, you will want to use authentication and possibly a message digest.

The simplest way to apply authentication is to use `HttpChannel` because this class uses IIS, which can be configured to use authentication. If you use Windows authentication in IIS, your code will be able to access the identity of the authenticated client, as I will show in a moment. `HttpChannel` also supports access through the Secure Sockets Layer (SSL), but of course this means that IIS must have an installed certificate. With the `TcpChannel` class you can use Internet Protocol Security (IPSec) to protect the channel. IPSec can be used for authentication, which can be based on a certificate, or you can configure IPSec to use a preshared key or the Kerberos authentication protocol.[5] A preshared key is considered less secure than a certificate, but it has the advantage that it does not need you to purchase and administer a certificate.

If you use Windows authentication in IIS, your code will access the identity of the authenticated client through a `WindowsIdentity` object:

```
// C#
WindowsIdentity client;
```

---

5. Kerberos, of course, will work only with machines that use this method of authentication, so machines running Windows NT 4.0 and Windows 9x are excluded.

```
client = WindowsIdentity.GetCurrent();
Console.WriteLine("The client is "
    + client.Name);
```

`WindowsIdentity` allows you to perform checks during a method call to determine the identity of the client and decide the actions that the client is allowed to perform. This class also has properties that allow you to determine if the client is authenticated and, if so, what authentication was used. You can also find out whether the client is anonymous, a guest, or the system account, and you can impersonate the client's identity.

Of course, .NET remoting allows you to add sinks into extensibility points, so you can design your own custom sinks that encrypt the contents of the message when it is being sent with sensitive data and decrypt the data when a message is received from the server. If you use `TcpChannel` and do not have access to IPSec, this is the only way to encrypt the contents of the channel packets.

3.4 Web Services

Web Services are a protocol for providing access to code on a server machine. Web Services are not a .NET innovation; indeed, they are not even a Microsoft-specific protocol. They use a well-defined protocol, and in essence any platform that has (1) an HTTP server that can take custom HTTP headers and (2) an XML parser can provide a Web Service. Web Services are the solution to the arguments over distribution technologies that have been raging in the last few years. They have the potential of being the de facto standard simply because they are *not* a proprietary solution.[6]

Visual Studio.NET has two solutions for Web Services—one managed and the other unmanaged. The managed version uses ASP.NET; the unmanaged version is called ATL Server.

3.4.1 Architecture

Web Services rely on a protocol that can take a payload to the service that will then perform the action and return results to the client. Inclusion of the word

---

6. You would not believe the number of conversations I have had with people who refuse to use DCOM simply because it is produced by Microsoft. Such vehemently anti-Microsoft people refuse to accept DCOM even when it is described as a DCE protocol (which is more than partially true).

Web implies that the protocol should assume that the network is inherently unreliable and thus should not rely on a long-lived client/server connection. Of course, the Web has a protocol designed for such a situation: HTTP. What's more, this protocol is implemented by all servers on the Web. HTTP is typically used to access static HTML pages and Web applications through GET and POST requests. However, the protocol can be extended by the addition of extra headers, and an HTTP server extension can check for specific headers and act on them. For example, here is a POST request made to a Web Service as an extension to IIS:

```
POST /TimeService/TimeService.dll?
   Handler=Default HTTP/1.1
Content-Length: 384
Content-Type: text/xml
SOAPAction: "#GetTime"
Accept: text/xml
Host: mars
User-Agent: Microsoft-ATL-Native/7.00
```

This request calls a Web Service called TimeService on a machine called mars. The service has a method called GetTime(), which is invoked through an HTTP header called SOAPAction. The user agent given in this packet—Microsoft-ATL-Native/7.00—is interesting. This is the ActiveX Template Library (ATL) Server SOAP client code generated by the sproxy tool, but as you can see, this code is native x86 code; that is, it is *not* .NET code. This example illustrates again that Web Services are *not* a .NET technology, but are available to all platforms.

The Web Service illustrated in the following code executes the requested method and packages the results as a SOAP packet. Here the GetTime() method returns a string containing the time:

```
<soap:Envelope
  xmlns:soap="http://schemas.xmlsoap.org/soap/envelope/"
    xmlns:xsi="http://www.w3.org/2001/XMLSchema-instance"
    xmlns:xsd="http://www.w3.org/2001/XMLSchema"
    xmlns:soapenc="http://schemas.xmlsoap.org/soap/encoding/">
   <soap:Body
    soap:encodingStyle=
```

```
     "http://schemas.xmlsoap.org/soap/encoding/">
     <snp:GetTime
      xmlns:snp="urn:TimeService">
        <return>01/10/27 20:14:53</return>
     </snp:GetTime>
   </soap:Body>
 </soap:Envelope>
```

This code uses documentation from the XML Schema Definition (XSD); I'll come back to this later. It is interesting to compare this packet with the packets generated for client-activated objects via .NET remoting: First, client-activated objects live on the server after a method call is made, so they have a distributed identity represented through an `ObjRef` object (essentially, although not exclusively, containing a URI for the object). Second, .NET remoting distributes the context of the object, to allow for any special handling of this context in the client application.

Web Services do not allow you to have a reference to an object on another machine, so there is no need to have a distributed identity. If a Web Service method returns an object, the state of the object is returned. For managed Web Services the state is the data in the public fields of the class, and the class does not have to be serializable because the returned object merely acts as a repository of data and has no functionality. The client code that accepts the SOAP packet may take the data and use it to initialize a client-side object.

In addition to handling Web Service requests, each Web Service should provide a description of itself so that tools can query it to see which methods it supports and the descriptions of those methods. There is a standard XML-based type description language called Web Services Description Language (WSDL) that your Web Service can use to describe itself. ATL Server Web Services expose an additional handler to return the WSDL for the Web Service. (This is why, in the earlier example, the Web Service is called through the `Default` handler—i.e., to distinguish it from the handler that generates WSDL.) ASP.NET Web Services generate WSDL when you call them and pass `WSDL` as a query string, as I'll explain later.

Of course, you need to know the address of a Web Service before you can call it, so Web Services provide a mechanism to allow you to publish the Web

Services that are available on a server, through files called *discovery* (or *disco*) *files*. A discovery file is an XML file that lists information about implemented Web Services—for example:

```
<?xml version="1.0" encoding="utf-8"?>
<discovery
 xmlns:xsi="http://www.w3.org/2001/XMLSchema-instance"
 xmlns:xsd="http://www.w3.org/2001/XMLSchema"
    xmlns="http://schemas.xmlsoap.org/disco/">
  <contractRef
   ref="http://myserver/TimeService
        /TimeService.dll?Handler
        =GenTimeServiceWSDL"
   docRef="http://myserver/TimeService
        /TimeService.htm"
   xmlns="http://schemas.xmlsoap.org/disco/scl/" />
</discovery>
```

This file indicates that there is a single Web Service with a summary HTML page and shows how to generate the complete WSDL for the Web Service. You can use the `Disco` tool to query a particular server for the Web Services that it supports. The tool will extract information from the discovery file, including the WSDL for all the exposed Web Services, which you can pass to the `WSDL` tool to generate a managed client, or to the `Sproxy` tool to generate an unmanaged client that talks to the Web Service.

If you know that a particular server exposes its Web Services through discovery files, the `Disco` tool is useful. But what happens if you have to use a Web Service with a particular desired functionality but you do not know where such a Web Service is installed, or indeed, whether such a service exists? You need a tool that will allow service providers to publish their services in a form that you can search. Such a facility exists, and it is called *Universal Description, Discovery and Integration (UDDI)*. UDDI is a publicly available Web Service that you can query for services by providing the criteria that interest you (see Figure 3.12). You can get more information about UDDI at *www.uddi.org*.

Web Services are loosely coupled and stateless. They are loosely coupled in the respect that requests are self-describing, so the client and service do not have to be developed in tandem. Indeed, the Web Service developer does not need to

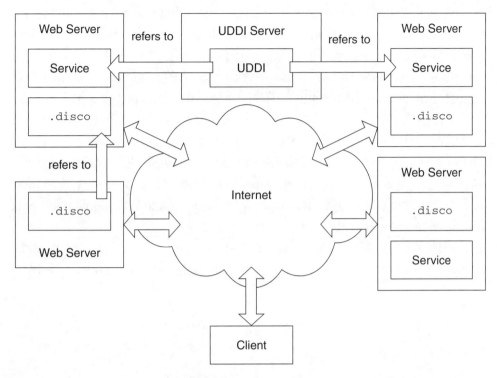

Figure 3.12 Schematic showing how to get information about Web Services. Individual Web servers can publish the services they expose through a .disco file, and they can publish services on other machines. Publicly available UDDI servers have information about Web Services.

have any knowledge about the clients that will use the service. They are stateless because the requests are not necessarily made to objects using session state; in this respect they behave like .NET remoting singleton objects. It is possible to hold session state as long as the Web Service has access to some persistent storage, as well as a mechanism to pass session information to the client. Managed Web Services can hold session state through ASP.NET session management, and ATL Server Web Services can use ATL session state management.

3.4.2 Managed Web Services

Managed Web Services are provided by the ASP.NET extension to IIS. But don't worry, doing Web Service development does not make you an ASP developer because you do not have to do it by writing scripts and you are not constrained to scripting languages (as was the case with unmanaged ASP), nor are you denied C++ (as is the case with developing pages with ASP.NET).

Figure 3.13 shows a schematic of ASP.NET: IIS processes HTTP requests, which may be for static HTML pages, dynamic pages generated by ASP.NET, or SOAP requests for Web Services or remote objects. IIS runs in the native world and handles ASP.NET requests through a native code ISAPI called `aspnet_isapi.dll`. This ISAPI talks to the ASP.NET worker process (`aspnet_wp.exe`) via a named pipe. The worker process is a native process that hosts the .NET Runtime, which loads each Web application and Web Service in a separate application domain.

ASP.NET uses a mixture of script and compiled code. The script code resides between `<%@` and `%>` tags in a similar fashion to ASP code. When the

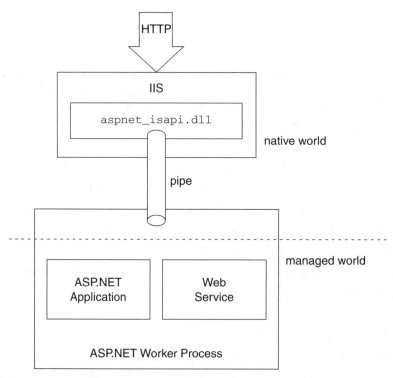

Figure 3.13 Architectural overview of ASP.NET

page is first loaded, the ASP ISAPI compiles the script page and caches the generated assembly so that subsequent calls to the same page will use the compiled version. The script page has the extension `.asmx`.

There is an inherent weakness in this scheme: Any errors in the script will appear only after the script has been deployed. As mentioned in Chapter 1, ASP.NET solves this problem with *code-behind*, which allows you to split the presentation tags of the page from the code that will generate presentation data dynamically. The code can be placed in a separate file and compiled into an assembly before the application is deployed. You can then indicate in the `.asmx` file that the page inherits from the class in your compiled assembly so that now when the page is first accessed, ASP.NET will compile the script and derive it from the class that you indicate. The code that you provide in this separate assembly is called *code-behind*.

ASP.NET Web Services use this code-behind concept, too, in that you provide an `.asmx` file identifying the assembly that contains the actual Web Service code. For example, here is a script *without* code-behind:

```
<%@ WebService Language="C#"
    Class="MyServices.TimeService" %>
using System;
using System.Web.Services;
namespace MyServices
{
    [WebService(Namespace
        ="http://myserver.com/TimeServer")]
    public class TimeService
    {
        [WebMethod]
        public string GetTime()
        {
            return DateTime.Now.ToString();
        }
    }
}
```

This script code gives a class that returns the current time through the Web method `GetTime()`. When the class is accessed with a URL like this:

```
http://myserver.com/TimeService/TimeServer.asmx
```

the ASP.NET ISAPI will compile the `.asmx` file using the compiler indicated by the `Language` attribute. Note that with Visual Studio.NET, the languages you can use are C#, VB.NET, and JavaScript. You *cannot* mix languages in `.asmx` files, and you *cannot* use managed C++.

The `[WebService]` attribute provides the default namespace that is used in the generated WSDL files, as you'll see later. The `[WebMethod]` attribute indicates the particular method that will be exposed through the Web Service. If you put the code in a separate source file, you can compile the file to a library assembly and use this as code-behind. In this case the `.asmx` file looks like this:

```
<%@ WebService Class="MyServices.TimeService" %>
```

That's it. The ASP.NET ISAPI will look for the assembly in a directory called `bin` that is a child of the directory containing the `.asmx` file. The extra step of compiling an assembly gives you the added bonus of getting the compiler to check the code at compile time, rather than when the code is first accessed. It also gives you the ability to use code written in C++ because the code has already been compiled, so the script compiler does not care what language was used to create the assembly.

Your Web Service assembly does not have to concern itself with the code to interpret the request packets, nor does it need to format its returned data into XML. All of this is done by the ISAPI, and all your Web Service class should do is implement the actual Web Service methods. Because your Web Service assembly has metadata, the ISAPI can determine if the Web method is supported and, if so, call it with the parameters from the request packet. In addition, the metadata in a Web Service allows the ISAPI extension to generate WSDL for the Web Service.

As long as the Web method has parameters that are primitive types, the ASP.NET ISAPI provides access to the Web Service through HTTP GET and POST, as well as SOAP. In addition, the ASP.NET ISAPI generates WSDL from the metadata in the assembly. For example, using the Web Service I showed earlier, you can invoke the Web Service method `GetTime()` using HTTP GET with the following URL:

```
http://myserver.com/TimeService/TimeServer.asmx/GetTime
```

Each Web method is provided in this way. Because the `GetTime()` method takes no parameters, the URL merely has the method name. If the method takes parameters, they should be passed to the Web Service via a GET query string. So if the `TimeServer` class has the following method:

```
// C#
[WebMethod]
public string GetTimeF(string format)
{
    return DateTime.Now.ToString(format);
}
```

it can be invoked with this URL:

```
http://myserver.com/TimeService
    /TimeServer.asmx/GetTimeF?format=dd-MM-yy
```

The ASP.NET ISAPI also provides information about the Web Service. To get the WSDL for the Web Service, you pass WSDL as a query string to the `.asmx` file:

```
http://myserver.com/TimeService/TimeServer.asmx?WSDL
```

You can get information about an individual Web method through the query string parameter `op`:

```
http://myserver.com/TimeService/TimeServer.asmx?op=GetTimeF
```

This URL will generate a Web page that describes the method and gives you a form to invoke the method through HTTP GET. It will also document how to call the method through SOAP and HTTP GET and POST.

3.4.3 SOAP Invocation

Before going into details about how Web Services are accessed, I will make some comments about SOAP.

As I have already shown, Web Services can be accessed through SOAP requests (they can also be accessed through HTTP GET and POST requests). The SOAP packet packages the request in XML, which makes SOAP packets self-describing. However, the SOAP specification is not prescriptive about the encoding used in these XML documents, and .NET supports two versions, which it calls *Literal* and *Encoded.* The former follows an XSD schema; the latter follows the guidelines in the SOAP specification. The SOAP specification allows for methods to be invoked either according to an XSD schema (which .NET refers to as *Document style*) or according to the guidelines in the SOAP specification (which .NET refers to as *RPC style*). In both cases all parameters of a method have a named element wrapped in a single element that is named after the method.

Web Services implemented by ASP.NET will use the XSD schema by default (Literal parameters, Document methods). You can change this specification on a method-by-method basis using either `[SoapRpcMethod]` or `[SoapDocumentMethod]`, or for the Web Service as a whole using the `[SoapRpcService]` or `[SoapDocumentService]` attribute. The Document (XSD) style supports both Literal and Encoded parameter encoding, and this support can be expressed as a named parameter called `Use` passed to the `SoapDocument*` attributes. The RPC style supports only Encoded, so the associated attributes do not have a `Use` parameter.

Your Web Service client must be written to use the appropriate method invocation type and parameter encoding. I'll show an example in the next section.

3.4.4 Web Service Clients

The WSDL for a Web Service allows you to write client code to access the Web Service programmatically. Of course, such client code is essentially boilerplate, so the .NET SDK provides a tool called `WSDL` to generate the code for you:

```
wsdl http://myserver.com/TimeService/TimeServer.asmx?WSDL
```

When you run this command from the command line, the tool will use the WSDL data returned to generate a C# file with a class to access the Web Service. I have used the default values here. You can use command-line switches to change the language of the code that will be generated, the protocol used to access the service, and information about how to access the server. The following is an edited version of the class that `WSDL` will generate from the command I've given here (I have omitted the method's implementation):

```csharp
// C#
public class TimeService
    : SoapHttpClientProtocol
{
    public TimeService();
    [SoapDocumentMethod(
        "http://myserver.com/TimeServer/GetTime",
        RequestNamespace="http://myserver.com/TimeServer",
        ResponseNamespace="http://myserver.com/TimeServer",
        Use=SoapBindingUse.Literal,
        ParameterStyle=SoapParameterStyle.Wrapped)]
    public string GetTime();
    public IAsyncResult BeginGetTime(
        AsyncCallback callback,
        object asyncState);
    public string EndGetTime(
        IAsyncResult asyncResult);
}
```

The `SoapHttpClientProtocol` class allows you to access a Web Service through SOAP. It has members to invoke methods synchronously or asynchronously, and the `WSDL` tool creates wrapper classes that call these methods—for example:

```csharp
// C#
[SoapDocumentMethod(
    "http://myserver.com/TimeServer/GetTime",
    RequestNamespace="http://myserver.com/TimeServer",
    ResponseNamespace="http://myserver.com/TimeServer",
    Use=SoapBindingUse.Literal,
    ParameterStyle=SoapParameterStyle.Wrapped)]
public string GetTime()
{
    object[] results;
    results = this.Invoke(
        "GetTime", new object[0]);
    return ((string)(results[0]));
}
```

The WSDL will document the type of encoding that should be used for the SOAP body for method invocation and parameter encoding. Your Web Service client must be written to use the appropriate encoding, and this is done by

[SoapRpcMethod] or [SoapDocumentMethod] for individual methods, and by [SoapRpcService] or [SoapDocumentService] for the service as a whole. The example shown here indicates that GetTime() should be invoked by an XSD schema, and the parameters are wrapped in a single element.

3.4.5 ASP.NET Services

ASP.NET will implement all that is needed to accept requests and encode the returned data. All your Web Service class needs to do is implement the methods and mark them with [WebMethod]. However, your Web Service may want to use some of the facilities of ASP.NET; it should be derived from System.Web.Services.WebService.

I mentioned earlier that as they stand, Web Services are essentially stateless. Through the WebService class, however, you can have application and session state; application state is maintained across all sessions. These state services are accessed through the Application and Session properties. The session state can be configured by the <sessionState> element in the web.config file for the service.

By default, ASP.NET uses cookies to identify which requests belong to a particular session. If the client does not allow cookies, a session can be tracked by the addition of a session identifier to the URL, which requires that the cookieless element be set to true. In addition, you can use the mode element to configure how a session is stored—in SQL Server, on a remote server, or held in memory. If the session is stored in SQL Server, you have to specify a sqlConnectionString node so that the session can access the database. If you are using a remote server, you need to supply a connectionString node that provides the address and port of the server.

If the Web Service is configured with IIS to support authentication, and authentication is also enabled by the web.config file for the service (see the next section), then you can access the client principal through the User property. The Server property is an instance of the HttpServerUtility class that provides utility methods to encode and decode pages and URLs, create COM objects, and forward execution to other pages.

All of the properties I have mentioned are part of the HTTP context for the request and can be accessed through the Context property.

3.4.6 Web Services and Security

The whole point of a Web Service is to expose functionality to the Web. However, you may decide to allow only specific users to use your server, or you may decide that you want to audit who uses the service so that you can charge for the usage. Managed Web Services allow you to access authentication and authorization. The more important of these two facilities is authentication because without the ability to confirm who a client is, there is no point in determining whether that user is authorized to perform a particular action. Indeed, authentication implies that the identity of a client is known and available, so you can even perform your own authorization scheme.

Even after a client has passed the initial authentication/authorization checks to see if it is allowed access to the Web Service, the security does not stop. .NET code access security still applies.

To enable authentication, you first have to configure IIS to support it. Figure 3.14 shows how to do this: First disable the default, which is to enable anonymous access, and then decide the type of authentication to use: basic, digest (for a domain controller), or Windows authentication. In the figure I have decided to use integrated Windows authentication.

After IIS has been configured, you have to configure the Web Service through its `web.config` file. Two sections are relevant here: `<authentication>` and `<authorization>`. Here is an example of the first:

```xml
<?xml version="1.0" encoding="utf-8" ?>
<configuration>
   <system.web>
      <authentication mode="Windows"/>
   </system.web>
</configuration>
```

This file indicates that the Web Service will use integrated Windows security. IIS can use basic, digest, or Windows (NT Lan Manager [NTLM]) authentication set in the **Authentication Methods** page in IIS. Be very careful when writing the configuration file; the value of the `mode` attribute is case sensitive, so `Windows` (capitalized) is fine, but `windows` (all lowercase) is not. .NET then has the authenticated identity and will use this identity when accessing secured

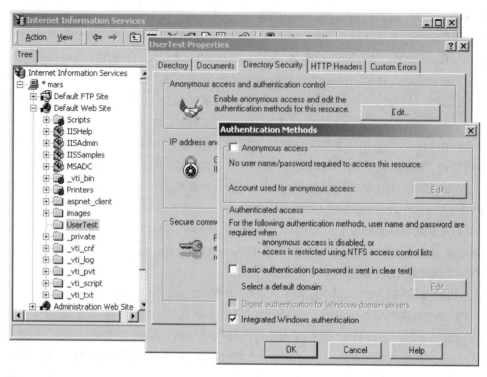

Figure 3.14   Configuring authentication for IIS

resources (e.g., files). If the application allows anonymous access, the `IUSER_<MachineName>` account (where `<MachineName>` is the name of the machine) will be used.

If you choose, you can impersonate another identity, and this identity will be used when NT File System (NTFS) ACL checks are performed to determine whether the authenticated client can access a particular resource. To indicate whether you are using impersonation, you should provide the `<identity>` tag with the `impersonate` attribute set to `true`, as well as `name` and `password` attributes to give details about the account you are impersonating. Here is an example:

```
<identity impersonate="true"
          name="mars\Richard"
          password="secret">
```

DEVELOPING APPLICATIONS WITH VISUAL STUDIO.NET

The `<authorization>` tag allows you to list the authenticated accounts that are allowed access to the Web Service or denied access. The authorization status is indicated by the `<allow>` and `<deny>` elements, as illustrated here:

```
<authorization>
    <allow users="mars\Richard"/>
    <deny users="*"/>
</authorization>
```

This authorization allows access only to the domain account `mars\Richard`; the special account `*` means all users (you can also use the special account `?` to represent anonymous users). These values refer to all access to the Web Service, but you can use the `verb` attribute to indicate the specific access method (e.g., `GET` or `POST`) that the authorization applies to.

The settings I have mentioned here apply to the folder where the file is installed and to all child folders. If you choose to use different settings for child folders, you can use the `<location>` element, which has a `path` attribute that indicates the subfolder to which the settings apply. Figure 3.15 illustrates this.

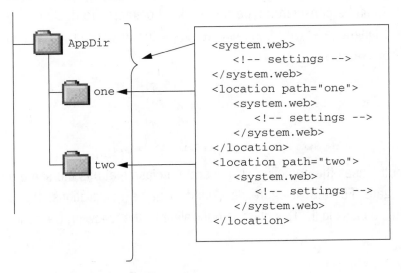

Figure 3.15 Configuration files and the `<location>` **tag**

3.5 Asynchronous Programming

By default, method calls are synchronous; that is, the code that calls a method blocks on the method call until the method has completed. Synchronous method calls suit most programming tasks, but they may not suit all cases. For example, if a thread makes a call to a complicated, lengthy algorithm, the thread will block and do no work. In another situation, if the thread calls a method on a remote object and then waits for the method to complete but the Web is particularly slow at the time, or the connection somewhere down the line breaks, what happens? With a synchronous call you have no way to make the call time out so that you have an opportunity to cancel it.

An asynchronous call is made on a different thread from the one that initiated the call. This means that the caller thread is free to do other work and is able to check periodically that the call has completed. The nice thing about asynchronous calls in .NET is that they are part of the design of the runtime. You do not have to write your classes specifically to be called asynchronously, and the caller code is straightforward.

3.5.1 Asynchronous Delegates

Asynchronous calls in .NET are based on delegates. Recall from Chapter 1 that delegates can be considered type-safe method pointers. To declare a delegate, you use a language keyword. In managed C++ this keyword is __delegate; in C#, it is delegate:

```
// C#
public delegate int DoAction(string msg);
```

```
// C++
public __delegate int DoAction(String* msg);
```

In both cases the compiler will generate a class that has the same name as the delegate. For the delegate described in these declarations, the compiler generates a class in IL. This class is equivalent to the following C# code:

```
// C#
public class DoAction
   : MulticastDelegate
{
```

```
    public DoAction(object, unsigned int);
    public virtual int Invoke(string);
    public virtual IAsyncResult BeginInvoke(
        string, AsyncCallback, object);
    public virtual int EndInvoke(IAsyncResult);
}
```

This class has synchronous (`Invoke()`) and asynchronous (`Begin-Invoke()` and `EndInvoke()`) methods for calling the method. You do not see the implementations of any of these methods; ILDASM does not show their contents. The compiler generates a `BeginInvoke()` method with the in parameters of the delegate (in this case the first parameter, `string`). `EndInvoke()` returns the results of the method.

The idea is this: The data that the method needs in order to start its work is passed in through parameters of `BeginInvoke()`, and the results of the method are returned by `EndInvoke()`. Using out and in/out parameters makes the situation a little more complicated, but the basic idea is the same.

An exception that is generated by a method called asynchronously is returned when the client calls `EndInvoke()` because in effect the exception is an out parameter. In any case the caller must place exception handling somewhere to catch the exceptions thrown by the method. The call to `Begin-Invoke()` is not a good place for exception handling because the method may take a long time to execute, and by the time the exception is thrown the caller thread may be executing other code outside of the `try` block.

Let's take a closer look at these asynchronous methods. When `Begin-Invoke()` is called, the runtime will create a new thread and call the delegate's method on this new thread. This means that the calling thread is not blocked and can do other work. When the method has completed, it must inform the caller, so interthread communication will be involved.

With that in mind, I will now discuss `IAsyncResult`. An object with this interface is returned from `BeginInvoke()`, and this reference is the last parameter of `EndInvoke()`. The interface looks like this:

```
// C#
public interface IAsyncResult
{
```

```
        object AsyncState {get;}
        WaitHandle AsyncWaitHandle {get;}
        bool CompletedSynchronously {get;}
        bool IsCompleted {get;}
}
```

The `IsCompleted` property is set to `true` when the method has completed, so this is one way that a client can test for completion of a method. Here is an example:

```
// C#
class Complicated
{
    public int LongMethod(string s)
    {
        int result = 0;
        /* do something complicated with result */
        return result;
    }
}
// use the class
Complicated x = new Complicated();
DoAction c = new DoAction(x.LongMethod);
IAsyncResult ar;
ar = c.BeginInvoke("data", null, null);
// do some work
// now poll for completion
while (!ar.IsCompleted) Thread.Sleep(0);
int i = c.EndInvoke(ar);
```

After the call to `BeginInvoke()`, the calling thread can do some other work while `LongMethod()` is executing. When the calling thread is available, it can check whether the method has completed by checking `IsCompleted`. In the `while` loop I call `Sleep(0)` while the method has not yet completed to allow another thread to perform its work (hopefully, the thread that is executing `LongMethod()`). This mechanism of polling for completion is quite efficient (the call to `Sleep()` ensures that the thread does not consume too many resources), but if your thread wants to do some work, there is a better mechanism to check for method completion.

`AsyncWaitHandle` is a synchronization object. When the method is executing, `AsyncWaitHandle` is nonsignaled, so a call to `AsyncWaitHandle.WaitOne()`

will block. When the method has completed, the synchronization object becomes signaled and `WaitOne()` will return. When `WaitOne()` blocks, the thread is put into an efficient wait state. However, it may not be convenient to wait indefinitely, so one overloaded version of `WaitOne()` takes a timeout in milliseconds, and another one takes a `TimeSpan` object. With either version you can allow your caller thread to wait a limited amount of time for completion. The code now looks like this:

```
// C#
Complicated x = new Complicated();
DoAction c = new DoAction(x.LongMethod);
IAsyncResult ar;
ar = c.BeginInvoke("data", null, null);
// do some work
// now wait for completion
ar.AsyncWaitHandle.WaitOne();
int i = c.EndInvoke(ar);
```

There is another way to handle method completion. `BeginInvoke()` for this delegate takes three parameters, and in general the last two parameters are (1) a delegate that will be called when the method has completed and (2) a state object. The delegate looks like this:

```
// C#
public delegate void
    AsyncCallback(IAsyncResult ar);
```

The parameter is the asynchronous call object that `BeginInvoke()` returned. When the asynchronous method completes, this delegate is called *on the thread that executed the asynchronous method*. It may seem obvious to finish the call by calling `EndInvoke()`, but there is a problem: How do you access the delegate that was called asynchronously? It turns out that `IAsync-Result` is the interface on a class called `AsyncResult`, which has a property that has the delegate. So now you can change your code to the following:

```
// C#
Complicated x = new Complicated();
DoAction c = new DoAction(x.LongMethod);
IAsyncResult ar;
ar = c.BeginInvoke(
        "data",
```

```
          new AsyncCallback(this.callback),
          null);
// do some work
```

The `callback()` method looks like this:

```csharp
// C#
void callback(IAsyncResult iar)
{
    AsyncResult ar = (AsyncResult)iar;
    DoAction d;
    d = (DoAction)ar.AsyncDelegate;
    int i = d.EndInvoke(iar);
}
```

Now the calling code does not have to concern itself with the result of the delegate call. It is handled by the `callback()` method. Of course, once `callback()` has gotten the result, it needs to do something with it. Here's one solution:

```csharp
// C#
class Results
{
    public int result;
    public void callback(IAsyncResult iar)
    {
        AsyncResult ar;
        ar = (AsyncResult)iar;
        DoAction d;
        d = (DoAction)ar.AsyncDelegate;
        result = d.EndInvoke(iar);
    }
}
```

The `Results` class is used like this:

```csharp
// C#
Complicated x = new Complicated();
DoAction c = new DoAction(x.LongMethod);
IAsyncResult ar;
Results ret = new Results();
ar = c.BeginInvoke("data",
    new AsyncCallback(ret.callback), null);
// do some work
if (ar.IsCompleted){ /* use ret.result */ }
```

If you want to supply the method with an object—maybe to help process the results, or maybe even to accept the results—you can pass the Results object as the final parameter to BeginInvoke(). This object is then accessible in the callback() method through IAsyncResult.AsyncState. Be careful what you do with this object because the code that allocates it (i.e., the code that calls BeginInvoke()) will be a different thread from the one that calls the callback, so you may need to use synchronization when reading data from this object and writing data to it.

3.5.2 Fire and Forget

Asynchronous delegates that do not return values allow you to perform fire-and-forget programming. In other words, your code needs to notify another object that something has happened, but your code does not want an acknowledgment that the notification has been successful. For example, here is a class used to log messages to a file:

```
// C#
class Logger
{
    private delegate void
        WriteDelegate(string s);
    private static void WriteString(string s)
    {
        TextWriter tw;
        tw = File.AppendText("log.txt");
        tw.Write(s + "\n");
        tw.Close();
    }
    public  static void Write(string s)
    {
        WriteDelegate d;
        d = new WriteDelegate(WriteString);
        d.BeginInvoke(s, null, null);
    }
}
```

This class has a single public method that a client will call to log a message to a file. It does this by creating a delegate and calling it asynchronously with

`BeginInvoke()` before returning immediately. Because `WriteString ()` is called asynchronously, it will be called on a different thread from the code that called `Logger.Write()`. Because the delegate returns no values, there is no point in checking if the delegate call has completed, so the `Write()` method returns without calling `EndInvoke()`.

When the delegate is called remotely, the remoting infrastructure will still set up the necessary sinks to accept the return from the method call. The infrastructure does this even if there is no return value and there are no `out` or `ref` parameters because the method could throw an exception, which would be treated as an implicit return value. The fire-and-forget pattern does not care about *any* return values from a method; indeed, it does not care if the call was successful. To indicate that you really do not want *any* return values, you can mark the method with the `[OneWay]` attribute, as illustrated here:

```
// C#
[OneWay]
private static void WriteString(string s)
{
    TextWriter tw;
    tw = File.AppendText("log.txt");
    tw.Write(s + "\n");
    tw.Close ();
}
```

Finally, a delegate that is called asynchronously must *not* be multicast. The reason, of course, is that there is no mechanism to identify the particular delegate of a multicast that an `EndInvoke()` call will refer to. Using `[OneWay ]` on the delegate method does not change this situation because the asynchronous infrastructure will set up sinks to make the call, and this sink chain will be specific to a particular target (a closer look at the problem makes this clear). If you have a multicast delegate and you wish to call the constituent delegates asynchronously, you should access each delegate individually by calling `Delegate.GetInvocationList()` and then call each delegate asynchronously. Here is an example with a multicast delegate called `d`:

```
// C#
Delegate[] list;
```

```
list = d.GetInvocationList();
foreach(Delegate del in list)
{
    writeDelegate writeDel;
    writeDel = (writeDelegate)del;
    writeDel.BeginInvoke(null, null);
}
```

3.5.3 Delegates and Remoting

By their nature, calls to remote objects take longer than calls within the application domain. They are therefore good candidates for calling asynchronously—for example:

```
// C#
// for this class:
// class MyClass { public string CallYou(); }
delegate string myClassDelegate();
RemotingConfiguration
    .RegisterActivatedClientType(
        typeof(MyClass),
        "tcp://TESTMACHINE:4000");
MyClass c = new MyClass();
myClassDelegate del;
del = new myClassDelegate(c.CallYou);
IAsyncResult ar;
ar = del.BeginInvoke(null, null);
// do some other work
ar.AsyncWaitHandle.WaitOne();
Console.WriteLine("results: ", del.EndInvoke(ar));
```

You can also pass a delegate to a remote object. The delegate itself is marshaled by value, but the method passed through the delegate should be on a marshal-by-reference object. If you do not use a marshal-by-reference object, when the delegate is called it will be called in the remote object's context, which is not necessarily what you want. Of course, for a callback to go to the client, the client must register a *server* channel to accept this call, as I mentioned earlier in this chapter.

3.6 Summary

Contexts are important to the execution of objects. Indeed, without the correct context an object cannot run. .NET provides a flexible framework not only for accessing an object's context, but also for *extending* it. Contexts can be extended across machines with .NET remoting, which is extremely flexible, providing many extensibility points where you can insert your own custom code. Because .NET remote components need .NET on both the client and server machines, these machines are tied to the .NET Framework. Not every machine on the Internet will have .NET, but .NET provides the facilities to write Web Service clients and servers—based on standard protocols—thereby enabling all machines on the Internet to interoperate.

Chapter 4

Interoperation and COM+

.NET is not an operating system, and Microsoft contends that it is not an extension of its operating systems.[1] This means that .NET must use the host operating system to perform its work; hence it needs to interoperate with the operating system's code.

Like other developers, you have code that you have written for your current applications, and you may have purchased libraries to help you do your work. These libraries consist of unmanaged code and typically are in the form of static libraries, DLLs, or COM objects. A new framework, even one as wide-ranging as .NET, will never be able to cover every aspect of programming, so libraries of tools are vitally important. Without a mechanism to use existing libraries, the only option is to port them or do without them, and if you do not have access to the library source code, you are at the mercy of the library vendor to port the library.

With interoperation you are more likely to get a ported version of a library than you are without it. A software house is unlikely to invest in the resources to port an existing library unless it is sure that the market will exist. If the framework has interoperation, developers will continue to develop with existing libraries, and the rise in the number of applications that use the framework will improve its popularity. A framework without interoperation will attract only the most devoted of developers with the resources to develop for an unproven technology. Interoperation is vitally important.

---

1. I only partially believe this because Fusion is an important part of .NET and performs tasks so similar to those of an operating system that it is provided as part of Windows XP/Windows Server.NET for use with unmanaged DLLs.

The good news is that .NET comes with a whole host of interoperation solutions for all developers and all languages. In this chapter I will cover three main forms of interoperation: It Just Works is provided for C++ developers; Platform Invoke and COM Interop are provided for all developers.

I have also decided to cover COM+ in this chapter. On the one hand COM+ fits in here because of its close association with COM. On the other hand, it is inappropriate because the implication may be that COM+ is a legacy technology and that you need to have a "bridging" technology to access COM+ code. This could not be farther from the truth. COM+ is the future of .NET because .NET is used to write *components* and COM+ provides *component* services. The argument that COM+ and COM are closely related is compelling, so I decided to keep COM+ in this chapter near to where I describe how to use COM objects in .NET.

4.1   Interoperation

Interoperation (commonly referred to as *interop*) allows you to access components written for platforms other than .NET from your .NET components. Before I continue, I need to distinguish among managed code, managed data, native code, and unmanaged data. When you compile C# code (or VB.NET code for that matter), you will get IL code. The code will be intermediate language—that is, JIT-compiled by the runtime—and the instances of your types will be managed by the garbage collector. When you compile C++ code with the `/clr` switch, *most* of the code will compile to IL. The types marked with `__gc` or `__value` will be compiled to IL code and will be managed by the garbage collector; types marked with `__nogc` (or without a modifier) will be compiled to IL but will be unmanaged; and finally, types linked in from static libraries will be native and hence unmanaged. C++ is the only language that allows you to mix managed and unmanaged types, IL, and native code. (I will go into more details about managed C++ in Chapter 7.)

Of course, C++ is not the only language that is allowed access to native code. C# and even VB.NET can also access native code, as long as that code is packaged in a DLL or a COM object. .NET provides all the facilities you need. In the following sections I will look at each of the various interop technologies and explain how to use them.

DEVELOPING APPLICATIONS WITH VISUAL STUDIO.NET

4.1.1 Interop with Native Code

The C++ compiler allows you to call native code linked in from static libraries—for example, as follows:

```
// C++ compiled with /clr
#using <mscorlib.dll>
#include <stdio.h>
class Hello
{
public:
    int x;
    void SayHello(){ puts("hello"); }
};
void main()
{
    Hello* hello = new Hello;
    hello->x = 0;
    hello->SayHello();
    delete hello;
}
```

This looks like ordinary C++ that you are used to compiling to native code. I have written it like this deliberately because I want to indicate that normal ANSI C++ can be compiled by the managed C++ compiler. The interesting point is that the code you see here will be compiled to IL. The class is not modified by __gc, so the type is not managed by the garbage collector. Thus when an instance is created on the heap with a call to the new operator, the heap that is used is the C++ unmanaged heap and the operator is the unmanaged new operator. This means that you have the responsibility to call the unmanaged delete operator to ensure that the memory does not leak. The SayHello() method calls the C runtime library function puts(), which is linked in from a static library. The static library contains *native* code, so when your code calls puts(), it is executing native code even though your code is compiled to IL.

The IL does not call the native code directly. Instead, it calls through thunk code generated by the compiler. If you look at the assembly generated from the previous code with ILDASM, you'll see something like the screen shot in Figure 4.1. The items in this screen shot are explained in Table 4.1.

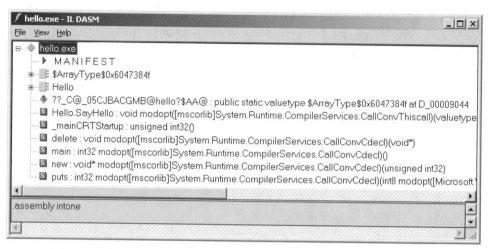

Figure 4.1 Thunk code generated for calls to native code

Table 4.1 Thunks generated for native code

Item	Description
`$ArrayType$0x6047384f`	A `char` array type to hold the literal string
`??_C@05CJBACGMB@hello?$AA@`	A global instance with the literal string
`_mainCRTStartup`	The thunk for the CRT (C runtime library) initialization code; contains native code
`delete`	The thunk for the unmanaged delete operator; contains native code
`Hello`	The unmanaged class, compiled to IL
`Hello.SayHello`	The IL for the `SayHello()` method
`main`	The managed entry point
`new`	The thunk for the unmanaged new operator; contains native code
`puts`	The thunk for the unmanaged `puts()` function; contains native code

DEVELOPING APPLICATIONS WITH VISUAL STUDIO.NET

Because the class is not managed by the garbage collector, the compiler generates a value type to hold the data for the class member x. If you look in the Hello type, however, you will see something like this:

```
// IL
.class private sequential ansi sealed Hello
   extends [mscorlib]System.ValueType
{
    .pack 1
    .size 4
    .custom instance void [Microsoft.VisualC]
    Microsoft.VisualC
        .DebugInfoInPDBAttribute::.ctor()
    = ( 01 00 00 00 )
}
```

This code indicates that the size of the class is 4 bytes because it is allocating space for the int member. The code in main() that initializes the data member looks like this:

```
// IL
.locals (valuetype Hello* V_0)
            // initialize the local variable here
            // (omitted for clarity)
ldloc.0  // load the address of the local variable
ldc.i4.0 // load constant 0 onto the stack
stind.i4 // store the item at the top of the stack
            // in the address pointed to by the next
            // item on the stack
```

In other words, the IL reads and writes data in the non-garbage-collected type using direct memory access. If the type is GC managed, the .size directive is not used because the class will contain fields and the code to set the x member to zero looks like this:

```
// IL
.locals (class Hello V_0)
                        // create the __gc class
newobj instance void Hello::.ctor()
stloc.0                 // store as the first variable
ldloc.0                 // load address of the first
                        // variable on the stack
ldc.i4.0                // put 0 on the stack
stfld int32 Hello::x   // store the item at the top of
```

```
                              // the stack in the x member of
                              // the item pointed to by the
                              // next item on the stack
```

This explains the oddly named `$ArrayType$0x6047384f` type. A global instance of this type (called `??_C@05CJBACGMB@hello?$AA@`) holds the literal string `"Hello"`. This type is intended *only* to hold this particular string because ILDASM shows that it has a size of six bytes indicated by the `.size` directive.

Going back to the unmanaged code, the `SayHello()` method calls `puts()`, so the compiler generates a thunk method that is also called `puts()` that IL can call. The thunk looks like this:

```
// IL
.method public static pinvokeimpl(/* No map */)
 int32 modopt([mscorlib]System.Runtime
                 .CompilerServices.CallConvCdecl)
 puts(int8 modopt([Microsoft.VisualC]Microsoft
                 .VisualC.NoSignSpecifiedModifier)
modopt([Microsoft.VisualC]Microsoft
                 .VisualC.IsConstModifier)* A_0)
     native unmanaged preservesig
{
  .custom instance void
   [mscorlib]System.Security
     .SuppressUnmanagedCodeSecurityAttribute::.ctor()
     = ( 01 00 00 00 )
  // embedded native code
  // disassembly of native methods is not supported.
  // managed TargetRVA = 0x571b
}
```

Note first that the method is marked `native unmanaged`, and that ILDASM has included some helpful comments indicating that the method contains native code and that ILDASM cannot decompile it. The embedded native code is the code for `puts()` linked from the CRT. The thunk code is an IL wrapper for the native code, and if you compile this with debugging information, the PDB will have information for `puts()`. This means that you can use the VS.NET debugger to single-step through IL code and seamlessly step into the native `puts()`. And if you have the CRT source installed, you will be able to single-step through the C source code. This is important: The VS.NET debugger allows you to move between the managed and unmanaged worlds as if you were merely stepping into a function.

The thunk is declared with `pinvokeimpl()`. I will come back to this later, but basically it indicates to the runtime that the method is called by Platform Invoke—the technology to call platform-specific code. The `pinvokeimpl()` modifier can have parameters. In particular, it can indicate the DLL that contains the method, but because in this case `puts()` is static linked, this is not necessary and, as the comment indicates, the mapping to a DLL function is not given. Next the method is decorated with `modopt()`, which modifies a method or parameter. In this case `modopt()` modifies the method with `CallConvCdecl`, which indicates that the wrapped native function is called with the C calling convention (__cdecl). Table 4.2 shows the other calling conventions that may be used.

The native method will have parameters and a return value, and the thunk gives the IL equivalents to the types of these. In the case of `puts()`, the return value is the native `int` value, which is equivalent to the IL `int32` member, whereas the parameter type is `const char*`. There is no direct equivalent to `const char*` in IL, so the compiler uses `int8*` and the modifiers `NoSign-SpecifiedModifier` and `IsConstModifier`.

Table 4.2 Method-calling conventions

Modifier	Calling Convention	Description
CallConvCdecl	__cdecl	Stack cleaned up by the caller; arguments passed right to left on the stack
CallConvFastcall	__fastcall	Stack cleaned up by the called function; registers may be used for arguments; otherwise arguments passed right to left on the stack
CallConvStdcall	__stdcall	Stack cleaned up by the function; arguments passed right to left on the stack
CallConvThiscall	thiscall	Stack cleaned up by the method; this pointer pushed last onto the stack

Note that the thunk method is decorated with the `[SuppressUnmanaged-CodeSecurity]` attribute. This attribute turns off the demand for the `UnmanagedCode` permission at runtime when the call is made to the native code. This attribute does present a possibility of a security hole, but there are safeguards: First, as a developer you are unlikely to link to code that you do not know about. Second, the code that performs the JIT compilation must have the `UnmanagedCode` permission.

The thunk presents an IL view of the native code. The compiler has done the necessary declaration for you so that the correct values are passed as parameters. The static library has all the information that the native compiler needs to call the method, and thus the managed compiler has enough information to generate the thunks. You do not have to provide any other information, which is why Microsoft calls this technology *It Just Works* (IJW).

4.1.2 Calling DLLs

If you can call code in static linked libraries, what about calling DLL functions through an export library? No problem, because yet again the export library has type information that the C++ compiler can read and use to generate the appropriate thunks. Take a look at the following code, which creates a DLL:

```
// C++ compiled with cl /clr /LD
#using <mscorlib.dll>
#include <windows.h>
#include <string.h>
#include <stdlib.h>
#pragma comment(lib, "user32.lib")

public __gc class MyMessageBox
{
public:
   static void SayHello()
   {
      wchar_t* name = _wgetenv(L"USERNAME");
      wchar_t str[256];
      wcscpy(str, L"hello ");
      wcscat(str, name);
      MessageBoxW(NULL, str, L"Test", MB_OK);
   }
};
```

Here I define a `__gc` class called `MyMessageBox` with a method, `Say-Hello()`, that obtains the user that called the method through the CRT function `_wgetenv()`. `SayHello()` concatenates this user name with a greeting and puts it in a Unicode buffer before calling `MessageBoxW()` in `user32.dll`. Because `MyMessageBox` is a `public __gc` class, it can be called by C# or VB.NET code. The library assembly will have a Win32 import table for `MessageBoxW()`, just as this code would if it had been compiled as an unmanaged DLL. The thunk for `MessageBoxW()` looks like this:

```
// IL
.method public static pinvokeimpl(/* No map */)
  int32 modopt([mscorlib]System.Runtime
                  .CompilerServices.CallConvStdcall)
  MessageBoxW(valuetype HWND__* A_0,
    unsigned int16 modopt([Microsoft.VisualC]Microsoft
                  .VisualC.IsConstModifier)* A_1,
    unsigned int16 modopt([Microsoft.VisualC]Microsoft
                  .VisualC.IsConstModifier)* A_2,
    unsigned int32 A_3) native unmanaged preservesig
{
 .custom instance void
  [mscorlib]System.Security
    .SuppressUnmanagedCodeSecurityAttribute::.ctor()
  = ( 01 00 00 00 )
// embedded native code
// disassembly of native methods is not supported.
// managed TargetRVA = 0x5818
}
```

Much of this code will be familiar to you from the `puts()` example. Because I am calling the Unicode version of this function, the parameter is `LPCWSTR`. Hence the C++ compiler has chosen `unsigned int16*` with `IsConstModifier` for the string parameters. Notice that again `pinvokeimpl()` has no parameters; the reason is that the information about the location of the function is held in the module's DLL import table.

In this code I don't use any of the Framework Class Library classes. If I did, I would be tempted to include a `using namespace` statement so that I could use the Framework Class Library class names without fully qualified names. However, this approach can cause problems because many of the Framework Class Library classes have members with names similar to those of functions in Win32. For example, if the first few lines of the preceding example looked like this:

```
// C++ compiled with cl /clr /LD
#using <mscorlib.dll>
using namespace System;
#include <windows.h>
```

then the types sucked in from `mscorlib.dll` and shorn of their `System` namespace will clash with types prototyped through `windows.h`. The solution is quite simple: position the `using namespace` statement after the `#include <windows.h>` statement. However, there is another potential problem: the C++ preprocessor. Take a look at the following code, which constructs a managed string with the name of the user that called the code:

```
// C++
Text::StringBuilder* sb;
sb = new Text::StringBuilder;
sb->Append("hello ");
sb->Append(Environment
    ::GetEnvironmentVariable(S"USERNAME"));
```

I call the static method `GetEnvironmentVariable()` on the `System::Environment` class. If I have an `#include <windows.h>` statement in this file, `winbase.h` will be included, and this includes the following lines:

```
// C++
#ifdef UNICODE
#define GetEnvironmentVariable GetEnvironmentVariableW
#else
#define GetEnvironmentVariable GetEnvironmentVariableA
#endif // !UNICODE
```

The C++ preprocessor essentially does text substitution, but it does not take into account the context of the code it is substituting. As a consequence, it will blindly change the previous code to this:

```
// C++
Text::StringBuilder* sb;
sb = new Text::StringBuilder;
sb->Append("hello ");
sb->Append(Environment
    ::GetEnvironmentVariableW(S"USERNAME"));
```

and this code will not compile. The only solution is to undo the effects of the preprocessor as follows:

```
// C++
#ifdef UNICODE
#define GetEnvironmentVariableW GetEnvironmentVariable
#else
#define GetEnvironmentVariableA GetEnvironmentVariable
#endif
```

The moral here is to be careful about mixing unmanaged C++ with code that uses the Framework Class Library. The C++ compiler is very good at compiling unmanaged C++, and you *should* use it because doing so is the first step to moving your applications over to .NET. To avoid name clashes, however, try to keep your unmanaged code in different translation units from your managed C++.

4.1.3 Platform Invoke

IJW makes C++ the ideal way to use existing code in new .NET applications. However, not all developers use C++; to allow non-C++ developers to use existing code, Microsoft has provided *Platform Invoke* through attributes.

The major issue with calling DLL functions is that usually there is no type information. If you export a C++ function from a DLL, the name will be C++ mangled with the parameter types and the return type, and the correct compiler can read this and link to it. However, C++ name mangling is compiler specific, so other languages have the problem of importing functions with C++ names. As a consequence, DLL developers take the lowest-common-denominator approach and export unmangled names (in C++ this means using `extern "C"`). Without type information, .NET knows nothing about the parameters and return type of a function, and it does not know how to set up the stack when calling the exported function.

As a developer, however, you know the signature of the method; you have the documentation provided by the library developer. To provide this documented type information to .NET, you must convert it into metadata; to do this you define the function prototype in managed code and mark it with the

[DllImport] attribute. Defining the method as a managed function has the added advantage of allowing you to provide a description of the method using .NET types, and as long as you provide conversion information, the runtime will convert managed types to the appropriate unmanaged types.

Let's see how this works:

```cpp
// C++
#using <mscorlib.dll>
using namespace System;
using namespace System::Runtime::InteropServices;
public __value enum MBFlags
    : unsigned int {MB_OK};
public __gc class MyMessageBox
{
public:
    [DllImport("user32.dll",
            CharSet=CharSet::Auto,
            EntryPoint="MessageBox")]
    static int MsgBox(int hWnd, String* strCaption,
                String* strTitle,
                unsigned int flags);
};
```

This class defines a static function called MsgBox() that is used to call MessageBox() in user32.dll. Note that I do not use the import library user32.lib. Instead, the DLL is truly dynamically linked; it is loaded at runtime using the information provided by the [DllImport] attribute. The equivalent code in C# is as follows:

```csharp
// C#
using System;
using System.Runtime.InteropServices;
public enum MBFlags : uint {MB_OK};
public class MyMessageBox
{
    [DllImport("user32.dll",
            CharSet=CharSet.Auto,
            EntryPoint="MessageBox")]
    public static extern int MsgBox(
                int hWnd, string strCaption,
                string strTitle, uint flags);
}
```

As before, the compiler generates a thunk for the unmanaged function, and the IL for the `MsgBox()` method from the C++ example looks like this:

```
// IL
.method public static pinvokeimpl(
    "user32.dll" as "MessageBox" autochar winapi)
    int32  MsgBox(int32 hWnd,
                    string strCaption,
                    string strTitle,
                    unsigned int32 flags)
                cil managed preservesig forwardref
{ }
```

Yet again the `pinvokeimpl()` modifier is used, but now it has parameters to indicate the name of the DLL and the imported function. The parameters are managed parameters, and Platform Invoke will convert them to unmanaged types. However, the `string` parameters present a problem because the conversion could be to an ANSI or Unicode string, so `pinvokeimpl()` has a parameter to indicate which one is used. I will come back to this in a moment. The modifiers after the function signature indicate that the function will be handled by the runtime with code implemented elsewhere (Platform Invoke is, of course, managed code) and that the function that Platform Invoke will call will have the same signature (notwithstanding the conversions to native types) as the thunk has.

The two most important members of the `[DllImport]` attribute are the name of the DLL (the attribute class's constructor parameter) and the name of the imported function (the `EntryPoint` field) because these are required by `pinvokeimpl()`. The DLL name is a mandatory parameter because without it, the function cannot be imported. The function name is optional (an attribute field) because you have to give a name for your .NET code to call, and you can use the same name as the exported function. In my example I have chosen to use a different name for the .NET method, so I have to use the `EntryPoint` field. This field can also be used to import a function by ordinal rather than by name. `MessageBoxW()` is exported as ordinal `457`, so the following code will import `MessageBoxW()`:

```
// C++
[DllImport("user32.dll",
            CharSet=CharSet::Unicode,
            EntryPoint="#457")]
```

```
static int MsgBox(int hWnd, String* strCaption,
                  String* strTitle,
                  unsigned int flags);
```

The additional fields of `[DllImport]` are listed in Table 4.3.

4.1.4 String Conversions

The `CharSet` property is interesting. Consider the following code:

```
// C++ compiled with cl /LD print.cpp
#include <stdio.h>
extern "C" __declspec(dllexport)
void PrintStringA(char* str)
{ printf("ANSI %s\n", str); }
extern "C" __declspec(dllexport)
void PrintStringW(wchar_t* str)
{ wprintf(L"UNICODE %s\n", str); }
extern "C" __declspec(dllexport)
void PrintANSI(char* str)
{ printf("ANSI %s\n", str); }
```

You can choose to print an ASCII string or a Unicode string, depending on the suffix to `PrintString()`, which can be called like this:

Table 4.3   Fields for `[DllImport]`

Field	Description
`CallingConvention`	Defines the calling convention used; these are defined in `System.Runtime.InteropServices.CallingConvention`.
`CharSet`	Defines how string parameters are converted and, if the DLL has multiple versions of a function depending on the character set, which version is called.
`EntryPoint`	Gives the name or ordinal of the exported function.
`ExactSpelling`	Specifies that a character set suffix should not be added.
`PreserveSig`	Specifies whether the runtime translates HRESULT results into .NET exceptions.
`SetLastError`	Specifies whether the runtime should call Win32's `GetLastError()` after calling the method.

```
// C#
[DllImport("print.dll",
        CharSet=CharSet.Auto,
        EntryPoint="PrintString")]
public static extern void PrintString(string s);
```

Notice that the name of the function put in the `EntryPoint` field does not have a suffix. Instead I give a value to `CharSet` that Platform Invoke uses to choose the suffix. In this case I use `CharSet.Auto`, which means that the runtime will choose the character set appropriate to the platform: For 32-bit systems like Windows NT, 2000, XP, and CE, this will be Unicode; for partially 32-bit systems[2] like Windows 95, 98, and Millennium Edition (Me), this will be ANSI.

Thus, if I run this code on Windows Me, `PrintStringA()` will be called; the runtime will add an `A` to the entry point name. If I run this code on Windows XP, `PrintStringW()` will be called. In both cases the appropriate conversion of the data in the managed `string` parameter will be performed. If you prefer, you can explicitly specify the character set to be used by specifying `CharSet.Ansi` or `CharSet.Unicode`, in which case the runtime will add the specified suffix and perform the necessary conversion.

The runtime does not add these suffixes unreservedly. Thus in the preceding example the `PrintANSI()` function can be accessed with the following code:

```
// C#
[DllImport("print.dll",
        CharSet=CharSet.Ansi,
        EntryPoint="PrintANSI")]
public static extern void PrintANSI(string s);
```

The parameter is `string`, so the runtime must be told how to convert the string. Thus I have explicitly told the runtime that the imported function is an ANSI string. Even so, the runtime will *not* add the suffix `A` to the name of the function; it will call `PrintANSI()`. For ANSI methods, Platform Invoke first tries the method name without adding the `A` suffix. If the call to `GetProcAddress()` fails for the raw method name, Platform Invoke tries to access the method with

---

2. These operating systems *still* contain 16-bit code as part of the core operating system. The 32-bit operating systems I mentioned are 32-bit in the core operating system, but all except Windows CE have the facility to run 16-bit code.

the A suffix. For Unicode methods, the algorithm works in the opposite way: Platform Invoke first tries the name with the W suffix, and if this fails it attempts to access the method without the suffix.

The rationale here is straightforward: ANSI strings have been used much longer than Unicode strings, so an API written to use ANSI strings was most likely written when Unicode was not an option. On the other hand, a developer writing a Unicode method typically will create an ANSI version (that merely converts the strings before calling the Unicode version) for the convenience of users of older, less capable operating systems. The ExactSpelling field allows you to specify whether these tests are performed. If you set this field to true, you are asserting that you know exactly what the name should be and that the runtime should not attempt to add a suffix. The default is false.

Of course, if you import a function using an ordinal, clearly the suffix is irrelevant. Be careful if you do this because if you choose to call a Unicode version of a Win32 function, your code will run only on the versions of Windows that support Unicode.

In general, you should make the signature of the managed function as similar to the unmanaged version as possible. It is your responsibility to provide the managed equivalents to the unmanaged data types. In this process you do not have to worry about C++ niceties like const, which is actually just an instruction to the compiler to do some checking for you. You do have to take special care about pointers and structures, and I'll go into more details about this in the next section. Note that the C concept of varargs (i.e., the ... syntax for variable numbers of arguments) is not yet supported.

4.1.5 Errors and Exceptions

.NET has complete support for exceptions, and you are actively discouraged from writing methods that return status code in preference to using exceptions. As I outlined in Chapter 2, most Win32 methods take one of three approaches:

1. Returning a status code
2. Returning a Boolean value and calling SetLastError()
3. Returning an HRESULT

DEVELOPING APPLICATIONS WITH VISUAL STUDIO.NET

If you call a method of the first type, you have no option in .NET but to explicitly check for the appropriate status code. If the method is of the second type, you can set the `SetLastError` field to `true` to indicate to the runtime that on every call to the function it ought to call the Win32 method `GetLast-Error()`. You can then obtain the value read by the runtime through a call to `Marshal.GetLastWin32Error()`. However, note that if you call a method with this field set to `true`, you should always check the error code because you are recognizing that the error code has information about the success of the function. Nevertheless, the runtime merely stores the status code; it does not act on it. If you choose, you can get an `HRESULT` for the error by calling `GetHRForLastWin32Error()`, but to be honest there is little point in doing so because all this will do is add `0x80070000` to the value.

In the case of the third type, the runtime will do some work for you. If the method is a COM-style method—that is, it returns an `HRESULT` (and possibly creates an error object)—any return values from the method must come through an out parameter. Programmers who write unmanaged Visual Basic code will recognize that such methods appear in VB code as if the method returned the value and the `HRESULT` were used to initialize the `Err` object. The field `DllImportAttribute.PreserveSig` affects whether the .NET Runtime does a similar translation. If this field is set to `false` (the default is `true`), the runtime will use the return value from the method to initialize an exception that will be thrown if the return value is a failure value (i.e., the top bit is set). In addition, the runtime will make the *last* out parameter the return value of the method. Here is an example:

```
// C++
extern "C" __declspec(dllexport)
    HRESULT ComMethod(int* val1, int* val2);
```

The declaration in C# could look like this:

```
// C#
[DllImport("commethods.dll",
           EntryPoint="ComMethod",
           PreserveSig=false)]
public static extern int ComMethod(out int i);
```

If the unmanaged method returns a success `HRESULT`, the calling code will get `val2` returned from the method and `val1` through `i`. If the unmanaged method returns a failure `HRESULT`, there will be no return value (because execution will be passed to the exception handler), but `i` will still be set to the value that was set by the method. If an exception is thrown, you can access the failure code by calling `Marshal.GetHRForException()`.

There is a gotcha here that is serious enough to persuade you not to use this approach. The `HRESULT` returned by a method can contain success codes as well as failure codes, but if you use `PreserveSig=false`, the `HRESULT` is accessible only if an exception is thrown, which clearly will not happen if the method succeeded! Take heart, though, because the COM specification says that if a method can return a success code, these status codes should be documented as part of the method's interface. Therefore, if the method's documentation does not mention success codes, you can be assured that you will need to know the return code only when the method fails. If the method's documentation *does* mention success codes, you have no option but to use `PreserveSig=true`. In this case you can manually throw an exception for failure `HRESULT` results by calling `Marshal.ThrowExceptionForHR()`. This method does the right thing; that is, it will throw an exception only for a failure `HRESULT`, and it will ignore the call for a success `HRESULT`.

4.1.6   Data Flow Direction

Some parameters of unmanaged functions take data into the function, other parameters take data out of the function, and occasionally a single parameter can take data in both directions. The interop runtime must know the direction of the data flow to marshal parameters correctly. Primitive types that are passed by value (i.e., parameters that are not passed through a pointer) will always be in parameters. The runtime assumes that all parameters passed by reference (through pointers on the unmanaged signature) will be in/out parameters. To mention the data direction flow explicitly, you can use the `[In]` and `[Out]` attributes, although these are not mandatory and in most cases the defaults will be satisfactory.

Reference types, of course, are always passed through pointers, which means that a reference type passed by reference will be accessed in an unmanaged function through a pointer to a pointer.

4.1.7 Structures

Many Win32 functions take data or return results through structures. This makes sense for two reasons: First, it allows you to organize your data as records, thereby making the data easier to read and manipulate. Second, it allows you to pass potentially many data items through a similar parameter. There is another reason, too: A pointer to a structure may refer to a chunk of memory, and the structure allows the programmer to access the memory in a more convenient form—for example, as follows:

```
// unmanaged C++
// from winnt.h
typedef union _ULARGE_INTEGER
{
    struct {
        DWORD LowPart;
        DWORD HighPart; };
    struct {
        DWORD LowPart;
        DWORD HighPart; } u;
    ULONGLONG QuadPart;
} ULARGE_INTEGER;
```

The union allows you to treat a 64-bit number as an __int64 type (through QuadPart) or as two 32-bit integers. This technique relies on the following: (1) that the 64-bit integer will be in 8 consecutive bytes, (2) that the two 32-bit integers will each be made up of 4 consecutive bytes and will be next to each other in memory, and (3) that the DWORD members are in the order given.

In .NET, structures are value types, but there is no guarantee that the individual members will be in the order given or that they will be consecutive; .NET decides these details. If you want to create a structure and pass it to unmanaged code, you must take steps to ensure that the memory layout is as the unmanaged code expects. To do this you have to use the [StructLayout] attribute. Here is an example in C# (which makes the attribute usage a little clearer):

```csharp
// C#
[StructLayout(LayoutKind.Sequential)]
public struct SYSTEMTIME
{
    public short wYear;
    public short wMonth;
    public short wDayOfWeek;
    public short wDay;
    public short wHour;
    public short wMinute;
    public short wSecond;
    public short wMilliseconds;
    public override string ToString()
    {
        return String.Format(
            "{0:0000}-{1:00}-{2:00} "
            + "{3:00}:{4:00}:{5:00}",
            wYear, wMonth, wDay,
            wHour, wMinute, wSecond);
    }
    [DllImport("kernel32.dll")]
    public static extern void
        GetLocalTime(out SYSTEMTIME st);
}
```

The data members of this struct mimic the Win32 SYSTEMTIME structure. I have added two methods to this struct—one to provide formatted output for the struct, and the other to fill it using the Win32 GetLocalTime() function. The struct is used like this:

```csharp
// C#
SYSTEMTIME st;
SYSTEMTIME.GetLocalTime(out st);
Console.WriteLine(st);
```

Using the [StructLayout] attribute, I am making an explicit assertion about the memory layout that the struct takes. The LayoutKind enum has three members: Auto, where the runtime chooses the memory layout; Sequential, where the memory layout will be as declared; and Explicit, where you use the `[FieldOffset]` attribute to give the offset (in bytes) of the member from the beginning of the structure.

You can manually marshal structures using methods in the `Marshal` class. In this case your managed structure should be a reference type rather than a value type.

4.1.8 Arrays and Buffers

Arrays are buffers of memory that contain one or more items of the same type. If the type is a primitive type (`int`, `double`, and so on), the buffer will contain the type. If the type is a complex type (a struct) or a buffer (like a string), typically the array will be an array of *pointers* to that type. Consider the following example:

```
// unmanaged C++
#include <stdio.h>
typedef struct _Person
{
    char* name;
    int age;
} Person;
extern "C" __declspec(dllexport)
void PrintPerson(Person* p)
{
    printf("%s is %ld\n", p->name, p->age);
}
extern "C" __declspec(dllexport)
void PrintPeople(Person* p, int size)
{
    printf("there are %ld items\n", size);
    for (int x = 0; x < size; x++)
        printf("%s is %ld\n",
                p[x].name, p[x].age);
}
```

Here I define a structure that holds information about a person: the name and age of that person. Single instances of this structure are passed to `Print-Person()`, which prints the information to the console. Notice that the instance is passed through a pointer. The second method, `PrintPeople()`, takes an array of `Person` structures, and the number of items in the array is passed as the second parameter.

The array is passed to the method along with a pointer to the first item; that is, in C++ there is no distinction between a pointer to a single item and an array. When the data is marshaled from the managed world to the unmanaged world, the marshaler must know whether the pointer points to a single item or indicates the start of an array so that it knows how much data to marshal.

To determine the size and type of data that will be marshaled, you use the [MarshalAs] attribute in the declaration of the thunk. This attribute specifies that a parameter is an array and identifies the size of the array. Thus for the following managed struct:

```
// C#
[StructLayout(LayoutKind.Sequential)]
public struct Person
{
    public Person(string s, int a)
    {name = s; age = a;}
    public string name;
    public int age;
}
```

I define the access to the unmanaged code as follows:

```
// C#
public class PersonMethods
{
    [DllImport("exp.dll")]
    public static extern
        void PrintPerson(ref Person p);
    [DllImport("exp.dll")]
    public static extern void PrintPeople(
        [
          MarshalAs(UnmanagedType.LPArray,
                    SizeParamIndex=1,
                    ArraySubType=UnmanagedType.LPStruct)
        ]
        Person[] p,
        int size);
}
```

[MarshalAs] is a general-purpose attribute; I'll come back to it in detail later. In this code I am using it like the Microsoft Interface Definition Language

(MIDL) unmanaged `[size_is()]` attribute. The mandatory constructor parameter indicates the type of the item being marshaled—in this case an array whose size is determined by another parameter. The parameter that holds the size is indicated by the `SizeParamIndex` field, which gives a zero-based index of the parameter. Of course, this still isn't enough because the marshaler will need to know what data the array holds so that it knows to what type to convert the data. The information about the data type is provided through metadata in the `Person` type, which is why the `ArraySubType` field is set to `Unman-agedType.LPStruct`.

4.1.9 Marshaling

As I mentioned earlier, Platform Invoke uses a marshaler to pass data between the managed and unmanaged worlds. By default, the marshaler assumes that parameters passed by reference are in/out parameters, and that other parameters are in parameters. A parameter that is a `StringBuilder` reference is the exception, as I'll discuss later. In parameters are passed from the caller to the callee, out parameters are passed from the callee to the caller, and in/out parameters are passed in both directions. You can use the `[In]` or `[Out]` attribute to suggest to the runtime explicitly the direction of data flow; however, these are just suggestions, and the runtime can choose to ignore them.

You use the fields of `[DllImport]` or `[MarshalAs]` to give information to the marshaler about the data type on the unmanaged side. The marshaler can read the metadata of the method signature to get information about the data type on the managed side. If the default marshaler is inadequate, you can write your own, as I'll explain shortly.

Data types can be *isomorphic* or *nonisomorphic*. Isomorphic types are the same in the managed and unmanaged worlds; the documentation calls them *blittable* because such types passed by value can be copied bit by bit. Isomorphic types are the integer types (both signed and unsigned), `float`, `double`, and `void`. In addition, single-dimensional arrays of isomorphic types and "formatted" structures that contain only isomorphic types (i.e., those that use `[StructLayout]`) are also isomorphic. A formatted isomorphic type has the same layout and data representation in the managed and unmanaged worlds; thus the marshaler passes to the unmanaged code a pointer to the isomorphic type. All other types are nonisomorphic and require conversion when being passed between the managed and unmanaged worlds.

When an object reference is passed to unmanaged code, there is a problem: The object in the managed world is subject to the garbage collector's determination of whether there are any references on the object. The garbage collector makes this determination by checking whether the object is reachable, and it can do this only with references held in the managed world; references passed to the unmanaged world are beyond the reach of the garbage collector. Furthermore, even if the object is reachable in the managed world, when a garbage collection occurs the object could be moved to compact memory. Because the garbage collector cannot change the pointer passed to the unmanaged code, this pointer will become invalid. To avoid this problem, the marshaler uses two approaches: *copying* and *pinning*.

When a managed object is pinned, the garbage collector is told that the object is locked in memory; it cannot be moved or garbage-collected. An isomorphic type on the garbage-collected heap (e.g., a single-dimensional array of an isomorphic type) will be pinned before a pointer is passed to the unmanaged code. Because the type is isomorphic, it is the same in the managed and unmanaged worlds, so a pointer can be passed. But because the type is allocated on the managed heap, the memory occupied by the object must be pinned to ensure that the pointer remains valid.

When a nonisomorphic formatted type is marshaled, a converted copy is made. If the parameter is passed by reference, a pointer to this copy is passed to the unmanaged code. Using the `[In]` attribute on the parameter indicates to the runtime that the copy is initialized before the parameter is passed to the callee. Using the `[Out]` attribute indicates that data in the copy will be used to initialize the object when the call returns. By default, when a parameter is passed by reference, copies are made in both directions, and using the `[In]` or `[Out]` attribute can suggest to the runtime the intended data flow and hence optimize the copies that are made.

4.1.9.1 Custom Marshaling

The `PersonMethods` example given earlier, in which the array is passed with an explicit size parameter, raises an interesting question: What happens if the array is not passed with an explicit size, but instead the array size is determined by iteration through each array item until the item is zero? Consider the following code:

```cpp
// C++
extern "C" __declspec(dllexport)
void PrintList(const char** str)
{
    while (*str)
    {
        puts(*str);
        str++;
    }
}
```

This code takes an array of strings—that is, an array of pointers to `char`. To indicate the end of the array, a `NULL` pointer is used for the string, so this code iterates through all the pointers, and if the pointer is zero the code knows that the end of the array has been reached. .NET does not have support for marshaling an array like this, so you have to write your own marshaler. It is not as difficult as it sounds. The first thing to do is use the `[MarshalAs]` attribute to specify the custom marshaler:

```csharp
// C#
[DllImport("printlists.dll")]
static extern void PrintList(
    [MarshalAs(
        UnmanagedType.CustomMarshaler,
        MarshalType="MyMarshaler")]
    string[] p);
```

The `UnmanagedType.CustomMarshaler` value indicates that the type indicated by the `MarshalType` field should be used. `MyMarshaler` is a class that implements the `ICustomMarshaler` interface. The marshaler object is created by Platform Invoke through a call to a static method called `GetInstance()` that returns an instance of the class:

```csharp
// C#
class MyMarshaler
    : ICustomMarshaler
{
    public static ICustomMarshaler
```

```
       GetInstance(string pstrCookie)
    { return new MyMarshaler(); }
    public IntPtr MarshalManagedToNative(
       object ManagedObj);
    public void CleanUpNativeData(IntPtr pNativeData);
    public object MarshalNativeToManaged(
       IntPtr pNativeData);
    public void CleanUpManagedData(object ManagedObj);
    public int GetNativeDataSize();
}
```

Because this class will be used to marshal data from the managed to the native world, the last three methods can have empty implementations. `Marshal-ManagedToNative()` takes a reference to the managed object that should be marshaled, and it should create a native buffer and copy the data into that buffer. The managed object will be a string array, and the native buffer should contain pointers to strings (allocated on the native heap). The method looks like this:

```
// C#
public IntPtr MarshalManagedToNative(
    object ManagedObj)
{
    string[] p = (string[])ManagedObj;
    int size = IntPtr.Size * (p.Length + 1);
    IntPtr array = Marshal.AllocHGlobal(size);
    int offset = 0;
    IntPtr str;
    for (int i = 0; i < p.Length; i++)
    {
        // allocate space for data
        str = Marshal.StringToHGlobalAnsi(p[i]);
        Marshal.WriteIntPtr(array, offset, str);
        offset += IntPtr.Size;
    }
    // for the last item, give a null pointer
    str = IntPtr.Zero;
    Marshal.WriteIntPtr(array, offset, str);
    return array;
}
```

First I create the array of string pointers. `IntPtr.Size` returns the size of pointers on the target platform, so I create space for one more pointer than there are strings in the array by using `Marshal.AllocHGlobal()` to allocate memory using the system memory allocator. Next I loop through the items in the array, and for each one I marshal the string into a native buffer with `StringTo-HGlobalAnsi()` and write the address of this buffer to the array. I use the ANSI version of this method because I have the privileged knowledge that the class will be used for arrays of ANSI strings.

The version of `WriteIntPtr()` I have used takes three parameters: The first is a pointer to the native buffer; the second is the offset from the start of this buffer where I want to write the data in the third parameter. Finally, I indicate the end of the buffer by writing a `null` pointer (`IntPtr` initialized to zero) to the array.

When the native method returns, the data allocated in `MarshalManaged-ToNative()` should be released, so `CleanUpNativeData()` looks like this:

```csharp
// C#
public void CleanUpNativeData(IntPtr pNativeData)
{
    // iterate through all the items
    // and release them
    int offset = 0;
    while (true)
    {
        IntPtr str;
        str = Marshal.ReadIntPtr(pNativeData, offset);
        if (str == IntPtr.Zero) break;
        Marshal.FreeHGlobal(str);
        offset += IntPtr.Size;
    }
    Marshal.FreeHGlobal(pNativeData);
}
```

In this code I iterate through the array and free the memory of each item until the end is reached. At this point the array itself is released.

In the `MarshalManagedToNative()` method, in addition, I convert from a managed `string` to an ANSI string. It would be better if the code were more generic (something I will leave as an exercise for the reader); if the code is more generic, the marshaler will need to have information about what character set to assume. This information can be acquired through a field of `[MarshalAs]` called `MarshalCookie`. The value of this field is passed to the static

`GetInstance()` method of the marshaler class, which could pass this value to the constructor of the marshaler—or could even create an object of a different class—depending on the value.

4.1.9.2 String Marshaling

Strings need special handling. First, they are arrays of characters, so they need allocating. Second, the characters used in a string could be single-byte or double-byte characters, so the marshaler must know the sizes of the characters for the method that is being called.

The .NET `System.String` type is immutable; you can never change the contents of a `String` object. If you call one of the string manipulation methods, the manipulated string will be a new string rather than an alteration of the original string. The `CharSet` and `ExactSpelling` fields of the `[DllImport]` attribute ensure that the correct character set is used. When a `String` object is passed to an ANSI parameter, the marshaler creates a temporary buffer with `CoTaskMemAlloc()` and fills it with the converted string. If the `String` object is passed *by value* to a Unicode parameter, a pointer to the object's internal Unicode buffer is passed. If a `String` parameter is passed *by reference,* the implication is that the callee could change the `String` object's contents.

To accommodate changing the contents of the `String` object, the runtime makes a copy of the `String` (converting it if necessary) and passes to the unmanaged code a pointer to the copy.[3] The unmanaged code can then write to the buffer. The runtime will use this altered buffer to initialize a `String` parameter, and a reference to this parameter will replace the reference passed to the unmanaged code. For the following unmanaged code:

```
// unmanaged C++
extern "C" __declspec(dllexport)
void SayHello(char** s)
{
    const char* str = "Hello";
```

---

3. From my tests (filling the buffer until the stack overflows), the runtime appears to allocate a buffer of about 2,500 *bytes*—that is 2,500 `char` values or 1,250 `wchar_t` values. However, this is an implementation detail; it is far better not to rely on this but to explicitly allocate the buffer using a `StringBuilder` reference.

```
    strcpy(*s, str);
}
```

the managed code could look like this:

```
// C#
class Test
{
    [DllImport("test.dll",
               CharSet = CharSet.Ansi)]
    static extern void SayHello(ref String s);
    static void Main()
    {
        string s = "";
        SayHello(ref s);
        Console.WriteLine("you say " + s);
    }
}
```

There are a couple of points to note here. The string should be passed by reference (ref); hence the parameter to the unmanaged method has the extra level of indirection, and you must allocate a String object in the managed code (even though it can be empty, as in this example).

To assume that the runtime will create a buffer of the correct size makes me uneasy; I prefer to allocate a buffer explicitly. There are several ways to do this, and passing a StringBuilder reference is the most straightforward. In this case StringBuilder can be passed by value (of course, StringBuilder is a reference type, so the *reference* to StringBuilder is passed by *value*), so the unmanaged code can look like this:

```
// unmanaged C++
extern "C" __declspec(dllexport)
int SayHello2(char* s, int size)
{
    const char* str = "Hello";
    int len = strlen(str);
    if (size > len)
        strcpy(s, str);
    else
        return 0;
    return len;
}
```

This time the parameter has a single level of indirection. This looks like many of the Win32 APIs in which you pass a pointer to a buffer, along with an indication of the buffer's size. The managed code looks like this:

```csharp
// C#
class Test
{
    [DllImport("test.dll",
                CharSet = CharSet.Ansi)]
    static extern int SayHello2(StringBuilder s);
    static void Main()
    {
        StringBuilder sb = new StringBuilder();
        sb.EnsureCapacity(6);
        SayHello2(sb, sb.Capacity);
        Console.WriteLine("result is "
                            + sb.ToString());
    }
}
```

Again the parameter to SayHello2() is a StringBuilder reference passed by value. Earlier in the chapter I said that parameters passed by value are treated as in parameters, and clearly in this example this parameter is returning data. StringBuilder is a special case in .NET. Passing a StringBuilder object by value actually passes a pointer to the internal buffer of that object.

In this code I call EnsureCapacity() to explicitly allocate a buffer in the StringBuilder object. It is my responsibility to ensure that I allocate a big enough buffer and that the unmanaged code does not overrun this buffer; this is the reason for the size parameter of SayHello2(). The StringBuilder class also has a constructor that takes a capacity value, so I could allocate the buffer using just the single step of calling this constructor. The advantage of using StringBuilder is that a large enough buffer will be allocated, no matter what character set the called method uses.

I can also explicitly allocate the buffer for a string by using the Marshal class, as described in the following section. However, the methods called will have to specify exactly the size of the required buffer, taking into account the size of the characters in the character set.

4.1.10 Explicit Allocation of Buffers

The `Marshal` class in the `System.Runtime.InteropServices` namespace has methods to allow you to allocate buffers, read and write data in unmanaged buffers, access COM objects, and access exception and error values from unmanaged code. In this section I will cover unmanaged buffers.

The `Marshal` class allows you to allocate buffers using two general-purpose allocators: the Win32 `HGLOBAL` allocator and the COM `IMalloc` allocator. In addition, it allows you to allocate `BSTR` values, which use the `BSTR` allocator. The `BSTR` allocator is essentially a third type of allocator, but it cannot be regarded as general-purpose allocator. Using these allocators is straightforward. The following code calls Win32's `MessageBoxW()` method using C++ and IJW:

```
// C++ compiled with cl /clr
#using <mscorlib.dll>
#include <windows.h>
using namespace System;
using namespace System::Runtime::InteropServices;
#ifdef UNICODE
#define GetEnvironmentVariableW GetEnvironmentVariable
#else
#define GetEnvironmentVariableA GetEnvironmentVariable
#endif
#pragma comment(lib, "user32.lib")
void main()
{
    Text::StringBuilder* sb;
    sb = new Text::StringBuilder;
    sb->Append(L"hello ");
    sb->Append(
        Environment::GetEnvironmentVariable(S"USERNAME"));
    LPCWSTR str;
    str = (LPCWSTR)(void*)
        Marshal::StringToCoTaskMemUni(sb->ToString());
    MessageBoxW(NULL, str, L"Test", MB_OK);
    Marshal::FreeCoTaskMem((int)str);
}
```

Much of this code will be familiar to you, but notice the code to call `MessageBoxW()`: Here I am using IJW and not `[DllImport]`, so I have to call the function using unmanaged data types. However, to construct the string I am using `StringBuilder`, so I must convert the string from the managed type to an unmanaged string. To do this I call `StringToCoTaskMemUni()`. Notice that the method name suggests that it will convert the `string` object to a Unicode string in a buffer allocated by `CoTaskMemAlloc()`. Thus I have to ensure that the unmanaged method takes a Unicode string, and when I am finished with the string I have to call `FreeCoTaskMem()`. Table 4.4 lists the complete set of functions for allocating and converting strings.

All of these methods return an instance of `IntPtr`, which is the .NET structure to hold a native pointer. `IntPtr` can be converted to a 32-bit number, a 64-bit number, or a `void*` pointer, depending on the current operating system. Thus in the code earlier I cast the `IntPtr` structure to a `void*` value to do the conversion before casting to an `LPCWSTR` so that it matched the type of the parameter to `MessageBoxW()`. In a similar vein, an unmanaged method may return a pointer to a string:

```
// C++ compiled with /clr
#using <mscorlib.dll>
#include <stdlib.h>
using namespace System;
using namespace System::Runtime::InteropServices;
```

Table 4.4   String allocation and conversion methods

Method	Description
StringToBSTR()	Creates a BSTR based on the string.
StringToCoTaskMemAnsi()	Creates an ANSI string using the COM allocator.
StringToCoTaskMemAuto()	Uses the COM allocator. On Unicode systems creates a Unicode string; on ANSI systems creates an ANSI string.
StringToCoTaskMemUni()	Creates a Unicode string using the COM allocator.
StringToHGlobalAnsi()	Creates an ANSI string with the Win32 allocator.
StringToHGlobalAuto()	Uses the Win32 allocator. On Unicode systems creates a Unicode string; on ANSI systems creates an ANSI string.
StringToHGlobalUni()	Creates a Unicode string with the Win32 allocator.

```
void main()
{
    wchar_t* p = _wgetenv(L"USERNAME");
    String* s;
    s = Marshal::PtrToStringUni((IntPtr)p);
    Console::WriteLine(s);
}
```

The CRT function `_wgetenv()` returns a pointer to the requested environment variable. You do not have to allocate space for this string, nor do you have to free it. The string pointer is then cast to an `IntPtr` value, which is then passed to `PtrToStringUni()` to convert it to a managed `String` object. Because the conversion is to a managed type, you do not have to release the buffer that is created (the GC does that), but you do have to specify the character set used by the unmanaged string. Table 4.5 shows all the methods for converting native strings to managed strings.

If you wish, you can perform allocations using the general-purpose methods. So if you wanted to pass an ANSI string to `puts()`, you could allocate it like this:

```
// C++
#using <mscorlib.dll>
#include <stdio.h>
using namespace System;
using namespace System::Runtime::InteropServices;
void main()
{
    IntPtr p = Marshal::AllocHGlobal(27);
    for (unsigned char x = 'a'; x < 'a' + 26; x++)
        Marshal::WriteByte(p, x - 'a', x);
```

Table 4.5   Methods for converting native strings to managed strings

Method	Description
PtrToStringAnsi()	Converts an ANSI string to a managed string.
PtrToStringAuto()	Depending on the operating system, converts an ANSI or a Unicode string to a managed string.
PtrToStringBSTR()	Converts a BSTR to a managed string.
PtrToStringUni()	Converts a Unicode string to a managed string.

```
    Marshal::WriteByte(p, 26, 0);
    puts((char*)p.ToPointer());
    Marshal::FreeHGlobal(p);
}
```

The call to `AllocHGlobal()` creates a buffer through the Win32 allocator. Then, using `WriteByte()`, I loop and write individual 8-bit characters into the buffer.

Table 4.6 shows the other methods that you can use to access native buffers. You are allowed to access the native buffer for read and write operations, and to access integral types or pointers. `ReadIntPtr()` and `WriteIntPtr()`, respectively, will read and write a pointer whose size depends on the processor type. These methods are useful if you are passed a complicated structure type (e.g., the instance of `EVENTLOGRECORD` from `ReadEventLog()`) and have to read the values from the structure item by item. Each of these methods is overloaded and can either read or write directly from the pointer, or (as I have done here with the second parameter) you can pass an offset from the pointer.

The methods in Table 4.6 allow languages that do not have pointer types (like VB.NET) to access items in a native buffer. In C++ I could simply do this:

Table 4.6 Methods for reading and writing values to and from a native buffer

Method	Description
ReadByte()	Reads an 8-bit value from a native buffer.
ReadInt16()	Reads a 16-bit value from a native buffer.
ReadInt32()	Reads a 32-bit value from a native buffer.
ReadInt64()	Reads a 64-bit value from a native buffer.
ReadIntPtr()	Reads a processor-relative pointer (32- or 64-bit) from a native buffer.
WriteByte()	Writes an 8-bit value to a native buffer.
WriteInt16()	Writes a 16-bit value to a native buffer.
WriteInt32()	Writes a 32-bit value to a native buffer.
WriteInt64()	Writes a 64-bit value to a native buffer.
WriteIntPtr()	Writes a processor-relative pointer (32- or 64-bit) to a native buffer.

```
// C++
IntPtr p = Marshal::AllocHGlobal(27);
char* pp = (char*)(void*)p;
for (unsigned char x = 'a'; x < 'a' + 26; x++, pp++)
    *pp = x;
*pp = 0;
puts((char*)p.ToPointer());
Marshal::FreeHGlobal(p);
```

The conversion to a `void*` pointer is important because it calls the conversion operator on `IntPtr`. Once the `IntPtr` value has been converted, I can use unmanaged pointers to perform normal pointer arithmetic. Table 4.7 lists the general-purpose methods for allocating memory.

A managed array initialized with data can be copied into a native buffer with the `Copy()` method:

```
// C++
IntPtr p = Marshal::AllocHGlobal(27);
char c __gc [] = new char __gc [27];
for (char x = 'a'; x < 'a' + 26; x++)
    c[x - 'a'] = x;
c[26] = 0;
Marshal::Copy(c, 0, p, 27);
puts((char*)p.ToPointer());
Marshal::FreeHGlobal(p);
```

Table 4.7 General-purpose memory allocation methods

Method	Description
`AllocCoTaskMem()`	Allocates a buffer using the COM allocator.
`ReAllocCoTaskMem()`	Resizes a buffer created with the COM allocator.
`FreeCoTaskMem()`	Frees a buffer created with the COM allocator.
`AllocHGlobal()`	Allocates a buffer using the Win32 allocator.
`ReAllocHGlobal()`	Resizes a buffer created with the Win32 allocator.
`FreeHGlobal()`	Frees a buffer created with the Win32 allocator.
`FreeBSTR()`	Frees a `BSTR`.

Manual marshaling of structures presents a problem because structures may contain embedded structures or types. `Marshal` contains several methods that allow you to pass structures between managed and unmanaged code. Consider the `Person` class I showed earlier:

```csharp
// C#
[StructLayout(LayoutKind.Sequential)]
public struct Person
{
    public Person(string s, int a)
    {name = s; age = a;}
    public string name;
    public int age;
}
```

Instead of using Platform Invoke to do the marshaling, I will do it explicitly:

```csharp
// C#
public class PersonMethods2
{
    [DllImport("exp.dll")]
    public static extern void PrintPerson(IntPtr p);
    public void SendPerson(string name, int age)
    {
        IntPtr p;
        p = Marshal.AllocCoTaskMem(
            Marshal.SizeOf(typeof(Person)));
        IntPtr n;
        n = Marshal.StringToCoTaskMemAnsi("Richard");
        Marshal.WriteIntPtr(p, 0, n);
        Marshal.WriteInt32(
            p, Marshal.SizeOf(typeof(IntPtr)), 36);
        PrintPerson(p);
        Marshal.FreeCoTaskMem(n);
        Marshal.FreeCoTaskMem(p);
    }
}
```

Here I allocate memory for the structure using the `SizeOf()` method to get the size of the memory that I need (`Person` is a formatted structure). Next I allocate memory for the string, and then I initialize the memory with the values before calling `PrintPerson()`. The signature of this method has an instance

DEVELOPING APPLICATIONS WITH VISUAL STUDIO.NET

of `IntPtr` as the parameter because an instance of `IntPtr` is essentially a `void*` pointer. Manually walking through the structure takes up code and is error prone. Because we have the metadata for the structure, you can pass this structure to `StructureToPtr()`:

```
// C#
IntPtr p;
p = Marshal.AllocCoTaskMem(
        Marshal.SizeOf(typeof(Person)));
Person per = new Person("Richard", 36);
Marshal.StructureToPtr(per, p, false);
PrintPerson(p);
Marshal.DestroyStructure(p, typeof(Person));
Marshal.FreeCoTaskMem(p);
```

In this case you still have to allocate memory for the native structure, but you do not have to allocate memory for embedded types, nor do you need to initialize the fields because `StructureToPtr()` does that. The managed `Person` object has both the metadata and the actual values that `Structure-ToPtr()` needs. When the native method returns, you have to clear up the memory that you allocated. The top-level structure can be freed with a call to `FreeCoTaskMem()`; however, you do not know which allocator the call to `StructureToPtr()` will use.

To handle this problem, I call `DestroyStructure()`. This method goes through all the members of the structure and frees the buffers that may have been allocated for subitems. Incidentally, the last parameter to `Structure-ToPtr()` is a Boolean value that determines whether the subitems within the buffer should be freed before the buffer is initialized with the new data. In my example, this parameter is set to `false` because I pass in an uninitialized buffer. However, if I decide to call `PrintPerson()` another time with another instance of `Person`, I could marshal in the values with a call to `Structure-ToPtr()` with `true` for the third parameter, which would essentially call `DestroyStructure()` for me before marshaling in the values.

Finally, a native method may return a `Person` structure, so managed code can use `PtrToStructure()` to convert this to a managed version. Note that you should check the documentation of the native function to see how the structure is allocated and perform the necessary deallocation in the managed code.

4.1.11 Unmanaged Exceptions

Unmanaged code may throw exceptions. When your code calls unmanaged code, any SEH (structured exception handling) exception thrown by this code will be caught by the runtime, which will attempt to convert the exception into an exception type it understands. The following code, for example:

```
// native C++
int* p = 0;
*p = 0;
```

will throw an exception of the type `System.NullReferenceException` in the managed code that called the function. In some cases the runtime cannot convert the exception type (e.g., if you throw a C++ exception), so instead it throws `System.Runtime.InteropServices.SEHException` in the managed code. SEH exceptions have an associated exception code that can be obtained with a call to `Marshal.GetExceptionCode()`. Note that this method can be called only in a `catch` block.

When you call the native code displayed here, `GetExceptionCode()` returns `0x80004005`, which represents the value `EXCEPTION_ACCESS_VIOLATION`. In addition, Win32 gives detailed information about an exception through the intrinsic `GetExceptionInformation()` method, and the same information is available through `Marshal.GetExceptionPointers()`. However, be aware that the Framework Class Library does little work for you; this method just returns an `IntPtr` value, and you have to decipher what it points to.

The reason why the Framework Class Library does not go to greater lengths is that `IntPtr` returns the equivalent of the Win32 `EXCEPTION_POINTERS` structure, which (among other things) contains a pointer to a `CONTEXT` structure. The `CONTEXT` structure has different members, depending on the processor that is used. If you are interested in the information in the `CONTEXT` structure, you should first call the Win32 `GetSystemInfo()` function through interop and check the `SYSTEM_INFO.wProcessorArchitecture` item before interpreting the context items.

The first item in EXCEPTION_POINTERS is a pointer to an EXCEPTION_RECORD structure, and the first item of that structure is a DWORD that has the exception code. Thus the following code gets the same exception code that is returned from Marshal.GetExceptionCode():

```
// C#
try
{
    CallNativeCode();
}
catch(Exception)
{
    IntPtr exceptionPointers
        = Marshal.GetExceptionPointers();
    IntPtr exceptionRecord
        = Marshal.ReadIntPtr(exceptionPointers);
    Console.WriteLine(
        "Exception Code is {0:X}",
        Marshal.ReadInt32(exceptionRecord));
}
```

As I mentioned earlier, if the [DllImport] attribute metadata has the SetLastError field set to true, you can call Marshal.GetLastWin32Error() to get the Win32 error code that the native function may have set with SetLastError(). You can also call Marshal.GetHRForLastWin32Error() to have this status code translated to an HRESULT (but this merely sets the top WORD to 0x8007 for an error). Once you have an HRESULT, you can throw it as a .NET exception with ThrowExceptionForHR(). This method will throw either an exception specific to the error or the more general COMException type. If the native method is a COM-style method, it makes more sense to set the [DllImport] PreserveSig field to false to indicate that the runtime should throw the exception for you.

4.1.12 Unsafe Code

C++ gives you complete flexibility when you are accessing native code and unmanaged data. As always, however, flexibility comes with complexity and the potential for foul-ups. These are "features" that C# was designed to eliminate, so it removes most of the more dangerous actions. However, you are still able to access native data (outside of the facilities provided by the `Marshal` class) through *unsafe* code.

The idea of unsafe code is that you can access memory through C-style pointers and manipulate them in a C-like way. However, because this means that you are effectively rejecting the runtime's safety net, you have to mark the method with the `unsafe` keyword and compile with the `/unsafe` switch. The `/unsafe` switch causes C# to set the `System.Security.UnverifiableCodeAttribute` on the assembly and adds a permission set that sets the `Flags` property to `SecurityPermissionFlag.SkipVerification`. The net effect is to indicate that the code is not verifiable and hence should not be verified; thus the code *cannot* be downloaded.

One use for unsafe code is to access native buffers through pointer syntax—for example, as follows:

```
// C#
enum AllocType : uint
{ MEM_COMMIT = 0x001000,
  MEM_RESERVE = 0x002000 }
enum ProtectType : uint
{ PAGE_READWRITE = 0x004 }
[DllImport("kernel32.dll")]
static extern IntPtr VirtualAlloc(
    IntPtr start, uint size,
    AllocType type, ProtectType protect);
static unsafe IntPtr AllocMem(uint size)
{
    IntPtr m = VirtualAlloc(
        IntPtr.Zero, size, AllocType.MEM_RESERVE,
        ProtectType.PAGE_READWRITE);
    VirtualAlloc(
        m, size, AllocType.MEM_COMMIT,
        ProtectType.PAGE_READWRITE);
    byte* start = (byte*)(void*)m;
    for (byte* b = start;
         b < start + size; b += sizeof(uint))
    {
        *(uint*)b = 0xd00fdaab;
    }
    return m;
}
```

This method uses the Win32 `VirtualAlloc()` method to allocate some memory and initialize every 32-bit segment of data in it with the value `0xd00fdaab` to indicate that it has not been used yet (I have reversed the bytes so that it appears as `0xbaadf00d` when viewed with a debugger). I could have used the `Marshal.WriteInt32()` method to write to this memory, but I prefer to initialize the memory using pointer syntax. I have chosen to return the pointer from `VirtualAlloc()` in an `IntPtr` structure to accommodate the use of 64-bit pointers. To convert this pointer to a pointer that I can use, I first cast to `void*` so that `IntPtr.op_Explicit()` for `void*` is called. Then I cast to the `byte*` pointer type. In the `for` loop I cast the `byte*` pointer to a `uint*` pointer before assigning it to the appropriate value. Notice that C# supports C-style pointer arithmetic (see the `for` statement), assignment, and dereferencing, as long as these appear in an unsafe method.

In the preceding code the memory buffer is unmanaged. If the memory buffer is on the managed heap, you should pin it first before accessing it with pointers. The reason is that during the time that you are using an unsafe pointer, the garbage collector may move the memory to which the pointer points, and unlike references, the garbage collector cannot change the value in an unsafe pointer. For pinning the buffer, C# provides the `fixed` keyword:

```
// C#
static unsafe void Copy(byte[] src, byte[] dest)
{
    if (dest.Length < src.Length)
        throw new Exception(
            "destination is smaller than the source!");
    fixed (byte* pdest = dest, psrc = src)
    {
        byte* pd = pdest; byte* ps = psrc;
        for (int x = 0; x < src.Length; x++, pd++, ps++)
            *pd = *ps;
    }
}
```

This method copies one array to another using unsafe pointers. The `fixed` statement ensures that the arrays are fixed in memory during the scope indicated by the braces. Note that these fixed pointers are read-only, so they cannot be incremented. This is why I have used an extra pair of temporary pointers (`pd` and `ps`).

4.2 COM Interop

Earlier in this chapter I covered interop with native code, and I showed how this worked with Win32 APIs. The .NET Framework also has support for accessing COM components, and for native code to access .NET components as if they were COM components. This access is seamless in both directions, and the VS.NET debugger has been written to take COM Interop into account, so stepping from managed code to unmanaged code and vice versa also happens seamlessly.

In this section I will outline how to use COM Interop, including the attributes and the tools that you can use. I will also describe some of the pitfalls that can occur, especially with the various interface types that are available in COM.

4.2.1 Interop of COM and Managed Code

COM is based on interface programming; that is, COM objects provide their behaviors through interfaces, and COM clients access COM objects through those interfaces. COM clients access COM objects *only* through interfaces. These interfaces are usually well known[4] and are registered. They also have type information in the form of a type library or *fast-format strings* embedded in a proxy DLL (one that has been compiled with `/Oxcf`).

Every COM object must implement `IUnknown` so that the COM infrastructure is able to place an object with this interface between the client and the object. When the client requests an interface—and the object supports it—this intermediate ("proxy") object can simulate the requested interface, and the client cannot distinguish between the real object and the proxy. DCOM owes its existence to this arrangement because the proxy object can be in an apartment on a different machine from the actual object, and the proxy has the responsibility of talking to the remote object through the remoting infrastructure.

---

4. COM interfaces don't have to be well known. Indeed, a COM interface could be known only by the object and a single, trusted client. For example, much of the VS6 user interface is implemented by interfaces that are known only by Microsoft and the Visual Studio Integration Partners. There are no type libraries and no mechanism to deduce what these interfaces are. This is yet another advantage of COM interface programming.

Interface programming in .NET does not have such an important role because .NET has complete metadata: The runtime creates proxies based on .NET metadata. COM also has metadata, but it is not as complete as .NET metadata. .NET has an interop mechanism, which, as you have seen, effectively describes methods with a managed signature and gives the runtime hints about how to convert these to their native equivalents. For Win32 methods you had to construct these methods yourself, but because COM interfaces have type information, a tool could read this type information and construct the managed signature.

There is such a tool, `tlbimp`, and for almost all objects that you are likely to use, this tool will suffice. I will talk more about `tlbimp` in a moment. In a few cases, `tlbimp` is not sufficient to access a COM object, but all is not lost. You can write your own managed interfaces and use attributes to describe how COM Interop should be applied.

Recall that when you use Win32 interop, you effectively have two method signatures: the managed signature and the native signature. Platform Invoke performs the conversion between the two, which involves conversion of parameter types and sometimes extra actions, like reading error values and throwing managed exceptions. COM interfaces are collections of methods, and a COM object has one or more of these interfaces. The situation is more complicated because of the increased number of methods, but there is still the same concept of a managed signature and a native signature.

However, COM objects have another level of complication: COM objects have *identity* and *lifetime*. Both are handled through the `IUnknown` interface. `AddRef()` and `Release()` alter the reference count on the object that implements the `IUnknown` interface. If this object is the actual object, then when this reference count falls to zero, the object is allowed to destroy itself. If the object is a proxy object, there will be a corresponding stub object in the real object's apartment, which manages the real object's lifetime. When the reference count on the proxy object falls to zero, the stub object is informed, and it determines whether the real object should destroy itself.

The lifetime of a .NET object is determined by the garbage collector. Clearly, then, if managed code has access to a COM object, the lifetime methods of `IUnknown` must be called. In particular, when the garbage collector determines that the reference to the COM object is no longer needed, there must be a mechanism to call `Release()` on that object. Conversely, if a COM client has access to a .NET component through COM Interop, the lifetime of the .NET component should be determined by the COM client (or at least influenced by it). .NET has a solution, as you'll see shortly.

Each COM object has an identity, allowing a client to determine which object it is talking to. From the client's perspective, the identity is obtained by examination of the absolute value of the object's `IUnknown` pointer. The value of this pointer should be the same for a single object, so whenever an object is queried for `IUnknown`, it should *always* return the same pointer (this is a requirement only for this interface).

COM marshaling ensures that a proxy will always be a proxy to a single object. When an interface pointer is marshaled to another apartment, the new proxy will be a proxy to the real object, even if the original interface pointer that was marshaled was on a proxy: You can never have a proxy to a proxy. In this case the absolute value of the `IUnknown` pointer obtained on one proxy will be different from the absolute value of the `IUnknown` pointer obtained on another proxy. But to compare the two interface pointers, they have to be marshaled into the same apartment, and the marshaling infrastructure will ensure that if these `IUnknown` pointers are proxies for the same object, when they are marshaled into the same apartment they will have the same value.

There are several clearly important issues here. If managed code accesses a COM object, it should maintain the COM reference count so that when the garbage collector decides that there are no more references to the COM object, it can release the COM reference that the managed code has on the object. If the managed code requests an interface on the COM object, `Query-Interface()` must be called, and this method must be presented to the managed code as a managed interface. Finally, if the managed reference to the COM object is passed through remoting, the identity of the object should also be passed.

Looking at the problem from another point of view, if a COM client has access to a .NET component through COM Interop, it will expect to access the object's behavior through interfaces. The .NET component may implement .NET interfaces, but it may not, in which case COM Interop must concoct a COM interface from the .NET component's noninterface methods. The .NET component must live as long as the COM client thinks it has a reference; thus something in the managed world must ensure that a .NET reference is maintained on the component and that when the COM client releases its last reference count, the .NET reference is freed.

Finally, during the time that the COM client holds an interface pointer to a .NET component, that interface pointer must remain valid. The COM client will hold a proxy pointer, which will remain valid as long as the proxy lives, but the object to which the proxy points must also remain valid. If the garbage collector decides to move the object around in memory, a call from the COM client should reach the .NET component. The GC will fix up all managed references, but clearly there must be some code to ensure that the COM proxy will be "connected" to such a reference in such a way that the "connection" always remains valid.

.NET performs all of this through two runtime objects: the *COM callable wrapper* (*CCW*) and the *runtime callable wrapper* (*RCW*).

4.2.2 COM Callable Wrapper

Figure 4.2 shows the COM callable wrapper in action. The COM client calls `CoCreateInstance()` with the appropriate CLSID (which I will talk about later) and gets the COM callable wrapper with the interface that the client requested.

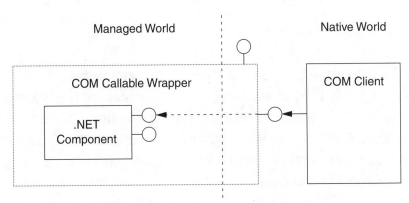

Figure 4.2 COM callable wrapper

The CCW conceptually has two parts: a managed part and a native part. The COM client accesses the native part, which implements `IUnknown` and hence has a COM identity. The managed part of the CCW holds a managed reference to the component and hence keeps the component alive. If the GC moves the component on the managed heap, the reference held by the CCW will be changed accordingly. The CCW ensures that the calls from the COM client will be passed through the managed reference.

In addition, the CCW will implement other COM interfaces on demand when the client requests them. The .NET component has complete metadata, so the CCW allows COM late binding by implementing `IDispatch` and using this metadata. You can access this metadata as COM type information using the following code:

```
// unmanaged C++
IProvideClassInfo* pclassInfo = NULL;
HRESULT hr = S_OK;
hr = CoCreateInstance(
    clsid, NULL, CLSCTX_INPROC_SERVER,
    IID_IProvideClassInfo, (void**)&pclassInfo);
if (SUCCEEDED(hr))
{
    ITypeInfo* ptypeInfo;
    hr = pclassInfo->GetClassInfo(&ptypeinfo);
    if (SUCCEEDED(hr))
    {
        // use ITypeInfo here
        ptypeInfo->Release();
    }
    pclassInfo->Release();
}
```

The CCW implements `IProvideClassInfo` automatically. This interface returns an object that implements `ITypeInfo` to provide the type information.

The CLSID that is used in this example is either one that is generated for the .NET component, or one that you assign to it. To assign a CLSID, you use the `[GuidAttribute]` attribute from the `System.Runtime.InteropServices` namespace (in this case it is best to use the complete name, rather than the abbreviated name without the `Attribute` suffix, because there is a value type called `Guid` in the `System` namespace). If you do not assign a CLSID explicitly, the `regasm` tool will do this automatically for you.

```csharp
// C# compiled with csc /t:library Person.cs
using System;
using System.Reflection;
using System.Runtime.InteropServices;
[assembly:AssemblyKeyFile("person.snk")]
namespace RTG
{
    [GuidAttribute(
        "31D7DFC2-051E-422b-869F-D85A7F724DC7")]
    public class Person
    {
        public Person() { Name = ""; Age = 0; }
        private string name;
        private short age;
        public string Name
        { get{ return name; } set{ name=value; } }
        public short Age
        { get{ return age;  } set{ age=value; } }
        public string GetPersonInfo()
        {
            if (Name == "" && Age == 0)
                return "unassigned";
            return Name + " is " + Age + " years old";
        }
    }
}
```

This simple class represents a person. It merely gives access to name and age properties, and to a simple method that summarizes the person. When the class is used via COM Interop, the assembly is loaded by the runtime, so Fusion is used to locate the assembly. As you will remember from Chapter 1, Fusion will load an assembly if it is in the current directory or in a subdirectory according to the various rules applied through the configuration files. This makes sense if the class is to be used by only a single application, and it helps solve the COM versioning problems outlined in Chapter 1 by allowing side-by-side COM components.

If you intend to use the class via COM Interop from a directory other than the ones that Fusion will search, the runtime will not be able to load the assembly and hence the class will not be loaded. There are two ways to solve this problem: You can provide a code base that will identify the location of the assembly (which I'll explain later), or you can make the class global and put its assembly in the GAC. In both cases you have to give the assembly a strong name. This is why I have used the `[AssemblyKeyFile]` attribute. To register this class in the GAC I need to invoke the following:

```
regasm Person.dll
gacutil /i Person.dll
```

The first statement adds COM entries to the system registry; the second adds the assembly to the GAC. The `Person` class is defined in the `RTG` namespace, so the `regasm` tool will generate a ProgID (programmatic ID) of `RTG.Person.1` for this class. If you want to specify the ProgID explicitly, you can use the `[ProgId]` attribute.

The `regasm` tool adds an entry for the ProgID and CLSID of the class, and it registers the class as an `InprocServer32` type, giving `mscoree.dll` as the server.[5] To allow the runtime to locate the class, `regasm` also adds a value called `Assembly` that has the full assembly name (name, version, culture, strong name) and a key called `Class` that identifies the class in the assembly.

If I obtain the `ITypeInfo` interface for the object using the C++ code shown earlier and iterate through the types defined, I get the following type information:

```
// IDL
[
  uuid(FB678ED9-B901-3903-A108-24B85F10505B),
  version(1.0),
  custom(90883F05-3D28-11D2-8F17-00A0C9A6186D,
         "Person, Version=0.0.0.0,
         Culture=neutral,
         PublicKeyToken=958ab0ba2a5b045a")
]
library Person
```

---

5. It does this whether the assembly is a library (DLL) or an executable (EXE). This makes sense because the assembly must be loaded by `mscoree.dll` to provide the CCW. If you want process isolation, you should load `mscoree.dll` in a surrogate.

DEVELOPING APPLICATIONS WITH VISUAL STUDIO.NET

```
{
    [
        uuid(31D7DFC2-051E-422B-869F-D85A7F724DC7),
        version(1.0),
        custom(GUID_ManagedName, "RTG.Person")
    ]
    coclass Person
    {
        [default] interface IDispatch;
        dispinterface _Object;
    };
};
```

This code gives the assembly information through the `library` statement, and it indicates that the class has a managed name of `RTG.Person` applied through a custom Interface Definition Language (IDL) attribute (`GUID_ManagedName`). In addition, this code indicates to automation clients that the class implements `IDispatch`, and that the class represents a managed object because it derives from `System.Object`. The class implements the `_Object` interface:

```
// IDL
[   uuid(65074F7F-63C0-304E-AF0A-D51741CB4A8D),
    dual, hidden, nonextensible,
    custom(GUID_ManagedName, "System.Object") ]
interface _Object : IDispatch
{
    [id(DISPID_VALUE), propget,
     custom(GUID_ManagedName, "System.Object")]
    HRESULT ToString(
        [out, retval,
         custom(GUID_ManagedName, "System.Object")]
        BSTR* pRetVal);
    [id(0x60020001),
     custom(GUID_ManagedName, "System.Object")]
    HRESULT Equals(
        [in,
         custom(GUID_ManagedName, "System.Object")]
        VARIANT obj,
        [out, retval,
         custom(GUID_ManagedName, "System.Object")]
        VARIANT_BOOL* pRetVal);
```

```
    [id(0x60020002),
     custom(GUID_ManagedName, "System.Object")]
    HRESULT GetHashCode(
        [out, retval,
         custom(GUID_ManagedName, "System.Object")]
         LONG* pRetVal);
    [id(0x60020003),
     custom(GUID_ManagedName, "System.Object")]
    HRESULT GetType(
        [out, retval,
         custom(GUID_ManagedName, "System.Object")]
         _Type** pRetVal);
};
```

You will recognize these methods from the `System.Object` class. They use straightforward COM types except for `GetType()`, which returns the `_Type` interface, which is defined in the `mscorlib.tlb` library. However, there is a problem: Where are the properties and methods that I defined on the class?

The `Person` class does not implement a specific `IPerson` interface. .NET does not require that you access your class behavior through interfaces, but COM does. To accommodate this requirement, .NET has an attribute, `[Class-Interface]`, that indicates that the class members should be accessible through an interface with the same name as the class prefixed with an underscore:

```
// C#
namespace RTG
{
    [GuidAttribute(
     "31D7DFC2-051E-422b-869F-D85A7F724DC7"),
     ClassInterface(ClassInterfaceType.AutoDual)]
    public class Person
    { /* members */ }
}
```

When this code is compiled and the assembly is run through `regasm`, type information will be generated for the class members (the properties `Name` and `Age`, and the method `GetPersonInfo()`). Now when the type information is extracted, the coclass will implement the following interface:

```
[ uuid(7CFA5A32-2243-3B26-9416-56E04A36710A),
  dual, hidden, nonextensible,
  custom(GUID_ManagedName, "RTG.Person") ]
interface _Person : IDispatch
{
    [id(DISPID_VALUE), propget,
     custom(GUID_ManagedName, "RTG.Person")]
    HRESULT ToString(
        [out, retval,
         custom(GUID_ManagedName, "RTG.Person")]
         BSTR* pRetVal);
    [id(0x60020001),
     custom(GUID_ManagedName, "RTG.Person")]
    HRESULT Equals(
        [in,
         custom(GUID_ManagedName, "RTG.Person")]
         VARIANT obj,
        [out, retval,
         custom(GUID_ManagedName, "RTG.Person")]
         VARIANT_BOOL* pRetVal);
    [id(0x60020002),
     custom(GUID_ManagedName, "RTG.Person")]
    HRESULT GetHashCode(
        [out, retval,
         custom(GUID_ManagedName, "RTG.Person")]
         LONG* pRetVal);
    [id(0x60020003),
     custom(GUID_ManagedName, "RTG.Person")]
    HRESULT GetType(
        [out, retval,
         custom(GUID_ManagedName, "RTG.Person")]
         _Type** pRetVal);
    [id(0x60020004), propget,
     custom(GUID_ManagedName, "RTG.Person")]
    HRESULT Name(
        [out, retval,
         custom(GUID_ManagedName, "RTG.Person")]
         BSTR* pRetVal);
    [id(0x60020004), propput,
     custom(GUID_ManagedName, "RTG.Person")]
    HRESULT Name(
        [in, custom(GUID_ManagedName, "RTG.Person")]
         BSTR pRetVal);
```

```
[id(0x60020006), propget,
 custom(GUID_ManagedName, "RTG.Person")]
HRESULT Age(
   [out, retval,
    custom(GUID_ManagedName, "RTG.Person")]
    short* pRetVal);
[id(0x60020006), propput,
 custom(GUID_ManagedName, "RTG.Person")]
HRESULT Age(
   [in, custom(GUID_ManagedName, "RTG.Person")]
   short pRetVal);
[id(0x60020008),
 custom(GUID_ManagedName, "RTG.Person")]
HRESULT GetPersonInfo(
   [out, retval,
    custom(GUID_ManagedName, "RTG.Person")]
    BSTR* pRetVal);
};
```

Now the COM client can access the object's methods through early binding because the _Person interface is a dual interface. However, there is another problem: COM clients that use early binding expect the interface to remain fixed because this is a requirement of COM interfaces. If the .NET component is changed to have another member, the class interface will have another member and the early-binding clients will be broken because the interface will have changed. Late-binding (automation) interfaces do not fare better because the dispatch identifiers (DISPIDs) of the members may change between versions. Another option is to use ClassInterfaceType.AutoDispatch as the class interface type. Although this interface type is version proof because the DISPIDs of the methods are generated at runtime, the downside is that these methods can be accessed only through late binding.

Clearly the solution to successful COM Interop is to follow COM's rules and define immutable interfaces on your classes. If a later version of Person adds more members, these should be part of a new interface so that older COM clients can still access the class.

One interesting exercise is to trawl through all of the interfaces registered in the system registry, extract the interface IDs (IIDs), and then query an object to see if it supports each interface (this is effectively what OLEView does). If you do this on the `Person` class (without a dual class interface), you will find that it supports the following interfaces:

```
IUnknown
IMarshal
IDispatch
_Object
IProvideClassInfo
IConnectionPointContainer
IManagedObject
IObjectSafety
ISupportErrorInfo
```

The `Person` class supports `IConnectionPointContainer` so that it can generate events through managed delegates. This class does not have any managed events, so the implementation of this interface does not allow clients to attach to it. The `IManagedObject` interface is interesting. It is defined in `mscoree.tlb` and looks like this:

```
// IDL
[ uuid(C3FCC19E-A970-11D2-8B5A-00A0C9B7C9C4),
  oleautomation ]
interface IManagedObject : IUnknown
{
    HRESULT GetSerializedBuffer(
        [out] BSTR* pBSTR);
    HRESULT _stdcall GetObjectIdentity(
        [out] BSTR* pBSTRGUID,
        [out] int* AppDomainID, [out] int* pCCW);
};
```

As the name suggests, if the class is serializable (i.e., has the `[Serializable]` attribute or implements `ISerializable`), then `GetSerializedBuffer()` will obtain the serialized state of the object and return it in a `BSTR` (this is not the case with my object). The `GetObjectIdentity()` method returns a GUID as the identity of the object. This ID should be unique and can be compared with other references to managed objects of the same type. In addition, there is an identifier for the application domain where the managed object is running, and an identifier for the CCW. Because the runtime creates exactly one CCW for an object, you can use the identifier for the CCW as the identity of the .NET object.

4.2.3 Exporting Type Information

There are two tools for generating type information from assemblies: `tlbexp` and `regasm`. The `tlbexp` tool is straightforward: It takes an assembly and from the metadata generates type information, which it puts in a type library. The `regasm` tool does more than this: It registers components and interfaces according to the metadata they contain, and it can also generate COM type information and register it as a type library. Using `regasm` without any switches will add a ProgID and a CLSID entry for the classes in the assembly. As I mentioned earlier, `regasm` identifies the runtime as the in-process server, but it also gives information about the assembly and the name of the class. At runtime, the CCW will read the metadata in the assembly so that it can generate the type information for the interfaces (for `IDispatch` and `ITypeInfo`) and implement the actual COM interfaces that will delegate to the .NET component.

Along with the classes, `regasm` will register an application ID (`AppID`) for the assembly. This means that you can use OLEView to specify a surrogate process so that the class is created out of process, and hence you can also specify COM launch and access permissions for the server.

Interfaces defined in the assembly will *not* be registered because COM Interop supports type library–marshaled interfaces or automation interfaces, and by default it assumes that interfaces are accessed as automation (i.e., late-binding) interfaces. If you want to register an interface as a type library–marshaled interface, you have to use `regasm` to create and register a type library:

```
regasm /tlb:person.tlb person.dll
```

This command will extract the type information, put it in the type library `person.tlb`, and then register it in situ. Note, however, that the registration does not add a `TypeLib` entry for the class because as far as .NET is concerned, the type information for components should be accessed only at runtime. You should not rely on cached information. However, interfaces are a different issue: If you expressly define an interface and export it to a type library, you are making the assertion that the interface is immutable, so you are happy to have a definition of the interface in the registry.

One of the reasons for not using type libraries to describe classes in an assembly is that you will have two descriptions on your machine: the type library and the assembly. The presence of two files means that the two may go out of sync, and one of the reasons for .NET metadata was to keep type descriptions with the types they describe to prevent a mismatch. Of course, if the type library is generated whenever an assembly is generated, the two will never go out of sync. And if the type library is part of the same code module as the assembly, there will be no problems with deployment. The .NET Framework SDK has a sample project called `TlbGen` that does this.

This tool relies on the fact that assemblies are PE (portable executable) files, and PE files have a resource section. The tool generates a type library from the assembly using a class called `System.Runtime.InteropServices.TypeLibConverter`. The `ConvertAssemblyToTypeLib()` method on this class takes the assembly, generates a type library, and returns the unmanaged `ICreateTypeLib` interface for the type library that was created. `TlbGen` uses COM Interop to call this unmanaged interface and save the changes to a temporary file. To add the type library as a resource, the tool first creates a copy of the assembly and then uses the Win32 `UpdateResource()` API on the copy.

The newly generated assembly will have objects accessible through COM, so it needs to have a strong name and needs to be signed. The signing involves the strong name and a hash of the code and resources in the assembly, so these items must be generated. `mscoree.dll` is an unmanaged shim to the .NET Runtime. In addition, it exports native functions for creating strong names and signing assemblies. The `TlbGen` tool uses these functions through Platform Invoke. Finally, the tool registers the newly generated assembly as a type library. The Win32 `LoadTypeLibEx()` function accesses the type library resource, adds an entry for it, and registers the interfaces described in it.

If an assembly is associated with a specific type library, it should be marked with the `[PrimaryInteropAssembly]` attribute to indicate that users of the types in the type library should use this specific assembly whenever possible. If you choose, you can also export a REGEDIT file with information about the components in an assembly using the `/regfile` switch on `regasm`. However, be aware that this file will not generate registry information about interfaces (because if interfaces need registry entries, they are type library marshaled) or about type libraries (because it cannot guarantee that a type library has been generated).

I mentioned earlier that Fusion is used to locate the assembly. However, this means that the assembly must be either in the same directory as the COM client or in the GAC. A third option is to explicitly give the location of the assembly COM-style—that is, using the `/codebase` switch with `regasm`, which adds a `codebase` value with the current location of the assembly. Finally, `regasm` has an `/unregister` switch, which you can use to remove the registration entries added by a previous call to `regasm`.

4.2.4 Registration

The `regasm` tool will register the types in an assembly. If you choose, you can do the same thing programmatically. The .NET Framework provides the necessary tools in the `RegistrationServices` class in the `System.Runtime.InteropServices` namespace. You can register all types in an assembly by calling `RegisterAssembly()`, and you can unregister an assembly with `UnregisterAssembly()`. Both methods take an `Assembly` object; you can also register just one type using `RegisterTypeForComClients()`. In addition, you can get information from the class about the types in the assembly (`GetRegistrableTypesInAssembly()`) and about individual types (`TypeRepresentsComType()` and `TypeRequires-Registration()`).

If you have a specific COM registration requirement for the types in your assembly, you can provide a registration method. This is a static method that takes either a single `Type` or a `string` parameter, returns `void`, and is marked with `[ComRegisterFunction]`. If your version takes a string, then the runtime will pass a string giving the registry key path where the object is being registered; it is in this format:

```
HKEY_CLASSES_ROOT\CLSID\{GUID}
```

If your version has a `Type` parameter, then the type of the object being registered will be passed. You can get the registry path from the type because the GUID of a type is generated by `regasm` by a call to `Marshal.GenerateGuidForType()`, which always returns the same GUID for a type.

The antithesis of the registration method is the unregistration method, which is a static method that takes a `Type` parameter, returns `void`, and is marked with `[ComUnregisterFunction]`.

4.2.5 Runtime Callable Wrapper

The runtime callable wrapper (RCW) is illustrated in Figure 4.3. The .NET client requests an instance of the COM component, and the runtime creates the RCW, which acts as a bridge between the managed and native worlds. The RCW has the interface that the .NET client requests. When the .NET client casts this interface reference to another interface reference corresponding to an interface that the COM component supports, the RCW will return a reference to that interface, too. The question arises: How does the runtime know how to create these interfaces on the RCW?

The answer lies in metadata. To use a COM component through interop, you must create a managed version of the interfaces that the COM component implements—much in the same way that you create a managed signature for the native function that you access through Platform Invoke. There are two ways to create these managed interfaces: by hand or using `tlbimp`.

The `tlbimp` tool takes COM type information and generates an assembly. The VS.NET IDE does much of this work for you. It is interesting to see what this

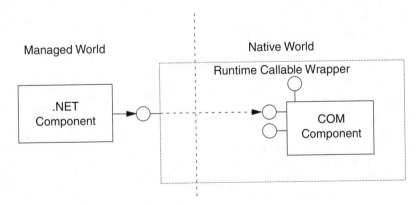

Figure 4.3   Runtime callable wrapper

tool does. As an example, here is a COM object (the C++ code uses the new Visual C++ attributes in VS.NET; for details, see Chapter 7):

```cpp
// unmanaged C++ compiled with cl /LD person.cpp
#define _ATL_ATTRIBUTES
#include <atlbase.h>
#include <atlcom.h>
[ module(dll,
    uuid="31D7DFC4-051E-422b-869F-D85A7F724DC7",
    name="PersonLib") ];
[ dual,
  uuid("31D7DFC3-051E-422b-869F-D85A7F724DC7") ]
__interface IPerson : IDispatch
{
    [id(1), propget]
    HRESULT Name([out, retval] BSTR* pRetVal);
    [id(1), propput]
    HRESULT Name([in] BSTR Val);
    [id(2), propget]
    HRESULT Age([out, retval] short* pRetVal);
    [id(2), propput]
    HRESULT Age([in] short Val);
    [id(3)]
    HRESULT GetPersonInfo(
        [out, retval] BSTR* pRetVal);
};
[ coclass,
    uuid("31D7DFC2-051E-422b-869F-D85A7F724DC7"),
    threading("Both"),
    vi_progid("RTG.Person.1"),
    progid("RTG.Person") ]
class Person : public IPerson
{
    CComBSTR name; short age;
public:
    Person() : age(0) {}
    HRESULT get_Name(BSTR* pRetVal)
    { return name.CopyTo(pRetVal); }
    HRESULT put_Name(BSTR Val)
    { name = Val; return S_OK; }
    HRESULT get_Age(short* pRetVal)
    { *pRetVal = age; return S_OK; }
    HRESULT put_Age(short Val)
    { age = Val; return S_OK; }
```

DEVELOPING APPLICATIONS WITH VISUAL STUDIO.NET

```
      HRESULT GetPersonInfo(BSTR* pRetVal)
      {
          CComBSTR bstr;
          if (name.Length() == 0 && age == 0)
              bstr = L"unassigned";
          else
          {
              bstr = name;
              bstr += L" is ";
              WCHAR strAge[12];
              swprintf(strAge, L"%d", age);
              bstr += strAge;
              bstr += L" years old";
          }
          return bstr.CopyTo(pRetVal);
      }
};
```

This class is essentially the same as the .NET class shown earlier. The attributes are used by the Visual C++ attribute provider to generate ATL code to implement the COM object. When compiled, this code will create a COM DLL server. To use this server in managed code, you have to create an assembly using `tlbimp`:

```
tlbimp person.dll /out:netperson.dll
```

This command generates a library DLL that contains metadata for the COM object:

```
// pseudo C# from IL
[ assembly: GuidAttribute(
    "31D7DFC4-051E-422b-869F-D85A7F724DC7") ]
[ assembly: ImportedFromTypeLib("PersonLib")]
namespace netPerson
{
    [ TypeLibTypeAttribute(
        TypeLibTypeFlags.FDispatchable |
        TypeLibTypeFlags.FDual),
      GuidAttribute(
        "31D7DFC3-051E-422b-869F-D85A7F724DC7")]
    public interface IPerson
    { /* see later */ }
    [ ClassInterfaceAttribute(
        ClassInterfaceType.None),
        TypeLibTypeAttribute(
```

```
        TypeLibTypeFlags.FCanCreate),
      GuidAttribute(
        "31D7DFC2-051E-422b-869F-D85A7F724DC7")]
  public class Person : IPerson
  { /* see later */ }
}
```

Here I have rewritten the IL as C# to illustrate what is happening: The tool creates an assembly and marks it with the LIBID (library ID) from the COM server. It then creates a namespace with the same name as the COM server's `library` statement, and within this namespace it creates managed definitions for the types defined in the type library (in this case an interface and a coclass). These types are marked with attributes that indicate to COM Interop how it can call the types: These are analogs of the type library attributes used by the type library marshaler, so both types have a GUID and the class is indicated as being creatable (i.e., the opposite of `[noncreatable]`), and the interface is shown to be a `dual` interface.

The definition of the interface is fairly straightforward; it lists the properties and methods just as if they were managed properties and methods. The difference is that each item has a `[DispId]` attribute that gives the DISPID read from the type library. The class is more interesting. As you might imagine, this class has a constructor and methods for the method and properties of the class. Here is the IL for the method:

```
// IL
.method public hidebysig newslot virtual
   instance string marshal(bstr)
   GetPersonInfo() runtime managed internalcall
{
   .custom instance void
     [mscorlib]System.Runtime.InteropServices
     .DispIdAttribute::.ctor(int32)
       = ( 01 00 03 00 00 00 00 00 )
   .override netPerson.IPerson::GetPersonInfo
}
```

The `tlbimp` tool has essentially generated what would be described in C# as follows:

```
// C#
using System;
```

```
using System.Runtime.InteropServices;
using System.Runtime.CompilerServices;
[ DispId(3),
  MethodImpl(
     MethodImplOptions.InternalCall,
     MethodCodeType=MethodCodeType.Runtime) ]
[ return: MarshalAs(UnmanagedType.BStr) ]
public extern virtual string GetPersonInfo();
```

In other words, the method is implemented by the runtime, so you cannot see the code that does the implementation. The assembly has sufficient metadata for another .NET assembly to be able to use the COM component as if it were a managed .NET component.

Notice that the method returns a `string` object rather than an HRESULT. The `tlbimp` tool has read the type information and determined the parameter marked with `[retval]`. If an error occurs, COM Interop will create an exception based on the HRESULT that the COM method returns. This will be one of the exceptions in the Framework Class Library (`COMException`).

The type created by the `tlbimp` tool is a .NET type, and as such it can be used as a base type in .NET inheritance. That is, your code can derive from this type, so in effect you will derive from the COM object. This is a facility that does not exist in COM.

COM Interop creates an apartment when calling a COM object. This can be a single-threaded apartment (STA) or a multithreaded apartment (MTA), and you can read `Thread.ApartmentState` on the current thread to determine which one is used (by default it will be MTA). If you create the thread, you can use this property to specify the apartment type before any calls are made. If you want all of your calls to assume a specific apartment type, add the `[STAThread]` or `[MTAThread]` attribute to the entry point of the application. VS.NET will apply this attribute to the `Main()` function of a C# Windows application. This attribute is necessary if the application used COM components, but in this case do not be tempted to change it to `[MTAThread]` because any thread that has user interface code *must* run as a single-threaded apartment.

Usually the type library approach using `tlbimp` is sufficient, but sometimes you may not have a type library, in which case you have to construct the metadata yourself. When you do this, you have to shift your thinking from .NET mode, in which programming is carried out on types, to COM mode, in which programming is carried out by interfaces. The primary task is to define the interfaces that the COM object supports. Here is the interface definition defined for the COM object I showed earlier:

```csharp
// C#
[ ComImport,
  GuidAttribute(
      "31D7DFC3-051E-422b-869F-D85A7F724DC7" )
]
public interface IPerson
{
    [DispId(1)] string Name {get; set;}
    [DispId(2)] short Age {get; set;}
    [DispId(3)] string GetPersonInfo();
}
```

This definition looks remarkably like a `dispinterface` definition in Object Description Language (ODL). The interface is marked with the `[ComImport]` attribute to indicate to the runtime that COM Interop should be used, and because it is a COM interface it *must* have a GUID. We know that a type that implements this interface is the `Person` coclass. But we have to remember COM interface programming: The only interface that an object *must* support is `IUnknown`, and since that is assumed, we don't have to specify it explicitly. The only time we know for certain the interface(s) that a coclass supports is at runtime, when we ask for an interface through a call to `IUnknown::QueryInterface()`. Don't be fooled by a type library; it is just a suggestion about the interfaces that the object supports. With this in mind, here is the definition for the managed `Person` class:

```csharp
// C#
[ ComImport,
  GuidAttribute(
      "31D7DFC2-051E-422b-869F-D85A7F724DC7" )
]
public class Person { }
```

Again, the `[ComImport]` attribute is used and the type has a GUID, but notice that the type has no members and does not derive from the `IPerson` interface. To use this class you have to follow interface programming semantics and explicitly ask for the interfaces that you want:

```
// C#
Person person = new Person();
IPerson richard = (IPerson)person;
if (richard != null)
{
    richard.Name = "Richard";
    richard.Age = 36;
    Console.WriteLine(richard.GetPersonInfo());
}
```

By calling `QueryInterface()` when the cast is made, COM Interop determines at runtime whether the `Person` object supports the `IPerson` interface.

4.2.6 COM Automation Types

Automation types are essentially an evolution of the types used by early versions of Visual Basic. There are four main complex types to consider: BSTR, VARIANT, SAFEARRAY, and CURRENCY.

The BSTR type is a length-prefixed string—or more accurately, a size-prefixed buffer because the prefix gives the size of the buffer in *bytes,* not characters. The runtime will happily convert a BSTR value to a managed String type during marshaling, but because the BSTR contains no information about the type of string it holds (it can even hold a binary buffer), you have to provide information through [MarshalAs]. UnmanagedType.BStr is used for BSTR values generated on Win32 systems (and hence Unicode), and UnmanagedType.AnsiBStr is used for Win16 BSTR values and binary buffers.

The VARIANT type has a member that contains the type of the data held in the VARIANT, so when a VARIANT parameter is passed to managed code, the marshaler will convert it to the appropriate managed type. The tlbimp tool will convert a VARIANT parameter to an Object reference, which you can cast to the appropriate type (checking the type by calling Object.GetType() if necessary).

Managed arrays contain information about their rank and bounds. In this respect they are much like the SAFEARRAY type. The difference is that SAFE-ARRAY objects are generic and contain the type of the data they hold as a data member, whereas a managed array is typed to the type of data that it holds. Because of the close similarity between SAFEARRAY objects and managed arrays, COM Interop is quite straightforward. For example, this IDL:

```
// IDL
[id(1)] HRESULT GetArray(
    [out, retval] SAFEARRAY(BSTR)* sa);
// Visual C++ COM attributes
[id(1)] HRESULT GetArray(
    [out, retval, satype(BSTR)] SAFEARRAY** sa);
```

is imported into managed C# as follows:

```
// C#
[DispId(1)] string[] GetArray();
```

The automation CURRENCY data type presents something of a problem because it is defined as a 64-bit integer data type and is scaled by 10,000 to give four decimal places and 15 digits to the left. The problem occurs when you are marshaling a CURRENCY value from the managed world to the unmanaged world, particularly if the conversion is done through a VARIANT or Object parameter, because you need to indicate that the data you pass to such a method is the automation type VT_CY, and not VT_R8 (if you use a managed double type) or VT_I8 (if you use a managed long type). The solution lies in the framework class CurrencyWrapper. When this class is passed as a parameter, the marshaler knows that the data type is CURRENCY and hence ensures that the VARIANT value is initialized accordingly:

```
// IDL
[id(1)] CreditAccount(VARIANT v);
// C#
decimal cheque = 100.23;
account.CreditAccount(new CurrencyWrapper(cheque));
```

Similarly, if you want to pass a managed object via a VARIANT so that the COM code can call the object through an IDispatch pointer (VT_DISPATCH), you can use the DispatchWrapper class. If you want to pass an object as an IUnknown pointer (VT_UNKNOWN), you can use the UnknownWrapper class. Finally, if you want to pass an error value (VT_ERROR), you can use the ErrorWrapper class.

DEVELOPING APPLICATIONS WITH VISUAL STUDIO.NET

4.2.7 COM Interface Types

COM essentially has three types of interfaces: RPC-like interfaces; `dispinterface` interfaces, which are named implementations of `IDispatch`; and `dual` interfaces, which have a vtable with `IDispatch` followed by the methods of the interface so that a client can access the methods either through `IDispatch::Invoke()` or through the vtable. RPC-like interfaces are typically marshaled through separate proxy-stub DLLs, although if they use automation-compatible types (and are marked with `[oleautomation]`), they can be marshaled by the type library marshaler. Dual interfaces are typically type library marshaled (`[dual]` implies `[oleautomation]`), but can be proxy-stub DLL marshaled, although there are usually few reasons to want to do this. Automation interfaces are always type library marshaled.

Managed code needs to know the type of interface that a COM component implements particularly to distinguish between automation interfaces and early-bound interfaces because with a `dispinterface` COM Interop needs to make a call to `IDispatch::Invoke()` rather than to the actual method. If you know that the interface is type library marshaled, you can use the `[Automation-Proxy(true)]` attribute on the managed interface.

When exporting an interface from a managed assembly, you have to specify the type of interface that will be exported. The `[InterfaceType]` attribute does this. For example, take a look at this code:

```csharp
// C#
using System;
using System.Runtime.InteropServices;
[ GuidAttribute(
    "8AF805BF-152F-4cba-9610-79D9FA79108D") ]
public interface ITester
{
    void CallMe();
}
[ GuidAttribute(
    "8AF805BE-152F-4cba-9610-79D9FA79108D") ]
public class Tester : ITester
{
    public void CallMe()
    { Console.WriteLine("you called me"); }
}
```

By default, the `ITester` interface will be exported as a dual interface, which implies the following native C++ code to access it:

```cpp
// unmanaged C++
#include <objbase.h>
#include <stdio.h>
#pragma comment (lib, "ole32.lib")
struct __declspec(
    uuid("8AF805BF-152F-4cba-9610-79D9FA79108D"))
ITester : IDispatch
{
    virtual HRESULT __stdcall CallMe() = 0;
};
class __declspec(
    uuid("8AF805BE-152F-4cba-9610-79D9FA79108D"))
Tester;

void main()
{
    CoInitialize(NULL);
    HRESULT hr;
    ITester* p = NULL;
    hr = CoCreateInstance(
        __uuidof(Tester), NULL,
        CLSCTX_INPROC_SERVER,
        __uuidof(ITester), (void**)&p);
    if (SUCCEEDED(hr))
    {
        p->CallMe();
        p->Release();
    }
    CoUninitialize();
}
```

For convenience I have used the `__declspec(uuid())` operator to "attach" GUID values to symbols in my project. Doing this means that I can extract the GUID later by using the `__uuidof()` operator. I have also defined the interface in the C++ file so that I can change the definition if necessary. Because the object is loaded in process and all .NET components have the `ThreadingModel` value `Both`, the CCW will be created in the same apartment as the calling code; thus COM marshaling is not used.

This code essentially calls the eighth function pointer in the `ITester` vtable (before `CallMe()` there are the seven methods of `IDispatch`, including the three methods of `IUnknown` at the beginning). Because COM marshaling is not used and I don't need to support scripting clients, it does not make sense to have the `IDispatch` methods. Thus I could be tempted to define the interface as follows:

```
// unmanaged C++
struct __declspec(
    uuid("8AF805BF-152F-4cba-9610-79D9FA79108D"))
ITester : IUnknown
{
    virtual HRESULT __stdcall CallMe() = 0;
};
```

I have highlighted the change. Of course, what I have just done is a cardinal sin in COM interface programming because I have completely changed the layout of the interface: Now the interface has only the three `IUnknown` methods and `CallMe()`. If I run the code now, the line that calls `CallMe()` through the interface pointer will actually execute `IDispatch::GetTypeInfoCount()` (the first method in `IDispatch` after the `IUnknown` methods). To remedy the situation, the managed code should be changed to this:

```
// C#
[ GuidAttribute(
      "8AF805BF-152F-4cba-9610-79D9FA79108D"),
   InterfaceType(ComInterfaceType.InterfaceIsIUnknown)
]
public interface ITester
{
    void CallMe();
}
```

`InterfaceType` indicates to COM Interop the type of interface to create.

Most of the COM interfaces that you use you have to define yourself. However, some COM APIs are supported through framework classes, so the COM interfaces that these use are defined in `System.Runtime.Interop-Services`. In general, these interfaces have the prefix UCOM to indicate that

Table 4.8   Wrappers to OLE unmanaged interfaces

Interface	Description
UCOMIBindCtx	Access to the bind context for a moniker
UCOMIConnectionPoint	Access to a connection point for COM events
UCOMIConnectionPointContainer	Connection pointer container to manage several connection points
UCOMIEnumConnectionPoints	Access to an enumeration object that enumerates connection points
UCOMIEnumConnections	Access to an enumeration object that enumerates the connections to a connection point
UCOMIEnumMoniker	Enumeration of monikers in a collection
UCOMIEnumString	Enumeration of strings in a collection
UCOMIEnumVARIANT	Enumeration of VARIANT values in a collection
UCOMIMoniker	Moniker interface
UCOMIPersistFile	Interface to the persistence of objects to a file
UCOMIRunningObjectTable	Access to running objects registered with the running object table (ROT)
UCOMIStream	Access to data via a stream
UCOMITypeComp	Interface to type library compilation
UCOMITypeInfo	Interface to type information in a type library
UCOMITypeLib	Access to a type library

they are managed interfaces that give access to *unmanaged COM* interfaces. Table 4.8 lists these interfaces.

In general, if you access a COM object that can generate connection point–based events, you do not need to worry about IConnectionPointContainer because the tlbimp tool will take care of translating connection points into managed delegates and vice versa, as you'll see in the next section.

4.2.8 COM Events

COM events are different from .NET events in that they are interface based. That is, for a COM object to generate a single event, the developer has to create a whole interface just for that event and the event handler has to implement the entire interface. If an existing interface has the specific event, it can be used, but the client will have to implement the entire interface just to support the single event. One solution is to use a `dispinterface` as the event interface—so that late binding is used—but this requires the handler to implement `IDispatch`, so it still has to support four methods to handle a single event.

Typically, methods that can generate events are marked with the `[source]` ODL attribute, and the `coclass` entry lists the event interface as a `[source]` interface. This entry in the `coclass` statement adds type information to a type library to allow clients to construct the necessary sink objects. In addition, COM objects can support the `IProvideClassInfo2` interface, which provides the GUID of the default event source interface.

In contrast, .NET events are delegate based, and delegates are effectively method pointers. This means that a .NET component has the best of both worlds: If it supports a single event, it can use a single delegate. And if it supports multiple events, it can have multiple delegates and can even manage them as event members of an interface.

COM events and .NET events are similar in that they are tightly coupled. That is, the event source object has to be running for the event handler object to register its interest in handling an event, and the event handler object has to be running when the event source object generates the event. In COM, the protocol of "registering" to handle an event is performed through connection point objects that are managed by the event source object implementing `IConnectionPointContainer`. In .NET this protocol is managed through language-specific "events" that provide support for adding and removing event handlers to the delegate and raising the event.

If a class supports event generation, it does so through a language-specific "event" construct that adds the `.event` IL to the class. Clients can use reflection to query for the events that a class supports and hence determine the handler method to implement. To allow the two event systems to interoperate, calls to `IConnectionPointContainer` and `IConnectionPoint` must be converted to calls to methods that add and remove delegates (and vice versa), and calls to sink interface methods must be converted to a delegate invocation (and vice versa).

In the following example a COM client catches an event from a .NET component:

```
// C#
using System;
using System.Threading;
public delegate void Tick();
public interface ITicker
{
    void Start();
    void Stop();
}
public class Ticker : ITicker
{
    public event Tick OnTick;
    Timer timer = null;
    public void Start()
    {
        if (timer != null)
            throw new Exception("already started");
        timer = new Timer(this);
        Thread t = new Thread(
            new ThreadStart(timer.TimerProc));
        t.Start();
    }
    public void Stop() { timer.Stop();}
    public void Tick() { OnTick(); }
}
internal class Timer
{
    Ticker ticker;
    AutoResetEvent mre = new AutoResetEvent(false);
    public Timer(Ticker t) { ticker = t; }
    public void Stop()      { mre.Set(); }
    public void TimerProc()
    {
        while (!mre.WaitOne(1000, true))
            ticker.Tick();
    }
}
```

`Ticker` is a simple class that produces a tick every second and informs interested clients that this has happened. It does this by exposing an event to which handlers can add delegates. The class is controlled by methods on the `ITicker` interface: The `Start()` method starts the ticking, and the `Stop()` method stops it. Although this is a simple class, I have decided to use a helper class to do the work on another thread. A complete implementation of `Ticker` could do some other work while the ticking was happening. In any case, including a helper class here helps me look at threading issues, as you'll see.

The thread is started when `Start()` is called and is passed the `TimerProc()` method of the helper class. This class has an `AutoResetEvent` object that is set when the thread is told to die. `TimerProc()` waits one second on this event object, and if the thread has not been told to die, the thread generates the .NET event by calling the `OnTick` event on the instance of the `Ticker` class. Notice that the event is passed directly to the thread within the `Ticker` instance that is passed to the constructor of the `Timer` class. Because the event represents the client sink interface that will be called by COM, an interface pointer is passed from one thread and used on another. In COM this is safe only if the two threads run in the same apartment, the MTA. The `Ticker.Stop()` method merely tells the `Timer` object to stop, which it does by setting the `AutoResetEvent` object.

To use this code from COM, the COM client must create a sink object that supports an interface containing the event method. To provide this interface to COM Interop, there must be metadata. This metadata should be provided on a managed interface with the event method and associate it with the event source:

```csharp
// C#
using System.Runtime.InteropServices;
[ GuidAttribute(
     "E9BF6F44-F2F9-4103-9B17-0FE4692173DF"),
  InterfaceType(
     ComInterfaceType. InterfaceIsIDispatch)
]
public interface ITick
{
   [DispId(1)] void OnTick();
}
```

```
[ ComSourceInterfaces("ITick") ]
public class Ticker : ITicker
{ /* other members */ }
```

Look at the ITick interface: The name of the method is the name of the event member, *not* the name of the delegate. The interface is marked with [GuidAttribute] so that it has a COM name (an IID is a COM interface name), as well as with [InterfaceType] to indicate to COM Interop the type of COM interface to which it refers (the options are dual interface, non-dual type library–marshaled interface, or dispinterface; in this case the interface will be a dispinterface).

The final part is to associate the interface with the event source class, which is done with the [ComSourceInterfaces] attribute. This attribute can associate up to four source interfaces with a class (each interface is specified through a constructor parameter). Each interface must have methods with the same names and signatures as the events that the class can generate. The parameter to the attribute is the fully qualified name of the source interface, so in this case I specify that the source interface is ITick.

This assembly can now be put through regasm or tlbexp, and the type information will be as follows:

```
// IDL
[ uuid(E9BF6F44-F2F9-4103-9B17-0FE4692173DF),
  version(1.0),
  custom(GUID_ManagedName, "ITick") ]
dispinterface ITick
{
properties:
methods:
    [id(1)] void OnTick();
};
[ uuid(2D45078C-7D1A-3225-AC1B-435F22899DB7),
  version(1.0),
  custom(GUID_ManagedName, "Ticker") ]
coclass Ticker
{
        [default] interface _Ticker;
        interface _Object;
        interface ITicker;
        [default, source] dispinterface ITick;
};
```

The tool creates type information for the sink `dispinterface` and for the event source object specifying that `ITick` is a source interface. In addition, the tool generates a COM wrapper for the `Tick` delegate. This is not needed by the COM event handler but is generated because the delegate is a public type. To prevent this class from being exported to the type library, you can use the `[ComVisible]` attribute:

```
// C#
[ComVisible(false)] public delegate void Tick();
```

A value of `false` indicates to `tlbexp` that type information for the delegate should *not* be generated. The client can now implement the `dispinterface` and use the normal COM connection points to attach to the type. Here is an implementation using ATL event sinks:

```
// unmanaged C++
#import "..\ticker.tlb" no_namespace
_ATL_FUNC_INFO TickInfo
    = {CC_STDCALL, VT_EMPTY, 0, NULL};
class Handler
    : public IDispEventSimpleImpl<99, Handler,
                                 &__uuidof(ITick) >
{
public:
    STDMETHOD_(ULONG, AddRef)()  { return 0; }
    STDMETHOD_(ULONG, Release)() { return 0; }
    STDMETHOD(QueryInterface)(
        REFIID iid, void ** ppvObject)
    {
        *ppvObject = 0;
        if (iid == IID_IUnknown || iid == IID_IDispatch
            || iid == __uuidof(ITick))
            *ppvObject = this;
        return *ppvObject == 0 ? E_NOINTERFACE : S_OK;
    }
    void __stdcall OnTick()
    { printf("tick\n"); }
BEGIN_SINK_MAP(Handler)
    SINK_ENTRY_INFO(99, __uuidof(ITick),
                    1, OnTick, &TickInfo)
END_SINK_MAP()
};
```

The details of this code are not too important. Basically, because the object cannot be created through a class factory, it has no class factory support and does not need reference counting. The object implements `IDispatch` (through `IDispEventSimpleImpl<>`) and a sink map. The `Handler` class requires descriptions of the methods that it will support, and this is the reason for the `TickInfo` variable (which says that the handler has no return value and no parameters). `IDispEventSimpleImpl<>` provides an implementation of `IDispatch::Invoke()` based on the sink map so that when the method with a DISPID value of 1 is invoked, the `OnTick()` method is called. Because this object is not created by a class factory and hence its lifetime is determined by the C++ code that creates it, I can create it on the stack:

```cpp
// unmanaged C++
void main()
{
    HRESULT hr;
    hr = CoInitializeEx(NULL, COINIT_MULTITHREADED);
    if (SUCCEEDED(hr))
    {
        CComPtr<ITicker> clock;
        hr = CoCreateInstance(__uuidof(Ticker), NULL,
            CLSCTX_INPROC_SERVER,
            __uuidof(clock), (void**)&clock);
        Handler handler;
        CComPtr<IConnectionPointContainer> pCPC;
        clock->QueryInterface(&pCPC);
        CComPtr<IConnectionPoint> pCP;
        hr = pCPC->FindConnectionPoint(
            __uuidof(ITick), &pCP);
        if (SUCCEEDED(hr))
        {
            DWORD dw=0;
            CComPtr<IUnknown> punk;
            handler.QueryInterface(
                __uuidof(punk), (void**)&punk);
            hr = pCP->Advise(punk, &dw);
            if (SUCCEEDED(hr))
            {
                clock->Start();
                // make sure that some events are
```

```
            // generated before we go away
            Sleep(5000);
            clock->Stop();
            pCP->Unadvise(dw);
        }
        else
            printf("advise failed %08x\n", hr);
    }
    else
    {
        printf("cannot get cp %08x\n", hr);
    }
}
CoUninitialize();
}
```

Much of this code is straightforward COM connection point code. First I create an instance of the object, and then I query for the `IConnectionPoint-Container` interface. Because the managed object has an event, it *should* support this interface. Next I see if there is a connection point for the specific event interface, and once this connection point is returned I can hook up to it and call a method that will generate events.

Look at the `Ticker.Start()` function again: The client will connect to the connection point on the thread (and apartment) that the `Ticker` object runs (which of course is where the delegate is created to add to the `OnTick` delegate). The event is actually generated in the `TimerProc()` function, which is called by a different thread. The .NET component is registered as `Threading-Model = Both`, and because the server is loaded in process, the component is loaded into the same apartment as the caller. When a new thread is created, it is automatically created in the MTA, so there are no marshaling issues with respect to generating the event (i.e., calling the sink object in the native code).

Now consider what happens if the calling code is in an STA: In this case the connection point is attached and `Start()` is called in the STA, but the new thread will be created in another apartment and the callback will be made from there. Because this is a different apartment and the interface pointer to the sink object has not been explicitly marshaled, the callback will not work. I used this extra class and thread to make this point: You have to be careful about COM marshaling issues.

Now let's look at events from the opposite point of view: A .NET component can implement a sink interface and handle events generated by a COM component. In essence you access individual event methods as if they were delegates. COM event interfaces contain multiple methods, so to identify the specified event you must append the event name with the interface. For example, if you have the following source interface:

```
// ODL
dispinterface DMyEvents
{
properties:
methods:
    [id(1)] void Started();
    [id(2)] void Ended();
};
```

you need to provide delegates called DMyEvents_Started and DMyEvents_Ended. So if a COM object generates events using the DMyEvents interface and is imported via COM Interop as the EventSource object, you can use code like this:

```
// C#
class UseCOMObject
{
    void OnStarted(){}
    void OnEnded(){}
    public void UseObject()
    {
        EventSource eo = new EventSource();
        // hook up to the events
        eo += new DMyEvents_Started(OnStarted);
        eo += new DMyEvents_Ended(OnEnded);
        // now do something that generates events
        eo.DoSomething();
    }
}
```

The tlbimp tool will generate the metadata for these delegates for you.

4.2.9 COM Aggregation

COM aggregation allows one object to expose the interfaces implemented by another COM object. Aggregation is not about code reuse per se; it is about providing a single COM *identity* for the code implemented by multiple objects. The canonical example is COM proxies (see Figure 4.4), where the COM-provided

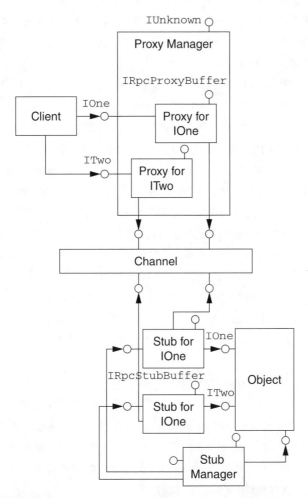

Figure 4.4 COM aggregation used in COM proxies. Unlike usual COM aggregation, the outer object—the proxy manager—holds on to the `IRpcProxyBuffer` **interface on the aggregated proxies rather than the IUnknown interface, but this is the only difference.**

proxy object provides the identity, and individual interface proxy objects are aggregated into the proxy object to provide the marshaling support for those interfaces. When a client queries for `IUnknown` to access other interfaces, it is the `IUnknown` interface of the outer object—the proxy object—that is returned. And when the client performs the query for an interface, the proxy object can pass the query to the `IUnknown` interfaces of the aggregated interface proxies, or it can handle the query itself, perhaps by aggregating other objects. As with outer aggregated objects, the proxy does not need to know the implementation of the aggregated object.

Thus the outer object holds the `IUnknown` interface of the aggregated objects but exposes only its own `IUnknown` interface. When the outer object gets a request for an interface, it can either pass the request to the aggregated objects—*blind aggregation*—or it can pass requests for specific interfaces to selected aggregated objects. In general, blind aggregation is not a good idea because the outer object loses control over the implementation that it exposes.

The RCW can be aggregated as an inner object; that is, a COM object in the unmanaged world can aggregate a .NET object exposed as a COM object through COM Interop. The RCW follows the COM rules of aggregation, returning the outer object's `IUnknown` interface when queried for it and passing reference-counting requests to the outer object. This facility is important for COM+ because if you want to use an object in an object pool, that object must be aggregatable; that is, .NET objects can be used as COM+ pooled objects.

4.2.10 COM Interop and the CRT

When you call a .NET component through COM Interop, the client process loads the .NET Runtime into its process space. The client process does not do this explicitly; it merely loads what it sees as a COM object. However, the .NET component server is registered as `mscoree.dll`, which will load the runtime before loading the .NET component's assembly.

.NET components are created on the managed heap and may have finalizers; the implication is that at some point the finalizer thread should call these finalizers. When the client process exits, it will shut down all threads, including the .NET finalizer thread. To make sure that the finalizer thread completes its work before the process goes away, `mscoree.dll` exports a function called `CorExitProcess()` as a replacement for `ExitProcess()`. This function delays process termination until the finalizer thread has completed its work. The CRT process termination code in `__crtExitProcess()` ensures that `CorExitProcess()` is called.

4.3 Component Services

Any discussion about .NET and COM+ component services must start with this statement:

COM+ component services are .NET component services.

.NET does not replace COM+ because .NET does not provide component services! This implementation has always been the intention, and the reason that we had COM+ when Windows 2000 was released is that Microsoft decided that that part of the component framework was ready for release and would be useful to COM but the managed runtime part (what we call .NET) wasn't.

When a .NET component needs transaction support, loosely coupled events, role-based security, or activity-based synchronization, it gets what it needs through COM+ component services. In general, the component indicates the support that it requires through attributes that the framework provides through the `System.EnterpriseServices` namespace.

4.3.1 Serviced Components

A .NET component that uses component services is a *serviced component*. Such a component must be derived from `ServicedComponent`:

```
// psuedo C# generated from IL
public abstract class ServicedComponent
   : ContextBoundObject,
     IRemoteDispatch, IDisposable,
     IManagedObject
{
   public ServicedComponent();
   public static void DisposeObject(
     ServicedComponent);
   // IObjectControl-like methods
```

```
public virtual void Activate();
public virtual bool CanBePooled();
public virtual void Deactivate();
// IObjectConstruct-like methods
public virtual void Construct(string);
// MarshalByRefObject methods
public virtual ObjRef CreateObjRef(Type);
public object GetLifetimeService();
public virtual object
    InitializeLifetimeService();
// IRemoteDispatch methods
string RemoteDispatchAutoDone(string);
string RemoteDispatchNotAutoDone(string);
// IManagedObject methods
string GetSerializedBuffer();
void GetObjectIdentity(out string,
    out int, out int);
// IDisposable methods
void Dispose();
}
```

Because all serviced components derive from the `ServicedComponent` class, they can take part in just-in-time activation and object pooling. The framework does not need to provide separate `IObjectControl` and `IObjectConstruct` interfaces.[6] As one would expect, a serviced component is context bound because component services are applied as part of a COM+ context. Deriving from `ContextBoundObject` also means that the component derives from `MarshalByRefObject`, so the resulting component is accessible through remoting.[7]

The class implements `IDisposable`, which means that it can be used with the C# `using` pattern, but of course it makes more sense to use serviced components with just-in-time activation (and as-soon-as-possible deactivation), in which case the object is activated and deactivated during the lifetime of a method call.

---

6. To use object construction strings, the serviced component must have the [Construc-tionEnabled] attribute.
7. Note that you need COM+ 1.5 in Windows XP/Windows Server.NET to get a .NET remoting listener. For other operating systems, COM marshaling is used under the covers.

DEVELOPING APPLICATIONS WITH VISUAL STUDIO.NET

Note that if you want non-.NET clients to use your serviced component, you should provide the `[ClassInterface]` attribute or—better—provide a separate interface that can be exported as a COM interface.

4.3.2 Assemblies and Applications

A COM+ application is a unit of isolation, configuration, and deployment. It contains the components that will be subject to the same application settings (e.g., security access control) and, when the application is configured to be a server application in COM+ 1.0, will run in the same process. COM+ applications also represent a unit of deployment in that an application is exported as a unit from the component-services explorer, and the Microsoft Installer (MSI) file that is created represents all that needs to be installed on another machine. A .NET assembly is also a unit of isolation, configuration, and deployment: Components in an assembly are subject to the same security settings, and assemblies are deployed as a unit.[8]

Thus there is a one-to-one mapping between .NET assemblies and COM+ applications. An assembly must be registered with COM+ as an application, which means that the application must have a strong name to make the assembly unique, and it must have an application ID—for example, as follows:

```
// C#
using System;
using System.Reflection;
[ assembly: AssemblyKeyFile("strongname.snk") ]
```

To register the assembly, you should use the `regsvcs` tool: For now simply pass the assembly name to this tool; I will come back to the other options later. First, this tool registers all the public types in the assembly just as `regasm` does: then it scripts the COM+ catalog and adds entries for those components. Finally, it generates a type library with the types that it has added to the COM+ application. The `regsvcs` tool will generate an application ID from the public key, and the application name from the assembly name; indeed, you can even

---

8. True, modules mean that not all of the assembly may be *physically* deployed at a particular time, but this can be regarded as delayed deployment because when a module is required, it will be downloaded accordingly.

pass to the tool the application name that it should generate. However, it is far better to provide these as part of the assembly:

```csharp
// C#
using System.EnterpriseServices;
[ assembly: ApplicationID(
    "650C19B1-D5C8-4988-86EB-4BE03672003D") ]
[ assembly: ApplicationName("Test Application") ]
```

The `regsvcs` tool can be told to update an application, so while you are developing COM+ components, you can add the following as a build step:

```
regsvcs /reconfig $TARGET⁹
```

where `$TARGET` is the assembly name.

Next you can use the component-services snap-in to configure the application and determine the application type (by default `regsvcs` will create a library type), the services used by the types in the application, the security access control that will be used, and extras like roles and subscriptions. If you decide that the COM+ application should be activated as a server application, you must add the assembly to the GAC so that Fusion can find it.

The problem with this approach is that pieces of information that are vital to how these components work are held in separate storage from the components, and an errant administrator can change the values in the catalog and destroy how your components will work. It makes far more sense to add this information to the assembly so that the information is held with the types that it describes.

Perhaps the most important piece of information is the COM+ application type: Will it be loaded in a separate process (using `dllhost`), or will it be loaded in process, in the process that calls the configured components? This is determined by the `[ApplicationActivation]` attribute:

```csharp
// C#
[ assembly: Application(ActivationOption.Server) ]
```

---

9. Be careful with the command line to this tool: You must give the switches first; otherwise the tool will give you some odd errors that appear unrelated to the assembly and application that you want to install.

I will look at other assembly attributes later, but now let's look at the component attributes. COM+ allows you to run a component under the context of a transaction, and this can be applied to a .NET component using the [Transaction] attribute:

```
// C#
[ GuidAttribute(
    "A3F3C8C5-A379-43b1-9BDC-4BFE4E468B66"),
  Transaction(TransactionOption.Required) ]
public class Account : ServicedComponent, IAccount
{ /* other members */ }
```

The TransactionOption enumeration has all the options that are familiar from the component-services snap-in: Requires, RequiresNew, Supported, NotSupported, and Disabled.

If a component runs under a transaction, it must run in an activity and it must be activated via COM+ just-in-time activation (JITA), and regsvcs will make these changes for you. If you have a nontransactional object and you want to run it using JITA, you can use the [JustInTimeActivation] attribute (with a value of true or false) to add support—again, such a component must run in an activity, so the tool will automatically add a synchronization setting of Required. Finally, if you have a nontransaction, non-JITA component that you want to run in an activity (perhaps it is used by a transactional object), you can specify its activity membership with the [Synchronization] attribute, which takes a SynchronizationOption enumerated value.

If the component is transactional, you can specify details about the transaction. The [Transaction] attribute has a property called TimeOut that allows you to override the global transaction timeout value for the current component. If you are running Windows XP (and hence have COM+ 1.5), you can also change the transaction isolation value to one of the TransactionIsolationLevel values: Any, ReadCommitted, ReadUncommitted, RepeatableRead, or the default, which is Serializable.

Now when you run regsvcs on an assembly with the assembly or class attributes (and the other attributes that I'll mention later), the catalog will be updated with the COM+ attribute values.

If the assembly is loaded in process as a library application and the assembly and the client application are in the same directory, the assembly need not be installed in the GAC. In this case you can use the autoregistration feature of .NET. This feature is used when the client uses a serviced component and the assembly has not been registered with COM+. The runtime will see that the component is serviced and will effectively run `regsvcs` on the assembly (but *not* add the assembly to the GAC). There will be a short delay during this registration, but as a result, an application will be added to the COM+ catalog and the component will be activated as expected.

4.3.3 COM+ Context

COM+ configured components are run in a COM+ context where the COM+ component services required by the components are applied. You can get information about the context through the `ContextUtil` class:

```
// C#
string ctxInfo = "the component is running "
    + "in the following context: "
    + ContextUtil.ContextId;
```

This code will return a GUID that represents the current COM+ context. In addition, you can get a GUID for the current application instance, the activity ID, and the application ID. Later I will mention some other properties.

If a component is part of a COM+ library application, it can be marked with the `[MustRunInClientContext]` attribute to ensure that the component runs in the creator's context (or is not created if the contexts are incompatible). If you want to get information about a component, you can mark it with the `[EventTrackingEnabled]` attribute, which indicates that the component supports events and statistics collection during its execution that will be shown in the component-services snap-in.

I have already mentioned the `[JustInTimeActivation]` attribute. This attribute indicates that the component is just-in-time activated, which means that when the client creates an instance of the component, it is not activated; instead the component is activated only when the client makes a method call. JITA is required for transactional components because it ensures transactional isolation.

A component that has `[JustInTimeActivation]` set will be activated only when a method is called on the component, at which point its `Activate()` method will be called. The object's context will have been created before `Activate()` is called, so you can perform context-specific initialization. The requested method will then be called. The method will need to decide whether the object has completed its task; typically JITA objects are designed so that each method is a complete work item and no state should remain after the end of the method. The object indicates to COM+ that it has completed its task by setting `ContextUtil.DeactivateOnReturn` to `true`. If this property is set to `false`, the object will not be deactivated and its state will survive until a subsequent method call.

When a component is deactivated, its `Deactivate()` method is called. After `Deactivate()` has been called the object is destroyed, but the infrastructure of connecting to the object—the client proxy, the stub object, and the object's context—will remain. This means that the client can make a new call through the proxy, at which point the object will be activated in the same context that was used before.

The object exists between the `Activate()` and `Deactivate()` calls, and the context exists until the client proxy is finally released. Thus you can use the `Activate()` method to initialize the object's state from persistent storage and the `Deactivate()` method to persist that state before the object is deactivated. Between method invocations the object's state will exist in persistent storage rather than in the object. This is the so-called *stateless object* scenario.

If you know that a component should always be deactivated when a method completes, you can mark the method with the `[AutoComplete]` attribute. If the component runs under a transaction, this attribute ensures that the transaction has completed before the component is deactivated.

4.3.4 Object Pooling

Components can also be marked as being pooled. Object pooling allows you to create a pool of objects *before* they are needed, thereby allowing you to initialize objects that otherwise will need lengthy initialization. The `[ObjectPooling]` attribute allows you to set the minimum and maximum pool size and a timeout that, if exceeded, will cause an exception to be thrown:

```
// C#
[ObjectPooling(MinPoolSize=10,
    MaxPoolSize=50, CreationTimeout=200)]
public class MyComponent : ServicedComponent
{ /* members */ }
```

If you omit any of these values, the default COM+ settings will be used (minimum pool size of 0, maximum pool size of 1,048,576, and creation timeout of 60 seconds). This example sets a lower limit of 10 so that when the application starts, a pool of ten objects will be created. When the client requests an object, COM+ will first check the pool for an available object. If all of these objects are in use, COM+ will create new objects up to a maximum of 50. The minimum can be used as an optimization if you have an idea of the typical number of concurrent clients. If you make the minimum value too great, you will waste resources. If you make it too small, the benefits of precreating objects will be lost. The maximum value can be used to "throttle" the number of clients.

When a client has finished using a pooled object, the object will not be destroyed but will be returned to the pool. This means that a single object could be used by different clients (over its lifetime and *not* at the same time)

The context of an object is largely determined when it is executed: A transactional component has the transaction ID as part of its context; a synchronized component has the activity ID as part of its context. This means that while the object is in the pool it is in a default context, and only when the object is taken out of the pool will the context be fully created (because only then does COM+ know the full details of the client's context). This means that over its lifetime, the object can live in many contexts. The process of moving from the object's default context to its running context is called *activation*.

When a pooled object is created (i.e., when its constructor is called), the object will be in the default context. Thus you should not perform any context-specific initialization because when the component is executed it will be in a different context. When a client requests a pooled object, COM+ checks the pool to see if an object is available. If so, that object will be activated—moved from the pool to the context where it will be used. COM+ will call the object's `Activate()` method to allow you to do any context-specific initialization before the reference is returned to the client. When the client has finished with the object, it will be deactivated; that is, COM+ will call `Deactivate()` on the object to allow it to perform any context-specific cleanup; then it will call `CanBePooled()`. This last method is provided for the object to indicate whether it is happy to be placed back in the pool. If the deactivation was not completely successful, an object should not be returned to the pool.

One rule of thumb that you should use when deciding whether an object should be pooled is how long the context-specific initialization is compared to the context-neutral initialization. If it takes longer to perform the context-neutral initialization, the object is a good candidate for pooling. If the context-specific initialization takes longer, the object is not a good candidate unless you specifically need to control the number of instances that will be created, in which case you can use the `MaxPoolSize` property.

Of course, a .NET component will be deactivated only when the garbage collector does a collection, and you have no guarantee how frequently—or infrequently—this will occur. If the time between garbage collections is a long time, the object will not be available for use by another client, and the whole point of putting the object in a pool is effectively negated. This is why `ServicedComponent` derives from `IDisposable`: You are actively encouraged to call `Dispose()` when a client is finished with an object. When `Dispose()` is called, the object is deactivated and returned to the pool; the implementation calls it the static `ServicedComponent.DisposeObject()`.

.NET components can have constructors with parameters; COM objects cannot. However, COM+ objects may be passed construction parameters, and this facility is useful for initializing pooled components. To take a construction parameter, the object should have the `[ConstructionEnabled]` attribute and implement the `ServicedComponent.Construct()` method. This method is passed a string that can be configured on a per-class basis by the COM+ component-services snap-in.

Pooled objects can be marked as using JITA, in which case the object can be activated just for a single call—and then placed back into the pool when the call completes. In this case the client will still hold a reference to the object (in fact, a proxy), and the context will still remain between method invocations. `Activate()` and `Deactivate()` will be called when the object is activated and deactivated, respectively—in this case just before and after the method is invoked.

4.3.5 Transactions

Perhaps the most convenient of the COM+ component services is *transactions*. COM+ allows you to specify that a component should run in a transaction (either its own, or inheriting a transaction from its creator), and any resource managers will be enlisted in the transaction before doing any work. The whole point of a transaction is that it represents a unit of work, so if several resource managers are enlisted and one performs some work that fails, the transaction will be aborted, and the work performed by all the resource managers will be rolled back to the state before the transaction occurred.

If your component is transactional, it will use JITA to ensure that no transactional state survives longer than the transaction. Your component's methods can influence the transaction state by changing `ContextUtil.MyTransactionVote` to a value of `TransactionVote.Commit`, which will indicate that the transaction should be committed. A value of `TransactionVote.Abort` (or the method throwing an exception) indicates that the transaction should abort. The `MyTransactionVote` property is independent of the `DeactivateOnReturn` property, so committing the transaction does not necessarily deactivate the object. To do this in one call (commit the transaction and mark the object for deactivation), you can call `ContextUtil.SetComplete()`. Marking a component's method with `[AutoComplete]` is equivalent to the runtime's calling `SetComplete()` when the method finishes.

An object can be marked with `TransactionOption.Supported`, which means that it can use a transaction if one exists. Such an object can check the context to see if it has inherited a transaction from its creator by examining `ContextUtil.IsInTransaction`. If the transaction exists, then its ID can be obtained through `ContextUtil.TransactionId`.

4.3.6 COM+ Security

Perhaps the most useful part of COM+ was that it finally allowed VB6 programmers to write secured applications because it allowed access checks to be performed against role names (which are strings) rather than using access token checks against access control lists (both binary structures). .NET allows you to define roles and to have access to role-based access checks.

The top-level attribute is the assembly attribute `[ApplicationAccess-Control]`, which is used to turn on or off access checks on the application. In addition, it is used to give the authentication and impersonation levels. The `ApplicationAccessControl.AccessChecksLevel` property indicates whether the access checks are performed at the process level (`AccessCheck-LevelOption.Application`) or on both process and component levels (`AccessCheckLevelOption.ApplicationComponent`). The latter case takes into account the situation in which an object is activated and attempts to activate another object in the application. The `ApplicationAccess-Control.Authentication` property is used to configure the authentication that is required to access components in the application. The client call must be made at the level set in this property or at a higher level. Finally, the `ApplicationAccessControl.ImpersonationLevel` property specifies the impersonation level used when outgoing calls are made.

You can determine whether access checks are made on the objects of a class by using the `[ComponentAccessControl]` attribute:

```
// C#
[ComponentAccessCheck(true)]
public class Account
   : ServicedComponent, IAccount
{ /* members */ }
```

This attribute indicates that when calls are made into the component—on any interface—an access check is performed. The access check consists of determining the role membership of the caller and checking whether it is one of the roles that is allowed access to the component. Note that COM+ security is *inclusive:* You cannot explicitly deny access to a role, although a role that is not expressly given access is denied.

COM+ roles are essentially named groups of users. The roles are part of the application and are good candidates for attributes. The contents of a role are an administration issue, and this administration should be performed when the application is deployed. The developer knows nothing about the users that will be added to a role; consequently, you cannot determine role membership with attributes (there is one exception). To create a role, you use the assembly attribute [SecurityRole]:

```
// C#
[assembly: SecurityRole("Managers")]
[assembly: SecurityRole("Clerks")]
[assembly: SecurityRole("AllEmployees")]
```

This attribute has (1) a `Description` property that allows you to give a text description of what the role members are allowed to do and (2) a Boolean value called `SetEveryoneAccess`. If `SetEveryoneAccess` is set to `true`, when the assembly is registered with COM+ the `Everyone` group is added to the role (the one exception I mentioned earlier). This is fine for unit testing, when you want to test a component without security issues, but when the component is deployed, this property should be set to `false`. As a consequence, I prefer not to use this property, which always requires me to configure the role to allow my account to have access.

Once you have defined the roles, you can perform access checks. There are two ways to do this: programmatically or through attributes. Confusingly, the [SecurityRole] attribute is used to specify the roles that are granted access so that these roles can execute code in a component. This attribute can be applied on the component, an interface, or a method:

```
// C#
[SecurityRole("Clerks")]
interface IAccount
{
    int GetBalance();
}
[ ComponentAccessCheck(true),
  SecurityRole("Managers") ]
public class Account
    : ServicedComponent, IAccount
{
```

```
    public int GetBalance(){}
    public void ExtendCredit(int x){}
}
```

In this code the `Managers` role can do anything to an `Account` object, but a member of the `Clerks` role can call methods only in the `IAccount` interface. As a consequence, only members of the `Managers` role will be able to call the `ExtendCredit()` method. The framework also has an attribute called `[SecureMethod]`. If you apply this attribute to a method, the registration will add a special role called `Marshaler` to your application and give this role access to the method. This attribute indicates that the method must be called through an interface so that security is applied.

Thus attributes allow you to specify access checks to be made on components, interfaces, and individual methods, but a finer-grained level of access control can be performed with programmatic access checks. To achieve this finer control, your code calls the `SecurityCallContext` object. This class has methods to perform access checks and properties to get additional information. To make an access check, you can call `IsCallerInRole()`, which will check whether the caller is a member of the specified role:

```
// C#
SecurityCallContext ctx;
ctx = SecurityCallContext.CurrentCall;
if (ctx.IsCallerInRole("Managers"))
{
    SanctionParty();
}
else
{
    PleadForParty();
}
```

When a call is made into a component, it can be the result of a chain of calls involving several COM+ components and several accounts. The `Security-CallContext.Callers` property gives access to an object of type `SecurityCallers` that is a collection of `SecurityIdentity` objects and represents the accounts of the callers through the call chain. A `SecurityIdentity` object identifies the name of the account, the authentication and impersonation levels it used to make the call, and the authentication service it used. The name can be passed to `SecurityCallContext.IsUserInRoll()` to test the account's role membership.

Although the `Callers` property gives access to all the accounts used in the call chain, you may find it more convenient just to check against the immediate caller or the caller that started the call chain, in which case you can use the `DirectCaller` and the `OriginalCaller` properties.

Finally, if an application does not have security set, `IsCallerInRole()` will give a false result, so your code should call `SecurityCall-Context.IsSecurityEnabled` to verify that you can make security checks.

4.3.7 Queued Components

COM+ allows you to make object calls through MSMQ (Microsoft Message Queuing), whereby a method call is serialized into a message and posted in a queue. A COM+ application can be configured to listen on the queue, and when a message appears in the queue, COM+ will create an object, deserialize the message, and make the call. The assembly attribute `[ApplicationQueuing]` indicates that the application has queued components; thus COM+ will create a public queue with the application name. The attribute has two properties: `QueueListenerEnabled`, which indicates that the application should listen for messages on the queue; and `MaxListenerThreads`, which sets the maximum number of threads that will be used.

Queued components must have interfaces that can be queued, so the methods must have only in parameters and not return values. The interface also must have the `[InterfaceQueuing]` attribute. A client of queued components accesses the component through a moniker. Luckily, the Framework Class Library designers recognized this requirement and supplied the `Marshal.BindToMoniker()` method:

```
// C#
IQueuedObject qo;
qo = (IQueuedObject)Marshal.BindToMoniker(
    "queue:/new:QueuedObject");
qo.DoSomething();
```

4.3.8 Loosely Coupled Events

COM+ comes with a service that provides *loosely coupled events*. .NET events are tightly coupled; that is, the event source and the event handler must be running when the handler indicates its interest in accepting events and when the events are generated. COM+ events are loosely coupled; that is, when an application generates an event, the client does not have to be running; the client application will already have made its requirement known through an entry in the COM+ catalog called a *subscription*.

To allow loosely coupled events, you have to provide an event class. This is just an indication of the event methods that the source application can call and should not contain any implementation. When the event source generates the event, it creates an instance of the event class, and COM+ will create a class that has the same methods. When the event source calls the event class, the COM+ event service checks the subscriptions that have been made for that event and calls the subscribed components. I won't go into all the details here; suffice it to say that all event classes are marked with the [EventClass] attribute.

4.3.9 Catalog Configuration

The Framework Class Library has little support for accessing the COM+ catalog. The little support it gives is in the RegistrationHelper class, which has methods that allow you to install or uninstall assemblies into the catalog—essentially the actions of the regsvcs tool. If you want to have programmatic access to the COM+ catalog (which is essential if you want to make transient COM+ subscriptions), you have to access the COM+ administration APIs through COM Interop.

4.4 Summary

Interop is vital for a framework because it allows a smooth transition from legacy frameworks to the new framework. .NET has been built with interop as an integral part, allowing interoperation with COM and functions exported from Win32 DLLs. Taking this a step further, the managed C++ compiler allows developers to use existing static libraries and unmanaged types. This means that investment now in unmanaged libraries will not be wasted, and it allows library vendors the time to develop the library as .NET code.

Chapter 5

Visual Studio.NET Environment

So far in this book I have concentrated on the .NET Framework. In this chapter I will introduce a .NET application: Visual Studio.NET. VS.NET is where you will most likely start when developing .NET code. The IDE makes editing code easier; it manages compiler options and assembly references for you and it hosts the Visual Studio.NET debuggers to give you an integrated environment to do all of your application development.

In this chapter I will give an overview of VS.NET and its tools. I will show you how the IDE manages projects and how to use the IDE features to add classes and to configure the VS.NET compilers.

5.1 The Visual Studio Environment

VS.NET is a managed application—well, mostly. Some parts of the IDE, like the **Properties** window, are managed code, whereas others, like add-ins, use COM. You should take this as an example of how managed and unmanaged code can coexist and complement each other. The VS.NET IDE borrows a lot from its predecessors—Visual Studio 6.0, Visual J++, and Visual InterDev—and you'll find some familiar tools and some new ones. In this section I will describe the user interface (UI) features of the IDE as a precursor to describing the VS.NET facilities, starting with Section 5.2, titled Projects and Solutions.

5.1.1 Menus, Commands, and Shortcut Keys

Initially you will access most of the facilities in VS.NET through the menus, simply because it is the most obvious way. These menus are dynamic and have items that are pertinent to the work you are doing and the editor you are using. The menus may look like classic Win32 window menus, but in fact they are toolbars that have been docked permanently.

When you click on a menu item, the menu bar creates a toolbar (the class is called `MsoCommandBarShadow`) with the names of the items on the menu. As with classic Win32 menus, these toolbar menus list the shortcut keys that you can press to perform a command, and they place check marks next to selected items (e.g., with a document open in the IDE, in the **Window** menu you'll see a check mark next to the name of the document).

However, these menus have more functionality than classic Win32 menus. Many of the menu items are also available through toolbars and thus have an associated toolbar button. When a menu with such items is shown, the toolbar button will also be shown next to the item. Furthermore, the context menus that are accessible in the VS.NET editors or tools (like Solution Explorer or Class View) by right-clicking the mouse are also toolbar windows and will show these items' toolbar buttons.

Toolbars are created and manipulated through the **Customize Toolbar** dialog. You can access this window by selecting **View | Toolbars | Customize**, or by right-clicking on any toolbar (including the menu bar) and selecting **Customize**. This will give you a dialog with three tabs: **Toolbars**, **Commands,** and **Options**. The first tab allows you to select which toolbars should be shown, and it allows you to create a new toolbar. Any new toolbar you create will float in the IDE next to the dialog, but it will not have any buttons.

To add buttons, you should use the **Commands** tab, which contains two list boxes: The left-hand box lists categories (which, in part, correspond to the menus that can be shown). When you select a category, the right-hand box will be filled with the commands that are available. This list box gives the names of the commands and the associated toolbar buttons, if applicable. To add a command to a toolbar, you merely have to select the command from this list box and then drag and drop the command onto the toolbar. If the command has a toolbar button, this will be shown on the toolbar; otherwise a standard pushbutton will be shown with the name of the command.

If you hold the mouse over a toolbar button, a tool tip can be shown that has the command name and the shortcut key for the command. The **Options** tab of the **Customize Toolbar** dialog allows you to specify whether the command name will be shown (**Show ScreenTips on toolbars**) and whether the shortcut key will be displayed (**Show shortcut keys in ScreenTips**). At the bottom of the dialog is a button marked **Keyboard...**, which will open the **Options** dialog (which I will describe later) that allows you to change the keyboard mappings you will use.

The **Options** dialog will allow you to select one of the standard keyboard schemes, and from one of these you can create your own scheme. At the top of the dialog is an edit box called **Show commands containing** and an associated list box. As you type in the edit box, the dialog will list the commands that fit the command that you have typed; if you leave the edit box empty, all commands will be listed.

When you select a command in the list box, the other controls below it will be filled with details about the command. The **Shortcut(s) for selected command** edit box will show the currently assigned shortcuts. These shortcuts can be global, in that the shortcut key can be used anywhere within the IDE, or they can be specific to a particular context or window. You can also add a shortcut to a command by clicking on the **Press shortcut key(s)** edit box and then pressing the key that you want to use. Once you have done this, the edit box will list the key you pressed. To make this a shortcut for the selected command, you have to click on the **Assign** button. If the shortcut has already been assigned to another command, the list box at the bottom of the dialog will list the command.

The commands that are listed will be in the form `<Category>.<Command>`. An example is `File.OpenFile`; this command can be used in several contexts. The command name typically refers to the menu where it can be accessed, so `File.OpenFile` is accessed through the **File** menu item on the **Open** submenu of the **File** menu. You can use the command in macros through the `DTE.ExecuteCommand()` method:

```
' VBS macro
Sub MyMacro()
   DTE.ExecuteCommand("File.OpenFile", "\data\test.txt")
End Sub
```

The `DTE` object is the design-time environment—that is, the IDE. The first string parameter of `ExecuteCommand()` is the name of the command; the second parameter is the parameter of the command. In this example the file `test.txt` will be loaded in the source code editor. If the command takes multiple parameters, these should be concatenated to form the parameter string. For example, the `File.OpenFile` command can have a switch specifying the editor that will be used (I will describe this command in more detail later in this chapter), so the macro specifying that the binary editor should be used could look like this:

```
' VBS macro
Sub MyMacro()
   DTE.ExecuteCommand("File.OpenFile",
      "\data\test.txt /e:""Binary Editor""")
End Sub
```

The `/e` switch gives the name of the source editor to use, and because this name includes an embedded space, it has to be given in quotation marks. In VBScript, double quotation marks (`""`) are required. You can execute any of the commands in this way. Some of the more common commands are available through other `DTE` properties; for example, the `File.OpenFile` command can be executed directly by a call to the `DTE.ItemOperations.OpenFile()` method. You can experiment by recording a temporary macro and selecting a command through a menu item and then editing the macro to see the code that is executed. I will have more to say about macros later in this chapter.

The other two contexts in which you'll use a command are in the **Command** window and through the `devenv.exe` command line. I will give more details about both of these later in this chapter, but in brief, the **Command** window allows you to type command names, some of which will generate output that will be shown in the **Command** window. The IDE can be started through inclusion of the `/command` switch on the command line: When the IDE starts, the specified command will be executed. Incidentally, both the **Command** window and the `/command` switch allow you to execute custom commands that are add-ins or macros.

5.1.2 Docking Windows and Toolbars

The new toolbars and windows that make up the IDE have several features to maximize the screen real estate that you can use. Toolbars can be docked to the edges of the IDE, and dockable windows can be docked together as groups that

DEVELOPING APPLICATIONS WITH VISUAL STUDIO.NET

can then be docked to the edges of the IDE. When windows are docked as groups, each window has a tab with the window name and an icon. Figure 5.1 shows an example; the tabs at the bottom refer to the **Solution Explorer** and **Class View** windows, which give information about the current project.

To add a new dockable window to the group, you drag the window and drop it on the tabs of the group. If you have two separate dockable windows (i.e., not already grouped), to dock them you drag one window over the caption bar of the other window. When you do this, the drag outline will change from a rectangle to a tabbed rectangle. Figure 5.2 shows the effect of dragging the **Solution Explorer** floating window over the caption of the **Class View** window: When you drag the **Solution Explorer** window over any other part of the **Class View** window, you see just the

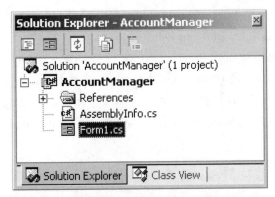

Figure 5.1   A floating docked group of dockable windows

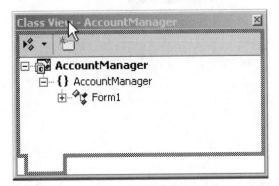

Figure 5.2   Docking one window onto another to form a group

rectangular outline. When you drag it over the caption, the outline becomes tabbed, indicating that you can drop the window to create a group.

To separate a window from a group, you have to drag it by its tab. And if you want to change the tab order, you drag and drop windows within a group using the tabs.

Dockable windows may also be grouped as a tiled group. Figure 5.3 shows an example. To get a tiled group, you drag one window and drop it on another dockable window near one of the edges of the bottom window, but not on its caption bar. As you drag a window over another one, you'll see its drag outline change to the tiled docked window outline, which indicates when to drop the window. You can tile windows vertically (as in Figure 5.3) or horizontally. If you have two tiled windows, you can drop another window on top either as another tile or to create a tabbed group.

Any combination is possible, but you may have to rearrange the existing windows first. For example, with the window arrangement shown in Figure 5.3 you can add a third window above, between, or below the existing ones (to get three in a vertical stack); or you can add the third window to the right or left of one of the existing windows (so that the other window has the complete width). What you cannot do is drop a window on this tiled group so that it is to the left or right

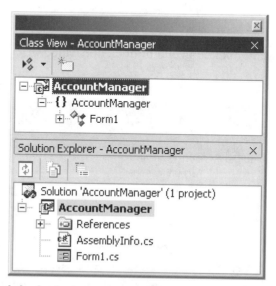

Figure 5.3   A tiled docked window group

of *both* of the existing windows; to do this you have to remove one window from the existing tiled group, add the window so that it is to the right (or left) of the remaining window, and then add the removed window back to the group so that it is above (or below) its original partner. Figure 5.4 shows how to do this.

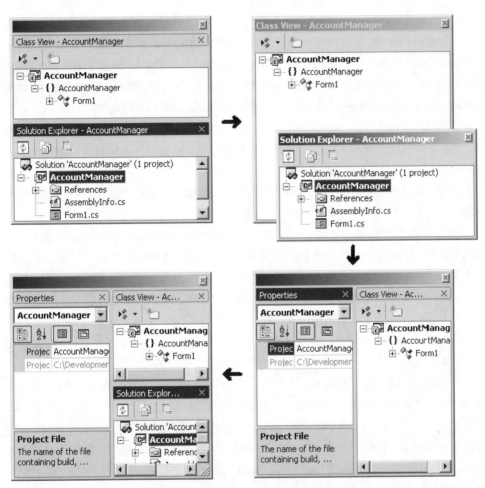

Figure 5.4   Adding a third window to an existing tiled group. The intention is to add the Properties window so that it is to the left of both of the existing windows. The process is shown in steps, clockwise from upper left: First the Solution Explorer window is removed, then the Properties window is tiled to the left of the Class View window, and finally Solution Explorer is tiled underneath Class View.

When you create a group, you essentially get an extra window that acts as a container for the windows of the group. Adding a window to the group can only split the real estate taken up by one of the tiled windows. This is the reason you have to go through the steps just described to get a window tiled to the left or right of two vertically tiled windows. The windows in a tiled group are separated by splitter bars so that you can change their relative widths and heights. In a tiled group the container window is always completely filled with the tiles.

In some cases you'll want the window to float and not dock. This arrangement is useful, for example, when you want the window to be a particular size. To change a window from dockable to floating, you right-click on the window caption bar and change the selection from **Dockable** to **Floating**.

The IDE itself acts as a container, except that when you dock windows they do not fill the entire area of the container. You can dock individual windows or groups to the IDE, and you can dock toolbars, too. When a dockable window is docked to the IDE, the thumbtack icon appears. The thumbtack indicates whether or not the window has autohide set.

Figure 5.5 shows the thumbtack for a window that has autohide turned off; the thumbtack indicates that the window is "pinned" open on the IDE. Clicking on the thumbtack turns autohide on, in which case the thumbtack will be rotated 90 degrees to indicate that the window is no longer pinned to the IDE area. When the mouse moves away from an autohide window, the window will "slide" to the edge of the IDE and show a tab. Holding the mouse over the tab will cause it to slide out again.

Visual Studio.NET defines hot keys to allow you to show a hidden window. The default values of the hot keys for the most common IDE windows are shown in Table 5.1. You can change the key assignment through the **Tools | Options | Environment | Keyboard** property page. If you have set your keyboard layout to one of the other layouts (e.g., VS6, VB6, VC++6, VC++2), the hot keys will be different.

Figure 5.5   The thumbtack for a window docked in the IDE

Table 5.1 Keyboard mappings to show various common VS.NET IDE windows[*]

Window	Key
Class View	Ctrl-Shift-C
Code	F7
Command	Ctrl-Alt-A
Designer	Shift-F7
Find Symbol	Ctrl-Alt-F12
Macro Explorer	Alt-F8
Object Browser	Ctrl-Alt-J
Output	Ctrl-Alt-O
Properties	F4
Resource View	Ctrl-Shift-E
Server Explorer	Ctrl-Alt-S
Solution Explorer	Ctrl-Alt-L
Task List	Ctrl-Alt-K
Toolbox	Ctrl-Atl-X

[*]*Note:* The keyboard mapping is the VS.NET default value.

If you have several windows in a tabbed group and then turn autohide on for one window in the group, by default all windows in the group will autohide: The tabs now will show just an icon, except for the topmost window in the group, which will show an icon and its title. If you autohide two groups against the same IDE edge, you'll have two groups of tabs against the edge. If you have a tiled group docked to an edge and you turn autohide on for one window, only that window will autohide. All this sounds complicated, but after a few experiments of docking and grouping windows, you'll get the hang of it. Only a docked window can be autohidden; and conversely, to convert an autohide window to an un-docked (floating) window, you must first turn off autohide.

The main reason for autohide is that it gives you more space to work. The default window layout (you can configure this through the **Environment** options) is for the document window to take up the space within the IDE that is not taken up by docked windows and toolbars. A nonautohide docked window will take up space in the IDE that will not be available to the document window. When you autohide a docked window, you free this area for the document window. If you really do need lots of space, you can use the full-screen option (by selecting **View | Full Screen**). This will hide the IDE's caption, all docked windows, and all docked toolbars except the menu, and it will stretch the tabbed document window to cover the operating system's taskbar.

The default Visual Studio window layout has autohide set on the **Server Explorer** and **Toolbox** windows, and the other windows pinned to the IDE. Autohiding the **Toolbox** window can make it a little difficult to use Windows Forms designer, Web Forms designer, or the dialog editor because a tabbed document (e.g., the dialog) will treat the area taken up by the autohide window (except for its tab) as free space, so the document will occupy that space. Consequently, when you open the **Toolbox** window to grab a control, it will obscure the document. When I use **Toolbox**, I usually turn off autohide so that the dialog or form is not obscured by the **Toolbox** window.

Using autohide windows allows you to maximize the central area of the IDE. However, if you do something that will involve an autohide window—for example, start a build or perform a search—the autohide window will automatically slide out to show you the output.

You can change how autohide works through the **General** page of the **Environment** options. You can change the animation speed of the autohide windows, and you can determine if the autohide feature (the thumbtack icon) and the close buttons affect just the active window or all the windows in the group.

5.1.3 Documents

The VS source code editor is used to edit documents. Typically, when you open a document it will be one of the items in a project, but you can open any file you wish. If you choose, you can get the **Solution Explorer** window to show nonproject files in a tree view node called **Miscellaneous Files**. This collection of files can be saved along with the solution when the solution is closed; the **Documents** item of the **Environment** options allows you to determine if the

Miscellaneous Files node is used and how many of these files will be opened in the IDE when the solution is opened.

The IDE differentiates between the documents you can edit. When you open a document using the **File Open** dialog (`File.OpenFile`), the dialog will, by default, determine what editor will be used. Some documents will be edited with the standard VS.NET text editor; others will be edited with specific VS editors (e.g., HTML files are edited by the HTML editor, and XML files by the XML designer). If the document type is registered with the local system, then when you open the document, VS.NET will open it in the registered application. In addition, the **Open** button of the **Open File** dialog has a down-pointing arrowhead; if you click on this, you will get a context menu with the items **Open** (the default action of the **Open** button) and **Open With**. If you select **Open With**, the IDE will give you another dialog that has a list of the possible editors you can use. The editors listed in this dialog come from three sources: (1) a list of the default VS.NET editors, (2) a list of the applications registered to edit this document type, and (3) a list of applications that you have added through the **Add** button on this dialog. If you attempt to open a document that the IDE does not recognize and it cannot find a registered editor, it will load the document in the VS.NET binary editor.

It is interesting that if you specify the text editor to use with the opened file with **Open With** or through the `File.OpenFile` command with the `/e` switch, this information is also saved in the most-recently-used (MRU) list, so if later you select a file from the MRU list, it will be opened with the editor that you selected. If you open an executable file (`.exe` or `.dll`), by default the file will be opened in the **Resource View** window.[1]

The VS.NET text editor can be used to edit C++, C#, VB.NET, or SQL scripts. The **Environment** options allow you to specify the font used in the text editor and the colors of the various items in the text. The **Text Editor** options offer the ability to specify general formatting options and *IntelliSense* (the technology by which list boxes of relevant options—like class members and function parameters—appear as you type). If you type a URL in the text editor, by

---

1. Note that this is the Win32 resource view, so if you open a .NET assembly you will not see the .NET resources in the file.

default it will be treated as a hyperlink. This means that if you to single-click on the link, it will be opened in your browser (the browser is configurable with the **Environment** options). Personally I find this facility irritating and wish it were not the default, so I usually turn it off through the **Text Editor** options by selecting the rather confusingly named **Enable single-click URL navigation** option.

As you type in the text editor, the editor will look at the text that you are typing and will make decisions about the formatting; in particular it will determine how tabs and indentation are handled. When you press the **Tab** key, the text editor can interpret it as a tab character or as a series of spaces. If you want tab characters, the editor needs to know how many character spaces a tab character represents (it assumes that you are using a fixed-width font). These settings—whether to insert spaces and how many, and how wide a tab character should be—are configurable through the **Text Editor** options, either as a global setting for all languages or for each individual language.

In addition, you can determine how indentation is applied by the text editor. When you finish typing one line and press the **Enter** key, the text editor can either move the caret to the beginning of the next line (**None** indenting), or it may indent according to the last line of text typed (**Block** indenting), or it may use language rules to determine how to indent the next line (**Smart** indenting). If you choose smart indenting, some of the rules for indenting will be given in the associated **Formatting** item of the language's **Text Editor** options.

5.1.4   Start Page

The first time that you run the IDE, you will get the start page, which is hosted by Internet Explorer within the IDE and gives various pages of information. If, like me, you dismiss this page after the first few minutes of examination (or by selecting **Show empty environment** from the **At startup** list box), you can show this page again by selecting the **Show Browser** option on the **View Browser** item of the **View** menu.[2]

---

2. The **Environment** options also give the **At startup** options, so that you can change the options at a later stage.

Perhaps the most important piece of information when you first start is the **My Profile** page. This page allows you to specify the keyboard layout and general window layout that you prefer (which you can change later using the **Environment** options). Of the other pages, some configure the help system and give general information. Three other pages stand out as particularly useful: **Get Started**, **Downloads,** and **Web Hosting**.

The **Get Started** page lists the recent projects that you have been working on in a table, giving the name of each project and the date of the last change. This is slightly more information than what the solution MRU list on the **File** menu provides, but it is presented in a more pleasing way.

The **Downloads** page lists the resources that Microsoft has decided you will find useful. To use this page, you must have a connection to the Internet, so the page will automatically update according to the current tools. In a similar way, the **Web Hosting** page also attaches to a page at msdn.microsoft.com to give a list of the current "Web host partners" that you can use to host your Web Services. Be aware that the list of "partners" that Microsoft gives are not free hosts; you have to pay for their services.

5.2 Projects and Solutions

Visual Studio.NET uses the terms *project* and *solution* as containers for the code that you'll write. A project has an output, typically a DLL or an EXE; a solution is a collection of projects that are interrelated in some way. So a solution could contain one project that produces an EXE and other projects that produce DLLs used by the application. Another solution could contain a single output (an EXE or a DLL) that is encompassed by one project, and an additional project to "deploy" that output.

Projects contain the files that will be used to generate the output: C++ files, C# files, resource files, and so on. Projects contain code in a single language: You cannot mix languages in a single project. A solution, however, can have projects of any language. The project maintains information about the tools used to build it, as well as dependency information between the files it contains and its output. A solution maintains the dependency information of the projects it contains.

You can choose to build a single project in a solution or all projects. One project in a solution is designated as the *start-up project,* meaning that when you open the solution this will be the default project. More importantly, when you debug your solution, the output of the start-up project is what will be treated as the primary code module to debug. Thus if you have a solution with an EXE that loads several DLLs, it makes sense to make the EXE project the start-up project. As you'll see in Chapter 9, you can have a solution with multiple executables and start all of these executables under the debugger, but to do this you will have to explicitly start the executables other than the one identified as the start-up project.

5.2.1 Project Types

To create a new project, you select the **New Project** item from the **File** menu. If you don't have a solution open, the project will be created in its own solution. Otherwise you will be given the option to add the project to the current solution or to create a new solution. If you opt to create a new solution, by default the project will be created in a folder with the same name as the solution, but you are given the option to create a separate folder within the solution folder.

Most projects will be stored in a folder on your hard disk (the default location is configurable via the **Projects and Solutions** item of the **Environment** options). However, some projects (C# **Web Applications** and **Web Services**, for example) can be created on a remote machine if the FTP log-on details are specified. I will discuss the various types of projects in Chapter 6.

5.2.2 Project Wizard Files

When you create a project, the project wizard will create the initial files for you from project template files. You can write your own project wizards by providing templates of the files that should be created for the new project, along with a script to perform any other configurations.

Each language folder will have a folder with a name something like `<Language>Projects` and a folder called `<Language>ProjectItems` (where `<Language>` is the specific language); two examples are `VCProjects` and `CSharpProjects`. The first folder contains the wizard files to create projects, and the second folder contains the wizard files to add new items to a project.

Within these folders are one or more `.vsdir` files with information about the wizards described in the folder. The entries in the `.vsdir` file indicate a `.vsz` file, and the name, description, and icon for the wizard. If the name, description, or icon is a resource in a file, the file must be a VS package[3] and registered as such, in which case the GUID of the package is given along with the resource ID.

Within the project directory are the `.vsz` files—one for each of the wizards. Each `.vsz` file contains information about the wizard, including the name of the folder that contains the wizard code. There are essentially two types of wizards: those that have a UI, and those that do not. If the wizard has a UI (as C++ wizards do), the user will be presented a dialog with a series of pages that will contain pages of controls used to enter the parameters of the project (e.g., class names and facilities). If the project wizard lacks a UI (as C# wizards do), the wizard will create the project using default values for the project parameters.

For example, the C# Console Application project wizard lacks a UI and has a file called `CSharpConsole.vsz` that indicates that the wizard is called `CSharpConsoleWiz`. In `VC#\VC#Wizards` in the VS.NET folder you'll find a folder called `CSharpConsoleWiz`. This folder contains two subfolders—`Templates` and `Scripts`—each of which has a folder with the locale ID of the version of VS.NET that you have installed (in decimal). Within the `Templates` folder is a text file called `Template.inf` that lists all the template files for this project; these template files are found in the same folder as the `.inf` file. The `Scripts` folder contains a script file that is used to do processing when the project is being created. For example, the main file in the project is created from a template file called `file1.cs` that looks like this:

```
// C#
using System;

namespace [!output SAFE_NAMESPACE_NAME]
{
    /// <summary>
    /// Summary description for [!output SAFE_CLASS_NAME].
```

---

3. Visual Studio packages are DLLs that are used to extend the IDE. Microsoft provides the APIs for creating packages to their integration partners only.

```
        /// </summary>
        class [!output SAFE_CLASS_NAME]
        {
            /// <summary>
            /// The main entry point for the application.
            /// </summary>
            [STAThread]
            static void Main(string[] args)
            {
                //
                // TODO: Add code to start application here
                //
            }
        }
    }
```

The items in the `[!output]` placeholders will be filled with strings when the project files are generated. In this case SAFE_NAMESPACE_NAME and SAFE_CLASS_NAME are "safe" insofar as they are legal C# names. The wizard maintains a collection of such symbols that can be accessed through code.

If the wizard has a UI, there will be an HTML page for each page of the UI. The first page will be called `default.htm`, which is shown first when the wizard starts. This page should be used to present project summary information, and like all the other pages, it contains a table of links (actually implemented through the `<span>` HTML element) to the other pages. Thus the actual user makes the choice to actively select additional pages, rather than adhering to the previous Visual Studio model, which was to guide the user through the process page by page. The controls on these pages are named according to the symbols that they will add to the symbol table, and the `<head>` section of each page has a list of these symbols. When the **Finish** button is clicked on the wizard, the values in these controls are added to the symbol table.

Two mechanisms control generation of the project files: the template files and the script. The `.inf` file for the project wizard can have simple scripting directives (`[!if]` and `[!loop]`) based on symbols and can thus determine which files are generated for the project. As you have seen, the template files themselves contain code in the specified language, and they can have custom or optional text specified by directives based on symbols.

You can also write a script file to perform tasks when the wizard requires extra information or generates an event. Thus you'll find that most of the project wizards will have a script file that defines an `OnFinish()` method, which is called when the **Finish** button is clicked. This method should create the project, either through your own custom code or by calling the methods defined for the specific language and located in the `common.js` file in a subfolder of the wizards folder. You can use this method to add symbols that may be used in the template files. Indeed, the method itself initiates processing of the template files (through a method on the `Project` object called `AddFromTemplate()`) either explicitly or through calls to methods in `common.js`.

As you can see, there are several tasks involved in creating a wizard. To simplify the process, Microsoft has provided a project type: Called **Custom Wizard**, it can be found in the **Visual C++ Projects** category of the **New Project** dialog.

5.2.3 Project Files

The project files that are generated depend on the project and the language. I will give a brief overview of the files generated for C# and C++ projects to give you a basic understanding of what is contained in these files.

C++ projects are created with a configuration file with the extension `.vcproj`. This is an XML file with the build and dependency information, and there are sections for the platform; for the configuration (e.g., Release or Debug), which defines the tools that can be used; and for the files in the project defining the tool that will be used on files of a specific type (specified through a *filter*).

Each project is given a GUID, which is referenced in the `.sln` file, which gives the relative paths of the project files to the solution file and the configurations that the projects contain. The `.vcproj` and `.sln` files are as important to your project as the source code files that you'll compile; thus you should not delete them. In addition, you'll find `.suo` and `.ncb` files in the project folder. These are not so important and will be generated if they do not exist. Indeed, if you are storing your solutions in a source control database or distributing them to a coworker, you should make sure these files are *not* saved. The reason is that the

`.suo` file contains information about the current solution options you have selected, such as the files that you had open when you closed the solution (can you *guarantee* that your coworker will have *that* particular file, in *that* particular path?).[4]

The `.ncb` extension stands for *no compile browser,* and `.ncb` files contain information about the classes that you have in your project—which is used by the **Class View** window—and information used by statement completion. All of this information can be generated if the `.ncb` file is missing. And because these files can become quite large, it is often a good idea to delete them before distributing a project.[5]

C# projects have two project files: `.csproj` and `.csproj.user`. The former holds information about the build process: the files that should be built, the assemblies to reference, and the compiler switches. The `.csproj.user` file holds user settings like debugging options. The `.csproj` file is required, and you should *not* delete it. The `.csproj.user` file will be generated from defaults if it is missing.

5.2.4   Solution Configurations

When you open a project, you will get two views of it: **Solution Explorer** and **Class View**. As the names suggest, one gives a view of the files in a solution, and the other gives a view of the classes (types) in the solution.

The two views have similar context menus. However, because **Solution Explorer** shows the files in the solution arranged in folders, its context menu will have items to create folders and to add, remove, and move files between folders. Note that with a C++ project, these folders *do not* represent actual folders in your project folder; they are just a notational device to group the files logically in your project. With a C# project, these *do* represent folders within your project folder.

---

4. Of course, it can be interesting for the coworker to see what files *you* have been using.
5. One of my pet peeves is receiving a project e-mailed from a coworker with the `.ncb` and `.pch` files—both potentially huge files—attached. I have to pay the telecom charges to download these files, which are of no use to me. A project that contains these files often ends up being sent directly to the Recycle Bin.

The C# **Solution Explorer** window goes one step further: It has a button that the C++ equivalent does not have: **Show All Files**. By default this button is off, so you see only the files that the **Solution Explorer** wants you to see and the folders that you have added. However, if you click on the **Show All Files** button, it will populate the **Solution Explorer** window with the files and folders in the project directory (it ignores the solution and project files and the options files). The files and folders that the **Solution Explorer** thinks you should not see are shown as gray items.

The **Class View** window, on the other hand, shows the types in the solution, so it has context menu items that allow you to manipulate the symbols shown in the **Class View** window and to alter how they are arranged. You can create folders in **Class View** (both C# and C++ projects), but these folders are purely logical and have no relation to the project folder. The **Class View** window shows the types that you have defined in your project in a hierarchical view: The top level is the namespace; then there are the types, and below those the members of the type, including any nested types that you may have defined. With a large project, the **Class View** window can become quite cluttered, especially when you have to traverse several layers in the tree view to get to a type member. **Class View** folders allow you to organize your classes in whatever order you choose; you can even nest folders. **Class View** folders represent your personal view of the classes in the project, so information about them is stored in the .suo file.

I will come back to the differences between **Class View** and **Solution Explorer** in a moment. First I want to cover the common context menu items. When you right-click on the solution in the **Solution Explorer** window, you'll get a context menu containing items that allow you to build the solution (**Class View** does not show the solution). Among the items you'll see are **Build** and **Rebuild** for both C# and C++ projects, as well as **Clean**, **Link**, and **Deploy** for C++ projects.

Build will start the build process according to the project dependencies, ignoring any items that are up-to-date. **Rebuild** will remove any build outputs and intermediate files and start the build process as if for the first time. C++ solutions can do a "clean" build; that is, delete outputs and intermediate files. It is usually a good idea to do this before zipping up a project to send to a coworker, to reduce the size of the files. C# projects do not have a separate link process (assemblies are referenced through metadata that is compiled into the referring assembly, so no link step is needed[6]). C++ projects, of course, do have a separate link step, so you can specify that already compiled object files should be linked.

If a C++ solution contains a deployment project or has deployment options set in its project options, you can use the **Deploy** menu item to deploy the solution, which will most likely involve copying build outputs to another machine and performing some installation steps (more details will be given in Chapter 6 in the section on deployment).

Both C++ and C# solutions have an **Add** context menu item in the **Solution Explorer** window. The **Add** context item for a solution allows you to add a new project to the solution or an existing project on your hard disk or elsewhere on the Web. In addition, it allows you to add new (or existing) items as *solution items*. So, for example, you may decide to add a Word document that contains documentation for the solution.

The property pages for a solution have two sections: **Common Properties** and **Configuration Properties**. The properties in the **Common Properties** section are used to configure which project is started up when the debugger runs, the interdependencies of the projects in the solution, and the location of the source files and symbol files used during debugging. If you have your own framework class library, you will want to include the path to the source files to this library so that when you step into functions during your debug session, you'll see the source code for the library.

You do not get the source code with the Framework Class Library, but you do get the symbols for the main assemblies, so you should add the address of these files (they'll be in the `Microsoft.NET\FrameworkSDK\Symbols` folder in `Program Files`) to your list of symbol files. Although it appears that you are setting the debug source files and symbols for a solution, you are actually

---

6. In addition, Visual Studio.NET does not have support for multimodule assemblies, so the Assembly Linker tool, `al.exe`, is not used.

making global changes, and these paths will be set for all solutions that you debug. **Startup Project** and **Project Dependencies** are specific to the solution.

The **Configuration Properties** section allows you to determine the current configuration that you'll use. This section lists each project in the solution and for each project the configuration (e.g., Release or Debug), the platform (e.g., .NET or Win32), and whether the project should be built. If you decide that you do not want the project built when the solution is built, you can use this page to indicate this preference. You can add new build configurations through the **Configuration Manager**, either by clicking on the appropriate button on the property page, or through the context menu for the solution.

Figure 5.6 shows the **Configuration Manager** for a solution with two projects. You can change the active configuration through the list box at the top of the dialog. This dialog also allows you to create new configurations by selecting the **<New...>** item. Once you have added a new configuration, you can select the project properties to specify the details of the configuration.

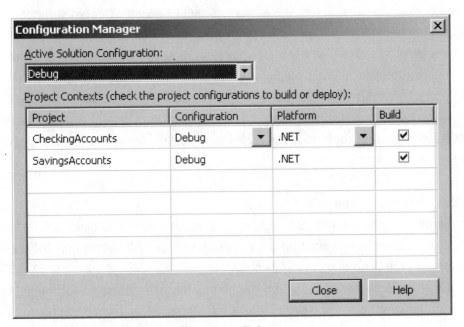

Figure 5.6 The Configuration Manager dialog

The last context menu item to mention here is **Batch Build**. Selecting this option will list all the configurations in the solution, and next to each will be a **Build** check box. You use this list to determine the configurations that you want built and to initiate the batch build.

5.2.5 Project Configurations

When you right-click on a project in the **Solution Explorer** or **Class View** window, you'll get the project context menu. This menu gives you the option of building the specific project (and of doing a clean build or a deployment if the project is C++), and it allows you to determine the project dependency and build order with respect to other projects in the solution.

When a project has been built, you have an output file that can be debugged. I will give more details in Chapter 9 about debugging. Basically, executables and libraries can be debugged, but if the target is a library (DLL) then there must be an executable to host it. The project properties can be used to specify the path to this executable. Pressing **F5** (or selecting the **Start** item from the **Debug** menu) will start a debug session. The IDE will start the output of the start-up project under the debugger; the start-up project can be selected through the project context menu.

For projects other than the start-up project, you can initiate a debug session through the project context menu. The items on the **Debug** submenu will start the project's output under the debugger. If you select **Start new instance**, the debugger will run until a breakpoint is reached. Alternatively, you can select **Step Into new instance**, in which case the debugger will stop in the entry point of the executable.

5.2.6 Project Properties

The project context menu also allows you to change the project properties. These properties are specific to the project type, so I will outline only the more important project settings in this section.

C++ projects have many more options than C# projects. Through the project options you can specify the C++ compiler and linker options, the switches passed to the resource compiler and MIDL (Microsoft Interface

DEVELOPING APPLICATIONS WITH VISUAL STUDIO.NET

Definition Language) compiler, and whether the browser database is built. In addition, you can configure the build events—that is, specify a tool that is run before a build is started, before the linker is run, and after the build occurs. You can also specify a tool that will be run after the linker has been run—a custom build step—and specify the outputs and dependency of the outputs of this tool.

C# project properties are relatively simple compared to C++ properties, reflecting the fact that the C# compiler has fewer command-line switches than the C++ compiler and that creating C# assemblies does not involve a separate link step. Furthermore, you cannot create multimodule assemblies through the IDE. All of this means that the C# project properties are pretty Spartan: You can set the assembly name, the assembly key file and key name, the default namespace, and the start-up object (if more than one class has a static `Main()` method). These are described as "common" properties, but they apply to the current project *only*. In addition, the **Build** page of **Configuration Properties** allows you to configure build options like the conditional compilation symbols (like TRACE and DEBUG), allowing you to configure unsafe code and set warning levels of the build.

5.3 Configuring Code

Once you have a solution with one or more projects, the next thing that you'll want to do is write code. This code will be made up of classes (types) and will use resources. The IDE, through the **Solution Explorer** and **Class View** windows, allows you to add these items to your project and configure them through the **Properties** window.

5.3.1 Adding Items to C++ Projects

The C++ **Add** context menu for projects has two pertinent items: **Add Class** and **Add Resource**. Each has a corresponding dialog containing the items that you can add. The **Add Resource** dialog lists the standard resources (icons, dialogs, and so on) and will add the item you select to the project's .rc file. The resource file (and the associated resource.h file) is added to the project. After this you'll be able to manipulate the resources through the **Resource View** window; I'll come back to this window later.

The **Add Class** dialog is more interesting: It lists the ATL and MFC types that you can add to the project. The wizards accessed in this dialog can be found in the `ClassWiz` folder under the `VCWizards` folder. Again, the wizards are HTML based and generate the appropriate files using template files and scripts. These wizards are explained in more detail in Chapter 6. I will mention just one here: the Generic C++ Class wizard. As the name suggests, this wizard will add a C++ class to the project, it will add a header file, and it can also add a `cpp` file (if the **Inline** check box is checked, all the code will be in the header file). When you add a class through this wizard, its files will be added to the project, but *no* other file in the project will be changed. The reason is that the wizard does not know where in the project you'll want to use the class, so it leaves it up to you to add the header to the appropriate file.

Once you have added a class to a project, the **Class View** window will be updated with the class and any types added along with the class, such as interfaces, structs, macros, and so on. I will explain these tools in a moment.

5.3.2 Resource View

The **Resource View** window has effectively remained unchanged as far as unmanaged C++ is concerned. You have all the tools that you were used to using in VS6, and the **Resource View** window looks the same as it did before. However, the big difference becomes clear when you add code to message handlers for an ATL or MFC control or dialog: The message handlers now appear on the **Messages** page of the **Properties** window. Adding message handlers involves selecting the message that you want to handle and typing the name of the handler method. The **Properties** window will then add the appropriate class and map entries. I'll come back to the **Properties** window later.

5.3.3 Adding Items to C# Projects

The context menu items to add items through the **Solution Explorer** and **Class View** windows are similar, but the **Solution Explorer** has additional items. Although both context menus have an **Add Class** item, the two **Add Class** dialogs are totally different. Selecting this item from the **Solution Explorer** context menu will start the Add New Item wizard, whereas selecting it from the **Class View** context menu will start the true Add Class wizard.

The Add Class wizard (see Figure 5.7) is detailed, and it is the preferred wizard to use. It allows you to create a class that may inherit from other classes and may implement existing interfaces. The first page is quite straightforward: It merely allows you to define the name of the class, its file, and its namespace (the **Namespace** combo box contains the current namespaces in your project, and you can create a new namespace by typing it in the edit control). The interesting parts of this wizard are the other two pages: **Base Class** and, in particular, **Inheritance**.[7]

The **Base Class** page allows you to select the base class for the new class. The page has two drop-down list boxes. The top one, **Namespace**, lists the

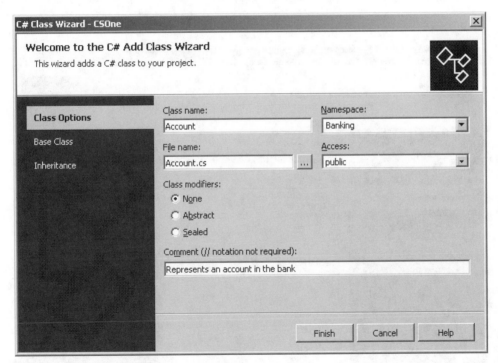

Figure 5.7   The C# Add Class wizard

7. Don't ask me why the **Inheritance** page is not called *Interfaces*, which seems more appropriate.

current namespaces in the project and all the namespaces of the Framework Class Library. Once you have selected a namespace, the bottom list box, **Base class**, contains all the classes in the selected namespace. Selecting a class from the **Bass class** list box will make that class the base class of the new class.

The **Inheritance** page (Figure 5.8) allows you to select the interfaces that your class will implement. At the top of the page is a drop-down list box with the namespaces in your project and all the namespaces in the Framework Class Library. If you select a namespace in your project, all the public and internal interfaces will be listed in the **Available interfaces** list box, If you select a Framework Class Library namespace, only the public interfaces will be listed. To get support for an interface, you should select the interface from the **Available interfaces** list box and add them to the **Selected interfaces** list box. When you dismiss the wizard, it will add the specified class. And if that class derives

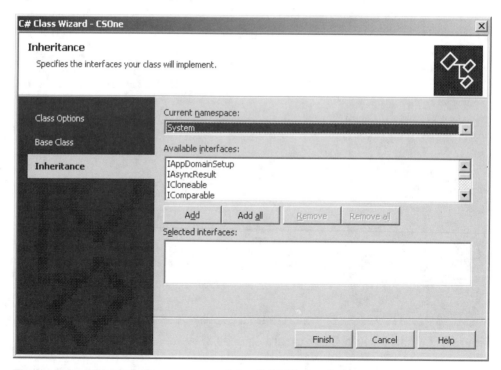

Figure 5.8   The Inheritance page of the Add Class wizard

DEVELOPING APPLICATIONS WITH VISUAL STUDIO.NET

from a base class or implements an interface, the wizard adds the assembly reference for that base class or interface.

When you select **Add Class** from the **Solution Explorer** window, you'll start the C# Add New Item wizard, which allows you to add items other than classes (some of the more useful items, like forms and controls, have a separate item on the **Add** submenu). I'll give more details about this wizard in Chapter 6; here I will just mention one item: C# Class. As the name suggests, this wizard will add a new class. First it will add a new file to the project, and then it will add the class to the namespace that has the same name as the project. It does not give you any options about the class, so if you want to derive the class from a base class or implement interfaces, you have to add this support yourself, by hand.

5.3.4 Adding References

The **Solution Explorer** context menu has items not found on the **Class View** context menu: C# has **Add Reference**, and both C# and C++ have **Add Web Reference** (in spite of the names, the two are unrelated). The **Add Reference** item allows you to add an assembly reference to a project; the dialog contains three tabs: **.NET**, **COM**, and **Projects** (see Figure 5.9). The **.NET** tab lists the Framework Class Library assemblies and the primary interop assemblies (PIAs). (PIAs are the "standard" way to access COM objects described by standard type libraries, as explained in Chapter 4.) If the assembly that you want to reference is not in this list, you can use the **Browse** button to locate it.

When you select an assembly and close the dialog, the assembly will be added to the assembly references list in **Solution Explorer**, and this will be added to the list of assembly references passed to the C# compiler through the /r switch. If the assembly is not installed in the GAC, it will be copied to the output path defined for the current configuration (**Project Options | Build Configuration Properties**) and to the obj folder under the project folder. Note that when you change to another configuration, the IDE will create the correct folder format and copy the referenced assemblies. The **Projects** tab lists the other projects in the solution that you can reference, and you can use this list to select the assembly—or COM server—that was created.

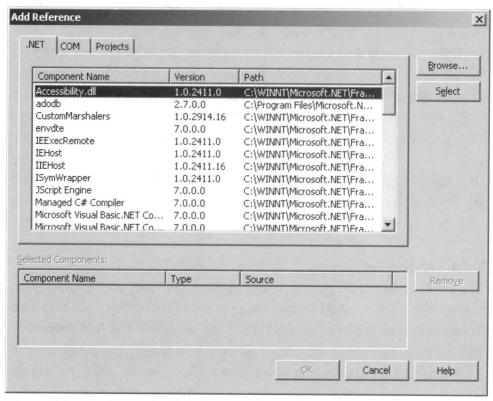

Figure 5.9   The Add Reference dialog to add assembly references

The **COM** tab lists the type libraries that have been registered with the system. When you select a type library from the list (or locate one using the **Browse** button), the wizard will attempt to find a PIA for the type library. If it cannot find a PIA, the wizard will generate a wrapper assembly for the type library (essentially running `tlbimp`) and add it as a reference. You will then be able to use the objects defined in the type library through COM Interop. The wrapper assembly will be installed in the output path and in the `obj` folder.

5.3.5   Class View

As the name suggests, the **Class View** window gives an overview of the types in the solution. These types are displayed as items in a tree view; the icon next to the item indicates the item type (Table 5.2) and its access level (Table 5.3).

Table 5.2 Class View icons for various types and their members

Icon	Type
	class
	delegate
	enum
	event
	field
	const field
	method
	interface
	COM library
{}	macro
	namespace
	C++ project
	C# project
	property
	struct
	union

Table 5.3 Member and type protection*

Icon	.NET Protection Level
	public
	family, famandassem
	assem, famorassem
	private

*Note: This table shows the icons for a field.

Although there are seven levels of protection in .NET (including the `private-scope` level used on method static members), there are only four icons used to show access levels in **Class View**. These are added to the icon for a class member, and Table 5.3 shows them applied to a non-`const` field member of a class.

5.3.5.1 Changing Types with Class View

The **Class View** window also allows you to change types. If you click on a type you will get an **Add** item on the context menu that will allow you to add various items to the type. The items that you can add depend on the actual type, as summarized in Table 5.4.

When you add a method or a function, essentially the same wizard will be run (see Figure 5.10). The same wizard is used for classes, structs, interfaces, and (in the case of C++) unions. There are some language and type differences; for example, for C++ classes you have the option of determining whether the function is in line and specifying the file where it will be saved, and in C# classes you can specify `virtual` method hiding. The Add Method wizard allows you to build up the parameter list for the function by creating a parameter and adding it to the list box on the right-hand side. When you close this dialog, the function is added to the item.

Table 5.4   Adding items to types using Class View

Type	Items You Can Add
C++ ATL classes	Interface, function, variable, connection point
C++ managed and native classes	Function, variable
C# classes	Method, field, property, indexer
C++ managed and COM interfaces	Method, property
C# interfaces	Method, property, indexer
C++ managed and native structs	Function, variable
C# structs	Method, field, property, indexer
C++ native unions	Function, variable

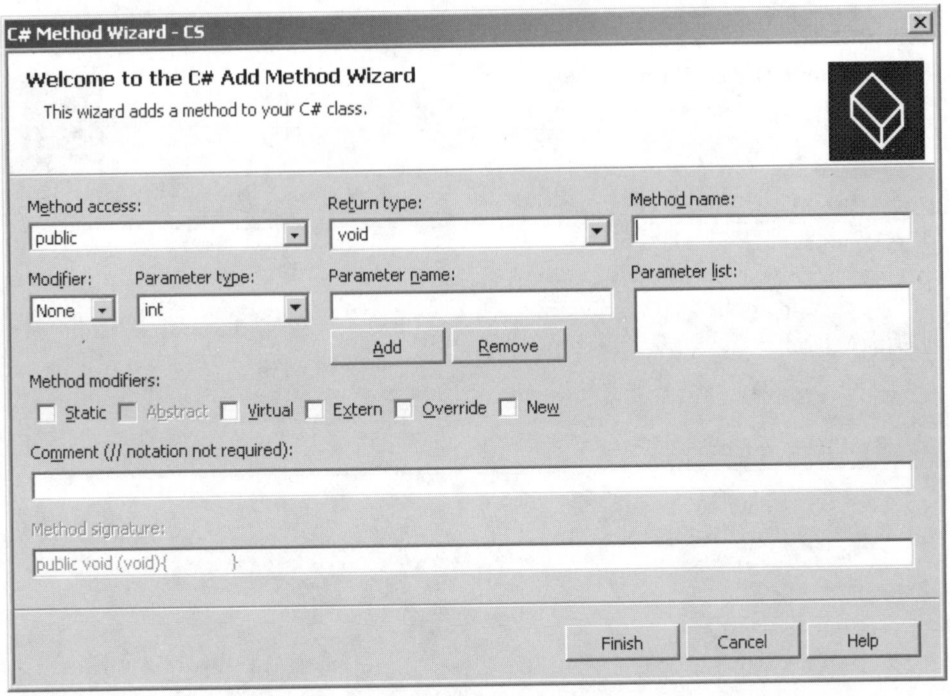

Figure 5.10 The Add Method wizard for C#. The C++ version is similar.

Adding methods to a COM interface uses a two-page wizard, where one page allows you to build up the parameter list, and the second page allows you to determine the IDL attributes for the method. The Add Variable wizard is used by C++ classes, and it is used to add variables to an MFC `CDialog`-derived dialog class. Consequently, the wizard has controls to associate the variable with a control on the dialog and to perform value validation through MFC's dialog data validation (DDV) macros.

The C# Add Property (Figure 5.11) and Add Field wizards are similar in that they allow you to specify the name, type, and access level for the item. The Add Property wizard gives you the option of specifying whether the property is read-only, write-only, or read/write through `get` and `set` methods. The Add Indexer wizard is essentially a cross between the Add Property and Add Method wizards: An *indexer* is a property that can take parameters. You use this wizard to create the parameters for the indexer—one for each of the indexer's indices—and to specify the type that the indexer will return.

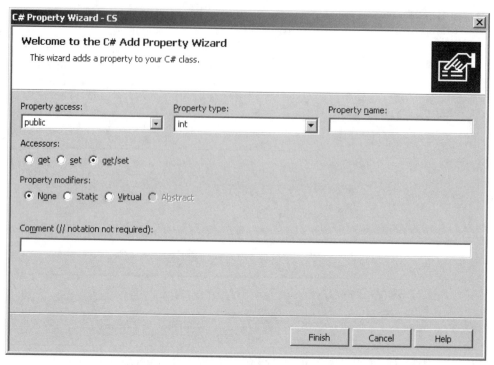

Figure 5.11   The C# Add Property wizard. The Add Field wizard is similar.

The COM interface Add Property wizard is similar, but (like the Add Method wizard) it has an extra page to specify the IDL attributes of the property, and of course, the property type is one of the COM types as opposed to the .NET types.

The most complicated wizards that you can use through **Class View** are the Implement Interface and Add Connection Point wizards used for ATL classes. The Implement Interface wizard allows you to select a type library (either by choosing a registered library or by browsing for a library), and the wizard will list all the interfaces that are described. When you select the interface, the wizard adds it to the class, and (unlike the C# Add Class wizard) it provides stub implementations for the interface methods. The Add Connection Point wizard uses the same dialog, but it shows only the interfaces in the type library that have been marked with the `[source]` IDL attribute.

5.3.6 Properties

The **Properties** window is used to identify the properties for an item and in some cases change those properties. The IDE is a little inconsistent in this respect. For example, the C# Add Class wizard allows you to specify whether the class is abstract. This capability is shown as the read/write **IsAbstract** property in the **Properties** window so that after you have created this class, you have the option of changing its abstractness. The inconsistency comes with C++ classes, for which there is no wizard allowing you to specify whether the class is abstract but you can still use the **Properties** window to change the `IsAbstract` property of the class.

The **Properties** window has icons along the top that you can use to change the data that the grid is used to display. Table 5.5 shows the icons; there are essentially three types. The first two icons indicate how the entries in the **Properties** window are displayed (alphabetically or by category). The next four show the data that can be displayed, and the final icon is used to generate a property page showing the particular item. Property pages are useful to get a quick view of a resource selected in **Resource View** for unmanaged C++ projects.

Message handlers are appropriate only for C++ ATL and MFC classes. The **Properties** window allows you to specify the message handlers for these

Table 5.5 Properties window icons

Icon	Meaning	Description
	Alphabetical listing	Lists the items (properties, messages, events, overrides) alphabetically.
	Categorical listing	Lists the items by category.
	Event handlers	Lists the events that can be handled by the class.
	Message handlers	Lists the Windows messages that can be handled by the class.
	Overrides	Lists the base-class methods that can be overridden.
	Properties	Lists the class properties.
	Property pages	Shows a property page for the item.

classes, and adding a method name to a message will add that method to the class and to the message map. In addition, the event list for an MFC class lists the menu and other UI update items and allows you to add the idle handlers and the `WM_COMMAND` handlers.

5.3.6.1 General Properties

Managed types (C++ and C#) have an `Access` property that determines whether the type is visible outside of the assembly. Common C# and C++ properties are shown in Table 5.6.

5.3.6.2 Attribute Properties

If a type—whether an unmanaged C++ class, or a managed C++ or C# type—has attributes, the **Properties** window shows the attributes. For example, if you have an unmanaged C++ class, you can specify that it should be compiled as a COM `coclass` by applying the `[coclass]` Visual C++ attribute:

```
// native C++
[coclass]
class Person : public IPerson
{
```

Table 5.6 Common C# and C++ class properties

Property	Description
Access	Specifies the visibility of the managed type.
File	Specifies the file where the type is implemented.
FullName	Specifies the name of the type, including the namespace.
IsAbstract	Specifies if a managed type is abstract.
IsInjected	Specifies if the native type has been generated through Visual C attributes.
IsManaged	Specifies if the type is managed or native.
IsSealed	Specifies if the managed type is sealed.
IsTemplate	Specifies if a C++ class has templates.
IsValue	Specifies if the managed type is a value type.

```
/* members of Person */
};
```

If you view the class with the **Properties** window, you'll see the entries in Figure 5.12. The C++ compiler will generate ATL code for this class, so the **Messages** and **Overrides** icons are enabled. But because the class is not a control, there are no messages that you can handle, and the only methods you can override are `FinalConstruct()`, `FinalRelease()`, and `ObjectMain()`.

The **Properties** page shows the properties that the IDE has "assumed" you'll want when you specify the `[coclass]` attribute. Notice that these properties will be read-only. For example, if you want to change the threading model from the default of `Apartment`, you cannot use the **Properties** window; instead you have to explicitly add the `[threading]` attribute and add the threading model either in code or through the **Properties** window.

Figure 5.12 Properties for the `Person` **class**

A managed C++ or C# class will have its attributes listed in the **Properties** window. When you select an attribute, you'll see the attribute class's properties listed (the optional attribute parameters), as well as its constructor parameters (the mandatory attributes, listed as "default"). For example, when you apply this custom attribute to a class:

```
// C++
[AttributeUsage(AttributeTargets.All)]
public __gc class TestAttribute
{
public:
   TestAttribute(int value, String* string)
   { /* use the values */ }
   __property void set_Value(int i)
   { /* use the value */ }
};
[Test(42, S"Test Data", Value = 99)]
public __gc class MyClass
{
};
```

you'll get the **Properties** window shown in Figure 5.13. As you can see, the constructor parameters are merely called **default** in the window, whereas the `Value` property is named.

5.3.6.3 Events

If the class is a UI class (a form or a control), you can use the **Properties** window to list the events that the class can handle. Because events are associated with controls and forms, you can see the events for a form only when you view the form open in the Windows Forms designer.

The **Properties** window and the Windows Forms designer work hand in hand as far as events are concerned. You add event handlers by supplying the name of the event handler to the event in the **Properties** window. When you do this, the designer adds the handler to the class (note that if you have two handlers for an event, the **Properties** window will show only one of them).

DEVELOPING APPLICATIONS WITH VISUAL STUDIO.NET

Properties	✕
MyClass VCCodeClass	▼

⊟ **Attributes**	
⊟ Test	42
(Name)	Test
default	42
default	S "Test Data"
File	c:\development\
Index	1
IsInjected	False
Value	99
⊞ C++	

Test

Figure 5.13   Properties window for a class with a custom attribute

5.3.7   C# Resources

Resources in managed applications are treated totally differently from resources in unmanaged applications. In an unmanaged file, resources are added to a segment of the PE file; in a managed file, resources are added to the manifest, either embedded or as links to external files. Information about the resources that should be added to a manifest are held in an XML file, an `.resx` file. The framework comes with a tool called `resgen` that compiles an `.resx` file to a `.resource` file that can be added to an assembly through the `/res` switch of the C# compiler.

Thus, in general, C# applications do not use the **Resource View** window because resources like icons, cursors, and bitmaps are added to the project through the **Add Item** dialog (much in the same way that new classes are added to a project), and the IDE adds information about these resources to the project's `.resx` file. You do not have to worry about creating any of these files; the IDE will do the work for you. I will come back to the issues of managed resources in Chapter 8.

There is one small area where the managed and unmanaged worlds cross: Windows Explorer. When you view a folder with Explorer, it will show an icon for the file (this is true for all of the view types). The icon will be the registered icon for a data file, or if the file is an executable file, Explorer will use the first icon that it can find in the file. Because managed applications have their own way of storing icons, Explorer will not be able to find an icon in the file, so it will use a generic icon for the application. To avoid this problem, you can add a Win32 resource to a managed executable. The C# compiler allows you to do this through the `/win32res` switch, which lets you add an already compiled Win32 `.res` file to the file, or through `/win32icon`, which lets you add just an icon. The project **Properties** dialog allows you to specify the icon through the **Application Icon** property on the **General** page of the **Common Properties** section.

Another area where Explorer has influenced the information that is put into an assembly is the file `VERSIONINFO` information. A seasoned C++ developer will recognize this resource; it is used to add version and copyright information to a file. This information is shown in the **Properties** dialog shown for the file by Explorer. When you use the various version and information attributes, the C# compiler will generate a `VERSIONINFO` resource using this information.

5.4 Editing Code

One of the most important features of the IDE is its ability to edit code and to integrate this editing with the build process. Visual Studio comes with a capable text editor that you can use to edit C++ and C# code. However, it is more than just this. The text editor is integrated with the help system so that you have **F1** and dynamic help, it is integrated with the type information of the libraries that you are using so that you can use IntelliSense, and it will format your code as well!

In addition, Visual Studio comes with "visual" editors so that you can edit HTML as if it were a rendered document and XML as if it were real data and not a mess of angle brackets. All of these tools are integrated into the IDE.

5.4.1 The Text Editor

On the surface the editor is a text editor, but it is far more sophisticated than that. For starters, it applies color to the text to identify specific code types, it provides various tools to allow you to view your code (outlining), and it is your interface to code completion (IntelliSense).

Code coloring makes code more readable by showing keywords and comments in a different color from the rest of the code. Keyword coloring is also a helpful hint as you type: You can tell if you have typed a keyword correctly because it will change color. When you scroll through code, you can quickly identify commented sections by their color. Furthermore, if you have a color printer, you can even amaze your friends and show that writing code can be artistic (well, colorful). The colors that the text editor will use can be specified through the **Environment | Fonts and Colors** options page.

When you copy sections of text, the formatting that the source code editor has applied (the font and the colors) will be copied into the Clipboard data. The editor copies three versions of the code to the Clipboard: `CF_TEXT`, Unicode, and Rich Text Format (RTF). The first two do not have formatting code; the last one has the font and color information. Depending on your point of view, pasting font and color information to the Clipboard is either a great idea or a lousy one. In my case, I prefer to edit code in Lucida Console at a large font size (to accommodate my less than perfect eyes), but this book does not use Lucida Console or the point size I used for the code sections, and in any case, it is not printed in color. Because Word automatically pastes in the RTF data from the Clipboard, I have to go through the extra step of telling Word to paste the unformatted data. I find this feature irritating and I wish I could turn it off. On the other hand, if you use the same font in VS.NET that you have defined for the code in your documentation styles, this feature will save you the tedium of formatting your code.

As you type code, the editor will perform some syntax checking according to the type of the document. For example, if you type the following code as part of a C# class:

```
// C#
public void f(
{
}
```

you'll find several things happening. First, when you press **Enter** after typing the method signature, the caret will align itself one tab stop to the left of the `public` keyword that you typed (this is smart indenting; the editor has recognized that there is a closing parenthesis missing and assumes that you want to type the parameters on a new line). When you type the opening brace, the editor will automatically align it with the `public` keyword. After a brief pause, the opening parenthesis and opening brace will be underlined with *squigglies,* as shown in Figure 5.14.

Squigglies indicate that there is a problem. You can get a summary of these problems in the task list. I will talk about the task list more in Chapter 6—because it is important in the build process—but basically in this case it will list three problems:

1.) expected
2. Identifier expected
3. Type expected

All three problems are caused by the missing parenthesis. The editor has identified that the opening parenthesis should be followed by either a closing parenthesis or a parameter list. Double-clicking on the error in the task list will place the caret on the offending code.

The editor is an interface to the code completion technology. When you type a namespace, class name, or object variable, IntelliSense will obtain information about the namespace or the class of the object. When you type a scope operator (i.e., . for C#; ., ->, or :: for C++) code completion will create a list box with the members of the item. You can scroll through this list box and select the item you need. If you start to type an item, you can persuade the editor to select the appropriate member (i.e., complete the code for you) by pressing **Alt–<right arrow>** (for the default keyboard mapping scheme). If the editor does not have enough information to complete the code, it will bleep at you. You can

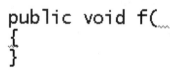

Figure 5.14   Squigglies

DEVELOPING APPLICATIONS WITH VISUAL STUDIO.NET

also get a list of the members of a type by placing the caret within a method of that type and selecting **List Members** on the context menu.

When you type the opening parenthesis of a method, IntelliSense will list the signature of the method in a tool tip, and as you type the parameters, it will make the current parameter bold. If the method is overloaded, the tool tip will have up and down arrows to allow you to scroll through the signatures (with the mouse or the arrow keys). Furthermore, you can place the caret in a method or on the type of a member field and select **Quick Info** from the context menu to get a tool tip summary of the type.

IntelliSense also has a code commenting feature. When it shows you the list of members for the current item, IntelliSense will display for the selected item either the comment associated with the item, or a summary that it creates from the item's description. The comment can appear immediately before the definition of the item in line in the class or, if it is a C++ method, immediately before the method definition if defined out of the class. Note that for C# code, only the comments applied as `<summary>` XML comments (starting with `///`, as explained later) will appear as comments for the item; C++ allows you to use both `//` and `/* */` comments.

This brings up another topic for which the source code editor has a nice solution: block comments. If you are writing C++ code, you will typically type a description of an item before the item in the code (C# code can use XML comments to do this). If the item is a method, the comment will typically take up many lines, including descriptions of the parameters and the return value. The source code editor allows you to type a block of text like this as normal text and then comment the entire block at once: To do this you select the text and click on **Edit | Advanced | Comment Selection** (`Edit.CommentSelection`). This feature is also useful for commenting out blocks of code, especially because there is an **Uncomment Selection** action (`Edit.UncommentSelection`) that will remove the single-line comment symbol from all lines in the selection. This feature does not work with multiline comments (`/* */`).

The text editor also allows you to view and change the formatting that is used. Tabs are displayed as spaces, and you can select **Text Editor** options to specify how many spaces will be used. This means that when you view some text, you do not know if the indentation is done with tabs or spaces, which could be a problem if the code is viewed by a coworker who has a different tab setting. The solution is to make sure that formatting is done either with only tabs or—better—with only spaces.

The **Edit | Advanced | View White Space** menu item (**Shift-Ctrl-8**) shows tabs and spaces using symbols: → for a tab, for a space. You can convert all tabs to spaces using **Edit | Advanced | Untabify** (`Edit.UntabifySelection`), and all spaces to tabs using the **Tabify** item (`Edit.TabifySelection`). Note that **Tabify** does not always work the way you expect. It reads the number of spaces set for the tabs and uses this information to define a tab stop. If text appears at a tab stop with a space before it, the command will replace this space with a tab.

Finally for tabs, if you select some text and press **Tab**, the entire block will be indented by one tab (either by a tab character or by spaces, depending on the options you have selected). If you press **Shift-Tab**, then the text will be unindented by a tab. The same action can be performed by the **Increase Line Indent** and **Decrease Line Indent** menu items on the **Edit | Advanced** menu (`Edit.IncreaseLineIndent` and `Edit.DecreaseLineIndent`).

As with most other text editors, if you hold the left mouse button down as you move over some text, you'll select that text, including all leading and trailing tabs and spaces. If you just want to select a block within the text (e.g., to ignore the leading tabs and spaces), you can do so by holding the **Alt** key down before you press the left mouse button down and keeping the **Alt** key down as you select the text (see Figure 5.15). When you press **Ctrl-C**, only the selected text will be copied.

```
int·_tmain(int·argc,·_TCHAR*·argv[])
{
···printf("hello, everyone");
···return·0;
}
```

Figure 5.15 Block selection in action. Note that this shows the code with View White Space turned on.

A related facility is *virtual space*. Virtual space allows you to place the caret *anywhere* in the document and start typing. If the caret happens to be after the end of a line, the editor will pad out the space between the caret and the previous end of the line with white space. To use this facility, you have to turn it on through the **Text Editor | All Languages** options page. By default, the text editor does not have a limit to line lengths (contrast this with VS6, which had a 2,000-character limit). This can be a problem if you have a large font and small windows, so the text editor allows you to turn on word wrap through the **Text Editor | All Languages** options page (`Edit.ToggleWordWrap`), and word wrap will wrap a line if it extends past the current edge of the window.

The text editor supports mouse wheel browsing and autoscrolling. Autoscrolling is turned on when you press the middle button (or the wheel for a wheel mouse), at which point you can move the mouse forward or backward to scroll up or down and alter the scroll rate. This is a feature that has been present in Office and Internet Explorer for quite a while, but unlike IE, the text editor does not allow you to scroll sideways.

5.4.1.1 *Outlining*

Outlining is designed to make your code easier to read. When turned on (via **Edit | Outlining | Start Automatic Outlining**, or `Edit.StartAutomaticOutlining`), outlining groups sections of code that can be contracted to show only the first line of the code (`Edit.CollapsetoDefinitions`). Code blocks are identified in the indicator margin by gray markup lines and a **+** or **–** check box at the top of the block. Clicking on the **+** check box expands a contracted code block, and clicking on a **–** check box contracts an expanded code block. The same action can be performed with the `Edit.ToggleOutliningExpansion` command, which will expand a collapsed definition and collapse an expanded definition at the caret. `Edit.ToggleAllOutlining` will do the same for all text in the document.

When a code block is contracted, the outliner shows a summary line in gray and may also show an ellipsis. Table 5.7 shows the types of code blocks and the summary lines that are shown in contracted view. When you hold the mouse over

Table 5.7   Code regions that you can outline

Code Block Type	Contracted View
Blocks of comments	`/* */`
Namespaces	Namespace name and ellipsis
Blocks of using statements	`using` and ellipsis
Classes	Class name and ellipsis
Functions	Function signature and ellipsis
Mixed blocks of code	`[]`
Regions	Region name

the gray summary line or the ellipsis (if it is shown), a tool tip window will be created with the expanded outlined code.

The entries in Table 5.7 need more explanation. Regions are available in C# (and VB.NET) but not in C++. They are identified through the `#region/#endregion` (in VB.NET, `#Region/#End Region`) directives. The `#region` directive gives a title for the region so that when the block is contracted, the title is shown in gray. This directive can be used to outline code within a method, or it can group several methods and typically is used by the Windows Forms designer around code that is generated by the designer. This directive is used to hide code that the designer has decided only it should know about. When you print code that has outlining, the code will be expanded except for the sections marked by `#region`, which will appear on the printed page as the region title.

C++ code is usually more difficult to outline than C# code, principally because functions don't have to be in line and you can have global variables. This is the reason for the `[]` outlining symbol; it is used to group together "orphaned" code like global and class static variables.

5.4.1.2   *XML Comments*

C# allows you to document your code with XML tags. These tags are placed in code with the C# comment symbol followed by an extra slash (`///`) and will be stripped out by the compiler and placed in an XML file. It is then just a matter of processing the XML using XSLT (Extensible Stylesheet Language Transformations) to transform the XML into a documentation format like HTML or RTF. Table 5.8 shows the tags that can be used.

How the XML is interpreted depends on the transformation being applied. The IDE comes with a transformation through the **Tools | Build Comment Web Pages** menu item (`Tools.BuildCommentWebPages`). This transformation goes through the solution and extracts a list of classes, the members of the classes, and the parameters of the methods contained in the classes. It applies the comments that you have added with the XML tabs, and it creates HTML documentation pages in a subfolder called `CodeCommentReport`.

Table 5.8   XML comment tags

Tag	Description
`<c>`	Identifies sections of a comment that should be displayed as code.
`<code>`	Identifies multiple lines of a comment that should be displayed as code.
`<example>`	Identifies an example within the comment.
`<exception>`	Identifies an exception class.
`<include>`	Includes documentation from a file referenced via `XPATH`.
`<list>`	Defines a bulleted or numbered list, or a table.
`<para>`	Defines a paragraph.
`<param>`	Provides a description for a method parameter.
`<paramref>`	Indicates a parameter in a comment.
`<permission>`	Specifies the permission set for a member.
`<remarks>`	Creates a remarks section.
`<returns>`	Indicates the return type of a method.
`<see>` and `<seealso>`	Creates a link to another topic.
`<summary>`	Creates a summary for the item.
`<value>`	Describes a property.

5.4.2 HTML Editor

When you open an HTML page as a document in the IDE, you'll get the option of two views: **Design** or **HTML**. The **HTML** view shows the HTML tags of the page as text. Code completion works in this view so that as you type tags, the attributes that you can use will appear in list boxes. When you type the opening tag, the editor will insert the closing tag. One nice feature is that if you type < for a tag, you'll get a list of the tags that are relevant to the current context, and if you have a tag that has been opened but not yet closed, the list box will include it. Indeed, once you have saved the page to disk, you can run the HTML page validator from the HTML Editor toolbar, which will check tags and put any validation errors in the task list.

The **Design** view renders the HTML as a Web page, but it also allows you to edit the page. The Formatting toolbar can be used to select fonts and colors, create lists, and indent text. In addition, the **Toolbox** window has an **HTML** section containing the HTML controls that you can drag and drop onto the page. When you place the caret on an element in **HTML** view or **Design** view, you'll see the properties of the element in the **Properties** window, and this gives you a quick way to set the attributes of the element. Some elements (e.g., list boxes and tables) will also have a property page that groups together similar properties.

If you are developing an ATL Server project, the HTML editor will be used to edit the `.srf` stencil files. Stencil files have placeholders identified with double braces (`{{ }}`), and if you right-click on a placeholder you'll get the option of adding a handler method for the placeholder or editing an existing one.

5.4.3 XML Editor

Similarly, when you edit XML files, you will have two views of the data: the **XML** view and the **Data** view. The **XML** view shows the XML as text. If you right-click on **XML**, you'll get a context menu that contains the item **Create Schema**; selecting this item will create a schema and open it. Schemas are shown in an **XML** view or a **DataSet** view. The **DataSet** view shows the schema in tabular form—in a similar way to defining tables in Microsoft Access. If you start with an empty schema (through the **Add New Item** context menu) or an empty `DataSet`, when you have the schema open in **DataSet** view you can build up the schema using the items on the **XML Schema** tab in the **Toolbox** window. This tab has items that allow you to define simple types, complex types, and the relationship between those types by dragging and dropping the appropriate items from the **Toolbox** window.

Once you have a defined a schema for an XML file, you can view the XML data using **Data** view. Again, the **Data** view shows a data grid, with a column for each attribute and a column for the element text, through which you can enter the data. If you have added the schema as a `DataSet` to a C# project, the DataSet editor will also add a class to your C# project derived from `System.Data.DataSet` that uses the schema.

5.4.4 Data

I will give more details about the **Server Explorer** window in Chapter 6, but it is pertinent to mention here the data grid for data sources. When you open a table (or a view) of a data source, you will get a data grid through which the results of the view or the entire table will be shown. You can use this data grid to enter new data, and as you move to a new row in the grid, the appropriate INSERT or UPDATE operation will be performed.

5.4.5 Designers

The VS.NET designers give you a visual image of the type that you are developing. It works in tandem with the **Toolbox** and **Properties** windows: You drag and drop items from the **Toolbox** window onto the designer window and use the **Properties** window to change the properties of the items that you have dropped. When you open a file that contains a form, control, or component, the IDE will automatically start the designer window for you, but you can start it manually through the **View | Designer** menu item (`View.ViewDesigner`). When you do this, the designer will read the currently loaded file and the class in the file, and will create a RAD image. This image will be either a visual representation of a form or a control, or it will show the components that make up the item.

The various designers will show C# and VB.NET code. C++ is not supported for the simple reason that the C++ language is too complicated and has too many quirky rules for it to be parsed effectively. The forms designer will show a visual representation for controls derived from `UserControl`—that is, a composite control that is made up of other controls. The forms designer will not show an image for noncomposite controls (those derived from `Control`); instead, you'll see the component designer.

The reason is that a noncomposite control is responsible for painting its surface, and the Windows Forms designer is simply not clever enough to show the image. To get around this restriction, you have to create a separate Windows Application project within your solution that has the sole purpose of showing the control that you are designing. As you edit the code for your own purposes, you should periodically compile the assembly and use the test project to view the effect on the control. I'll show an example in Chapter 8.

Another example of a designer is the component designer. When you use the **Add Component** context menu item, you'll get a class derived from `IComponent`, and you'll see a blank sheet onto which you can drag and drop components from the **Toolbox** window—for example, `EventLog`, `MessageQueue`, or `PerformanceCounter`. Components do not have a user interface, so these components will be shown on the designer surface with just their object name. You can use the **Properties** window to set the properties and add event handlers for these components, but the only mechanism to make these components interact is to switch to code through the **View Code** context menu item and type the code by hand.

The forms designer also allows you to drag and drop components from the **Toolbox** window. Controls are components with a user interface, and the location and size of a control are important. Thus, with controls you should be careful where you drop the control and either use the **Properties** window to specify an exact position and size of the control or use one of the tools on the **Layout** toolbar to resize or align a control with respect to other controls on the form. Once you have determined that a control's size and location are final, you should "lock" the control.

Controls can be locked one by one or together as part of the form. Each control will have a `Locked` property. When this property is changed from the default value of `false` to `true`, you will not be able to change the control's size or location through the designer window (i.e., by dragging it with the mouse), but you can continue to change these properties through the **Properties** window. Forms, too, can be locked through their `Locked` property, but if you change this to `true`, you indicate that the designer cannot be used to change the form's size. This does not mean that the sizes and positions of its child controls cannot be changed. To lock the form *and* its controls, you select one of the controls and then choose **Lock Controls** on the **Format** menu (`Format.LockControls`).

As I mentioned earlier, turning off autohide from the **Toolbox** window during the time that you are dragging and dropping controls makes it easier to design a form. As you make changes to a form or control in the designer window, the designer will write these changes to the associated code file. However, not all items in the **Properties** window represent properties that are part of a control class. The `Locked` "property" is such an item: It is not a property of `Control` or any of its derived classes. Because it is not a proper property, it cannot be added to the code file. Instead it is written to the `.resx` file associated with the form. Normally you do not see this file; the **Solution Explorer** window will hide it from you. You can click on the **Show All Files** button to make this file visible in **Solution Explorer**, but you cannot view it in the IDE while the form is open. I will return to `.resx` files in Chapter 8; in essence, an `.resx` file is used with a form to hold values needed by the designer for the form.

The Web Forms designer is a cross between the Windows Forms designer and the HTML editor. Like the Windows Forms designer, it shows a UI view of code—in this case an ASP.NET page—and like the HTML editor, it allows you to view the underlying HTML that will be rendered in a Web browser. For more details about using the Web Forms designer, I recommend that you read one of the excellent texts currently available about ASP.NET.

5.4.6 Binary Editor

If you open an EXE or a DLL with VS.NET and the file has standard Windows resources, VS.NET will open the file in the **Resource View** window. If the file does not have resources, or if the file is in a format that VS.NET does not recognize, the file will be opened in the **Binary View** window.

Binary View shows the file with the actual bytes and a hex representation of the data. You can edit the file in either view, by typing the actual characters that you want to be placed in the file, or by typing the hex. You can overwrite the bytes that are there, or if you press **Insert** you can add extra bytes. There is one irritating feature with **Binary View**: If you select part of the view and copy it to the Clipboard, the actual bytes from the file will be copied to the Clipboard instead of the formatted view from **Binary View**. You do not have the choice of whether the formatted text is copied.

5.5   Searching and Browsing Code

Searching and browsing are very important with large software projects because they allow you to see the relationship of one piece of code to another, and they allow you to locate code that may interest you. *Searching* involves trawling through one or more files to see if there is text that matches a specified pattern. *Browsing* is more sophisticated: Browsing accesses information about types, about their relationships to other types, and about where they are implemented and used. Visual Studio has excellent support for both searching and browsing.

5.5.1   Find In Files

The **Find In Files** command allows you to search for specific text or to match patterns within files in a path. When you specify text, you can indicate whether matches should occur for text that has the same case or differing case, and you can specify whether the text refers to a whole word or to part of a word. In addition, you can specify a pattern to match against—either a regular expression or a pattern with wild-card characters.

The files that are searched are identified by path and name. The path can be the current solution, or you can browse for a folder on your hard disk or on a file share—or all of these: The browse dialog allows you to select more than one path. You can provide the exact name for a file or a pattern using wild-card characters, and you can specify that the search should be conducted only in the folders you have selected or should include their subfolders.

Once you have initiated a search, you can stop the process by bringing up the search dialog again. If a search is in progress, the **Stop** button will be enabled. When the search has completed, the results will go to one of the **Find Results** windows. There are two—**Find Results 1** and **Find Results 2**—and by default the results will go to the first window. If you want the results to go to the second window, you can indicate your preference by using the check box on the **Find in Files** dialog. Once the search has produced results, you can load the file at the location of the matched text by double-clicking on the entry in the **Find Results** window.

The same dialog can be used to replace text; however, you should be careful because if you select **Replace All**, you could change lots of files. The dialog does warn you when you select this action—it says that the undo feature does not work unless the files remain open—but it is safer to leave this action alone. If you use the **Replace** button, the files will be searched and when a match is made, the search will pause to allow you to decide if you really want to make the replacement.

Searches can be performed against a regular expression, and if you specify this option, the right arrow button next to the search text edit control will be enabled. Clicking on this button gives a list of regular-expression matching patterns to enable you to build up your own pattern. Regular-expression pattern matching can perform several searches at once, and you can get the results of the subexpressions saved as tagged expressions. To identify a subexpression, you use braces in the regular expression.[8] When you replace text, you can indicate that the matched text should be replaced with text made up of the results of the subexpressions; these results are in the form \1, \2, and so on, according to the location of the subexpression within the main expression. The tagged expression \0 is the original text that is found.

5.5.2 Find In Project

The **Find** dialog is similar to the **Find In Files** dialog, but there are a few important differences. The first is obvious: The search will occur in the files opened within the current project (the default action is to search the current opened document). The second is more subtle: There is a button called **Mark All** that will place a bookmark against all the matches rather than sending the results to the **Find Results** window. A bookmark is a cyan rounded rectangle in the indicator

---

8. Many regular-expression evaluators use parentheses for subexpressions.

column, and the IDE allows you to move through a document from bookmark to bookmark. A third difference is that the current document can be searched from the current caret position, and you can specify that the search should be directed upward.

The **Find in Project** functionality can also be accessed through the **Find in Files** combo box from the Standard toolbar. Although it is called **Find in Files**, when you type text in this edit control and press **Enter**, the search will be performed on the current file.

5.5.3 Command Window

The **Find in Files** combo box has another interesting property: It gives access to the IDE commands. You can access these commands by typing > and then the command. This edit control supports IntelliSense, so as you type a command it will provide a list box with the possible commands, as Figure 5.16 shows.

To get a more complete view, you can show the **Command** window (e.g., by typing `>View.CommandWindow`). This window allows you to type commands in what is known as *command mode,* and to print out results during a debugging session in the *immediate mode.* I will explain how to use immediate mode in Chapter 9. Command mode is the default when you are not in a debugging session (otherwise you can access it by typing `>cmd` in the **Command** window when in immediate mode; note the > character); it allows you to type commands and their parameters. To switch from command mode to immediate mode, you type `immed` at the > prompt.

Figure 5.16   The Find in Files combo box

DEVELOPING APPLICATIONS WITH VISUAL STUDIO.NET

To perform a case-sensitive search for the text "Class" in the current folder, you can type the following in the **Command** window:

```
>Edit.FindInFiles /case Class
```

The command mode also supports IntelliSense, so you will be presented with a list box showing the commands you can select. The **Command** window is even more helpful than this. For example, if you type `File.OpenFile`, you get the command-line version of the **File Open** dialog, and if you press **Enter** at this point, the IDE will present you with the dialog. However, you can also type the name of the file that you want to open, and the **Command** window helps to browse for a file. So if I type, for example, `\Documents and Settings`, the **Command** window will give me a list box with the files and folders in the specified folder and I can browse the list for the file that I require.

As another example, consider creating a new file. The **File | New | File** menu gives you a dialog that lists the types of files that you can create. Each of these types is a *template,* as I mentioned earlier. In the **New File** dialog, these templates are categorized in a tree view on the left-hand side. To create the file, you click on the **Open** button, which will create a file of the specified type with a default name. However, this button will let you do more. If you click the down arrow on the **Open** button and select **Open With...**, you'll get a list of all the current editors, so you can specify an editor other than the one that is the default for the file type. All of these facilities are available when you type the command in the **Command** window, but unlike the **New File** dialog, the **Command** window lets you give the name of the file, as the following example illustrates:

```
File.NewFile test.bin /t:"General\Text File"
    /e:"Binary Editor"
```

This command will create a file called `test.bin` through use of the `Text File` template in the `General` category (which merely creates an empty file). The command will then open the file using the binary editor. Unfortunately, the **Command** window IntelliSense is not clever enough to list the command switches as you type or the options that each switch supports, so to use this useful facility of specifying command options you have to know what switches a command supports. The documentation for Visual Studio lists all commands and their formats.

A quick way to type the command to create a new file is to use `nf`, which is an *alias* for `File.NewFile`. Aliases are shortened commands that you are allowed to use in the **Command** window. You can create your own aliases for commands that you use often. To do this you use the `alias` command; for example, you could type the following at the command line to define an alias called `newBin`:

```
alias newBin File.NewFile /t:"General\Text File"
    /e:"Binary Editor"
```

The `newBin` alias will create a new empty binary file in the binary editor. Typing `newBin` will create a file with the default name, whereas `newBin test.bin` will create a file called `test.bin`. In other words, the **Command** window will append your additional parameters to the end of the text of the alias. To delete an alias, you simply use the following format:

```
alias newBin /delete
```

The Visual Studio IDE has many predefined aliases, and you can view these by typing `alias` at the **Command** window. Note that often there are two aliases for what appear to be the same thing. The reason is that one refers to a UI element, and the other is pertinent to the **Command** window. So the alias `threads` will show the **Threads** window, whereas ~ will print the list of threads in the **Command** window.

The `shell` alias (for `Tools.Shell`) is interesting. It will execute a command, so `shell notepad` will start Notepad. Any output from the command can be piped to the **Command** output pane of the **Output** window through the `/output` switch, whereas the output can be piped to the **Command** window with the `/command` switch. If you want to execute a command-line utility like `dir` or `del`, you need to launch the command in the command-line processor using `cmd /c` (on NT)—for example, as follows:

```
shell /command cmd /c dir
```

This command will list the files in the current directory in the **Command** window. Other command-line utilities do not need a command-line processor. For example, to send the list of the switches for the C# compiler (i.e., `csc /?`) to the **Output** window, you can use the following command:

```
shell /output csc "/?"9
```

5.5.4   Incremental Searches

Incremental searches are performed on the current document, and they do not use a dialog. To initiate a search, you select **Edit | Advanced | Incremental Search** (or press **Ctrl-I** for the standard keyboard layout), at which point the cursor will change to a pair of binoculars with a downward-pointing arrow. Now you should start to type the item that you are looking for, and a search will be performed on a character-by-character basis. That is, when you type the first character, the caret will move to the first match for it, and when you type the second character, the caret will move to the first match for those two characters, and so on. Once you have typed the entire search text, you can perform more searches for that text by pressing **Ctrl-I**.

5.5.5   Bookmarks

There are three types of bookmarks: temporary, named, and comment bookmarks. *Temporary bookmarks* are shown as a cyan rounded rectangle in the indicator column, *named bookmarks* are shown as a blue curved arrow, and *comment bookmarks* do not have a special indicator because the comment acts as the indicator.

Temporary bookmarks can be applied and removed individually by toggling, or they can be applied in a group through the **Find** dialog. Once you have set bookmarks in a document, you can remove them individually by toggling them, or you can remove all bookmarks in a document at once. The **Edit | Bookmarks** submenu has items to add, remove, and move between bookmarks.

You add named bookmarks by right-clicking on the indicator column and selecting **Add Task List Shortcut**, or by selecting **Edit | Bookmarks | Add Task List Shortcut**. Adding a named bookmark will add the current line to the task list, and the contents of the current line will be used as the name. To see the bookmark, you have to make sure that you have the filters set to **Shortcut** (or to **All**) by right-clicking on the task list and selecting the filter through the **Show**

---

9. I have enclosed the /? switch in quotation marks because without these the Command window will interpret the switch as requesting help on the shell command.

Tasks submenu. When you double-click on an item in the task list, the caret will move to that line.

Comment bookmarks are lines that start with a designated comment. By default, four comment bookmarks are predefined (and all except TODO can be removed): HACK, TODO, UNDONE, and UnresolvedMergeConflict. You can view the current comment bookmarks and their settings on the **Task List | Environment | Task List** options page. When you type a comment that starts with the designated bookmark comment, the line will be added to the task list. You must have the filter set to **Comment** or to **All** to see them, and as with named comments, when you double-click on an item the caret will be moved to that point in the document.

Bookmarks—both temporary and named—are saved in the solution file and hence are persisted from session to session. A comment bookmark, of course, remains until the comment is deleted from the source file.

5.5.6 Braces

The text editor has automatic brace matching; that is, when you type a closing brace, it and the matching brace are highlighted. This feature allows you to make sure that the braces are correctly matched. Such matching is carried out for braces ({ }), parentheses (( )), square brackets ([ ]), angle brackets (<>), and quotation marks (" "), but interestingly, not for single quotes (' '). In addition, matching is used with the #if/#else/#endif conditional construct.

If you have code that already has braces, you can move between them by placing the caret on one brace and pressing **Ctrl-]** (for the default keyboard mapping). Again, this works with all of the brace types listed here. Note that the matching is "smart": If a brace character is contained within a string in your code, the brace matching will ignore it.

5.5.7 Object Browser

The **Object Browser** window allows you to browse objects, their base classes, and their interfaces. To be able to show this information it needs *type information,* and the source of this information depends on whether the code is managed or unmanaged. The **Class View** window also needs type information (so

DEVELOPING APPLICATIONS WITH VISUAL STUDIO.NET

that it can show you the types in your project), and this information will be held in the project's `.ncb` file. The **Object Browser** window also has access to the `.ncb` file, so it will show the same information. In fact, the only difference that you'll see between the two is that the **Class View** window shows all types in a single tree view, whereas the **Object Browser** window uses a list view as well.

If your project is managed, the assemblies that your code uses will have type information in the form of metadata. This means that the **Object Browser** window has enough information to display all the public and protected types and their members in the assembly. When you select a member of a type in the **Object Browser** window, the associated description window will give information about the selected item, including any attributes applied to it and a summary. Because metadata has complete information about each type and about the types that each type uses, you can search other assemblies to see if they use a type, or a member of that type. To do this you select **Quick Find Symbol** from the context menu for the symbol. This command will give a list of the files that use the selected symbol in the **Find Symbol Results** window in a tree view. All available source files are listed, and if you double-click on an item in this list, the source file will be loaded and the caret placed on the symbol.

Unmanaged C++ code does not have metadata, and the information in the `.ncb` file is not sufficient for you to be able to search for the use of a symbol. Instead you have to provide type information, and to do this you have to create a *browser information* file. The browser information file is created in a separate build step, and by default this facility is turned off. To turn it on, you have to use the project's property pages, and on the **General** page set the **Build Browser Information** option to **Yes**.

The source code browser tool will generate a browser file that by default will have the same name as the project, with the `.bsc` extension. Be aware that if the project has many classes—if it is an ATL or MFC project—the browser build step could take a long time. Therefore, it makes sense to keep this option turned off, turning it on only when you specifically want to use the object browser. You can open the `.bsc` file as a document or by selecting **Browse Definition** from the **Class View** window (or using the command `View.Ob-jectBrowser`).

You are not restricted to the code in the current solution and the libraries that it uses. You can use the **Object Browser** window to browse any assembly or type library. To do this you click on the **Customize** button on the **Object Browser** window's toolbar, which will bring up the **Selected Components** dialog (Figure 5.17). This dialog lists the referenced assemblies and code files in the solution in the **Projects and references** node. Other assemblies and type libraries are listed in the **External Components and Libraries** node. To load an assembly or type library you click on the **Add** button of this dialog, which brings up a dialog listing the shared assemblies and registered type libraries.

Once you have browser information, there are several ways you can use it. First, you can simply browse through the information, looking at base classes, methods, and properties. On the other hand, if you are interested in a type that

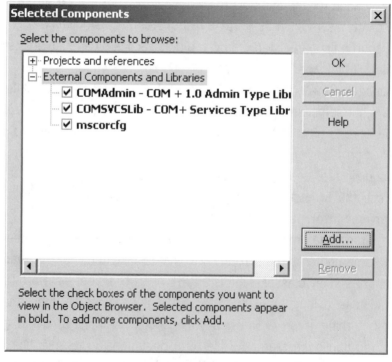

Figure 5.17   Configuration of external tools

you have defined in your project, you can select that type in the **Class View** window and select **Browse Definition** in its context menu (`View.BrowseDefinition`), which will open the **Object Browser** window with the type located. At this point you can view the members of the type in the right-hand **Members** pane.

To see the actual definition of the type, you can use the context menu: You select **Go To Definition** (`Edit.GoToDefinition`), and the source file (if available) will open with the caret at the selected type. In addition, each type will have a node called **Bases and Interfaces** that will allow you to view the base classes and interfaces implemented by the type. In an unmanaged project, all of the browser information will be searched when you search for a symbol, so if you have a class called `Test` and you select **Quick Find Symbol** from the **Class View** window, the results window will list all occurrences for `Test` in all the source files and header files (including those contained in `#include` statements through headers like `windows.h` and `atlbase.h`), whether or not the symbol is what you are looking for. Managed projects are less of a problem because they do not have header files.

You can also find symbols through the **Command** window using the `Edit.FindSymbol` command. This command takes the name of the symbol as a parameter, along with switches that allow you to refine the search to whole words and case-sensitive searches, or to widen it to say that the search string is the first part of an item name or a substring within the item name.

5.6 Tools

The **Tools** menu gives access to several tools provided with Visual Studio.NET, and it allows you to install your own tools.

5.6.1 External Tools

Visual Studio comes with a whole host of tools. You'll find these in the `Common7\Tools` folder under the main Visual Studio folder. I won't describe the tools that are supplied or outline the tools accessible through the **Tools** menu (they may change according to the version of Visual Studio you have). Instead I'll explain how to add an external tool of your own to this menu.

To add your own tools to the **Tools** menu, you run the **External Tools** dialog through the **Tools | External Tools** menu item or the `Tools.External-Tools` command (see Figure 5.18). Each tool has a title that will be added to the **Tools** menu, and a command line. When you add a title, you can use an ampersand to indicate the mnemonic that will be used on the menu item, but be aware that the tool does not check whether that mnemonic has already been used. Note also that you can use a command to execute the external tool, but because the IDE will not know the name that you give to the external tool, the command to use is `Tool.ExternalCommand<n>` where <n> is a number between 1 and 24 (the number indicates the position of the command in the **External Tools** dialog).

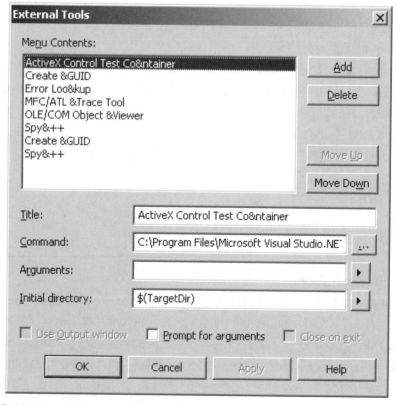

Figure 5.18 Configuration of external tools

DEVELOPING APPLICATIONS WITH VISUAL STUDIO.NET

The command line that you use for the external tool is made up of the path to the tool and the argument to pass to the tool. The argument can be made up of the targets within the current project; the right arrow button next to the **Arguments** edit box gives you the various predefined macros. For example, to add the message compiler tool (so that I can compile custom messages for the event log), I can use the values in Table 5.9.

The `ItemFileName` macro will provide the name of the file that is currently open. This macro will place the outputs in the same directory as the input file (`ItemDir`). Because the message compiler is a command-line tool, I also check the **Use Output** window box to indicate that the output from the tool should go to the Visual Studio **Output** window. In this case I have decided that the arguments are sufficient, but I could check the **Prompt for arguments** option to allow the user to decide which switches to use.

The **Output** window has several panes, which are accessed through a drop-down list box. By default you will get two panes—**Build** and **Test Run**—but if you use an external tool that uses the **Output** window, the IDE will create a pane with the name of the tool. This pane behaves just as the **Build** pane does (see Chapter 6): If errors or warnings are generated, you can double-click on the error report in the **Output** window, and the file will be loaded and the caret placed on the offending line. To get this behavior, the external tool must generate errors and warnings with the following format:

```
<filename> (<linenumber>) : <error text>
```

Table 5.9   External Tools settings for the message compiler

Property	Value
Title:	&Message Compiler
Command:	C:\Program Files\Microsoft Visual Studio.NET\Common7\Tools\Bin\MC.Exe
Arguments:	-v $(ItemFileName)
Initial directory:	$(ItemDir)

Here `<filename>` is the source file that caused the problem (e.g., the name produced by the `$(ItemPath)` macro), and `<linenumber>` is the line. If you include some error description (here, `<error text>`), that will be shown on the status bar when you double-click on the error in the **Output** window.

5.6.2   The Help System

There are essentially two types of help: **F1** help and dynamic help. When you press **F1**, help will be shown for the currently selected item. If that item is a tool window, you'll get the help for that window. On the other hand, you can use this facility while you are typing code to get help on a keyword or a class: When you press **F1**, the help will be shown for the code that is currently under the caret. You can use the **Environment | Help** options to configure the **F1** help system to specify whether help is shown within the IDE or in a separate window.

As the name suggests, the **Dynamic Help** window shows links to help topics relevant to what you type. As you type some text, the contents of the **Dynamic Help** window will change. The help is not always as relevant as you would expect. For example, as I type `printf()`, I see the following help topics in the **Dynamic Help** window:

I type:	**Dynamic Help** shows:
p	`CHtmlGenBase::p`
	`CComPtrBase::p`
print	`IMTMLWindow3::print method`
printf	`printf Type Field Characters`
	`printf, wprintf`
	`Format Specification Fields`
	`printf Width Specification`
printf(	`Cast Operator ()`
	`Function Call Operator ()`
	`Explicit Type Conversion Operator ()`
	`locale::operator()`

DEVELOPING APPLICATIONS WITH VISUAL STUDIO.NET

I can understand why I get the topics I get as I type the characters from `p` to `print` because the help system does not know that I intend to type `printf`. However, typing the parenthesis after `printf` should be interpreted as part of the function call, and *not* as a cast operator. In general, I find dynamic help distracting as I type, so I usually close this window.

The **Environment | Dynamic Help** options page allows you to configure what dynamic help is shown. By default, dynamic help will show all relevant help on the current context. The options page shows two checked list boxes: **Categories**, which has the groups of the links that dynamic help will show (you can limit the number of links per category); and **Topic**, which identifies the type of the documentation. You can also define the *context* in which dynamic help is given: (1) for the UI element that has the focus, (2) for all UI elements open, or (3) for any link relevant to the work you are doing.

5.6.3 Toolbox

The **Toolbox** window usually appears as an autohide window on the left-hand side. It contains tabs, and the items in these tabs slide vertically into view when you click on them. The **Toolbox** window will show the tabs relevant to the current context, but you can specify that all tabs should be shown through the **Toolbox** window's context menu.

You can add components to a tab by opening the **Toolbox** window, selecting a tab, and then using the **Tools | Customize Toolbox** dialog (or simply by executing the `Tools.CustomizeToolbox` command). This command lists the registered COM controls on your system and the .NET Framework components that have their assembly in the GAC, or the controls that already have been added to the **Toolbox** window. The **Toolbox** window allows you to add and remove components. To add a component, you should check the check box next to the component (if its assembly is in the GAC), or if the component is not shown, use the **Browse** button to locate the component's assembly, before checking its check box. To remove a component from the **Toolbox** window, you merely have to clear the component's check box. In Chapter 8 I will return to the issue of adding components to the **Toolbox** window.

5.6.4 Clipboard Ring

Whenever you copy or cut code from a document, it will be added to the Clipboard ring, which is accessed through the **Toolbox** window. The Clipboard items are named here according to the text they contain, but you can rename them through the context menu. You can paste an item from the Clipboard ring by selecting it and then dragging and dropping it at the appropriate place in the document. The items in the Clipboard ring are saved as part of the VS.NET application (*not* as part of a solution), so the same items will be available whenever you start VS.NET, no matter which solution you load.

5.6.5 The Macro Explorer and Editor

The Visual Studio IDE can be scripted with macros. The IDE's facilities are available through automation commands. There are general objects for the IDE, which are part of the `DTEEnv` type library and give access to items like documents, windows, and facilities like the **Find** dialog. VB.NET and C# projects are manipulated by objects in the `VsLangProj.dll` assembly, and C++ projects are manipulated by objects in the `vcpkg.dll` type library.

You can view the available macros with the **Macro Explorer** window: This is a window within Visual Studio that displays the macro modules stored in the `Visual Studio Projects\VSMacro` folder in your `My Documents` folder. These modules are edited with the Macro Editor—which is a separate application—through the **Edit** context menu item. To run a macro, you can simply double-click on it in the **Macro Explorer** window or use the command format `Macros.<namespace.class>.<method>` in the **Command** window, where `<namespace.class>` is the macro's class name and `<method>` is the macro's name.

The Macro Editor looks very much like Visual Studio, with windows like VS.NET's **Toolbox** and **Properties** window. You can do some quite sophisticated things with macros, especially because there are objects available to access the file system, and other parts of the system like the event log, from automation script. On the other hand, you can also use scripting to perform repetitive tasks with the IDE. Your starting point in this case is the **Tools | Macros | Record Temporary Macro** menu item (`Tools.RecordTemporaryMacro`). This command allows you to perform tasks, and the actions will be recorded in the Macro Editor within a class called `RecordingModule`. You can then copy this code to a method in another class and edit the code.

You can use .NET components and COM components within a macro script, but first you have to add a reference to the assembly or type library that describes the component, just as you would with a .NET managed project. The Macro Editor supports only VBScript, so you have no choice, sadly, but to use VB.NET syntax. In this case you use the VB.NET keyword `Imports` to indicate that you want to use code in a particular namespace of an assembly in the GAC.

5.6.6 Add-In Manager

Add-ins extend the Visual Studio IDE. They can have commands that have a UI or that lack a UI. If a command lacks a UI, it can be started from the command line through the `/command` switch. The Add-In Manager displays the currently installed add-ins and allows you to specify whether the add-in should be loaded when the IDE is started and whether the add-in's commands can be run from the command line.

Add-ins are COM objects that implement various automation interfaces defined in the `dte.olb` type library. You can write an add-in object using ATL or C# (and register it through `regasm` so that the IDE can access your add-in through COM Interop). You do not have to worry too much about the details of writing the basic files for an add-in because there is a project type—`Visual Studio.NET Add-In`—in the `Other Projects\Extensibility Projects` folder in the **New Project** dialog. This project will create the necessary start-up files and a deployment project (I'll go into more details about these in Chapter 6).

However, the add-in wizard is unusual in that when you run it to create your project, it will register your add-in. I find this odd, and rather irritating, because registration should be performed as a deployment step (which you will be able to choose to do as part of your build process). Indeed, once the add-in wizard has completed, it has only part of the required registration information because you need to register the actual COM object, through either `regsvr32` or `regasm`. If you don't mind manipulating the registry, here are the details of the registration that the add-in wizard performs.

If the add-in can be used by all users of your machine, the registry settings will be made in the `HKEY_LOCAL_MACHINE` hive. If you decided that only your account can use the add-in, the registration values will appear in the `HKEY_CURRENT_USER` hive. The following key:

```
Software\Microsoft\VisualStudio\7.0\AddIns
```

contains a key for each of the registered add-ins, with its ProgID. The add-in's key contains values for specifying the name (`FriendlyName`) and description (`Description`) of the add-in; whether the add-in has an about box and if so what it will show (`AboutBoxDetails`, `AboutBoxIcon`); and whether the add-in should be loaded at start-up (`LoadBehavior`). Finally, the add-in's key has a value that specifies whether the command can be run from the command line (`CommandLineSafe`).

All of these values are documented in MSDN, so I think it is far, far better for your component to do this registration itself than for the wizard to do it. It is better because your component should have this responsibility, and it is better because it allows your component to be used on other machines. For an ATL project, this registration should be performed through the RGS script or in the `UpdateRegistry()` method. For a C# project, this code should be in the method identified by the `[ComRegisterFunction]` attribute, as I mentioned in Chapter 4.

5.6.7 The VS.NET Command Line

The Visual Studio application is `devenv.exe`. You can run `devenv` as a command-line application, which is particularly useful for building solutions as part of an automated build process. The build command-line switches are summarized in Table 5.10. You have the option of building a project within a solution or the entire solution. If you choose to build just a project in a solution, then you need to use the `/project` switch to indicate which project. Each of the various build command-line switches takes a parameter that is the name of the solution configuration that you want to build. If you want to build a project, you can use the `/projectconfig` switch to identify the specific project configuration.

The `/build`, `/clean`, `/deploy`, and `/rebuild` switches will perform the build from the command line, so all output will appear on the console. You may de-

Table 5.10 `devenv` **command-line switches for building projects and solutions**

Switch	Description
/build	Builds either a project or a solution of a specified configuration.
/clean	Cleans a project or a solution of a specified configuration.
/deploy	Deploys a project or a solution of a specified configuration.
/rebuild	Cleans and then builds a project or solution of a specified configuration.
/run	Builds a project or solution of a specified configuration through the IDE.
/runexit	Builds a project or solution of a specified configuration through the IDE and then exits.

cide that you want to see the build occur in the IDE. To do this you use the /run or /runexit switches; the difference between the two is that the IDE will be left open after the build has completed with /run, whereas with /runexit it will close down. Neither of these run switches takes a configuration; instead the active solution configuration set in the configuration manager (see Figure 5.6) is built.

You can also start the IDE by specifying a particular command that should be run. After the command has run, the IDE will remain open so that you can see any results from the command. For example, if you want to search all .cpp files in the \Dev folder and its subfolders for the string "data", you can use the following command line:

```
devenv /command "Edit.FindinFiles data /looking:\Dev
   /sub /ext:*.cpp"
```

This command will perform the search, and you can use the **Find Results 1** window to see the results. Note that the command should be in quotation marks so that devenv knows the full command, and for this reason the use of the command can be impaired. For example, if you run Edit.FindinFiles from the **Command** window, you can use quotation marks around the search text or the search path to allow you to have text that contains spaces. The /command switch does not allow you to use embedded quotation marks (or to use single quotes), so in the case of Edit.FindinFiles, you are restricted to single-word search texts and to the short forms of paths that have spaces (e.g., `\Docume~1` for `\Documents and Settings`).

5.7 Summary

The first .NET application that you will use will be Visual Studio.NET. The IDE is a rich environment; it gives you many tools and facilities to help you create your application. The IDE allows you to add projects in any of the languages supported by VS.NET as dependent projects in a solution. The build process can be configured to create some or all of the outputs of the projects in the solution. The IDE gives you tools to organize your solution that you can view on either a file or a type basis.

The IDE allows you to open the source files in one of the standard VS.NET editors. These are fully featured, equipped with facilities to search, view, and organize the code. Some of the editors (like the HTML and XML editors) will also render the data. Again, this makes writing these document types much easier. In the next chapter I will describe the details of creating and building applications.

Chapter 6

Creating and Building Solutions

Your primary aim, of course, is to write software. To do this you have to write code and compile it into an executable or a library to be used by an executable. To do this you need to create your projects and add code to them. Visual Studio.NET helps here by providing code generation wizards that will create the starting code and **Class View** wizards to allow you to change that code. If your code is part of a distributed environment, you'll want to be able to add code that accesses remote servers. The Visual Studio.NET IDE provides several tools for browsing a server and for generating code to access a remote resource.

If you work as part of a team—or simply if you want to control how changes are made to your code—you should protect your code using source control. Doing so allows you to maintain a database with all the changes made to your code and to control who can change the code. Clearly, source control is an important part of an integrated development environment.

Once you have created a project, you need to build it. The build process is not as simple as just pressing **F7**; there are more steps involved. For a start, you may have changed only part of the code in an application, so you will want to compile only the files that have been changed. This means that you will want to set up file dependencies to indicate which files should be compiled when one source file changes. If the build fails with errors or warnings, you will need to find out where those errors occur so that you can fix them. The IDE passes errors and warnings to the **Build** pane of the **Output** window and to the **Task List** window so that you can determine how to fix the related problems.

Once you have successfully built a solution, you will need to test it. For a distributed application, testing involves installing the application on another machine. Again, Visual Studio.NET helps here by adding deployment to your projects that allows you to configure the installation.

In this chapter I will concentrate on the following solution configuration and building tasks: generating code in solutions, maintaining the code in solutions, and building solutions.

6.1   C++ and C# Project Types

I mentioned in Chapter 5 that you can use Visual Studio's wizards to create projects and to add items to those projects. In this section I will outline the C# and C++ project types that are provided, and the types that you can add to them. The majority of this section will cover C++ projects, partially because VS.NET has inherited a rich range of C++ projects from VS6. Reflecting the fact that C++ can be used for both managed and unmanaged code, there are C++ project wizards for both native code and .NET code. I have decided to split these into four groups of projects: ATL (ActiveX Template Library), MFC (Microsoft Foundation Classes), managed C++, and what I'll describe as "other." After I have described C++ projects, I will describe C# sharp projects in a single section.

6.1.1   ATL Projects

ATL has undergone a total revamp since VS6. There are essentially three main changes: VC (Visual C++) attributes, the ATL7 library, and ATL Server. The ATL7 library consists of many new utility classes and owes its existence partially to ATL Server and partially to the tighter integration between ATL and MFC. Indeed, many MFC features, such as `CString`, are now implemented by ATL classes. So rather than having to import MFC to use those classes in an ATL project, as the ATL3 developer must do, the MFC developer effectively imports ATL classes into her project. All of this is done seamlessly, of course: An MFC project created with VS6 can be used in VS.NET and will compile with the new integrated ATL and MFC libraries.

There are three ATL project wizards, two of which (ATL Server Project and ATL Server Web Service) are essentially the same; the third (ATL Project) is generic. All three ATL project wizards can produce code that is based on ATL maps and templated classes, but the default is to produce attributed code. VC attributes indicate that the compiler should generate code and inject it into the code that you have typed. Attributes are not like C++ macros. Whereas macros are a simple text substitution performed by the C++ preprocessor, attributes are handled by the compiler, which will generate code based not only on the attribute, but also on the other attributes that may be present and on the code to which the attribute is applied. I will explain what I mean by attributed code in more detail in Chapter 7.

6.1.1.1 ATL Project Wizard

The ATL Project wizard looks very similar to the ATL3 equivalent. The first change is that it has an **Attributed** check box to determine if the code uses VC attributes. The other change is that one of the options for DLL servers is now called **Support COM+ 1.0** (which replaces the **Support MTS** option in ATL3), but all that this option does is add `comsvcs.lib` to the list of linked libraries. As in the ATL3 version, you have the option of creating a COM server in a DLL, in an EXE, or installed as an NT service. Clearly the option you choose determines the entry point(s) that the server should have, as well as how class objects (class factories) are provided to the system (EXE servers call `CoRegisterClassObject()`; DLL servers give access to class objects through `DllGetClassObject()`).

Attributed projects have a single entry in the main `.cpp` file: the `[module()]` attribute applied to an anonymous code block. For a DLL server it looks like this:

```
// native C++
[ module(dll,
         uuid = "{EDE17D65-85CF-42EB-8D3F-4F0DC067E46F}",
         name = "TestModule" ) ];
```

This code looks straightforward, but a lot is going on here. The first thing to note is that VC attributes have the same structure as .NET attributes: They can have mandatory *unnamed parameters* and optional *named parameters*.[1] The

---

1. Interestingly, although the documentation lists the `name` parameter of `[module()]` as optional, the compiler treats it as mandatory.

unnamed parameter specifies the type of server that will be generated: `dll`, `exe`, or `service`. If the server is of the `service` type, the `[module()]` attribute should also have a `resource_name` parameter that gives the resource symbol for a string that has the service name. If you inadvertently click on the **Executable** option when you wanted the **Service** option, all you have to do is change the `[module()]` parameter to `service` and provide the `resource_name` parameter. This example eloquently shows the power of attributes. If you made this error with an ATL3 project, you would most likely opt to start again because there would be so many changes that you would need to add support for deployment as an NT service.

To see the generated code, you can pass to the C++ compiler the `/Fx` switch. For an IDE project you do this through the project options: On the **C/C++** item, select the **Output Files** page and change the **Expand Attributed Source** option to **Yes**.

The `[module()]` attribute will generate the entry points for the module. Usually a DLL project exports its entry points by identifying the exported functions in a `.def` file and then passes this file to the linker. ATL attributed projects no longer use `.def` files; instead they use the alternative method: the `/EXPORT` switch of the linker, which can be placed in C++ code through the `comment()` pragma. The following is taken from the code generated for a DLL:

```
// generated unmanaged C++
#pragma comment(linker,\
    "/EXPORT:DllMain=_DllMain@12,PRIVATE")
#pragma comment(linker,\
    "/EXPORT:DllRegisterServer=_DllRegisterServer@0,"\
    "PRIVATE")
#pragma comment(linker,\
    "/EXPORT:DllUnregisterServer=_DllUnregisterServer@0,"\
    "PRIVATE")
#pragma comment(linker,\
    "/EXPORT:DllGetClassObject=_DllGetClassObject@12,"\
    "PRIVATE")
#pragma comment(linker,\
    "/EXPORT:DllCanUnloadNow=_DllCanUnloadNow@0,PRIVATE")
```

The right-hand side of the equal sign is the actual name of the function in the code; the left hand-side is the name that is used to export the function from the

DLL. Table 6.1 shows the entry points generated for the various module types. The functions that are generated to implement these entry points merely delegate the call to a method in the global _AtlModule object. This object is an instance of the C<name>Module class, where <name> is the name you pass to the [module()] attribute. The base class of this class (and hence the implementation of the entry point) is also given in Table 6.1.

Because the [module()] attribute generates module type–specific code, the ATL designers decided to factor out this code into the module classes given in Table 6.1. These entry points need to register COM classes with the system, as well as to provide the class object for a class. The registration information and information about its class factory are part of the class definition. In the ATL3 days, the object map acted as a central repository for this information and was accessible by the ATL3 classes. In ATL7, this information still has to be accessed by the ATL code (in the various module classes), so there must be an equivalent of the object map. If you look through the code generated for [module()], you will not be able to find an object map. In Chapter 7 I will look at how ATL7 solves this problem.

An ATL project produces a COM server that provides instances of COM objects, and COM objects implement one or more interfaces. These interfaces may be system-defined interfaces (e.g., IPersistStream or IDispatch), but they are more likely to be interfaces that you have defined. If the interface is a dispinterface, a dual, or an oleautomation-compatible custom interface, you *should* use type library marshaling. If the interface is not

Table 6.1 Generated entry points

Module Type	Entry Points	Module Base Class
dll	DllMain, DllGetClassObject, DllRegisterServer, DllUnregisterServer, DllCanUnloadNow	CAtlDllModuleT<>
exe	_tWinMain	CAtlExeModuleT<>
service	_tWinMain	CAtlServiceModuleT<>

`oleautomation` compatible, you *must* use a proxy stub if the interface is marshaled. By default, the project wizard will add a proxy-stub DLL project to your solution when you create an ATL project. As a rule of thumb, you should leave this project as part of your solution *only* if your code has interfaces that are marshaled with it; otherwise you should delete this project.

6.1.1.2 *ATL Server Project and ATL Server Web Service Wizards*

The ATL Server Project wizard can be used to generate a Web application or a Web Service, which is why I am also covering the ATL Server Web Service wizard in this section. ATL Server is a collection of non-COM classes that you can use to write an ISAPI extension. ISAPI is used to extend IIS to handle HTTP requests. Those requests can be made through the standard HTTP verbs of `POST` and `GET`, or through extended HTTP headers. I will defer a detailed explanation of the architecture until Chapter 7; in this chapter I will simply introduce each project wizard and briefly describe the options it offers.

The ATL Server Project wizard allows you to create an ISAPI extension DLL to handle requests for Web Services via SOAP or Web applications that will return rendered output, typically as HTML. The wizard has five pages, and you can get a summary of the options that you have selected by selecting the **Overview** page.

Whether you are developing a Web Service or a Web application, the final result will be a DLL that will be installed as part of IIS, and the **Project Settings** page is your entry into this process. The various check boxes that this page presents may appear a bit confusing at first, especially because the first two—**Generate Web application DLL** and **Generate ISAPI extension DLL**—are interconnected: You can check either or both of the boxes, but you cannot leave both unchecked. I will ignore these for the moment and start with the check box on the right-hand side of this page: **Deployment support**.

The **Deployment support** box is checked by default, and it will have the name of the solution as the virtual directory of the ISAPI. If you leave this box checked, it will create a virtual root in IIS with the specified name when the solution is deployed (which occurs as part of the build process of the solution), and it will copy all the output DLLs of the project to this virtual directory. I will describe the deployment options later.

The other check boxes on this page specify how many DLLs will be created. If both the **Generate Web application DLL** and the **Generate ISAPI extension DLL** boxes are checked, two DLLs will be generated. If only one of these two boxes is checked, then only one DLL will be generated. Furthermore, if just the **Generate combined DLL** box is checked, a single DLL will be created, and this DLL will contain code for both the ISAPI and the application.

The ISAPI extension code handles the initial request and will do all of the initial work of parsing the URL (for GET) or the POST stream to determine the request that is being made. The ISAPI extension code is managed by a class derived from CIsapiExtension<>, which implements the ISAPI to search the URL and extract the name of either the request handler DLL or a server response file (.srf file). A request handler DLL contains the code that will be called at runtime to provide the Web Service implementation, or code that will be called for placeholders in the .srf file. The ISAPI will load the request handler and will either call the requested Web Service method in the request handler DLL or render the .srf file by calling the handler code in the request handler DLL.

If you want a rendered output (typically an HTML page), you can base this output on a combination of static text and commands in the .srf file, which acts as a template for the page. This information is processed by an object called the *stencil processor,* which generates an object called a *stencil* that can be cached in the ISAPI application so that the .srf file is not parsed every time the page is requested. The stencil object is rendered to produce the output.

If you want a Web Service, you do not need a .srf file, but because the Web Service code is implemented in a request handler DLL, you still need to select the **Generate Web application DLL** option (either for a separate DLL or as part of the combined DLL).

If **Generate ISAPI extension DLL** is checked, the **Server Options** page will be enabled, allowing you to specify the services that the ISAPI will implement. These services will be available to any request handlers loaded by the ISAPI. I will explain these services in Chapter 7, but briefly, the ISAPI can implement various caches: It can cache the request handler DLLs that it loads so that they are loaded only once, it can cache data source connections, and it can provide a generic memory cache within which request handlers can store data. In addition, the ISAPI can implement session state—that is, hold data associated with client sessions either within memory or in a database table.

If the **Generate Web application DLL** box is checked, the **Application Options** page will be enabled, allowing you to specify the facilities that the request handler DLL will be able to access. This page has a check box that you can use to indicate that the request handler implements a Web Service.

Typically, you will create both an ISAPI and a request handler DLL, either as separate DLLs or as a combined DLL. However, if later you decide to add another Web Service, or you want to add additional `.srf` pages with associated handlers, you can choose just to develop the request handler DLL and leave **Generate ISAPI extension DLL** unchecked.

The final page of the wizard is called **Developer Support Options**. This page allows you to specify if you want attributed code to be generated. If you do not select this option, the wizard will generate code with macro-based maps that indicate the handler code in the classes that are generated. It will also generate macros that indicate the handler classes that your request handler DLL implements. In general, nonattributed code is harder to read than attributed code, and as I'll discuss in Chapter 7, if you use attributes you can still add code and maps to your code because the compiler will recognize when you do this and will add the attribute's code to your code.

6.1.1.3 *ATL Server Deployment Options*

I will discuss deployment projects later in this chapter, but ATL Server deployment is worth a look here because deployment projects are part of the project options. The **Web Deployment** page of the project options allows you to specify where the project outputs will be copied when the project is built. You can use this page to specify (1) the IIS virtual directory name used for the ISAPI application where the DLL will be deployed on the local machine and (2) the process isolation level that will be used (in other words, whether the ISAPI will be run in the IIS process or in `dllhost.exe`). If the DLL is an ISAPI, you can also specify the extensions of pages that IIS will handle with the ISAPI by selecting **Application Mappings**. Finally, because there are several deployment options, this page has a general master switch, **Exclude From Build**, that you should change from the default of **Yes** to **No**, to allow the DLL to be deployed.

If **Exclude From Build** is set to **No**, when the project is built and is successful, the DLL and other outputs from the project will be copied to the specified virtual directory. If the DLL is a request handler, VS.NET will locate the physical folder for the specified virtual folder by querying IIS. It will then check the modified time of the file in the virtual directory against the modified time of the file in the project folder, and if the file has changed, it will be copied to the virtual directory.

If the DLL is an ISAPI DLL, the same process is carried out, except that the DLL cannot simply be copied to the virtual directory because if the ISAPI application has been run, the DLL may be loaded into IIS, so you will not be able to overwrite it. To get around this problem, the deployment step will stop the Web server, so that it unloads the ISAPI DLLs it has loaded, and then restart the Web server before copying the ISAPI file.

If you have Internet Services Manager running when you deploy an ISAPI DLL, you will get a dialog informing you that the connection to IIS has been lost. This dialog is triggered by the restarting of the Web server. The dialog is harmless because the connection will be made again when you attempt to perform some administration.

I said earlier that the DLL and "other outputs" from the project are deployed to the Web application's folder. These other outputs are the `.srf` file for a Web application and the `.disco` and descriptive `.htm` files for a Web Service. You can also indicate that other files from the project should be deployed. To do this you should select the file in the **Solution Explorer** window and then view its properties with the **Properties** window. You should *not* use the **Properties** context menu because this gives access to the custom build step for the file (by default there will not be one). The **Properties** window for the file will show a property called **Content**. If this property is set to **True**, the file will be deployed.

6.1.2 MFC Projects

There are two principal changes in MFC: the integration of the MFC and ATL libraries, and the new support in the IDE. There are also some new classes and updates to other classes, but these are fairly minor changes. The MFC project wizards are shown in Table 6.2. To be honest, all of these projects—with the exception of the MFC application—are redundant because ATL provides far better solutions.

The MFC project wizards follow the style of the other VS.NET project wizards: You configure the project by actively selecting the pages rather than by being led through the process page by page. Although this mechanism makes MFC appear more integrated with the new-style IDE, it means that unlike VS6, MFC offers no preview of the application as you work through the options. Some new options have been added to the wizards (e.g., the MFC Application wizard has a page that lists the UI features that will be used by the main frame and the MDI child windows).

There is no longer a class wizard in the IDE. Instead the actions have been moved to the **Class View** and **Properties** windows.

6.1.3 Managed C++ Projects

The project wizards for managed C++ (listed in Table 6.3) lack user interfaces; they do not give you any options. Each wizard (except the Empty Project wizard) will create a main-class .cpp file and a file called AssemblyInfo.cpp that has

Table 6.2   MFC project wizards

Wizard	Description
MFC ActiveX Control	Creates a DLL that implements ActiveX controls.
MFC Application	Creates an EXE based on the MFC document-view architecture.
MFC Dll	Creates a DLL that exports MFC functions used by other MFC applications.
MFC ISAPI Extension Dll	Creates a DLL containing an ISAPI extension or filter.

Table 6.3   Managed C++ project wizards

Wizard	Description
Managed C++ Application	Creates a console-based EXE.
Managed C++ Class Library	Creates a DLL.
Managed C++ Empty Project	Creates a project with no source files.
Managed C++ Web Service	Creates an ASP.NET-based Web service.

assembly-level attributes for assembly information, versioning, and the assembly strong name.

The Managed C++ Application wizard creates a console application. If you decide that you want a GUI application, you need to remove the `main()` function and replace it with `WinMain()`:

```
// managed C++
int __stdcall WinMain(long hInst, long hInstPrev,
                      char* cmdLine, int n)
{
    return 0;
}
```

You do not have to change the linker options when you change a project from a console to a GUI project because the compiler will tell that you have a `WinMain()` entry point and pass the linker the appropriate option for you. Bear in mind that you will not be able to use the Windows Forms designer to write a C++ project, although it is quite straightforward to adapt C# generated by the designer to managed C++.

6.1.4 Other C++ Projects

There are four other wizards in the C++ category, although only two of them—the Extended Stored Procedure Dll wizard and the Win32 Project wizard—really produce C++ projects. The Custom Wizard wizard creates the HTML pages and JScript scripts for a VS.NET project wizard, and the Makefile Project wizard allows you to create a custom makefile to make any type of project.

The Win32 Project type allows you to create an unmanaged C++ console or GUI application, a DLL, or a static linked library. The console and GUI projects have the option of containing a bare minimum of code or being empty projects; the VS6 option of producing a "Simple" or "Hello, World" application no longer exists. In addition, the console project can have support for ATL and/or MFC, which adds the appropriate headers to `stdafx.h` and appropriate project options.

6.1.5 C++ Project Options

Once you have created a C++ project, you can use the context menu in the **Class View** or **Solution Explorer** window to access the project options. These options are the same for all of the C++ application types; they differ only by the default settings. The default values, incidentally, are held in `.vcstyle` XML files in a folder called `VCProjectDefaults`.

The project options dialog has several sections. There is a section for the various compilers that are used—**C/C++** (for the compiler), **Resources**, **Browse Information**, and **MIDL**—and there is a section called **Linker** for the linker. There are also sections for the build process in general (**Build Events**, **Custom Build Step**), a section for the parameters passed to `sproxy` when you are adding a Web reference (**Web References**), and a section for parameters to use when you are deploying Web applications (**Web Deployment**). Finally, there are general sections to specify the type of code that is generated and for debugging options.

6.1.6   C# Project Types

Like the managed C++ wizards, C# project wizards lack a user interface and hence offer no options for the code that is generated. Table 6.4 shows the C# project wizards. The Web projects are created in a virtual directory on a Web server.

6.2   C++ Classes

The C++ **Add** context menu option has two items—**Add Class** and **Add Resource**—each of which has a corresponding dialog that presents the items you can add. The **Add Resource** dialog lists the standard resources (icons, dialogs, and so on). When you select an item from this dialog, it will be added to the project's `.rc` file. If the project does not already have an `.rc` file, a new one will be added to the project, along with the associated `resource.h` file. The **Add Class** dialog is more interesting: It lists the ATL and MFC types that you can add to the project. The wizards accessed in this dialog can be found in the `Class-Wiz` subfolder of the `VCWizards` folder. Again, the wizards are HTML based and generate the appropriate files using template files and scripts. These wizards are outlined in Table 6.5.

Once you have added a class to a project, the **Class View** window will be updated with the class and any types added along with the class, such as

Table 6.4   C# project wizards

Wizard	Description
ASP.NET Web Application	Creates a Web Forms–based application, stored on a Web server.
ASP.NET Web Service	Creates a Web Service, stored on a Web server.
Class Library	Creates a DLL library.
Console Application	Creates a simple class compiled as a console application.
Empty Project	Creates a console application with no code.
Empty Web Project	Creates a class library, stored on a Web server, with no code.
New Project to Existing Folder	Specifies an existing folder for the project.
Web Control Library	Creates a control that can be used on a Web form.
Windows Application	Creates a GUI forms-based EXE application.
Windows Control Library	Creates a DLL with a `UserControl` class.
Windows Service	Creates an NT service, EXE GUI module.

Table 6.5   C++ class wizards

Wizard	Description
Add ATL Support to MFC	Adds the necessary initialization code and headers to an MFC project.
ATL Active Server Page Component	Creates a COM class that can be used by an ASP script; caches pointers to the request, response, session, and server objects.
ATL COM+ 1.0 Component	Creates a COM class that can support `IObjectControl` and `IObjectConstruct`.
ATL Control	Implements a standard windowed or windowless control, a composite control, or a control based on Dynamic HTML (DHTML).
ATL Dialog	Creates a dialog class based on the ATL `CDialogImpl<>` class.

(continued)

Table 6.5   (continued) C++ class wizards

Wizard	Description
ATL OLEDB Consumer	Creates a class to access an OLE DB data source.
ATL OLEDB Provider	Creates classes to implement an OLE DB provider.
ATL Performance Monitor Object Manager	Adds support for performance monitoring. Adds the manager object; the objects and counters have to be added separately.
ATL Property Page	Adds support for property pages.
ATL Server Web Service	Creates an unmanaged Web Service implemented through ISAPI.
ATL Simple Object	Creates a basic COM class.
Generic C++ Class	Adds a header (and possibly a `.cpp` file) for a simple C++ class.
MFC Class	Creates a `CWnd-derived` class.
MFC Class From ActiveX Control	Creates a wrapper class to access an ActiveX control.
MFC Class From TypeLib	Creates a wrapper class to access an object described in a type library.
MFC ODBC Consumer	Creates an MFC class for accessing Open Database Connectivity (ODBC) data sources.
WMI Event Provider	Creates a class to provide Windows Management Instrumentation (WMI) events.
WMI Instance Provider	Creates an instance of a WMI Common Information Model class.

interfaces, structs, macros, and so on. I explained these tools in Chapter 5. Many of these wizards have been ported from VS6, so I will not describe them here. Instead I'll just explain a few of the new wizards

6.2.1   Simple Object

Although the simple object type is not new to VS.NET, I will describe it here because the wizard has changed and I want to use it as a general example of the class wizards. The main change in the ATL Simple Object wizard from VS6 is the **Options** page, which allows you to specify details of the COM class that you want created. The **Threading model** group has been extended to include the **Neutral** threading model for COM+, which is treated like the **Free** threading model in terms of the ATL synchronization that is used, differing only in its registration.

As you select the threading model, other options on the page will be enabled or disabled. This is a great improvement over VS6 because it prevents you from selecting an option that is inappropriate (e.g., aggregating the **Free threaded marshaler** [FTM] is appropriate only for **Both** and **Neutral** threaded objects). The **Interface** group still gives the option of a **Dual** or **Custom** (i.e., nondual) interface, but it also has the option of marking the custom interface as being oleautomation compatible (**Automation compatible**) so that type library marshaling is used.

Note that there is no explicit option to write a pure automation interface—that is, to implement IDispatch and use IDispatch::Invoke() to delegate to specific methods in your class. Don't be fooled by this: If your class is *not* attributed, it will derive from IDispatchImpl<>, and the interface will be implemented in terms of the default CComTypeInfoHolder, which uses information in the project's type library to dispatch the dual method call to the appropriate method. However, if your class is attributed and has a dual interface *and* the methods have an [id] attribute, the class will have an implementation of IDispatch that implements GetIDsOfNames() and Invoke() to dispatch invocation requests to the methods in the class. In this case the type library is not used.

A proxy-stub project will always be added to your solution when you add an ATL project, even if your objects will be marshaled only through type library marshaling. Registering a proxy-stub DLL and a type library can produce inconsistent values in the registry and should be avoided. It is best, therefore, to decide at design time which type of marshaling your objects should use. If you decide that they will use only *type library* marshaling, then remove the proxy-stub project from your solution.

If you decide that your objects will use only *proxy-stub* marshaling, you should remove the type library from your project and turn off the code that registers the type library. Unfortunately, you cannot do this for attributed code, in which case you have no option but to make the project and classes nonattributed; after doing so, you can use the **Resource Includes** dialog to remove the type library. This dialog is accessible through the **Resource View** window: You need to use the context menu for the `.rc` file, not the project.

The code generated for an attributed project is straightforward: The wizard creates an interface and a class using the names you supply. Many of the options in the wizard are associated with one or more attributes. For example, the **Threading model** option determines the value for the `[threading()]` attribute, and the **Aggregation** option specifies the value passed to `[aggregatable()]`. Others do more work. The **Support Connection Points** option will generate an additional interface—a `dispinterface`—as the outgoing, or source, interface. Note the new syntax used here:

```
// native C++
[ dispinterface,
  uuid("AB276DF8-AC4E-4286-8A45-EFEA1A2C4480") ]
__interface _IErrorEvents
{
  [id(1)] void OnError([in] BSTR bstrDesc);
};
```

This code occurs in the header file where the COM class is defined; attributed COM code no longer uses IDL (Interface Definition Language) files. This interface is called to generate an event that indicates that an error has occurred. The significant point is that if this were ODL (Object Description Language), the interface definition would look similar but would display the ODL syntax of having `properties` and `methods` sections. The generated class is marked with the `[event_source("com")]` attribute to indicate that the class should implement `IConnectionPointContainer` and have an interface map. In addition, the class declares an event:

```
// native C++
[ coclass, event_source("com") ]
class ATL_NO_VTABLE CMyObject : public IMyItf
{
public:
  __event __interface _IErrorEvents;
  // other members
};
```

This is *not* a .NET event. In effect, it indicates that the interface should be added to the class's connection point map, and therefore that the object can create a connection point for this interface. In addition, the class implements `IProvideClassInfo2` by deriving from `IProvideClassInfo2Impl<>`, and the compiler will provide this event interface as the default source interface for the class. The compiler will also add the event's methods to the class, using the name of each method. Thus, in one of `CMyObject`'s methods I can generate the `OnError` event by calling a method called `OnError()` (in nonattributed code this method would be called `Fire_OnError()`).

Attributed code hides many of the macros that were used in ATL3 to indicate class factory support, aggregation, and registration. If you look at an attributed project, you will notice that the object map is also missing. In fact, however, ATL7 still has an object map, and in Chapter 7 I'll show how it is implemented.

6.2.2 COM+ Component

This class type is essentially a cut-down version of the simple object class, without the **Options** page, but with a page called **COM+**. I find it curious that the ATL team decided not to allow the **Options** page because this means that you cannot use the wizard to specify the COM+ component's threading model, aggregation, or use of the FTM. Instead the COM+ wizard deduces values for threading and aggregation from the values that you specify from the **COM+ 1.0** page, and if you disagree with these values you have to edit the generated code. The **COM+ 1.0** page allows you to specify your component's transaction and queuing requirements; these values merely use custom IDL attributes to add information to the type library.

6.2.3 Control

The ATL Control wizard aggregates the various control wizards that were in VS6, so you can choose among standard, composite, and DHTML controls and whether the control has full support for the control interfaces or implements the minimum. The interfaces that this wizard supports are shown on the **Interfaces** page, which has one list box with the interfaces that are supported and another with the interfaces that can be supported. If you click on the **Minimal control** box on the **Options** page, the **Supported** list box on the **Interfaces** page will be emptied, and you can choose which of the interfaces you want to support.

You can create an attributed control, but there isn't a `[control]` attribute, so you'll find that the class will be derived from the various `Impl` classes for the interfaces you have selected. In addition, controls need more registration than other COM classes, so this extra registration information is provided through the `[registration_script()]` attribute. The interesting point here is that the script that is used is `control.rgs` (the template file from the wizard), and not a generated file. This file has `[!]` directives and placeholders, so presumably the code that implements `[registration_script()]` understands what these directives mean and can deduce values for the symbols.

6.2.4 Performance Monitor

Performance monitor code can be added only to DLL projects because it will be loaded by both your code and the performance monitor. I described the performance monitor in Chapter 2—in particular the rather archaic and complicated way that the performance monitor accesses data from your code. The ATL performance monitor code makes this straightforward. When you create an ATL performance monitor project, a manager object is created (derived from `CPerfMon`) that manages the performance monitor objects, and these objects provide their data through memory-mapped, file-based shared memory.

If you create a nonattributed project, you'll see that the manager object will have a map that references performance objects (derived from `CPerfObject`). If you create an attributed project, you'll find that the wizard will create a class marked with `[perfmon]`. It will mark any performance object classes with `[perf_object]`, but because the map is hidden by the attributed code, you will not see that the performance object classes are associated with the manager class. However, this is not a problem because there should be only one manager class in a project, and this class will manage *all* performance objects in the project. Indeed, once you have added a manager object to a project, you can use the **Class View** window to add more performance objects: Through the context menu of the manager object, you'll see that there is an **Add PerfMon Object** menu item.

As you may recall from Chapter 2, *performance monitor objects* are actually categories of the type of data that can be provided. The performance data itself is provided through *counters*. You can add a counter through the context menu in **Class View** for a performance object; doing so will start the performance counter wizard, as shown in Figure 6.1.

In this wizard, **Variable type** is the data type of the member that will be added to the performance object class, and **Counter type** is the type of data that is being provided and that determines how the performance monitor shows this data. **Variable name** is the name of the data member, which is displayed to the user in the **Add PerfMon Counter Wizard** window in the **Name string** and **Help string** fields (you must provide values for these). For a nonattributed project, the counter will be added as a data member and as part of the counter map. For an attributed project, the counter will be added as a data member with the [perf_counter] attribute.

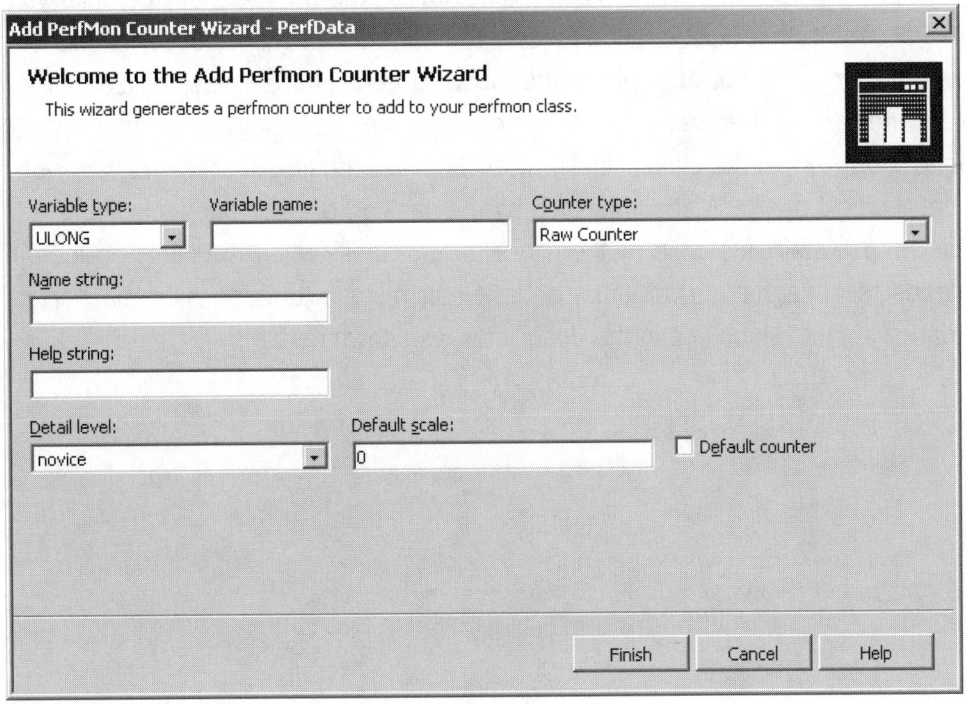

Figure 6.1   The Add Perfmon Counter wizard

Generating performance data is straightforward: You create a global instance of the manager object in your project so that all of your project code has access to it. Then you initialize the manager object by calling its `Initialize()` method before any code that can generate performance data is called (before your DLL is unloaded you should also call `Uninitialize()`). Once you have done this, your code can access a performance object through the manager object's `CreateInstance()` method. I mentioned in Chapter 2 that performance objects can have *instances,* and you can decide whether or not your objects can have instances, but in either case you still call `CreateInstance()`. This method returns the `CPerfObject` that you request, and you can cast this object to its specific class type so that you can access its counter data members.

Because performance counter data is accessed by both your code and the performance monitor, two threads can try to access the same data at the same time. To prevent simultaneous access attempts from becoming a problem, ATL provides a class called `CPerfLock` that "locks" the manager object while you are accessing the performance object. You can then cache a pointer to this object in your class. For example, in the following code I have a class called `COrders` that can generate performance data by caching a pointer to a `CPerfObject` in the class. Initializing this pointer requires that the manager object be locked, a task accomplished by the passing of the manager object's address to a stack instance of the `CPerfLock` class. When the class no longer needs to generate performance data, it can release its access to the performance object, which I do in the destructor, as shown here:

```
// native C++
// myPerfMonObject is a global object
COrdersStatistics* m_pStatistics;
COrders()
{
   CPerfLock lock(&myPerfManObject);
   myPerfManObject.CreateInstance(
      1, L"Orders Statistics", &m_pStatistics);
}
~COrders()
{
```

```
    CPerfLock lock(&myPerfManObject);
    myPerfManObject.ReleaseInstance(m_pStatistics);
}
```

Generating performance data is as simple as writing to the data members of the cached performance data object. However, because this will involve writing to shared data, you must use thread synchronization, so if the `COrderStatistics` class has a counter called `m_orderCount`, the `MakeOrder()` method could look like this:

```
// native C++
bool MakeOrder(int itemID, int count)
{
    InterlockedIncrement(
        &(m_pStatistics->m_orderCount));
    return DoOrder(itemID, count);
}
```

If you are writing an ATL Server application, you can use standard counters defined by the library. The use of such counters is enabled through the ATL Server wizard and provides performance monitor data for an ISAPI through a struct called `CPerfRequestStatObject` that provides statistics about the ISAPI requests:

- Total number of requests to date
- Total number of failed requests
- Number of requests per second
- Average response time per request
- Number of requests waiting
- Maximum number of requests waiting
- Number of active threads

The `CIsapiExtension<>` class is the base class of all ATL Server ISAPI extensions and will generate performance monitor data as it performs its work. The second template parameter to `CIsapiExtension<>` indicates the performance-monitoring class that will be used. By default this class is `CNoRequestStats`, which has stub functions that do not export data to the performance monitor, but if you change this class to `CPerfRequestStatObject`, your ISAPI will provide the required data.

6.3 C# Classes

In Chapter 5 I described the Add Class wizard of the **Class View** window, which allows you to build up a new class on the basis of existing classes and interfaces. In this section I will explain the items that you can add through the C# **Solution Explorer** window. The **Add** context menu item gives you three options of items to add—forms, controls, and components—which are actually individual items of the more generic **Add Class** menu item. As Table 6.6 shows, only a few of these can actually be described as classes.

Table 6.6   C# "class" types

Category	Wizard	Description
Code	Class	Adds a generic class to your project.
	Code File	Adds an empty `.cs` file to the project.
	Windows Service	Adds a class derived from `ServiceBase`; this will be displayed by the designer tool.
	Installer Class	Adds a class derived from the `Installer` class.
	Component Class	Adds a class derived from `Component`.
UI code	Windows Form	Adds a class derived from `Form`; this will be displayed by the Windows Forms designer.
	Inherited Form	Allows you to choose the class to derive from—either a form in your assembly or one in another assembly.
	Data Form	Builds up a form based on a data source.
	User Control	Adds a class derived from `UserControl`, which allows you to build a composite control based on other controls.
	Inherited User Control	Allows you to choose the class to derive from—either a control in your assembly or one in another assembly.
	Custom Control	Adds a class derived from `Control`; this is a totally new control.

(continued)

DEVELOPING APPLICATIONS WITH VISUAL STUDIO.NET

Table 6.6   (continued) C# "class" types

Category	Wizard	Description
	Web Custom Control	Adds a class derived from `WebControl`.
Web	HTML Page	Adds an empty HTML file to the project.
	Frameset	Adds an HTML file based on a frame set. This wizard gives you basic templates on which to base your frame set.
	Style Sheet	Allows you to build up a cascading style sheet.
XML	XML File	Runs the XML editor.
	XML Schema	Runs the XML Schema editor.
	Data Set	Runs the XML Schema editor to create an `.xsd` file and a DataSet class based on it.
	XSLT File	Adds an XSL Transformations file.
Resources	Assembly Resource File	Adds an `.resx` file containing localized strings.
	Bitmap File, Cursor File, Icon File	Adds the appropriate resource to the project.
Utility	JScript File, VBScript File	Adds the appropriate script file.
	Windows Script Host	Adds a `.wsf` file (Windows Script file) XML file. This is a container for multiple "jobs" using multiple script files in multiple script languages.
	Text File	Adds a file containing text.
	Crystal Report	Adds a report based on data sets in your project or other data sets.

In Chapter 5 I mentioned adding resources, and I will give more details in Chapter 8. In the remainder of this chapter I will explain some of the items I have not covered already.

6.3.1 Components, Controls, and Forms

A *component* is a .NET class that has design-time support; that is, it can be used by a tool like the VS.NET IDE as a RAD component used by classes in your application. All components implement the `IComponent` interface:

```
// C#
public interface IComponent : IDisposable
{
    ISite Site { get; set; }
    event EventHandler Disposed;
    // IDisposable members
    void Dispose();
}
```

Thus a component maintains a reference to the site within the container that contains it, and it allows explicit management of its resources. The `System.ComponentModel.Component` class provides a default implementation of `IComponent` and derives from `MarshalByRefObject`, so the component can be accessed by code in another application domain. Forms and controls are components, but they are more wide-ranging than this; components can be items that lack user interfaces, like data sets and timers. Components integrate with the UI features like the Windows Forms designer and the **Toolbox** and **Properties** windows, and you give details of this interaction using attributes. I will explain more about how to do this in Chapter 8.

Controls are reusable UI RAD components that can be used on forms. Controls cannot exist on their own; they need a container. There are two types of controls that the wizard allows you to create: controls and user controls. The names are a little misleading; they are both controls that can be placed on a site in a container. The difference is that a user control is what ATL calls a *composite* control; that is, it is made up of existing controls, and hence the `UserControl` class needs to have the extra functionality of routing messages from the child controls. In addition, you'll find that when you create a `UserControl` class in your project, you will get a borderless, captionless "form" in the Windows Forms designer so that you can drag and drop items from the **Toolbox** window; with a control, there is no designer support.

A *form* is a container to provide a site for controls (and components in general). Each form is a window in its own right. You can add menus to forms, write to the surface of a form, and add controls. The Windows Forms designer makes adding controls and setting their properties simple, but it is not mandatory. In addition, the **Add Class** dialog gives you the Data Form wizard, which will take you step-by-step through the process of creating a form with a data grid bound to a data source.

6.3.2 Inherited Forms and Controls

Forms and controls are .NET classes. They provide their behavior by overriding the methods and providing handlers to events of their base classes. Because they are classes, you can extend the functionality of an existing control or form by deriving from it and adding more code. The .NET Common Language Infrastructure (CLI) means that it does not matter what language was used to write the original form or control; you can still derive from it. This is why you have the **Inherited Form** and **Inherited Control** items in the **Add Class** dialog. These items add a class that is derived from an existing class, and the IDE will start the **Inheritance Picker** dialog (see Figure 6.2) so that you can choose the class from which you want to derive.

Inheritance Picker will list the suitable classes in the current project that you can use as a base class. To get this list you must have already compiled your assembly. In addition, you can click on the **Browse** button and select another assembly (which will be added as a reference to your project).

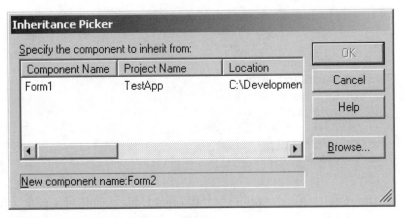

Figure 6.2 The Inheritance Picker dialog

6.3.3 Data

The various data items do a lot of work and yet hide much of it from you. Much of the database code in .NET depends on `DataSet` objects. A `DataSet` object holds data and a schema of that data. `DataSet` objects can be persisted as XML files, which is the purpose of the **DataSet** type in the **Add Class** dialog. On the surface this just appears to be a way to edit an XSD schema file, but it does more than this.

Once the designer has started, you can use the XML schema items in the **Toolbox** window to build up your schema. The following schema shows a complex type:

```
<xsd:schema id="dbCDs"
    targetNamespace="http://www.tempuri.org/dbCDs.xsd"
    xmlns="http://www.grimes.demon.co.uk/dbCDs.xsd"
    xmlns:xsd="http://www.w3.org/2001/XMLSchema"
    xmlns:msdata="urn:schemas-microsoft-com:xml-msdata"
    attributeFormDefault="qualified"
    elementFormDefault="qualified">
    <xsd:element name="dbCDs">
        <xsd:complexType>
            <xsd:sequence>
                <xsd:element name="id"
                 msdata:ReadOnly="true"
                 msdata:AutoIncrement="true"
                 type="xsd:int" />
                <xsd:element name="Artist"
                 type="xsd:string" />
                <xsd:element name="Title"
                 type="xsd:string" />
                <xsd:element name="Year"
                 type="xsd:int" />
            </xsd:sequence>
        </xsd:complextype>
        <xsd:key name="Constraint">
            <xsd:selector xpath="." />
            <xsd:field xpath="id" />
        </xsd:key>
    </xsd:element>
</xsd:schema>
```

This code defines a schema for a database table called `CDs` with a primary key called `id` and fields called `Artist`, `Title`, and `Year`. Once you have typed in the XSD, you can change from the **XML** view to the **DataSet** view and you'll see the `DataSet` shown in a table. You can add new items to this table. Once you have saved the `DataSet` object, the designer will generate code based on the schema. If you look at the **Solution Explorer** window, all you will see is the `.xsd` file (see Figure 6.3). However, clicking on the **Show All Files** button will show that in addition to the `.xsd` file, the designer has generated an `.xsx` file and a code file. The `.xsx` file contains layout information used by the XSD designer.

The code file contains a class derived from `DataSet`, and nested classes derived from `DataTable` and `DataRow`, which reflect the information in the schema. Although the **Solution Explorer** window purposely hides this file, you'll be able to see these classes in the **Class View** window. You can use a data adapter class as the bridge between a data source and the `DataSet` class. I will come back to this issue later in this chapter.

Once you have defined a data set, you have a schema of the data that you want to use. VS.NET has several tools that will read this schema and generate code for you. The Data Form wizard leads you step-by-step through the process of creating a form with data-bound controls. The wizard allows you to select the

Figure 6.3 Solution Explorer with generated data set files. The Show All Files button (second icon) has been clicked to show the generated files.

tables and fields read from the `DataSet` object. The wizard gives you the option of displaying the data in individual data-bound controls, or in a `DataGrid` control. If you provide connection data for the `DataSet` object, then once you have completed the wizard you will have a fully working form that will connect to the data source and allow your users to browse, edit, delete, and insert data.

6.4 Enterprise Template Projects

Enterprise template projects are available only in the Enterprise Edition of Visual Studio.NET. They allow a development team to customize the IDE so that new solutions that follow the enterprise template are restricted in the projects and items that can be added to the solution. Creating an enterprise template is not a straightforward task because it involves creating several descriptive files, as well as templates for the projects that you can add to the solution. The MSDN documentation has an enterprise template walk-through that illustrates how to do this, so I will not replicate that here. Instead, I will describe the various parts of an enterprise template and the enterprise solution that it is used to create, and compare this with the solution and project files that I described in Chapter 5.

6.4.1 Enterprise Solutions

Visual Studio.NET gives you many facilities and options. It allows you to generate both managed and unmanaged code, libraries, and applications. You can add various types of objects to these projects and configure those projects through the **Properties** window. To a technogeek like me, this is programming nirvana: I can create a solution with both managed and unmanaged, Web-based or locally installed code. So if I decide that my Web client pages need extra client-side functionality, I could add an ActiveX control and write it using an ATL control project.

This may sound like a wonderful idea, but it may not be the best solution. Imagine that the enterprise I work for has the policy that it does not want client-side ActiveX controls used, preferring a Web control solution instead. However, as a typical developer who is more interested in technology than bureaucracy, I rarely read the decrees issued from my managers and choose instead to use the best available solution to the specific problem. My time will be wasted, and my error of judgment will most likely become clear only when the application is being system-tested.

Enterprise templates are a mechanism to prevent enthusiastic developers like me from creating code that does not fit with the enterprise guidelines. On the surface, an enterprise template solution appears to be a solution full of projects, representing each stage in a multitier distributed application: Data Access, Business Rules, Business Facade, and Presentation layers (Web, or fat-client based). In fact, you do not need all of these projects, and you can delete the ones that you do not need. Furthermore, these projects are not the essence of enterprise templates.

You will see the differences between creating the solution from an enterprise template project, and creating it yourself by adding projects one by one, only when you try to add another project to the solution. For example, if you create a Visual C# distributed application and try to add another project to the solution, you'll find that the number of projects you can add has been reduced significantly. For example, the C++ projects that you can add will merely be managed C++ empty projects; you will not see any of the unmanaged projects (neither ATL nor MFC), and consequently you cannot add unmanaged code to your solution.

Enterprise template solutions involve two new types of files: the *enterprise project files* (`.etp`) and an *enterprise template policy file* (`.tdl`). Each solution will have an `.etp` file in addition to the `.sln` file. The `.etp` file lists the `.etp` files of the constituent projects and has a reference to the policy file that specifies the items that can be added to the solution and its projects. The *policy file* is global in that it describes the rules for all solutions of that particular type; it lives in the `EnterpriseFrameworks\Policy` folder under the main Visual Studio folder. Each project in an enterprise solution also has an `.etp` file, which is used to identify the policy file.

6.4.2 Enterprise Template Files and Proxy Projects

Before I talk more about policy files, it is worth describing how enterprise solutions are created. Recall from Chapter 5 that projects are described by `.vsz` files in a folder that has a `.vsdir` file. The `.vsdir` file indicates how the project is displayed in the **New Project** dialog (its descriptive text, the icon, and so on), and the `.vsz` file indicates the wizard that will be called. In general, the wizards for managed projects lack user interfaces, and the indicated wizard folder will have the template files, each with a placeholder and a script that creates some (or all) of the values that will be inserted into the placeholder.

Enterprise template files are based on a different structure. Within the `EnterpriseFrameworks` folder is a folder called `ProxyProjects` that contains `.vsdir` files listing the items that will be added to the **New Project** dialog. The entries in this file reference `.etpproxy` files in this folder that are XML files giving the location of the template for the enterprise solution. This template is essentially an entire solution with start-up projects, and a new solution created from the template is effectively a copy of these files.

Of course, the developer may not want these projects and may want to add other projects. Figure 6.4 shows the **New Project** dialog for the enterprise solu-

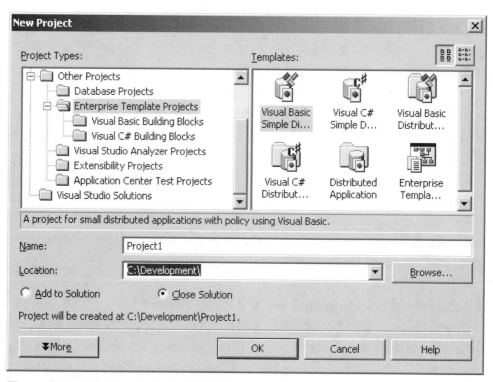

Figure 6.4 The New Project dialog for enterprise solutions

tions. Within the **Enterprise Template Projects**[2] folder are solutions for distributed applications for Visual Basic and C# (each has a distributed application and a simple distributed application). Beneath this folder are two others—**Visual Basic Building Blocks** and **Visual C# Building Blocks**—which are effectively the enterprise template solutions returning to the model used by other projects. These two folders are represented by folders under the `ProxyProjects` folder with `.vsdir` and `.vsz` files. They represent the project types that can be added to the current solution.

Note that the test solution I used to take the screen shot has few restrictions applied in the policy file. If you create your own enterprise templates, you may restrict the projects that are added to the solution. Specifying these restrictions is the purpose of the policy file.

6.4.3 Policy File

Policy files are XML files written to the Template Description Language (TDL) schema. They can be quite large because they are used to hold information about every project that could be added to the specific solution. The VS.NET XML editor knows about the TDL schema, so if you edit a TDL file with VS.NET, you will be able to use code completion.

The root node of a TDL file is called `<TDL>`, and below this there are four possible child nodes: `<DEFAULTSETTINGS>`, `<ELEMENTS>`, `<CATEGORIES>`, and `<FEATURES>`. As its name suggests, `<DEFAULTSETTINGS>` gives default values that are used by the items defined in the file. `<FEATURES>` defines the menus and **Toolbox** items shown by the IDE for this solution. The `<ELEMENTS>` collection is the core of a policy file; it contains `<ELEMENT>` items that represent projects, project items, references, classes, and controls. The `<CATEGORIES>` collection, not surprisingly, holds `<CATEGORY>` items, which are used to create groups of items (consisting of `<ELEMENT>` items and other `<CATEGORY>` items) with a common name.

---

2. This really should be **Enterprise Template *Solutions***.

Here is a simple policy file showing an `<ELEMENT>` item:

```
<!-- TDL -->
<TDL>
<ELEMENTS>
    <ELEMENT>
        <!-- identifier used to reference
             this item -->
        <ID>projMyCSharpProject</ID>
        <CONTEXT>
            <!-- use this section to provide
                 context help -->
            <CTXTKEYWORD>C#</CTXTKEYWORD>
        </CONTEXT>
        <IDENTIFIERS>
            <IDENTIFIER>
                <!-- identifies the IDE item -->
                <TYPE>PROJECT</TYPE>
            </IDENTIFIER>
        </IDENTIFIERS>
        <PROTOTYPES>
            <!-- provide the item(s) from which
                 this project can be created -->
            <PROTOTYPE>
                [VC#]\CSharpProjects\CSharpDLL.vsz
            </PROTOTYPE>
            <PROTOTYPE>
                [VC#]\CSharpProjects\CSharpEXE.vsz
            </PROTOTYPE>
        </PROTOTYPES>
        <CONSTRAINTS>
            <!-- define restrictions on menus,
                 properties, and toolbox items -->
        </CONSTRAINTS>
        <ELEMENTSET> <!-- see later --> </ELEMENTSET>
    </ELEMENT>
</ELEMENTS>
</TDL>
```

The `<ELEMENT>` tag defines a project type called `projMyCSharpProject`. The `<IDENTIFIER>` tag indicates the IDE item type that is being described. The possible values are PROJECT, PROJECTITEM, REFERENCE, CODE, CODEVARI-ABLE, and HTMLELEMENT. In this case I have used PROJECT to indicate that `projMyCSharpProject` is a project type. This project can be either a DLL or an EXE project as defined by the `<PROTOTYPES>` node, where each `<PROTOTYPE>` item gives the path to the wizard that can be used. So that absolute paths are not used, the values used in each `<PROTOTYPE>` node indicate the VC# folder with the [VC#] symbol; the VB7 folder can be identified with [VB], the VC7 folder with [VC], and the `EnterpriseFrameworks` folder with [EF].

The item can be associated with help items through the `<CONTEXT>` node so that when dynamic help is used, these help items will be displayed. The `<CONSTRAINTS>` node can be used to apply constraints to the menus and **Toolbox** items that can be used with the defined item, as well as to the values of the properties that the item can have. One constraint that you may decide to define is the identity of the items that can be added to a project, or the project that can be added to a solution. To do this you need to add an `<ELEMENTSET>` node to your `<ELEMENT>` item.

An `<ELEMENTSET>` node is used to identify other `<ELEMENT>` items defined in the policy file that either can or cannot be used with your `<ELEMENT>` item. These items are identified through the definition of included and excluded elements—for example:

```
<!-- TDL -->
<ELEMENTSET>
    <INCLUDE>catCommonProjectItems</INCLUDE>
    <INCLUDE>codeCSClasses</INCLUDE>
    <EXCLUDE>codeVBClasses</EXCLUDE>
</ELEMENTSET>
```

This definition indicates that the items described by `catCommonProject-Items` and `codeCSClasses` can be used in this project, but the items described by `codeVBClasses` cannot. As it stands, however, this description is probably not very useful. If the `<DEFAULTSETTINGS>` node in the policy file defines the `<DEFAULTACTION>` item with `INCLUDE`, for example, all the other possible items will be included automatically. Thus you need to override this behavior in your `<ELEMENTSET>`, as illustrated here:

```
<!-- TDL -->
<ELEMENTSET>
    <DEFAULTACTION>EXCLUDE</DEFAULTACTION>
```

```
<ORDER>INCLUDEEXCLUDE</ORDER>
<INCLUDE>catCommonProjectItems</INCLUDE>
<INCLUDE>codeCSClasses</INCLUDE>
<EXCLUDE>codeVBClasses</EXCLUDE>
</ELEMENTSET>
```

Now the description says to exclude all items and build up the new list of items starting with the items explicitly identified for inclusion and then from that list remove the items explicitly identified for exclusion. The items that can be included or excluded are <ELEMENT> items or collections of <ELEMENT> items defined as <CATEGORY> items. The <ELEMENTSET> just defined implies that catCommonProjectItems is a <CATEGORY> item:

```
<!-- TDL taken from DAP.tdl -->
<CATEGORY>
    <ID>catCSCommonProjectItems</ID>
    <CATEGORYMEMBER>
        codeClass
    </CATEGORYMEMBER>
    <CATEGORYMEMBER>
        projItemCSharpFile
    </CATEGORYMEMBER>
    <CATEGORYMEMBER>
        codeComponent
    </CATEGORYMEMBER>
    <CATEGORYMEMBER>
        codeInstallerClass
    </CATEGORYMEMBER>
    <CATEGORYMEMBER>
        codeGlobalApplicationClass
    </CATEGORYMEMBER>
</CATEGORY>
```

Given that codeCSClasses and codeVBClasses are <ELEMENT> items, here's a possible definition for codeCSClasses:

```
<!-- TDL -->
<ELEMENT>
    <ID>codeClass</ID>
    <FEATURELINKS>
        <MENULINKS>
            <MENULINK>menuProject.AddClass</MENULINK>
```

```
      </MENULINKS>
    </FEATURELINKS>
    <PROTOTYPES>
      <PROTOTYPE>
        [VC#]\CSharpProjectItems\CSharpAddClassWiz.vsz
      </PROTOTYPE>
    </PROTOTYPES>
  </ELEMENT>
```

This `<ELEMENT>` item is associated with the C# Add Class wizard. If this item is included, menu items associated with it should be enabled. To be enabled, the `<ELEMENT>` item has a `<FEATURELINKS>` node (`menu-Project.AddClass` is a `<MENU>` item defined elsewhere in the policy file).

Constraints defined in a policy file are applied when the developer drags and drops an item described by an `<ELEMENT>` item, or adds or deletes such an item through the **Solution Explorer** window. The IDE will validate the item, and any item that fails validation will be added to the task list.

As you can see, building up a policy file for an entire solution involves creating descriptions for all the possible projects and all the possible items that can be placed in the project. Then you need to define the menu items, **Toolbox** items, and any property constraints and finally link all this information together. As a consequence, TDL policy files tend to be quite large and quite complicated. The `Policy` folder contains a file called `VSIDE.tdl` that has descriptions of all the projects provided by VS.NET and of all the IDE items. If you decide to write your own policy file, it is a good idea to use a copy of this file as your starting point.

6.5 Server Explorer

The VS.NET window configuration will place the **Server Explorer** window to the left of the IDE as an autohide window. This is your portal to the wide world outside of your current machine. **Server Explorer** serves two purposes: It gives information about the servers to which you have access, and it is integrated with the various VS RAD designers. By default, **Server Explorer** will show just your machine, but you can use the context menu to add other servers on which your account has administrative privileges.

6.5.1 Data Connections

The **Data Connections** node shows the OLE DB connection that you have made. You can create a new connection by right-clicking on the **Data Connections** node and selecting **Add Connection**. This will give you the OLE DB **Datalink** dialog, which you can use to locate the data source. Once you have selected a data source, Server Explorer will query it for the tables, views, and stored procedures that are available. You can select items in these nodes and drag and drop them onto a form, control, or component in the designer, and the designer will create a connection object and a data adapter. The data adapter is the link between a `DataSet` object and a data connection.

6.5.2 Servers Node

The **Servers** node shows the servers to which you have connected; you can access other servers through the context menu. The particular items you see in the **Server Explorer** window depend on the access that your account has to the server machine you are accessing. In the following sections I will outline these items.

6.5.2.1 *Event Logs*

The **Event Logs** node lists the event logs on the server machine presented in a tree view. Each event log shows the event log sources that have generated events, and under these tree view nodes are the actual events. Recall how the event log works: When the event is reported, the event ID and parameter strings are put in the event log. The event ID identifies a format string in a resource DLL that is used to generate the final formatted event message. This is wonderful because the message that is displayed on the client machine is formatted on the basis of the resource strings in the DLL installed on the client machine; hence the formatted messages will be formatted in the locale of the local machine. Sadly, the .NET classes that handle event logs place the entire message into the event log, so the onus of internationalization is on the developer (assuming that the developer knows the locale of the client machine that will read the event logs).

To be fair to the .NET class designers, they appear to have tried to solve a problem with the event log; that is, if the client does not have the message resource DLL installed, it cannot format the message and the event log viewer displays a message like this:

```
The description for Event ID ( 1 ) in Source
( TestSource ) cannot be found. The local computer
may not have the necessary registry information or
message DLL files to display messages from a remote
computer. The following information is part of the
event: TEST_SVR.
```

Unless you know what message 1 of the source `TestSource` is, you cannot make any sense of this. All you have is the parameter string `TEST_SVR`, which gives little information about what is going on.

If the parameter string is the entire message, you will have a message like this in the event log viewer:

```
The description for Event ID ( 1 ) in Source
( TestSource ) cannot be found. The local computer
may not have the necessary registry information or
message DLL files to display messages from a remote
computer. The following information is part of the
event: Tried, but failed to access TEST_SVR.
```

This is better. You now know what event message 1 is reporting, but clearly the message still looks ugly.

I mention this issue because the event log entry in the **Server Explorer** window suffers from this problem: If you access the event log on another machine and the source's message resource file is not available locally, the **Server Explorer** window will give you a message saying so.

Sometimes it is more useful to see the event log messages in the order that they are generated, rather than categorized as sources. To do this you should use the context menu of the event log node to launch the event log viewer.

The event log node exists in the **Server Explorer** window for two main reasons: First, it allows you to monitor the event log of another machine when you are developing a distributed application to see the events that are generated by your application. Second, you can drag and drop individual event logs (e.g., **Application** or **System**) to a component in the designer and an instance of `System.Diagnostics.EventLog` will be added and initialized to the specified server.

6.5.2.2 *Performance Counters*

The **Performance Counters** node lists the objects that are available on the server, and under each object it lists the counters that you can read. If you drag and drop a counter to a form, you'll get a `System.Diagnos-tics.PerformanceCounter` object, initialized to the specific server and counter type.

6.5.2.3 *Services*

The **Services** node shows the services that are installed on the specific machine. Note that this particular node gives access to the service control manager, so if you drag and drop a service onto a component, the designer will add a `System.ServiceProcess.ServiceController` object to the component. The `ServiceController` class allows you to start, stop, pause, and resume services on the server machine. In addition, it allows you to pass a command to the service; this command is an integer and is defined by the service. If you have written the service using .NET, the custom command will be passed to the service's `OnCustomCommand()` method. If the service has been written with the Win32 API, the control message will be passed to the service's handler function.

6.6 The Build Process

In this section I will outline the tools in Visual Studio.NET to use source control and to perform the build.

6.6.1 Source Control

VS.NET has support for source control programs, and the Enterprise Edition is supplied with Visual SourceSafe (VSS). VSS allows you to store source files in a database, which can be on a central enterprise server giving the entire development team access to the source. Simply sharing files among team members is not good enough because without proper control, two developers could edit the same source file at the same time, bringing into question which change should take precedence. Another issue that needs to be addressed is maintaining a list of changes. Such a list is important for tracking bug fixes and to allow a rollback if code changes cause a problem.[3]

Source control solves these problems. A source control application maintains the code in a database, and when the code is checked out by one developer, it becomes read-only to other developers. When a developer checks code back into source control, the changes are stored along with the identifier of the developer so that the changes can be rolled back if necessary, and metrics can be performed on the changes made by each developer.

When you install Visual SourceSafe, the IDE will be updated to reflect that the code can be put under its control. There is a **Source Control** option in the **Options** dialog that allows you to configure how the source control (VSS and other applications) is used with VS solutions. In addition, you will get menu items in the **File | Source Control** menu. This facility allows you to add projects to and open projects from source control, and it allows you to get information about code (the history of the code changes) and to make comparisons. Finally, the **Solution Explorer** and **Class View** windows are updated to show the status of items under source control.

Table 6.7 shows the icons for a class in **Class View** after it has been under source control. The source control adds a little blue padlock for an item that has been checked into the source control database, and a tick mark and an exclamation point for an item that has been checked out. At the same time, the **Pending Checkins** window (see Figure 6.5) is updated to remind you of the items that have been checked out. You can use this window to select the items that should be checked in (using the **Check In** button), to add a comment for a

Table 6.7   Icons for a class under source control

Icon	Description
	Item checked in
	Item checked out

---

3. At one company I worked for, a contractor developed a technique of solving bugs by merely commenting out the offending code! When that developer left the company, we rolled back to the previous version of the code and had a proper developer fix the bugs.

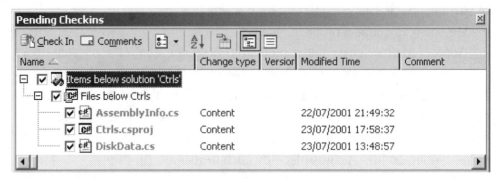

Figure 6.5   The Pending Checkins window

check-in (using the **Comments** button), or to view a difference between the current version and the previous version under source control (by double-clicking on an item).

When your code is checked in, a copy is kept on the local disk, which means that you can view the code. The local file will have the read-only attribute, so you cannot write to the file. If you attempt to write to a checked-in file, the IDE will pop up a dialog asking if you want to check out the file. If a coworker changes a file, your local copy will not reflect the change. You can update your local copy by selecting the **Get Latest Version** menu item.

6.6.2   Customizing Builds

C++ projects have far more options to customize builds than C# projects. Part of the reason is that the C++ build process is more complicated (it always has a link step, which is missing from the IDE in the build process for C# projects). In addition, the build tools have a much longer pedigree, so there are more command-line switches. I like to think that the main reason is that C# projects have been simplified to make them easier to understand, whereas C++ projects keep their complexity to offer you the most flexibility.

The most obvious difference, to a VS6 developer, is that C# projects do not have *build events*. A C++ project can define prebuild, prelink, and postbuild events, as well as a custom build step. C# projects built with the IDE do not have a separate link step, so you can understand the lack of a prelink event, but pre- and postbuild steps like those of C++ projects would be nice.

You can use the build events to run a command; for example, you can copy a file to specific location. Custom build steps are a little more complicated because you can specify them both on the project and on individual files. Custom build steps can be used to provide an output that will be used in the build process, so you have to add information about the outputs generated by the build step and any other files that the build step depends on. For example, your code may use custom event log messages, so you could add a custom build step to build an `.mc` file in the project. The outputs in this case will be the header file created by MC with the event IDs.

One fairly important aspect of not having a separate link step is the issue of rebuilding projects. In a C++ project, source files are compiled to `.obj` files by the compiler, and the linker creates the final output by linking these files and any static (or import) libraries that you want to use. If just one C++ source changes, then only that file will be compiled and the link step will use the new `.obj` file with the `.obj` files from the previous builds.

Visual C++ goes a step further, allowing you to create precompiled headers (so that large header files are compiled only once) and incremental linking (to cut down on the time of subsequent linking). The C# compiler has an `/incremental` switch that turns on incremental compilation (using this switch generates an `.incr` file with details about the compilation). However, you do not have an incremental output like the C++ `.obj` files have, so you cannot create libraries similar to the CRT `setargv.obj` or static libraries, in which you can change the behavior of your code by linking to a specific file.

In general, it makes sense in C# projects to keep assembles fairly small—remember that versioning is done at the assembly level—or possibly to divide large assemblies into modules. Note that with the VS.NET IDE, multimodule assemblies are not allowed with C# projects. However, you can create multimodule assemblies with C# if you are willing to write a makefile and use the Makefile Project from the C++ projects node.

6.6.3 Building and Task List

To start a build you select **Build Solution** or **Rebuild Solution** from the **Build** menu (the `Build.BuildSolution` command). You can start a build for a C#

or C++ solution through the **Solution Explorer** window with the **Build Solution**, **Rebuild Solution**, or **Clean Solution** context menu item for a solution or through the **Build** or **Rebuild** option for a project. For a C++ project you can also perform a link and compile individual C++ files.

The IDE will go through the outputs in the projects and look at the files that they depend on. If those files have changed (i.e., their modification dates are later than those of the files that depend on them), they are compiled. Errors and warnings are sent to the **Build** pane of the **Output** window and also to the task list. The items in the **Output** window will indicate where the problem occurred—the source file and line number—including an error number and description. If you double-click on an error or warning in the **Output** window, the file will be loaded and the caret will be placed on the offending code.

The **Task List** window contains information about things that you should do. It contains the named and unnamed bookmarks that you set, as well as errors and warnings from a build. If you double-click on an item in **Task List**, you'll be taken to the position of the error. (The error text is shown in the task list, as well as the status bar, but to be honest, usually neither one of these shows the full description.) Typically, you should use the **Output** window to view the build errors.

6.7 Deploying Solutions

Once written, projects must be tested, and with a distributed application this may mean installing project outputs on a remote machine. To accommodate this action, Visual Studio comes with deployment projects and (with the Enterprise Edition) Visual Studio Analyzer projects to allow you to monitor the interaction of each piece of code in a distributed application.

6.7.1 Deployment Solutions

To deploy a solution, you copy appropriate files to a specific location, register those files (in the registry, or maybe make configuration changes to another file), create shortcuts and **Start** menu entries, and possibly make changes to a log file that can be viewed later. However, it does not end there because well-behaved code will also provide uninstall information so that the user can completely remove the code from her system. Removing code is often far more difficult than installing it because after you have installed your code, another application may use a file that you have installed, so removing your code may well break the later, dependent, application. A well-behaved uninstall program will perform checks and remove only code that is no longer being used.

Visual Studio.NET provides deployment projects for two installation technologies: CAB (cabinet) files and Windows Installer. CAB files are the older of the two technologies; in essence they contain one or more compressed files and typically are used to install ActiveX controls from a remote location.

Microsoft Windows Installer is more sophisticated. It maintains a database of information about what is installed, what registration is performed, and the other applications that depend on the installed item. This means that code installed with Windows Installer supports repair—where you can "mend" an installation using the original installation information, and the code can be uninstalled safely without breaking another application. Windows Installer also supports *rollback,* whereby the code is either installed in its entirety or, if the installation fails for some reason (it could not create a folder or write to a file, for example), the entire installation is removed so that the system is restored to the state it was in before the installation was performed.

Shared code is a distinct problem with installation because you have to make sure that the shared code is installed only once[4] and that the code is uninstalled only once, but only when all dependent code has been uninstalled. Visual Studio provides a project type called *merge modules* for shared components. These deployment units are not intended to be installed on their own. Instead they are expected to be added to other Windows Installer projects so that the code will be installed when the containing package is installed, but only if the component has not already been installed. Merge modules contain unique versioning information about the components they contain. This means that a specific merge module should be used with the Windows Installer file for the code that uses that specific version of the component.

---

4. Unless, of course, you install the code as side-by-side components, in which case the code can be installed many times on the same machine. However, side-by-side installation presents additional problems to an installer.

Visual Studio provides project types for CAB file installation and for Windows Installer, for both Web applications and non-Web applications. You can add one of these to your solution and configure it, or you can optionally run the Setup wizard, which will do the work for you.

6.7.1.1 CAB Project

You should add a CAB project to solutions that produce ActiveX components, which for Visual Studio.NET means that the solution contains a C++ project (typically an ATL or MFC project). The **Add** context menu item allows you to add files to the CAB project. There are two options: **Files** allows you to add any file to the CAB, which is fine if you have an existing file. The problem with this option is that if you want to add the output of the compilation of a project, that output will not necessarily exist when you create the CAB project. To avoid this problem, you can use the **Add Project Output Group** context menu item to specify the files created from the project that should be added to the CAB file (see Figure 6.6).

The top drop-down list box gives the projects in the current solution; the **Configuration** drop-down list box allows you to determine the configuration that will provide the output. You can choose one or more of the following options: **Primary Output** (EXE or DLL), **Debug Symbols** (the debug symbols created during compilation), **Content Files** (e.g., HTML files), and **Source Files**. Of course, you may have some items in your project that fit the description of "project outputs" or "content files," so once you have added the item to the CAB project, you can use the context menu to filter out files (by either file name or file name pattern) to *exclude* from the CAB file.

When you build a CAB project, it will create a CAB file and add to it the files that you've specified. The project also will add an Open Software Description (OSD) file, which is an XML file that holds a description of the code files in the CAB file (VS.NET merely provides the name of the CAB file). You can also specify whether the CAB file should be signed, as well as the type of compression that should be used through the CAB project's properties.

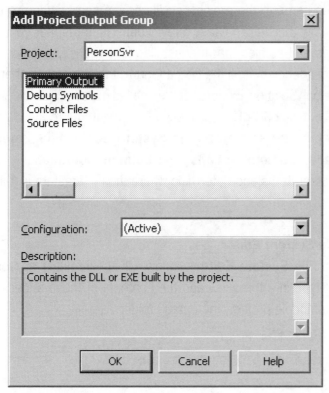

Figure 6.6   The Add Project Output Group dialog for CAB projects

6.7.1.2   Windows Installer Projects

Like the CAB project, the Merge Module project allows you to add project out-puts and individual files to the installation file. In addition, you can add assemblies (a system assembly or your own assembly) and references to other merge modules. This last option is interesting because Visual Studio comes with merge modules for the common redistributable parts of Visual Studio: MFC, ATL, STL (Standard Template Library), CRT, GDI+, and the .NET redistributables.

The Setup project type will create a complete Windows Installer (.msi) file. As with the Merge Module project, this file can contain project outputs, individual files, and merge modules, but it cannot itself be added to another setup project. The Web Setup project is used to deploy Web applications and Services and will install the files in a virtual directory of a Web server.

As you add items to the project, you'll see the items added to the **Solution Explorer** window (but *not* to **Class View**), both as items that you add from the various dialogs and as files that the installed files require. Solution Explorer will check the dependencies of all the files added to the setup project and add these files to a special Solution Explorer folder called `Detected Dependencies`. However, this is only part of the process of adding items to the installer project. Visual Studio provides six views—**File System Editor**, **File Types**, **Registry**, **User Interface**, **Custom Actions**, and **Launch Conditions**—through which you can add other items and determine where those items are installed on the final machine.

6.7.1.3   *File System Editor*

By default the **File System Editor** window will show folders appropriate to the Setup project type in a tree view and the contents of those folder in a list view. For the Merge Module project, the default folders are

- `Common Files Folder`
- `Global Assembly Cache Folder`
- `Module Retargetable Folder`

For a Setup project the defaults are

- `Application Folder`
- `Global Assembly Cache Folder`
- `User's Desktop`
- `User's Programs Menu`

Finally, for a Web Setup project the defaults are

- `Global Assembly Cache Folder`
- `Web Application Folder`

These are all child nodes of the **File System on Target Machine** node in the list view. You can add additional folders through the context menu of this root item, as shown in Table 6.8. You can use this view to create new folders on the target machine, so for example, when you add the outputs of the solution to a merge module setup project, they will be added to the **Common Files Folder** node, for

Table 6.8   Special folders that you can add to File System Editor[*]

Folder	Description
Common Files Folder	The common files folder, `CSIDL_PROGRAM_FILES_COMMON`
Custom Folder	Any folder
Fonts Folder	The system fonts folder, `CSIDL_FONTS`
Global Assembly Cache Folder	Location of the GAC
Module Retargetable Folder	A custom folder for the location of merge modules
Program Files Folder	Location of installed applications, `CSIDL_PROGRAM_FILES`
System Folder	Location of the system files, `CSIDL_SYSTEM`
User's Application Data Folder	Location of application data, `CSIDL_LOCAL_APPDATA`
User's Desktop	The root of the Windows namespace, `CSIDL_DESKTOP`
User's Favorites Folder	The user's favorite items, `CSIDL_FAVORITES`
User's Personal Data Folder	Documents folder, `CSIDL_PERSONAL`
User's Programs Menu	Location of the **Start** menu `Programs` folder, `CSIDL_PROGRAM`
User's Send To Menu	Folder for items on Explorer's **Send To** menu, `CSIDL_SENDTO`
User's Start Menu	Location of the **Start** menu folder, `CSIDL_STARTMENU`
User's Startup Folder	Location of applications that are started at start-up, `CSIDL_STARTUP`
User's Template Folder	File template folder, `CSIDL_TEMPLATES`
User's Windows Folder	`%windir%` or `%systemroot%` folder, `CSIDL_WINDOWS`
Web Application Folder	A folder on an HTTP server
Web Custom Folder	A folder on an HTTP server

[*]*Note:* Where relevant, I have given the identification flag used by the Win32 Shell functions.

a setup project they will be added to the **Application Folder** node, and for a Web setup project they will be added to the **Web Application Folder** node. This means, for example, that with a merge module, during installation these files will be added to the special folder `CSIDL_PROGRAM_FILES_COMMON` (typically `Program Files\Common Files`). Of course, it is far better to create your own subfolder within this folder, and you can do this through the context menu for this folder in the **File System** window.

You can also create shortcuts to a folder. If you do this, you are given the option of adding a shortcut to an item that you have already added to the project. Thus you are likely to add files to an application folder, and then add shortcuts to all or some of these files to a **Start** menu folder for the application.

You can use the properties of the items you add with this editor to control how the items are added to the target machine. For example, you can add a `Condition` property to an item. The condition is a Boolean expression based on properties provided by the installer (like `WindowsBuild` for the build number, `ServicePack-Level` for the currently installed service pack) or by other items in the project. If the conditional expression evaluates to `false`, the item is not installed. The `Transitive` property specifies whether the `Condition` property is checked on subsequent reinstallation. The documentation for Visual Studio lists the properties for each item type that you can install and the properties that Windows Installer provides.

6.7.1.4 Registry

The **Registry** window presents a view of the possible hives on the target machine. Again you have a tree view and a list view, and through these you can add keys and values to those keys (to add the default value for a key, you give it a blank name). Through the properties you can determine whether a key is removed at uninstall. Furthermore, through the context menu of the top-level node you can import a `.reg` file; doing so will add the items in the `.reg` file to the list of items to create in the registry.

6.7.1.5 File Types on Target Machine

This editor is provided so that you can specify file associations. If your application uses a custom data file type with a specific extension, you can use this editor to associate files that have the specified extension with your application. When you use this editor, you need to specify the file type in the **Name** field (which will be added to HKCR and will contain the command association), the extension (which will also be added to HKCR and is used to associate the extension with the file type name), and the command—that is, the application—that will be used to open files of that type.

6.7.1.6 Custom Actions

The **Custom Actions** window is divided into four nodes—**Install**, **Commit**, **Rollback**, and **Uninstall**—representing four possible types of installation actions. When the installation has completed, the custom action will be performed. When you add a custom action, you have to provide an executable item (an EXE or a script); you can provide information for this item through the CustomActionData property.

6.7.1.7 User Interface

The Setup and Web Setup projects produce an output with which the user installs code on a machine. Consequently, you can provide a UI to inform the user what is happening. This interface is provided through the **User Interface** window.

The view appears as a tree control with a series of events that can happen during the installation: **Start**, **Progress**, and **End**. In each of these nodes are default items that will be shown—for example, a welcome screen or a banner to confirm installation. You can even add your own UI element, and the view gives you a dialog box with the items that you can add, such as check boxes, radio buttons, and text boxes. Items used to obtain user input will have a property associated with them, and you can access these property values during the installation to determine, for example, whether a particular item will be installed or will ask for the installation location.

6.7.1.8 Launch Conditions

The **Launch Conditions** window is available only to the Setup and Web Setup projects. It allows you to perform searches and conditional checks that will be performed when the installer begins. You can check for a particular file, registry entry, or component, and the results will set a property that can be checked at a later stage in a condition. By default, Web setup projects will perform a search for IIS on the target machine because clearly there is no point in installing a Web application without IIS!

6.7.2 Visual Studio Analyzer

Visual Studio Analyzer (VSA) is a powerful testing tool, and I don't have enough space to provide a complete appraisal here. VSA comes in two parts: machines that can generate VSA events (also called VISTA events) have to have the VSA components installed; machines that monitor VSA events have to have Visual Studio Analyzer installed. VISTA events are wide-ranging, covering almost all aspects of COM, MTS, COM+, ODBC, OLE DB, and the performance monitor, but sadly, .NET is excluded.

The machine that will gather the VISTA events—the *target*—initiates the event generation process by specifying that it can receive events and identifying where the events will be generated (the *source* machine). Without this initiation by the target machine, no events will be generated. Custom VISTA events can be generated by your COM code, but typically you will allow the COM infrastructure to generate events for you. In addition, many of the system DLLs will generate VISTA events. There is no documentation on how to catch VISTA events or initiate the generation process, so your only option is to use VSA. Although a target machine can receive events from many source machines, events from one source machine cannot be sent to multiple target machines.

VSA can catch events at quite a fine level (e.g., you get multiple events from each COM call, as the call is made through the stub and the actual object code), and the sheer number of events that will be captured causes a problem. These events can inundate you, making it possible that you will miss a vitally important event among the other less important events. However, Visual Studio Analyzer does allow you to define filters, and you are well advised to use these to remove events that do not interest you.

Visual Studio.NET provides VSA projects under **Other Projects** on the **New Projects** dialog for the Enterprise Edition. You can create a project and configure it yourself, or you can take the simplest route and use the Analyzer wizard.

This wizard has four dialogs that allow you to configure your project step-by-step: First you select the machines that can generate the events, then you select the event sources (e.g., OLE DB or COM objects), and finally you specify the filters that will be applied. At this point the project will start up and gather events. Now you should start your distributed application and perform your test scripts. Once you have collected enough events, you can stop collection and view the results.

VSA provides several views of the data—as a chart, or tabulated—and it can analyze the data to give a view of the machines, processes, and components that were running when the events were captured.

6.8 Summary

Creating an assembly or application file involves more than merely writing the code. Your code may depend on other code, and you may use resources. A project contains the files that will be compiled, and a solution contains the dependencies of each project, so that when you build a solution only the files that have been changed will be compiled. The Visual Studio.NET IDE allows you to identify these dependencies through the solution properties. In addition, the IDE integrates with the source control application that you use so that any changes you make will be recorded and so that in a multideveloper team, only one developer will have access to a file at a time.

Chapter 7

Visual C++ .NET

OK, I have to admit it. So far in this book I have been flirting with that newcomer on the block: C#. It is time that I returned to my true love, C++, and hope that my flirtations have not damaged our relationship too much. I think that many of you will come to feel the same. C# is a wonderful language, but it often leaves you wondering if you can do more, and when you discover that you have reached the limits of the language, you realize it is time to get back to C++.

In this chapter I will cover two main aspects of Visual C++.NET that are new to VS.NET: First there is ATL Server, along with the new ATL7 library, which provides new tools to develop unmanaged applications. I will describe the ATL Server architecture in detail and explain how it is used to develop Web applications and Web Services. Second, C++ has been extended to allow you to develop managed code: the managed extensions for C++. I will explain the changes to the language that have been made to allow you to do this.

7.1 ATL

Since it was first released, the ActiveX Template Library has always been the library of choice for developing COM objects and controls. ATL was designed to be efficient and flexible, but until ATL7 the library has had few utility classes. The developer had two options: either call the Win32 API directly, or import MFC and use its utility classes. Microsoft Foundation Classes is an application framework, so it is not designed to provide small, efficient code. Importing MFC into an ATL3 project was a problem. So the ATL team decided that if it was a problem to import MFC into an ATL project, it would implement utility classes in ATL and allow

MFC to benefit from them. In VS.NET the utility classes are implemented in ATL with the ATL ethos of thread-safe, efficient code; these classes are shared by both MFC and ATL code.

Another new feature in Visual C++.NET is VC attributes. Attributes are used by the native C++ compiler to generate code—COM code, event code, and ATL Server code. ATL Server is an extension of the ATL library to develop ISAPI extensions to implement Web applications and Web Services. In spite of the name, ATL Server is not used to generate COM code, but like the rest of the ATL library, it generates efficient and flexible code.

7.1.1   A Few New Keywords

The ATL library is based on C++ templates. Template parameters can be used by the developer to provide code for a templated class. The ATL classes typically have default values for their parameters so that there is a default implementation.

One pattern that ATL uses is to allow the developer to provide code for its classes as a *mix-in class*. The developer provides this class through a template parameter:

```
// native C++ from atlcom.h
template <class Base>
class CComObjectGlobal : public Base
{
public:
    typedef Base _BaseClass;
    CComObjectGlobal(void* = NULL);
    ~CComObjectGlobal();
    STDMETHOD_(ULONG, AddRef)();
    STDMETHOD_(ULONG, Release)();
    STDMETHOD(QueryInterface)(REFIID iid,
                                void ** ppvObject);
    HRESULT m_hResFinalConstruct;
};
```

This class provides an implementation of IUnknown for the class that you pass as the parameter to the template (Base). As you can see, CComObject-Global derives from the template parameter and hence has access to the public and protected members.

The problem with ATL deriving from your class is that it does not know what methods your class has implemented. If the ATL class requires that your class implement a method, this requirement should be documented, and if you have no need for the method, you can provide an empty implementation. This was the approach taken in ATL3, and these empty implementations were often provided by the classes that were used as base classes.

ATL7 takes a different approach. It introduces two new directives: __if_exists and __if_not_exists. These directives identify a class or a class member, and they provide code if the item exists or if it does not exist, respectively. For example, look at the constructor and destructor of CComObjectGlobal:

```cpp
// native C++ from atlcom.h
CComObjectGlobal(void* = NULL)
{
    m_hResFinalConstruct = S_OK;
    __if_exists(FinalConstruct)
    {
        __if_exists(InternalFinalConstructAddRef)
        {
            InternalFinalConstructAddRef();
        }
        m_hResFinalConstruct = FinalConstruct();
        __if_exists(InternalFinalConstructRelease)
        {
            InternalFinalConstructRelease();
        }
    }
}
~CComObjectGlobal()
{
    __if_exists(FinalRelease)
    {
        FinalRelease();
    }
}
```

ATL3 would require the Base parameter to implement FinalConstruct(), FinalRelease(), InternalFinalConstructAddRef(), and InternalFinalConstructRelease(). When this code is compiled, the compiler checks whether these methods exist in the class you have provided. If so, the compiler can generate the code that calls the method; otherwise this code is not generated.

Another place where these directives are useful is CComControlBase. As the name suggests, CComControlBase is used as a base class for ActiveX controls and provides default implementations for many of the control interfaces and for facilities like ambient properties. Your control can also implement stock properties, and if it does, you should provide get and put methods for the property and implement the put method so that it indicates that the control's state has changed and hence that the control should be treated as dirty. If the control is part of a document, the document will need updating and the control may need redrawing. ATL provides CStockPropImpl<>, which you can use as a base class to provide these get and put methods for *all* stock properties. But this presents a problem because the get and put methods should access the state of the property, meaning that CStockPropImpl<> would have to have data members for the state of all stock properties, and thus your code would inherit this bloated data.

ATL3 took the approach that the data members for the state should be declared in the class that you pass as a template parameter to CStock-PropImpl<>, one of the base classes of your class. The methods in CStockPropImpl<> assume that your code provides the data members, so the following code from ATL3 casts the this pointer to the T class pointer to access your class members (a down cast):

```
// native C++ from atlctl.h in ATL3
// T is a template parameter of the class
HRESULT STDMETHODCALLTYPE get_Font(
    IFontDisp** ppFont)
{
    T* pT = (T*) this;
        *ppFont = pT->m_pFont;
    if (*ppFont != NULL)
        (*ppFont)->AddRef();
    return S_OK;
}
```

If your class does not have a member called m_pFont, this code will not compile. To get around this problem, ATL3 added an anonymous union to CCom-ControlBase in which all of the data members were needed by all of the stock property implementations, so if your class did not provide the data member, the member of the union would be used. Because a union is used, your code has storage for only the largest member of the union added to it. This was a bit of a hack job, but it worked. However, it still meant that when you derived from CStockPropImpl<>, you got implementations of the get and put methods for properties that you did not want to support.

The ATL7 version of get_Font looks like this:

```
// native C++ from atlctl.h in ATL7
// T is a template parameter of the class
HRESULT STDMETHODCALLTYPE get_Font(
    IFontDisp** ppFont)
{
    __if_exists(T::m_pFont)
    {
        if (ppFont == NULL)
            return E_POINTER;
        T* pT = (T*) this;
        *ppFont = pT->m_pFont;
        if (*ppFont != NULL)
            (*ppFont)->AddRef();
    }
    return S_OK;
}
```

If your class does not provide m_pFont, none of the code will be added to your class. You will see the directives __if_exists and __if_not_exists throughout ATL7, and you can also use them in your own code.

C++ is a very flexible language, and you can do some very interesting things with it. One of the important features of C++ is the ability it offers you to develop a class library and to provide implementations in base classes. Your code can override the implementation inherited from a base class, and—provided that it has the access—it can call the base-class implementation. When your code calls a method in a base class, the compiler has to know which method you intend to call. It will do this by looking at the method name and the parameters you pass. If the derived class has a method with the names and parameters that you give, the compiler will call your method. To ensure that the base-class method is called, you have to use the base-class name:

```
// native C++
class MyBase
{
public:
    void f(){}
};
class MyDerived : public MyBase
{
public:
    void f(){}
    void g()
    {
        f();            // call MyDerived::f
        MyBase::f(); // call MyBase::f
    }
};
```

This is fine and very useful, but it assumes that when you write the derived class, you know the name of your base class. As you'll see in a moment, attributes can add a base class, but unless you have detailed knowledge of the classes that an attribute will add, you will not know the name of the base class. Of course, this is not a problem if you are not overriding a base-class method. The new C++ compiler provides the __super keyword to avoid this problem:

```
// native C++
class MyDerived : public MyBase
{
public:
    void f(){}
    void g()
    {
        f();            // call MyDerived::f
        __super::f(); // call MyBase::f
    }
};
```

This implementation of g() is the same as the earlier version, except that I have not explicitly used the name of the base class. The compiler will check all the accessible base-class members and will choose the method that best fits the signature you call. If you have multiple base classes and more than one of these provides a method that fits the signature you call, the compiler will issue an error.

7.1.2 ATL Attributes

The raison d'être for ATL was to bring together boilerplate code in a template library. Before ATL existed, every COM developer had to start writing his COM class by writing the implementation of `IUnknown`. For example, here is a simple COM class:

```
// native C++
class CMyObject : public IMyItf
{
    LONG m_uRef;
public:
    CMyObject() : m_uRef(0){}
    STDMETHODIMP QueryInterface(
        REFIID riid, void** ppv)
    {
        if (riid == IID_IMyItf
            || riid == IID_IUnknown)
            *ppv = static_cast<IMyItf*>(this);
        else
        {
            *ppv = 0;
            return E_NOINTERFACE;
        }
        reinterpret_cast<IUnknown*>(*ppv)->AddRef();
        return S_OK;
    }
    STDMETHODIMP_(ULONG) AddRef()
    {
        return InterlockedIncrement(&m_uRef);
    }
    STDMETHODIMP_(ULONG) Release()
    {
        LONG res = InterlockedDecrement(&m_uRef);
        if (res == 0) delete this;
        return res;
    }
    STDMETHODIMP DoSomething()
    {/* do something */return S_OK;}
};
```

Note that in Windows 9x, the `Interlocked*()` methods do not necessarily return the actual value after the increment or decrement. They will, however, return `0` if that is the result, so although `Release()` will work the way that you expect, you cannot rely on the absolute value returned from these methods. This is only part of the implementation; if this COM class is cocreatable, the class factory is an intimate part of the class implementation. Because only the class factory knows how to create instances of the class, and only the class knows how to destroy instances, the class and class factory have to be written at the same time. I will assume that such a class factory class exists for `CMyObject`.

Notice that practically all of the code for `CMyObject` can be used by another class. The only new requirement is that the interfaces supported by `QueryInterface()` have to be changed. Some developers, bored with writing essentially the same code for every class, produced base classes, templates, or even macros to reuse the code. The advantage of putting boilerplate code into such libraries was that the developer could concentrate on the task at hand—writing a COM class—rather than on the plumbing to use that class.

Some libraries of code were more successful than others. MFC, for example, provided code to write COM objects but suffered from the fact that it was essentially a thread-unaware library that had been made thread aware halfway through its lifetime. MFC was developed to write UI classes, which by definition had to have a message map, so if the class exposed a COM interface, it could run only in an STA (single-threaded apartment). ATL did not suffer the constraints that MFC had because it was built from the ground up as a COM class library and hence had support for all the features of COM built in. Furthermore, ATL was designed to be flexible and extensible so that if COM changed, new code could be "plugged" into the ATL classes to accommodate the new features without breaking existing code.

ATL became the de facto method to write COM classes; VB6, for example, could be used only to create trivial COM classes because it did not have the power of C++ to access features like security, and it was hamstrung because it could produce only STA-based objects (which prevented the classes from using the full features of COM+). However, ATL's success soon emphasized that it was actually contributing to the problem that it was designed to prevent. Consider the following code:

```
// native C++ using ATL
class ATL_NO_VTABLE CMyObject :
    public CComObjectRootEx<CComMultiThreadModel>,
    public CComCoClass<CMyObject, &CLSID_MyObject>,
    public IMyItf
{
public:
    CMyObject() { }
    DECLARE_REGISTRY_RESOURCEID(IDR_MYOBJECT)
    DECLARE_PROTECT_FINAL_CONSTRUCT()
BEGIN_COM_MAP(CMyObject)
    COM_INTERFACE_ENTRY(IMyItf)
END_COM_MAP()
public:
    STDMETHODIMP DoSomething()
    {/* do something */return S_OK;}
};
```

This is the previous class (CMyObject), this time implemented through ATL. Notice that you no longer get to see the innards of the IUnknown methods and that class factory support is provided by derivation from CComCoClass<>. CComCoClass<> takes the derived class as a template parameter so that the class can access the public methods of your class by downcasting the this pointer as I showed earlier. Most ATL classes look like this. There may be differences—such as implementing multiple interfaces or providing dual interface support—but in essence most ATL classes start by deriving from CComCoClass<> and CComObjectRootEx<> and have an interface map. In other words, much of this code is boilerplate! (Actually, I am being rather unfair to ATL, especially if you consider the code that it provides for implementing ActiveX control.)

Visual C++ attributes are a natural progression from ATL. The idea is that one or more attributes could be used to say, "This is a COM class that needs a class factory, implements these interfaces, and is designed to be run in this apartment type." VC attributes are *code* attributes and not *type* attributes; that is, they are part of the C++ code, and once that code is compiled the attributes no longer exist. .NET attributes are part of a type, so when that type is compiled to IL, the attribute is still part of the type and is available through the type. The native C++ compiler recognizes VC attributes and will generate code at compile time according to the attributes that it sees. However, it does not do this using simple text substitution as the C++ preprocessor does. The compiler can check other code being compiled and make changes to the code that it generates. For example, the `[coclass]` attribute indicates that a class is a COM class:

```
// attributed native ATL code
[coclass]
class CMyObject :
   public IMyItf
{
public:
   HRESULT DoSomething()
   {
       // do something
       return S_OK;
   }
};
```

This code is essentially all you need to generate the ATL code that I showed earlier. The C++ compiler will determine that the class should derive from `CComCoClass<>` and `CComObjectRootEx<>` and have an interface map with an entry for `IMyItf`. By default, the C++ compiler will assume that instances should run in the STA. I can change this by using the `[threading("Both")]` attribute, which will ensure that the class derives from `CComObjectRoot-Ex<CComMultiThreadClass>`. If I wanted to use my own threading class, I could specify this preference by derivation:

```
// attributed native ATL code
[coclass, threading("Both")]
class CMyObject :
   public IMyItf,
   public CComObjectRootEx<CMyThreadingClass>
{
public:
   HRESULT DoSomething()
   {
       // do something
       return S_OK;
   }
};
```

The C++ compiler is clever enough to realize that although `[threading("Both")]` implies that the class derives from `CComObjectRoot-`

`Ex<CComMultiThreadClass>`, this implication is unnecessary because I have specified my own class. But the other benefits of using `[threading("Both")]` (like registration for an in-process server) still apply.

In a similar way, the C++ compiler will generate an interface map for the class. If I add one myself, however, the compiler will test whether the interfaces from which the class derives are in the explicit interface map, and if so, it will not generate its own interface map. If the map that I provide is not sufficient, the compiler will chain its interface map to the end of the one that I provide.

In earlier chapters I stated that .NET metadata means that type information for a class is part of the class. .NET attributes are used to extend this metadata. COM has always been deficient in this respect because type information was held in several places. Take ATL as an example: A class can be implemented in line in a C++ header file, but the definition of the interface is in a separate IDL (Interface Definition Language) file, which also has the information that generates the type library definition for the class. However, type libraries do not contain threading models or ProgIDs, so ATL has another file, the `.rgs` file, that contains this information. ATL3 servers used the object map to indicate the class factory that should be used to create instances of the COM class, so this is yet another piece of information about the implementation of the class, held in yet another location.

Thus, in an ATL3 project an ATL class contains information in its implementation header file, its `.rgs` file, the IDL file, and the main `.cpp` file of the project that contains the object map. As the class author, it is *your* responsibility to ensure that all of these files are consistent. So if you change the class so that instead of running in an STA, it can run in both an STA and an MTA, it is not sufficient merely to derive the class from `CComObjectRootEx<CComMulti-ThreadClass>`; you have to make sure that you edit the `.rgs` file so that the `ThreadingModel` value is changed to `Both`.

VC attributes ensure that the information about a COM class is held in just one location: next to the class. So if you decide that `CMyObject` should run only in the MTA, all you have to do is change the `[threading()]` attribute parameter to `Free`, and the compiler will do the rest.

Attributed ATL projects do not have an IDL file, but when you build an attributed ATL project you'll see that there is still a separate MIDL (Microsoft Interface

Definition Language) step. However, this step occurs *after* the C++ files have been compiled because there is enough information in the attributed code for the compiler to compile the code. To understand why, you have to understand the reason for the separate MIDL step for an ATL3 project.

In the old days, IDL defined interfaces, and classes implemented those interfaces. The IDL compiler generated a C++ header file from the IDL that had the interface definition in a format that the C++ compiler would recognize. This was a C++ abstract struct that the implementation class would derive from and implement. Because the implementation used this interface definition, the compilation of the IDL file had to occur *before* the C++ files were compiled.

With attributed code, the interface can be defined in C++ files, and thus C++ files that use the interface can be compiled without a separate MIDL step. Attributed C++ projects have a separate MIDL step to generate the proxy-stub files and the type library, but because C++ classes do not depend on the proxy stub and the type library, the MIDL step appears after the compilation of the C++ files. An ATL server may have a type library as a resource, so the MIDL step occurs before the server is linked. All of the IDL items and attributes have equivalent VC attributes, and some attributes allow you to import type information from type libraries and IDL files.

7.1.3 Interfaces

Interfaces are declared in C++ files through the new __interface keyword. You can use this keyword to define dual interfaces, dispinterface interfaces, and "custom" interfaces. Unlike MIDL (which requires the old ODL format for dispinterface interfaces), all of these interfaces use the same syntax. Here are some examples:

```
// native C++, compile with cl /LD test.cpp
#define _ATL_ATTRIBUTES
#include <atlbase.h>
[ module(dll, name="test") ];
[ dispinterface ]
__interface IDisp
{
   [id(1)] void One();
};
[ dual ]
```

```
__interface IDual : IDispatch
{
    HRESULT Two();
};
[ dual ]
__interface IDual2 : IDispatch
{
    [id(1)] HRESULT Three();
};
[ object ]
__interface ICustom : IUnknown
{
    HRESULT Four();
};
```

Notice that to use VC attributes, I have to define the _ATL_ATTRIBUTES symbol and include `atlbase.h` (typically, these will be in the `stdafx.h` file). Because these are interfaces, they can derive from other interfaces (indeed, an interface can derive from more than one interface), and the derivation is implicitly public. I can derive a class from any of these interfaces, and as with the previous version of C++, I will have to implement the methods in the interface. The interface effectively contains pure virtual functions.

If my class derives from the `IDisp` or `IDual2` interface (i.e., an interface derived from `IDispatch` in which the methods are marked with the `[id()]` attribute), the compiler will implement the class with an in-line implementation of `IDispatch`. In this case it will implement `GetIDsOfNames()` with arrays that map the specified DISPIDs to the function names, and it will implement `Invoke()` on the basis of the DISPID. If the class derives from a `dual` interface that does not have `[id()]` applied to its methods, the class will derive from `IDispatchImpl<>`, and the `IDispatch` methods will be implemented by an implementation of `ITypeInfo` generated from the type library.

The `__interface` keyword can be used to define native (COM) interfaces and managed interfaces (if marked with `__gc`, as you'll see later). Interfaces defined with this keyword:

- Inherit from zero or more base interfaces
- Contain public pure virtual functions
- Can contain properties

- Cannot derive from a class
- Cannot contain constructors, destructors, or operators
- Cannot contain static methods
- Cannot contain data members

7.1.4 ATL Object Map

There is one nagging issue that I need to address at this point: the object map. In the old ATL3 days, the *object map* was a map implemented in the main `.cpp` class. The Object wizard would update this map when it added a class to a project, but if you changed the class or indeed removed it from your project, the onus was on you to change the class's entry in the object map. This meant that a piece of information about the class was stored in a location completely separate from the class. This situation has been improved in ATL7: Now—whether or not the code is attributed—the object map does not even exist until the project is compiled.

The registration and class factory code in ATL is centralized in one place—the `_AtlModule` global variable—so the information about all of your ATL classes must be centralized too. This is why the object map in ATL3 was located in a central location: the main `.cpp` file of the project. ATL7 has a similar, centralized map for the registration information, and the end of the file generated by the wizard for a nonattributed class offers a clue about how this map is achieved:

```
// native C++
OBJECT_ENTRY_AUTO(__uuidof(MyObject), CMyObject)
```

The first parameter is a CLSID, and for a nonattributed project the CLSID is obtained from `MyObject`, not `CMyObject`. This is an inconsistency, not a bug. `MyObject` is generated by MIDL and associated with the CLSID with the `__declspec(uuid())` directive. For an attributed project the MIDL step occurs *after* the code is compiled, so the equivalent macro call will get the CLSID from `CMyObject`. This is OK because the class will be associated with a CLSID through the `[uuid()]` attribute.

The `OBJECT_ENTRY_AUTO()` macro defines a global variable called `__objMap_CMyObject` of type `_ATL_OBJMAP_ENTRY`:

```
// native C++
#define OBJECT_ENTRY_AUTO(clsid, class) \
__declspec(selectany) ATL::_ATL_OBJMAP_ENTRY \
    __objMap_##class = \
{ &clsid, class::UpdateRegistry, \
  class::_ClassFactoryCreatorClass::CreateInstance, \
  class::_CreatorClass::CreateInstance, NULL, 0, \
  class::GetObjectDescription, \
  class::GetCategoryMap, class::ObjectMain }; \
// more to come...
```

This is the ATL structure that, among others, holds information about (1) the function that is called to add information about the class to the registry, (2) a function to create a class factory object, and (3) a function to create an instance of the class. But this variable is declared in the class's header file, so the question of how the registration code in the `_AtlModule` object accesses this code remains unanswered. The answer lies in the next line of the `OBJECT_ENTRY_AUTO()` macro:

```
// native C++
extern "C" __declspec(allocate("ATL$__m")) \
    __declspec(selectany) ATL::_ATL_OBJMAP_ENTRY* \
        const __pobjMap_##class \
        = &__objMap_##class; \
// more to come...
```

The `__declspec(allocate())` declaration indicates that the pointer `__pobjMap_CMyObject` is added to a data segment called `ATL$__m`. Data segments are global items, so the linker will collate all the items that have been declared as residing in the same data segment in a contiguous area of memory. In effect, the linker will create a table of pointers, and each of these pointers will point to an `_ATL_OBJMAP_ENTRY` entry. The `atlbase.h` file contains the following code:

```
// native C++
#pragma section("ATL$__a", read, shared)
#pragma section("ATL$__z", read, shared)
#pragma section("ATL$__m", read, shared)
extern "C"
{
    __declspec(selectany)
        __declspec(allocate("ATL$__a"))
        _ATL_OBJMAP_ENTRY* __pobjMapEntryFirst = NULL;
    __declspec(selectany)
```

```
            __declspec(allocate("ATL$__z"))
            _ATL_OBJMAP_ENTRY* __pobjMapEntryLast = NULL;
}
#pragma comment(linker, "/merge:ATL=.rdata")
```

The `#pragma section()` statements declare the `ATL$__m` segment and two others: one named alphabetically before `ATL$__m`, the other named alphabetically after it. The `/merge` line effectively merges these segments with the `.rdata` segment in the final PE module. The linker will place the segments in alphabetical order, so the `__pobjMapEntryFirst` pointer, allocated in the `ATL$__a` segment, will always be in the memory location immediately before the first pointer in the `ATL$__m` segment. Correspondingly, the `__pobjMapEntryLast` pointer will be in the memory location immediately after the last pointer in the `ATL$__m` segment. These two pointers are accessible by any of the ATL code, which can access the `ATL$__m` segment by taking the address of the `__pobjMapEntryFirst` pointer. Thus the `ATL$__m` segment is a centralized table of `_ATL_OBJMAP_ENTRY` pointers, mirroring the purpose of the ATL3 object map.

The final part of the `OBJECT_ENTRY_AUTO()` macro calls the `OBJECT_ENTRY_PRAGMA()` macro, which is defined as follows:

```
// native C++
#define OBJECT_ENTRY_PRAGMA(class) \
    __pragma(comment(linker, \
            "/include:___pobjMap_" #class));
```

This definition tells the compiler to pass the `/include` switch to the linker, which tells the linker to add the specified symbol (the pointer added to the segment) to the symbol table.

Part of the reason for the `ATL$__m` segment is to give access to the registration function of each of the COM classes that you define. As in ATL3, this function is called `UpdateRegistry()`. If you write a nonattributed class, you use the ATL3 `DECLARE_REGISTRY_*` macros to implement this function. If you write an attributed class, the compiler will generate this function for you—for example, as follows:

```
// native C++
static HRESULT WINAPI UpdateRegistry(
    BOOL bRegister)
```

```
{
    CRegistryVirtualMachine rvm;
    HRESULT hr;
    if (FAILED(hr = rvm.AddStandardReplacements()))
        return hr;
    rvm.AddReplacement(_T("FriendlyName"),
                        GetObjectFriendlyName());
    return rvm.VMUpdateRegistry(GetOpCodes(),
                GetOpcodeStringVals(),
                GetOpcodeDWORDVals(),
                GetOpcodeBinaryVals(),
                bRegister);
}
```

The generated class holds the registration information in four static arrays: a binary array that is accessible through `GetOpCodes()` and has information about the registration actions to perform; and three additional arrays that are accessed by `GetOpcodeStringVals()`, `GetOpcodeDWORDVals()`, and `GetOpcodeBinaryVals()`, respectively, and hold string, DWORD, and binary values that are added to the registry. The contents of these arrays are generated by the compiler from the attributes that you added to the class. This means that you no longer have to support an `.rgs` file, although if you have an `.rgs` file that you want registered, you can indicate this using the `[registration_script()]` attribute on the class. The compiler reads this `.rgs` file at compile time and adds the information to the static arrays.

7.1.5 ATL Server Project and ATL Server Web Service

The **C/C++** category of the Project wizard includes the following two entries for creating wizards: **ATL Server Project** and **ATL Server Web Service**. In fact, these wizards are the same, which is why I am covering both of them in this section.

Figure 7.1 shows the relationship between the ATL Server ISAPI and IIS. When an HTTP request comes into IIS, it is handled by a thread taken from a pool maintained by IIS. This thread will locate the ISAPI DLL that has been registered in the IIS metabase to handle the request, and it will call the ISAPI's entry point. Clearly, the longer this thread takes to handle the request, the more it is delayed from handling other requests. When the IIS thread pool is exhausted, IIS will create more

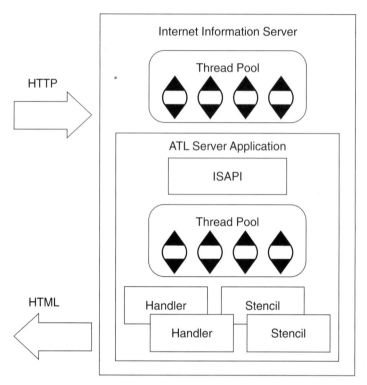

Figure 7.1 ATL Server

threads to handle requests, but this is only a stopgap measure; a higher number of threads means greater resource usage and hence slower performance.

The ATL Server solution is to rationalize the use of threads by implementing its own thread pool. When the IIS thread calls the ISAPI entry point, it does so merely to queue the request in the ISAPI's thread pool. The IIS thread then returns to the IIS thread pool. When a thread becomes available in the ISAPI thread pool, it reads the request and extracts the name of the file that is requested through the URL. If the call is to a Web application, the file will be a *stencil* file with the extension .srf. If the call is to a Web Service, the file will be the request handler DLL encoded with the Web method name.

A stencil is essentially a template for the rendered output that the application will generate—typically, but not restricted to, HTML. The stencil file contains static text and commands; the commands are identified by double braces ({{ }}) surrounding the command name. These commands are provided by the ATL Server stencil processor, or they are placeholders for commands provided by your Web application. The stencil processor loads the handler DLL (identified in the stencil by a command) and parses the .srf file to collate these commands into an object called a *stencil object*. The stencil object is cached so that the .srf file is parsed only once, even for subsequent requests. When the stencil object is *rendered*, the code in the handler associated with the placeholders is called. Consider the following stencil:

```
{{//Stencil File}}
{{handler MyHandler.dll/TimeClass}}
<html>
<head>My First ATL Server Application</head>
<body> The time is {{CurrentTime}} </body>
</html>
```

This stencil indicates that `MyHandler.dll` implements a handler class called `TimeClass` that has a handler method associated with the `Current-Time` placeholder. The stencil processor will locate the handler method identified by `CurrentTime` and generate an HTML page with the static HTML in the stencil and the placeholder replaced with the output from the handler code. An implementation of this handler class could look like this:

```
// native C++
[request_handler("TimeClass")]
class MyHandler
{
public:
    HTTP_CODE ValidateAndExchange()
    {
        m_HttpResponse.SetContentType("text/html");
        return HTTP_SUCCESS;
    }
    [tag_name("CurrentTime")]
    HTTP_CODE GetCurrentTime()
    {
        CTime t = CTime::GetCurrentTime();
        CString tt = t.Format("%H:%M:%S");
        m_HttpResponse<<tt;
        return HTTP_SUCCESS;
    }
};
```

This implementation uses VC attributes to mark the class as the `TimeClass` handler; the handler code for the `CurrentTime` placeholder (`GetCurrent-Time()`) is identified by another attribute. This code inserts the output data into the stream member variable `m_HttpResponse`. However, this variable has not been declared in this class, and there does not appear to be a base class. This is an illusion because under the influence of the `[request_handler()]` attribute, the compiler will derive the class from `CRequestHandlerT<>`, which declares the member variable `m_HttpResponse`. This is why earlier, when I was describing the `__super` keyword, I said that when you use attributes, you often do not know what base classes your class has.

When a request comes in for the stencil file given earlier, the pool thread handling the request loads the stencil file and determines that the handler is located in `MyHandler.dll`. This thread then loads the DLL and locates the handler class identified by `TimeClass`. The request handler class derives from `CRequestHandlerT<>`, and this class derives from `CHtmlTagReplacer`, which has the responsibility of loading and caching stencil processor objects and associating each stencil processor object with a single stencil.

The stencil processor parses the stencil file, separating the static data from the directives and the placeholders, and stores this information. The pool thread then requests that the handler render the stencil, which the stencil processor does by iterating through its parsed results and calling the handler code associated with each placeholder. The pooled thread then returns the constructed page to the client via IIS.

The stencil cache means that a stencil file is parsed only once, and that on subsequent requests for the same page, the stencil processor uses the cached results. Because the cached results contain directives and calls to handler code, on subsequent page requests these handlers are called again, so the data put into the placeholders is always generated. The stencil cache is just one of the several caches that ATL Server provides.

Figure 7.2 shows the various facilities that ATL Server provides. The thread pool maintains a pool of threads by using an NT IO Completion Port. Requests are queued by the completion port, and threads are chosen to handle requests on a first-in, first-out basis. The threading code avoids synchronization as much

DEVELOPING APPLICATIONS WITH VISUAL STUDIO.NET

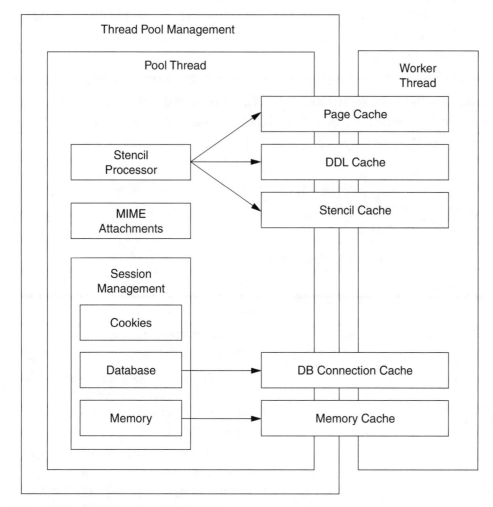

Figure 7.2   ATL Server facilities

as possible to try to prevent a pool thread from becoming blocked; threads are kept as busy as possible. Some of the facilities—for example, the stencil processor—cache results in one of ATL Server's caches. These caches are checked periodically by a single worker thread (which is not part of the pool), and stale items are removed. The caches can be configured as to what constitutes a "stale" item.

ATL Server also provides code for session management. It has code to generate unique session keys that can be passed back to the client through a cookie, a hidden control, or the URL. The session key is used to identify session state for the client, which is held either in a memory cache or in a database accessed through OLE DB.

The `CStencil` and `CHtmlStencil` stencil processor classes provide the basic directives shown in Table 7.1. Of course, if you want to use more directives, you can implement your own stencil processor and provide it through one of the template parameters of `CRequestHandlerT<>`, as illustrated here:

```
// native C++
[request_handler("TimeClass")]
class MyHandler :
    public CRequestHandlerT<
```

Table 7.1 Stencil file directives

Directive	Description
`{{!--}} {{//}}`	Identifies a comment.
`{{while h}} {{endwhile}}`	Performs a loop while the handler `h` returns `HTTP_SUCCESS`.
`{{if h}} {{else}} {{endif}}`	Includes the items between `{{if}}` and `{{else}}` if the handler `h` returns `HTTP_SUCCESS`; otherwise the items between `{{else}}` and `{{endif}}` are used.
`{{locale}}`	Indicates the locale to be used for the generated response; when the stencil is rendered, `SetThreadLocale()` is called. This directive can be used multiple times in a stencil file.
`{{codepage}}`	Indicates the code page that was used to write the stencil file.
`{{handler dll/class}}`	Indicates that handlers used in directives and placeholders are in the specified class within the specified DLL.
`{{subhandler sub dll/class}}`	Indicates the class and the DLL for the directives and placeholder that are called with the specific subhandler (`sub`).
`{{include f}}`	Inserts the stencil file `f` into the current file.

DEVELOPING APPLICATIONS WITH VISUAL STUDIO.NET

```
      MyHandler, CComSingleThreadModel,
      CHtmlTagReplacer<MyHandler, MyStencilProcessor> >
{
// members
};
```

Handlers can also take parameters, thereby allowing you to produce more generic code. The parameters can be one of the following common data types:

```
char            unsigned char
short           unsigned short
int             unsigned int
__int64         unsigned __int64
double
float
bool
```

Alternatively, you can define your own parameter type using a structure and a `parse_func` method. In both cases the data is passed to the handler via the placeholder through parentheses, but it appears through a *pointer* parameter to the handler code. The following command in an `.srf` file:

```
{{GetVolName(C)}}
```

could be used to return the volume name for a particular disk, and the handler could look like this:

```
// native C++
[tag_name("GetVolName")]
HTTP_CODE OnGetVolName(char *pszParam)
{
   TCHAR strDisk[10];
   USES_CONVERSION;
   lstrcpy(strDisk, A2T(pszParam));
   lstrcat(strDisk, _T(":\\"));
   TCHAR strName[32];
   DWORD sn, mcl, fsf;
   TCHAR strFsn[32];
   if (!GetVolumeInformation(
         strDisk, strName, sizeof(strName),
         &sn, &mcl, &fsf, strFsn, sizeof(strFsn)))
   {
```

```
        ATLTRACE("cannot get volume info, error %ld",
                GetLastError());
        return E_FAIL;
    }
    m_HttpResponse.Write(strName);
    return HTTP_SUCCESS;
}
```

In the stencil file example shown earlier, the disk name is passed as c, but in the handler a pointer is passed. The reason is that the stencil processor has to allocate memory for this parameter using the ATL memory manager (although this memory is allocated on a heap, your code does not need to free it). This is more obvious when you use a parse function. For example, the following command returns the disk name, in a particular color:

```
{{GetVolName2(C, red)}}
```

Because there are two parameters to the command, you need to do some more processing. The associated handler code looks like this:

```
// native C++
typedef struct _tagVals
{
    TCHAR strName[5];
    TCHAR strColor[20];
} Vals;

[ tag_name("GetVolName2",
            parse_func="OnGetVolName2Param") ]
HTTP_CODE OnGetVolName2(Vals* strVals)
{
    m_HttpResponse.Write(_T("<font color="));
    m_HttpResponse.Write(strVals->strColor);
    m_HttpResponse.Write(_T(">"));
    OnGetVolName(strVals->strName);
    m_HttpResponse.Write(_T("</font>"));
    return HTTP_SUCCESS;
}

DWORD OnGetVolName2Param(IAtlMemMgr *pMemMgr,
    LPCSTR szParams, Vals** strVals)
{
    *strVals = (Vals*)pMemMgr->Allocate(sizeof(Vals));
```

```
    int i = 0;
    LPSTR ptr = const_cast<LPSTR>(szParams);
    while (*ptr != ',')
    {
        (*strVals)->strName[i] = *ptr;
        i++;
        ptr++;
    }
    (*strVals)->strName[i] = 0;
     ptr++;
    lstrcpy((*strVals)->strColor, A2T(ptr));
    return HTTP_SUCCESS;
}
```

This code assumes that the color has a name of 20 or fewer characters (including the NUL character). The OnGetVolName2Param() function is called by the stencil processor and passed the parameters of the placeholder through the single szParams string. The parse function extracts the disk name and color and places them in an instance of the struct Vals. This code allocates the memory for the structure using the ATL memory manager, but it includes no explicit code to free the memory because ATL Server takes care of freeing this memory.

Web Services are also extensions of IIS. A Web Service accepts requests via HTTP and returns the reply as structured results using XML. Thus much of the code used for Web applications can be used for Web Services. When you create a Web Service (either one of the ATL Server wizards can be used), you will get a request handler class created just as before. However, there are several important differences. Web Services should provide a description through WSDL (Web Services Description Language). The ATL Server architecture requires that your Web Service request handlers implement an interface. This does not mean that they are COM objects or that the interfaces are published as interfaces. The interface is essentially used to group together the methods that will be exposed through the Web Service and to allow the compiler to generate the WSDL for the Web Service at compile time. Here is an example:

```
// native C++
[ uuid("018C4A76-0605-4F20-B006-D7951E2A343F"),
  object ]
__interface IInfoSvrService
{
```

```
    [id(1)] HRESULT GetVolName(
        [in] BSTR bstrDisk,
        [out, retval] BSTR *bstrName);
};
[ request_handler(name="Default",
                   sdl="GenInfoSvrWSDL"),
   soap_handler(name="InfoSvrService",
                namespace="urn:InfoSvrService",
                protocol="soap") ]
class CInfoSvrService :
    public IInfoSvrService
{
public:
// members
};
```

This is a Web Service version of the method I showed earlier. The method is a member of the interface IInfoSvrService. Notice that the interface does not derive from IUnknown or IDispatch, and thus it is not a proper COM interface. IInfoSvrService is used to generate the WSDL for the Web Service, and the [request_handler] attribute indicates that *two* handlers should be generated: one called Default, and another called GenInfoSvrWSDL. You can obtain the WSDL by querying for this handler using the following URL:

```
http://servername/InfoSvr/InfoSvr.dll
   ?Handler=GenInfoSvrWSDL
```

The WSDL handler will return the WSDL for the Web Service, which is essentially a description of the IInfoSvrService interface. Because WSDL is XML, you can call this URL with a Web browser, which will display the results. In addition, you can pass the URL as a parameter to the sproxy tool:

```
sproxy http://servername/InfoSvr/InfoSvr.dll
   ?Handler=GenInfoSvrWSDL
```

This command line will generate a file called InfoSvrService.h that will have the client code for accessing the Web Service. Note that this client code uses the Microsoft XML parser, so you should initialize an apartment before calling the code it declares. In addition to [request_tag], the class has the [soap_handler()] attribute, which gives details of the SOAP code that will be generated. The Web Service methods should have the `[soap_method]` attribute to tell the compiler to generate SOAP code, as illustrated here:

```
// native C++
[ soap_method ]
HRESULT GetVolName(BSTR bstrDisk, BSTR *bstrName)
{
    TCHAR strDisk[10];
    USES_CONVERSION;
    lstrcpy(strDisk, W2T(bstrDisk));
    lstrcat(strDisk, _T(":\\"));
    TCHAR strName[32];
    DWORD sn, mcl, fsf;
    TCHAR strFsn[32];
    if (!GetVolumeInformation(strDisk, strName,
            sizeof(strName), &sn, &mcl,
            &fsf, strFsn, sizeof(strFsn)))
    {
        ATLTRACE("cannot get volume info, error %ld",
                GetLastError());
        return E_FAIL;
    }
    CComBSTR bstrRet = T2BSTR(strFsn);
    return bstrRet.CopyTo(bstrName);
}
```

In addition, when you create a Web Service project, a `.disco` file and a descriptive HTML page will be created. These are used to identify the Web Services available in the handler and to provide the URL that a client can call to generate the WSDL. When you want to add the client code to call the Web Service, typically you call the `.disco` file by selecting **Add Web Reference** in the **Solution Explorer** window.

7.2 Managed Extensions for C++

The managed extensions for C++ extend the language with a pragma, some new keywords (see Table 7.2), and a new compiler switch. When you use the `/clr` switch, you indicate to the compiler that *all* code should be compiled to intermediate language. In effect, you have two types of dynamically allocated classes: GC managed and native heap allocated. Applying the __gc keyword to

Table 7.2   New C++ keywords

Keyword	Description
__abstract	Indicates that the class is abstract; it can be used only as a base class. This doesn't imply that the class is managed. If this is what you want to indicate, you should use __gc as well. An __abstract class may have method implementations.
__box	Creates a managed object from a value type. The managed object will be allocated on the managed heap and managed by the garbage collector (GC).
__delegate	Declares a .NET delegate.
__event	Declares an event, which is a delegate member of a class.
__finally*	Identifies an exception finally block.
__gc	Indicates that instances of a class or struct are managed by the .NET GC.
__identifier	Allows you to use a C++ keyword as a class member.
__interface	Declares an interface. Managed interfaces have to be marked with __gc.
__nogc	Indicates that instances of a class or struct are not managed by the .NET GC.
__pin	Works on a managed pointer to tell the CLR that it shouldn't move the managed object referred to during the GC process.
__property	Indicates that the method is a get or set method of a property.
__sealed	Indicates that a class can't be a base class because it's the bottom class in any class hierarchy. You can also apply __sealed to a virtual method to indicate that the method can't be overridden.
__try_cast	Throws System::InvalidCastException if the cast can't be performed.
__typeof	Returns the Type object for a class.
__value	Indicates that the data in a managed class or struct is stored on the stack and not on the heap. Such a class is implicitly sealed and can't derive from another class or struct.

* I include __finally here because managed C++ allows it to be used with the C++ try/catch construct. In native C++, __finally can be used only with structured exception handling (SEH) with the __try/__except keywords.

a class indicates to the compiler that the class can be created only on the GC-managed heap; such a class cannot be created on the stack. The keyword indicates that the class is part of the .NET object model and not part of the ANSI C++ object model. This means that the syntax to declare classes is different, and the rules of inheritance and member access are the .NET rules and not the C++ rules.

7.2.1 Class Declaration

The __gc and __value keywords have a profound effect on C++ classes. Without either of these, a C++ class will be allocated according to normal C++ rules: When you declare the variable as an auto variable, it will be allocated on the stack; and when you explicitly allocate it with the C++ new operator, the object will be created on the C++ heap. This is true even if the code is compiled with /clr.

Applying __gc indicates that instances of the class are allocated on the GC-managed heap, which means that you can create instances only by using the new operator (you cannot create auto variables of the class) and the operator that will be used will be the managed new. Applying the __value keyword indicates that the class is intended to be created on the stack or as a member of a class, but that it should follow the rules of .NET types. The compiler enforces this requirement because if you try to create a __value type on the GC heap, you'll get an error (C2716). Here is an example:

```
// managed C++
__value class A{};
void f()
{
    // OK, created on the stack
    A a1;
    // OK, use unmanaged new
    A* a2 = __nogc new A;
    delete a2;
    // Error! Will not compile C2716
    A* a3 = new A;
}
```

The class A is marked as being a .NET type; thus when you use the new operator, the managed new is used by default. However, because the type is marked as __value, instances should not be created with the managed new operator; they should be created only on the stack or as class members. So attempting to create an instance on the GC heap (with the pointer a3) will result in a compiler error—the GC will explicitly manage only types marked with __gc. Allocation of the __value type with the native C++ new operator is fine (hence the line allocating an object and assigning it to a2), but of course you should question why you really want to create a .NET type on the C++ heap.

The fact that all __gc types must be created with new implies that instances will always be accessed through pointers. The compiler will enforce this requirement and issue an error if you attempt to access a __gc type through the dot syntax. The operator new that will be called is *always* the managed new operator, so you cannot define a __gc type (or for that matter, a __value type) that has an operator new or operator delete member.

__gc types can have constructors, including a default constructor, but if you do not define a default constructor, the compiler will *not* generate one for you. You cannot define a copy constructor or an assignment operator (operator=()), simply because they will never be called! __gc types will always be accessed through pointers, so the only assignment that will occur will be the assignment of pointers.

Consider the following code:

```
// managed C++
__gc class B{};
void f()
{
    B* b1 = new B;
    B* b2 = b1;
    B* b3(b1);
}
```

The pointer b1 will point to an instance of B on the managed heap. Assigning b1 to b2 means that b2 will point to the same object instance. Similarly, b3 will be initialized with the value of the pointer b1, so it will point to the same object.

__gc types can contain __value types and unmanaged primitive types. A __gc type can also contain pointers to unmanaged classes, but in this case the class designer has the responsibility of ensuring that the unmanaged heap object is destroyed—most likely by implementing a destructor of the containing class that destroys the embedded object. The code in the destructor is called by a `Finalize()` method generated by the compiler. This method will be called by the finalizer thread, perhaps a long time after the object was last used.

The rules of writing .NET classes are different from those for native classes. The current version of .NET does not support generics, so you cannot write templated `__gc` or `__value` types. .NET supports only single inheritance, so a class marked `__gc` can have only a single base class. The base class must be another `__gc` type, and it supports only public inheritance:

```
// managed C++
__value class A{};
__gc class B{};
class C :          // Error: native type cannot
    public B       // derive from __gc type
{};
class U {};
__gc class D :     // Error: __gc type cannot
    public U       // derive from native type
{};
__gc class E :     // Error: cannot derive
    public A       // from __value type
{};
__gc class F :     // Error: only public
    private B      // inheritance allowed
{};
__gc class G :     // OK
    public B
{};
```

Inheritance means that the derived class will hide the base-class implementation of a method when called through the derived-class pointer. However, when the derived-class pointer is cast to a base-class pointer, the methods that will be called will be those implemented in the base class. The standard C++ mechanism to override this behavior is to make the method virtual so that the binding of the function pointer is performed through a vtable, and thus when the virtual method is called through a base-class pointer, the derived version will be called. This behavior also works in .NET, and of course, it works irrespective of the language used to write the base or derived class—for example:

```
// managed C++
__gc class B
{
public:
    virtual void f()
    { Console::WriteLine(S"B::f"); }
};
__gc class D : public B
{
public:
    virtual void f()
    { Console::WriteLine(S"D::f"); }
};
void g()
{
    D* d = new D;
    d->f();    // prints D::f
    B* b =d;
    b->f();    // prints D::f
}
```

A .NET type can be marked __abstract, which means that the designer in-
tends the type to be used only as a base class (hence __abstract cannot be
used with a __value type):

```
// managed C++
__abstract __gc class A1 { };
__gc class C1 : public A1 { };
void g()
{
    // Error: class is abstract
    A1* a1 = new A1;
    // OK, derived class is concrete
    C1* c1 = new C1;
}
```

Here, the class A1 is abstract, so you cannot create an instance of it. However, the class C1 is derived from the abstract type and hence is a concrete
type, so you can create an instance of this type. C++ methods can be declared
as *pure virtual*, which means that the class does not contain an implementation.
A class that has pure virtual methods is implicitly __abstract:

```
// managed C++
__gc class A2
{
public:
    virtual void f() = 0;
};
__gc class C2 : public A2
{
public:
    virtual void f()
    { /* implementation */ }
};
```

Here the class A2 has a pure virtual function, so the class is abstract (if you look at the IL generated for this code, you'll see that both the class and the method are marked with the abstract IL modifier). Note that the error generated when you try to instantiate A2 is concerned with the lack of an implementation of f() rather than with the fact that the class is implicitly abstract.

The antithesis of an abstract class is a sealed class, one that is marked with the __sealed modifier. A sealed class is one that is completely finished and can't be modified. Users can create instances of this class but cannot derive from it. The __sealed modifier can also be used on a virtual method in a non-sealed class to indicate that the method is complete and cannot be improved on, but __sealed does not "seal" the rest of the class.

The __gc modifier means that the type is managed by the garbage collector, which will ensure that when the object can no longer be reached, it will be available for garbage collection (see Chapter 1). __gc types do not have destructors in the C++ sense because you do not call the operator delete to free an instance. Instead, you can instruct the compiler to define a Finalize() method that will be called sometime after the type has been garbage-collected (I say *sometime after* because once the object has been garbage-collected, it will be moved to the finalizer queue, and the finalizer thread will determine when Finalize() is called).

Managed C++ allows you to define a "managed" destructor that the compiler will interpret as your desire to implement Finalize(). The compiler will copy the code that you have put in the destructor into the Finalize() method and add a new destructor that will suppress finalization. If your class is derived from another class that has a `Finalize()` method, the compiler will call this code after it has called the code in your destructor. Thus the following class:

```
// managed C++
__gc class A
{
public:
   ~A(){ Console::WriteLine(S"dtor"); }
};
```

will generate code as if you had written the class like this:

```
// managed C++
__gc class A
{
public:
   void Finalize()
   { Console::WriteLine(S"dtor"); }
   ~A()
   {
      GC::SuppressFinalize(this);
      Finalize();
   }
};
```

I said *as if* because the compiler prevents you from implementing `Finalize()`; implementing a destructor is the only way to do this. If you call the operator `delete` on a pointer to a __gc type, the destructor will be called for the object pointed to. However, the memory for the object will not be deallocated, so the pointer to the object will still be valid. Thus you can reuse the object reference after calling `delete`—as long as you make sure that any resources freed in the destructor are reinitialized:

```
// managed C++
__gc class A
{
public:
   char* s;
   A() : s(0) { }
   void Init()
   {
```

```
        s = __nogc new char[6];
        strcpy(s, "hello");
    }
    void SayHello()
    {
        if (!s) Init();
        Console::WriteLine(s);
    }
    ~A(){ delete [] s; s = 0; }
};

void g()
{
    A* a = new A;
    a->SayHello();
    delete a;
    a->SayHello();
    a = 0;
}
```

Notice that `SayHello()` first checks whether the embedded member, s, is NULL. If it is, the method `Init()` is called to initialize it. `Init()` allocates memory from the unmanaged heap and copies the string `"hello"` into the buffer. Look at how this object is used: First I create an instance on the managed heap and call `SayHello()`; then I call `delete` before calling `SayHello()` again! This does not cause a problem because `delete` only calls the destructor; it does not release the memory occupied by the object, so the pointer is still valid. The call to `GC::SuppressFinalize()` in the compiler-generated destructor ensures that the object will not be finalized. Right at the end of the method I change the value of the pointer (I assign it to 0); this means that the object will no longer be reachable, so it can be collected (and finalized).

If a class derives from a class with a destructor, the base-class destructor will be called after the derived-class destructor is called. As I mentioned in Chapter 4, the CRT cleanup code will ensure that before a process terminates, the finalizer thread is allowed to perform its work. Thus for any object of a class that has a destructor, the destructor will be called even if the process is about to terminate. So you should be aware that if your destructors take a long time to perform, your application may take a long time to terminate.

One commonly used pattern in unmanaged C++ is to define a class that obtains a resource in the constructor and then free the resource in the destructor. An instance of such a class can be created on the stack so that the C++ scoping rules will define the lifetime of the instance and hence how long the resource is held. The lifetime of a GC-managed type is determined by the GC, so a resource released in a destructor (hence the finalizer) may be released when the variable goes out of scope (as you would expect with unmanaged code) or it may be a long time later, maybe even not until the process terminates.

You must alter the way you program to take this nondeterministic destruction into account. One way to do this is to use the dispose pattern—that is, add a `Dispose()` method to the class specifically for instance resource cleanup. Of course, this means that you have to write the code that uses such a class to specifically call this method. Another scheme is to totally rethink how you use resources, and as I mentioned in Chapter 2, it is often possible to rewrite your code to obtain resources as late as possible, and then to free them as soon as they have been used.

`__value` types are declared as stack-based instances. However, you cannot use a `__value` type to overcome this issue of deterministic destruction because `__value` types cannot have destructors. `__value` types are implicitly sealed, so you cannot use them as base classes, nor can they have base classes. A `__value` type is intended for small items, which are usually created on the stack. However, a `__value` type can be part of a `__gc` type, and if it is, it will be created in memory allocated on the GC-managed heap:

```
// managed C++
__value class H{};
__gc class J { public: H h; };
```

Here instances of the class `J` are created on the GC-managed heap, so the managed operator `new` will allocate space on the heap for an instance of `H`. If `H` were a `__gc` type, the `new` operator would allocate space for a *pointer* to `H` and not an instance of `H`.

7.2.2 Member Access

To specify accessibility, managed and unmanaged C++ use the same keywords, but managed C++ is far more expressive than unmanaged C++ or, indeed, any

DEVELOPING APPLICATIONS WITH VISUAL STUDIO.NET

other .NET language. There are two main issues to consider: First, can code outside your assembly access a type in your assembly, and can this external code derive from your class? Second, can types inside or outside the assembly access members of a type within the assembly?

To express type accessibility, you must decorate the type declaration with the `public` or `private` keywords. Accessibility occurs on the assembly level, which means that you can make types accessible from both DLLs and EXEs. Member accessibility is further complicated because it must combine a member's accessibility from another assembly with the accessibility from a derived class. Combining these issues has created a new accessibility syntax for managed C++.

Type accessibility is expressed with the `public` and `private` keywords; for example, the following managed C++ code declares three classes (see Figure 7.3):

```
// managed C++ compiled into assembly X.dll
public __gc class A  { /* code */ };
private __gc class B { /* code */ };
__gc class C         { /* code */ };
```

Here code outside the assembly class can see class A because it's declared with the `public` access specifier, and this external code can also access class A. Class B is visible outside the assembly, but because it is marked `private` it is not accessible; only code in the current assembly can access class B. Class C doesn't have a modifier, so by default it is treated as having `private` access, so external code can't access it.

The `public` and `private` modifiers can be applied to any .NET type (i.e., those marked with __gc or __value): `class`, `struct`, `enum`, `__delegate`, and `__interface`. However, note that .NET types (classes, enums, and interfaces) can derive only publicly from other .NET types.

Note that you apply `public` and `private` only to classes, but you can export global methods because the compiler treats them as members of a `Module` type. In this case global methods are treated as accessible outside of the assembly by default. To hide such a method you have to use the keyword `static`. I will describe accessing global methods later.

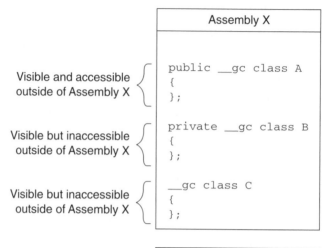

Assembly X

```
public __gc class A
{
};
```
Visible and accessible outside of Assembly X

```
private __gc class B
{
};
```
Visible but inaccessible outside of Assembly X

```
__gc class C
{
};
```
Visible but inaccessible outside of Assembly X

Assembly Y

```
#using "X.dll"
public __gc class D
{
public:
    void f()
    {
        A* a = new A;
    }
};
```

Figure 7.3   Type visibility and accessibility. The C++ `public`, `private`, **and** `static` **modifiers affect the accessibility and visibility of a type outside of the assembly where that type is declared. This figure illustrates two assemblies—X and Y—and shows the types defined in them.**

An assembly that wants to use exported types must import the metadata of those types from their assemblies. This metadata is imported with a `#using` statement, as shown in Figure 7.3. The `#using` directive brings in metadata from an assembly, and the compiler stores information about the imported assembly's location, its version, and the version of the types used. The compiler puts this information into the assembly it is generating, thereby guaranteeing type safety. The `#using` directive can specify the assembly using angle brackets or quotation marks, and either it should have a fully qualified path or the compiler will use the following search algorithm:

1. The current folder
2. The folder that has the .NET Framework assemblies
3. The folders specified by the `/AI` switch
4. The `LIBPATH` environment variable

In addition, you can pass an assembly using the `/FU` compiler switch. I have used the term *assembly* with respect to `#using`, and this is the most common use for the directive (both EXEs and DLLs). However, the compiler also supports the importation of types in an `.obj` file produced by compilation with the `/clr` switch. In this case both `public` and `private` types are imported.

.NET defines levels of access to members within a type. These access levels are similar to but more flexible than the access specifiers that are part of the C++ language. .NET defines seven levels of accessibility, as shown in Table 7.3.

The final access level in the table is `privatescope`, which the compiler applies to something a C++ programmer wouldn't regard as a class member: static variables within a method. These access specifiers determine how external code accesses class members, but note that managed C++ does not allow you to use the `friend` keyword.

You can use combinations of the C++ `public`, `protected`, and `private` access specifiers to provide the seven access levels required by .NET. These access specifiers look odd because on first inspection, a specifier such as `public private` appears to be a contradiction. However, when you read the first half as the *internal* accessibility and the second half as the *external* accessibility, you can read `public private` as "accessible by code in the current assembly only," which makes sense.

Of the other types in .NET, enums and interfaces can have only public members, and struct members are public by default. Indeed, the only difference between structs and classes is that if you don't specify otherwise, members in a class are `private private` by default, whereas members in a struct are `public public` by default.

7.2.3 Properties and Fields
Data members in .NET types are called *fields,* and you use the .NET access specifiers to determine which code can access them. *Properties* allow you to

Table 7.3   Member access levels in .NET

Managed C++ Access Specifier	CLS Equivalent	Meaning
`public public` or `public`	`public`	Accessible by any code
`public protected`	`famorassem`	Accessible by types in the same assembly, or by types derived from the containing type, whether in the same assembly or not
`public private`	`assem`	Accessible by code in the same assembly
`protected protected` or `protected`	`family`	Accessible by code in types derived from the containing type, whether in the same assembly or not
`protected private`	`famandassem`	Accessible by code in types derived from the containing type only if they are in the same assembly
`private private` or `private`	`private`	Accessible only by code in the containing type
(used on method static variables)	`privatescope`	Accessible only by code in the method where the static variable is declared

provide values through a method that are called as if they were fields. There are several advantages to properties: You can provide just a getter to make the property read-only, or just a setter to make the property write-only. In addition, you can use code in a getter to make sure that the value returned by the property is completely up-to-date, or you can put code in a setter so that code that uses the value can be informed that the value has changed (e.g., changing the `Height` property of a form will generate the `SizeChanged` event).

Properties are indicated by the `__property` keyword and are implemented through `get_` and `set_` methods—for example, as follows:

DEVELOPING APPLICATIONS WITH VISUAL STUDIO.NET

```
// managed C++
__gc class CMyData
{
    int m_x;
public:
    __property int get_Data()
    { return m_x; }
    __property void set_Data(int i)
    { m_x = i; }
};
```

Here I've declared storage for one integer (m_x), which is `private` and hence inaccessible by external code. This is the local storage for the `Data` property, which is an implementation detail of my class; the property could generate the value dynamically. I've defined two accessors for this property—a `get_` method and a `set_` method—which implies that the property is readable and writable. The name after `get_` (or `set_`) is the name of the property, so you can access that property like this:

```
// managed C++
CMyData* p = new CMyData;
p->Data = 4;
Console::WriteLine(S"Data is {0}",
                    __box(p->Data));
```

In the second line the `set_Data()` method is called; in the last line, `get_Data()` is called. If you want to have a read-only property, you can simply implement the `get_Data()` method.

7.2.4 Compiling to IL

When you compile a C++ file with the `/clr` switch (and the `#using <mscorlib.dll>` statement), all functions, including global functions, will be compiled to IL. However, there are exceptions. Native code will be generated if the function has `__asm` code blocks, if it uses `setjmp`, or if it has `varargs` in its parameter list. In addition, you can specifically instruct the compiler to generate native code using `#pragma unmanaged` (and turn generation of IL back on with `#pragma managed`).

7.2.5 .NET Pointers

Managed C++ provides two types of pointers: __gc pointers, which point to the managed heap and hence are tracked by the GC; and __nogc pointers, which are not tracked by the GC. __gc pointers are automatically initialized to zero, so you do not have initialize them. For example, the following code:

```
// managed C++
String* s;
s = S"hello";
```

will generate the following IL:

```
// IL
.locals (string V_0)
IL_0000:    ldnull
IL_0001:    stloc.0
IL_0002:    ldstr "hello"
IL_0007:    stloc.0
```

The first line declares a reference, and this is immediately assigned to zero by the following two lines. After that a reference to the managed string `"hello"` is assigned to the reference.

__gc pointers are tracked by the GC when it determines whether an object is reachable. All pointers to __gc types are __gc pointers, so you do not need to use a modifier. Pointers to __value types may be __gc pointers or __nogc pointers, depending on where the type has been allocated. Of course, __value types are generally accessed through instances rather than pointers, so a pointer is assigned only when the address operator (&) is used. If the __value type is created on the stack, the address operator will return a __nogc pointer because the GC does not track the object. If the __value type is a member of a __gc type, the address operator will return an *interior* pointer into an object allocated on the stack. This pointer is effectively a reference on the object because while this pointer is being used, the object cannot be collected, and if a collection occurs that moves the object, then this interior pointer must be changed to point to the new location of the __value type data member. Thus the address operator will return a __gc pointer. In both cases it is safe to use the __gc modifier on the pointer because it will be ignored if the address operator returns a __nogc pointer. Interior pointers can be only local variables, function parameters, or function return types.

This issue of the GC tracking object references is an important one, and it affects the casts that you are allowed to perform. A __gc pointer cannot be cast to a __nogc pointer because doing so would create a reference to the object that the GC cannot manage. If you really want to get a __nogc pointer to a managed object, you have to tell the GC that references to the object exist that the GC cannot track and therefore the object cannot be collected. And because the GC cannot manage the reference, the GC must keep the object in the same position on the managed heap. This mechanism is called *pinning*.

In managed C++ you pin an object by declaring a pinning pointer and assigning it to the object. These steps declare an IL `pinned` reference, which is declared as a C++ `volatile` pointer, so that the C++ optimizer is careful what it does to code that uses the pointer:

```
// managed C++
String* s;
s = S"hello";
String __pin* p = s;
void __nogc* c;
c = reinterpret_cast<void __nogc*>(p);
```

The pointer `p` is a pinning pointer. Pinning pointers are *always* local, stack-based variables. Once the object is pinned, you can use it to assign a __nogc pointer. As you can see, I have done this to get a `void*` pointer into the managed heap. However, note that this pointer will point into the internal workings of the `String` type and not necessarily to the data held by the `String` object. The character array held by a `String` object is a fixed offset from the start of the object, and this offset can be obtained by a call to the `OffsetToStringData` property:

```
System::Runtime::CompilerServices
    ::RuntimeHelpers::OffsetToStringData
```

Thus the following code will give access to the character array in the string:

```
// managed C++
unsigned offset;
offset = System::Runtime::CompilerServices
```

```
::RuntimeHelpers::OffsetToStringData;
wchar_t* cc = (wchar_t*)(offset + (char*)c);
_putws(cc);
```

This action is so useful that the Visual C++ team has provided a function called `PtrToStringChars()` to return an interior pointer to the characters in a managed string. This function is declared in the `vcclr.h` header file.

If you pin a pointer to a subobject (an interior pointer, or a pointer to a member of an array), the entire object will be pinned.

IL has two casting opcodes: `castclass` and `isinst`. `castclass` will convert an object reference to a reference of one of the parent classes in the class hierarchy. If the cast fails, `InvalidCastException` will be thrown; otherwise the stack will contain the reference to the object. To access this opcode in managed C++, you can use the `__try_cast<>` operator, which I will explain in more detail in the next section. `isinst` will check whether the reference on the stack is of the specified type, and if it isn't, the item on the stack will be replaced with 0. Again, this means that a runtime check is performed, and if the check fails, the return value is 0. This is the same behavior that you would expect from the C++ `dynamic_cast<>` operator, and indeed, this is how you access this opcode in your managed C++ code.

You use `dynamic_cast<>` in the same way that you would for unmanaged types, except that `dynamic_cast<void*>` is not allowed. In unmanaged C++, performing a `dynamic_cast<>` operation to a `void*` pointer will return a pointer to the start of the object in memory, whatever type that object is. The equivalent in managed C++ is to perform a `dynamic_cast<Object*>` operation instead. A `static_cast<>` can be used to cast between related pointer types without a runtime check; in effect the IL will initialize the new pointer with the pointer being cast. This is a dangerous action, so it should be carried out only in performance-critical code. Even if you are sure that the cast will succeed, it is a good idea to use `__try_cast<>` in the debug build to catch the possibility that the cast will fail.

7.2.6 Managed C++ and Interfaces

You can declare an interface in VC++ 7.0 using the `__interface` keyword. In previous versions `interface` was declared as a struct, which meant that you could derive an interface from another struct, and you could add method implementations

and data members (i.e., storage for data). To a certain extent declaring `interface`
as a struct could be beneficial; the following is an excerpt from `unknwn.h`:

```
// native C++
struct __declspec(
    uuid("00000000-0000-0000-C000-000000000046"))
IUnknown
{
public:
    virtual HRESULT STDMETHODCALLTYPE QueryInterface(
        REFIID riid, void** ppvObject) = 0;
    virtual ULONG STDMETHODCALLTYPE AddRef(void) = 0;
    virtual ULONG STDMETHODCALLTYPE Release(void) = 0;
    template<class Q>
    HRESULT STDMETHODCALLTYPE QueryInterface(Q** pp)
    { return QueryInterface(__uuidof(Q), (void **)pp); }
};
```

This is the native C++ binding to the `IUnknown` interface. The Win32 designers have added the type-safe templated implementation of `QueryInter-`
`face()` to prevent C++ programmers from adding a common bug to their
code: a mismatch in the IID and interface pointer type passed to this method.
However, although this is good C++ (and a good idea), it looks odd when you
consider that COM interfaces should have only public, pure virtual methods.
However, this is not an interface definition; it is merely the C++ binding.

Managed interfaces are declared like native interfaces, but they also have to
have the __gc keyword—for example, as follows:

```
// managed C++
__gc __interface IScanner
{
    __property Point get_ImageTopLeft();
    __property void set_ImageTopLeft(Point tl);
    __property Point get_ImageBottomRight();
    __property void set_ImageBottomRight(Point tl);
    void Start();
    __property Byte get_Image()[];
};
__gc class DesktopScanner
    : public IScanner
{ /* members */ };
```

This code defines (1) an interface with two read/write properties to define the area to scan, (2) a method to start the scan, and (3) a property that returns the scanned image (I will explain the strange syntax used for arrays later). All of the interface's members are implicitly public and implicitly virtual. A class that derives from this interface must implement the three properties and the method. The `DesktopScanner` class derives from the `IScanner` interface. As I have already mentioned, .NET supports only public inheritance, but you still need to use the `public` keyword. The class can be used like this:

```
// managed C++
DesktopScanner* ds = new DesktopScanner;
ds->ImageTopLeft = Point(0, 0);
ds->ImageBottomRight = Point(500, 500);
ds->Start();
// use a method of some sort to save the image
SaveImage(ds->Image);
```

The main use of an interface is to allow you to request a particular behavior from an object. If the object does not support the behavior, then asking for the interface will fail. To test for a specific behavior, you should cast the object to the interface:

```
// managed C++
DesktopScanner* ds = new DesktopScanner;
IScanner* scanner = dynamic_cast<IScanner*>(ds);
if (scanner != 0)
{
    // use the scanner interface
}
```

In this code I am explicitly asking for the specific behavior through the cast (I will return to this issue of casting in a moment). Another advantage of using interfaces is that the type of the object you are calling does not matter. If the object supports the interface, you'll be able to access that behavior. For example, you could have another `IScanner`-derived class, `ScannerPrinter`. You can put instances of each class into a generic container, such as `Collections::ArrayList`, and when you extract instances from the container, you can cast to the interface to get the behavior you require:

```
// managed C++
ArrayList* scanners = new ArrayList;
scanners->Add(new DesktopScanner);
scanners->Add(new ScannerPrinter);
for (int i = 0; i < scanners->Count; i++)
{
    IScanner* p;
    p = static_cast<IScanner*>(scanners->Item[i]);
    p->ImageTopLeft = Point(0, 0);
    p->ImageBottomRight = Point(500, 500);
    p->Start();
}
```

You know that each object in `scanners` implements `IScanner`, but be-cause the `Item[]` property returns a `System::Object` object, you must cast this to get the interface. Because I am confident that the objects implement `IScanner`, I have used `static_cast<>`, which merely takes the `Object*` pointer and places it in an `IScanner*` pointer without a runtime check to see if the conversion is legal. This is fine if the objects in the container hold objects that implement this interface, but can you *always* guarantee this?

If the object does not implement the interface, the cast will still succeed, but an exception will be thrown when an attempt is made to call code through this pointer. Of course, if you use `dynamic_cast<>`, then a runtime check will be made, and if the cast fails, the interface pointer will be assigned to `0`, which means that you can check the interface pointer after the cast is made. However, even in this case sometimes you think such a check is unnecessary because you know that the objects will support the interface for which you are casting and a check will take up CPU cycles that could be used by other code.

An intermediate solution is to use the `__try_cast<>` operator in debug builds. This operator will throw an `InvalidCastException` exception when a cast fails. Here is an example:

```
// managed C++
try
{
    IScanner* p;
#ifdef _DEBUG
    p =__try_cast<IScanner*>(n);
```

```
#else
   p = static_cast<IScanner*>(n);
#endif
   p->Start();
}
catch(InvalidCastException* e)
{
   Console::WriteLine(e->ToString());
}
```

This code will check the debug version to see if the cast succeeds. The advantage with this check is that it is clear through the exception type that the cast failed.

7.2.7 Multiple Interfaces

.NET types can implement more than one interface and hence have more than one behavior. The advantage of interfaces is that users of a type can request the specific behavior they require by casting to the appropriate interface. The `ArrayList` class, which I used earlier, is a good example of a class that has multiple interfaces. This class derives from four interfaces, three of which give you different ways to access `ArrayList`'s data: `IEnumerable`, `IList`, and `ICollection`.

`IEnumerable` enables the class to implement `GetEnumerator()`, which returns a reference to an enumerator object that you can use to traverse all the items in one direction starting with the first item. The `ICollection` interface provides the `Count` property. `IList` provides the `Item` property I used earlier to randomly access the data. You can access the objects in the `scanners` container like this:

```
// managed C++
IEnumerator* pEnum;
pEnum = scanners->GetEnumerator();
while (pEnum->MoveNext())
{
   IScanner* p;
   p = static_cast<IScanner*>(pEnum->Current);
   p->Start();
}
```

Now consider the situation in which two interfaces have a method with the same name and signature—for example, `IPrinter`:

```
// managed C++
__gc __interface IPrinter
{
    __property int get_Pages();
    __property void set_Pages(int num);
    void Start();
};
```

This interface also contains a `Start()` method, with the same signature as `IScanner::Start()`. The `PrinterScanner` class implements both the `IScanner` and the `IPrinter` interfaces:

```
// managed C++
__gc class PrinterScanner :
    public IScanner, public IPrinter
{
public:
    void Start()
    { Console::WriteLine(S"Start what?"); }
    // other members
};
```

Both interfaces have a method called `Start()` with the same signature, but the two methods clearly do something different. The `PrinterScanner` class contains a single implementation of `Start()`, so if an instance of `Printer-Scanner` is created and cast to either interface, the same method will be called regardless of the interface used. This problem was experienced by VC6 programmers developing COM objects and has spawned several solutions. MFC uses nested classes to implement each interface, but although this approach solves the problem, it introduces the complexity of managing nested classes. ATL's approach is to use multiple inheritance and provide one solution through separate C++ classes accessible as tear-off interfaces. This ATL solution suffers from the complexity of coupling the tear-off class and object class and the confusion of spreading a COM class's implementation over several C++ classes.

The new C++ compiler solves this problem by allowing you to identify the interface to which the method belongs, and this facility is available in both managed and unmanaged C++. You can implement the `PrinterScanner` class as follows:

```
// managed C++
__gc class PrinterScanner :
   public IScanner, public IPrinter
{
public:
   void IScanner::Start()
   { Console::WriteLine(S"Start scanning"); }
   void IPrinter::Start()
   { Console::WriteLine(S"Start printing"); }
   // other members
};
```

Here the first implementation of `Start()` will be accessible only through an `IScanner` pointer. When you use explicit interface implementation like this, you must do so for *all* versions of the method with the same signature. I have shown this in the code here by implementing `Start()` twice—once for each interface that defines it. (But I can add an overloaded version of `Start()` as long as the signature is not the same.)

Because these methods have been identified as being called only through an interface pointer, any code that tries to call `Start()` through a `PrinterScanner` pointer will not compile. The metadata generated for the `PrinterScanner` class will indicate that there are two `Start()` methods: `IPrinter.Start()` and `IScanner.Start()`. Thus, other languages also have this restriction: The methods can be accessed through only the specified interface pointer. This works if the object implements a single interface, or even if it implements multiple interfaces that do not have name clashes.

I mourned the loss of interface programming when .NET first appeared because interface programming is a precise way to obtain behavior from an object, and it is clear to both the client and the object developer what the code means. The .NET (or if you like, the CORBA-like[1] or VB-like) mechanism of accessing behavior through object references leads either to objects with a single behavior (as in the case of CORBA objects) or to a confusing mishmash of

---

1. CORBA stands for Common Object Request Broker Architecture.

methods representing different behaviors (as with VB objects). Because of all the advantages of interface programming, I urge you to consider implementing your objects by explicitly marking methods as interface methods.

It is worth pointing out that interfaces can add a small performance penalty on object calls. My empirical tests indicate that calls made in process (within the current domain or across domains) take between 5 and 16 percent longer when made through an interface than a similar method call on an object reference takes. For out-of-process calls through .NET remoting, however, I have found that calling a method through an interface rather than an object reference is slightly quicker (by about 1 percent). These figures are purely empirical and you may obtain different results, but because calling interface methods is not a significant performance hit (and in some cases gives a slight performance advantage), it is worthwhile implementing interfaces on your classes. Doing so will ensure that your developers—whether they are C++, C#, or VB.NET programmers—will have to use interface programming. You know that it is good for them to do so.

7.2.8 Managed Arrays

An array is an ordered group of items accessed through one or more indices. Arrays in unmanaged C++ are flexible, but they are potentially dangerous because C++ does not check that the indices actually refer to a value within the array. .NET has two types of arrays: vectors (which are one-dimensional arrays) and multidimensional arrays.

The C++ syntax to create, initialize, and access both types of arrays is the same. Whether you use a vector or a multidimensional array, the object will implicitly derive from `System::Array`, so you get the benefits of being able to access array information (number of elements per dimension, rank, and so on) and doing searches within the array. Apart from the number of dimensions, there is no difference between the two array types in this release of .NET, so I won't distinguish between the two in the following discussion.

In the following code I create an array and initialize it with the first ten items of the Fibonacci series:

```
// managed C++
Array* fib = 0;
```

```
// create the array
fib = Array::CreateInstance(__typeof(int), 10);
// initialize the first two values
fib->SetValue(__box(1), 0);
fib->SetValue(__box(2), 1);
// fill the rest
for (int x = 2; x < 10; x++)
{
    // obtain the two previous values
    Object* o1 = fib->GetValue(x-1);
    Object* o2 = fib->GetValue(x-2);
    // convert to int values
    int i1 = Int32::Parse(o1->ToString());
    int i2 = Int32::Parse(o2->ToString());
    // initialize the current value
    fib->SetValue(__box(i1 + i2), x);
}
for (int x = 0; x < 10; x++)
    Console::WriteLine(fib->GetValue(x));
```

If using .NET arrays were this involved, few people would want to use them! The `Array::CreateInstance()` method creates an array of `int` elements (`System::Int32`), which has ten items indexed from zero. These items can be accessed through `Array::GetValue()` and `Array::SetValue()`, but even though the array has been declared explicitly as holding `int` elements, these access methods deal only in `System::Object` references, so you must box the values you want to insert into the array, and use a parse method to get the values out of the array.

Thankfully, there is a better way. Managed C++ provides access to managed arrays through array syntax that is similar to that of C++ arrays, but with significant differences. For example, consider the following unmanaged C++ code:

```
// unmanaged C++
int i[3][2];
int val = 1;
for (int x = 0; x < 3; x++)
{
    for (int y = 0; y < 2;   y++, val++)
        i[x][y] = val;
}
printf("%ld\n", i[2][1]);
```

DEVELOPING APPLICATIONS WITH VISUAL STUDIO.NET

The first line creates an array with six elements (a rectangular array), but notice the syntax: Square brackets enclose the size of each dimension. Accessing individual items in the array requires the same syntax: `i[2]` retrieves the array `{5,6}`, and `i[2][1]` gets the second item, `6`. Now compare this example to the equivalent code in managed C++:

```
// managed C++
int j __gc[,] = new int __gc[3,2];
int val = 1;
for (int x = 0; x < 3; x++)
{
    for (int y = 0; y < 2; y++, val++)
        j[x,y] = val;
}
Console::WriteLine(S"{0}", __box(j[2,1]));
```

The main difference between the two sets of code is the array syntax. Instead of allocating the storage with `int i[3][2]`, you use the syntax `int __gc[3,2]`. This code uses a C++ primitive type (`int`) as the array's base type, so by default the unmanaged `new` operator will be used. To ensure that the managed `new` operator is used, you declare the array as `int j __gc [,]`. Whenever you use the square-bracket syntax for managed arrays, the lower bound of every dimension is zero, in contrast to arrays created by `Array::CreateInstance()`, which allow you to use an overloaded version to specify the lower bound. However, note that an array created with `CreateInstance()` cannot be used with the square-bracket array syntax.

Array members are accessed in managed C++ in much the same way as in unmanaged C++, except that instead of using `i[2][1]` to get the first item of the second row, you use `i[2,1]`. This new syntax takes a bit of getting used to, especially because you can have both the managed and unmanaged syntax in the same code. In unmanaged C++, you can obtain each row in the array like this:

```
// unmanaged C++
int* k = i[1];
```

When you dereference the pointer `k`, you obtain the value of `i[1][0]`; however, C++ pointer arithmetic allows you to get the value of `i[1][1]` by incrementing the pointer `k` like this: `*(k+1)`. In managed C++, you can't do this because .NET enforces type safety, and the managed variable j is a two-dimensional array, not a one-dimensional array of arrays. This is an important distinction, and it means you must access the variable j with two indices.

In unmanaged C++, you can pass arrays as parameters to functions—for example, as follows:

```
// unmanaged C++
void f(int a[3][2])
{
    for (int x = 0; x < 3; x++)
        for (int y = 0; y < 2; y++)
            printf("[%ld,%ld] = %ld\n",
                    x, y, a[x][y]);
}
// in main, i initialized as before
f(i);
```

Because the parameter a is accessed through the multidimensional array syntax, you must declare the parameter with the exact dimensions of the arrays you will pass. This is where managed C++ improves on unmanaged C++: Because arrays are instances of System::Array, you can call Array::GetUpperBound() to get the upper bound of a specified dimension:

```
// managed C++
void f1(Int32 i[,])
{
    for (int x = 0; x <= i->GetUpperBound(0); x++)
        for (int y = 0; y <= i->GetUpperBound(1); y++)
            Console::WriteLine(S"[{0},{1}] = {2}",
                    __box(x), __box(y), __box(i[x,y]));
}
```

In this example the parameter to f1() is passed by value, which means that a copy of the array reference is made. So although you can change the values within the array, you cannot change the array reference itself (e.g., if you want to alter the size of the array). If you want to pass an array reference by reference, you can use the following syntax:

```
// managed C++
void f2(int (*i) __gc[])
```

```
{
    // indexed from zero, so GetUpperBound()
    // returns one less than the number of items;
    // create another array with one extra item
    int j __gc[];
    j = new int __gc[(*i)->GetUpperBound(0) + 2];
    for (int x = 0; x <= (*i)->GetUpperBound(0); x++)
        j[x] = (*i)[x];
    // initialize last item to 99
    j[j->GetUpperBound(0)] = 99;
    (*i) = j;
}

void main()
{
    // create five items
    int k __gc[] = new int __gc[5];
    // initialize those items with values
    // from 0 to 4
    for (int x = 0; x <= k->GetUpperBound(0); x++)
        k[x] = x;
    // change the array
    f2(&k);
    // this should print out five items:
    // 0, 1, 2, 3, 4, 99
    for (int x = 0; x <= k->GetUpperBound(0); x++)
        Console::WriteLine(S"k[{0}]={1}",
                           __box(x), __box(k[x]));
}
```

Managed functions can also return arrays, but here the syntax looks strange because you must suffix the function header with the array rank. For example, the following function returns a two-dimensional array:

```
// managed C++
Int32 Get2DArray() [,]
{
    return new Int32[2,3];
}
```

This code creates a 2×3 array of Int32 elements and returns a reference to the calling code. Again, if you want a managed array of primitive types, you need to prefix the square brackets with __gc. This format appears strange because with unmanaged C++ you usually return a pointer to the first item in the array, and the calling code has to know what this pointer means, so in this case managed extensions have made C++ a richer language. If this syntax makes you uneasy, you can make it more palatable using a C++ `typedef` statement:

```
// managed C++
typedef Int32 TwoD [,];
TwoD Get2DArray()
{
    return new Int32[2,3];
}
```

The elements in an array can be __value types or pointers to __gc types, as illustrated here:

```
// managed C++
String* comments[] = new String*[3];
comments[0] = S".NET ";
comments[1] = S"Rocks";
comments[2] = S"!";
```

When you allocate an array, the items will automatically be initialized to zero. So in the case of an array that takes __gc types, you should initialize the members, as I have done in the preceding code. If the array elements are __value types, the default constructor of that type will be called for each element, or the elements will be initialized to zero. You can also provide an initializer list, as you do in unmanaged C++:

```
// managed C++
String* comments[] = {S".NET ", S"Rocks", S"!"};
```

7.2.9 Managed Strings

The C++ compiler allows you to specify explicitly that a string literal is a managed string. The means for doing this is the s prefix:

```
// managed C++
Console::WriteLine(S"hello");
```

This syntax will create a managed string literal, which will be loaded with the IL `ldstr`:

```
// IL
ldstr "hello"
call void [mscorlib]System.Console::WriteLine(string)
```

If you use an ANSI or Unicode string, the compiler will perform a conversion for you. For example, for the code shown here:

```
// managed C++
Console::WriteLine(L"hello");
```

the compiler will generate the following:

```
// IL
ldsflda valuetype $ArrayType$0xe68a7113
    '?A0x098f0d63.unnamed-global-0'
newobj instance void [mscorlib]System.String::.ctor(char*)
call void [mscorlib]System.Console::WriteLine(string)
```

There is a lot going on here. The first line loads the address of a static field that has the data for the string. This address is put on the stack as a *transient pointer*. Transient pointers are intermediate between unmanaged pointers and managed pointers. The memory specified by a transient pointer is not managed by the GC, so the address can be passed to a native function like `wcslen()`. However, it can also be passed to a method (like the constructor of `String`) that expects a managed pointer.

`$ArrayType$0xe68a7113` is a value type that has no members but is declared to be 12 bytes in size (the Unicode string `L"hello"` occupies 12 bytes). `?A0x098f0d63.unnamed-global-0` is a module static variable and is declared as follows:

```
// IL
.field public static valuetype $ArrayType$0xe68a7113
    '?A0x098f0d63.unnamed-global-0' at D_00008030
```

This declaration indicates that the contents of the value type can be found at location `D_00008030`:

```
// IL
.data D_00008030 = bytearray (
    68 00 65 00 6C 00 6C 00    // h.e.l.l.
    6F 00 00 00)               // o...
```

The data at `D_00008030` is the Unicode string that should be converted. The `String` class has several constructors, including pointers to arrays of 8-byte characters (`int8*`) and 16-byte characters (`char*`, which is the one that is called here). These constructors perform the conversion from the unmanaged array of characters to a `String` object.

Clearly, passing a managed string literal as a parameter to a managed method does not require this extra IL to convert the string, and you should use a managed string literal where possible. You will want to use nonmanaged string literals if there is a possibility of passing the pointer to unmanaged as well as managed methods. There is no implicit conversion from a managed string; you will have to do this yourself with a call to the `Marshal` class.

The CLR maintains a table called the *intern pool,* which has an entry for each unique literal string that you use. This means that if you use the same literal string twice, you'll get a reference for the same managed string—for example:

```
// managed C++
String* s1 = S"hello";
String* s2 = S"hello";
String __pin* v1 = s1;
String __pin* v2 = s2;
assert((int) v1 == (int) v2);
```

Here `s1` and `s2` are pointers to two managed strings. When `s1` is declared, it is interned; and when `s2` is declared, the CLR tests whether the string is already in the intern pool, and because it is a reference to the interned string, that string is returned. Finally, I pin both pointers so that I can compare their absolute values.

7.2.10 Exceptions

The managed C++ exception syntax is similar to unmanaged C++ syntax. The only difference is that managed code has a concept of a `finally` block: The code in a `finally` block is called when the `try` block is exited, in whatever way this occurs. C++ does not have a keyword for this, but unmanaged Visual C++ has the `__finally` keyword for Win32 SEH exceptions, so managed C++ has borrowed this keyword.

Exceptions are passed to the exception handler through a pointer to a class derived from `Exception`, and unlike unmanaged C++, you cannot pass any other type, nor can you pass C++ references. If you do throw another type of exception, it will be treated by the compiler as the code throwing a native C++ exception:

```
// managed C++, compiled with /clr /EHsc
__nogc class invalid_argument
{
public:
    invalid_argument(const char* s) : str(s){}
    const char* str;
};
void Test(int x)
{
    try
    {
        if (x <= 0)
            throw new invalid_argument(
                "value must be greater than 0");
    }
    catch(Exception* e)
    {
        Console::WriteLine(e->ToString());
    }
}
```

Here I have created an unmanaged class called `invalid_argument` (which mirrors the behavior of the standard library `std:invalid_argument` class). The `throw` line here is not the managed `throw`; instead the compiler generates code that calls a native function called `_CxxThrowException` that generates a native SEH exception. The output from this code will be the following:

```
System.Runtime.InteropServices.SEHException:
External component has thrown an exception.
    at _CxxThrowException(Void* , _s__ThrowInfo* )
    at Test(Int32 x)
```

Unfortunately, the `SEHException` object, which is generated by the CLR, loses the native exception. The only way to get around this problem is to explicitly catch the native exception:

```
// managed C++
void Test(int x)
{
   try
   {
      if (x <= 0)
         throw new invalid_argument(
            "value must be greater than 0");
   }
   catch(invalid_argument* ia)
   {
      Console::WriteLine(ia->str);
   }
   catch(Exception* e)
   {
      Console::WriteLine(e->ToString());
   }
}
```

This code looks innocuous, but the compiler actually does a lot of work here: It has to create code to catch both native exceptions and .NET exceptions. This ability to catch both types of exceptions is needed to allow libraries like STL (the Standard Template Library) to compile as IL. The preceding code shows the managed C++ equivalent of the unmanaged C++ catch(...) code to catch all exceptions. As I have shown, you can provide more than one exception handler for a guarded block of code, but clearly you should provide more specific handlers before the more generic ones.

7.2.11 Operators

Table 7.4 lists the .NET operators that you can define on your .NET types. Each of these is a static method and returns a new object with the operation performed on the parameter. There is no difference between postfix and prefix increment and decrement operators (remember, .NET does not support the concept of friend).

As an example, here is a __value class that defines an addition operator:

```
// managed C++
__value class Complex
{
   int x, y;
public:
   Complex(int i, int j) : x(i), y(j) {}
```

```
static Complex op_Addition(Complex l, Complex r)
{ return Complex(l.x + r.x, l.y + r.y); }
String* ToString()
{
    return String::Format(S"{0} + {1} i",
                          __box(x), __box(y));
}
};
```

Table 7.4   .NET operators

.NET Operator	C++ Operator	Description
op_Implicit		Converts to a type that does not lose information.
op_Explicit		Converts to a type that does lose information.
op_Addition	+	Adds two objects of the same type.
op_Subtraction	–	Subtracts two objects of the same type.
op_Multiply	*	Multiplies two objects of the same type.
op_Division	/	Divides one object by another object of the same type.
op_Modulus	%	Generates the remainder from the division of one object by another object of the same type.
op_ExclusiveOr	^	Performs a bitwise exclusive OR on two objects of the same type.
op_BitwiseAnd	&	Performs a bitwise AND on two objects of the same type.
op_BitwiseOr	|	Performs a bitwise OR on two objects of the same type.

(continued)

Table 7.4 (continued) .NET operators

.NET Operator	C++ Operator	Description
op_LogicalAnd	&&	Performs a logical AND on two objects of the same type.
op_LogicalOr	||	Performs a logical OR on two objects of the same type.
op_Assign	=	Creates a new object with the same value of another object.
op_LeftShift	<<	Produces a bitwise shift left (divides by 2).
op_RightShift	>>	Produces a bitwise shift right (multiplies by 2).
op_SignedRightShift		Produces a bitwise shift right on a signed type.
op_UnsignedRightShift		Produces a bitwise shift right on an unsigned type.
op_Equality	==	Tests two objects to see if they have the same value.
op_GreaterThan	>	Tests if one object is greater than another.
op_LessThan	<	Tests if one object is less than another.
op_Inequality	!=	Returns true if two objects have different values.
op_GreaterThanOrEqual	>=	Returns true if one object is greater than or equal to another.
op_LessThanOrEqual	<=	Returns true if one object is less than or equal to another.
op_MultiplicationAssignment	*=	Assigns a reference with its product with another object.

(continued)

Table 7.4 (continued) .NET operators

.NET Operator	C++ Operator	Description
op_SubtractionAssignment	-=	Assigns a reference with its value minus another object.
op_ExclusiveOrAssignment	^=	Assigns a reference with its value exclusive-ORed with another object.
op_LeftShiftAssignment	>>=	Assigns a reference with its value shifted to the left.
op_RightShiftAssignment	<<=	Assigns a reference with its value shifted to the right.
op_ModulusAssignment	%=	Assigns a reference with the remainder of its value divided by another object.
op_AdditionAssignment	+=	Assigns a reference with its value plus another object.
op_BitwiseAndAssignment	&=	Assigns a reference with its value bitwise ANDed with another object.
op_BitwiseOrAssignment	|=	Assigns a reference with its value bitwise ORed with another object.
op_DivisionAssignment	/=	Assigns a reference with its value divided by another object.
op_Comma	,	Defines the sequencing operator.
op_Decrement	--	Decrements the object.
op_Increment	++	Increments the object.
op_UnaryNegation	-	Negates the object.
op_UnaryPlus	+	Makes the object positive.
op_OnesComplement	~	Returns the ones complement of the object.

When you add two instances of `Complex`, the compiler will call the `op_Addition()` function:

```
// managed C++
Complex a = Complex(1, 2);
Console::WriteLine(a.ToString());
Complex b = Complex(3, 4);
Console::WriteLine(b.ToString());
Complex c = a + b;
Console::WriteLine(c.ToString());
```

7.2.12 Global Methods

The `main()`, `wmain()`, `WinMain()`, or `wWinMain()` function in a source file is treated as the entry point of a .NET executable assembly. By default, you do not write a `DllMain()` function for library assemblies, although you can do so, as shown here:

```
// managed C++
__declspec(dllexport) unsigned int
    __stdcall DllMain(unsigned int hinstDLL,
                      unsigned int fdwReason,
                      void* lpvReserved)
{
    return 0;
}
```

When the library assembly is loaded, the operating system will call the exported `DllMain()`. The interesting point is that this function will be IL and needs the runtime to be called. Indeed, you can use `__declspec(dllexport)` to export other managed functions and call them from native code. For example, here is a managed method:

```
// managed C++, compiled to a library assembly test.dll
__declspec(dllexport) void __stdcall Test()
{
    Console::WriteLine("in Test()");
}
```

This code is managed, and when you compile the library assembly, the compiler will generate an export library. The following native code can call this method:

```
// unmanaged C++
#pragma comment(lib, "test.lib")
__declspec(dllimport) void __stdcall Test();

void main()
{
    Test();
}
```

This code will compile, and when you run it the string will be printed on the console. In this case the calling code is native, and there is no code that loads and initiates the runtime. Later in this chapter I'll show you the code to explicitly start the runtime.

As with unmanaged C++ projects, the `main()` function for console applications can have zero parameters, or it can have parameters that give access to the command-line parameters and the environment variables (as mentioned in Chapter 1). The parameters of the entry point are unmanaged; managed parameters are *not* supported. In addition, if you indicate that `main()` returns a value, the compiler will return `0` by default, so the following is accepted:

```
// managed or unmanaged C++
int main()
{
}
```

The C++ compiler also allows you to write global methods that can be exposed as public .NET methods—for example:

```
// managed C++
String* GetTime()
{
    return DateTime::Now.ToString();
}
```

This method is not part of a class. It is a global method; consequently, you cannot access it through an object. You can call this method within the assembly where it is declared and just use the normal C++ function binding. If the method is declared in another assembly, the global method is treated as a module method. Every assembly is made up of modules. One module will have the name of the assembly. .NET treats a module as the object that implements global methods, but unfortunately, there is no direct method to call these methods, so you have to use reflection.

The `Module` class has a method called `GetMethod()` that will return a `MethodInfo` object for the global method that you identify. If the preceding code is compiled into a library assembly called `TimeFunc.dll`, the following code will locate and invoke the `GetTime()` method:

```
// managed C++
Assembly* as = Assembly::Load(S"TimeFunc");
Module* mod = as->GetModule(S"TimeFunc.dll");
MethodInfo* mi = mod->GetMethod(S"GetTime");
Console::WriteLine(mi->Invoke(mod, 0));
```

If `GetTime()` is the only global function in the library, you can shorten this code because the method will be treated as the entry point of the assembly, so you can access this method through the `EntryPoint` property. However, it is better to explicitly locate the method. You can use the keyword `static` to hide a global method so that it is not accessible through reflection:

```
// managed C++
static String* GetMachineName()
{
    return Environment::MachineName;
}
```

7.3 Using Managed Code in Unmanaged Code

In Chapter 4 I wrote about calling unmanaged code from managed code—but what about the opposite situation: calling managed code from unmanaged code? There are two issues to address: First, how do you call managed code from unmanaged code? Second, how do you manage the lifetimes of managed objects within unmanaged code? I will address the latter first.

7.3.1 Using Managed Types within Unmanaged Types

Imagine that you have a managed project. You know that the code will be compiled to IL, and you have code that runs in the .NET Runtime. Part of your code is unmanaged; it is compiled to __nogc types, which means that the code is IL but the data is created on the unmanaged C++ heap. Some of these types may be mixed; that is, they are created on the unmanaged heap (or the stack) but want to maintain pointers to managed objects. The problem here is that a reference will be maintained in the unmanaged world far out of the reach of the GC. Here is an example:

```
// managed C++
__nogc class F
{
    int* i;
public:
    F()
    {
        String* str = new String(S"hello");
        i = new int;
    }
};
```

This class is not managed, so the GC will not track the usage of instances of this class. Although the constructor is IL and hence the local variable `str` will be tracked by the GC (and released at the end of the constructor), the data member `i` will not be tracked, and this represents a memory leak. Indeed, if you look at the IL for this constructor, you'll find that `str` is created with the keyword `newobj`—the managed `new` operator—whereas `i` will be created with the C++ unmanaged `new` operator.

If you try to make `str` a class member, you'll get error C3265, which says that you cannot declare a managed type in an unmanaged type. The reason is that data members of the `__nogc` class will not be tracked by the GC, and thus the class itself has the responsibility to release its resources. This is fine for `i`, which was created by the unmanaged `new` operator because you can provide a destructor and call the unmanaged `delete` operator. However, there is no managed `delete` operator because the GC does that work.

The solution is to use the value type `System::Runtime::InteropServices::GCHandle`. This class allows you to create a type on the managed heap, and the pointer is held as an integer (hence a value type). The class has an operator that allows you to convert a managed pointer to an integer. The class also has a `Free()` method that you can use to release the managed object. The

`GCHandle` class has the combined advantages that you want: The compiler is happy that the unmanaged object does not have a managed pointer (because `GCHandle` holds an integer) and has the code to allow you to allocate and free managed objects. The VC team has provided a convenient C++ templated class called `gcroot<>` (in the `gcroot.h` header) that makes using `GCHandle` simple. For example, the following version of the class compiles fine, and there are no longer any memory leaks:

```
// managed C++
#include <vcclr.h> // includes gcroot.h
__nogc class F
{
   gcroot<String*> str;
   int* i;
public:
   F()
   {
      str = new String(S"hello");
      i = new int;
   }
   ~F()
   {
      delete i; // dtor of gcroot<> releases String
   }
};
```

The `gcroot.h` header is included by the `vcclr.h` header, which is a generic header created by the VC team for .NET utilities. This header also defines `PtrToStringChars()` to return an unmanaged (a pinned) `char*` pointer to the character array held by a `String` object, so you do not have to bother with getting the buffer offset or doing the pinning that I showed earlier.

7.3.2   Calling Managed Code

Your unmanaged code is allowed to *host* the .NET Runtime.[2] That is, Microsoft has provided the code that allows you to load and initialize the runtime, create an application domain, and load .NET objects. This code is—naturally—provided

---

2. For a more complete description of this mechanism, see Steven Pratschner's article "Implement a Custom Common Language Runtime Host for Your Managed App," *MSDN Magazine*, March 2001.

through a COM API. The prototypes for these functions and interfaces can be found in `mscoree.h`, and they are exported from `mscoree.dll`.

The first task is to load the runtime. To do this you need to call `CorBindTo-RuntimeEx()`. This function has five input parameters, and it returns an interface pointer in the final, out, parameter. The input parameters are used to specify (1) the CLSID of the runtime COM object, (2) the REFIID of the interface that interests you, and (3) the version of the runtime and details about it:

```
// unmanaged C++
CorBindToRuntimeEx(
    NULL, NULL,
    STARTUP_LOADER_OPTIMIZATION_SINGLE_DOMAIN,
    CLSID_CorRuntimeHost,
    IID_ICorRuntimeHost,
    (void**)&pHost);
```

The first parameter is a string that specifies the version, and the fact that I have used `NULL` indicates that I want the most current version installed on the machine. The second parameter is also a string and can be `L"wks"` or `L"svr"`, for the workstation or server version. Again I have used `NULL`, which will load the workstation version. Next come some flags that indicate the number of application domains I will use. I intend to have only one application domain.

Once you have created an instance of the runtime, you can use the `ICor-RuntimeHost` interface to create an application domain or to access an existing domain. Here is an example using ATL:

```
// unmanaged C++
#import <mscorlib.tlb> raw_interfaces_only
using namespace mscorlib;
#include <atlbase.h>
#include <stdio.h>
#pragma comment(lib, "mscoree.lib")

void main()
{
    if (SUCCEEDED(CoInitialize(NULL)))
    {
        CComPtr<ICorRuntimeHost> pHost;
        CorBindToRuntimeEx(
```

```
                NULL, NULL,
                STARTUP_LOADER_OPTIMIZATION_SINGLE_DOMAIN,
                CLSID_CorRuntimeHost,
                IID_ICorRuntimeHost,
                (void**)&pHost);
        pHost->Start();
        CComPtr<IUnknown> pDef;
        pHost->GetDefaultDomain(&pDef);
        CComPtr<_AppDomain> pAppDomain;
        pDef->QueryInterface(&pAppDomain);
        // see later...
    }
    CoUninitialize();
}
```

This code starts the CLR and then requests the default domain. The interface returned can be queried for the `dual` interface `_AppDomain`, which is the COM equivalent of `System.AppDomain`. You can use this interface to create instances of types from assemblies and then, through those types, call their methods. Earlier in this chapter I showed how to access a global method through the module of an assembly, so let's see how to do the same thing in unmanaged C++. Once you have the application domain object, you can load an assembly with the following code:

```
// unmanaged C++
CComPtr<_Assembly> pAssembly = NULL;
CComBSTR bstrAssembly(L"TimeFunc, Version=0.0.0.0, "
        L"Culture=neutral, PublicKeyToken=null");
pAppDomain->Load_2(bstrAssembly, &pAssembly);

CComPtr<_Module> pModule = NULL;
CComBSTR bstrModule(L"TimeFunc.dll");
pAssembly->GetModule(bstrModule, &pModule);
```

Through the pointer to the application domain object, we can load a specific assembly by calling `Load_2()`, passing the display name of the assembly. The display name is the complete name of the assembly, so it includes the version, culture, and public key hash from the strong name. If you check `System._AppDomain`, you'll see that there is no method called `Load_2()`. Instead there are seven versions of `Load()`. COM interfaces do no allow you to overload methods, but .NET does allow you to have overloaded methods on a class. To get around this inconsistency between COM and .NET, the `#import` directive adds a numbered suffix to distinguish between methods that are imported. Once the assembly has been loaded, the code calls `GetModule()` with the module name, and as I mentioned earlier, the default module has the name of the file that contains it. Although `GetModule()` appears to return a `dual` interface, `_Module` contains no methods, so instead you have to call `IDispatch::Invoke()`. The following code queries for `Module.GetMethod()`:

```
// unmanaged C++
OLECHAR* method = L"GetMethod_3";
DISPID dispid = 0;
pModule->GetIDsOfNames(IID_NULL, &method, 1,
                    LOCALE_SYSTEM_DEFAULT, &dispid);
CComVariant varRes;
CComVariant varArg(L"GetTime");
DISPPARAMS dp = {&varArg, NULL, 1, 0};
pModule->Invoke(dispid, IID_NULL, LOCALE_SYSTEM_DEFAULT,
                DISPATCH_METHOD, &dp, &varRes, NULL, NULL);
```

Again, because `GetMethod()` is overloaded, a suffix is used. This code obtains the DISPID of the method and then calls the method through `Invoke()`, passing the name of the module method that we wish to call. If the module has a method called `GetTime()`, the `VARIANT` will contain an `IUnknown` pointer to a `MethodInfo` object that describes the method. To call the method, the interface must be cast to a `_MethodInfo` interface, and then the appropriate `Invoke()` method can be called:

```
// unmanaged C++
CComPtr<_MethodInfo> mi;
varRes.punkVal->QueryInterface(&mi);
CComVariant varMod(pModule);
CComVariant varRet;
mi->Invoke_3(varMod, NULL, &varRet);
printf("the time is %S\n", varRet.bstrVal);
```

I hope you can see from this sample code that it is possible to call .NET types from unmanaged C++ code. However, I hope you can also see that doing so is not always straightforward. This code shows some inconsistencies: Some methods return `dual` interfaces (`Load_2()`), whereas others return a `dispinterface` (`GetModule()`). This complicates the code and means that you have to trawl through type libraries carefully to see what is being returned. Indeed, at one point while writing this code, I had to write some code to dump the type information of the returned interfaces before I could determine which method I could call! Once you have overcome these quirks, the code to access .NET objects resembles typical automation code.

7.4 Summary

.NET is a rich runtime environment. Visual Studio offers several options for writing .NET code, but most of the languages are deficient in one way or another. The language that gives you the best access to the .NET Runtime is C++. As you have seen in this chapter, C++ gives you better options for exporting code from assemblies and importing metadata than the other languages, and it gives you access to all of the .NET access specifiers. In addition, C++ is the only language that allows you to mix GC-managed and C++ heap objects, as well as native and IL code, in the same code module.

All in all, C++ is *the* language for .NET development, and I hope that you, like me, will recover from a brief flirtation with other .NET languages and return to the best language for the job: C++.

Chapter 8

Application Development

In this chapter I want to discuss the issues that will arise when you come to develop applications. A .NET application that lacks a user interface typically is made up of components, and UI applications consist of forms that have components and controls. Visual Studio.NET has been designed to make developing applications simple and to aid rapid application development (RAD) by allowing you to generate code simply by dragging and dropping components.

I will start by explaining what constitutes a component and what extra facility you get with controls. I will then show you how to develop a control that will integrate with the IDE's **Toolbox** and **Properties** windows, and how you can make it easier for the users of your controls to change their properties.

The world we live in moves day by day to a single global market, so it is extremely important that your application, components, and controls not be tied to a single locale. Internationalization in .NET is carried out with locale-specific resources. The VS.NET IDE has been designed to make the internationalizing process as simple as possible, and I'll show you how this works and how the localized resources are deployed. .NET resources are handled differently from Win32 resources, so I will show you how to create resources and how to include Win32 resources in your assemblies when .NET resources are deficient.

8.1 Developing Components

I mentioned in Chapter 6 that components are items that implement `ICompo-nent`. This interface derives from `IDisposable`, which means that components allow explicit management of their resources, and will inform interested classes when they are disposed of. In addition, the `IComponent` interface has a `Site` property that is initialized to the site of a container:

```csharp
// C#
public interface IComponent : IDisposable
{
    ISite Site { get; set; }
    event EventHandler Disposed;
    // IDisposable members
    void Dispose();
}
```

A container implements the `IContainer` interface:

```csharp
// C#
public interface IContainer : IDisposable
{
    ComponentCollection Components { get; }
    void Add(IComponent component);
    void Add(IComponent component, String string);
    void Remove(IComponent component);
    // IDisposable members
    void Dispose();
}
```

As the name suggests, the `ComponentCollection` class is an enumerable collection. The `Add()` and `Remove()` methods allow you to add components to this collection and remove them. The fact that `IContainer` derives from `IDisposable` is important because containers are used to hold resources (the components), so when an object that uses components is disposed of, the components should be disposed of, too, through the implementation of `IContainer.Dispose()`.

When you create a Windows Forms application you'll find that a container is created for you, as in this example:

```csharp
// C#
public class MyForm : System.Windows.Forms.Form
{
    private System.ComponentModel.Container
        components = null;
    public MyForm() { InitializeComponent(); }
```

```
    protected override void Dispose(bool disposing)
    {
        if (disposing)
        {
            if (components != null) components.Dispose();
        }
        base.Dispose( disposing );
    }
    private void InitializeComponent()
    {
        this.components =
            new System.ComponentModel.Container();
        this.Size = new System.Drawing.Size(300,300);
        this.Text = "My Form";
    }
}
```

The `container` member is not required. Indeed, if you write forms code by hand (e.g., in C++), you can dispense with the `container` member as long as you call `Dispose()` on each component.

The VS.NET **Toolbox** window contains a tab with standard components: classes for the event log, MSMQ queues, performance counters, and of course the timer component. These components lack a user interface, but you can still drag and drop them onto a form in the Windows Forms designer, which will generate code to add the component to the form class and will display that you are using the component by showing an icon at the bottom of the **Designer** window. You can access a component's properties by selecting the component in the **Designer** window and then switching to the **Properties** window.

Creating components is relatively straightforward. Your component, of course, must derive from `IComponent`, and the best way to do this is to derive from `Component`. The component will most likely be used as an item in the **Toolbox** window, so it will need a **Toolbox** image (which I'll explain later).

When you drag a component from the **Toolbox** window and drop it on a form in the **Designer** window, you are actually creating an instance of the component. It is important therefore that the component does not rely on constructor parameters; instead, your component should be initialized through properties. For example, look at how the `System.Timers.Timer` component is used.

When you drag and drop a timer onto a form, the generated code will create the component using its default constructor, and the interval of the timer is initialized through the `Interval` property, even though the `Timer` class has a constructor that takes an interval parameter.

Some components—for example, `EventLog` and `MessageQueue`—allow you to access resources. Such components are great examples of components because they consist of code that GUI applications will use, but they themselves do not have a UI. Your components are likely to give access to similar resources.

8.2 Developing Controls

I find the process of developing a control rather odd. The whole point about a control is that it has a visual element, but the Windows Forms designer does not show the visual representation of a class derived from `Control`. Instead it gives a schematic showing the components that the control uses that you've dragged from the **Server Explorer** or **Toolbox** window. This makes developing the visual aspect of a control a bit of a nuisance: In effect you have to add a forms project to your control solution with a form that contains the control so that as you develop the control, you can see the effects as you make them. You do not have this problem when developing a `UserControl` class because the designer shows the control as a captionless, borderless form onto which you can drag and drop controls from the **Toolbox** window.

In this section I will describe the process of developing a simple control and point out some of the issues you will face. `UserControl` is composed of other controls, so developing a `UserControl` object is similar to developing a `Control` object, except that you have the additional steps of adding controls from the **Toolbox** window and adding event handlers generated by these constituent controls.

8.2.1 Developing a Sample Control

The control that I'll develop, called `DiskSpace`, is shown in Figure 8.1. This control has a property called `Disk` that holds the logical name of a disk on your machine. The control will display in its area the name of the disk and either the size

Figure 8.1 **The** `DiskSpace` **control**

of the disk or the amount of free space available to the current user on the disk. Which of these sizes will be displayed is determined by another property, called `Display`. These properties can be changed at design time in the **Properties** window.

The first step is to create a control library. I will use C# as the development language so that I can use the designer tool for some of the work. The project type to use is the Windows Control Library project, and I will call my project `DiskData`. Once you have created the project, the first thing you'll notice is that the **Designer** window will start up showing a gray, borderless box. Don't be fooled; you get this because the project wizard has generated control code derived from `UserControl`. In this example the control should derive from `Control`, and you can make this change in a moment.

While the control is visible in the **Designer** window, you should select its properties (through the context menu) and change its name (in the **Name** field) to `DiskSpace`. Now switch to code view by selecting **View Code** from the control's context menu, and edit the code so that the `DiskSpace` class derives from `Control`. Because the designer is not much use for this code, and because the control will not use other components, it is safe to remove the code that the wizard added for the designer. Finally, by selecting **Rename** in the context menu of the **Solution Explorer** window, change the name of the code file from `UserControl1.cs` to `DiskSpace.cs`.

After all these changes, the class should look like this:

```
// C#
namespace DiskData
{
    public class DiskSpace : Control
```

```
    {
        public DiskSpace()
        {
        }
    }
}
```

If you now switch back to the designer, you'll see that the gray surface of the control has been removed, and there will be a message telling you to add components from the **Server Explorer** or the **Toolbox** window. The control has a UI and hence needs to draw itself. To do this it has to implement the OnPaint() method:

```
// C#
protected override void OnPaint(PaintEventArgs pe)
{
    Graphics g = pe.Graphics;
    g.FillRectangle(new SolidBrush(BackColor),
                    0, 0, Size.Width, Size.Height);
    g.DrawRectangle(new Pen(ForeColor),
                    0, 0,
                    Size.Width - 1, Size.Height - 1);
}
```

This code accesses the inherited properties BackColor and ForeColor; it fills the area of the control with the color specified by BackColor and draws a rectangle within the inside edge with the color specified by ForeColor. The area of the control is accessed through the Size property. Even though this control clearly has a user interface, the **Designer** window *still* does not give a visual representation, so the only way you can see what you are creating is by adding the control to a form.

Before doing this, you should close the **Designer** window, compile the project and then use **Solution Explorer** to add a new **Windows Application** project to the solution (I call my project CtrlTest). When this project is created, you'll see an empty form, and if you open the **Toolbox** window, you'll see **Components** and **Windows Forms** tabs. Select one of these tabs (or even create your own tab), and while the **Toolbox** window is open, switch to Windows Explorer, drag the DiskData.dll file from the bin\Debug folder of the project folder, and drop it on the **Toolbox** window. You'll see that the control will be added to the **Toolbox** window as shown in Figure 8.2. Notice that the image next to the control name is a cog. This is a standard image used when components don't specify a particular image; I'll explain how to change this later.

Now you can drag the `DiskSpace` control from the **Toolbox** window and drop it on the form, and you should see a gray square bordered by a black edge. As a quick test, grab one edge of the control and reduce the width or height; you'll see that the control does not repaint the edge that you have moved. Furthermore, if you increase the control's size, you'll see that the edge is moved but the interior is not repainted. The result is that lines appear on the control surface as the control is resized, as Figure 8.3 shows.

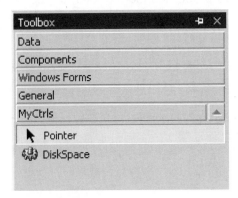

Figure 8.2   A control added to the Toolbox window

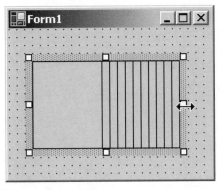

Figure 8.3   Resizing the control

The solution to this problem is to ensure that when the control is resized, it is redrawn. To do this you need to add the following method:

```csharp
// C#
protected override void OnSizeChanged(EventArgs e)
{
    Invalidate();
    base.OnSizeChanged(e);
}
```

When the control is resized, this method will be called. I handle the resize event by indicating that the entire control should be redrawn. I could be more sophisticated and track the size of the control and then invalidate only the area that has changed, but for this example my code is sufficient.

The control has two properties, so the following code needs to be added to the class:

```csharp
// C#
public enum DisplayOptions {TotalSize, FreeSpace};
private string disk = "C:\\";
private DisplayOptions
    display = DisplayOptions.TotalSize;
public string Disk
{
    get { return disk; }
    set
    {
        disk = value;
        Invalidate();
    }
}
public DisplayOptions Display
{
    get { return display; }
    set
    {
        display = value;
        Invalidate();
    }
}
```

The Display property indicates whether the size of the disk or its free space is shown, as identified by the enum. The Disk property indicates the drive to be displayed. If you compile the project at this point and then select the control on the test form, you'll see that the **Properties** window has been updated with the new properties (Figure 8.4). Furthermore, the **Properties** window reads the metadata of the control to see that the `Display` property can have one of two named values, and it will insert these values in a drop-down list box.

By default the **Properties** window allows you to either type in a value (as in the case with `Disk`) or select a value from a list, and the **Properties** window will do the appropriate *coercion* from the value you input to the type needed by the property. You can change this behavior by applying the `[TypeConverter]` attribute to the property and pass the type (or name) of a class derived from `TypeConverter` as the attribute parameter. In addition, you can provide values for a drop-down list box, or even provide a dialog to edit the property, as I'll show later.

Figure 8.4 shows the properties in alphabetical order. The properties can also be listed by category; to do this you need to use an attribute on the property—for example:

```
// C#
[Category("DiskSpace")]
public string Disk{/* code */}
[Category("DiskSpace")]
public DisplayOptions Display{/* code */}
```

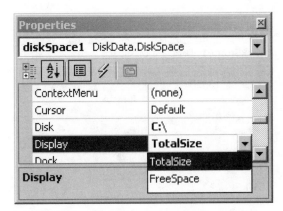

Figure 8.4   Properties window showing the new properties

The category can be one of the predefined categories documented in the MSDN entry for `System.ComponentModel.CategoryAttribute`, or you can create your own category, as I have done here. When you compile the assembly and look at the control's categorized properties, you'll see a new category called **DiskSpace**. Under this category are the two properties (see Figure 8.5).

The properties are shown in the **Properties** window because by default, all properties are browsable. If you want to indicate that the property should not be shown in the **Properties** window, you can use the `[Browsable(false)]` attribute. In a similar way, if you write code that uses an instance of the `DiskSpace` control, IntelliSense will show the property names in a list box when you type a period after the name of a variable of `DiskSpace` (for C#). You can use the `[EditorBrowsable]` attribute to alter this behavior: The parameter is `EditorBrowsableState`, and if you use the value `Never`, the property will not be shown in the IntelliSense list box; the default is `Always`. At the bottom of the **Properties** window is a space for a description of the property, and because these properties do not have descriptions, just the property name is given. To add a description to a property, you should use the `[Description]` attribute. Here are the changes:

```csharp
// C#
// initialized to default value
private string disk = "C:\\";
[ Category("DiskSpace"),
```

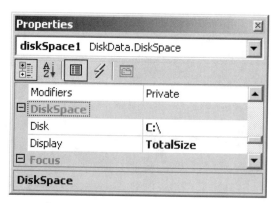

Figure 8.5 Categorized properties

```
      Browsable(true), EditorBrowsable,
        Description("The name of the disk") ]
    public string Disk  { /* code */ }
    [ Category("DiskSpace"),
        Browsable(true), EditorBrowsable,
        Description("Whether the total size or free "
                    + "space on the disk is shown") ]
    public DisplayOptions Display { /* code */ }
```

The name of the property given in the **Properties** window will be the name of the property in the class. You can use the [ParenthesizePropertyName] attribute to indicate that the name should be shown in parentheses, which means that the property will appear near the top of the **Properties** window when properties are shown in alphabetical view, or near the top of the category when they are shown in categorized view. You will notice that all of the screen shots of the **Properties** window that you have seen here show the values of the Disk and Display properties in bold. The **Properties** window uses the convention of showing in bold any properties that have been changed from their default values. This poses the question, How do you specify a default value?

There are two ways to do this. The first is to use the [DefaultValue] attribute on the property, passing the value as the constructor parameter. This option is fine for primitive types (the attribute constructor is overloaded for all of the base types). If the type is more complex, you can provide a string version of the default value, as well as the type to which the value should be converted, and the system will attempt to find a TypeConverter class to do the conversion. If there is no type converter, you can use the second way to specify a default value: adding two methods to the class with the names Reset<property>() and ShouldSerialize<property>(), where <property> is the property name. Reset<property>() should change the property to its default value, and ShouldSerialize<property>() should return a bool value indicating whether the property has a value other than its default. This last method gets its name from the fact that if the property does not have its default value, the value should be stored so that it can be used at runtime (for a form generated by the C# or VB.NET designer, this means initializing the control's property with the value).

If the property has a default value, the value does not need to be serialized because when the control is created, the property will have the default value.

Your implementation of the property must be initialized to the default value. Examples of the `Reset<property>()` and `ShouldSerialize<property>()` methods are shown in the following code:

```csharp
// C#
// initialized to default value
private string disk = "C:\\";
[  Category("DiskSpace"),
   Browsable(true), EditorBrowsable,
   Description("The name of the disk"),
   DefaultValue("C:\\") ]
public string Disk  { /* code */ }
// default value
private DisplayOptions
    display = DisplayOptions.TotalSize;
[ Category("DiskSpace"),
   Browsable(true), EditorBrowsable,
   Description("Whether the total size or free "
              + "space on the disk is shown") ]
public DisplayOptions Display { /* code */ }
public void ResetDisplay()
{ display = DisplayOptions.TotalSize; }
public bool ShouldSerializeDisplay()
{ return display != DisplayOptions.TotalSize; }
```

In both cases you'll find that the property value will be shown in normal text if it is the default value.

Properties can be changed at runtime, and the change in a property value can have effects on other code. A good example is the `Size` property of a control: If the size changes, in most cases the control will need to be redrawn; thus you need to catch the event of the property changing. This is what I showed earlier with the code that overrides the `OnSizeChanged()` method. You should also add events that are generated when your properties change, by adding an event and an event generation method, as illustrated here:

```csharp
// C#
public event EventHandler DiskChanged;
public event EventHandler DisplayChanged;
protected virtual void OnDiskChanged(EventArgs e)
{ if (DiskChanged != null) DiskChanged(this, e); }
protected virtual void OnDisplayChanged(EventArgs e)
```

DEVELOPING APPLICATIONS WITH VISUAL STUDIO.NET

```
{
    if (DisplayChanged != null)
        DisplayChanged(this, e);
}
```

The event generation method should be named `On<property>Changed()` and should generate the event. The `set` methods for the properties should call this method:

```
// C#
public string Disk
{   get { return disk; }
    set { disk = value;
          OnDiskChanged(null);
          Invalidate(); }
}
public DisplayOptions Display
{   get { return display; }
    set { display = value;
          OnDisplayChanged(null);
          Invalidate(); }
}
```

Sometimes several properties may depend on one property. If that is the case, when that property changes the dependent properties will change too. In this case the **Properties** window should refresh all the values. To indicate this requirement, such a property should be marked with the `[RefreshProperties]` attribute.

The next task that needs to be carried out for this control is to make it actually do something! The first thing is to implement the `Disk` property so that it checks that the value passed to the property is valid:

```
// C#
public string Disk
{
    get { return disk; }
    set { string str;
          str = Char.ToUpper(value[0]) + ":\\";
          string[] disks
              = Environment.GetLogicalDrives();
          if (Array.BinarySearch(disks, str) < 0)
              throw new IOException(value
                       + " is not a valid drive");
```

```
        disk = str;
        OnDiskChanged(null);
        Invalidate(); }
}
```

For this code to compile, you will need to add a `using` statement for the `System.IO` namespace at the top of the file. First I construct the disk name; then I obtain the list of logical drives on the current machine and perform a binary search to see if the requested disk is within the array of logical drive names. Now that I have a valid drive name, I need to obtain the size of the disk. I do this through interop to call the Win32 `GetDiskFreeSpace()` method:

```csharp
// C#
[ DllImport("kernel32", CharSet=CharSet.Auto,
  SetLastError = true) ]
static extern bool GetDiskFreeSpace(
    string strRoot, out uint sectersPerCluster,
    out uint bytesPerSector, out uint numFreeClusters,
    out uint totalClusters);
protected override void OnPaint(PaintEventArgs pe)
{
    Graphics g = pe.Graphics;
    g.FillRectangle(new SolidBrush(BackColor),
                    0, 0,
                    Size.Width, Size.Height);
    g.DrawRectangle(new Pen(ForeColor),
                    0, 0,
                    Size.Width-1, Size.Height-1);
    uint spc, bps, fc, tc;
    GetDiskFreeSpace(disk, out spc, out bps,
                     out fc, out tc);
    long free, total;
    long bPerCluster = (spc*bps);
    free = bPerCluster*fc/(1024*1024);
    total = bPerCluster*tc/(1024*1024);
    StringFormat sf = new StringFormat();
    sf.Alignment = StringAlignment.Center;
    sf.LineAlignment = StringAlignment.Center;
    string str;
    if (display == DisplayOptions.FreeSpace)
        str = disk + " " + free + "Mb";
    else
```

```
            str = disk + " " + total + "Mb";
      g.DrawString(str, this.Font,
                   new SolidBrush(ForeColor),
                   new RectangleF(0, 0,
                         Size.Width, Size.Height),
                   sf);
  }
```

For this code to compile, you should add a `using` statement for the `System.Runtime.InteropServices` namespace to the top of the file. The `OnPaint()` method calls the imported `GetDiskFreeSpace()` function and passes the `Disk` property. Depending on the value of `Display`, the string printed on the control is formatted as showing the total space on the disk or just the free space. Notice again how the control's properties are used. In the `DrawString()` method at the end of `OnPaint()`, I draw the string in the color specified by `ForeColor`, using the default font for the control.

Once you have rebuilt the control, you should be able to view it on the test form, and you should be able to change the `Disk` and `Display` properties and see the control on the form change its view at design time. Before I leave this section, I ought to explain one property that you'll see in the **Properties** window: the parenthesized `DynamicProperties` complex property, which will have a subproperty with the parenthesized name `Advanced`. If you select this property, you get a list of most of the properties that the control supports and a check box next to each. If you check a property in this list, the designer will add a section for the property in the application's `.config` file (an XML file that is installed in the same folder as the application), and at runtime when the control is loaded, its values will be set according to the values in this `.config` file. For example, if I use `DynamicProperties` to select the `Disk` property, the `.config` file will look like this:[1]

```
<configuration>
  <appSettings>
    <add key="diskSpace1.Disk" value="D:\" />
  </appSettings>
</configuration>
```

---

1. You will need to build the project to get the values written to the `.config` file.

Here I have specified that the `Disk` property of the control `diskSpace1` should have the value `D:\` when the control is loaded. The code on the form can still change this property; however, this is a useful facility because it allows you to give your users some control over how the controls on your forms are initialized.

8.2.2 Property Editor

When you type a value into the **Properties** window, what you are actually typing is a text value. Some types—for example, `Point`—are complex and are made up of subtypes. The **Properties** window reads the type of the property, recognizes that the property has subtypes, and displays these subtypes in the grid as nodes in a tree view. The grid allows you to edit each subobject individually or, through an editor class, the entire property as one.

When the values of the property have been edited, the values are converted to the appropriate types through a converter class. The framework type converter classes are shown in Table 8.1. If your type is not covered by one of these converters, you can create your own converter by deriving from `Type-Converter` and then pass the type of this class to the constructor of the `[TypeConverter]` attribute, which you should apply to the definition of the type that is converted.

Table 8.1 Type converter classes

ArrayConverter	DecimalConverter	SByteConverter
BaseNumberConverter	DoubleConverter	SingleConverter
BooleanConverter	EnumConverter	StringConverter
ByteConverter	ExpandableObjectConverter	TimeSpanConverter
CharConverter	GuidConverter	TypeConverter
CollectionConverter	Int16Converter	TypeListConverter
ComponentConverter	Int32Converter	UInt16Converter
CultureInfoConverter	Int64Converter	UInt32Converter
DateTimeConverter	ReferenceConverter	UInt64Converter

DEVELOPING APPLICATIONS WITH VISUAL STUDIO.NET

Imagine that you have developed a control class that has an array property:

```
// C#
int[] b = new int[4];
public byte[] Data
{
    get { return b; }
    set { b = value; }
}
```

When you view the property in the **Properties** window, you'll see it shown as its constituent parts, and you can edit each item. If you select the property itself, an ellipsis button will appear (see Figure 8.6); and when you click this button, an appropriate UI editor will be shown. In the case of an array of Int32 members, the **Int32 Collection Editor** will be shown (Figure 8.7). This editor allows you to edit the values in the array, and to add and remove items in the array.

You can also write your own editor. For example, imagine that you want to create an editor for the Disk property so that it gives you only the option of the disks that are available on the current machine. The first action is to design an appropriate editor dialog, by adding a form to the project called DiskEditor.cs through the **Solution Explorer** window. Next you edit the class to look like this:

```
// C#
public class DiskEditor : Form
{
    private ComboBox cbDisks;
    private Button btnOK;
    private Container components = null;
    private string str;
    public string Value { get { return str; } }
```

Data	Int32[] Array ...
[0]	0
[1]	0
[2]	0
[3]	0

Figure 8.6   Array property in the Properties window

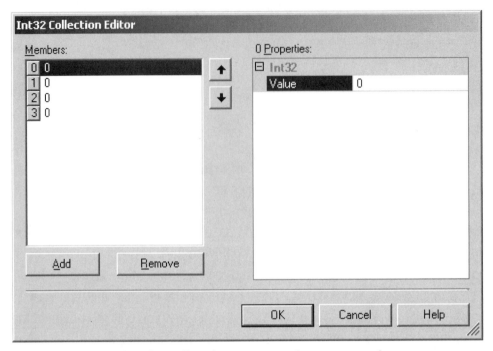

Figure 8.7   The collection editor for an array of `Int32` **members**

```
public DiskEditor(string currentVal)
{
    str = currentVal;
    ClientSize = new Size(120, 70);
    components = new Container();
    cbDisks = new ComboBox();
    components.Add(cbDisks);
    cbDisks.DropDownStyle
        = ComboBoxStyle.DropDownList;
    cbDisks.Location = new Point(10, 10);
    cbDisks.Size = new Size(100, 20);
    string[] disks
        = Environment.GetLogicalDrives();
    cbDisks.Items.AddRange(disks);
    cbDisks.Text = (string)cbDisks
                    .Items[cbDisks.FindString(str)];
    btnOK = new Button();
    components.Add(btnOK);
    btnOK.Location = new Point(30, 40);
    btnOK.Size = new Size(60, 20);
```

```
        btnOK.Text = "OK";
        btnOK.Click += new EventHandler(OnOK);
        Controls.AddRange(
            new Control[] {btnOK, cbDisks});
        FormBorderStyle = FormBorderStyle.FixedDialog;
        Text = "Disks";
    }
    protected override void Dispose( bool disposing )
    {
        if (disposing)
            if (components != null)
                components.Dispose();
        base.Dispose( disposing );
    }
    private void OnOK(object sender, EventArgs e)
    { Close(); }
    protected override void OnClosing(CancelEventArgs e)
    { str = (string)cbDisks.SelectedItem ; }
}
```

The `DiskEditor` constructor takes the current value of the property. The dialog has two controls: a drop-down list box that is initialized to the logical disk drives on the machine, and an **OK** button that, when clicked, will close the dialog. The form has a property called `Value` that is initialized to the disk that you selected, and this property is updated when the dialog closes.

Next you need a class derived from `UITypeEditor` that will be called to determine how the type should be edited. The `GetEditStyle()` method is called by the **Properties** window to determine how the value should be edited. `UITypeEditorEditStyle` has three values: `None`, which means that no UI element will be used to edit the value; `DropDown`, which means that a drop-down list will be shown; and `Modal`, which means that a modal dialog will be shown. I will first show an example of using a modal dialog. In this case the type editor class in `DiskEditor.cs` should be edited to look like this:

```
// C#
public class DiskTypeEditor : UITypeEditor
{
    public override object EditValue(
        ITypeDescriptorContext context,
        IServiceProvider provider, object value)
```

```
    {
        IWindowsFormsEditorService edSvc;
        edSvc = (IWindowsFormsEditorService)
                provider.GetService(
                    typeof(IWindowsFormsEditorService));
        DiskEditor editorForm;
        editorForm = new DiskEditor((string)value);
        edSvc.ShowDialog(editorForm);
        return editorForm.Value;
    }
    public override
        UITypeEditorEditStyle GetEditStyle(
            ITypeDescriptorContext context)
    { return UITypeEditorEditStyle.Modal; }
}
```

For this code to compile you need to add a `using` statement for both the `System.Drawing.Design` and `System.Windows.Forms.Design` namespaces to the top of the file. After the `GetEditStyle()` method is called, the **Properties** window will show either an ellipsis button (for the modal dialog) or a down-arrow button (for a drop-down list). When this UI button is clicked, the `EditValue()` method will be called to create the dialog to fill the list. The code here shows how to create the form. The first parameter of `EditValue()` provides information about the container, the **Properties** window. The second parameter gives access to the services that the **Properties** window provides, and in this case I request `IWindowsFormsEditorService`, which I use to call `ShowDialog()` to show the modal form. The final parameter of the method is the actual property that is being edited, so this parameter is used to initialize the form. When the modal form is closed, `ShowDialog()` will return; I access the value that the user selected through the `DiskEditor.Value` property. The final step is to indicate that a property will be edited with this particular editor; for this purpose the `[Editor]` attribute is used as follows:

```
// C#
[ Editor(typeof(DiskTypeEditor),
  typeof(UITypeEditor)) ]
public string Disk { /* code */ }
```

You will need to add a `using` statement for the `System.Drawing.Design` namespace to the top of the `DiskSpace.cs` file. Now when the ellipsis box of the `Disk` property is clicked, the dialog will be shown (Figure 8.8). When the dialog is dismissed, the selected value will be written to the property.

It may seem a little over the top to have a whole dialog to present this data; the alternative is to use a drop-down list box, which the following class does, and you should add to the `DiskEditor.cs` file:

```csharp
// C#
public class DiskTypeEditor2 : UITypeEditor
{
    private IWindowsFormsEditorService edSvc;
    public override object EditValue(
        ITypeDescriptorContext context,
        IServiceProvider provider, object value)
    {
        edSvc = (IWindowsFormsEditorService)
                provider.GetService(
                    typeof(IWindowsFormsEditorService));
        ListBox cbDisks;
        cbDisks = new ListBox();
        string[] disks = Environment.GetLogicalDrives();
        cbDisks.Items.AddRange(disks);
        cbDisks.Text = (string)cbDisks
            .Items[cbDisks.FindString((string)value)];
        cbDisks.SelectedValueChanged
            += new EventHandler(TextChanged);
        edSvc.DropDownControl(cbDisks);
        return cbDisks.Text;
    }
    public override UITypeEditorEditStyle
        GetEditStyle(
            ITypeDescriptorContext context)
    { return UITypeEditorEditStyle.DropDown; }
```

Figure 8.8 The disk editor dialog

```
      private void TextChanged(
         object sender, EventArgs e)
      { if (edSvc != null) edSvc.CloseDropDown(); }
   }
```

The GetEditStyle() method of the DiskTypeEditor2 class returns UITypeEditorEditStyle.DropDown to indicate that the **Properties** window should show the down arrow button. The EditValue() method creates a list box and initializes it with the names of the logical disks. This list box is shown by a call to the blocking method IWindowsFormsEditorService.Drop-DownControl(), and it is removed by a call to CloseDropDown(). The user expects to have drop-down list box behavior; that is, when an item is selected, the drop-down box should be removed. To get this behavior I add a handler to the list box that calls CloseDropDown(), which makes the blocked Drop-DownControl() method return. At this point I can access from the list box control the item that was selected and return it from EditValue().

8.2.3 Licensing

Controls can be licensed; therefore you can add code to check whether the control is being used in a context where it is permitted. The licensing model recognizes two contexts: *design time* and *runtime*. Design time is the time when the control is being used in a designer (such as the Windows Forms designer) and as part of other code, such as a form. A developer must have a design-time license to be able to integrate your control into his application. Once the application has been compiled, it will be distributed to users and run, creating a new situation: The licensed control will perform a check for a runtime license when the application is run; if the runtime license is valid, the control can be created.

Having two licenses like this means that you can have a licensing scheme that is more secure for the design time than for the runtime. The licensing is based on a class called a *license provider* that is called to generate a license when an attempt is made to instantiate the object. Here is a license provider class:

```
// C#
public class LicProvider : LicenseProvider
```

```
{
    public override License GetLicense(
        LicenseContext context,
        Type type, object instance,
        bool allowExceptions)
    {
        if (context.UsageMode
                == LicenseUsageMode.Designtime)
        {
            if (!CheckForLicense())
            {
                if (!allowExceptions)
                    return null;
                throw new LicenseException(GetType());
            }
            return new MyLic(type.Name
                            + " design time");
        }
        else
            return new MyLic(type.Name
                            + " runtime time");
    }
}
```

This provider is passed a `LicenseContext` object that indicates the context in which the license is being requested—either `LicenseUsage-Mode.Designtime` or `Runtime`. Your license provider can then check whether the license is available (as my method `CheckForLicense()` does)—for example, by looking for the location of a valid license file or a registry value. If the check succeeds, a new license can be created. If the license check fails, the license provider should throw a `LicenseException` exception if `allowExceptions` is `true` or just return `null` if it is `false`. In this example I have decided that the control should be freely available at runtime, so I don't perform any runtime checks; I merely return the license.

The license object should derive from `License` and provide implementations of the `LicenseKey` property and the `Dispose()` method. In my implementation I simply store a string:

```
// C#
public class MyLic : License
```

```
    {
        string str;
        public MyLic(string t){ str = t; }
        public override string LicenseKey
        { get { return str; } }
        public override void Dispose(){}
    }
```

The `LicenseKey` property is not intended to be a secure key. Instead it should be treated as an opaque cookie—an encoded string perhaps—that gives access to other data. This string could be stored as a resource in an assembly.

The license provider is associated with the control through the `[LicenseProvider]` attribute, and the control should call the `LicenseManager` object to check that the license is valid:

```
// C#
[LicenseProvider(typeof(LicProvider))]
public class DiskSpace : Control
{
    public DiskSpace()
    {
        LicenseManager.Validate(
            typeof(DiskSpace), this);
    }
    // code
}
```

If the control is not licensed, the call will throw an exception. If this happens in the Windows Forms designer, you'll get a message like the one shown in Figure 8.9. If the call to `Validate()` fails at runtime (a runtime license was not available), a `LicenseException` exception will be thrown. In the code I show

An error occurred while loading the document. Fix the error, and then try loading the document again. The error message follows:

An exception occurred while trying to create an instance of DiskData.DiskSpace. The exception was "An instance of type 'DiskData.DiskSpace' was being created, and a valid license could not be granted for the type 'DiskData.DiskSpace'. Please contact the manufacturer of the component for more information.".

Figure 8.9   Error message received if a form opened in the Windows Forms designer has a control that is not licensed

here I do not catch this exception because I want to make sure that if `Vali-date()` fails, the control will not load.

The Framework Class Library comes with one implementation of `License` called `LicFileLicenseProvider`. `LicFileLicenseProvider` will check for the existence of a license file, in much the same way as many ActiveX controls are licensed today.

8.2.4 Toolbox Items

The **Toolbox** can take any item derived from `IComponent`. When you add a control to the **Toolbox** window, the control will be shown with the standard control bitmap image, a cog. To change this image you have to apply the `[ToolboxBitmap]` attribute to the control class. The image should be a 16×16 bitmap embedded as part of your assembly, and it should have the same name as your class; for example, if your class is called `DiskSpace`, the bitmap should be called `DiskSpace.bmp`. To add the bitmap you use the C# **Solution Explorer** window's **Add New Item** on the **Add** context menu. The bitmap should be an embedded resource (which I'll explain later), so through the bitmap's **Properties** window you should change its **Build Action** property to **Embedded Resource**. Finally, the constructor parameter of the `[ToolboxBitmap]` attribute should take the type of the class to which it is applied:

```
// C#
[ToolboxBitmap(typeof(DiskSpace))]
public class DiskSpace : Control
{
    // code
}
```

For this new bitmap to be shown in the **Toolbox** window, you will need to remove the old control (from the context menu, select **Delete**) and then add it again by dragging and dropping it from Windows Explorer to a tab in the **Toolbox** window.

8.3 Resources and Internationalization

.NET supports a different model of resources from that supported by Win32. In Win32, resources are held in a section that is part of the PE (portable executable) file format; the resources are embedded within this segment. .NET resources are part of an assembly, but they can be embedded within the assembly or supplied as separate files. In this section I'll explain how resources are generated with Visual Studio.NET and how your code can access them.

8.3.1 Resources and .NET

.NET has been designed with internationalization in mind. Imagine that you download an application from a Web site that you trust and the Web site is in a locale different from yours. You would expect the application's developers to have created the application in their own locale. However, if the language is different from yours, you will hope that the application has been localized to your locale and that the Web site gives you the option of downloading different localized versions. Win32 applications typically used this scheme. It is possible in Win32 to create resource DLLs for locale-specific resources, but this means that the developer has to explicitly load the resource from the DLL.

.NET allows you to create locale-specific resources, but it is far more sophisticated than Win32 because the Framework Class Library provides a class (`ResourceManager`) that will automatically load the resources for the current locale. These resources can be part of the current assembly, or they can be part of a separate assembly called a *satellite assembly*.

8.3.2 Locales, Cultures, and Languages

.NET uses the naming convention defined in RFC 1766. Cultures are named with the following pattern: `xx-yy`, where the two letters `xx` represent a language (e.g., `en` for English, `de` for German, or `fr` for French), and `yy` represents an area where that language is used (e.g., `GB` for the United Kingdom, `AU` for Australia, and `US` for the United States). Together, a language and an area represent a particular *culture*, so `en-US` represents English spoken in the US and implies hamburgers, Coke, and baseball. Whereas `en-GB` is the Queen's English and implies roast beef, tea in china cups, and cricket. (Well, you get the idea.) Without the area (e.g., `en`), a resource is area neutral; without a language, a resource is both language and area neutral. Most cultures can be represented by this four-letter style, but if further delineation is required, you can add extra pairs of letters.

The Framework Class Library provides the `CultureInfo` class to represent a particular culture. You can initialize this class by passing to the constructor either the RFC 1766 string or a locale ID (LCID). As I mentioned in Chapter 2, a culture can be used to format items like dates:

```
// C#
CultureInfo ci = CultureInfo("en-GB");
Console.WriteLine(DateTime.Now.ToString(
    "F", ci.DateTimeFormat));
```

Here the date is printed at the command line in the UK format. Because different cultures that use the same language have different rules for formatting, the `CultureInfo` class must be initialized with enough information, and a language identifier is not enough. If you do not specifically use a culture in format code, the current culture will be used. This culture is a per-thread value and is a read/write property of the current thread:

```
// C#
CultureInfo ci = CultureInfo("en-GB");
System.Threading.Thread
    .CurrentThread.CurrentCulture = ci;
Console.WriteLine(DateTime.Now.ToString());
```

.NET resources are not as strict as formatting code, so the `ResourceManager` class (which is used to locate and load locale-specific resources) allows you to provide resources that are totally neutral, area neutral, or culture specific. Again, this information is set on a per-thread basis through the `Thread.CurrentUICulture` property.

8.3.3 Creating Resources

Assemblies contain either compiled resources or uncompiled resources, and these can be either embedded within the assembly or supplied as a separate file and a link provided within the manifest of the assembly. Resources in an assembly are named. For example, here is some IL:

```
// IL
.assembly App
{
```

```
   .hash algorithm 0x00008004
   .ver 0:0:0:0
}
.mresource public MyRes.resources
{
}
.module App.exe
```

This code indicates that an assembly called `App.exe` has a resource called `MyRes.resources`, which can contain several items, but ILDASM does not decompile the resource format, so these resources are not shown in IL. If the resource is a compiled resource, it can be read with the classes in `System.Resources`, as I'll explain in a moment. Otherwise the resource should be read as a single item, through the assembly object.

A resource can be embedded in an assembly with the C# compiler through the `/res` switch:

```
csc /res:MyRes.resources app.cs
```

This command will compile a C# file called `app.cs` and embed an already compiled resource called `MyRes.resources` in the assembly. The resource in the assembly will also be called `MyRes.resources`. If this is not what you want, you can append the switch with the name of the resource (separated by a comma).

The C++ linker has an `/assemblyresource` switch that you can use to embed a resource in an assembly. The resource will have the name of the resource file that you embed, and unlike the C# compiler, you cannot rename it through the switch:

```
link /out:app.exe
   /assemblyresource:MyRes.resources app.obj
```

If the resource is not compiled, it can be read only by explicit access of the resource through the assembly manifest:

```
// C#
Assembly assem
   = Assembly.GetCallingAssembly();
Stream stm;
```

```
stm = assem.GetManifestResourceStream(
    "MyRes.resources");
```

This code will return a stream that has all of the resource. It does not matter whether this resource is compiled, uncompiled, linked, or embedded. The following code will print out this stream to the command line:

```
// C#
while(true)
{
    int i = stm.ReadByte();
    if (i == -1) break;
    if (i < 32 || i > 127)
        Console.Write(".");
    else
        Console.Write((char)i);
}
Console.WriteLine();
```

An assembly can have a link to a resource. You can create this link with the C# compiler using the /linkres switch:

```
csc /linkres:data.txt,MyRes.resources app.cs
```

This command will compile the file app.cs, add a link to the file data.txt, and call the resource MyRes.resources. Clearly, if the resource is linked, it must be available through the link at runtime. Here is the IL produced by the preceding code:

```
// IL
.file nometadata data.txt
    .hash = (1E 7B 82 95 E5 DA 4B 04
             7A 56 47 DE EE C2 E7 7E
             1D 19 26 90 )
.mresource public MyRes.resources
{
    .file data.txt at 0x00000000
}
```

The resgen tool is used to compile or decompile resources. When resources are being compiled, the input can be either a text file (with the extension .txt) or an XML file (with the extension .resx). The text file can be used only for string resources; it is structured as a series of name/value pairs with the two separated by an equal sign. Here is an example:

```
; text resource file
ErrNoFile=File {0} cannot be found
MsgStarted=Application has started
```

The code that uses the resources refers to the first string with the identifier ErrNoFile. If you want to use binary resources (e.g., images), you have to use XML resources. The XML file equivalent to the name/value pairs just shown is as follows:

```
<?xml version="1.0" encoding="utf-8"?>
<!-- schema -->
<root>
  <data name="MsgStarted">
    <value>Application has started</value>
  </data>
  <data name="ErrNoFile">
    <value>File {0} cannot be found</value>
  </data>
  <resheader name="ResMimeType">
    <value>text/microsoft-resx</value>
  </resheader>
  <resheader name="Version">
    <value>1.0.0.0</value>
  </resheader>
  <resheader name="Reader">
    <value>
      System.Resources.ResXResourceReader
    </value>
  </resheader>
  <resheader name="Writer">
    <value>
      System.Resources.ResXResourceWriter
    </value>
  </resheader>
</root>
```

The <resheader> nodes give information about the format of the resources and the names of the classes used to read and write the resources. All of these <resheader> nodes except the Version node are required. For space reasons, I have not shown the schema, but in any case it is not needed. Although it is possible to write .resx files by hand, it is much easier to use the

VS.NET IDE, especially when you consider binary resources. Binary resources still have to have `<value>` nodes in the XML file, and to do this they must be converted to a readable format by something like base64 encoding. It is much easier to allow the IDE to do this for you, as I'll show in the next section.

`resgen` can also be used to decompile resources. If the input file has the extension `.resources`, `resgen` knows that it has to decompile resources. It determines the format that you require by the extension of the output file you specify. The general process of compiling resources is shown in Figure 8.10.

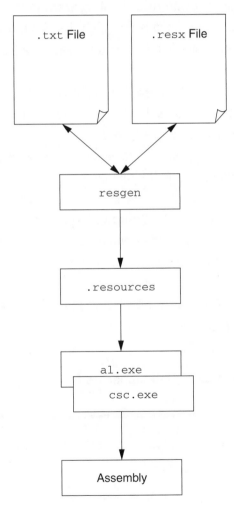

Figure 8.10   Resource compilation process

8.3.4 Managed C++ and Resources

Managed C++ projects allow you to add resources through the **Solution Explorer** or **Class View** window, but these will be Win32 resources. If you want to add your own .NET resources, you need to edit the project settings. Here are the steps: First you need to add an XML file to your project. To do this you should use the **Add New Item** dialog of **Solution Explorer**, and ensure that the extension of the file is `.resx` (the `resgen` utility insists that XML resource files have this extension). If you forget to give the file this extension, you will have to remove the file from the project, rename it using Windows Explorer, and add the renamed file to the project with **Add Existing Item** from the C++ **Solution Explorer** context menu. The reason is that the C++ **Solution Explorer** (unlike the C# **Solution Explorer**) does not allow you to rename a file that has been added to a project.

Once you have added the `.resx` file to the project, you should add the bare minimum of resource file contents: the `<root>` node and the three `<resheader>` nodes I mentioned earlier: `ResMimeType`, `Reader`, and `Writer`. After that it makes sense to add at least one `<data>` node (essentially as a template), and then you can edit the resource file using the XML designer.

The next task is to add the `.resx` file to the build. To do this you should select properties of this file from the **Solution Explorer** context menu by selecting **General Configuration Properties** and making sure that the **Tool** property option selected is **Custom Build Tool**. You can then set the tools command line through the **Custom Build Step** option (Table 8.2).

Choosing **Custom Build Step** will allow you to build the resource; however, you also need to embed the resource in the assembly, and to do this you need to edit

Table 8.2 Custom Build Step properties for an `.resx` file

Property	Value
Command Line	`resgen $(InputFileName)` `$(OutDir)\$(InputName).resources`
Description	`Building .NET resources`
Outputs	`$(OutDir)\$(InputName).resources`

the linker options. You select the properties of the project through the **Solution Explorer** window, and then in the **Property Pages** dialog you select the **Linker** node and then the **Input** node. Within the grid you'll see a property called **Embed Managed Resource File**; you change the value of this property as follows:

```
$(OutDir)\$(InputName).resources
```

This parameter assumes that the name of the `.resx` file that was compiled had the same name as the project. Once you have made these changes, you should be able to add string resources to the project through the `.resx` file.

Image files are not so easy; the problem is that you have to encode image files into a format that can be put in an XML file. A utility called `resxgen` will allow you to do this; it is supplied as an example in the .NET Framework `Samples` folder. However, the problem with this tool is that it will generate an entire `.resx` file from a single binary file. You cannot use it to add a binary resource to an existing `.resx` file.

8.3.5   C# and Resources

In this section I will give just a basic overview of using resources in C# projects; the sections that follow will go into more detail. To add a resource to a C# project you use the **Add Class** dialog of **Solution Explorer**. The **Resources** category shows that you can add bitmaps, icons, cursors, and string resource files. The resource files that it mentions here are `.resx` files that you'll typically use to add strings to the assembly, similar to adding a string table in a Win32 resource file. `.resx` files are XML files and are used as an input to the resource compiler, `resgen`, which I'll cover later. These resource files can also contain binary data like icons, but the data is stored in the `.resx` file as base64 encoded.

When you add one of the image files to the project, you can use the item's properties to see how the resource will be added to the assembly. **Build Action** gives the options of **None**, **Compile**, **Content**, and **Embedded Resource**. **Content** does not add the resource to the assembly, but it does indicate that the file should be deployed with the output of the project; **Compile** requires that you specify the compile tool through the **Custom Tool** property, and **Embedded Resource** will add the resource to the assembly without compiling.

For example, if you add an icon to your project and change its **Build Action** value to **Embedded Resource**, you will get the following IL when you build the assembly:

```
// IL
.mresource public myAssem.myIcon.ico
{
}
```

Here the icon file is called `myIcon.ico`, and the assembly is called `myAssem.` You can read this resource using `Assembly.GetManifest-ResourceStream()` and pass the stream as a construction parameter to the `Icon` class. For example, the following code loads an embedded resource as an icon for the `NotifyIcon` class that is used to create a tray icon:

```
// C#
// NotifyIcon trayIcon is a private class member
// this code is in constructor and components
// is the Container created in InitializeComponents
trayIcon = new NotifyIcon(components);
Assembly assem = Assembly.GetExecutingAssembly();
// assembly is called Tray; icon file is called MyIcon.ico
trayIcon.Icon = new Icon(
    assem.GetManifestResourceStream(
        "Tray.MyIcon.ico"));
```

Other resources, such as bitmaps and cursors, can also be loaded in this way. If you add a resource to a project as **Content**, it will be distributed with the output of the project as a separate file. Note that this is *not* the same as being part of a multifile assembly, as I mentioned in Chapter 1. When you add a link to an external resource file (through the `/linkres` switch to `csc`), the compiler will add a hash of the resource file to metadata in the assembly's manifest. To get the names of all such resources, you can use `Assembly.GetMani-festResourceNames()`, and the names returned can be passed to the constructor of `Icon`, `Cursor`, or `Bitmap` to load the resource. When you specify that the **Build Action** value of a resource is **Content**, there will be no information about this in the assembly's manifest, so your code needs to know the name of the file.

As you'll see in a moment, the icon for a form is shown as a property for that form when viewed in the **Designer** window. However, the **Cursor** property shows only standard cursors in the **Properties** window. If you want to use a custom cursor, you can simply add a cursor as an embedded resource and use code similar to that shown here to load the cursor and make it the cursor for the form.

When you add an icon to a project, the wizard will show a 32×32 icon with 16 colors. This size is fine for the large-icon view in Windows Explorer, but it is too large for the form's icon. Icon files can contain images of different sizes and color depth, and it turns out that the icon created by the wizard also has a 16×16 icon image with 16 colors. To switch between the two sizes, you should select **Current Icon Image Types** on the **Image** menu (or use the `Image.MoreIcons` command, which will list all the icons). If you want to add another icon type to the icon, there is a **New Icon Type** menu icon (for the command `Image.NewImageType`).

Form icons are a different situation. When you add a form to a C# project, the IDE will create a `.resx` file with the same name as the form specifically for the resources that the form will use. One of these resources, of course, is the form's icon. Normally you will not see this `.resx` file in the **Solution Explorer** window because it will be a hidden file. To view this file you need to click on the **Show All Files** button, and you need to close the form in the Windows Forms designer.

To add an icon to a form, first you have to add an icon to the project as I have shown here, but leave the icon's **Build Action** value as **Content**. Next you should select the form's properties in the Windows Forms designer and click on the form's **Icon** property. This will bring up a dialog that will allow you to browse for the icon you just created. When you have done this, the IDE will insert the icon as a node in the `.resx` file. In a similar way, if you add a background image (the `BackgroundImage` object) to the form, the image file will be added to the `.resx` file. These are just special cases: They are resources required by the form, so they have to be stored along with the form.

8.3.6 Forms and Localization

Every form has a property called `Localizable`. This is not a property inherited from the `Form` base class; it is a pseudoproperty created by the **Properties** window for `Form` objects and `UserControl` objects (but *not* `Control` objects). When you change this property from the default of `False` to `True`, the **Properties** window will copy all the form's properties to the form's `.resx` file. The `.resx` file with the form's name will have the default values for the form.

When you change the `Language` property (another pseudoproperty), the IDE will create a `.resx` file for the selected language, named according to the language (so if the form is called `myForm`, the UK English resource file will be called `myForm.en-GB.resx`). This resource file will contain the difference between the default resource and the localized resource. So if you have set the `Icon` property in the default resources, this value will be used by all cultures *unless* you explicitly change it for a specific culture. Thus, localizing your forms is as simple as generating the default resource for the form, then specifying the values for only those properties that you want to localize by changing the `Language` property in the **Properties** window, and finally changing the property to its localized value in the **Properties** window.

The effect of `Localizable` is recursive, so if you have controls on a form, you can change the properties of those controls for a specific culture, and those properties will be written to the appropriate `.resx` file. You are most likely to use this option if the form has a menu. You add a menu to a form by adding a `MainMenu` control, and the Windows Forms designer allows you to add submenus, handles, and embellishments like check marks and radio buttons. When you develop an application, you should start by building up the menu using the default `Language`. And once you have created the menu layout and the handlers, you can localize the menus by changing the form's `Language` property to a language other than the default and then changing the menu items' text values. The values that you change will be written to the resource file for the culture.

Of course, the Windows Forms designer generates code. When the form is not localized, the designer will add code to assign the property value to the property in the `InitializeComponent()` method. When you localize the form, the designer changes the code to use a `ResourceManager` object. I will go into more detail about this class in the next section, but as I have already mentioned, this class will locate the appropriate resources section in the assembly (or in satellite assemblies) and give access to the values. For example, here is some code that is generated for you:

```
// C#
private void InitializeComponent()
{
    System.Resources.ResourceManager resources =
        new System.Resources.ResourceManager(
            typeof(myForm));
    // some properties omitted
    this.Icon = ((System.Drawing.Icon)
        (resources.GetObject("$this.Icon")));
    this.Text = resources.GetString("$this.Text");
    this.Visible = ((bool)
        (resources.GetObject("$this.Visible")));
}
```

As you can see, `ResourceManager` is initialized with the type of the form, which gives the class one part of the information it needs to locate the resource in the assembly. This class reads the UI culture of the current thread, and using this and the name of the form, it can determine the name of the form's resources (i.e., it will search `myForm.resources` for the default resources, and `myForm.en-GB.resources` for UK English resources). It then accesses the string resources using `GetString()` (as shown here, with the `Text` property), and all other resources are accessed through `GetObject()`. The designer uses the convention of naming each resource `$this.<propertyname>`. Because `ResourceManager` determines the appropriate resources for the current locale, you do not need to write this locale-specific code.

When you compile the form, the project will add the default resources to the assembly that contains the form and will generate a satellite assembly for each of the other resource files. These satellites will be named according to the satellite convention: `<formAssem>.resources.dll`, where `<formAssem>` is the name of the form's assembly. Each satellite will be located in a folder named according to the locale of the satellite, as I'll describe later.

8.3.7 Resource Classes

The `System.Resources` namespace has the classes that are needed to read and write compiled resources. `ResourceReader` enumerates resources and gives access to them through an `IDictionaryEnumerator` interface. The constructor parameter takes either the name of a file or an already opened stream, which, conveniently, is what `Assembly.GetManifestResource-Stream()` will return:

```
// C#
System.Reflection.Assembly assem;
assem = Assembly.GetExecutingAssembly();
Stream stm;
stm = assem.GetManifestResourceStream(
    "myAssem.myResources.resources");
ResourceReader reader = new ResourceReader(stm);
foreach (DictionaryEntry de in reader)
    Console.WriteLine(de.Key +" = "+de.Value);
```

This code will look for a resource called `myAssem.myResources.resources` and will print the name/value pairs contained in it.

The `ResourceWriter` class is used to write compiled `.resource` files. It takes as a construction parameter either the name of the file or, if you have an already open file, a writable stream. You can then use one of the overloaded `AddResource()` methods to add a string or a binary value to the resource. If you choose to write a binary value, you can pass either a `byte[]` array with the object already serialized or a reference to the object. If you pass an object reference, it must be an instance of a serializable class. The actual resource is not created until you call the `Generate()` method, which is also called by the `Close()` method that closes the output stream. Thus you can write code like this:

```
// C#
ResourceWriter rw
    = new ResourceWriter("myResources.resources");
rw.AddResource("TestString", "Some string data");
byte[] b = new byte[]{0, 1, 2, 3, 4};
rw.AddResource("TestData", b);
rw.Generate();
rw.Close();
```

This code will add the resources to a file called `myResources.re-sources`. The ability to write resource files is useful when you consider the `ResourceManager` class. This class is used to provide convenient access to localized resources bound to an assembly or to satellite assemblies, or located

DEVELOPING APPLICATIONS WITH VISUAL STUDIO.NET

in separate files. As I have already mentioned, this class will read the UI culture of the current thread, and using this and a base name for the resource, it will locate the resource in the local file or in a satellite assembly. Typically you will add a resource for a form, so the base name of the resource will be derived from the form's type. This is why the type of the form was used as the constructor parameter in the code I showed earlier.

If you add a separate resource file to your project, you need to provide to the `ResourceManager` constructor the name of the resource that will be derived from the resource file's name. For example, if you add a resource file called `myRes.resources` to the project, the resource will be named `myRes.resources`, and the base name will be `myRes`. Thus the following code will initialize a `ResourceManager` object to load these resources:

```
// C#
ResourceManager rm
    = new ResourceManager("myRes", assem);
```

The `assem` reference is the `Assembly` object that contains the resource (or an assembly that has satellites that contain localized resources). You can get a reference through the type of an existing object (e.g., in a form you can call `this.GetType().Assembly`) or through the static members of `Assembly`: `GetAssembly()` to get the assembly for a particular type, `GetCallingAssembly()` for the assembly that loaded the current assembly, or `GetExecutingAssembly()` to get the current assembly.

If you have created resource files using a `ResourceWriter` object, you can load these resources using the static `CreateFileBasedResourceManager()` method of the `ResourceManager` class. In the previous example, then, you can load the resources in `myResources.resources` with the following code:

```
// C#
ResourceManager rm.
ResourceManager.CreateFileBasedResourceManager(
    "myResources", ".", null);
Console.WriteLine(rm.GetString("TestString"));
```

The first parameter is the name of the resource; the second parameter is the folder where the resources are located. You can use localized files, but note that the location of these files differs from how `ResourceManager` locates satellite files. If you localize the resources in `myResources` for, say, French spoken in France, the resource file will be called `myResources.fr-FR.resources`. Yet you load this resource using the same code I showed earlier (assuming that the UI culture of the thread is `fr-FR`). Because the culture is part of a resource file's name, you do not need to place the file in a separate localized folder, as you do with satellites.

The final parameter passed to `CreateFileBasedResourceManager()` is the type of the resource set (identified in `ResourceSet`) that will be used. In this case I have used `null`, which indicates that `System.Resources.ResourceSet` should be used. `ResourceManager` uses the resource set to read the resources from the resource file (the type of the resource set that this class uses is accessed through its `ResourceSetType` property). A resource set has a resource reader to do the actual reading; this reader is accessed through the resource set's `Reader` field. You create your own resource set class so that you can use resources that are held in a format other then the compiled format produced by `resgen`.

Resource sets contain only the resources for a specific culture. You can create a resource set through its constructor (by passing a resource stream or the name of a resource file), or you can obtain it through `ResourceManager` by calling `GetResourceSet()` and pass a `CultureInfo` object. Because resource sets are specific to a culture, there is no "fallback" to a neutral culture if the specified culture does not exist. When you create a resource set, it will load all the resources and cache them in a hash table.

In addition to classes for accessing `resgen`-compiled resources, the `System.Resources` namespace has classes for reading and writing `.resx` XML files: `ResXResourceReader` and `ResXResourceWriter`, respectively. It also has an implementation of `ResourceSet` called `ResXResourceSet`.

8.3.8 Satellite Assemblies

As the name suggests, a satellite assembly is separate from the assembly that will use its resources. Do not confuse satellite assemblies with modules. Modules are constituent parts of an assembly and hence are subject to the versioning of the assembly to which they belong. A satellite assembly is an assembly in its own right, but unlike normal assemblies, it does not have code and hence does not have an entry point. To create a satellite assembly, you use the assembly builder tool, `al.exe`. For example, imagine that you have resources localized to German in a resource file called `App.de.resources`. This file is embedded into a satellite assembly as a result of the following command line:

```
al /t:lib /embed:App.de.resources
    /culture:de /out:App.resources.dll
```

This command creates a library assembly called `App.resources.dll` localized to German. If you choose, you can create an empty code file with the `[AssemblyVersion]` attribute to give the satellite assembly a version:

```
// C#, file: ver.cs
[ assembly:System.Reflection
    .AssemblyVersion("1.0.0.1") ]
```

The assembly is now compiled with the following:

```
csc /t:module ver.cs
al /t:lib /embed:App.de.resources
    /c:de /out:App.resources.dll ver.netmodule
```

The assembly is still resource-only because the module that is linked in has only metadata. You could do the same thing with the `[AssemblyCompany]` and `[AssemblyDescription]` attributes to add information about the company that created the assembly and a description. The problem with this approach is that there are now two files to deploy: `App.resources.dll` and `ver.netmodule`. To get around this problem, the assembly builder tool allows you to pass some of this information through command-line switches, which are listed in Table 8.3.

Using the `/version` switch, you can tell the assembly builder to specify the version of the assembly. In the absence of other version switches (`/fileversion`, `/productversion`), the version you specify will be used to provide a Win32 FILEVERSION resource in the library and will be the basis of the PRODUCTVERSION and FILEVERSION fields.

Table 8.3 Assembly builder switches used to change the assembly's metadata

Switch	Attribute Equivalent	Description
/company	[AssemblyCompany]	The company that created the assembly
/configuration	[AssemblyConfiguration]	Typically Retail or Debug
/copyright	[AssemblyCopyright]	Your copyright notice
/culture	[AssemblyCulture]	The culture of the assembly
/delaysign	[AssemblyDelaySign]	Specification of whether the assembly can be signed later by sn.exe
/description	[AssemblyDescription]	A description of the assembly
/fileversion	[AssemblyFileVersion]	The Win32 version of the library
/keyfile	[AssemblyKeyFile]	The name of the file with the key
/keyname	[AssemblyKeyName]	The name of the key in a cryptographic container
/product	[AssemblyProduct]	The product's name
/productversion	[AssemblyInformationalVersion]	The version of the product
/title	[AssemblyTitle]	The friendly name of the assembly
/trademark	[AssemblyTrademark]	Your trademark
/version	[AssemblyVersion]	The assembly version

Now imagine that you have resources for the same application localized to French in `App.fr.resources`. This data is embedded into a satellite assembly by the following command line:

```
al /t:lib /embed:App.fr.resources
   /culture:fr /out:App.resources.dll
```

This command also creates a library assembly called `App.resources.dll`. The code in `ResourceManager` does not use the name of the assembly to determine its culture; instead it uses the `[AssemblyCulture]` attribute (the `.locale` metadata) to locate the correct satellite assembly. Because the satellites have the same name, they should be installed in subfolders of the folder containing the assembly that uses the satellite. These folders should have the name of the locale of the satellite; for example, the German resources should be in a folder called `de`, and the French resources should be in a folder called `fr`.

If your satellite files are to be shared by several applications, you should install the satellites in the GAC (global assembly cache). If you do this, the satellites should have a strong name. Remember that the full name of an assembly includes its culture, version, and public key, so there are no problems with installing several satellite files in the GAC because although the short name of the assembly will be the same, the full names will differ by the culture element.

When a `ResourceManager` object is created and tries to locate localized resources, the runtime first looks in the GAC for the satellite assembly with the correct culture and checks whether it has the resource. If this check fails, the current folder is checked for the culture-specific assembly in a named folder. If this search fails, the runtime starts the search again, but this time for an assembly that has the appropriate "fallback" culture—first in the GAC, and then in the current directory. Each culture will have a fallback culture that will be searched in this way, until finally the runtime will attempt to locate the resource in the default resources for the assembly, which will be in the main assembly. If this search fails, the resource cannot be found and an exception will be thrown.

Because satellite assemblies can have a different version from the version of the main assembly, satellite versions can get out of sync with the main assembly. To get around this problem, the main assembly can specify a *base version* of the satellite assemblies that it uses; it does this with an assembly-level attribute:

```
[assembly: SatelliteContractVersion("1.0.0.0")]
```

Unlike versions applied through `[AssemblyVersion]`, the string version must have all four parts. The satellite assembly can be versioned independently from the main version, and the changes can be reflected in the application's configuration file or, if it is installed in the GAC, through a publisher policy file.

The name that I have used for the satellite assembly is `<assem>.resources.dll`. This is a standard naming convention and is vital to how the `ResourceManager` class works. The `<assem>` part is the name of the assembly that will use these resources. This is the only mechanism that exists to tie a satellite to the assembly with which it is used.[2]

If you use satellite assemblies, I urge you to make sure that you also provide locale-neutral resources. A locale-neutral resource is named without a locale and is bound to the assembly that uses the resource. In the preceding example, the main assembly will be compiled with a command line that looks like this:

```
csc /res:App.resources /out:App.exe app.cs
```

The assembly is called `App.exe`. When it is run, `ResourceManager` will check for an appropriate resource for the current culture within the satellite assemblies, and if that resource is not present, it will load the locale-neutral resource from the main assembly. Locating satellite assemblies is not part of Fusion's work, so if `ResourceManager` cannot find a satellite assembly, there will be no binding-error message in the Fusion log (viewable with `FusLogVW.exe`), and if your main assembly has a locale-neutral resource, you'll have no indication that there has been a problem. (If you do not have locale-neutral resources, `ResourceManager` will throw a `MissingManifestResourceException` exception.)

8.3.9 The Event Log, Again

So I am back to the event log again. As I mentioned earlier in this book, .NET has a poor implementation of the classes to write messages to the event log. The principal reason I say this is that these classes put the onus on the user of the

---

2. If you are careful to name the satellite assemblies and folders correctly, then loading locale-specific resources is straightforward. However, because the location of the correct assembly is so dependent on these names, I regard it as quite a fragile mechanism.

`EventLog` class to localize the messages that are written to the event log rather than taking the correct approach, which is to put the onus on the reader of the event log. If the writer is responsible for localizing messages, the messages can be read in only one locale, which is fine if your distributed application runs in only one locale. In these days of globalization, however, your application could conceivably have components running in different locales, and if a message is localized when it is generated, it ties that message to that locale. Unfortunately, there is little one can do with the current framework classes, and one can only hope that this horrible throwback to the broken event log classes that were present in VB6 will be fixed in a later version of the Framework Class Library.

To localize event log messages, your code merely creates localized format strings in a resource file and then at runtime uses a resource manager to load the appropriate string:

```
// C#
ResourceManager rm
    = new ResourceManager(typeof(myForm));
string errMsg = String.Format(
    rm.GetString("errNoFile"), strFileName);
EventLog el = new EventLog("Application");
el.WriteEntry(errMsg);
```

8.3.10 Win32 Resources

Assemblies are PE files, so they can have Win32 resources. For a C++ developer this is not a problem because managed C++ projects use the standard linker, which will link a compiled Win32 (`.res`) file into a PE file. Indeed, as I mentioned earlier, when you add a resource to a managed C++ project, that resource will be a Win32 resource and not a .NET resource. C# developers can also include Win32 resources using either the C# compiler (`csc.exe`) or the assembly builder tool (`al.exe`). Both of these tools have a `/win32res` and a `/win32icon` switch, the first of which allows you to add an already compiled resource to an assembly. It is probably best to do this within a C++ project, where you can edit an `.rc` file and use the **Resource View** window to add and edit the resources. The unmanaged resource compiler, `rc.exe`, is used to compile a `.rc` file into a `.res` file.

One type of resource that can be described in an `.rc` file is the icon. The first icon in a file's resources will be used by Windows Explorer when displaying the file, and if the file is an executable, this icon will be the application icon.

The `/win32icon` switch is the only way that you can set the icon for an assembly. This switch takes the name of the icon (`.ico`) file; you do not compile it. It is prudent to add both a 32×32 bit image and a 16×16 bit image so that you can determine the icon that will be shown in Windows Explorer, no matter what view the user chooses.

.NET code does not understand Win32 resources, so if you need to read Win32 resources, you have to resort to interop through Platform Invoke. The code is straightforward, and there is even a sample in the Framework SDK samples (called `TlbGen`) that shows how to add a Win32 resource to an assembly programmatically, using the Win32 resource APIs.

8.4 Summary

Visual Studio.NET allows you to create applications, as well as controls and components that can be used as part of applications. Components are objects that can have a site and can be disposed of. The **Toolbox** window contains components. Controls are components that are derived from the `Control` class and have a user interface. Some controls are composites of other controls; these are derived from `UserControl`. The VS.NET IDE allows you to develop `UserControl` objects and `Form` objects with the designer, which lets you construct a user interface by dragging and dropping components and controls from the **Toolbox** window and then using the **Properties** window to provide property values and events. The designer also allows you to develop components and controls, but it does not allow you to develop the user interface of a `Control` class.

Applications and `UserControl` classes can be localized so that they can be used in different locales. Localization involves creating resources for each locale, and these resources can be stored in satellite assemblies. The IDE makes localization straightforward through the **Properties** window; you simply have to set the `Language` property, and then all the properties that you set will be stored in an `.resx` file for the locale. The IDE will build the satellite assemblies for each locale's `.resx` file in your project.

Chapter 9

Debugging

Of course your code is always well written and well behaved, so you don't have to debug *your* code. However, sometimes you will use code written by other people, which means that inevitably you will have to debug *their* code (and while you are doing this, it does no harm to look over your code too!).

The Visual Studio debugger has a lot of work to do. Clearly, .NET code needs a .NET debugger, and native code needs a native debugger, but Visual Studio also needs to take into account interop between .NET and native code and to allow you to step from the managed world to the unmanaged world and vice versa. In this chapter I will explain the features and facilities of Visual Studio.NET that allow you to debug your applications.

I will start by describing the UI features of the IDE debugger: the various windows that the IDE provides to give you information about the process that you are debugging. Then I will explain how to use the debugger: how to start a process under the debugger, how to attach to a running process, and how to step through the process.

9.1 IDE Tool Windows

I will start by explaining the various windows that Visual Studio provides for debugging code. In any debugging session, you will need to do one or more of the following: start the debugging session, step through code, set and run to breakpoints, view code, view memory, view values of variables, and stop the debugging session. Visual Studio has several tools that make each of these tasks easy.

9.1.1 Setting Breakpoints

There are several ways to set a breakpoint. The two simplest ways are to click in the gray margin at the left-hand side of the editor window (as illustrated in Figure 9.1), or to place the caret on the line and press **F9**. Both actions will add the breakpoint to the current list of breakpoints.

To view the currently set breakpoints you can open the **Breakpoints** window (Figure 9.2) through the **Debug | Windows | Breakpoints** menu option (or the `Debug.Breakpoints` command). While debugging the process, the debugger will stop when it hits a breakpoint. To remove a breakpoint you can use the delete button in the **Breakpoints** window or click on the breakpoint in the gray margin, but as you'll see in a moment, breakpoints can take a fair amount of setting up, so you won't want to lose that information. Instead, you can temporarily disable a breakpoint by unchecking the check box next to it in the **Breakpoints** window. Doing this retains all the information about the breakpoint but prevents the debugger from stopping at this point. The information about breakpoints is stored in the `.suo` file.

The **Breakpoints** window gives details about each breakpoint. The toolbar buttons allow you to change these breakpoints and how you view them: The

Figure 9.1 Setting breakpoints through the editor

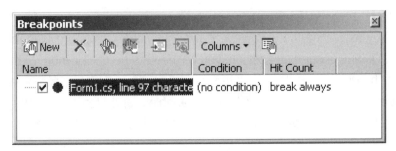

Figure 9.2 The Breakpoints window

Columns button determines how many columns are shown. The right-hand button on the toolbar (see Figure 9.2) gives the properties of the breakpoint, allowing you to make changes to a particular breakpoint. In addition, there is a **New** button, which allows you to create a new breakpoint; the same effect is achieved through the **Debug | New Breakpoint** menu item (the `Debug.NewBreakpoint` command).

9.1.1.1 File, Function, and Address

The location of a breakpoint is shown on three tabs of the **Breakpoint Properties** dialog. The **File** tab shows the name and path of the file, and the **Line** and **Character** text boxes indicate the actual position of the breakpoint. Typically, whatever value you set to the **Character** position, the breakpoint is treated as if it were at character position 1.

The **Function** tab gives details about the actual function where the breakpoint is to be found: The **Function** text box gives the fully qualified name of the function. If you have a function that is overloaded, you should identify which version you have by using its parameter list. If you do not do this, you will be presented with a dialog containing alternatives to allow you to select the function that interests you. The **Line** text box gives the line number with respect to the start of the function (the first line of the function signature is regarded as line 1). The **Language** list box lists the languages that are currently installed.

If you create a breakpoint through the **Function** tab, the **File** tab will be filled in, but the text boxes will be disabled. If you create a breakpoint through the **File** tab, the **Function** tab will be filled in and the text boxes will be disabled. In other words, after you have created a breakpoint, you can edit it only through the tab that you used to create it.

You use the **Address** tab differently, depending on whether the code is managed or unmanaged. Unmanaged code is compiled to native code at compile time, so the address of code is known at compile time (assuming that the code module will always be loaded at the same address; if it isn't, there will simply be an offset). In this case you use the **Address** text box to give the address where you want the breakpoint to be set (you can use the `.map` file to determine the address of a function). If the project is managed, the IL will be compiled to native code at runtime, so you cannot give an absolute address (because this will not be known until the JIT compiler has done its work). Instead you use the **Address** text box to give the byte offset from the beginning of the function—for example:

```
myNamespace.myClass.f() + 0x0000000d
```

You can use the **Address** tab also to set a breakpoint within a system DLL, or within another DLL that has an exported function you think your code may call. To do this you need to use the context operator ({}) to indicate that the breakpoint will be placed in the specified DLL on the specified function. If the project is managed, you have to make sure that native debugging is enabled through the **Enabled Unmanaged Debugging** option on the **Debugging** page of the project. Here is an example:

```
{,,kernel32.dll}_GetCurrentProcessId@0¹
```

This parameter indicates that a breakpoint should be placed on the first line of the `GetCurrentProcessId()` function exported from `kernel32.dll`. In this case I have the Windows 2000 symbols installed, so I have used the symbol name that is the name of the exported function prefixed with an underscore and postfixed with the number of bytes pushed onto the stack. If you do not have the symbols for a DLL, you can simply use the exported name (in this case `Get-CurrentProcessId`).

9.1.1.2 Data

If your project is unmanaged, you also have the option of checking whether a particular variable has changed. The **Data** tab (Figure 9.3) allows you to give the name of the variable and the context of that variable—in this case the variable x in a function called `CallMe()` in the DLL called `Lib.dll`. If the variable is an array (as in this case: x is a `char` array), you can indicate that the check is performed on more than one item in the array. Although this option is useful, it does

---

1. The syntax of the context operator is {function, source file, binary module}. Because the source of system DLLs is not available, you leave out the function and source file. If you do have the source, you can set a breakpoint on a particular line with {, source file, binary module}@linenumber.

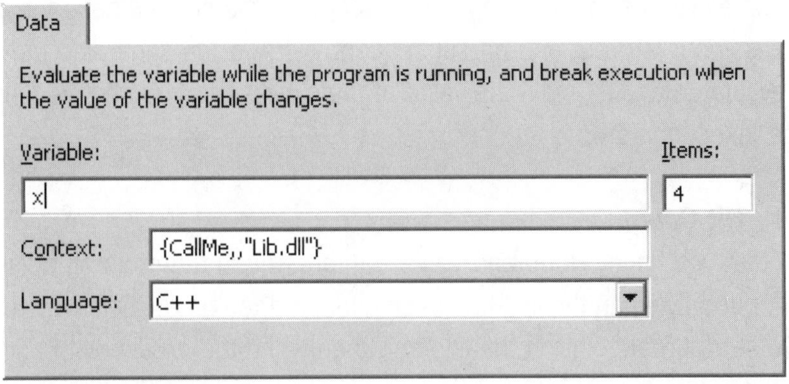

Figure 9.3 The Data tab

have its downside: The debugger attempts to use the CPU's debug registers to make the check, but these registers are limited in what they can check, so the debugger may simply resort to single-stepping through your code and checking the value of the variable at each step. Consequently, when you attempt to watch data, the debugger will warn you that the program may run very slowly.

When the variable changes, the debugger will pop up a dialog indicating that the variable has changed and will stop execution at the position of that change.

Because this mechanism involves checking the contents of a memory location, it is not supported for managed code. If you attempt to set such a break condition in a managed project, when you try to close the **New Breakpoint** dialog you'll get an error message saying that the breakpoint cannot be set. If you have an unmanaged DLL that is called by a managed process, you will expect to be able to set a **Data** breakpoint. You can, but only when you are running the unmanaged code. If you attempt to set the **Data** breakpoint while running managed code (or outside of a debugging session), the managed debugger will tell you that the **Data** breakpoint is not supported.

9.1.1.3 *Condition*
The **Condition** button in the **Breakpoints** window allows you to set a condition that will be checked when the line has been reached. You have two options: Break when the condition is `true`, or break when the condition has changed. In the first case the debugger just checks the expression (e.g., `x==4`), and if the

expression evaluates to `true`, execution stops. In the second case the value of the expression is stored, and on subsequent visits to the same line the expression is evaluated again, and if the value of the expression has changed since the last time, execution stops.

9.1.1.4 Hit Count

Imagine that you have a loop and you are interested in the code on a line within the loop, but only when the line has been executed ten times. One way to handle this is to set a breakpoint on the line and then when the breakpoint is hit, press **F5** to continue to run and repeat this nine times. However, this process can be very irritating, especially if the loop is executed a large number of times. The **Hit Count** button in the **Breakpoints** window allows you to set the number of times that the debugger should skip the execution of a line before stopping at a breakpoint. By default, the debugger will always break on a line, but you can specify that the debugger should break only when a count reaches a particular value or a multiple of a particular value (e.g., at every tenth execution of a line), or every time after a certain hit count has been reached (see Figure 9.4).

9.1.1.5 Unset Breakpoints

Sometimes the debugger will not be able to set the breakpoints that you specify through the **Breakpoints** window. The most common reason is if you add a

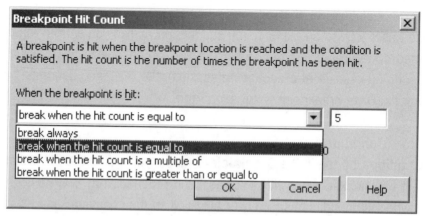

Figure 9.4   The Breakpoint Hit Count dialog

breakpoint for a DLL and that DLL is explicitly loaded by your code. Unmanaged projects typically use `LoadLibrary()` or `CoCreateInstance()` to explicitly load the DLL (in-process COM servers are always explicitly loaded). If the debugger cannot resolve the breakpoint when it starts, it will place the **Warning** glyph (a red spot with a yellow question mark inside it) next to the breakpoint in the **Breakpoints** window. When the DLL has been loaded, the debugger will try to resolve the breakpoint, and when it does the **Enabled** glyph will be shown (a red spot).

Managed projects that use library assemblies will show the **Warning** glyph for breakpoints set in the library. Similarly, if the project uses Platform Invoke (`[DllImport]`), the DLL will also be implicitly loaded, so the **Warning** glyph will be shown until the DLL is explicitly loaded. If the debugger cannot resolve a breakpoint at runtime (e.g., you've set a **Data** breakpoint in a managed project), the debugger will present you with a dialog telling you that the breakpoint cannot be set and will stop at the entry point of your process.

9.1.2 Threads and Modules Windows

You can get information about DLLs loaded by the process you are debugging through the **Modules** window (or the `Debug.Modules` command) (see Figure 9.5). If you are debugging more than one process (I will discuss the details later), you can opt to see just the DLLs for the current process or those loaded for all processes. The columns included in the **Modules** window are listed in Table 9.1.

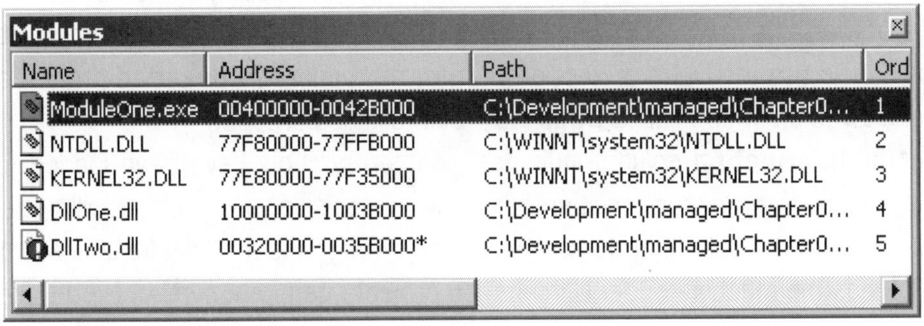

Name	Address	Path	Ord
ModuleOne.exe	00400000-0042B000	C:\Development\managed\Chapter0...	1
NTDLL.DLL	77F80000-77FFB000	C:\WINNT\system32\NTDLL.DLL	2
KERNEL32.DLL	77E80000-77F35000	C:\WINNT\system32\KERNEL32.DLL	3
DllOne.dll	10000000-1003B000	C:\Development\managed\Chapter0...	4
DllTwo.dll	00320000-0035B000*	C:\Development\managed\Chapter0...	5

Figure 9.5   The Modules window

Table 9.1   Columns in the Modules window

Column	Description
Name	The name of the code module
Address	The virtual address where the module is loaded
Path	The path identifying the location from which the module was loaded
Order	The order with respect to the other loaded modules at the time the **Modules** window was shown
Version	The module's version
Program	The program that loaded the version
Timestamp	The module's timestamp
Information	Information about whether symbols were loaded

When a DLL is loaded, the system attempts to load it at its base address. If another DLL already occupies that virtual address, the system will load it in an available address and take care of any necessary fix-ups of the DLL's exported functions. This mechanism will delay the loading of the DLL and hence should be avoided if possible.

In Figure 9.5, `DllOne.dll` is loaded at `0x10000000`, which is the default base address for DLLs produced with VS.NET. `DllTwo.dll` also has this as its base address, so when it is loaded, the system will move it in memory—in this case to `0x00320000`. To indicate this change, an asterisk is shown next to the load address and the module's icon is shown with an exclamation mark. These symbols indicate that you need to change the base address of at least one of the DLLs loaded by your process. (To do this for an unmanaged project you should use the DLL's project properties; the **Linker | Advanced** properties menu gives an option called **Base Address** for this purpose.)

The **Information** column indicates whether symbols have been loaded for the module. If the debugger cannot find the symbols for a module, it will not be able to show the source code when you step through the module. Instead all you will see is the machine code. Unmanaged projects generate symbol (`.pdb`) files in the output directory. Managed projects also generate symbol files; these are copied to the project's `bin\Debug` and `obj\Debug` folders, but the debugger will use the files in the `obj\Debug` folder. If the symbol file for an assembly cannot be found (e.g., the assembly is a Release build), you won't be able to step into source code in the assembly. The debugger will allow you to step into managed code using the **Disassembly** window. In other words, you are allowed to step through the code that has been jitted; the debugger does not show you IL.

If the module symbols are installed in a folder other than the symbols path (set through the **Debugging** page of the project's property dialog) or the folder containing the code module, you can tell the debugger to load the symbols from a new location by right-clicking on the module in the **Modules** window and selecting **Reload Symbols** from the context menu.

When you single-step through code under the debugger, you are essentially following the execution path of a single thread. If your application is multi-threaded, you may want to debug a specific thread, and to do this you will need to use the **Threads** window (Figure 9.6). This window is shown when the debugger is single-stepping through code through the **Debug | Windows | Threads** menu item (the `Debug.Threads` command). The context menu of a thread allows you to suspend ("freeze") a particular thread or switch to a particular thread.

9.1.3 Call Stack Window
As you step through a process in the debugger, you will step into and out of functions. The **Call Stack** window (`Debug.CallStack`) lists the functions that

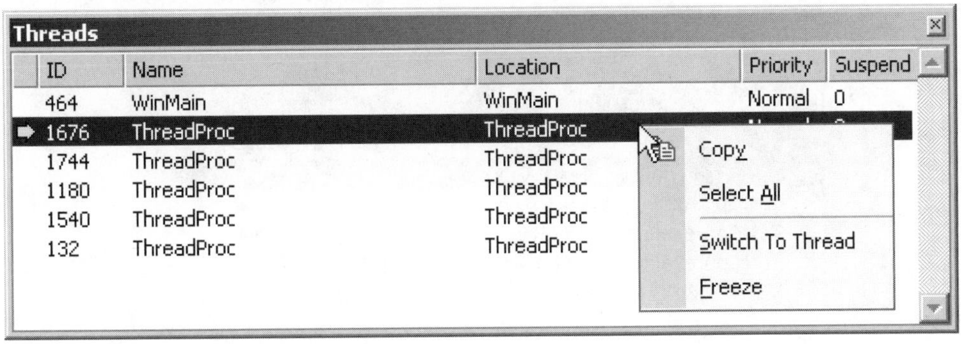

Figure 9.6 The Threads window

were called to get to the current location (see Figure 9.7). If symbols are available, the debugger will use the symbolic name of the function and will interpret the parameters on the stack, even showing the values of the parameters. If symbols are not available, the call stack will show the virtual address of the function. Consider the following code:

```
1:  // native C++
2:  #include <stdio.h>
3:  void g(int i)
4:  {
5:  }
6:
7:  void f()
8:  {
9:     g(0);
10: }
11:
12: void main()
13: {
14:     f();
15: }
```

If I put a breakpoint on line 4 and debug the process, the call stack in Figure 9.7 will be shown. As you can see, the window recognizes that g() takes an int value as its parameter, and that the value used as the parameter was 0. The call stack shows that the breakpoint occurs at line 4 in the file, and that the function g() was called in function f() at line 9 in the source file.

The left-hand column of the **Call Stack** window gives an indication about where the current execution point is and the function currently showing in the

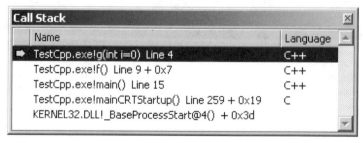

Figure 9.7   The Call Stack window

DEVELOPING APPLICATIONS WITH VISUAL STUDIO.NET

source editor. The current location is shown by a yellow arrow pointing right. If this location coincides with a breakpoint, you'll see the arrow superimposed over the red dot of the breakpoint. If the caret is moved to another function in the call stack, the source code editor will show a green triangle next to the location in the function that called the function in the **Call Stack**. The **Call Stack** window will show the green triangle next to the function where the caret is. To move the caret back to the execution point, you can click on the **Show Next Statement** button on the **Debug** toolbar.

9.1.4 Watch Windows

Visual Studio allows you to monitor variables in your process. The **Locals** window (see Figure 9.8) shows the local stack variables, which includes pointers to objects and parameters to methods. The **Autos** window shows the variables relevant to the current position in the code, so you'll see the values of the parameters that will be passed to the function at the current caret position in the code and the values used by the previous line in the code. If the code being executed is part of an object, this window will give access to the data members of the object. Finally, the IDE provides four watch windows (**Watch 1** through **Watch 4**) for identifying a particular variable to watch. These four types of windows are similar in that each one shows a grid with three columns—**Name**, **Value**, and **Type**—as well as values in the **Name** column using a tree view so that aggregated types can be expanded to see their members. For example, consider the following linked list class:

```csharp
// C#
class List
{
    public List(){ next = null; name = null; }
    public string name;
    public List next;
    static public List AddLink(List node, string s)
    {
        List current = new List();
        if (node != null) node.next = current;
        current.name = s;
        return current;
    }
}
```

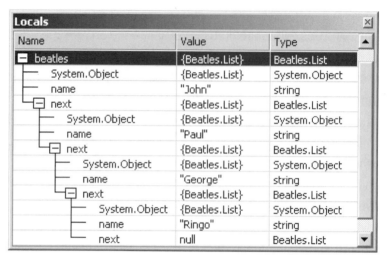

Figure 9.8 The Locals window showing a linked list

This class has a member that is a reference to another node in the linked list. The class could be used as follows:

```
// C#
List beatles = null;
List current = null;
beatles = current = List.AddLink(null, "John");
current = List.AddLink(current, "Paul");
current = List.AddLink(current, "George");
current = List.AddLink(current, "Ringo");
```

The linked list is shown expanded in Figure 9.8.

If you show an array in the watch windows, you will see all of the members in managed code (because the debugger will be able to determine how many items the array has). Unmanaged code will sometimes show the members, depending on how the array is allocated. If you allocate a native array on the stack, the debugger will know how many members there are and will list them. If you create an array on the unmanaged C++ heap, the **Locals** window will not know how many items were allocated and will show the value of only the first item.

However, if you look at the **Autos** window immediately after the array has been allocated, you'll see that it lists the members that were created. The reason is that the **Autos** window will track the return value from the call to the unmanaged C++ `new` operator. The **Autos** window does this for all functions that you call, which is useful if you have called a function without saving its return value. If you know that a pointer points to an array, you can specifically ask the watch windows to list a specified number of items—for example, as follows:

```
// native C++
int* i = new int[10];
memset(i, 0, sizeof(int) * 10);
i[1] = 1;
```

If you put a breakpoint on the line that assigns the second item to 1 and look in the **Autos** window, you'll see `i` listed as a pointer and not an array. The reason is that `memset()` was the last function to be called, so the debugger has "forgotten" that the pointer points to memory allocated with `new`. However, if you type `i,5` as the name of the variable (in the **Name** field) in a watch window, the window will treat `i` as an array and list its first five items.

The watch windows allow you to type an expression, and the debugger will show the value of the expression. This is useful if you want to watch a few values, and it helps keep the UI clear of the clutter that can appear in the other watch windows. Typically you will watch specific variables, but note that if you type the name of a local variable, when you step out of the method the debugger will not be able to show the variable (indeed the variable will no longer exist). Similarly, if you are within a class method and you watch a class member, when you step out of the class method the variable will be out of scope and the debugger will not be able to list its value. Conversely, if you watch an object member and fully qualify the member with an object variable, that variable will be out of scope when you step into a class method.

As you single-step through code, the watch windows will show you the values of the watched variables. And if a variable changes value while you are watching it, the value color will change (by default from black to red); this is a useful visual reminder. One particularly useful aspect of these windows is the ability to change values at runtime. Imagine that you are halfway through a particularly long debugging session, and you discover that a line of code generates an incorrect value. Rather than stopping the debugging session, fixing the code, and recompiling (or for native code using Edit and Continue, which I will discuss later), you can simply use one of the watch windows to change the value of the variable and continue single-stepping with the correct value.

You can add variables to a watch window by typing them directly into the grid, or through the editor window. To do this you should highlight the variable and through the context menu select **Add Watch**. You can also use this method to use the **Quick Watch** window, which I will talk about in a moment.

Managed and unmanaged code have different rules about what you can type in a watch window. Managed code allows you to type an expression using the arithmetic operators that you are accustomed to using in your code. In addition, you can call static methods and you can perform some manipulations on strings. Some examples are shown in Figure 9.9, which also shows strings being treated as arrays of `char` elements.

A watch window can also be used to run methods on existing objects. However, you have to be careful what you do. Imagine that you have a class like this:

```
// C#
class Test
{
    int x = 0;
    public int Inc(int i){ return x = x + i; }
}
```

Now imagine that you create an instance of `Test` in your code (call it `test`); you know that the member `x` will have a value of `0`. However, the watch window allows you to watch an expression like `test.Inc(2)`, and it will show the value of the expression as `2`, but of course, it has changed the value of the object.

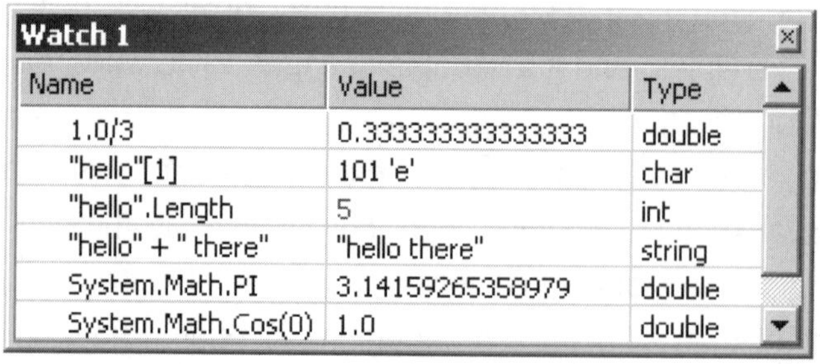

Watch 1			
Name	Value	Type	
1.0/3	0.333333333333333	double	
"hello"[1]	101 'e'	char	
"hello".Length	5	int	
"hello" + " there"	"hello there"	string	
System.Math.PI	3.14159265358979	double	
System.Math.Cos(0)	1.0	double	

Figure 9.9   Examples of watched variables

This may be what you want. If it is, you will be better off calling this function from the **Immediate** window (which will be discussed later).

Unmanaged C++ also allows you to access variables in the watch windows, and you can also call global functions, but you cannot call member functions. You can use most of the arithmetic operators, and you can use the BY, WO, and DW operators. These operators are typically used with the pseudovariables for the CPU registers. For example, esp will give you the value of the stack pointer, but the stack pointer is not a C pointer, so it does not have a type, and thus you cannot use *esp to get the contents at the position of the stack pointer. Instead, you can use BY esp to get the first byte, WO esp to get the first word, and DW esp to get the double word at that position. You can also increment the values obtained from these pseudoregisters, so BY esp+1 will give the second byte pointed to by the stack pointer.

Variables shown in the watch windows can be modified with the modifiers shown in Table 9.2. These modifiers affect how the value is shown in the watch windows. The hr postfix indicates that the variable should be treated as a COM status code, so the debugger will attempt to find the symbol for that variable. In a similar way, using wc as the modifier will show the appropriate symbol used for windows classes, and wm will show the symbol used for windows messages. Here is an example:

```
// native C++
HRESULT hr = 0x80070057;
ULONG w = 0x10000000L;
UINT m = 0x0001;
```

If you put a breakpoint after the line defining the variable m and add the following watch variables:

```
hr,hr
w,wc
m,wm
```

you'll see the following in the watch window:

```
hr,hr      E_INVALIDARG
w,wc       WS_VISIBLE
m,wm       WM_CREATE
```

Table 9.2   Format modifiers for variables in the watch windows

Modifier	Meaning
hr	Display the number as an HRESULT symbol.
wc	Display the number as a Windows class symbol.
wm	Display the number as a Windows message symbol.
x, X	Display the number in hex.
c	Display the lowest byte of the number as a character.
d, i	Display the number as a signed decimal number.
u	Display the number as an unsigned decimal number.
o	Display the number as an unsigned octal number.
l	Modifies the d, i, u, o, x, X modifiers for long numbers.
h	Modifies the d, i, u, o, x, X modifiers for short numbers.
f	Display the number as a signed floating-point number.
e	Display the number as a signed scientific number.
g	Display the number as signed floating-point or scientific number.
s	Display the data pointed to as single byte characters.
su	Display the data pointed to as Unicode characters.
ma	Display the 64 bytes at the memory address as ASCII.
m, mb	Display the first 16 bytes in hex and as the character equivalent.
mw	Display the first eight words in hex.
mu	Display the eight words at the memory address as Unicode.
md	Display the first four double words in hex.
mq	Display the first two quad words in hex.

The values used in any of the watch windows can be shown in decimal or hex format. To change between the formats, you can use the watch window context menu. If you select **Hexadecimal Display**, all numbers will be shown in hex. In this situation you can use one of the decimal modifiers (d, i, u, o) to show a specific value as a decimal without affecting the other values in the watch window. Conversely, if **Hexadecimal Display** is not selected, all numbers will be shown in decimal display, except those that you mark with `x` or `X`.

The `m` modifiers are interesting; they are used on pointers and will display the memory to which the pointers point in various formats. The `ma` modifier shows just the first 64 bytes as ASCII characters; the `mb` modifier shows just the first 16 bytes, both as hexadecimal display and as the ASCII characters that the hex values represent. The other modifiers display the memory as words, Unicode characters, double words, and quad (64-bit) words.

The IDE provides three other means for viewing values at runtime: the **Immediate** window, the variable tool tip, and the **Quick Watch** dialog. I'll leave discussion about the first two to later sections, and I'll describe the **Quick Watch** window here because it is essentially the watch grid in a dialog. This means that you can view aggregated types, expand them, and change their values. In addition, if you select a variable in the grid, you can click on the **Add Watch** button to add the variable to the currently visible watch window.

While you are paused in the debugger, you can use the **Registers** window (through **Debug | Windows | Registers** or the `Debug.Registers` command) to view the current CPU registers. By default the **Registers** window will show the basic CPU registers, but you can use the context menu to select the other registers you want to view (e.g., MMX [multimedia extensions] registers, floating-point registers, and the CPU flags register). You can even edit the values of these registers, but of course you need to be aware of the consequences of your actions before you make any changes. If you prefer, you can look at the register values through the watch window; the variable name that you type is the name of the register in the **Registers** window. If this name clashes with a variable in your code, you can prefix the register name with the `@` character (e.g., `@eax`).

The watch windows also support some special-purpose pseudovariables. The `err` variable will return the value of `GetLastError()` from the last time that the function was called, and `tib` gives access to the thread information block.[2]

---

2. For information about the cool things you can do with the thread information block, see John Robbins's book *Debugging Applications*, published in 2000 by Microsoft Press.

9.1.5 Memory Windows

The debugger supports four dockable memory windows. These are extremely useful for seeing exactly what is happening in unmanaged applications. The memory windows show the memory at a specified location in both hexadecimal and ASCII format in a multitude of combinations. The first option you have is how many columns will be shown: 1, 2, 4, 8, 16, 32, 64, or auto (fit to window). You can make this choice through the **Columns** list box on the memory window toolbar. Then you have the option of how the columns are displayed, which is specified through the context menu for the window: as 1-, 2-, 4-, or 8-byte integers, or as 32- or 64-bit floating-point numbers. The integers can be viewed as hexadecimal or as signed or unsigned decimal values. You also have the option of viewing the data as numbers, text, or both, and if you select text, the data can be interpreted as ANSI or Unicode. Finally, if you have write access to the memory, you can even change the values that are there!

The memory windows have a combo box for you to type the memory address that interests you. You can type the hexadecimal address (i.e., with the prefix `0x`), a decimal value, or for unmanaged code, the name of a variable. If the variable is a pointer, the memory window will show the address to which the pointer points (hence a quick way to look at the stack is to type `esp`). If the variable is not a pointer, you can pass its address (using the address operator, `&`), and the memory window will show the memory that it occupies.

9.1.6 Using the Command Window

The **Command** window is very useful during a debugging session. There are two ways to use this window: in command mode and in immediate mode. The first character of the line identifies the mode you're in: If it is >, you are in command mode; if your caret is at the first character of the line (so no > is present), you are in immediate mode. To switch from command mode to immediate mode, you type `immed` at the > prompt; to switch from immediate mode to command mode, you type `>cmd` (note the > character).

The Visual Studio IDE has many predefined aliases, which you can view by typing `alias` at the **Command** window. Table 9.3 lists the aliases that are pertinent to this chapter. Note that often there are two aliases for what appears to be the same

Table 9.3 Selected Command window aliases[*]

Alias	Meaning
? x	Print the value of the variable x.
?? x	Open the **Quick Watch** window for the variable x.
d m	Dump the 16 bytes of data at location m in hex and ASCII.
da m	Dump the 16 bytes of data at location m in ASCII.
db m	Dump the 16 bytes of data at location m in hex.
dc m	Dump the 16 DWORD items at location m in hex and ASCII.
dd m	Dump the 16 DWORD items at location m in hex.
df m	Dump the 16 32-bit float items at location m.
dq m	Dump the 16 quad (64-bit) words at location m in hex.
du m	Dump 16 Unicode characters at location m.
eval exp	Evaluate expression exp.
g	Start debugging ("go").
k, kb	List the call stack at the **Command** window.
log file /on	Turn logging on so that the commands will be written to a file.
log /off	Turn logging off.
p	Single-step the debugger.
pr	Step out of a function in the debugger.
q	Stop debugging ("quit").
rtc	Run to caret in the debugger.
shell app	Start the application app.
t	Step into a function in the debugger.
u m	Disassemble the next eight instructions at location m in the Command window.
|	List the programs being debugged.
~	List the threads in the process.

[*]*Note:* For a complete list, type alias at the **Command** window.

thing; however, one will refer to a UI element, and the other will be pertinent to the **Command** window. So the `disasm` alias will bring up the **Disassembly** window, and `u` will disassemble eight machine code instructions within the **Command** window. The `u` command will disassemble the code at the current instruction pointer by default, but you can give a specific address, or you can give a register name or a variable that is currently in scope. In a similar way, `threads` will show the **Threads** window, and `~` will print the list of threads in the **Command** window.

As their names suggest, command mode allows you to execute commands, whereas immediate mode gives you complete access to the variables in the current scope. In command mode you have read-only access to variables. For example, imagine you have a variable called `t`. In command mode you can view the value of this variable with the command `? t` (notice the space). You can get the **Command** window to print the value of a member of `t` using the usual access operators (`.` or `->`), and these operators will give access to members at all access levels.

You enter immediate mode by typing the `immed` alias at the **Command** window. Once in immediate mode, you can change the values of objects and even execute object and global methods. For example, imagine that you have an instance of the `Test` class (that I showed earlier) called `t`:

```
// C#
class Test
{
    int x = 0;
    public int Inc(int i){ return x = x + i; }
}
```

If you type `t` in immediate mode, the value of the object will be displayed (I'll talk about the formatting that is used in the next section). If you type `t.Inc(4)`, the instance will be incremented by 4 and the value of the object will be printed in the **Command** window. For managed projects you will be able to access any of the static members of the assemblies that have been loaded.

9.1.7 Formatting Values

When I mentioned viewing the values of variables, I deferred two of the methods of doing so for later discussion. These two are typing the name of the variable in the immediate window (which I just described) and using the variable tool tip. Both of these methods will present a compact, formatted view of an object. The variable tool tip is shown when you hold the mouse cursor over a variable in the source window while stopped in the debugger. If the variable is in the current stack frame, the IDE will show a tool tip with the value of the variable.

The format used to show types in the variable tool tips, the immediate window, and the watch windows is determined by three files in the `Common7\Packages\Debugger` subfolder of the `Microsoft Visual Studio.NET` folder: (1) `autoexp.dat` for native code, (2) `mcee_cs.dat` for C#, and (3) `mcee_mc.dat` for managed C++. These files document the format strings that you can use if you want to add your own formats.

9.1.8 Exceptions

The **Exceptions** dialog (Figure 9.10) allows you to determine how an exception type, or category of exceptions, is handled by various debuggers. At the top of the dialog is a tree control that lists the categories of exceptions relevant to the debuggers that are used by Visual Studio.NET.[3] You can select a category of exceptions or an individual exception and determine how that exception is handled when the exception is thrown while code is running under the debugger. The radio button group titled **When the exception is thrown** determines the action that will occur immediately after the exception is thrown. The options are as follows:

- **Use parent setting**, to use the settings set for the exception's immediate parent
- **Break into the debugger**, to tell the debugger to stop at the location where the exception occurred
- **Continue**, to ignore the exception and continue

The **Continue** setting is usually the best, especially if you think exceptions will be regularly thrown and caught. You will change this setting to **Break into the debugger** if an exception and the location where it is thrown particularly

---

3. It does not appear to matter which debugger is running. The same categories are always shown.

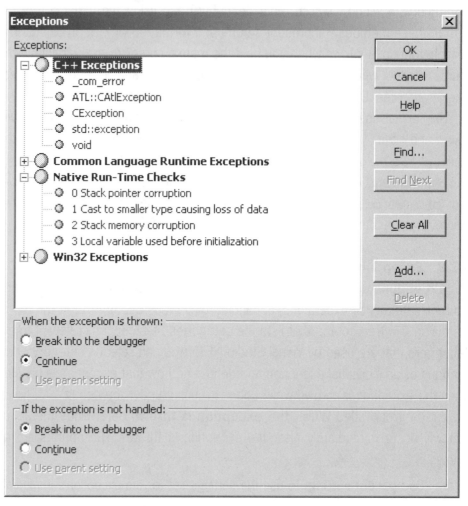

Figure 9.10 The Exceptions dialog

interest you. When an exception is thrown, it will propagate up the call stack until a handler handles it. If no handler exists, you can use the following options in the **If the exception is not handled** radio button group:

- **Use parent setting**, to use the settings of the immediate parent
- **Break into the debugger**, to stop the debugger at the location where the exception was thrown
- **Continue**, to continue execution

DEVELOPING APPLICATIONS WITH VISUAL STUDIO.NET

If you set an unhandled exception handler with `AppDomain.Unhandled-Exception` for the current domain, this event handler will be ignored.

You can add your own exceptions, but sadly you cannot add them in a hierarchical way as the CLR exceptions are in the **Exceptions** dialog. So if you want to add the options for your own managed exceptions, they will appear immediately below the **Common Language Runtime Exceptions** node. You cannot create your own namespace node.

9.1.9 Edit and Continue

Edit and Continue is a feature that I rarely use, but I will document it here just so that you know what it is all about. The idea of Edit and Continue is that while you are debugging code, you may notice that some of your code is incorrect and therefore the code will not work the way you intended it to work. The temptation is to change the code to rectify the error and continue your debugging session to take the code change into account. This approach may appear to save time, but really you should stop the debugging session and restart at such an occasion.

The reason you may think you will save time is that you may be a long way through a test script, and hence you may have entered lots of code before seeing the error. To stop the debugging session at this point means that you will have to go through the entire test script again. But when you think about it, the whole point of the debugging session and the test script is to find bugs like the one you have just identified, so the debugging session has been successful, and you should celebrate by stopping the session and having a cup of coffee while the application rebuilds. By continuing the debugging session with Edit and Continue, you are acting as if the bug had never happened, as if everything were nice and rosy and you could continue with impunity. If you are happy to change history like this, then go ahead and use Edit and Continue![4]

Edit and Continue works only with unmanaged, nonoptimized C++. If you attempt to change code in a C# project while in a debugging session, you'll get the

---

4. OK, I am being rather melodramatic, but honestly, why don't you celebrate the fact that you have found a bug and take that well-earned break from the debugging session? Even if you do not have the celebration, at least you can make sure that you change the code and update the source control—something you won't do with Edit and Continue.

Unable to Apply Code Changes dialog (Figure 9.11), which gives the option of building and restarting execution, or continuing execution. If you continue execution, the debugger will act as if the change were not made, but of course, the code in the source editor and the jitted code will be out of sync, so single-stepping will become difficult.

This is the default for C# projects. It is configured on the **Edit and Continue** page of the **Debugging** section on the **Options** dialog. There are three options for making changes to code in managed projects: First, the debugger can inform you that a change was made (the default, which will give the dialog in Figure 9.11). Second, the debugger can stop, recompile, and restart the application, or finally the debugger can simply ignore the change. If you uncheck the **Allow me to edit C# files while debugging** check box, the source editor will not accept any changes when you are debugging.

When you change code in an unmanaged C++ file during a debugging session, you'll get the **Edit and Continue** dialog (Figure 9.12), which gives you the option of applying the code changes (the **Yes** button), in which case the code is rebuilt and execution is continued at the current location, or not applying the changes (the **No** button), in which case execution continues but the source code and compiled code will be out of sync. Furthermore, if the code is under source control and you attempt to make a change, the source control will ask you to

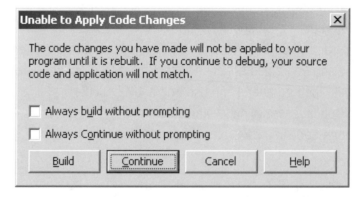

Figure 9.11   The dialog shown when you change C# source code during a debugging session

DEVELOPING APPLICATIONS WITH VISUAL STUDIO.NET

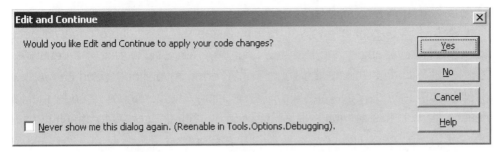

Figure 9.12   The Edit and Continue dialog shown when you change code in an unmanaged C++ project during a debugging session

check out the code before you make the change. Of course, once you have made the code change you must remember to document your change, and because it is easy to forget the details of the change, I think it is better to ignore the **Edit and Continue** dialog and stop the debugging session when you think a code change is needed.

Don't confuse **Edit and Continue** with the rebuild dialog. When you change a C+ project and press **F5** to start a debugging session, the IDE will go through the project dependencies to see if any files have changed, and if any have it will present the rebuild dialog (Figure 9.13). If you click **No** in response to the suggestion to rebuild the project, the source file and the code will be out of sync.

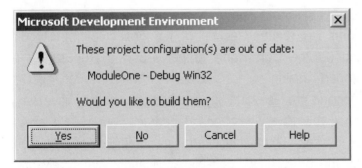

Figure 9.13   The dialog shown when the IDE has detected that a file in the project has changed and should be rebuilt before a debugging session is started

9.2 Using the Debugger

The VS.NET debugger allows you to single-step through source code, inspect values held in variables, and test how your program logic works. The debugger is invaluable in determining the source of an error in your code, and it is also a useful tool for code coverage (i.e., determining whether there is code that is never called). In this section I will go into some depth about how to attach the debugger to a process and how to step through code.

9.2.1 Starting Debugging

There are three ways to start a debugging session: (1) start a new process under the debugger, (2) attach to a running process, or (3) attach a debugger to a process that has an unhandled exception (just-in-time debugging).

Starting a process under a debugger is generally straightforward: You simply press **F5**, and the IDE will start the process and attach the debugger to it. The debugger attaches to a *process,* so if the code that you are debugging is not a process, the IDE will need to identify the process that will load your library. ISAPI extensions, for example, are loaded into IIS. Visual Studio.NET has a feature called *F5 deployment,* which means that if you are developing an ASP.NET application or Web Service, or an ATL Server application, the code will be deployed—that is, copied to the appropriate folder and installed in IIS—before the debugging session is started.

If you are developing a library (DLL), the debugger will need to know what process to use to load the library. You indicate the process that will load the library through (1) the **Start Application** property of the **Debugging** page of the **Configuration Properties** section of the project's property dialog for C# projects and (2) the **Command** property of the **Debugging** page of the project's property dialog for C++ projects. When the debugger starts, it will start the specified process, and any breakpoints you may have set in your code will be hit once your library has been loaded and your code is executed. In general, GUI processes are not launched with command-line arguments (but they can be). On the other hand, console applications are rarely started without command-line arguments. Process command-line arguments can also be specified through the project's options, both for process projects and for library projects (for the command line of the process hosting the library). I will go into more detail about project debugging options later.

Your code may already be executing—either a process or a library loaded by another process—so to debug your code in this case you'll need to attach to the process. There are two main ways to do this. If you are running an NT variant (NT4, Windows 2000, or Windows XP), you can bring up the task manager process. The **Applications** tab lists the applications with a visible window, and you can either select the application that interests you and through its context menu select **Go To Process**, or you can go directly to the **Processes** tab and select the appropriate process. From the context menu of the process you can select **Debug**, which will start the system-registered debugger and tell it to attach to the process. The system debugger is registered in the following registry key:

```
HKEY_LOCAL_MACHINE\SOFTWARE\Microsoft\Windows NT
    \CurrentVersion\AeDebug
```

Table 9.4 shows the values that you will find in this key. The `UserDebuggerHotKey` value is used when you are already running an unmanaged application under the debugger. When you press the hot key, the system will generate a `DebugBreak()` method within the process.

Table 9.4 Registered debugger key values

Value	Description
Auto	Value to determine if the debugger is automatically started. If this is set to 1, the debugger will be started without user intervention. If set to 0, the user will be queried as to whether the process should be debugged.
Debugger	Command line to start the debugger.
PreVisualStudio7Debugger	The debugger that was used before VS.NET was installed.
UserDebuggerHotKey	The virtual key code of the hot key when the process is running under a debugger.

The command line used to start the debugger will typically have the following parameters:

```
-p %ld -e %ld
```

The operating system will pass (1) the debugger the ID of the process to debug and (2) the value of an event that the debugger signals to indicate that it has attached to the process.

When you install VS.NET, it will replace the `Debugger` value with the path to the VS JIT debugger: `VS7Jit.exe`. This process lists the debuggers that you can use. Figure 9.14 shows an example of a debugger list. At the time that this

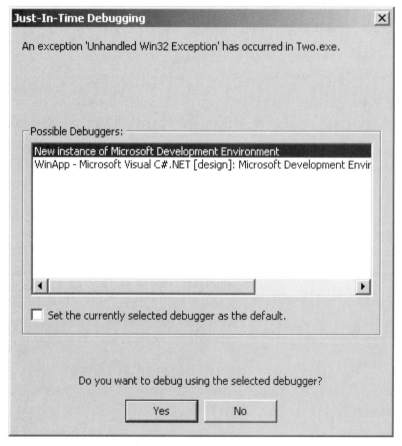

Figure 9.14 `VS7Jit` **in action**

list was generated, I had VS.NET running with a solution called `WinApp`. The window gives me the option of attaching the debugger from the existing instance of VS.NET to the faulted process, or to start a new instance of VS.NET.

When VS.NET is asked to debug a process, it needs to know which debugger to use. To get this information it will bring up a dialog like the one shown in Figure 9.15. In this example the process that faulted was a native process, so the dialog has the check box for the native debugger (**Native**) checked. If the faulting process is a .NET process, you'll also have the option of using the CLR debugger (**Common Language Runtime**). In this situation it makes sense to also select the **Native** debugger option so that if the process uses interop, you'll be able to debug that code too. The other difference that you'll see with JIT debugging of a managed application is the option of debugging the application with the Microsoft CLR Debugger.

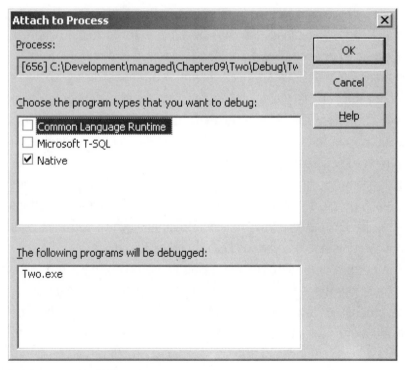

Figure 9.15   The VS.NET debuggers

Two debuggers are provided with the .NET Framework: `cordbg.exe` and `DbgCLR.exe`. The former is a command-line application, and the latter is a GUI debugger that is essentially a cut-down version of the VS.NET managed debugger.

If you select a new instance of VS.NET, `VS7Jit` starts the IDE by launching it as a COM local server. The IDE has the following CLSID:

```
{BC1046A0-CB44-4241-B8D9-0688243AFBC3}
```

If you look at the `LocalServer32` key for this server, you'll see that the development environment is started with the undocumented switch `/JITDebug`. `VS7Jit` obtains an interface called `IDebugJIT2` on the IDE, which it presumably uses to pass details about the process to debug (this interface is marshaled with a proxy-stub DLL, and there is no type library). Previous versions of the Visual Studio IDE allowed you to start the debugger through the command line by passing the process ID through a –`p` switch. This facility is no longer supported; you have to use `VS7Jit` instead.

The IDE also allows you to attach to a running process. If no solution is open, the **Processes** menu item will be on the **Tools** menu (where it will be called **Debug Processes**). If a solution is open, this menu item will be on the **Debug** menu. In both cases you'll get the **Processes** dialog shown in Figure 9.16. At the top of the dialog are options for remote debugging, which I will come back to later. The **Available Processes** list view control lists the processes running on the specified machine, which (if you have checked the **Show system processes** check box) will include services. You can select one *or more* processes from this list box and add them to the **Debugged Processes** list box. As each process is added to this list box, the debugger will attach to it. If you watch the **Output** window while this happens, you'll see as the debugger loads the symbols and the various DLLs used by the process.

At the bottom of the **Processes** dialog is a drop-down list box with the possible options for the debugger when the debugging session finishes: detach from the process or terminate it. This is a new feature of the VS.NET debugger. the VS6 debugger would always terminate a process when the debugging session finished; it could not detach from a process. To allow you to detach from a process, the Visual Studio Debugger Proxy Service must be started (through the

DEVELOPING APPLICATIONS WITH VISUAL STUDIO.NET

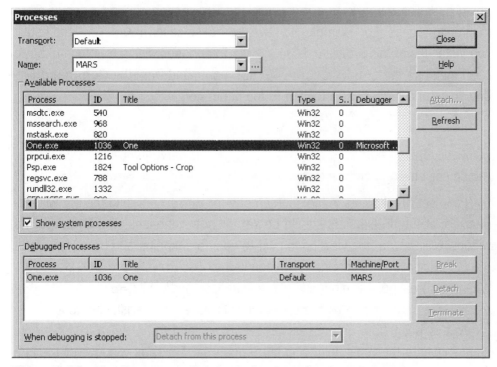

Figure 9.16   The Processes dialog used to attach to a running process

Services MMC [Microsoft Management Console] snap-in or through `net start dbgproxy` at the command line). As its name suggests, this service acts as a proxy for the Visual Studio debugger, so when you detach from a process the Debugger Proxy Service remains attached to it. You can use the three buttons to the right of the **Debugged Processes** list box to detach, terminate, or break into the process.

The option to detach is useful if you have a long-running process and you want to temporarily attach the debugger to test the behavior of the process to a particular action, but it is not a good idea if you want to make changes to the source code of the process. The reason is that when you detach, the proxy service is still attached, so you will not have write access to the process's file on disk. Consequently, any attempt to build the process will fail.

As I mentioned earlier, only one thread at a time can be single-stepped in the debugger; the other threads in the process are effectively frozen while you are doing this. The same is true if you use the **Processes** dialog to debug more than one process. For example, if I have a process called `test.exe` and I start two instances of this program, I can use the **Processes** dialog to attach to both. I can then use the `Debug.ListPrograms` command from the **Command** window to list the processes attached to the debugger:

```
Index  Id    Process          Program
-----------------------------------
  1    320   test.exe         Native
  2    1748  test.exe         Native
```

I can set breakpoints in the source code for `test.exe`, and the IDE will recognize that the breakpoints should be set for both instances. The **Breakpoints** window will show a tree view node next to each breakpoint, and below this node will be two *child breakpoints* corresponding to each of the process instances. When one breakpoint is hit in one of the instances and I call `Debug.ListPrograms`, the process that hit the breakpoint will have an asterisk next to it.

At this point *both* processes will be frozen, and I can get a list of the instances where the breakpoint was hit through the **Threads** window, or through the `Debug.ListThreads` command at the **Command** window:

```
Index  Id    Name             Location
--------------------------------------------------------
  1    1716  WinMain          _NtUserGetMessage@16
  2    2044  ThreadProc       _NtDelayExecution@8
  3    1540  ThreadProc       _NtDelayExecution@8
  4    1732  ThreadProc       _NtDelayExecution@8
 *5    792   ThreadProc       ThreadProc
  6    2040  ThreadProc       _NtDelayExecution@8
```

Here the process has six threads, five of them running in the thread procedure called `ThreadProc()`. In this example the breakpoint has been hit in the fifth thread. Neither the **Threads** window nor this list of threads in the **Command** window will list the threads for all of the processes being debugged. They both list the threads in the process where the breakpoint has been hit.

What I have described is the default action. However, you may decide that when the debugger has stopped on a breakpoint in one process, other attached processes should continue to run. To specify this, you should check the **In**

break mode, only stop execution of the current process option on the **General** page of the **Debugging** section of the **Options** dialog.

Now imagine another situation: a GUI client talking to a COM EXE server, as illustrated in Figure 9.17. When the GUI client starts up, it creates an instance of the object, and when the user clicks on a menu item, the client makes a cal to the object. I can put a breakpoint in the menu click handler that calls the object, and start the client process under the debugger. When the user clicks the menu item, the breakpoint will be hit. At this point `Debug.ListPrograms` will list just one process, `client.exe`.

If I step into the call to the COM object, one of two things will happen. Because the COM object is in another process, an interprocess call will be made. The default action is for the debugger to ignore the request to step into the call and to merely step over it. To change this behavior, you need to turn on RPC debugging through the native debugger options page (**Tools | Options | Debugging | Native**). With RPC debugging enabled, when you step into a COM call the debugger will step into the COM process that you are debugging. Because the COM object is in another process, the debugger will attach to the server process, and the IDE will present the **Attach to Process** dialog (see Figure 9.15) to allow you to specify which debugger you are likely to use. Once you have closed this dialog, you will have two processes attached to the debugger:[5]

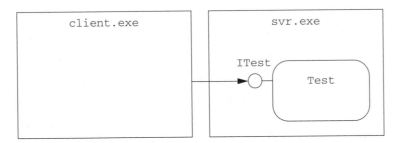

Figure 9.17   Interprocess communication using COM

---

5. I wish I could set default options here so that I could seamlessly step from the client to the server. At least this occurs only once per debugging session.

```
Index  Id    Process        Program
------------------------------------
*1     1852  Svr.exe        Native
 2     1864  Client.exe     Native
```

You can now single-step through the server code (assuming that the debugger can find the symbols and source code for the server), and when you step out of the COM method you'll appear in the client code that called the method. All of this occurs in a single instance of the VS.NET IDE.

Once the debugger has attached to the server process, you can set breakpoints in other parts of the server code. When you have finished debugging the server, you can use the **Processes** dialog to detach the server from the debugger. This is a huge improvement over the debugger in VS6, which also allowed RPC debugging but would load the server process in a separate instance of the IDE and would not allow you to detach the debugger from the server process, so that once the debugger was attached, it would remain so until the server process was terminated.

You can also start solution processes under the debugger. The project that is set as the start-up project will be started when you press **F5** or select the **Debug | Start** menu item. If the start-up project is a library, you can use the project options to specify the process that should be started to load your library. If your solution has more than one process project, pressing **F5** will not start all of them. Instead you can start each process individually through the **Debug** context menu item for the project in the **Class View** or **Solution Explorer** window. This context menu item gives two options: **Start new instance** and **Step Into new instance**. As the names suggest, these options will start a new instance of the process and either run under the debugger until a breakpoint is hit or start by stepping into the entry point for the process and breaking there.

Another option is to set the **Attach** property (on the **Debugging** properties page of the C++ project properties window). This property is usually set to **No**, which means that a new instance is started when a debugging session is started (**F5**). When it is set to **Yes**, the debugger will look for an instance of the debugging process for the start-up project and attach the debugger to that process.

9.2.2 Start-up Options

If the project is a DLL, you can use the **Debugging** properties **Command** property (C++) to identify the process to start for the DLL. This can be any process that you choose, or it can be one of the options in Table 9.5. You get these options whether the DLL is managed C++ or unmanaged C++, an ATL or MFC control, an ATL in-process server, or an MFC DLL.

If you create an ATL Server project, the **Debugging** properties page for the ATL Server DLL will give the URL to the `.srf` file for the HTTP URL property (e.g., `http://localhost/MyApp/MyApp.srf`). I will return to the issue of debugging ATL Server projects later.

If the project is a C# library, you can set the process to start through the **Start Application** property in the **Debugging** properties page, but all you get is a browse dialog to search for a process—whether the library has classes, controls, or Web controls, or is a Web Service.

If the project is a process, or if you have specified a process through the **Command** property (C++) or **Start Application** property (C#) of the **Debugging** properties page, you can pass the process command arguments. These arguments can be any parameter that the process needs and that is used typically by command-line (console) processes. Both C++ and C# console processes get the command line through the parameter passed to the process entry point:

Table 9.5 Commands to start the debugging process

Command	Meaning
Internet Explorer	Start Internet Explorer to debug an ActiveX control created through an `<OBJECT>` tag.
ActiveX Control Test Container	Either debug a control started through a `TstCon32` saved session, or use `TstCon32` to start a registered control.
regsvr32	Run `regsvr32` to call an in-process server's `DllRegisterServer()` or `DllUnregisterServer()` entry point.

```
// C++
void main(int argc, char** argv)
{
   printf("process called %s\n", argv[0]);
   puts("arguments:");
   for (int x = 1; x < argc; x++) puts(argv[x]);
}

// C#
class App
{
   static void Main(string[] args)
   {
      Console.WriteLine("process called: "
         + Environment.GetCommandLineArgs()[0]);
      Console.WriteLine("arguments:");
      foreach (string s in args)
         Console.WriteLine(s);
   }
}
```

Both managed and unmanaged C++ console arguments are passed command-line arguments through unmanaged parameters. The C++ `main()` method is passed the name of the process as the first parameter (so `argc` is always one greater than the number of arguments you pass on the command line), whereas the C# `Main()` method is passed only the command-line arguments, which are also accessed as a single string through the `Environment.CommandLine` property. The `Environment.GetCommandLineArgs()` method returns an array with all the command-line arguments, including the process name as the first argument.

C# GUI applications also have `Main()` as the entry point, so the command-line arguments are accessed through that parameter. C++ GUI applications are passed the command-line argument through the third parameter of `WinMain()`, or they can use the Win32 `GetCommandLine()` method to get the arguments as a single string or `CommandLineToArgvW()` to get the arguments in an array:

```
// native C++
int num;
LPWSTR* args;
args = CommandLineToArgvW(
   GetCommandLineW(), &num);
```

DEVELOPING APPLICATIONS WITH VISUAL STUDIO.NET

```
for (int y = 0; y < num; y++)
    _putws(args[y]);
```

The `GetCommandLine()` and `CommandLineToArgvW()` methods are available to managed projects through Platform Invoke, but it is far simpler to use the `System::Environment` class.

Both C++ and C# applications have a **Command Line Arguments** property on the **Debugging** properties page, through which you can pass the arguments that you want passed to the process.

By default, when you start a debugging session the debugger will make the *project* directory the current directory for C++ projects and the *build* directory the current directory for C# projects. That is, if you have a C++ project (managed or unmanaged) called `TestCpp` in `C:\TestCpp`, when you start the process it will be started in `C:\TestCpp`. If you have a C# project `TestCs` in `C:\TestCs`, it will be started in `C:\TestCs\bin\Debug` for debug builds and `C:\TestCs\bin\Release` for release builds. You can change the working directory through the **Working Directory** property of the **Debugging** properties page of both C++ and C# projects.

9.2.3 Stepping

Once you have started a process with **F5**, it will run under the debugger until a breakpoint is hit. The alternative is to start with **F11** (the **Step Into new instance** option I mentioned earlier), which will start the application at its entry point and break there. For a C# application the entry point will be the `Main()` function; for a console C++ application, the `main()` function; for a GUI application, `WinMain()`. Once the process has started, you can step through the project line by line in source code, or instruction by instruction in machine code. To do this you can type commands in the **Command** window (see Table 9.3 for a partial list of the possibilities), press the appropriate shortcut keys, or click on the buttons on the **Debug** toolbar (Figure 9.18). Personally, I find the shortcut keys the most convenient. When I install VS.NET on a machine, I usually use the **Customize** option (right-click on the toolbar to see this) to add the **Run To Cursor** button to the **Debug** toolbar because I use this button often.[6]

---

6. Although this command is called **Run To Cursor**, it actually means "run to caret" because the execution will run until the code is reached at the current insertion point—the caret.

Table 9.6   The default buttons on the Debug toolbar

Button	Key	Meaning
Continue	F5	Run until a breakpoint is hit.
Break All	Ctrl-Alt-Break	Break into a running process.
Stop Debugging	Shift-F5	Stop the process.
Restart	Ctrl-Shift-F5	Stop the process and restart the debugging session.
Show Next Statement		When stopped in the debugger, open the source window at the next statement that will be executed.
Step Into	F11	Step into the function at the caret.
Step Over	F10	Step over the function at the caret.
Step Out	Shift-F11	Step out of the current function.
Hexadecimal Display		Change the format of the tool windows between hex and decimal display.
Breakpoints	Ctrl-Alt-B	Show the **Breakpoints** window.

Figure 9.18   The Debug toolbar. These buttons are described in Table 9.6.

To single-step through code you use the **F10** key, which will execute a single statement. When you come to a function, pressing **F10** will step over the function—that is, execute it as if it were a single statement. If this is not what you want and you have symbols for the function, you can use **F11** to step into the function. You can use the **Call Stack** window to view and negotiate the call stack. The yellow arrow in the call stack (see Figure 9.7) indicates the current execution point—that is, the next statement that will be executed. The IDE allows you to move the execution point to another location. To do this you click on the yellow arrow with the cursor and then drag it to the location where you want to move the execution point. Consider the following code:

```
1: // native C++
2: #include "stdafx.h"
3: void main()
4: {
5:    int i = 1;
6:    i = 10;
7:    i *= 4;
8:    printf("%ld", i);
9: }
```

Imagine that you have put a breakpoint on line 6 and then started the debugger. When the breakpoint is hit, the yellow arrow will be on line 6 and i will have a value of 1 (i.e., the assignment at line 6 will not have occurred). If you move the execution point to line 7, you indicate that any lines between the old execution point and the new one should not be executed. Thus when you single-step (i.e., press **F10**), line 7 will be executed without line 6 having been executed, and hence the value printed out will be 4, not 40.

Be very careful where you move the execution point. You are allowed to move it out of the current function in unmanaged code, even to a function that is not in the current call stack. But moving the execution point out of the current function will inevitably lead to an exception as the debugger recognizes that the stack has been corrupted. I have shown an example with unmanaged C++, but the debugger also supports this action with managed code. Under the .NET debugger, however, you are prevented from moving the execution point outside of the current function.

Typically, when you are debugging code you are interested in only small sections of code at a time. For example, you may be concerned with the first few lines of a function, and after you have checked that those lines have executed correctly, you may decide that you do not need to single-step through all the other lines in the function. You can use the **Step Out** button (**Shift-F11**) to tell the debugger to execute the remaining lines of the function and put the execution point on the line after the function call.

On the other hand, you may decide to skip forward a few lines. To do this you can place the caret on the next line that interests you and select **Run To Cursor**. The lines between the current execution point and the caret will be executed, and the debugger will stop at the location of the caret. If the caret happens to be above the execution point when you select **Run To Cursor**, the process will be restarted.

If you do not have the symbols for a function, you will be allowed to step through only the machine code for the function. For example, if you use `Debug-Break()` in a native C++ application, you'll find that if you run the application under the debugger, the actual execution point will be placed on an `int 3` opcode within the `DebugBreak()` function:

```
_DbgBreakPoint@0:
    int 3
    ret
```

In the previous version of Visual Studio this was a problem because the user saw that the debugger had stopped in some machine code and not the C++ code that they expected. To ease the anxiety that this caused, the VS.NET designers put the green triangle (next executed line in the calling function) in the C++ code that called `DebugBreak()`. The **Call Stack** window shows that the execution point is within code in `NTDLL.DLL`, and if you attempt to single-step, the IDE will tell you that there isn't any source code and will give you the option of viewing the **Disassembly** window. If you decide not to view the disassembly, the debugger will step over the call to `DebugBreak()`.

Another situation in which you'll see machine code disassembled is when you step out of a COM call to another process. Recall earlier that I said that if you step into a call to an out-of-process server, the IDE will magically load the server under the debugger in the same instance of VS.NET. You can then single-step through the COM method. However, when you single-step past a `return` call that leaves the COM method, you'll suddenly find yourself stepping through the machine code of the RPC marshaling code.

Technogeeks like me spend hours stepping through code like this (with symbols loaded, naturally) to get an idea of how COM marshaling works, but most developers are not interested in such fine details, so the way to avoid this is to make sure that when you leave a COM method, you use **Step Out** and not **Step Over** (i.e., single step).

9.2.4 Crashes

When a native application throws an exception, the system will start the default registered debugger (registered in the `AeDebug` registry key, as explained earlier) and allow the debugger to attach to the faulted application. When you install VS.NET, this debugger will be `VS7Jit.exe`, but most machines—the machines that will be running your code—will have Dr Watson (`drwtsn32.exe`) registered as the default debugger. Dr Watson will generate a crash dump by saving a copy of the memory used by the process at the point when the crash occurred. It will also generate a user-readable log file containing information about the threads that were running at the point of the crash, the contents of the stack, and the location of the fault. Dr Watson crash dumps can be loaded by the `WinDbg` utility,[7] which will load the crash dump and treat it as if it were the current state of the memory. The crash dump has full information about the modules that are loaded, and if the symbols are available you will be able to determine the name of the function that caused the fault, as well as its parameters and their values. You can also traverse the stack, and depending on the amount of information in the symbols, you may even be able to see values of local variables. This is wonderful information, and it makes determining the source of the fault an easier task. The downside is that Dr Watson crash dumps can be quite large.

Visual Studio.NET supports *minidumps*. As the name suggests, minidumps are crash dumps that are significantly smaller than full Dr Watson dumps, and Visual Studio.NET will both generate and load minidumps. You can generate a minidump when the debugger has stopped within a process through the **Debug | Save Dump As** menu item. The minidump you create can be shipped to another developer who has the same operating system and has the source and symbols for the application that faulted. This other developer can then load the minidump using the **File | Open | File** menu item, which will create a new solution that just contains the minidump.

At this point the developer can start a new debugging session by pressing **F5**, and the debugger will load the minidump as if the process were running in memory. This developer will be able to view the stack and (if she has access to

---

7. `WinDbg` can be installed from the Windows 2000 support CD.

the symbols for the modules identified in the minidump) will be able to see the function names and parameters. Furthermore, if the developer has the source code for the faulted process, she will be able to see the location in the source code where the fault occurred and the values of local variables.

9.2.5 Compile-Time Checks

I have already mentioned some of the compiler settings used in debugging, and I will mention more later in this chapter. In this section I will describe some of the compiler settings that you can use to persuade the compiler to do some work for you.

The compiler will do a lot of work for you to *prevent* a bug from occurring. When you compile an application, the compiler will check your source code for errors, looking for code that, although it compiles fine, may have a coding error and cause a fault at runtime. When the compiler encounters suspect code, it issues a warning because it cannot tell if the code is intended or not. In general, you should pay close attention to warnings. For example, look at the following code:

```
// C++
void printTotal(int i1, int i2, int i3)
{
    int il;
    i1 = i1 + i2 + i3;
    printf("total %ld", il);
}
```

Can you see what is wrong with this code? The function takes three `int` values, adds them together, and prints out the total. The intention is to assign a local variable `il` (the variable name is the two letters `i` and `l`) with the total of the three `int` values, and use this variable as the last parameter passed to `printf()`. However, the total is actually put into the variable `i1` (the variable name is the letter `i` followed by the number `1`), whereas the intended (but unassigned) variable `il` is passed to `printf()`. When this code is compiled, it will generate the following warning:

```
warning C4700: local variable 'il' used
without having been initialized
```

This warning indicates that you really ought to look at the code again. The suspect code could be an artifact left over from deleting code (but leaving one line that should have been deleted), or, as in this case, it could be a spelling mistake. Typically developers tend to ignore warnings during the initial development phase because they want to concentrate on more pressing issues, such as implementing business rules. However, a warning does indicate that there is something unusual in the code, so warnings should be acted on before the code is finally released.

Compiler errors are always acted on because the output file will not be generated if there are errors. Thus VS.NET compilers allow you to tell them to treat warnings as errors, and this should be the de facto setting for your release builds. The C# compiler supports two switches for how warnings are treated; both can be found on the project property pages, on the **Configuration Properties | Build** page. The **Warning Level** property (`/warn` switch) affects which types of warnings are displayed. There are five levels, and the default is the highest level (`/warn:4`), which lists all warnings that occur. As the warning level decreases, fewer warnings will be displayed. A value of `/warn:0` will list no warnings.

I rarely change the warning level, and if I do, I treat it as only a temporary change to remove some of the clutter from the **Output** window during a build when I am working on a section of code, when I know there is another section of code that needs my attention. After I have debugged the first section of code, I can increase the warning level and then give my attention to the other section of code. The C++ project properties give access to the warning level through the **Warning Level** property on the C/C++ property page. Again, there are five levels, from `/W0` (to turn off warnings) up to `/W4`.

Release builds should be bug free, so you should do your initial release builds by treating warnings as errors. The C# compiler has the `/warnaserror` switch, and the C++ compiler has the `/wx` switch (Visual Studio gives access to both of these through the **Treat Warnings as Errors** property).

9.2.6 Compiler Runtime Checks

In addition to the compile-time checks that I have just described, the C++ compiler can place diagnostic code in your debug builds to catch some of the more insidious bugs at runtime. As a language, C++ is elegant and flexible, but it has its roots in C, which was designed as a systems programming language in which developers often had to manipulate blocks of memory. So the C language allowed you to cast memory pointers to pointers to structures so that the memory could be accessed through members of the structure, or even to treat a pointer as an array of structures.

Pointer syntax makes C (and C++) very useful, but it has an implicit danger because there is nothing in the code to determine where the end of the array is. Instead the developer must know this and code accordingly. The most frequent case when this becomes a problem occurs when you use strings. In C++, strings are arrays of `char` items, and if you are likely to perform string concatenation, you must be sure to allocate enough space for the resultant string—for example:

```
// native C++
int i = 0;
char strGreeting[8] = "hello ";
strcat(strGreeting, "there");
puts(strGreeting);
```

This simple piece of code is a disaster waiting to happen. The reason is that the resultant string needs 14 characters, but the code allocates a buffer of only 8 characters. The compiler performs no checks on the code, so this error will show up only at runtime. Even at runtime it may not be immediately visible because auto variables are allocated on the stack in the reverse order that they appear in the code, so the buffer `strGreeting` will be at a lower memory location than the integer `i`. This means that the call to `strcat()` will cause a buffer overrun, and the excess data will be written into the integer `i` (so after the call to `strcat()`, this integer will have a value of `0x00657265`, the string "ere"). You will discover that there is a problem only when you perform a particular action with this integer, and even then it may not be immediately obvious.

A more serious situation occurs if the inadequate buffer is the first auto variable because if you use the C calling convention, the memory higher in the stack will contain the function parameters and the return address. Your buffer overrun

DEVELOPING APPLICATIONS WITH VISUAL STUDIO.NET

could overwrite the return address, causing, if you're lucky, an exception to occur because of a corrupted stack. However, because debug builds often put packing between auto variables on the stack, such an error may occur not in the debug build but only in a release build!

The following function:

```
// native C++
void f()
{
    char strGreeting[8] = "hello ";
    strcat(strGreeting, "there");
    puts(strGreeting);
}
```

will not show an error in debug builds but will throw an obscure exception (**The memory could not be "read"**) in release builds. Such a buffer overrun can be exploited by Trojan viruses and is a security risk. The new version of the compiler has a switch, /GS (that is applied by default for release builds on the **Buffer Security Check** property on the **C/C++ | Code Generation** page of the project property pages), and will check for buffer overruns that write over the return address of a function. In the case of such an overrun, a dialog will appear at runtime saying that a buffer overrun has happened and that it is so serious that the process will be terminated (Figure 9.19).

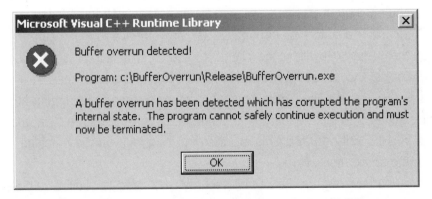

Figure 9.19   The dialog that will show in release builds if a buffer overrun occurs

This switch will not be set by default for debug builds. However, by default another new switch (called /RTC1) will be set for debug builds. This switch can be adjusted on the **C/C++ | Code Generation** page through the **Basic Runtime Checks** property. /RTC1 is a combination of two separate switches: /RTCs and /RTCu. The former (/RTCs) adds code that performs runtime checks on the stack. This code will initialize variables, filling them with one or more 0xCC bytes. If you find that your variables have odd values, it is likely that they have been used without initialization. The runtime check also places guard blocks before and after buffers. When the function finishes, the code checks whether these guard blocks are intact. If they are not, a dialog will appear telling you which variable had the problem. The final check is to see if the stack has been corrupted because the function was called with the wrong calling convention. The other new runtime check switch, /RTCu, performs checks on the variables in the function and will issue a dialog if a variable has been used without being initialized.

Finally, the /RTCc switch checks for data truncation, casting a variable to a type that will cause a data loss. This switch is configured through the **Smaller Type Check** property of the **C/C++ | Code Generation** page.

9.2.7 Remote Debugging

Visual Studio.NET supports two means of debugging remote applications: the Machine Debug Manager service and the VC remote debugging monitor. The Machine Debug Manager service (mdm.exe) is used to launch the JIT debugger. Visual Studio.NET talks to mdm through DCOM, so you have to make sure that you set up the security to allow the clients to attach. When mdm is installed, the DCOM launch and access permissions of the service give access to a group called Debugger Users. Thus when you set up a remote debugging session, the first action is to ensure that the account you'll be using on the client machine (where VS.NET will be running) is included in this group on the machine where the remote application will run.

After you have set up the DCOM security, you need to allow a remote machine to initiate JIT debugging, and to do this you have to configure the mdm service. This service is installed in the following path:

`Program Files\Common Files\Microsoft Shared\VS7Debug`

To configure the service, you should run `mdm` with the `/remotecfg` switch. Doing this will bring up the dialog in Figure 9.20. To allow a client machine to be informed when a process crashes, you have to check the **Enable Remote Just-In-Time Debugging** option and add the name of the client machine to the list box.

Once you have done this, you can run processes on the remote machine. When an exception occurs, you'll first get a dialog on the remote machine indicating that an unhandled exception has occurred, and when you dismiss this dialog using the **Retry** button, the debugger on the client machine that you specified on the `mdm` configuration dialog (see Figure 9.20) will be used. You'll get the familiar `VS7Jit` dialog (see Figure 9.14) asking you which debugger to use, which will then attempt to attach to the remote process and will give you a list of the debuggers that VS.NET can use. Furthermore, you can use the **Tools | Debug Processes** dialog to attach to a process on a remote machine.

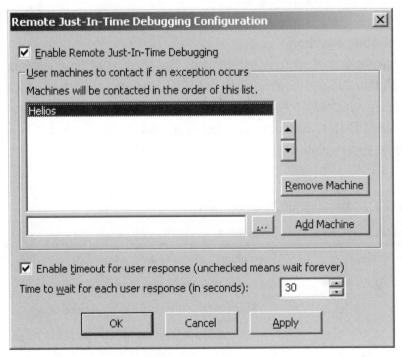

Figure 9.20   Machine Debug Manager

9.2.8 Disassembly Window

The **Disassembly** window is available both in managed and unmanaged projects. As I have already mentioned, although managed projects contain IL, the code that is executed is actually machine code that has been JIT-compiled at runtime. Hence when you use the **Disassembly** window, the code that is disassembled is the machine code and not the IL. Furthermore, there is no guarantee about where in virtual memory the JIT compiler will put the compiled IL, and for this reason the **Disassembly** window will show the address of managed code relative to the start of the function that is being disassembled. This gives the odd view of having code located at memory address 0x00000000: This is not virtual memory location zero, just zero with respect to the start of the function.

When you are in the debugger you can bring up the **Disassembly** window at any time through the source editor context menu item **Go To Disassembly**, and the current code will be shown in the assembly. The context menu of the **Disassembly** window allows you to determine how much detail is shown. This information is summarized in Table 9.7.

9.2.9 Debug Symbols

Debug symbols contain type information. The amount of type information depends on the compiler switches you use. Even though they are used for debugging, debug symbols do not necessarily imply that the source is compiled as a debug build. That is, you can have optimized code, and you do not need to define the DEBUG symbol.

Table 9.7   Disassembly window details

Context Menu Item	Description
Show Address	The memory address of the machine code
Show Source Code	The high-level source code (assuming it is available)
Show Code Bytes	The machine code that has been disassembled
Show Symbol Names	The names of symbols (assuming symbols are loaded)
Show Line Numbers	Line numbers of the source code (assuming it is available)

DEVELOPING APPLICATIONS WITH VISUAL STUDIO.NET

Visual Studio.NET creates a program database (.pdb) file, although the debugger recognizes three types of debug symbols. The amount of type information that is generated is controlled by the /z switch of the C++ compiler (see Table 9.8).

When you create symbol information, you have a choice of the amount of information you create. For your own use you should create full symbol information so that the debugger can step through machine code and relate that machine code to source code, associating memory locations with variables. In addition, you may want to generate symbol information for other users so that if an error occurs, your customers can debug your application and obtain a human-readable name of the function that generated the error. Such debug information should not contain complete symbol information because in that case information would be revealed that could be used to reverse-engineer your code. This is the purpose of the /zd switch.

The ability to step through code under a debugger requires enough information to interpret the stack. Typically, functions occupy a stack frame pointed to by the stack pointer (the EBP register points to the start of the stack frame). The return address and the function's parameters are pushed onto the stack, and local variables usually occupy the locations at lower memory. Being able to interpret the stack allows the debugger to get the previous stack frame and hence interpret what returning from a function means. Some code is optimized to remove the need for stack frames for some functions; hence so-called Frame Pointer Omission (FPO) records have to be generated in the symbols to enable the debugger to correctly interpret these situations.

Table 9.8 Compiler switches for generating symbol information

Switch	Description
/zd	Contains global and external symbols and line number information.
/z7	Contains full symbol information that is CodeView compatible.
/zi	Contains full symbol information in .pdb format.
/zI	Contains full symbol information in .pdb format and supports Edit and Continue.

The compiler will produce a separate program database file for the `/Zi` and `/ZI` switches. In addition, `/ZI` produces an `.idb` file with Edit and Continue information; for the `/Zd` and `/Z7` switches the symbol information is stored in the `.obj` file. The `.pdb` file created by the compiler is named after the version of the compiler (i.e., `vc70.pdb`) by default, but you can change this by using the `/Fd` compiler switch. When the `/debug` switch is used with the linker, it collates the debug symbols from the `.obj` and `.pdb` files (if they exist) and creates a single `.pdb` file with the name of the project (i.e., the output name of the file generated by `link.exe`) or a file specified by the `/pdb` switch. The output file will contain the full path to the `.pdb` file that was created. The debugger will use this path to determine the name of the program database, and either it will look in the same directory as the file that it is debugging for the program database, or if that fails, it will follow the path stored in the file.

As I have mentioned, you can use any of the compiler optimizer flags along with the flags to generate debugging symbols because the compiler will generate FPO records. This is generally the case with the linker when you use `/debug` to generate symbols, except that the linker uses `/ref:noref,noicf`, which indicates that the output module should include all functions, even if they are not referenced, and should include identical functions if they are referenced by different `.obj` files. You can use the `/ref:ref,icf` switch to remove both the functions (COMDAT records) that are not referenced and any duplicate COMDAT records.

As I have mentioned, debug symbols with full symbol information contain detailed information about your code, which can be useful for reverse-engineering your code. The linker supports the `/pdbstripped` option to produce a separate program database file that contains just public symbols and FPO data. You can ship this `.pdb` file to your customers so that they can get complete call stacks and information from Dr Watson logs out in the field. Microsoft does something similar with NT: It provides `.dbg` symbol files that contain FPO and public symbols.

VS.NET gives access to the generation of symbol files through the project's properties. The two main places to look are the **Linker** and **C/C++** nodes under **Configuration Properties**. The **General** node under **C/C++** properties gives access to the /z switches through the **Debug Information Format** property, whereas the **Output Files** node allows you to specify the program database produced by the C++ compiler (/Fd) through the **Program Database File Name** property. The linker options are all available on the **Debug** node: **Generate Debug Info** turns on the /debug switch, **Generate Program Database File** allows you to specify the name of the program database file (through the /pdb switch), and **Strip Private Symbols** allows you to specify the name of the private symbols file passed to the /pdbstripped switch.

9.2.10 Debugging ATL Server Projects

ATL7 has new facilities for providing tracing information and detecting memory leaks. ATL7 is now fully integrated with MFC, so MFC applications can use these facilities too. The development of these new facilities has been driven by the necessity to make ATL Server as robust as possible, and as you'll see, it has resulted in a rich API of debugging classes.

You make assertions in your code on expressions that *must* be true for the code to work. Assertions compile to nothing in release code, so they have no effect on the final output of your project. In debug builds, an assertion should check that the expression is true, and if it isn't, it should bring this to your attention in as obvious a way as possible. In native C++ the best way to perform an assertion is with the ATLASSERT() macro, and to use this you merely have to include atlbase.h. (ATLASSERT() is defined as the CRT _ASSERTE() macro, but you can define your own version if you wish, as long as you do it before including atlbase.h.) Here is a trivial example:

```
// unmanaged C++
void PrintName(LPCTSTR strName)
{
    ATLASSERT(strName != NULL);
    _tprintf("your name is %s\n", strName);
}
```

This code will generate a failed assertion in debug builds if PrintName() is called with a NULL pointer. In release builds the code will print

```
your name is (null)
```

at the console if a NULL pointer is passed, which will be an irritating but not earth-shattering bug. However, if your code performs some analysis on the pointer, then a NULL pointer will often cause a runtime access error. For example, the _tcslen() CRT function call will generate an access violation call at runtime for a NULL pointer. Consider the following version of the function:

```
// unmanaged C++
void PrintName(LPCTSTR strName)
{
    ATLASSERT(strName != NULL);
    _tprintf("your name has %ld characters\n",
             _tcslen(strName));
    _tprintf("your name is %s\n", strName);
}
```

This version of PrintName() will ensure that your customers do not see an access violation error because it will have been picked up by debug builds. (Of course, production code will check to make sure that the value passed to _tcslen() is not NULL.) By default, a failed assertion results in a dialog like the one shown in Figure 9.21. This dialog contains details of the process that performed the assertion, the location of the assertion, and the expression that was asserted.

Figure 9.21   The failed-assertion dialog

The failed-assertion dialog has three buttons. If you click the **Abort** button, the program will be aborted immediately. If you click the **Ignore** button, processing will continue, but you should be aware that something is wrong in the process, so an exception could occur later. The final button, **Retry**, will activate the just-in-time debugger, which will produce another modal dialog indicating that a breakpoint has been reached, and you must click on the **Cancel** button to debug the program. Debugging the process allows you to look at the stack with the debugger and find out why the assertion failed. Figure 9.21 shows that the expression that failed is `strName != 0`. You can make the message more expressive like this:

```
// unmanaged C++
ATLASSERT(strName != NULL && "string pointer is NULL");
```

This works because the string literal will always be nonzero and hence "true," so if `strName` is `NULL`, the entire expression will be `false`.

The assertion dialog is modal, which means that the thread that produces it will be blocked until the dialog is dismissed. This becomes a problem if the assertion occurs in code that is not running in the interactive user's window station: The dialog will not be visible.

`ATLASSERT()` is defined as `_ASSERTE()`, which calls the C runtime function `_CrtDbgReport()`. This function can create a dialog, or the assertion message can be diverted to a file or to the output stream by a call to `_CrtSetReportMode()`, which takes the type of report that you are changing (warnings, errors, or assertions) and where the report should be sent (debug stream, file, or dialog). If you direct the report to a file, you have to call `_CrtSetReportFile()` to pass the handle of an open file to write the assertion report:

```
// unmanaged C++
HANDLE hFile = CreateFile(_T("asserts.log"),
    GENERIC_WRITE, 0, 0, CREATE_ALWAYS,
    FILE_FLAG_WRITE_THROUGH, 0);
_CrtSetReportMode(_CRT_ASSERT, _CRTDBG_MODE_FILE);
_CrtSetReportFile(_CRT_ASSERT, hFile);
```

This code indicates that all assertions should be written to the file `asserts.log`. The code that includes this code should also have some code to close the file so that the assertion messages are flushed to disk. If you want to customize the message generated for an assertion (e.g., to log the time and date of the assertion or the process and thread ID where the assertion occurred), or if you want to apply a filter and log the assertions for only a specific class, you have to define a report hook. To do this you should create a function with the following prototype:

```
// unmanaged C++
int ReportHook(int type, char *message, int *retVal);
```

You register this method with the CRT by passing the function pointer to `_CrtSetReportHook2()`, so that when a report of any type is generated it will be passed to your report hook first. If your hook function returns TRUE, then no other processing will occur. However, if the hook returns FALSE, the report will be handled by whatever mode was set by `_CrtSetReportMode()`, and the default is the assertion dialog.

The first parameter to the hook function is the type of report (warning, error, or assertion), the second is the report string, and the final parameter is the value that should be returned by the `_CrtDbgReport()` function that called your hook function. If this value is 1, the JIT debugger will be started. The other possible values are 0 (if no errors are generated) and −1 (if an error occurred).

ATL7 has a solution to this problem with a class called `CDebugReportHook` (declared in `atlutil.h`). This class defines a hook function that sends all report messages to a named pipe called `AtlsDbgPipe`:

```
// unmanaged C++
class CDebugReportHook
{
public:
    CDebugReportHook(LPCSTR szMachineName = ".",
        LPCSTR szPipeName = "AtlsDbgPipe",
        DWORD dwTimeout = 20000) throw();
    ~CDebugReportHook() throw();
    BOOL SetPipeName(LPCSTR szMachineName = ".",
        LPCSTR szPipeName = "AtlsDbgPipe") throw();
    void SetTimeout(DWORD dwTimeout);
    void SetHook() throw();
    void RemoveHook() throw();
```

```
      static int __cdecl CDebugReportHookProc(
          int reportType, char *message,
          int *returnValue) throw();
};
```

The constructor calls SetPipeName(), which creates the pipe name from the parameters passed to it, which by default will assume that the pipe is located on the local machine. However, if you want to send reports to another machine, you can pass the machine name as the first parameter of the constructor. The constructor then calls SetHook(), which calls _CrtSetReportHook2() to install the static function CDebugReportHookProc as the hook function. The destructor also calls _CrtSetReportHook2(), but it removes the hook function.

The hook function writes information about the client (the process ID and the machine name), as well as the assertion message to the pipe. In response, the server at the end of the pipe will return 1 if it requires a stack dump, which the hook function will generate using a class called CReportHookDumpHandler. Finally, the hook reads from the pipe the possible responses to the assertion: ignore, retry (start under the debugger), or abort. To use the hook, all you have to do is declare a global instance of CDebugReportHook in one of the C++ files of your project, as shown here:

```
// unmanaged C++
#ifdef DEBUG
CDebugReportHook g_dbg;
#endif
```

Visual Studio.NET provides a named pipe server called WebDbg. You should run this utility on the machine that is specified in the constructor of CDebugReportHook. If you launch it from Windows Explorer or the command line, the utility will be run in the window station of an interactive user. When WebDbg is passed an assertion, it will add the message to its list box and present a dialog with details of the assertion (see Figure 9.22). The **View** menu of this utility has a checked menu item for the stack trace, and if this is checked it will write back to the source of the assertion that a stack trace is required. In Figure 9.22 this stack trace is shown in the list view at the bottom of the dialog. In addition, the

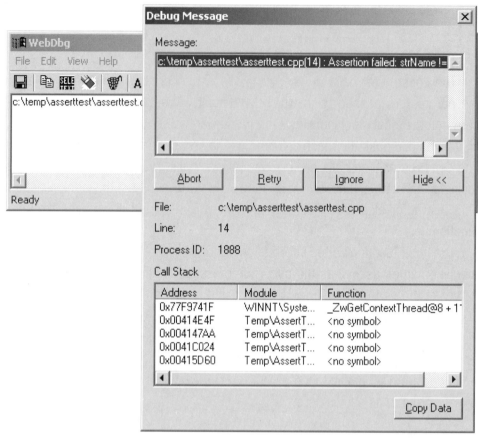

Figure 9.22 WebDbg

dialog has the familiar **Abort**, **Retry**, and **Ignore** trio of buttons. As I have already mentioned, when one of these buttons is clicked, its identity is sent back to the hook function. If the user clicks on **Retry**, the hook function calls `Debug-Break()` if a debugger is already attached to the process.

WebDbg allows you to specify the name of the pipe on which it is listening and to define the accounts that are allowed to access this pipe. This means that you can have more than one instance of WebDbg running on a machine, which is particularly useful if an application is made up of more than one process. You can choose whether all processes send assertions to the same pipe, or whether different processes report to different pipes.

WebDbg is also used to gather trace messages from processes generated through ATLTRACE(). This method has been improved significantly since ATL3. The ATLTRACE macro is defined as follows in atltrace.h:

```
#ifndef ATLTRACE
#define ATLTRACE \
    ATL::CTraceFileAndLineInfo(__FILE__, __LINE__)
#define ATLTRACE2 ATLTRACE
#endif
```

The first point to make is that ATLTRACE() and ATLTRACE2() are the same. In ATL3 the difference between the two was that ATLTRACE2() took extra parameters for the category of the trace message and a level of importance of the message. The definition of ATLTRACE() looks a little odd; all it does is declare a temporary instance of CTraceFileAndLineInfo, passing the current name of the source file and the line number. However, note that ATL-TRACE() is called like this:

```
// unmanaged C++
ATLTRACE("Test message\n");
```

for which the preprocessor will substitute the following:

```
// unmanaged C++
ATL::CTraceFileAndLineInfo(
    __FILE__, __LINE__)("Test message\n");
```

That is, operator() will be called on the temporary object. This function is overloaded for the various ways that it will be called: either with a Unicode string or with an ANSI string, with or without a category and level. These methods in turn call the overloaded TraceV() method on a static instance of a class called CTrace:

```
// unmanaged C++ from atltrace.h
class CTrace
{
public:
    typedef int (__cdecl *fnCrtDbgReport_t)
            (int, const char *, int,
             const char *, const char *, ...);
private:
```

```
        CTrace(
#ifdef _ATL_NO_DEBUG_CRT
        fnCrtDbgReport_t pfnCrtDbgReport = NULL);
#else
        fnCrtDbgReport_t pfnCrtDbgReport = _CrtDbgReport);
#endif
    ~CTrace();
public:
    bool ChangeCategory(DWORD_PTR dwCategory,
        UINT nLevel, ATLTRACESTATUS eStatus);
    bool GetCategory(DWORD_PTR dwCategory,
        UINT *pnLevel, ATLTRACESTATUS *peStatus);
    UINT GetLevel();
    void SetLevel(UINT nLevel);
    ATLTRACESTATUS GetStatus();
    void SetStatus(ATLTRACESTATUS eStatus);
    void __cdecl TraceV(const char *pszFileName,
        int nLine, DWORD_PTR dwCategory, UINT nLevel,
        LPCSTR pszFmt, va_list args) const;
    void __cdecl TraceV(const char *pszFileName,
        int nLine, DWORD_PTR dwCategory, UINT nLevel,
        LPCWSTR pszFmt, va_list args) const;
    DWORD_PTR RegisterCategory(LPCSTR pszCategory);
#ifdef _UNICODE
    DWORD_PTR RegisterCategory(LPCWSTR pszCategory);
#endif
    bool LoadSettings(LPCTSTR pszFileName = NULL) const;
    void SaveSettings(LPCTSTR pszFileName = NULL) const;
public:
    static CTrace s_trace;
protected:
    HINSTANCE m_hInst;
    DWORD_PTR m_dwModule;
};
```

First, this class has a private constructor because there is intended to be only
one instance: the public static instance `s_trace` (the allocation of the static variable
is in the file `externs.cpp`, which is used to build the `atls.lib` or `atlsd.lib` library). The constructor is passed either a pointer to `_CrtDbgReport` or `NULL`.
This pointer will be the function that will be called to generate the trace message.
The `CTrace` constructor registers this function pointer with a function called `Atl-
TraceRegister()`. Here's where the fun begins.

Each module in an application that has been written with ATL will have its own trace settings. Thus if you have an ATL server application that loads a COM DLL server written with ATL, the trace messages produced by the two DLLs can be individually configured. The `CAtlAllocator` class creates and manages a memory-mapped file, one per process. This memory-mapped file is used to provide a shared memory section that holds information about the trace settings for all of the ATL modules that are loaded. Access to this class is through a global instance called `g_Allocator`. This allocator hands out parcels of memory from this shared memory.

Figure 9.23 shows the relationships among the various types of information, and not necessarily the actual layout in memory. As you can see, a general instance of `CAtlTraceProcess` holds the trace settings for the process in general. This instance holds a collection of `CAtlTraceModule` objects—one for each ATL DLL loaded in the process. Each module (including the process) has a level, and only messages at or below this level will be traced. In addition, each module has a list of categories that can be reported, as well as a pointer to the function that will report the message.

This information can be changed at runtime by calls to the methods on the global allocator instance. In addition, you can use this global object to persist the settings to disk (`SaveSettings()`) or to load them from a disk file (`LoadSettings()`). If you call `LoadSettings()` without a file name, the name of the current module is used appended with `.trc`. However, you cannot call `SaveSettings()` without a file name.

Traversing the intricacies of the process, module, and category information is not straightforward, so the ATL team has provided a handy tool called the **ATL/MFC Trace Tool**.[8] This tool searches for the memory-mapped files created to hold trace settings information and presents them in a tree view. Under each node in the tree view are the trace settings for each module loaded into the process, and under these settings are the categories that can be traced. Figure 9.24 shows a screen shot of this tool; the debugging settings for the `Assert-Test.exe` process are being edited. Under the process is the list of modules

---

8. Or indeed the **MFC/ATL Trace Tool**, according to the **Tools** menu.

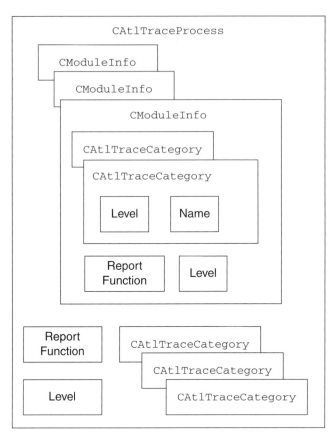

Figure 9.23 Schematic of trace settings

that it loads. Because this example does not load any other ATL DLLs, there is only an entry for the process. You can see the categories that can be traced, and for each one you can specify whether the category is enabled and if so, the level at which it will be traced. Categories can have their values specified globally (for the entire process), or they can have different values for each module.

When you change settings via the trace tool, you should click on the **Apply** button for each change you make. You can also use the trace tool to persist all the settings to a file and to load them from a persisted file.

In addition, you can create your own trace category, which you do by creating a global instance of the CTraceCategory class, passing the name and (optionally) the level of the category to the constructor:

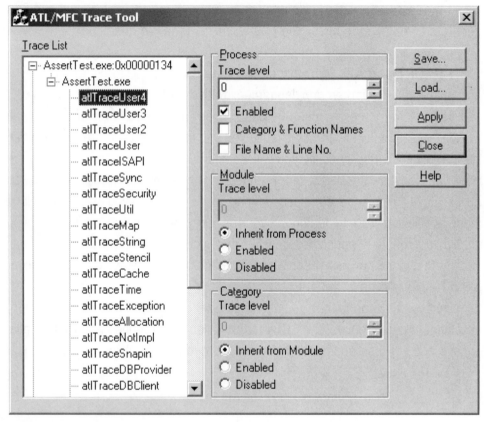

Figure 9.24   The ATL/MFC Trace Tool dialog

```
// unmanaged C++
CTraceCategory atlTraceGeneral("myInfo", 7);
CTraceCategory atlTraceCOM("myWarning", 3);
CTraceCategory atlTraceQI("myError", 0);
```

Using categories is straightforward:

```
ATLTRACE(myError, 0,
   _T("Cannot find file %s\n"), strFileName);
```

Here I am recording that the process cannot find a particular file. By default this information will be reported in WebDbg simply as the string passed to ATL-TRACE(). To get the category displayed in WebDbg, you need to check the **Category & Function Names** check box for the category (see Figure 9.24). If you would like to see the source file and line number where the trace message was generated, you need to check the **File Name & Line No** check box.

9.2.11 CRT and ATL Memory Debugging

ATL utilizes the CRT memory debugging routines to allow you to detect leaks and damage to memory caused by buffer overruns. The APIs to do this can be found in `atldbgmem.h`. To use this file you should include it before *any* included file that uses ATL, so typically you will include it before you include `stdafx.h`. However, because the debugging routines use the conversion routines in `atlconv.h`, which itself uses types defined in `wtypes.h`, you have to include these two files as well. In addition, if your project uses precompiled headers, you should turn off that option for any file that includes `atldbgmem.h` (you can specify that a file not use precompiled headers through its **C/C++ | Precompiled Headers** property page).

Once you have done this, you can add code to your files to perform memory checking. In debug builds, the CRT memory allocation routines will track all allocations and you can access this information through a call to `AtlDumpMemoryLeaks()`:

```
// unmanaged C++
#include <wtypes.h>
#include <atldbgmem.h>
#include <atlbase.h>
void LeakNew()
{
   char* p = new char[19];
   strcpy(p, "Allocated with new");
}
void main()
{
   LeakNew();
   AtlDumpMemoryLeaks();
}
```

This code calls a function called `LeakNew()` that allocates a buffer and initializes it but does not free it. The `AtlDumpMemoryLeaks()` function will produce the following output:

```
Detected memory leaks!
Dumping objects ->
c:\MemoryTest\memory.cpp(7) :
    {36} normal block at 0x002F0870, 19 bytes long.
Data: <Allocated with n>
    41 6C 6C 6F 63 61 74 65 64 20 77 69 74 68 20 6E
Object dump complete.
```

This output indicates where the allocation was made and dumps the memory that was leaked. The CRT memory allocation routines can call a user-defined hook function, and ATL defines such a function, called `_AtlAllocReportHook`. This hook function will record the memory allocation in a structure maintained by ATL. To indicate to the CRT that this function should be used, you should call `AtlSetAllocHook()`. Calling this function on its own indicates that you want to get a record of memory allocations sent to the output debug stream as they happen. To be able to view these allocations at a later stage you should call `AtlEnableAllocationTracking()`. To get these allocation statistics you can call `AtlDumpMemoryStats()`:

```
// unmanaged C++
AtlSetAllocHook();
AtlEnableAllocationTracking();
LeakNew();
AtlDumpMemoryStats();
```

This code results in the following output. The first line is generated when the call to `new` is made, and the last line indicates that an allocation has been made:

```
c:\MemoryTest\memory.cpp(7): Memory operation:
    allocating a 19-byte block (# 36)
1 records in dump:
c:\MemoryTest\memory.cpp(7): 1 operations of size 19
```

Allocation tracking does just that: It tracks the allocations that are made; it does not determine whether the memory block has leaked. The dump of the memory allocation gives the index of this allocation (in this case number 36). If you know that there is a problem with this particular allocation, you can specify that when the allocation is made, the debugger should stop by calling the following function:

```
// unmanaged C++
AtlSetAllocStop(36);
```

When the allocation is made, `_CrtDbgBreak()` will be called. At this point you should use the **Call Stack** window to see where `new` has been called.

You can also perform checks for writing operations to memory that overrun the buffer allocated for them. To do this you can call `AtlCheckMemory()`:

```
// unmanaged C++
char* MemOverrun()
{
    // should be one byte longer
    char* p = new char[14];
    return strcpy(p, "Memory overrun");
}
void main()
{
    char* p = MemOverrun();
    AtlCheckMemory();
    delete [] p;
}
```

The `MemOverrun()` function creates a buffer that is one character too small. This problem will be detected by the call to `AtlCheckMemory()`, which will write the following to the **Output** window:

```
DAMAGE: after Normal block (#36) at 0x002F0870.
Normal allocated at file c:\MemoryTest\memory.cpp(7).
Normal located at 0x002F0870 is 14 bytes long.
```

This output indicates the memory allocation index, the location of the memory problem in the source code, and the location of the actual overrun in memory. You can use `AtlSetAllocStop()` to break in the debugger and track the usage of the buffer to see if you can determine where the buffer overrun occurs. When the call to `delete` is made on such a buffer pointer, the debugger will break within the CRT `_free_dbg()` method.

The `atldbgmem.h` header also defines versions of the Win32 heap allocation routines that will record the heap allocations. These routines will allocate the memory using the debug version of `malloc()` rather than the actual heap method, so that memory leaks can be tracked. If you don't want tracking capability, you can define `_ATL_NO_TRACK_HEAP` before you include `atldbg-mem.h`, so the actual Win32 heap allocation function will be called and all you will get is a message in the output debug stream stating that the allocation has been made. Here is some code that uses these routines:

```
// unmanaged C++
void LeakHeapAlloc()
{
    char* p = (char*)HeapAlloc(
                      GetProcessHeap(), 0, 25);
    strcpy(p, "Allocated with HeapAlloc");
}
void main()
{
    LeakHeapAlloc();
    AtlDumpMemoryLeaks();
}
```

The `LeakHeapAlloc()` function looks as if it were calling the Win32 `HeapAlloc()` function, but in fact `_AtlHeapAlloc()` will be called. `AtlHeapAlloc()` allocates the memory with the CRT `_malloc_dbg()` function, and hence `AtlDumpMemoryLeaks()` will detect that the memory is actually leaked.

Finally, you can indicate that the ATL memory allocation messages and the output from `AtlDumpMemoryStats()` should be sent to a file rather than to the output debug stream. To do this you should open a file for writing and pass this handle to `AtlSetReportFile()`:

```
// unmanaged C++
HANDLE = CreateFile("data.log", GENERIC_WRITE, 0, 0,
                    CREATE_ALWAYS, 0, 0);
AtlSetReportFile(hFile);
AtlSetAllocHook();
AtlEnableAllocationTracking();
void* p = AtlAllocMemoryDebug(
                  20, __FILE__, __LINE__);
AtlFreeMemoryDebug(p);
AtlDumpMemoryStats();
CloseHandle(hFile);
```

Here I show another way to allocate memory: The `AtlAllocMemoryDebug()` function calls the CRT `_malloc_dbg()` function so that the allocation is recorded.

9.2.12 ATL Interface Debugging

One of the problems with COM is that it relies on the users of interface pointers to follow its rules. If a user omits a call to `AddRef()` when copying an interface pointer, there will be fewer references on the interface, so when other code correctly calls `Release()`, the object will be prematurely destroyed, and consequently an interface pointer that the user thinks is valid will point to a nonexistent object. On the other hand, if `AddRef()` is called more times than `Release()`, the object will remain in memory far longer than the developer intended. And if the process is long-lived, the result may be a resource leak.

ATL provides interface debugging facilities to help you track reference-counting bugs. To use these facilities you need to define the `_ATL_DEBUG_INTERFACES` symbol before you include any of the ATL headers. Defining this symbol changes the ATL implementation of `QueryInterface()` so that all requests for interfaces are recorded at the output debug stream. And if the object supports the interface, ATL will return a thunk object to the client. The thunk object traps each call to the interface, and delegates the call to the interface on the object. The thunk handles `AddRef()` and `Release()` by outputting the value of the interface reference count.

Notice I said *interface* reference count and not object reference count. ATL objects usually have one aggregated reference for all interfaces, but this is not as useful for debugging as having a count of the references on an individual interface on an object. ATL does this by maintaining an array of `_QIThunk` objects in the debug interface module object. When a client is queried for a new interface, a `_QIThunk` object is created for the interface and added to the array. When a call to `Release()` on the interface results in the interface's reference count falling to zero, the `_QIThunk` object for the interface is removed from the debug interface module object's array. Thus this array holds `_QIThunk` objects for all interfaces that have references, and if this array has items in it when the server closes down, they must be leaked interfaces:

```
QIThunk - 4 AddRef  : Object = 0x01003fe8 Refcount = 2
   CMyObj - IDispatch
QIThunk - 6 AddRef  : Object = 0x01003ed0 Refcount = 3
   CMyObj - IDispatch
QIThunk - 6 Release : Object = 0x01003ed0 Refcount = 2
   CMyObj - IDispatch
```

DEVELOPING APPLICATIONS WITH VISUAL STUDIO.NET

This snippet of code shows the part of the trace seen in the **Output** window during a debugging session. It refers to two objects of the same class; the class name is given at the end of each line along with the interface whose reference count is changing. You can determine the object by looking at the `Object` part of the trace. This is the value of the `IUnknown` interface, so this value will always be different for different objects. The first line increases the reference count of the first object to a value of 2; the following two lines increase the reference count on the other object and then decrease it back to 2.

The number that comes immediately after the `QIThunk` text is an index value, so in this case these `_QIThunk` objects are the fourth and sixth to be created. If you identify that a particular interface on a particular object is causing a problem, and that the problem is repeatable over several runs, you can use the appropriate index value to specify that you are interested in details about how this interface reference count is changed. The thunk array is held in a global instance of a class called `CAtlDebugInterfacesModule`. This global object is called `_AtlDebugInterfacesModule`. Thunks are added to the array by a call to `AddThunk()` on this object and are removed by a call to `DeleteThunk()` on this object. This object has a public property called `m_nIndexBreakAt`, and when a `_QIThunk` object with this index is created, `AddThunk()` will stop with a call to `DebugBreak()`. Furthermore, any changes to the reference count of the interface of this thunk will also result in a call to `DebugBreak()`.

9.3 Summary

Debugging is a vital part of developing a process. You can rarely guarantee that your application will work the way you intend it to the first time it is run. Therefore, you almost always need to debug it. Visual Studio.NET has a myriad of tools that allow you to debug code. You can debug managed code or unmanaged code, and you can even step between managed and unmanaged code seamlessly.

Index

casting pointers, 73
class wizards, 521–522
/clr switch, 601
code compiled with /clr switch, 29
coding, 84
combining delegates, 78
comments, 481
compiling to IL, 601
concatenating strings, 138
default constructor, 23
defining DEBUG symbol, 169
deploying solution, 460
destructor, 10
develop class library, 565
disambiguating attributes, 48–49
/DLL linker switch, 93
dynamic_cast<> operator, 74
entry points, 97
events based on delegates, 82
exceptions, 64, 135
__finally exception clause, 71–72
friend type, 39–40
__gc pointer, 263
general exception handler, 67
__identifier operator, 40
implementations of add_ and remove_ methods,
    85–86
interfaces, 572–574
keywords, 588
late binding, 203–204
/LD compiler switch, 93
lower bounds vectors and multidimensional
    arrays, 36
main() method, 714
managed code, 97
managed extensions, 587–626
mixing managed and unmanaged types, 348
name mangling, 357
new operator, 589
/NOASSEMBLY switch, 93
objects passed through pointers, 265
overflow checking, 139
pinning pointers, 11–12
pointer parameters, 263–264
pointer syntax, 25
prefixes, 48
primitive types, 29–30
pure virtual method, 24

regions, 484
rethrowing exception, 67
scoping rules, 596
struct as reference or value type, 29
/SUBSYSTEM switch, 93
System::Runtime::InteropServices::OutAttribute
    attribute, 264
templates, 562
text substitution, 356–357
throwing and catching exceptions, 66–67
__typeof() operator, 142, 195
unmanaged code, 11, 97
unmangled names, 357
Windows Forms designer, 222–223
C++ classes, 21, 520–529, 589–596
C++ compiler
    /Fx switch, 512
    /G3 - /G6 switches, 5
    IL (intermediate language), 3
    mscorlib assembly, 88–89
C++ projects, 519
    adding items, 463–464
    configuration file, 457
    folders, 458–459
    GUID, 457
    link process, 460
    manipulating, 504
    .ncb files, 457–458
    options, 462, 519–520
    properties, 462–463
    .sln files, 457
    .suo files, 457–458
    .vcproj file, 457
    Windows Forms designer, 519
CAB files, 551–552
Call contexts, 270–271
Call stack, 716
Call Stack window, 687–689, 716, 718
Callback() method, 342, 343
CallContext class, 271
CallContext.GetData() method, 271
CallContext.SetData() method, 271
CallMe() function, 682
CanBePooled() method, 433
CancelEventHandler delegate, 222
CAS (code access security), 18
Caspol.exe, 122
castclass casting opcode, 604

DEVELOPING APPLICATIONS WITH VISUAL STUDIO.NET

Results class, 342
Resume() method, 187
ResumeThread() function, 185
.resx extension, 661
.resx files, 477, 489, 662, 664–665, 667–668,
    672
Resxgen, 665
ResXResourceReader class, 672
ResXResourceSet class, 672
ResXResourceWriter class, 672
Return values
    attributes, 48
    returning errors, 66
Reusing code, 357–360, 568
RFC 1766 string, 659
RGB format, 212
.rgs file, 571, 577
Rogue processes, 118
Roles, 435–437
Rollback, 551
Rollback node, 557
<root> node, 664
Roots, 10
Rotate() method, 211
RotateTransform() method, 211
Round function, 160
RPC
    authentication, 290–291
    debugging, 711
    style, 332
RPC-like interfaces, 411
/RTCu switch, 724
RTF (Rich Text Format), 479
RTG namespace, 394
/run switch, 507
/runexit switch, 507
Run() method, 206
Runtime, xv
    context, 655
    probing, 116
    property changes, 644
    viewing values, 695
Runtime license, 654–657

S

SAFEARRAY type, 409–410
Satellite assemblies, 114–116, 658, 669, 672–676

Satellite files, locating, 672
Saving bookmarks, 496
Scale() method, 211
ScaleTransform() method, 211
ScannerPrinter class, 606
Schemas
    data, 534–536
    database table, 534–535
    DataSet view, 486–487
    reading, 535
    XML view, 486–487
SCM (Service Control Manager), 290
Scope operator, 480
Scoping variable, 13–14
Screen class, 227
Scripting, 505
Scripts, 456–457
Scripts folder, 455
Sealed classes, 25, 75, 593
__realed modifier, 593
Searching
    assemblies, 497–498
    code, 490–499
    with commands, 507–508
    incremental, 495
    projects, 491–492
    regular expressions, 491
    for symbols, 497–499
    for text, 490–491
    type library, 498
<section> tag, 112
<sectionGroup> tag, 112
Security, 122–126
    access checking, 18
    authentication, 18, 322, 335
    authorization, 335
    CAS (code access security), 18
    COM+, 435–438
    DCOM, 290–291
    evidence, 18–19
    message digest, 322
    permissions, 18
    remote objects, 320, 322–323
    remoting channels, 320, 322
    trust levels, 123
    Web Services, 335–337
    Win32, 17
Security API, 126

Uri class, 140
URIs (Uniform Resource Identifiers)
   for assembly, 117
   information about, 140
   local file, 182–183
   requested protocol, 182
   uniquely locating remote object, 309
URLs (Uniform Resource Locators), 451–452
User Control wizard, 530
User controls, 532
User interface
   C# projects, 520
   installation, 557
User Interface view, 554
User Interface window, 557
User32.dll file, 358
User32.lib library, 358
UserControl class, 532, 636, 637
User-created metadata, 408
User-defined hook function, 741
User-defined interfaces, 513
Ushort member, 28
Ushort type, 27
Using blocks, 14, 72–73
#using directive, 598
using namespace statement, 90, 355, 356
using statement, 72, 90, 646, 647, 652
Utility code permissions, 19
__uuidof() operator, 412

V

Validate() method, 656, 657
__value class, 620
__value keyword, 589–596
Value types, 6, 9
   arrays, 36
   converting to reference type, 34
   declaring instance, 27
   derivation from interfaces, 33
   events, 33
   fields, 23, 33
   implicitly sealed, 30
   initializing, 30–33
   managed C++, 29
   methods, 33
   properties, 33
   sealed, 33

   structures, 365
   ushort member, 28
   virtual methods, 33
__value types, 29
   arrays, 616
   __gc pointers, 602
   __nogc pointers, 602
   as stack-based instances, 596
Variable type, 527
Variables
   accessing in watch windows, 693
   adding, 471
   adding to watch window, 692
   checking for changes, 682–683
   complete access, 698
   modifying, 693
   out of scope, 15–16
   read-only access, 698
VARIANT type, 409, 410
VB (Visual Basic), 135
   Building Blocks folder, 539
   popularity, 130
VB6, 8–9
VB.NET, 8
   .asmx, 330
   COM objects, 9
   Framework Class Library, 8
   IL (intermediate language), 3
   late binding, 3, 203
   object references, 25
VBScript File wizard, 531
VC attributes, 511, 562
VC remote debugging monitor, 724
vcclr.h file, 604, 628
vcpkg.dll type library, 504
.vcproj file, 457
.vcstyle XML files, 520
VCWizards folder, 520
Vectors, 36, 611
Version checking, 113
/version switch, 673
VERSIONINFO resource, 104, 107, 478
VERSIONINFO resources, 247–248
Versioning
   before .NET, 103–105
   satellite assemblies, 114–116
View | Designer command, 487
View | Full Screen command, 450

X

Y

Z

DEVELOPING APPLICATIONS WITH VISUAL STUDIO.NET